# Lecture Notes of the Institute for Computer Sciences, Social Information and Telecommunications Engineering

Patrick Sénac   Max Ott
Aruna Seneviratne (Eds.)

# Wireless Communications and Applications

First International Conference, ICWCA 2011
Sanya, China, August 1-3, 2011
Revised Selected Papers

 Springer

Volume Editors

Patrick Sénac
LAARS, CNRS, Département de Mathématique
et Informatique, ENSICA
1 Place Emile Blouin
31056 Toulouse Cedex, France
E-mail: patrick.senac@isae.fr

Max Ott
NICTA, Australian Technology Park
Eveleigh, NSW 1430, Australia
E-mail: max.ott@nicta.com.au

Aruna Seneviratne
UNSW, Sydney, NSW 2053, Australia
and
NICTA
13 Garden Street, Eveleigh, NSW 1430, Australia
E-mail: aruna.seneviratne@nicta.com.au

ISSN 1867-8211                              e-ISSN 1867-822X
ISBN 978-3-642-29156-2                      e-ISBN 978-3-642-29157-9
DOI 10.1007/978-3-642-29157-9

Springer Heidelberg Dordrecht London New York

Library of Congress Control Number: 2012933994

CR Subject Classification (1998): C.2, H.4, I.2, H.3, F.1, K.6.5

*Typesetting:* Camera-ready by author, data conversion by Scientific Publishing Services, Chennai, India

Printed on acid-free paper

Springer is part of Springer Science+Business Media (www.springer.com)

# Preface

The market for wireless communications and the proliferation of mobile devices have enjoyed tremendous growth. Outdoor and indoor wireless communication networks are so successful that they lead to numerous applications in sectors ranging from industries and enterprises to homes and universities. No longer bound by the harnesses of wired networks, people are able to communicate with each other, interact with information-processing devices, and receive a wide range of mobile wireless services through various types of networks and systems everywhere, anytime.

The annual International Conference on Wireless Communications and Applications (ICWCA) aims to provide a forum that brings together researchers from academia as well as practitioners from industry to meet and exchange ideas and recent research work on all aspects of wireless communication networks.

For ICWCA 2011, we received around 90 papers from different countries including South Korea, UK, Iran, and Japan, but only 41 were accepted and presented.

Speakers primarily focused on mobile ad hoc networks, sensor networks, network architectural design, network protocol design, local area networks, MAC, routing, and transport protocols, quality of service provisioning, reliability and fault-tolerance issues, resource allocation and management, signal processing, medical imaging, data aggregation techniques, security and privacy issues, wireless computing and applications for wireless network, i.e., smart grid, agriculture, health care, smart home, conditional monitoring, etc.

We enjoyed working with our friends in the ICWCA 2011 Program Committee, with the authors of the papers themselves, and with the referees who reviewed papers. These researchers, who represent different countries and come from a variety of academic backgrounds and interests, have worked together because of a shared interest in wireless communications and applications.

We hope that the papers contained in these proceedings will prove helpful toward improving the development of wireless communication and expanding the scientific thinking of researchers.

Wencai Du

# Organization

## Chair

Wencai Du — Hainan University, China

## Co-chairs

Chong Shen — Hainan University, China
Kea Hsiang Kwong — MIMOS Berhad, Malaysia

## Publicity Chairs

Yonghui Zhang — Hainan University, China
Baodan Chen — Hainan University, China
Deshi Li — Wuhan University, China

## Technical Program Chairs

Dirk Pesch — Cork Institute of Technology, Ireland
Mengxing Huang — Hainan University, China
Ewe Hong Tat — UTAR, Malaysia

## Publication Chairs

Feng Du — Hainan University, China
Liew Soung Yue — UTAR, Malaysia
Lihua Wu — Hainan Normal University, China
Yaoting Wu — Qiongzhou University, China

## Steering Committee

Perry Ping Shum — NTU, Singapore
Quan Xue — City University of Hong Kong, Hong Kong
Robert Atkinson — University of Strathclyde, UK
Sidong Zhang — Beijing Jiaotong University, China
Wang Qi — University of the West of Scotland, UK
Kaiyu Yao — Nokia Siemens, USA
Susan Rea — Cork Institute of Technology, Ireland
Nanjie Liu — Nanjing University of Posts and Telecommunications, China

Yong Bai                    Hainan University, China
Youling Zhou               Hainan University, China
Goh hock Guan              UTAR, Malaysia
Liqiang Zheng              Tyndall National Insititute, Ireland

## Sponsorship Committee

Shipu Zheng                Hainan University, China
Gang Jiao                  China Unicom, China
Dongjun Zhu                China Telecom, China

# Table of Contents

## Applications

## Network Architectures

## Signal Processing

## Data Link and Network Layers

# Securities

# Locating Emergency Responders in Disaster Area Using Wireless Sensor Network

Abishek Thekkeyil Kunnath, Aparna Madhusoodanan,
and Maneesha Vinodini Ramesh

Amrita Center for Wireless Networks & Applications., AMRITA Vishwa Vidyapeetham
(AMRITA University), Kollam, India
{abishektk,maneesha}@am.amrita.edu,
aparna.mcse@gmail.com

**Abstract.** A worldwide increase in number of natural hazards is causing heavy loss of human life and infrastructure. An effective disaster management system is required to reduce the impacts of natural hazards on common life. The first hand responders play a major role in effective and efficient disaster management. Locating and tracking the first hand responders are necessary to organize and manage real-time delivery of medical and food supplies for disaster hit people. This requires effective communication and information processing between various groups of emergency responders in harsh and remote environments. Locating, tracking, and communicating with emergency responders can be achieved by devising a body sensor system for the emergency responders. In phase 1 of this research work, we have developed an enhanced trilateration algorithm for static and mobile wireless sensor nodes. This work discusses an algorithm and its implementation for localization of emergency responders in a disaster hit area. The indoor and outdoor experimentation results are also presented.

**Keywords:** Wireless sensor networks, Localization, Disaster area, Emergency Responders.

## 1 Introduction

The advent of Wireless Sensor Network (WSN) has marked an era in the sensing and monitoring field. The technology has made possible to monitor otherwise remote and inaccessible areas such as active volcanoes, avalanches and so on. WSN is widely being used in various areas, such as, environmental monitoring, medical care, and disaster prevention and mitigation. This paper details yet another application of WSN in the post disaster scenario and comes up with an algorithm for localization.

When a disaster has struck an area, it is important to act immediately to rescue and give first line help in the form of medical aid, food and so on to the people in that area. Thus the role of first line emergency responders becomes a vital part of the post disaster scenario. In a disaster scenario, locating and tracking the first hand responders is essential to organize and manage real-time delivery of medicine and food to disaster hit people. This requires effective communication and information

P. Sénac, M. Ott, and A. Seneviratne (Eds.): ICWCA 2011, LNICST 72, pp. 1–10, 2012.
© Institute for Computer Sciences, Social Informatics and Telecommunications Engineering 2012

processing between various groups of emergency responders in harsh and remote environments.

Locating, tracking, and communicating with emergency responders can be achieved by devising a body sensor system for the emergency responders. This project aims to locate the emergency responders in different locations. In a disaster hit area whole communication networks may get damaged and the communication between responders is not possible. So localization of responders is very difficult with other technologies other than WSN.

This research project is an application of Wireless Sensor Network in disaster management. The paper addresses the development of an algorithm that can perform precise localization and tracking of the responders with indirect line-of-sight. Responders will be randomly located in the area so an ad-hoc network will be formed between the sensor nodes. The following sections briefs the role of responders and the location tracking algorithms used.

## 2   Related Work

A lot of indoor localization algorithm has been developed using Received Signal Strength Indicator (RSSI). A method for distance measurement using RSSI has been discussed in [7]. The accuracy of RSSI method can be very much influenced by multi-path, fading, non-line of sight (NLoS) conditions and other sources of interference [11]. In a disaster prone area these effects are more pronounced and as such RSSI method cannot be used in our study. Coordinate estimation method of localization using the principle of GPS has been suggested in [1]. Since the GPS modules could be costly, it has been discarded for our study.

In this project work we focused on a category of localization methods which estimate coordinate based on distance measurement. Instead of considering signal strength, time of arrival of each packet is considered which increases the accuracy of location. The algorithm is based on the Time Difference of Arrival (TDOA) method the accuracy of which is much higher when compared to the RSSI and we also present optimization methods to decrease the error of estimating the location using TDOA.

## 3   System Architecture

As suggested in [13], creating a common operating picture for all responders in an emergency situation is essential to take appropriate action in the disaster hit area and the safety of the responders. Protective suits used by the responders to be safe from hazardous materials create unique problems for response teams because their protective suits often make it difficult to read instrument screens, and if subject-matter experts aren't on scene, responders must find ways to relay the information back to them.

The aim is to develop an algorithm that can perform precise localization of sensor nodes with indirect line-of-sight by utilizing location information and distance measurements over multiple hops. To achieve this goal, nodes use their ranging sensors to measure distance to their neighbors and share their measurement and location information with their neighbors to collectively estimate their locations. Multilateration is a suitable method for localization in outdoor navigation. As described in [10], when the receiver sends the signal to locate itself, it finds out at least three nearest anchor nodes which know their positions. The receiver then calculates the distance between one satellite and the receiver. If the distance is "X", then it draws an imaginary sphere with "X" as the radius from the receiver to the satellite and also the node as the centre [13]. The same process is repeated for the next two nodes. Thus three spheres are drawn with just two possible positions. Out of these one point will be in space and the other will be the location of the receiver. Thus the exact position of the receiver is found out. Usually the receivers try to locate more than four satellites so as to increase the accuracy of the location. The Earth is made as the fourth sphere so that two points converge with the imaginary spheres of the other three satellites. This method is commonly called 3-D Trilateration method. Here in this paper we have tried to implement a modified version of the above mentioned method.

Fig: 1 shows the entire architecture of the system. The entire wireless sensor network is formed by required number of MicaZ mote. MicaZ mote includes the program for Localization, tracking and monitoring the position of unknown node. Also it includes the program for time synchronization.

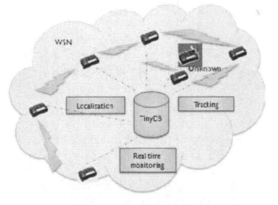

**Fig. 1.** System architecture

The TinyDB plays an important role here. Tiny database extract query information from a network of motes. TinyDB provides a simple Java API for writing PC applications that query and extract data from the network; it also comes with a simple graphical query-builder and result display that uses the API.

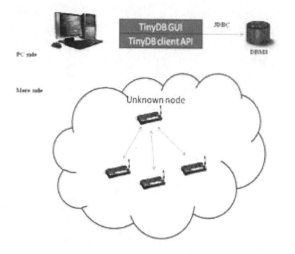

**Fig. 2.** TinyDB Architecture

## 4   Algorithm Design

The algorithm used here is a trilateration algorithm, and is implemented using TinyOS in the NesC language. This is the first step for responder's localization.

*Localization algorithm*

Trilateration is the method of using relative position of the nearby objects to calculate the exact location of the object of interest. Instead of using a known distance and an angle measurement as in normal triangulation methods, we used three known distances to perform the calculation. Here we use a GPS receiver to find out the coordinate points of three nodes.

The algorithm works as follows:

Step1: Set N numbers of nodes in the field and synchronize all the nodes.

Step2: Each of them continuously sent RF signals with packet containing a field for time stamp, i.e. whenever RF signal is sent by an unknown node, unknown node add the time of sending RF signal to the packet it broadcasts.

Step3: In addition there are B beacon nodes.

Step4: Each node $n_i, 1<=i<=N$ estimate its distance $d_{ij}$ from each     beacon $_j$ , $1<=j<=M$ where M is the no: of beacon nodes in its transmission range(assume M as 3 nodes)

Step5: Each beacon node will calculate the distance from node Distance=speed × time

Step6: Making this distance as radius each beacon create a circle.

Step7: The intersecting point of these 3 circles will be the position of unknown node.

Step8: Go to Step5 if the unknown node is moving and track its position at regular instance of time.

Step9: Stop

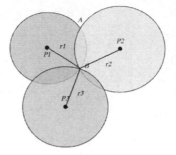

**Fig. 3.** Graphical Representation of Trilateration

For example (see Figure 2), point B is where the object of interest is located. The distances to the nearby objects *P1* and *P2* are known. From geometry, it can be concluded that only two possible locations, A and B, can satisfy the criteria. To avoid ambiguity, the distance of the third nearby object is introduced and now there is only one point B that could possibly exist [14].

If we apply the concept of 2-D trilateration to a GPS application which exists in 3-D space, the circles in Figure 2 become spheres.

In order for the receiver to calculate the distance from B, B send RF signals with time stamping. We know the speed of RF signal as $3 \times 10^8$m/s and we know the time of sending from the time stamping value. From this distance can be measured using equation 1.

$$\text{Distance} = \text{speed} \times \text{time} \qquad (1)$$

Using this calculated distance as radius and $p_1$ as center, draw a circle. Repeat the same steps for $p_2$ and $p_3$. We will get three circles. Solving the three equations of the circle we get one intersecting point.

Consider three circles with positions as $(x_1, y_1, z_1)$; $(x_2, y_2, z_2)$ $(x_3, y_3, z_3)$;

$$X = (4k_1 + 3k_2 - 2k_1)/6; \qquad (2)$$

$$Y = (2k_1 + 3k_2 - k_3)/6; \qquad (3)$$

$$Z = (k_1 + k_2 - k_3)/2 \qquad (4)$$

X, Y, Z are the co-ordinates of unknown node.

## 5 Implementation

With the entire setup field testing is also find out. The readings from the mote is calculated from the outdoor and find out the readings and they are tabulated which is shown in the table.

**Table 1.** The reading got from the field testing

| | | |
|---|---|---|
| | Without delay | 22m |
| Range(LOS) | With delay | 41m |
| | Obstacle human | 3.5m |
| Range(NLOS) | Obstacle Wall | 15m |
| Range(Environment with Vegetation) | | 30m |

The setup includes one unknown node and three beacon nodes. The beacon nodes calculate the distance of the unknown node from them and calculate the intersection point of the three circles formed by calculated distances. The actual distance, the time stamp and speed of the wave is tabulated in table1.

**Table 2.** Distance Information

| Receiver Nodes | Value of time stamp(s) | RF signal speed(m/s) | Radius' distance(m) |
|---|---|---|---|
| $p_1$ | 4 | $3 \times 10^8$ | $12 \times 10^8$ |
| $P_2$ | 6 | $3 \times 10^8$ | $18 \times 10^8$ |
| $P_3$ | 2 | $3 \times 10^8$ | $6 \times 10^8$ |
| $P_4$ | 10 | $3 \times 10^8$ | $30 \times 10^8$ |
| $P_5$ | 40 | $3 \times 10^8$ | $120 \times 10^8$ |
| $P_6$ | 8 | $3 \times 10^8$ | $24 \times 10^8$ |
| $P_7$ | 2 | $3 \times 10^8$ | $6 \times 10^8$ |
| $P_8$ | 4 | $3 \times 10^8$ | $12 \times 10^8$ |

The beacon node uses the time stamp to calculate the time of arrival. Knowing the speed of the RF waves the distance could be computed as discussed in section 3.1.1. This distance is calculated in beacon node which localizes the unknown node. The data from beacon node is viewed using XSniffer (figure 4).

A second method was tried out where the unknown node itself will act as a sink node. The beacon nodes calculate the distance and send it to the unknown node which does the localization calculations. This will avoid the use of more number of nodes. It was found that the accuracy of the calculation increases. The XSniffer output is as shown in figure 5.

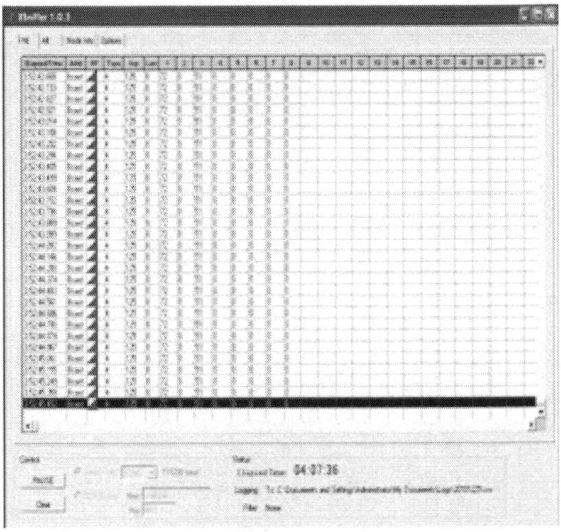

**Fig. 4.** Distance measurement as viewed using XSniffer

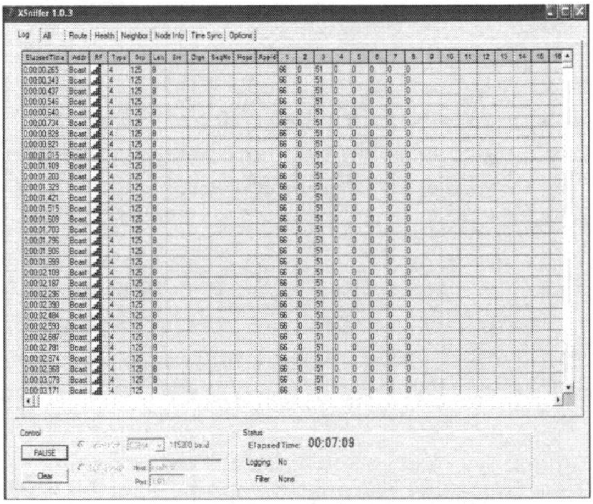

**Fig. 5.** Distance measurement

While experimenting, the actual distance was also calculated to find the percentage of the error. Figure 4 shows the error of the calculated distance from the actual values. The error occurs due to the dependency of distance calculations based on the time of arrival. If there is a delay introduced due to interference then there will be an error introduced.

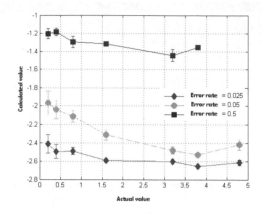

**Fig. 6.** Error Rate

Actual distance is measured using the measuring instruments. Using the micaz mote we calculated the distance and viewed the result using XSniffer. We did an analysis on actual distance and calculated distance which has been plotted in Figure 6 and came up with following three conclusions:

1. There are small differences in actual value and calculated values.
2. Error rate always remains in the range of 0.025%-0.5%.
3. The error rate is minimum when the unknown node and the beacon node are closer. When they are far from each other, error rate increases due to interference and delay.

Multilateration with a number of beacon nodes is a good method to reduce error in calculations. Multilateration, also known as hyperbolic positioning, is the process of locating an object by accurately computing the time difference of arrival (TDOA) of a signal emitted from that object to three or more receivers. It also refers to the case of locating a receiver by measuring the TDOA of a signal transmitted from three or more synchronized transmitters. In practice, errors in the measurement of the time of arrival of pulses means that enhanced accuracy can be obtained with more than four receivers. In general, N receivers provide N − 1 hyperboloids. When there are N > 4 receivers, the N − 1 hyperboloids should, assuming a perfect model and measurements, intersect on a single point. In reality, the surfaces rarely intersect, because of various errors. In this case, the location problem can be posed as an optimization problem and solved using, for example, least squares method or an extended Kalman filter. Additionally, the TDOA of multiple transmitted pulses from the emitter can be averaged to improve accuracy.

## 6 Advantages

Main advantage of the system is the use of distance measurements when compared to RSSI method which is based on the measurement of signal strength. The signal strength fluctuates every time as such accurate localization of the object in the plane may not be possible. In the above said algorithm the relationship between speed and time is used for measuring the distance. The time Stamping interface is used to keep track of the time. By knowing the speed of RF signal it is possible to calculate the distance.

## 7 Conclusion and Future Work

This project tries to develop a proper localization of first responders. Algorithm is implemented and tested; trilateration algorithm is used for localization and extracts the value of time from Time stamping. From this distance is measured. So there is no ranging problem. When we measure distance using strength of radio signal there is a problem like reducing signal strength due to different factors. Took the relationship between time and speed and calculated the distance. This method helps to locate the real coordinate of object in the plane.

This work could be extended by implementing the algorithm in a tag which has the capability to perform the functions of GPS receiver. So that exact location can be identified with great accuracy in an outdoor environment.

The developed algorithm could be extended to Mulilateration with minor changes. When the number of nodes increases the accuracy increases. Also the unknown node can act as a sink node and reduce the complexity of the network.

## References

1. Hu, L., Evans, D.: Localization of mobile sensor networks. In: IEEE InfoCom 2000 (March 2000)
2. Sabatto, S.Z., Elangovan, V., Chen, W., Mgaya, R.: Localization Strategies for Large-Scale Airborne Deployed Wireless Sensors. IEEE, Los Alamitos (2009)
3. Kang, Li, X.: Power-Aware Markov Chain Based Tracking. IEEE Computer 37(8), 41–49 (2004)
4. Park, J.Y., Song, H.Y.: Multilevel Localization for Mobile Sensor NetworkPlatforms. Proceedings of the IMCSIT 3 (2008)
5. http://www.tinyos.net/tinyos-1.x/doc/tutorial
6. Ramesh, M.V., Kumar, S., Rangan, P.V.: Wireless Sensor Network for Landslide Detection. In: Proceedings of the Third International Conference on Sensor Technologies
7. V.: RADER: An In-Building RF-based User Location and Tracking System. In: Proc. of IEEE INFOCOM 2000, pp. 775–784 (2000)
8. Biswas, P., Ye, Y.: Semidefinite Programming for Ad Hoc Wireless Sensor Network Localization. In: 3rd International Symposium on Information Processing

9. Bulusu, N., Estrin, D., Girod, L., Heidemann, J.: Scalable Coordination for Wireless Sensor Networks: Self-Configuring Localization Systems. In: Proceedings of the 6th IEEE International Symposium

10. Kannan, A., Mao, G., Vucetic, B.: Simulated Annealing based Localization in Wireless Sensor Network. In: Vehicular Technology Conference (2006), ieeexplore.ieee.org

11. Mao, G., Fidan, B., Anderson, B.D.O.: Wireless Sensor Network Localization Techniques. The International Journal of Computer and Telecommunications Networking (2007)

12. Sichitiu, M.L., Ramadurai, V.: Localization of Wireless Sensor Networks with a Mobile Beacon. In: Proceedings of the IEEE ICMASS (2004)

13. Ladd, M., Bekris, K.E., Rudys, A., Kavraki, L.E., Wallach, D.S.: Robotics-Based Location Sensing UsingWireless Ethernet. In: International Conference on Mobile Computing and Networking (2002)

14. Simic, S.N., Sastry, S.: Distributed Localization in Wireless Ad Hoc Networks. Tech. report, UC Berkeley, 2002, Memorandum No. UCB/ERL M02/26 (2002)

15. Evans, D., Hu, L.: Localization for mobile sensor networks. Proc. IEEE FGCN 2007 workshop chairs (2007)

# Research on the ZigBee Network Protocol Intelligent Meter Reading System

Qi Xia, Chong Shen, and Baodan Chen

College of Information Science & Technology
Hainan University, China
cbd@hainu.edu.cn

**Abstract.** Wireless Sensor Network, WSN to the exchange of data with each other must have the appropriate wireless network protocols, wireless protocols difficult to adapt to the traditional low-cost wireless sensors, low power, high fault tolerance requirements. In this case, ZigBee protocol came into being. ZigBee is an emerging short-range, low complexity, low-speed, low power, low-cost wireless networking technology, mainly for short-range wireless connection. It is based on IEEE 802.15.4/ZigBee protocol standards, in thousands of tiny sensors to achieve communication between the coordination. This background paper, based on ZigBee wireless meter reading system proposed routing algorithms and networking. In-depth analysis of several typical wireless sensor network routing protocols, through a network of some of the traditional routing algorithm feasibility, problems and improvement of, for the ZigBee standard in the meter reading system, designed for meter reading system Network routing algorithm, the test achieved the mesh point to point communication between modules[1].

**Keywords:** automatic meter reading, wireless sensor network, ZigBee, routing.

## 1 Introduction

With automation and the rapid development of measurement technology, people's lives, raising the level of intelligent home conditions, the indoor measurement instrument automatically Collecting data has gradually become the goal. Meanwhile, public utilities management also hopes that the new technology can solve the long plagued their meter reading difficult, difficult issues such as fees, in order to achieve savings in manpower, reduce corporate liquidity occupancy, user, and improve management purposes[2].

Existing wired meter reading system has many problems: to assume different functions of all kinds of cables, data lines on the one hand restrict the operator's hands and feet, on the other hand is a waste of electrical supplies. If installed in the indoor and outdoor long-term, likely to cause aging lines, there are short, the risk of disconnection, and the waste line, the cable will cause environmental pollution, in addition to improper due to aging and the layouts will be planted for the safety of no small risk.

P. Sénac, M. Ott, and A. Seneviratne (Eds.): ICWCA 2011, LNICST 72, pp. 11–22, 2012.
© Institute for Computer Sciences, Social Informatics and Telecommunications Engineering 2012

With the continuous development of wireless communication technology in recent years, low-cost equipment for the emergence of wireless networking requirements of the technical - ZigBee technology, it is a short distance, low complexity, low power, low data rate, low-cost Two-way wireless communications technology, mainly used in the field of automatic control and remote control. Although there are many successful development of the wireless meter reading system, but ZigBee's excellent performance, low power, high integration and low cost, has a very strong market competitiveness[3].

# 2 Backgrounds

## 2.1 ZigBee Protocol Architecture

As the wireless market and the high efficiency of the network growing demand for standardized, ZigBee protocol as to support low-rate, low power, secure and reliable wireless networking standards have emerged. A complete ZigBee protocol stack mainly application specifications component by the physical layer (PHY), media access control layer (MAC), network layer (NWK), security layer and high-level. Among them, the physical layer and MAC layers defined by the IEEE 802.15.4 protocol standard, the network layer and application layer developed by the ZigBee Alliance[4].

## 2.2 Network Layer

ZigBee network layer is the core protocol stack, which is responsible for the application layer to provide the right service interface, while on the IEEE 802.15.4 standard defines the MAC layer for proper operation. Including the network layer network layer data entity (NLDE) and network layer management entity (NLME) two service entities. Provide data transmission services which NLDE, NLME also responsible for providing management services and the network layer database - network information base, NIB[5].

Network layer will mainly consider technology-based Ad Hoc network protocols, is responsible for building and maintaining topology, naming and binding services, including the addressing, routing and security of these essential services, there are self-organizing, self-maintenance functions, to Minimize maintenance costs and consumer spending.

IEEE 802.15.4 network is the Personal Operating Space, POS use the same radio channel of mutual communication through the IEEE 802.15.4 standard set of a group of devices, also known as LR_WPAN (Low-Rate Wireless Personal Area Network) network, that is, low data rate Wireless personal area network. In this network, in accordance with the communication capabilities of the equipment can be divided into Full Function Device, FFD and Reduced Functions Device, RFD. And between the FFD and RFD FFD can communicate between; RFD cannot be communication between the only communication with the FFD, or forward the data out through a FFD.

In the IEEE 802.15.4 network, the one called PAN (PAN Coordinator) of the FFD, is LR_WPAN network master controller. PAN Coordinator in addition to direct applications, but also complete membership management, and link state information management and packet forwarding tasks. IEEE 802.15.4 WPAN has the following characteristics:

1. Scalable: excellent network capabilities, up to 254 network devices on dynamic device addressing.
2. Adaptability: The seamless integration of existing control network standard. Coordinated through the network automatically establish a network, using CSMA / CA channel access way.
3. Reliability: For reliable transmission, provide full handshake protocol.

## 2.3  Network Topology Structure

Zigbee standard specifies the network topology structure: star, tree and mesh structure. and they may be summarized as point-to-point network. as shown in Figure 1.

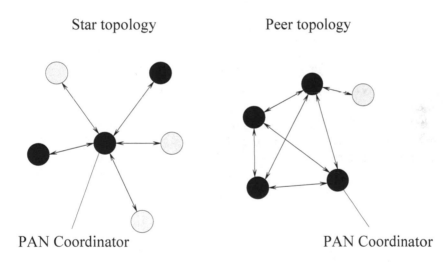

Star topology                         Peer topology

PAN Coordinator                    PAN Coordinator

**Fig. 1.** Star and mesh topology graph

In a peer-to-peer network, there is a pan coordinator, which is initiated and organized by the network. a device on the other communications equipment, they can communicate. on the internet, the various devices to send a message when using a lot of dance and to build the network coverage. each separate pan has a unique identifier paid to the same network nodes to identify and communicate with each other. This used to wait for the topology as a network; coordinator of the first node has initiated a pan, the node in the organizations to join[6].

# 3 Network Routing Algorithm

Routing protocols will be responsible for the data are from the source through a network node to node forwards the purpose, it mainly include two aspects of search function: source and destination node to node between; the path of data grouped along the path to the right forward. Sensor in wireless network, sensors network node numbers, and the nodes usually by energy limited battery operated, the routing protocols for the local network information on the basis of the ability to choose the path and the efficient use of energy. Wireless network to meet the sensor: energy efficient, reducing redundancies, information, extensible, robustness, and they can outdo and security, etc. In order to save costs and reduce energy consumption, ZigBee in a network of the functions are simplified, these nodes can only a simple transceivers, and cannot act as routers. Following are introductions to some sort of typical routing, and to proceed to the improved technology, combined with ZigBee applied to the wireless network list system[4].

## 3.1 Flooding Routing Algorithm

Flooding is a data in the center plane of the route is the traditional network of communication routing protocols. Its design philosophy is: node generates or receives data broadcast to all neighboring nodes, the data packets reach their destination until it expires or stop transmission. The protocol has serious flaws:

1. Implosion. Nodes also received a number of neighbor nodes from the same data, shown in Figure 2.
2. Overlap. Node has received a number of nodes in the same area sent the same data.
3. Blind use of resources. Node does not take into account their resource constraints, in any case forward the data.

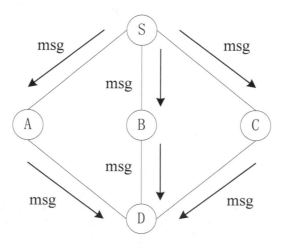

**Fig. 2.** Flooding implosion phenomenon

## 3.2   AODV Routing Algorithm and Its Improvement

AODV is on-demand routing algorithm, dynamic route discovery, maintenance mechanism and purpose of the sequence. AODV routing information obtained as follows: When a network node needs a route to reach another node, the source node broadcasts to all its neighbors a route request packet, the neighbor nodes in the network by way of Flooding in the dissemination of RREQ packets until the RREQ packet reaches the destination node or routing information can provide an intermediate node. In the dissemination process, the serial number is used to distinguish between the old and the new RREQ packet, to prevent routing loops. RREQ packet for each of the intermediate nodes forward it to create a temporary, to reach the source node routing, the route known as reverse route. When the RREQ packet reaches the destination node or a certain routing information to provide the intermediate nodes, a route reply packets at the path that RREQ packets sent back to the source node. When RREP transmit to the source node, for each of the intermediate nodes forward it to establish a route to the destination node, the route known as the forward routing. According to the source node receives the RREP packet to the destination node by its own route. When the source is moved, it will re-initiate route discovery algorithm; if the intermediate nodes move, then the adjacent nodes will find the link failure sends to its upstream node and link failure message has been spread to the source node, then the source node According to re-initiate route discovery process conditions[7].

Among the AODV algorithm, Flooding broadcast although improved, but the same node will repeat the broadcast packets redundant, so that power consumption greatly. And to receive intermediate nodes only handle the first RREQ, the RREQ packet received will be repeated regardless of how its performance, be discarded, which is equivalent to giving up the path later, then when the node failure on a route had to restart mechanism for routing the search request. This may lead to the efficiency of way finding and route efficiency not high.

For above, give a simplified version of the AODVgj. It has the main function of AODV, but taking into account cost, energy saving, ease of use and other factors, some of the features simplified AODV. This algorithm is characterized by the formation of the routing number after launch from the source node to destination node disjoint paths, when the path is interrupted for any reason, then the interrupt when the source node receives the report of the path, will first look for the results of the last route request whether there is a valid path, if it exists, the path to route data according to the new, if not a valid path, only to re-initiate route request command[8].

## 3.3   Cluster-Tree Algorithm and Its Improvement

Cluster tree algorithm is a typical cluster routing algorithm. In hierarchical routing, wireless sensor networks are usually divided into several clusters; each cluster consists of a number of cluster heads and cluster membership, the formation of multiple clusters of the first high-level network. In the high-level network, and can be divided into clusters, the formation of a higher level of network again until to the highest level of convergence node.

The core of the algorithm is to find whether the data to be transmitted is itself, if so, is no longer forwarded. If not, see if it came from a valid path, the so-called effective path is from the parent or the child came from, if the child node from the data, according to its destination to be reached, if it is a child of their own, then forwarded to the child node to the end, if not his own child, to reach the next address is the parent node, and thus a level, along the tree until you find the destination address.

Advantages of this algorithm is: clever use of the distribution of the various network nodes get the address properties of the tree was to select routes, equipment, do not keep in memory a routing table, nor take up the path to complete that operation, thus making the whole network traffic significantly reduced. Tree routing algorithm, but there are also many disadvantages, because according to an address on the routing tree structure, can not take the shortest path, the path to take longer than the actual.

The address allocation in improving the way is still assigned to the route for some address space to expand its child devices, and terminal equipment is assigned only a single address. Based on the above address assignment logic, by querying the destination address in the packet as long as a node to be able to easily move data packets transmitted to its destination. Way through this inquiry that is, the node simply decided to transfer its data packet to its child nodes, or terminal equipment of its routes to its parent node or child node.

The address allocation in improving the way, is still assigned to the router device to further a certain address space for its child devices assigned address, and terminal equipment is assigned only a single address, so it does not allow any child other equipment. Based on the above address assignment logic, as long as a node in the packet by querying the destination address to be able to easily move data packets transmitted to its destination. Way through this inquiry that is, the node can decide to pass its packet to its child nodes, or terminal equipment of its child nodes the router or its parent node. The data routing is to improve the cluster tree routing algorithm, the basic process algorithm shown in Figure 3, if the data transmitted from the FFD nodes (child nodes route), the first of the node to determine whether the data passed to itself, if it is received And by the upper handle, if not further to determine whether to pass to its child node that is to determine whether the packet destination address within its address space, and if it will forward the packet to its corresponding child nodes, if not in its address space Range, it will forward the packet to its parent node. When a packet is forwarded to its child nodes, and then determine whether the route of the child nodes of child nodes, if not the child node routing, that is the RFD node, packet processing directly by the upper node, if the child nodes for routing in accordance with the above Data processing to determine processing again.

### 3.4  Meter Reading System Routing Algorithm

Cluster tree-based routing algorithm, the device can be immediately passed to the first network packet to other devices without having to perform route discovery process. However, from the number of hops cost point of view, most of the cluster tree routing is not the best route. And the cluster tree routing can also lead to non-uniform flow distribution. Therefore, in the ZigBee wireless meter reading network, you can take the

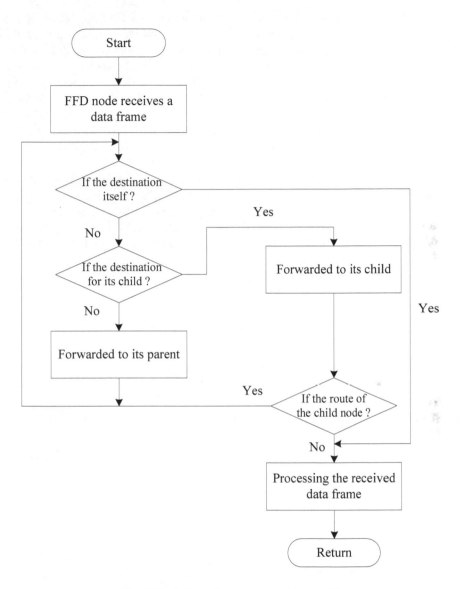

**Fig. 3.** Basic flow cluster tree routing algorithm

cluster tree routing table based on demand-driven routing algorithm for routing that AODVgj way to overcome the combination of the above-mentioned phenomenon.

Cluster-Tree AODVgj improved routing algorithm brings together the Cluster-Tree and the advantages of AODV. Each node in the network is divided into four types: Coordinator, RN, RN-and RFD, routing node; where RN is sufficient storage space and capacity to implement AODVgj node routing protocol, RN-is its storage space by limited agreement that does not have the ability to perform AODVgj node, RN-After receiving a packet with the Cluster-Tree algorithm can handle. Coordinator of the routing algorithm in which the same with the RN, Coordinator, RN and RN-are the FFD nodes, give the other nodes act as a routing node; RFD can only act as Cluster-Tree terminal child nodes. If the target node to send data to be their own neighbors, direct communication can be; the other hand, if not their neighbors, the three types of nodes to process the packet differently: RN to start AODVgj find the best route to the destination node , and it can play the role of the routing agent to help find other nodes route; RN-only use Cluster-Tree algorithm, which can be calculated to determine the packet is its own parent or a child node and forwarding; and RFD only the data to the parent node, please forward it.

Figure 4 for the Cluster-Tree + AODVgj diagram of the network layer data transmission. Nodes send packets to node N3 N4, figures represent the time sequence of all packets. It can be seen from the figure, the type of the node N3 is the RFD, it can only send packets to its parent node DATA N1. N1 is the type of RN +, so it first data into the cache, and then through the multicast request packet RREQ AODVgj find the routing node N2, node N4 and then through the shortest uncast path along the N4-N2-N1 to the node N1 Reply AODVgj reply packet RREP. Node N1 to find routes, the cache data along the N1-N2-N4 sent to the node N4, node N4 and then along the N4-N2-N1-N3 send a confirmation packet ACK to node N3, node N4 receive a confirmation packet, the entire communication process end.

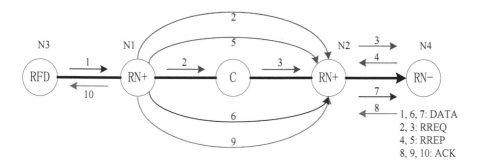

**Fig. 4.** Schematic diagram of network layer data transmission

## 4   Route Establishments

ZigBee routing protocols, RN-node needs to send packets to the network using a node in the Cluster-Tree routing to send packets.

RN + node sends a packet to the network but no access to the destination node in the routing table entry, it will initiate route discovery process:

1. Create node broadcasts a RREQ to the group around the node, the node if the received RREQ is a RN-node, it forwards by Cluster-Tree Routing in this group; If you receive a RREQ the node is a RN, is based on the information in the RREQ establish the appropriate routing table entries and routing table that entry and continue to broadcast this group.

2. Nodes will be calculated before forwarding the RREQ RREQ to its neighbor nodes send with the link cost between nodes and add it to the link stored in RREQ overhead, and then the link will be updated into the route discovery overhead table entry.
3. Once the RREQ reaches the destination node or destination node of the parent node, the node replies to the RREQ source node, a RREP packet, RREP should be established along the reverse path transmission to the source node, the node receives RREP to the destination node to establish forward path and update the corresponding routing information.
4. RREP before forwarding node will be calculated in the reverse path with the next hop link cost between nodes and add it to the link stored in RREP overhead. When the RREP reaches the corresponding RREQ initiator node, the route establishment process is complete.

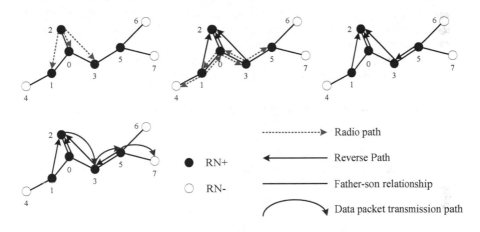

**Fig. 5.** ZigBee routing set up process

Figure 5 is an example of route establishment. Where node 0 is the focal point for ZigBee, if node 2 sends data packets to the node 7, but did not reach the node routing table 7 of the route, the node 2 is the RN nodes, so it will initiate route discovery process. Around node 2 to node broadcasts RREQ created (Figure a), nodes 0,1,3 established after receipt of RREQ reverse route to Node 2, and continue broadcasting RREQ (Fig. b), but not to the parent node broadcast sent, only the route to be broadcast the same level. Figure 3 c node has been forwarded RREQ, so it is no longer forward the packet; the node RN-4 is a node, does not have routing functions, it was found that they are not receiving RREQ the destination node, it will stop broadcasting; node 5 found RREQ the destination node is a child node of its own, it will replace the destination node along the reverse path to the newly created RREQ source node (Node 2) return a RREP, the establishment received RREP to the destination node node (node 7 ) positive route. RREP reaches the source node 2, the route establishment process is complete, the data packet along the path 2-3-5-7 just found transmission (Figure d). If the node 7 wants to send data packets to node 2, since node 7 is the RN-node, it only sends the packet to its parent node (node 5), initiated by the parent routing node, the process of building.

Network layer to achieve the following functions: power on any one node can work automatically join the network, automatically find their own parent; any one node of the power of information transmitted through a limited jump to reach the coordinator; any one node because leave the network for some reason, when the network does not affect other nodes, the network can automatically heal, that is, the original node to forward data through the nodes to find a new parent as a way to forward the data.

## 5   Comparison of Simulation Performance

Experiments using OMNet + + simulation tool, based on discrete event OMNeT + +, is a free, open source multi-protocol network simulation software, in the field of network simulation plays a very important position. OMNeT + + English name is Objective Modular Network Testbed in C + +, in recent years in the field of science and industry, an increasingly popular component-based open modular network simulation platform. In the simulation, defines the following scenario: A total of eight nodes 0, 1, 2, 3, 4, 5, 6, 7, parameter is set to: data rate = 1Mbps, delay = uniform (0.1ms, 1ms), packet length = uniform (128byte, 1024byte). However, the definition of routing protocols, respectively, using different protocols: AODV and AODVgj.

### 5.1   Figure 6 is Obtained Using Different Protocols with Different Data Plans

The experiment can be clearly seen that makes use of AODVgj overall network traffic routing protocol AODV routing protocol than with many stable and AODVgj routing protocols make the network link is more smooth, can send and receive large amounts of data packets.

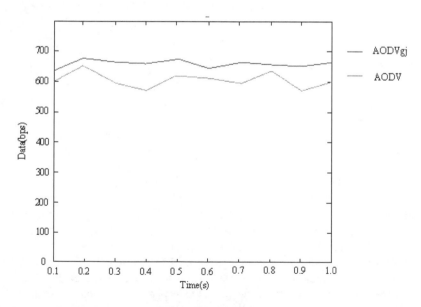

**Fig. 6.** Routing data

## 5.2  Figure 7 AODV Routing Overhead and AODVgj

Routing overhead: Every packet needs to send a data packet number of routing control. It reflects the degree of network congestion and node power efficiency, cost, the probability of a large great deal of congestion, and will delay sending the packet interface queue. Routing overhead for route discovery and route maintenance for the control group received the number and ratio of the number of data packets.

The experiment can be clearly seen that the routing protocol makes use of AODVgj overall network congestion is much smaller than that of AODV, routing protocol and makes the node AODVgj power efficient.

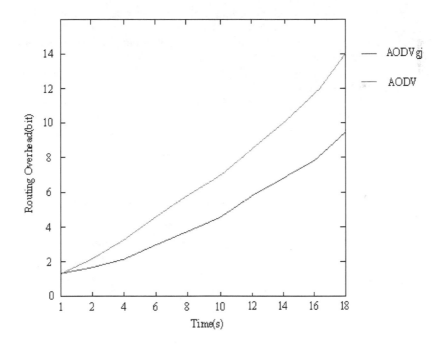

**Fig. 7.** Routing overhead

## 6  Conclusion

This study compared the traditional for wireless sensor network routing algorithm, in the ZigBee network layer protocol analysis, based on the characteristics of wireless sensor networks to improve it, make meter reading system for the routing algorithm. This article ZigBee standard implementation of the new wireless meter reading, and widen the scope of application of the ZigBee standard to solve the traditional manual meter reading and other drawbacks of the model. Experiments show that the performance indices in different embody AODVgj excellent than AODV, but not as good as the experience, there are many research and operational needs further. This paper is supported by " The 211 Project Central Special Fund of Hainan University " .

## References

1. Wang, S.-t., Zhou, H., Yuan, R.-m., Yi, Z.-I.: Concept and Application of Smart Meter. Power System Technology (2010)
2. Yang, H.-y., Zhang, Y., Lu, F.: The status prospect of communication schemes in AMRS. Electrical Measurement & Instrumentation (2001)
3. Cao, S.: Wireless Automatic Meter Reading System for Resident Power User Based on Smart Electricity Meter (2010)
4. Zhou, J., Shi, X.-c., Xu, C.: A Design of Multi-user Smart Meter Based on ZigBee. Electrical Measurement & Instrumentation (2010)
5. An, R.-r., Tong, N.: Application of Capacitance Grating Transducer in Test of Curtain Wall's Resisting Wind Press Capacity (2007)
6. Zhou, Y.-w., Ling, Z.-h., Wu, Q.-q.: ZigBee Wireless Communication Technology and Investigation on Its Application (2005)
7. Chakeres, I.D., Klein-Berndt, L.: AODVjr, AODVsimplified, Computing and Communications Review (2002)
8. Gareia-Luna-Aeeves, J.J., Spohnin Proe, M.: Source Tree Adaptive Routing in Wireless Networks (2010)

# Dairy Cattle Movement Detecting Technology Using Support Vector Machine

HaoEn Zhou*, Ling Yin, and CaiXing Liu

College of Informatics, South China Agricultural University,
510642 GuangZhou, China
`Terren.chow@gmail.com, scauyin@163.com, liu@scau.edu.cn`

**Abstract.** In this paper, the dairy cattle movement detecting technology based on 3-axis acceleration sensor information fusion is presented. For they show ideal performance in generalization and optimization, Support vector machines are used to build an information fusion model for dairy cattle's behavior classification. The data feature of the support vector machine fusion model is derived from 3-axis acceleration data. RBF function is used as the model's kernel function. The genetic algorithm is used to optimize the parameters of the kernel function. The training and testing results show that using genetic algorithm for kernel function parameter searching has good ability to optimize the fusion model.

**Keywords:** Dairy cattle movement detection, support vector machine, genetic algorithm.

## 1 Introduction

Automated animal behavior monitoring systems have become increasingly appealing for research and animal production management purposes [1]. Dairy cattle movement detecting plays a very important role in dairy cattle's physiology and health status monitoring.

There are already some approaches for dairy cattle movement detecting. Installing a pedometer on the cattle's leg is the most popular approach. By counting the number of the cattle's step in a specifically time, researcher can evaluate the active rate of that cattle [2-4]. This method has been implemented but its data model is not precise enough. Video-base Pattern recognition (PR) has been another hot point in the study of dairy cattle movement detecting. By applying PR algorithm on each video camera frame, Researcher can calculate the ratio of the cattle's active status and quiescent status based on the cattle's position changing rate. It has a precise data model but needs lots of computing resource and the deployment cost is too high. Object movement detecting using wireless sensor network and 3-axis acceleration sensor already received the attention in recent years.

---

* HaoEn Zhou is a graduate student in College of informatics, South China Agricultural University. He is interest in Wireless Sensor Network and Embedded System. This paper is supported by National 863 Fund under grant 2006AA10Z246.

Support vector machines (SVMs) are known as a suitable learning method, which is based on statistical learning theory, is gaining applications in the areas of machine learning, computer vision and pattern recognition because of the high accuracy and good generalization capability [5]. Unlike artificial neural network (ANN), which uses traditional empirical risk minimization (ERM) to minimize the error on the training data, SVM uses structural risk minimization (SRM) principle to minimize an upper bound on the expected risk. Using SRM as the risk minimization principle improve the SVM's generalization performance compared to ANNs and make it suitable to deal with the object movement detecting problems [6-7]. Some paper presents[8-10] that the combination of SVM and WSN with acceleration sensor was applied to human movement detection and recognition and SVM performs relatively well across different scene. In [1], the author made the first trail at detecting dairy cattle movement using SVM and WSN. 3-axis acceleration is acquired and transmitted back to data processing station from a sensor network node mounted on the target cattle's neck. A multi-class SVMs is used to setup the movement type classification model and it can recognize up to 6 types of cattle's movement. But the parameters of the SVM's kernel function are selected empirically and they have not been optimized. In this paper, a dairy cattle movement detection technology based on 3-axis acceleration sensor and binary SVM is present. Parameters and the feature set of the SVM are optimized separately in order to improve the accuracy and the performance. The remainder of the paper is organized as follows: chapter II describes the binary SVM model for cattle's movement detection, chapter III discusses binary SVM's parameter optimization algorithm, chapter IV focuses on the details of applying both SVM and GA to cattle movement detection, and chapter V is the conclusion.

## 2      Binary Classification SVMs

SVMs are derived from statistical learning and VC-dimension theory. The k-class classification SVMs construct a decision function $f(x) = \mathrm{sgn}(g(x, \alpha))$, given a training data set $T = \{(x_1, y_2), \ldots, (x_i, y_i), (x_j, y_j)\} \in (X \times Y)^l$, where $x_i \in X = R^n, i = 1, \ldots, l$ is a vector of length $d$ and $y_i \in \{1, \ldots, l\}$ is the class of the samples. After the training process, the decision function provides a specified class $y \in \{1, \ldots, k\}$ for an input $x \in R^n$.

In the case of binary classification problem, the main idea of binary classification SVMs is, given a training data set, constructing a hyper plane to separate the data set into two classes $y \in \{1, -1\}$ so that the margin between the two classes is maximal. It is equals to the optimization problem:

$$\min_{W \in H, b \in R, \xi \in R^l} \frac{1}{2} \| W \|^2 + C \sum_{i=1}^{l} \xi_i .$$

(1)

with constrains (2),

$$y_i\left(\left(W \bullet \Phi(x_i)+b\right)\right) \geq 1 - \xi_i, i = 1,\ldots,l$$

$$\xi_i \geq 0, i = 1,\ldots,l \tag{2}$$

where $W$ is the weight vector and $b$ is the bias term. $\Phi(x_i)$ is the non-liner mapping function which maps the input space $R^n$ to the high dimensional Hilbert space $H$ :

$$\Phi: X \subset R^n \to H$$
$$x \to \Phi(x) \tag{3}$$

In order to solve this problem, a dual problem is constructed:

$$\min_{\alpha} \frac{1}{2} \sum_{i=1}^{l} \sum_{j=1}^{l} y_i y_j \alpha_i \alpha_j K(x_i, x_j) - \sum_{j=1}^{l} \alpha_j \quad . \tag{4}$$

with constrains (5),

$$\sum_{i=1}^{l} y_i \alpha_i = 0$$
$$0 \leq \alpha_i \leq C, i = 1,\ldots,l \tag{5}$$

where $K(x_i, x_j)$ is the kernel function. It is the inner product of two $\Phi(x)$ mappings. That is $K(x_i, x_j) = \Phi(x_i) \bullet \Phi(x_j)$. In this pager, the radial basis function (RBF) :

$$R(xi, xj) = \exp\left(-\|xi - xj\|/2\delta^2\right) \quad . \tag{6}$$

is selected as the kernel function. $\delta$ is a kernel function parameter called kernel width and it must be selected by user in advance.

Suppose that $\alpha^* = \left(\alpha_1^*, \ldots, \alpha_l^*\right)^T$ is the optimal solution to optimization problem (4). The decision function is constructed:

$$f(x) = \mathrm{sgn}\left(\sum_{i=1}^{l} a_i^* y_i K(x, x_j) + b^*\right) \quad . \tag{7}$$

where $b^* = y_j - \sum_{i=1}^{l} y_i \alpha_i K(x_i, x_j)$ .

## 3    Optimizing SVM Parameters Using Genetic Algorithm

The genetic algorithm simulates Darwinian theory of evolution using highly parallel, mathematical algorithm that, transform a set (population) of mathematical object (typically string of 1's and 0's) into a new population, using operators such as reproduction, mutation, crossover. Genetic algorithms by their very nature consider a wide range of the search space for a particular problem. Unlike other techniques, they search from a population of pointes not from a single point. So they are less likely to become trapped on false optimization peaks. Using simple operations, genetic algorithm are able to rapidly optimize design parameter after examining only a small fraction of the search space.

In this paper, the SVM punishment parameter $C$ and the kernel width of the RBF kernel function $\delta$ are optimized by genetic algorithm. The values of the two parameters are directly code in the chromosomes with real data. The encoding form of the two parameters is $\left[[C_i][\delta_i]\right], i = 1, \ldots, m$, where $m$ is the number of sample the initial population. The proposed model used to select the parent chromosome is roulette-wheel method. Crossover and mutation method are used to modify the chromosome. The single best chromosome in each generation is survives to the next generation.

The function of adaptation value is used to advise the selection of the parent to produce the next generation. It also used to generate the probability of the crossover and the mutation operation during the reproduction process. The function of adaptation value is determined by the expectation output and the actual output of the SVM's decision function (7):

$$g(C, \delta) = \left( \sum_{i=1}^{m} |y_i| - \frac{1}{2} \sum_{i=1}^{m} |y_i - f(x_i)| \right) \bigg/ \sum_{i=1}^{m} |y_i| \ . \tag{8}$$

Crossover is a process which exchange the gene of two matching individual at a specified probability $P_C$. In this paper the $P_C$ is:

$$P_C = \max\left( g_i^t, g_j^t \right) \big/ g_{\max}^t \tag{9}$$

where $g_i^t, g_j^t$ is the adaptation value of the two individual parent and $g_{\max}^t$ is the maximum adaptation value in the parent's population.

Then the overlapping of two parent $\left[[C_i][\delta_i]\right]^t$ and $\left[[C_j][\delta_j]\right]^t$ is:

$$\left[[C_i][\delta_i]\right]^{t+1} = P_C \left[[C_j][\delta_j]\right]^t + (1 - P_C)\left[[C_i][\delta_i]\right]^t$$
$$\left[[C_j][\delta_j]\right]^{t+1} = P_C \left[[C_i][\delta_i]\right]^t + (1 - P_C)\left[[C_j][\delta_j]\right]^t \tag{10}$$

Since the $P_C$ is determine by the high adaptive value of the two parent, the individual who has higher adaptive value can keep more information about itself and pass it to the next generation.

Mutation is a process which changes some genes of an individual randomly at a specified probability $P_M$. In this paper, the $P_M$ is defined as:

$$P_M \begin{cases} 0.8 \times \left( g_a^t - g_i^t \right) \big/ g_a^t & g_i^t \le g_a^t \\ 0.2 \times \left( g_{\max}^t - g_i^t \right) \big/ g_{\max}^t & others \end{cases} \tag{11}$$

where $g_a^t$ is the average adaptation value of the parent's population. The $P_M$ is higher when the individual has lower adaptive value. It makes the individual more stable than the individual who has a lower adaptive value. It also give a larger chance to make the individual who has a lower adaptive value become better, or in other hands, make them be eliminated more faster.

# 4    Dairy Cattle Movement Detecting Using SVM and GA

The movement of dairy cattle is diversity and complicated, that has many kinds of action states, such as includes walking, canter, sprint, and so on. The dairy cattle movement detecting system is detecting action state of the cattle at all times. Sensor must be installed on the target cattle for action recording. The actions of the target cattle are then converted to a series of sensor output. These sensor data are transmitted to the background station. A classifier running on background station classifies automatically these data in to different classes so the action states of that cattle can be recognized. The behavior of the cattle in a specific moment can be recorded as moving when the action state falls into either walking, canter or sprint class at that time.

## 4.1    Data Collection Model

The cattle's actions data collection model is built on the Wireless Sensor Network (WSN) technology. There are three kinds of network node in the data collection network: sensor node, repeat node and the sink node. A sensor node is installed on the right hand side of the cattle's neck (figure 1). It captures the outputs of the sensor mount on it and sends them to the sink node deployed near the cattle at a rate of 10Hz. The sink node transmits the sensor data to the background station where the classifier is running on though wire network such as Ethernet or RS485 field network. The repeat node acts as a range extender and is placed between the sensor node and the sink node. It receives the data from the sensor node and sends them to the sink node simultaneously.

The radio system of the network nodes is a combination of a Texas Instrument (TI)'s CC2500 single-chip wireless transceiver and a CC2591 wireless signal amplifier. The radio system is running on 2.4GHz wireless channel at 15dBm power level. The maximum communication range between sensor node and sink node can beup to 400 meters if a repeat node is placed between them. The wireless network protocol stack that the nodes are running on is a reduced version of TI's SimpliciTI WSN protocol. The maximum data rate of the network is 250Kbit/s and the maximum hops between the sensor node and sink node are 2 when a repeat node is deployed between them. Data from sensor node can only be transmitted to the repeat node or the sink node. Data hops between two sensor nodes of the same kind not allowed.

In this paper, the sensor used for cattle's action recording is Analog Deceive International (ADI)'s AXD330L 3-axis acceleration sensor. Its measurement range is ±3g and its sensitivity is 300mV/g. The sensor is mounted on the center of the sensor node' PCB. After the installation of sensor node, the positive direction of the sensor's X-axis is point to the tail of the cattle and the Z-axis is point to the neck of the cattle (figure 2).

**Fig. 1.** Installation of the Sensor node

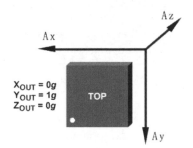

**Fig. 2.** The directions of the sensor's axes after installation

The central control unit of the network nodes is TI's ultra-low power MCU MSP430F169. The MCU keeps sampling the sensor's analog outputs of each axis and converts them digital results at intervals of 100ms. The mapping between the sensor's analog output and the MCU's digital result is:

$$N_{ADC} = 4095 \times \frac{V_{IN} - V_{R^-}}{V_{R^+} - V_{R^-}} \ . \tag{12}$$

Where $N_{ADC}$ is the MCU's digital output, $V_{IN}$ is the sensor's analog output, $V_{R^-}$ and $V_{R^+}$ are the reference voltages of the MCU. In MSP430F169, $V_{R^-}$ is 0Volt and $V_{R^+}$ is 2.5Volt.

### 4.2 Cattle's Behavior Classification

The cattle's behavior classification is performed by a binary SVM classifier running on the back ground station. After training and testing, the binary SVM classifies the sensor data received from the sink node into two classes: quiescence and movement using the decision function (7). In order to prevent the over fitting problem in the training process, a cross-validation procedure is performed. In the cross-validation procedure, the training set is divided into $n$ subsets of equal size. Sequentially one subset is tested using the classifier trained on the remaining $n-1$ subset. The parameters of the SVM in each subset training process are searched by the GA evolutionary process. These parameters include the SVM punishment parameter $C$ and the kernel width of the RBF kernel function $\delta$.

The data set used for the training process is the sensor data whose class labels are already know. The class labels of the data in the training set are marked up manually by examining the cattle's monitoring video. The features of the sensor data are $\left\{ax, ay, az, \sqrt{ax^2 + ay^2 + az^2}, \max, \min, \right\}$, where $ax, ay, az$ is the acceleration value for each of the three axes of the acceleration sensor. $\max$ is the maximum value of the three axes. $\min$ is the minimum value of the three axes.

The cross-validation procedure with the GA parameter searching process is achieved by VC++ program. The SVM training and classification process are achieved with the help of LIBSVM library version 3.0. The integrated process of the cattle's behavior classification is conducted as follows:

Step1: Divide the training set into $n$ subsets.

Step2: Select a subset of training data.

Step3: Generate an initial population of SVM parameter.

Step4: SVM is trained by the initial population of SVM parameter base on the remaining $n-1$ subsets.

Step5: Calculate the error and the adaptation value by (8).

Step6: $P_C$ and $P_M$ are calculated by (9) and (11). Inherit, crossover and mutate the parameters. The next generation population produces.

Step7: SVM is retrained by the new population of SVM parameter on the remaining subsets.

Step8: Repeat step5 to step7 until $m$ generations have been evolved.

Step9: SVM is test on the subset selected in step1. Calculate the classification error rate.

Step10: Step2 to step9 is repeated on another subset until all $n$ subset have been selected once.

Step11: Use the trained SVM of the lowest error rate test as the final SVM.

Step12: Use the final SVM to classify sensor data received from sink node.

The number of subsets $n$ is determined by the total number of the sensor data in the training set. Suppose the sample period of the sensor is $p$ and the number of the samples in a subset is $N$. The total sampling time $T$ of the subset is:

$$T = p \times N \qquad (13)$$

A larger value of $N$ will lead to better training accuracy but consume more time in the training process. The parameter $N$ should be chose carefully to keep the balance of the training time and the training accuracy.

## 4.3   Experiment

Experiments have been done on three individual dairy cattle. The number of data in the training set is 20480. They are divided into 10 subsets. The sampling period of the sensor node on each cattle is 100ms. In the training set, the movement class is label as 1 and the quiescence class is label as -1. The number of evolved generation is 500. Table 1 shows the training result of the three cattle.

**Table 1.** Training results of the three cattle

| No. | Movement samples | Quiescence samples | Best parameters $C, \delta$ | Best accuracy |
|-----|------------------|--------------------|-----------------------------|---------------|
| 1 | 15663 | 4817 | 0.55,0.27 | 97.5% |
| 2 | 9561 | 10919 | 0.47,0.34 | 96.8% |
| 3 | 7440 | 13040 | 0.56,0.31 | 98.1% |

After training, the classification SVM for each cattle is tested. 6 testing sets of different size are applied on each cattle and the accuracy is collected. The class labels of each data in the testing set are marked up manually by examining the monitoring video, just the same way as generating the training set. The number of the data in the test sets is selected randomly. The test results are show in table 2 to table 4.

**Table 2.** Test results of the cattle 1

| No. | Test data samples | Accuracy |
|-----|-------------------|----------|
| 1 | 33458 | 94.3% |
| 2 | 21757 | 94.1% |
| 3 | 22378 | 90.5% |
| 4 | 30145 | 91.0% |
| 5 | 20732 | 89.7% |
| 6 | 17681 | 93.2% |

**Table 3.** Test results of the cattle 2

| No. | Test data samples | Accuracy |
|-----|-------------------|----------|
| 1 | 11767 | 95.0% |
| 2 | 35233 | 83.1% |
| 3 | 14456 | 77.6% |
| 4 | 23788 | 92.3% |
| 5 | 33660 | 88.9% |
| 6 | 21100 | 97.7% |

**Table 4.** Test results of the cattle 3

| No. | Test data samples | Accuracy |
|-----|-------------------|----------|
| 1 | 14876 | 96.1% |
| 2 | 34332 | 96.4% |
| 3 | 32543 | 97.3% |
| 4 | 23266 | 92.2% |
| 5 | 17557 | 92.7% |
| 6 | 18684 | 94.5% |

The test results show that the accuracy of the classification is acceptable in most of the time. But there are some cases that the accuracy is rather low compared to other tests. For example, the accuracy of third test for cattle 3 is only 77.6%. One of the main reason is the network transmit error. Data packet lost makes some data in those tests become unavailable. Since all of the features of the unavailable data are zero, the classification SVM's output is fixed to -1. The action state of the cattle is fixed to quiescence when the sensor data is unavailable. Classification error occurs when the actual state of the cattle is movement but the sensor data is lost. The Quality of Service (QoS) of the network is important. The network stack still needs improvements to make the data transmit more reliable.

# 5 Conclusion

For better performance and higher accuracy, dairy cattle movement detecting technology base on 3-axis acceleration sensor information fusion is studied. The sensor data is collected through wireless sensor network. Binary classification SVM is used to build up the information fusion model. The Genetic Algorithm is used for SVM parameter searching in the crossover validation procedure. Test results show that the system has satisfactory accuracy and the quality of the data is a key external factor to improve the accuracy of the system.

# References

1. Paula, M., Mikko, J.: Cow behaviour pattern recognition using a three-dimensional accelerometer and support vector machines. J. Applied Animal Behaviour Science 119, 32–38 (2009)
2. Yoshioka, H., Ito, M., Tanimoto, Y.: Effectiveness of a Real-time Radiotelemetric Pedometer for Estrus Detection and Insemination in Japanese Black Cows. J. Journal of Reproduction and Development 56, 351–355 (2010)
3. Ungar, E., Schoenbaum, I., Henkin, Z.: Inference of the Activity Timeline of Cattle Foraging on a Mediterranean Woodland Using GPS and Pedometry. J. Sensors 11, 362–383 (2011)
4. van Eerdenburg, F.J.C.M.: The pedometer, an automated aid in the detection of estrous. J. Veterinary Quarterly 30, 49–57 (2008)
5. Cristianini, N., Shawe-Taylor, J.: Methodology of support vector machine. Machine press, Beijing (2005)
6. Hairong, W., Dongmei, L., Yun, W., Weiguo, Y.: Fire Detecting Technology of Information Fusion using Support Vector Machines. In: 2010 International Conference on Artificial Intelligence and Computational Intelligence, pp. 194–198 (2010)
7. Liu, X.W., Wang, H.: Multiclass Support Vector Machines Theory and Its Data Fusion Application in Network Security Situation Awareness. In: 3rd International Conference on Wireless Communications, Networking and Mobile Computing, ShangHai, pp. 6349–6352 (2007)

8. Zhao, M., Shi, Z.: Human Activity Recognition with User-Free Acceleration in the Sensor Networks. In: 2005 International Conference on Neural Networks and Brain, BeiJing, pp. 1212–1217 (2005)
9. Guraliuc, A.R., Serra, A.A., Nepa, P., Manara, G., Potorti, F.: Detection and classification of human arm movements for physical rehabilitation. In: 2010 Antennas and Propagation Society International Symposium, pp. 1–4 (2010)
10. Joohyun, H., Namjin, K., Eunjong, C., Taesoo, L.: Classification Technique of Human Motion Context based on Wireless Sensor Network. In: 27th IEEE Engineering in Medicine and Biology Annual Conference, ShangHai, pp. 5201–5202 (2005)

# How Network Reverse Engineering Differs from Software Reverse Engineering

Hui Zhou and Wencai Du

College of Information Science & Technology, Hainan University
Renmin Ave No.58, Haikou, China, 570228
h.zhou.china@gmail.com, wencai@hainu.edu.cn

**Abstract.** Software reverse engineering has undergone many milestones and stepped from research to industry quickly in recent ten years. By analogy, researchers have found that it is also possible to apply reverse engineering to computer networks. The goal of network reverse engineering is to annotate a living map of the networks, which exhibits node role, link connectivity, topology dynamics, and bandwidth usage. It is necessary, but also challenging, to employ reverse engineering to computer network. We present an comparatively analysis on the reverse engineering of both software and network from five fundamental perspectives: source, analysis, presentation, validation, and prediction. The comparison indicates that both software and network communities would benefit from the collaborative effort on reverse engineering.

**Keywords:** Network reverse engineering, software reverse engineering.

## 1 Introduction

Software reverse engineering is, in practice, one of the most important endeavors in software engineering. This stems from the fact that software systems are complex and often poorly specified and documented. As a result, software practitioners need to spend a substantial amount of time understanding the source code from a structural and behavioral perspective, before carrying out any maintenance task. In this context, most reverse engineering processes follow the same pattern: a program is analyzed through static or dynamic analysis and the collected low-level program information is transformed into a higher level, more abstract presentation. The presentation helps engineers better understand the rationale of the code and thus facilitate future refactoring.

From networking standpoint, reverse engineering is the process of analyzing a target network so as to identify the design of network and create presentations. Specifically, we take "design" to mean how its components, e.g. node, link and internal networks, are assembled and configured, as well as runtime properties including link available bandwidth, node congestion status, and end-to-end packet transmission delay.

It has become obviously necessary to employ reverse engineering to computer networks, and there have been a few experimental studies on this [1]. However,

P. Sénac, M. Ott, and A. Seneviratne (Eds.): ICWCA 2011, LNICST 72, pp. 33–43, 2012.

network reverse engineering is a challenging task. The key reason is that the design of the Internet can't provide explicit support for end nodes to obtain information about the network internals. A network typically consists of many small networks; such networks are under different administrative control, so there is no single place from which one can obtain a complete picture of the specified target network. Furthermore, the Internet is so heterogeneous that an approach found to be useful in a certain networks may not be effective elsewhere [2].

To reverse engineer the computer networks, we not only need to study network technology, but also need to understand software engineering. We argue that a collaborative effort of software and network domains would achieve significantly more than the isolated efforts of individuals. This paper tries to answer questions like "how does the reverse engineering of software and network differ?" and "can they benefit from each other?" To do so, we analyze both software reverse engineering and network reverse engineering from five basic perspectives: source, data analysis, presentation, validation, and prediction.

This paper is organized as follows. Section 2 first summarizes the recent progress on computer network reverse engineering. Section 3 analyzes the reverse engineering techniques of both software and networking, and then Section 4 concludes the paper with a short discusses.

## 2   Related Works

The field of software reverse engineering and its closely related fields, such as program comprehension or software analysis, have undergone many successes over the past 20 years. In addition, software reverse engineering environment has been equipped with various intelligent tools: extractors, analyzers, and repositories [3]. During the same time, along another thread, network community has introduced quite a few measurement systems to gathering and presenting the information of network properties [4]. The theories, protocols, techniques, tools, overlay framework, and the released data archives have initially make up the main body of network reverse engineering.

The reverse engineering of computer network mainly starts from measurement. Specifically, a router can be configured to passively record the information about its own performance, e.g. the number of packets received/sent by each of its network interface cards (NICs). A typical example is network traffic monitoring. Fig. 1 illustrates the bytes sent through the USENET bulletin board system, averaged over two-week intervals [5].

Furthermore, the measurement literature can further be classified according to different targets: node, link, topology, and packet pattern. Learning the role that a node plays is the first step to understand the network. Basically, each node has one of the following roles: client host; access router that aggregates the traffic from clients; and backbone router that transmits a large volume of traffic. The role problem has been frequently addressed, e.g. Rocketfuel [6] uses IP prefixes, DNS information, and topological ordering to identify role. In addition, many tools search for the bottleneck node with diverse heuristics [7].

Besides node, link is another important component. Generally, a link is the IP connection between two nodes that are only one IP-hop away from each other. Much research has been done to capture the usability, delay, and bandwidth capacity of a single link. Recently, the research community extends the study of link to end-to-end path, which can be regarded as a line of connected links. Measuring the properties of a path is very meaningful since it enables us to better understand how packets flow between nodes. For example, variation in the transmission delay of path is both a problem for time-critical traffic and a key indication of network congestion. Typically, tools use Internet control message protocol (ICMP) [8] timestamps to estimate the delay variation.

Finally, topology auto-discovery has strongly driven the study of active probing measurement. Network community has examined five categories of topologies: the graphs of connections between autonomous systems (ASs) [6], the point-of-presence (POP) topologies that interpret the structure of backbone using geography information, the IP-level topologies whose nodes are IP addresses and whose links are connections between the IP addresses, the router-level topologies that resolve IP aliases and group the IP addresses in the unit of router, and the connectivity of physical components, including routers, switches, and bridges. In particular, the router-level topology has attracted more interest than the others because it establishes the basis of AS and POP topologies, gives a more operational picture than the IP topology. As an example, Fig. 2 gives the result of a topology discovery work; the target network is Abilene backbone, i.e. an educational IPv6 network in America [9].

## 3  Comparative Analysis

We comparatively analyzed the reverse engineering of software and network from five basic perspectives: source, data analysis, presentation, validation, and prediction. The following analysis isn't exhaustive since we can't cover every aspect, but it offers a skeletal picture on the differences of software reverse engineering and network reverse engineering, and highlights the challenges faced by the network community.

### 3.1  Source

The source of software reverse engineering is code and code-related files such as log. Generally, software reverse engineering depends on performing some analysis of the source code in order to produce one or more models of the system under analysis. Generally, source code is written by software engineers according to the well-designed specification of programming languages, e.g. ASM, Pascal, C/C++, and Java. A language often comes with a specification, to which compiler developer and software engineer must conform. Furthermore, the coding process is supported by various integrated development environments. As a result, no matter how well (or bad) the code is organized, software reverse engineering tools is built on a solid basis, i.e. the tools do understand the exact meaning of each line of code.

USENET Traffic Volume

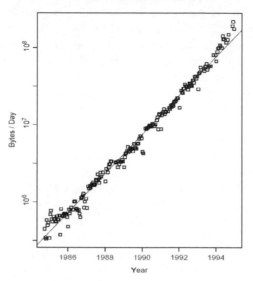

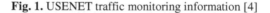

**Fig. 1.** USENET traffic monitoring information [4]

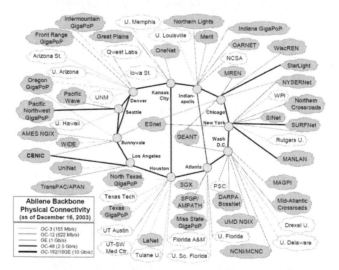

**Fig. 2.** The discovered topology of Abilene backbone [9]

Unlike the source of software reverse engineering, the one of network reverse engineering mainly comes from measurement, and it is highly volatile. The volatility can be perceived in almost every parameter that we attempt to measure. For example, the round-trip time (RTT) of a pair of nodes is an important metric of network performance. Generally, RTT can be used as an indicator of end-to-end transmission quality. Here we attempt to measure the RTT of a short path, i.e. two directly connected computers $C_1$ and $C_2$. First, $C_1$ sends an ICMP echo-request packet to $C_2$. When $C_2$ receives the packet, it immediately sends an ICMP echo-reply packet back to $C_1$. In each active probe, the time from sending out an ICMP echo-request to receiving the corresponding echo-reply is regarded as a candidate of RTT. As shown in Fig. 3, the RTT is ever-changing with network traffic and time.

## 3.2 Data Analysis

To analyze the source code, a software reverse engineering tool will first scan the source code. In most cases, reverse engineering tool assumes that the target source files won't undergo any change during the scan, which is done once and for all. In a very limited time interval, the source of software is safe to be regarded as static, while network is always a moving target. As a result, network tools must continuously collect the information about the designated network, in a never-ending style.

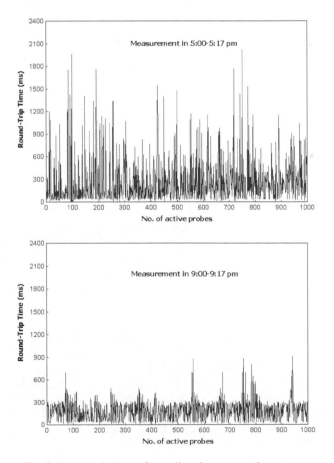

**Fig. 3.** Round-trip time of two directly connected computers

Moreover, as to network reverse engineering, analyzing the data source is challenging since it generally contains too much noises. But the analysis is valuable since it often provide insight into the network. For example, Faloutsos et al. discover some surprisingly simple power-laws of the network topologies [10]. These power-laws hold for three topologies between November 1997 and December 1998, despite a 45% growth of its size during that period. As shown in Fig. 4, log-log plot of the out-degree $d_v$ versus the rank $r_v$ in the sequence of decreasing out-degree.

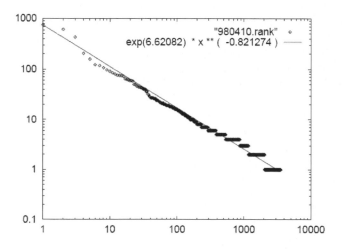

**Fig. 4.** The rank plots on dataset Intel-98 [10]

### 3.3 Presentation

After analyzing the source, software reverse engineering tools generally use UML diagrams to visualize the result. Historically, a rich set of diagrams have been introduced by the software research community, and then been applied by the industry. The diagrams, especially the class, activity and sequence diagrams, do provide an abstract and easy-to-understand picture of design, and lead to the prosperity of software modeling.

Software reverse engineering presentation tools support two significant features: design-code linkage and reuse. Specifically, in some reverse engineering tools, source code can be modified by changing the UML diagrams in the presentation. In this way, not only the code can be reorganized, but also some coding functions can be generated by changing the presentation. Besides design-code linkage, the presentation outputted by one tool generally can be reused by many others. For example, the UML diagrams of Java code from Eclipse plug-in can easily be loaded into Rational Rose since the presentations of both systems are UML-compatible.

Suppose that the presentation of software reverse engineering is a snapshot, the one of network reverse engineering can be regarded as a video. The parameters of target network can undergo changes as time passes, and thus lead to high dynamics. As shown in Fig. 5, the IP conversations of LAN captured by Sniffer Pro, which is a network packet sniffing tool installed in one node [11]. Since the target network is ever-changing, the presentation must trace the changes and output pictures that match.

Compared with software reverse engineering, the network reverse engineering tools can't support large-scale reuse since there isn't a universal accepted presentation standard. It is also hard to establish such a standard because each reverse engineering tool is built to study a specific question and work in a specific network environment.

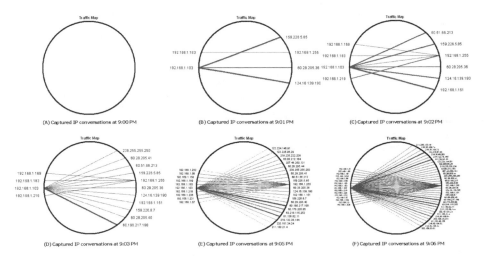

**Fig. 5.** IP conversations captured by Sniffer Pro in 9:00 – 9:06 PM

## 3.4 Validation

Usually, every reverse engineering tool needs to validate the correction of its result. Validation is necessary since it enables us to make sure that the data analysis and presentation is correct. However, validating the result of network reverse engineering is a challenging task. Almost all network reverse engineering tools use measurement, instead of the exact value, as data source to perform analysis and presentation. Thus, different reverse engineering algorithms and tools may obtain different result even if the target is the same. A step further, the key problem becomes: does the measurement exactly match the real network situation?

Now suppose that we are validating the available bandwidth of a path, which is defined as the minimum link available-bandwidth of all links along the path [7]. Therefore, the validation requires the information of all link available-bandwidth of target paths. But if the path crosses multiple administrative areas, or it is long enough (e.g. consist of more than six links), it becomes hard to obtain all link available-bandwidth at a specific time [1].

To validate the available bandwidth of a path, researchers have introduced many inspiring techniques. It seems that comparing the estimation result with closely estimated bulk TCP throughput over the same path is a good idea [12]. However, available-bandwidth and bulk TCP throughput are indeed different. The former gives the total spare capacity in the path, independent of which transport protocol attempts to capture it. While the latter depends on TCP's congestion control. Fig. 6 typically shows the measurement result of the available bandwidth of an end-to-end path, which starts from Hainan University and ends at Chinese Academy of Sciences. In particular, Cprobe [13] and BNeck [7] are installed on hosts inside Hainan, Pathload [14] is installed in both end points, while TCP throughput is tested by maximized the parallel TCP connections of Iperf [15]. It is apparent that there isn't a curve that can exactly match the other. Furthermore, since this end-to-end path traverses the confidential networks of several ISPs, we can't even validate which curve matches the exact situation.

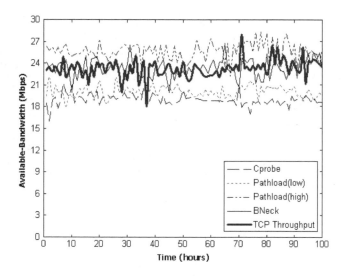

**Fig. 6.** Available-bandwidth measured by different tools

As a result, we are not able to completely validate end-to-end available bandwidth. Furthermore, it is very hard to make sure the data we collect reflects the exact network status, even if we have success experience on a limited number of networks. The same problem is faced by almost all measurement techniques that rely on active probing. And this thus makes the network reverse engineering more challenging than its software counterpart.

### 3.5  Prediction

Recently, there is a growing need of reverse engineering tools to support the prediction of changes in source. For example, through analyzing the history of the lines of code, managers can predict the code scale of a Java program in the next development iteration [3]. Surprisingly, though network contains much more noise than stationary software source code, many useful rules have been extracted, and used to predict the macro-behavior of networks.

**Diurnal Patterns of Activity:** It has been recognized for more than thirty years that network activity patterns follow daily patterns, with human-related activity beginning to rise around 8-9AM local time, peaking around 11AM, showing a lunch-related noontime dip, picking back up again around 1PM, peaking around 3-4PM, and then declining as the business day ends around 5PM. The pattern often shows activity in the early evening hours, rising around say 8PM and peaking at 10-11PM, diminishing sharply after midnight. Originally, this second rise in activity was presumably due to the "late night hacker" effect, in which users took advantage of better response times during periods of otherwise light load.

**Self-Similarity:** Longer-term correlations in the packet arrivals seen in aggregated Internet traffic are well described in terms of self-similar processes [16]. "Longer-term" here means, roughly, time scales from hundreds of milliseconds to tens of minutes. The traditional Poisson or Markovian modeling predicts that longer-term correlations should rapidly die out, and consequently that traffic observed on large time scales should appear quite smooth. Nevertheless, a wide body of empirical data argues strongly that these correlations remain non-negligible over a large range of time scales. While on longer time scales, non-stationary effects such as diurnal traffic load patterns (see previous item) become significant. On shorter time scales, effects due to the network transport protocols—which impart a great deal of structure on the timing of consecutive packets—appear to dominate traffic correlations [17].

**Heavy-Tailed Distributions:** When characterizing distributions associated with network activity, expect to find heavy tails. By a heavy tail, we mean a Pareto distribution with shape parameter a<2. These tails are surprising because for a<2 the Pareto distribution has infinite variance [17].

An important example is the application of best path selection. The availability of multiple paths between sources and receivers enabled by content distribution, multi-homing, and overlay or virtual networks suggests the need for the ability to select the "best" path for a particular data transfer. A common starting point for this problem is to define "best" in terms of the throughput that can be achieved over a particular path between two end hosts for a given sized TCP transfer [12].

# 4 Conclusions

*Can we reverse engineer the computer networks?* Network reverse engineering is the process of annotating a map of the designated network with properties such as: client populations, features and workloads; network ownership, capacity, connectivity, geography and routing policies; patterns of loss, congestion, failure and growth; and so forth. Naturally, the urgent need of exploring network internals gives birth to the network reverse engineering. The key challenge of network reverse engineering goes with the birth of Internet: the design of network doesn't provide explicit support for end nodes to gain the information of network internals. The measurement approach has led to many techniques, tools, and data, but it can't achieve the goal alone.

*Is the reverse engineering of software and network the same?* From a general perspective, the reverse engineering of both fields are the same in that it analyzes a subject system to (1) identify the system's components and their interrelationships and (2) create representations of the system in another form or a higher level of abstraction. Both software reverse engineering and network go through a roughly common process: reading source, carrying out analysis, creating presentation, validating result, predicting changes, and mining knowledge.

*Is the reverse engineering of software and network different?* Indeed, software reverse engineering and its network counterpart are not the same things. They come from different background, aiming at solving different problems, and have been supported by two lines of methods, techniques, tools, applications, and so forth. Specifically, their data sources come in two totally different forms, their analysis require different knowledge and techniques, their presentation are based on sharply different abstract models, their validation meets two domains of challenges, and finally their prediction and data mining focuses on different emphases.

*Can we benefit from the collaborative effort?* Both software and network fields have made an incredible number of contributions, and have learnt from each other at various points. For example, RichMap uses snapshot concept to optimize its models and fasten its presentation. Another example is that the patch dissemination system can also optimize its delivery strategies according to the traffic load measured by networking system [18]. We believe that both software and network communities can strongly benefit from the collaborative effort on reverse engineering computer networks, more than the hints illustrated by RichMap.

**Acknowledgment.** We gratefully acknowledge the financial support of the Project 211 supported coordinately by the State Planning Commission, Ministry of Education and Ministry of Finance, China.

# References

1. Zhou, H., Wang, Y.: RichMap: Combining the Techniques of Bandwidth Estimation and Topology Discovery. Journal of Internet Engineering 1(2), 102–113 (2008)
2. Zhou, H., Wang, Y., Wang, X., Huai, X.: Difficulties in Estimating Available-bandwidth. In: Proceedings of IEEE International Conference on Communications, pp. 704–709 (2006)
3. Kienle, H.: Building Reverse Engineering Tools with Components. Ph.D. Thesis, Department of Computer Science, University of Victoria, Canada, 325 p (2006)
4. Labovitz, C., et al.: Internet inter-domain traffic. In: Proc. ACM SIGCOMM (2010)
5. Thompson, K., Miller, G., Wilder, R.: Wide-area Internet Traffic Patterns and Characteristics. IEEE Network,10–23 (1997)
6. Spring, N., Mahajan, R., Wetherall, D., Anderson, T.: Measuring ISP Topologies with Rocketfuel. IEEE/ACM Trans. Networking 12(1), 2–16 (2004)
7. Zhou, H., Wang, Q., Wang, Y.: Measuring Internet Bottlenecks: Location, Capacity, and Available Bandwidth. In: Proceedings of International Conference on Computer Network and Mobile Computing, pp. 1052–1062 (2005)
8. Postel, J.: Internet Control Message Protocol. IETF RFC 792 (September 1981)
9. Abilene Network, http://www.internet2.edu/abilene
10. Faloutsos, M., Faloutsos, P., Faloutsos, C.: On Power-law Relationships of the Internet Topology. In: Proceedings of ACM SIGCOMM, Cambridge, USA (1999)
11. Sniffer Pro., http://www.netscout.com/
12. He, Q., Dovrolis, C., Ammar, M.: On the Predictability of Large Transfer TCP Throughput. Computer Networks 51(14), 3959–3977 (2007)

13. Carter, R., Crovella, M.: Measuring Bottleneck Link Speed in Packet-switched Networks. Performance Evaluation 27(28), 297–318 (1996)
14. Jain, M., Dovrolis, C.: End-to-end Available Bandwidth: Measurement Methodology, Dynamics, and Relation with TCP Throughput. IEEE/ACM Trans. Networking 11(4), 537–549 (2003)
15. Tirumala, A., Qin, F., Dugan, J., Ferguson, J., Gibbs, K.: Iperf - The TCP/UDP Bandwidth Measurement Tool
16. http://dast.nlanr.net/Projects/Iperf/
17. Zhang, Y., Duffield, N., Paxson, V., Shenker, S.: On the Constancy of Internet Path Properties. In: Proceedings of ACM SIGCOMM conference on Internet measurement, pp. 197–211 (2001)
18. Paxson, V.: End-to-end Internet Packet Dynamics. In: Proceedings of ACM SIGCOMM (1997)
19. Gkantsidis, C., Karagiannis, T., Vojnovi, M.: Planet Scale Software Updates. ACM SIGCOMM Computer Communication Review 36(4), 423–434 (2006)

# High-Voltage Equipment Monitoring System Based on IOT

Ye Cai[*], Xiao-Qin Huang, and Jie He

College of Electrical and Information Engineering, Hunan University,
ChangSha, 410082 Hunan Province, China
Caiye1988427@126.com

**Abstract.** The key to achieve intelligent is to introduce frontal information communication technology and integrate high-voltage equipment monitoring with the information system . High-voltage equipment system based on Internet of Things (IOT), including radio frequency technology, wireless sensor network and WISP environment monitoring technology, makes high-voltage equipment system,computer system and the network work together. It can realize the immediate response,analysis and control of the high-voltage equipment. This paper will lauch the research from following parts. First, it brings up a structural frame of high-voltage monitoring system based on the concept of IOT and characteristics of the high voltage equipment monitoring. Then main functions and core technology of the frane are introduced. Finally, the author elaborates the research problems and challenges of high-voltage equipment monitoring based on IOT from the aspects of the pivotal parts of IOT、 simulation algorithms and security assessment.

**Keywords:** Internet of Things (IOT), radio frequency technology, WISP, high voltage equipment.

## 1 Introduction

There is a wide range of high voltage equipments which mainly includes transformers, various types of switchgear、 arrester, insulation casing, current transformers, voltage transformers and so on. We can measure the parameters which reflect their characteristics according to different structural principles of the above-mentioned equipments. At present, high-voltage equipment maintenance working in China is done under the requirements of "Preventive test code for electrical equipment"[1] with regular preventive tests. Preventive tests play a significant part on the detection and diagnostic of equipment defection in time. But with the longer downtime period, the traditional preventive tests and and maintenance mode are fell behind[1-12]. So, a new maintenance mode based on the real-time device status and its trends prediction is being taking into consideration. From the 1990s, PC online monitoring system taking digital waveform acquisition and processing as core technology appeared. With this

---

[*] Corresponding author.

P. Sénac, M. Ott, and A. Seneviratne (Eds.): ICWCA 2011, LNICST 72, pp. 44–57, 2012.

system, we use high-tech like advanced sensors and computers to get more online monitoring parameters' data. Literature [35-37] introduced the UV applications on temperature and insulation monitoring. By studying the graphs and the data in different fault condition, we can find the places where are easy to breakdown. And then we can provide basis for malfunction analysis and optimal control. Literature [38-42] proposed a new monitoring model, communication protocols and fault location algorithm based on network topology.

Rising voltage level requires higher standard of security and reliability. Online monitoring has to confront mass of information(Structural features、 performance parameters and operating conditions are different among equipments. And components in the same kind of equipment are also different. As a result, there may be different macro signals for the same fault type. And vise verse, the same macro signal may reflect different fault types), which arise the need for new communication technology, sensor technology, network technology and optimal control methods. Thus, the existing theories, models, methods and algorithm system of high-voltage equipment monitoring system need a further development. And the key point for further development is to introduce new technology of computing、 communication and sensing [2-5].

As a new interconnected system, IOT integrates computing systems, large-scale communication networks, extensive sensor networks and control systems, by which it can achieve real-time monitoring, simulation, analysis and optimal control of large-scale physical system [10-20]. Internet of Things can improve the level of informationization and the efficiency of infrastructure utilization. Through IOT, we can achieve a high degree of cognitive and intelligentized decision-making control on high-voltage equipment. First, quick location of high-voltage equipment fault in transfomer substation is implemented. Then the information of high-voltage equipment identification and its attribute as well as the surrounding environment is obtained by automatic identification、 collection and induction. All the information is aggregated into a unified information network through various kinds of information transmission technology. Utimately, analysis and fusion of the relevant data is conducted by using some intelligent computing technology such as cloud computing, image recognition, data mining and semantic analysis. IOT technology makes the communication among different objects a possible thing, which also realize the communication between different types of entity and virtual body [3-20]. So, IOT is to meet the requirements of monitoring r different equipment and different control volume with different approaches.

This paper puts forword the structural frame and main funtions of high-voltage equipment monitoring system based on IOT. It elabarates the application of IOT on high voltage equipment monitoring from two aspects—wireless sensors frequency technology and information processing & optimal control. Meanwhile, the new sensing devices, simulation algorithms and security as core technologies are new trend for high-voltage equipment monitoring system based on IOT.

# 2  High-Voltage Equipment Monitoring System Based on IOT

## 2.1  Monitoring System Architecture

Specifically speaking, Internet of Things is a new technology which interrelates all kinds of sensors and the existing Internet. In IOT, all items will be linked with the network by installing information sensing equipments like RFID, infrared sensors, GPS, Laser scanner, which will facilitate the identification and management of the items [12-18]. Therefore, high-voltage equipment monitoring system based on LOT consists of three parts: 1. Perception of some high voltage equipment, to achieve "objects" identification with RFID and sensor; 2. Data transmission, data are transmitted and calculated through the new communication networks which is made up of the existing Internet, radio and TV networks, communication network; 3. Application, that is, the control terminal responsive for the input and output of signals.

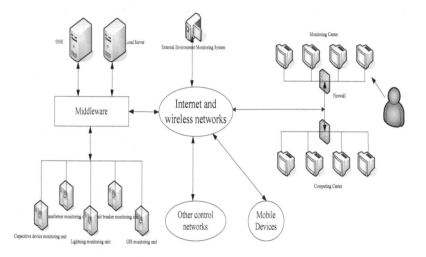

**Fig. 1.** architecture of high voltage equipment monitoring system based on IOT

High-voltage equipment monitoring system based on IOT should take the following characteristics into consideration:

1) The position of monitored equipment should be relatively fixed. The manifestation of macro-monitoring is different from communication.
2) There is a large number of wireless sensors and a large amount of information, what 's more, some sensors are in bad location. To ensure accurate communication among nodes, we need to consider problems with node topology, cluster and delay [5-8].
3) For external monitoring, we need to consider the location of equipment as well as the monitoring perspective to make sure we can clearly grasp external characteristics visually [33-36].
4) The monitored data can be divided into dynamic and static data. In order to achieve real-time monitoring and analysis with RFID, WISPS and wireless sensors, we need to consider power life and transmission distance.

## 2.2 System Function Analysis

1. Real-time monitoring and comprehensive simulation
As shown in Figure1, feedback information about the status of high-voltage equipment system is sent back to the monitoring center and computer center through wireless sensor networks and the wired network. With the acquired real-time information , the computer center constantly revises parameters so as to improve accuracy of simulation model. Then the simulation results conversely control the high-voltage equipment system via monitoring center. By this way, interaction and interoperability can be achieved. It seems that between the monitoring center and computer center we construct a virtual system co-existing with high-voltage equipment information collection. These two systems change synchronously and influence each other, which reflect the characteristics of actual condition of coexistence and interoperability of IOT [2-3].

2. Massive information Processing
High-voltage equipment monitoring system based on IOT can solve the problem of "funnel effect" [8] in system information(the larger monitoring scale and the more data traffic is, the more bottleneck pressure the "funnel" feels. This can cause a greater possibility of information blocking and congestion, which will seriously affect the safety of transformer substation. The functions of high-voltage equipment monitoring system based on IOT are shown in Figure2. In this system, data integration is divided into preliminary data processing, feature processing and fusion according to the characteristics of monitored objects. In Preliminary data processing, the collected data can stored with distributed or centralized control style selectively. In the process, real-time processing results can be transmitted to the monitoring center. It can also be made into backup data as history record future inquiries. In feature data processing, collected data with different characteristics are classified according to different requirements as well as various rules like data attributes, data packet length and data content. Useful information is targeted extracted and unwanted one is shielded through sorting and filtering. Fusion processing refers to data associating, transformation and encryption in monitoring [6-7] to ensure the security of transformer substation.

3. Adaptive and self-organization to external environment
With the rising voltage degree and increasing substation capacity, a lot of monitoring equipment access to the system, such as smart dust [5]. High-voltage equipment monitoring system based on IOT possesses the self-organization feature [10]of IOT. Any new device is connected to the system, the monitoring center can get all the information of the device and control the device at any time. Meanwhile, high voltage equipment monitoring system based on IOT possesses the adaptive function of IOT. Through the perception from sensors and electronic tags management, the system can grasp the dynamic environmental information and take corresponding measures. That is to say, according to the real-time environment information, the system can automatically remove all kinds of system failures (including the physical failure and information failure), guaranteeing the normal operation of system.

4. Mobile equipment and operator management
As is shown in Figure 2, any device accessed to high-voltage system may affect the security status of substation. With IOT, we can achieve tracking management on

mobile devices (operators) that is to be registered at any location through IOT before entering the high voltage system. With the development of perception technology and the popularity of electronic tags, we can know all the things we concerned. Each mobile equipment (maintenance personnel) is given a temporary ID. IOT can get detailed information of the device (basic properties, running state, the services to face) through the identification of the device ID. After mobile device (operator) entering the high voltage system, all information is back to the monitoring center through the wireless network. Once abnormalitis are discovered, monitoring center can remove connection between mobile equipment and network, cancel the given ID or take corresponding management . Mobile equipment(operator) can log-out through IOT in any place if permitted.

## 5. Scalability features

As a new generation of networks, IOT has better capacity to integrate different network elements. In high voltage equipment monitoring, when add or remove a monitoring device, we just need to follow the re-definition the generated object according to the IOT semantics or delete the object directory service. Object can get in touch with other devices or be removed easily.

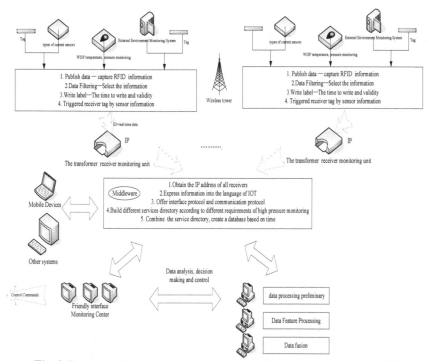

**Fig. 2.** Function of high voltage equipment monitoring system based on IOT

# 3   Key Technology

## 3.1   RFID Technology with Wireless Sensor

RFID, short for radio frequency identification,is often named as inductive electronic chips,proximity cards, non-contact card, electronic tags and electronic bar code, etc. The radio scanner transmits wireless electric wave energy in specific frequency to the receiver, driving the receiver circuit to send out its code which the scanner receives.

In IOT, RFID electronic tags store standard and interoperability-utilized information, which can be automatically collected into central information system through wireless communication network to achieve object identification. And through open computer networks for information exchange and sharing, we can achieve the "transparent" managemen of the objects.

1. RFID used in condition collection of high voltage equipment
In high-voltage equipment monitoring, each sensor is assigned a unique EPC (Electronic Product Code). This code is stored in the electronic tag attached to the wireless sensor. At the same time, the detailed information of the corresponding sensor is stored in the server of RFID information service system. Information and code collected through sensor is packed and flow to each link node along the communication path and eventually transmitted to receiving device of every monitoring unit. Through analysis of ONS(Object Naming Service),monitoring Center can acquire URI(Universal Resource Identifier) of information service system the very sensor belongs to. Put it in another way, it is to analyze the information carried by electronic tags, including the basic properties of the sensor (intrinsic information), location information (the location of the topology) and service information (the service directory for the next object) broken down. In this way, It can achieve automatic tracking of the status and quick positioning of device failure.

2. Wireless sensor
Wireless sensor network (WSN) is an comprehensive intelligent information system, which can collect, transmit and process information in one set. WSN possesses characteristics of low cost, low power consumption, low data rate and self-organizing network. WSN is a task-oriented wireless personal LA network consisting of a large number of distributed intelligent sensors nodes. It combines technologies in various fields, such as micro-motor technology, data acquisition technology, embedded computer technology, modern network and wireless communication technology, distributed information processing technology, the node energy-saving technology [15].

The deployment of wireless sensor based on high-voltage equipment monitoring should be closely related to its application. It involves network structure design, node selection and settings,etc. Researches on deployment strategies mainly focus on regional coverage and network connection problems. Figure 3 below is a typical WSN deployment which is frequently quoted[8]. Sensor nodes are arranged in the target area according to some strategic planning. And then all nodes are building the network in the form of self-organization. Each node has the same function, concluding information collection, RFID communication, routing from software and data processing. Each sensor node sends the useful information after preliminary processing and fusion. WSN data transmission is achieved by connecting the outside world with WSN through the Sink nodes. Information collected by nodes converge on Sink Nodes in multi-hop way. Then tne information is transmitted to the external world(the reader of the system).

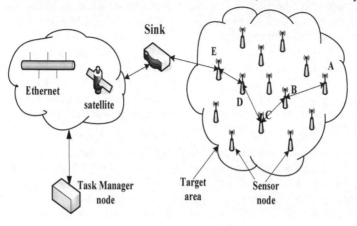

**Fig. 3.** a typical deployment of wireless sensor networks

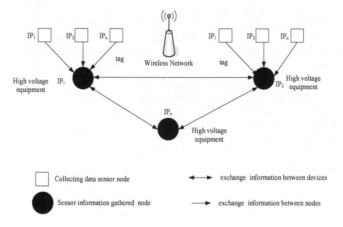

**Fig. 4.** The function of RFID with wireless sensor technology

## 3. Middleware

Middleware is to link the virtual network with the physical world。 It in essence is a software layer integrating different services and simplifying them. Therefore, it is the basis of IOT application. In the high-voltage equipment monitoring system based on IOT, all the data get in touch with monitoring center, computer center and other systems through the middleware in network to achieve commucation among "things". Information in middleware is processed in three layers: 1. Information abstract. Each monitoring unit is given a receiver IP, at the same time, through communication protocol, the gathered information are represented in the middleware language so as to communicate with the virtual world. Therefore, the redundancy of IP addresses and semantic standards are the difficult problems in IOT development. 2. Information management. Based on the computational simulation requirements, information management directory is made chronologically in the primary and secondary order according to specific rules. 3. Portfolio service. According to different requirements and the information management directory, we define a particular logical combination by specific semantics [39] and create a real-time database. In this layer, any complex process can be presented with a simple act. It is crucial for optimal control based on IOT.

4. WISP(wireless identification and sensing platforms)

WISP(Wireless Identification and Sensing Platform) bears the capabilities of RFID tags, supporting remote sensing and computing. Like any passive RFID tag, WISP is powered and read by a standard off-the-shelf RFID reader, harvesting the power it uses from the reader's emitted radio signals. WISPs have been used to sense quantities such as light, temperature, acceleration, strain and liquid level. Most of the work on WISP so far has involved single WISPs performing sensing or computing functions. We think the next phase of WISP work will involve the interaction of many WISPs based on LOT, and thus allow an exciting exploration of a new battery-free form of wireless sensor networking.

WISPs are powered by harvested energy from off-the-shelf UHF RFID readers. A WISP is just a normal EPC tag,but inside the WISP, the harvested energy is operating a 16-bit general purpose microcontroller[10-11]. The microcontroller can perform a variety of computing tasks, including sampling sensors, and reporting that sensor data back to the RFID reader. WISPs can write to flash and perform cryptographic computations. Furthermore, WISPs have these features: up to 10 feet range with harvested RF power, Ultra-low power microcontroller and Real-time clock.

WISP combined the advantages of wireless sensors and RFID. It can make the RFID static tags processing to dynamic data processing, connecting real-time data with electronic tags. The block diagram of the WISP platform just as Figure5[26-28].In this way, it can reduce the use of monitoring equipments and equipment investment. Therefore, using WISP widely in the future is the trend of combining wireless sensor technology and RFID technology.

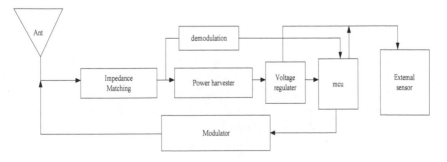

**Fig. 5.** block diagram of the WISP platform

## 3.2   Information Processing and Optimal Control

High-voltage equipment monitoring center is based on the technology of computer, communication, networks. Operators in monitoring center can get information of device operating conditions and parameters through the computer interface and achiece monitoring and controlling of high voltage equipments. With the application of IOT, high-voltage equipment monitoring system can achieve optimal coordination and remote control on "the distribution and concentration" of IOT.

High-voltage equipment monitoring system based on IOT will enhance ability to control the high-voltage system. Computer center process all the data from the whole region. The large variety and amount of data calls for high demanding of real-time analysis and simulation. So the computer center must have a high capacity of computing simulation. As a result, the large-scale distributed computing framework based on cloud computing is introduce to build a computing platform [18]. We need to build all the resources of high-voltage equipment monitoring into a huge resource library. Based on the requirements of simulation, cloud computing take real-time data、 images and temperature needed from the resource pool. It also matches the requirement of combining centralized control and decentralized control in IOT [3].

Based on IOT, high voltage equipment data simulations need a large number of experimental studies and field tests. By analyzing which parts of various types of equipment are easily to fall abnormal or adverse phenomenon as well as the mechanism of its occurrence, we obtain a large number of typical patterns, samples and data model. Then develop a corresponding database and corresponding evaluation rules. With the information aggregation technology of IOT, the mass of information can be processed, transmitted and integrated when it is transmitted [19]. We need to analyze and process the high-voltage equipment information from its the nature features. All the collected information high-voltage equipment includes large number of discrete redundancy data. Through the primary processing, feature processing and fusion, and compared to the corresponding evaluation rules, no concrete data and images but only the simple results are sent to monitoring center if the equipment is normal. otherwise, analysis results and alarm signal are displayed, and at the same time, detailed data and images will be sent to the monitoring center. Computer center record the change of important information with time scale information, which provides evidence for high-voltage equipment failure analysis. When abnomalites occurs, mass of information is generated ,recording data and images in chronological order. Then we conduct failure analysis according to specific algorithms to investigate causes and eliminate potential danger.

Electrical signals of high-voltage equipment can be acquired through various types of sensors and WISP environmental monitoring. Some operating status which are very difficult to detect by electrical signals, such as oil spill in transformer, crack of high voltage bushing, fire and theft,etc. we can use other technology, such as camera, infrared, ultraviolet, to achieve monitoring of these external circumstances[25-26].

Table 1. principal monitoring of high-voltage equipment

| Equipment | principal monitoring |
|-----------|---------------------|
| Transformer | Dissolved gas  partial discharge  Core ground current  Pipe insulation |
| | Vibration spectrum |
| Capacitive Equipment | insulation Capacitive current  value of capacitance  $\tan \delta$ |
| Lightning rod | Full current  Resistive current  Capacitive current  Leakage current |
| | Action times |
| Breaker | Gas density of $SF_6$  Partial discharge monitoring  circuit breakers feature |
| GIS | Gas density of $SF_6$  Partial discharge monitoring  circuit breakers feature |

## 4  Main Research Difficulties and Challenges

Based on IOT, developing a high-voltage equipment monitoring system is a new study. There are large number of problems both on theories of IOT and monitoring technology.

Challenges can be summarized as follows:
1. RFID tag management for high-voltage equipment monitoring
RFID technology is the backbone of IOT, which is used radio waves to identify objects. Combine the RFID technology with new two-dimensional code and other software technologies, just like WISPs, RFID can track and analyze data automatically. And it can widely used in high voltage equipment monitoring. RFID is an advanced non-contact automatic identification technology. It is transparent through the two-dimensional codes. It is urgent to establish a standard to develop RFID technology with the increased requires. EPC system is the most typical solution in the world now[32-33].But it is not completing. Hence, we need a scalable standard specification and protocol to regulate the standards of coding tag and the corresponding identification technology

We can use completely wireless sensor network with the application of UHF radio frequency technology. Extending UHF RFID tag technology agreement to extend range of reader and the receiver. The purpose is to analyze real-time data tag while long-distance wireless transmission.

2. Wireless Sensor Networks Topology
Based on IOT, A typical feature of wireless sensor networks in high-voltage equipment monitoring system is coverage of a large area. Therefore, redundant nodes and complex communication links are problems. Due to the radio frequency interference, humidity, vibration, dust and dirt, wireless link will change. At the same time the changing of wireless sensor nodes lead to wireless connection failure. Some sensor nodes can not collect information or its misuse void, it will also affect the accuracy of electronic tags.

Second, energy of high side sensor node has a strict limit . The energy need to supply sensor nodes and the launch of electronic tags. Especially some sensor node in bad location. The agreement on self-organizing wireless network now(Ad Hoc wire-less networks) is difficult to adapt to the needs of sensor network technology based on IOT. Therefore, we need to be design a balanced and reliable data transmission protocol to accommodate the new features of wireless sensor networks

3. Simulation platform

High-voltage equipment monitoring system and control system constantly transfer data to the computer center while collecting huge data. Computer center needs to establish a dynamic real-time data model and information model. Computer center needs to recursive use and verify the correctness simulation model. And then continue to modify the simulation model and give the relationship between environmental change and simulation model. Take measures when environment model changes and get the risk of switching model. With assessment of switching model, the result provides the basis for dynamic adjustment of the model. Especially for the "smart dust", data acquisition network transfer a huge data, computer center requires a suitable algorithm for large-scale simulation. Ultimate goal are to enhance capacity of controlling high-voltage equipment and provide the theoretical basis of optimal control strategy for the monitoring center.

4. Security and reliability

As technology advances, RFID tag in high-voltage equipment monitoring holds detail information. When the wireless network is in a random attack or failure, information reliability is the issue to be examined. At the same time, LOT links high-voltage equipment monitoring system and network information systems. Therefore, information system security and safety of high-voltage monitoring system is not an isolated problem. Attacks on information systems may also lead to large-scale monitoring system failure, failure of information systems will lead to loss control of physical systems, which led to failure of the monitoring system.

# 5 Conclusion

High-voltage equipment monitoring based on IOT will promote the development of intelligence of transformer substations. Taking advantage of information aggregation technology of IOT to process massive terminal information that can be collected, sensed and identified, we can eliminate data redundancy and provide more accurate and comprehensive information through a series of key technologies such as data fusion. From the angle of IOT, this paper mainly describes modeling and failure analysis, equipment monitoring and equipment maintenance, network security and risk assessment, stand-alone computing and optimal control of distributed computing integration. This paper also discusses the still unsolved issues of high voltage equipment monitoring based on IOT from the aspects of the theoretical basis, the simulation algorithm, safety and reliability.

# References

1. National Grid 2008, 269 documents:"On the issuance of State Grid Corporation of equipment condition-based maintenance management (Trial)" And on the "standard advice to carry out condition-based maintenance work" \\ State Grid Corporation of equipment, maintenance rules and regulations and technical standards for the state assembly. China Electric Power Agency, Beijing (2008)
2. Zhao, J., Xue, Y., Li, X., Dong, C.: Cyber:Physical Power System: Implementation Techniques and Challenges. Automation of Electric Power Systems 34(16), 1289–1291 (2010)
3. Atzori, L., Iera, A., Morabito, G.: The Internet of Things: A survey. Computer Networks 54(15), 2787–2805 (2010)
4. Cantoni, V., Lombardi, L., Lombardi, P.: Future scenarios of parallel computing: Distributed sensor networks. Journal of Visual Languages & Computing 18(5), 484–491 (2007)
5. Jabeur, N., McCarthy, J.D., Xing, X., Graniero, P.A.: A knowledge-oriented meta-framework for integrating sensor network infrastructures. Computers & Geosciences 35, 809–819 (2009)
6. Bakken, D.E., Hauser, C.H., Bose, A.: GridStat:A Flexible QoS-Managed Data Dissemination Framework for the Power Grid. IEEE transations on power delivery 24(1), 136–143 (2009)
7. Broll, G., Rukzio, E., Paolucci, M., Wagner, M., Schmidt, A., Hussmann, H.: Perci: Pervasive Service Interaction with the Internet of Things. Internet Conputing 13(5), 74–81 (2009)
8. Luo, J., Chen, Y., Tang, K., Luo, J.: Remote Monitoring Information System and Its Applications Based on the Internet of Things. Internet Computing 13(6), 74–81 (2009)
9. Smart Home Mobile RFID-based Internet-Of-Things Systems and Services: Advanced Computer Theory and Engineering 20, 116—120 (2008)
10. Ngai, E., Riggins, F.: RFID: Technology, applications, and impact on business operations. Production Economics 112, 507–509 (2008)
11. Wanga, B., Tanga, H., Guoa, C.: Entropy optimization of scale-free networks' robustness to random failures. Physica A 363, 591–596 (2006)
12. Darianian, M., Michael, M.P.: Smart Home Mobile RFID-based Internet-Of-Things Systems and Services. In: International Conference on Advanced Computer Theory and Engineering (2008)
13. Darianian, M., Michael, M.P.: A Low Power Pervasive RFID Identification System for Medication Safety in Hospital or Home Tele-Care. Wireless Pervasive Computing 7, 143–146 (2008)
14. Kortuem, G., Kawsar, F., Fitton, D.: Smart Objects as Building Blocks for the Internet of Things. Internet Computing 14, 44–51 (2010)
15. Akyildiz, I.F., Weilian, S., Sankarasubramaniam, Y., et al.: A Survey on Sensor Networks. IEEE Communications Magazine 40(8), 102–105 (2002)
16. Hydra Middleware Project, FP6 European Project,
    http://www.hydramiddleware.eu
17. Welbourne, E., Battle, L., Cole, G.: Building.:the Internet of Things Using RFID. Internet Computing 13(3), 48–55 (2009)

18. Schmidt, L., Mitton, N., Simplot-Ryl, D.: Towards Unified Tag Data Translation for the Internet of Things. In: 1st International Conference on Wireless Communication, Vehicular Technology, Information Theory and Aerospace & Electronic Systems Technology, 2009. Wireless VITAE 2009, pp. 332–335 (2009)
19. Spiess, P., Karnouskos, S.: SOA-based Integration of the Internet of Things in Enterprise Services. In: IEEE International Conference on Web Services, pp. 968–975 (2009)
20. Alanson, P.: A Capacitive Touch Interface for Passive RFID Tags. In: 2009 IEEE International Conference on RFID, pp. 103–109 (2009)
21. Riekki, J., Salminen, T., Alakarppa, I.: Requesting Pervasive Services by Touching RFID Tags. Pervasive Computing 5(1), 40–46 (2006)
22. Qing, X., Chen, Z.N.: Proximity Effects of Metallic Environments on High Frequency RFID Reader Antenna: Study and Applications. IEEE Transactions on Antennas and Propagation 55(11), 3105–3111 (2007)
23. Sample, A.P., Yeager, D.J., Powledge, P.S., Mamishev, A.V., Smith, J.R.: Design of an RFID Based Battery Free Programmable Sensing Platform. IEEE Transactions on Instrumentation and Measurement 57(11), 2608–2615 (2008)
24. http://seattle.intel-research.net/wisp/
25. Floerkemeier, C., Roduner, C., Lampe, M.: RFID application development with the Accada middleware platform. IEEE System Journal 2, 82–94 (2007)
26. Smith, J.R., Sample, A., Powledge, P., Mamishev, A., Roy, S.: A wirelessly powered platform for sensing and computation. In: Proceedings of Ubicomp 8th International Conference on Ubiquitous Computing, Orange Country,USA, pp. 495–506 (2006)
27. Sample, A., Smith, J.R.: Experimental Results with two Wireless Power Transfer Systems. In: Radio and Wireless Symposium, Jap, pp. 16–18 (2009)
28. Shin, D.-B., Choi, G.-Y., Kim, D.-Y.: Design and Implementation of Wireless Sensing Platform based on UHF RFID Technology. In: Digest of Technical Papers International Conference, Jap, pp. 297–298 (2010)
29. Yeager, D.J., Sample, A.P., Smith, J.R.: WISP: A Passively Powered UHF RFID Tag with Sensing and Computation. In: Ahson, S.A., Ilyas, M. (eds.) RFID Handbook: Applications, Technology, Security, and Privacy, pp. 261–278. CRC Press, Boca Raton
30. Sample, A.P., Yeager, D.J., Powledge, P.S., Mamishev, A.V., Smith, J.R.: Design of an RFID-Based Battery-Free Programmable Sensing Platform. IEEE Transactions on Instrumentation and Measurement 57(11), 2608–2615 (2008)
31. Lin, F.: High Voltage Engineering. China Electric Power Press, Beijing (2006)
32. Sekine, C., Jiang, Y., Xu, X.: Analysis on the Error of On-line Monitoring of HV Apparatus Insulation in Substation and Processing Method. High Voltage Engineering (2), 34–37 (2003)
33. Zhu, S.L., Zhang, J., Wu, G.W.: Substation computer monitoring system and application. China Electric Power Press, Beijing (2008)
34. Xiaowei, L., Xu, Y., Fengyuan, R.: Wireless sensor network technology. Beijing Institute of Technology Press, Beijing (2007)
35. Shanghai Municipal Electric Power Company. Power equipment and application of infrared detection and diagnosis of map specification. China Electric Power Press, Beijing (2009)
36. Li, N., Chen, X., Wu, F., Li, X.: Study of Information Aggregation Technology on the Internet of Things for Smart Grid. ICT 2, 21–28 (2010)
37. Shi, B., Shi, Y.: Analysis of the Principles on On-Line Monitoring andDiagnostic Systems for HV Apparatus. High voltage engineering 31(6), 24–28 (2005)
38. Chen, Y., Cheng, P.o., Jiang-bo: A Real-time Monitoring System of Inmates in Prisons Based on RFID and WSN. Microcomputer Information 26(7), 185–188 (2010)

39. Lv, L., Wang, W., Bu, T.R.: Design of Precision Agriculture Environment Monitoring System Based on Wireless Sensor Network. Compter systems and applications (8), 5–9 (2009)
40. Liu, W., Huang, X., Zhang, Y.: Design of Field Sampling Unit of an On-line Monitoring System of Dielectric Loss in Capacitive High-voltage Apparatus. Computer Measurement & Control 18(1), 233–238 (2010)
41. Mu, J.-g., Chen, X.-x.: Study and application of online temperature wireless monitor system used in transformer substation at Laigang. Metallurgical Industry Automation 33(4), 53–58 (2009)
42. Ning, H.-s., Zhang, Y., Liu, F.-l.: Research on China Internet of Things' Services and Management. Acta Electronica Sinica 34(12), 2514–2518 (2006)
43. Zhao, S., Li, B., Cui, G., Yuan, J.: Remote state monitoring anddiagnosis of substation based on computer vision. Power System Technology 29(6), 63–67 (2005)
44. Wang, S., law, F.C., Li, Y.: Application of UV Imaging Method to Corona Discharge Detection in Substation. High Voltage Apparatus 46(2), 15–23 (2010)
45. Hu, Q.X., Cheng, Z.: The design of wireless sensor network platform positioning system based on ZigBee. Application of Electronic Technique. 25(7), 82285 (2007)
46. Fan, Y., Xu, J., Yang, D.: A high-performance multi-hop and synchronous time-division protocol for wireless sensor networks of equipment monitoring. Journal of University of Science and Technology Beijing 29(7), 750–755 (2007)
47. Yuan, S., Sheng, M.-s., Song, Z.-y.: Analysis and Improvement of Key Problems of HV Equipment On-Line Monitoring System in Substation. Transformer 42(8), 44–49 (2005)
48. Gan, Y., Zheng, F.E., Ji, X.: Research of RFID middleware key technology. Application of Electronic Technique 9, 130–132 (2007)
49. Yan, W., Tong, Z.-g., Liao, X.-l.: Research & application of novel real-time equipment monitoring method. Computer Integrated Manufacturing Systems 8, 1288–1293 (2006)
50. Wang, C.-L., Wang, K., Wang, L.-m.: Study on Corona Performance of Insulators Based on the UV Pulse Detecting Method. In: Proceeding of the CSEE, vol. 27(36), pp. 19–28 (2007)

# A New K-DOPs Collision Detection Algorithms Improved by GA*

Wei Zhao and Lei Li

XinCheng Street, Changchun City, Jilin Province, China 2888,
College of Information Technology, Jilin Agricultural University, 130118, China
prince1205@163.com,
521klqf@163.com

**Abstract.** In collision detection algorithm based on bounding volume hierarchies, the update cost of the bounding volume hierarchies tree when the collision detection object motion or deformation directly influenced speed of collision detection. According to this trait, the update of bounding volume hierarchies was optimized by utilizing temporal-spatial coherence in virtual environment, to reduce the cost when the collision detection object motion or deformation that coused the update of the bounding volume hierarchies tree by using the genetic algorithm instead of traditional approximate method and improve the speed of collision detection greatly. The emulation experimental of the collision between cars show that this algorithm can solve the complexity and improve the property of the collision detection algorithm effectively.

**Keywords:** collision detection, bounding box, K-DOPs, genetic algorithms(GA), virtual reality.

## 1 Introduction

The collision detection is the base of interaction between dynamic objects and static objects or dynamic objects and dynamic objects in virtual environment. Collision detection is such an important issue in the fields of computer animation, physical simulation, computer graphics, virtual reality, and so on. The fast and precise collision detection has a vital role in improving the authenticity and increase customer immersed sense of the virtual environment. And the virtual environment own

* **Foundation item:** Supported by the Key Projects in Scientific and Technological Development Program of Jilin Province (20100214); the science and technology development planning of Jilin Province(20100155, 20100149, 201101113, 201101114, 201101115); the National Science Foundation of Jilin Province (20101521, 201115188); the Doctor Programs Foundation of Jilin Agricultural University (201022).
**Brief introduction of author:** Wei Zhao (1967 - ), male, born in ChangChun City of Jilin Province, Postdoctoral, the member of CCF, the main research fields are data base system, virtual reality technique and so on; Lei Li(1987- ), male, born in Shuicheng City of Guizhou Province, Master(521klqf@163.com), the main research fields are virtual reality technique, data base system and image processing.

P. Sénac, M. Ott, and A. Seneviratne (Eds.): ICWCA 2011, LNICST 72, pp. 58–68, 2012.
© Institute for Computer Sciences, Social Informatics and Telecommunications Engineering 2012

complexity and real-time, that put forward higher request for collision detection. The key problem of the collision detection is that how to improve the real-time and accuracy whom are contradictory, need to consider the equilibrium relationship of them according to the need. Many experts and scholars come from home and abroad have already had a productive research and application for collision detection problem[1-2].

The frequently-used algorithm of the collision detection fields can be mainly divided into three categories: bounding box algorithm, distance algorithm and space subdivision algorithm[3].The bounding box algorithm is the most widely used, such as: AABB, spherical hierarchies, OBB, K-DOPs algorithm etc. The tightness of AABB is poor, but the overlap test is simple; The tightness of spherical hierarchies is worst, seldom use; The tightness of OBB is good, but the randomicity of OBB direction makes the overlap test complex; K-DOPs' tightness is better than AABB, and it's complexity of overlap test is less than OBB, so K-DOPs has already admittedly been the better collision detection method that had been widely used.

Yingmei Wei [comes from NUDT (National University of Defense Technology)] used the temporal-spatial coherence of the virtual environment object to accelerate collision detection on the basis of bounding box algorithm. She puts forward a kind of traverse tracking strategy: track the traverse process of the current object in other active object tree last time point, then make sure the traverse way of the active object current time. Optimized the K-DOPs tree using the temporal-spatial coherence of the virtual environment object, reduced the bounding box number greatly, thus improved the efficiency of collision detection effectively[4]. Later, a collision detection algorithm based on parallel is presented by Wei Zhao, Jilin Agricultural University, which mainly uses the partition strategies to build the balanceable bounding box tree, traverse the assignment tree comprises the bounding box tree, using the pipelining to accelerate the collision detection, and this algorithm can be in common used on both monoprocessor and multiprocessor[5]. In this paper, it can reduce the cost when the collision detection object motion or deformation that coused the update of the bounding volume hierarchies tree by using the genetic algorithm instead of traditional approximate method and improve the speed of collision detection greatly.

## 2    Rationale

### 2.1    Definition of K-DOPs

K-DOPs (Discrete Orientation Polytopes) bounding box is a kind of convex polyhedron, it's surface is composed of a set of half space Hi determined, these half space can so said: $H_i=\{x \in RmlnTix \leq b_i, n_i \in N, b_i \in R\}$, type: $n_i$ are the outer normal vectors of the half space, which are discrete, and they constitute the set N= $\{n_1, ..., n_k\}$ . In order to detect overlapping polyhedra into simple interval test, usually choose k/2 vector pairs , collinear and opposite in direction, as the element of set N, therefore, actually there are only k/2 direction in K-DOPs, thus it just need k/2 times interval test in 2 K-DOPs' detect overlapping[6]. Because of that these k/2 directions are settled and foreseeable, it's needless to save these directions when we should save a K-DOPs, only k numerical values should be saved, every numerical value corresponds to the position of one plane.

There are four K-DOPs (6-DOPs, 8-DOPs, 14-DOPs, 18-DOPs) of different direction vector listed in figure 1.

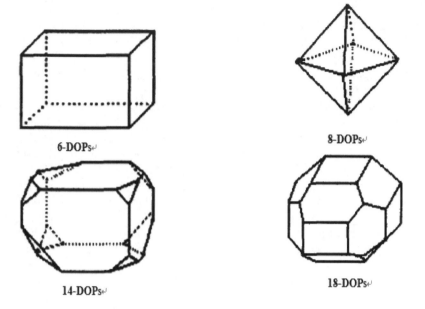

Fig. 1. K-DOPs of different direction vector

## 2.2   Intersection Test of K-DOPs Bounding Box

The intersection test of K-DOPs bounding box can be accomplished by overlap testing of the projections, we can determine the 2 K-DOPs bounding box are not intersectant if their projections in a certain direction of N are not overlapping; if all of the projections in any direction of N are overlapping, consider conservatively them are intersectant[7].

Presume that we had built two bounding box trees for objects A and B respectively. In the bounding box tree, the bounding box on every node correspond to a subset of the set which is comprised of the basal geometrical element of the object, the root node is the bounding box of the whole object[8]. Through traverse the two trees effectively in order to make sure whether some parts of object B collide with some parts of object A current location. This is process of double traverse. Algorithm let the root node of the object B's bounding box tree traverse object A's bounding box tree firstly, if reach a leaf node, then let this leaf node traverse object B's bounding box tree. If it can reach object B's leaf node, then do the intersection test of the basic geometrical element further. The basic idea is that use the bounding box of simple geometric characteristic symbols instead of the complicated geometry object to intersection test, if the bounding boxes of the two nodes are not intersect, the subsets of their basic geometrical element are not intersect, thus it has no use for intersection test to the elements of the subsets further.

The implementation algorithm of K-DOPs collision detection is under: (for example while K=2)

```
Void CollisionDetection(K-DOPs Tree)
{
  if (p_Root->angle< π /2)
    {
    return;
    }
  else
    {
    if (p_Root->p_FirstChild->angle> π /2)
    {CollisionDetection (p_Root->p_FirstChild)
    }
    if (p_Root->p_SecondChild->angle> π /2)
  {CollisionDetection (p_Root->p_SecondChild)
    }
    if(*p_Child1=Max(p_Root->p_FirstChild->angle,p_Root->p_SecondChild-
>angle)<=  π  /2&&*p_Child2=SecondMax(p_Root->p_FirstChild->angle,p_Root-
>p_SecondChild->angle)<= π /2)
    CollisionDetection(p_Child1,p_Child2);
    }
    }
```

## 2.3  Updating of K-DOPs Tree

Because of that the shape of deformable objects would vary continually in the simulation process, the creating bounding box tree quondam would be disabled after every simulation time step and it's need to update. There are two methods to complete the updating for the bounding box tree:

(1) Rebuilding. Rebuild bounding box tree on the basis of the new position of the basic geometric element, the combination condition of these elements would vary if we use the top-down generator function. The generative process is time-consuming especially when the model is meticulous, so the weakness of this method is obvious, the calculation burden is too hard to be fit for real time application and interactive application.
(2) Updating. Saving the element's combination condition of the current bounding box tree is just that update the bounding box which is contained in the all nodes of the tree, thereby update the total bounding box tree. The speed of this method is very fast but it also has a shortcoming: it would make the bounding box incompact and affect the efficiency of collision detection[9-11].

## 2.4  Genetic Algorithms(GA)

Genetic algorithm is presented by an American scholar Holland J H. The GA is a computation model that simulate the evolutionaryprocess of biological in nature. Its essence is parallel, it does not require derivation or other auxiliary knowledge, only need to determine the objective function of search direction and the fitness function of response, it emphasizes that transform probability to rule, but not determinate rules of conversion.

When solving problems by genetic algorithm, at first create a group of initial candidate solutions of the problem randomly, namely the initial population; Every individual in a population (each solution) should be transformed to binary code, such a binary code is called a chromosome; then calculate each individual's fitness, eliminate the individuals of smaller fitness. Then must inject the same numbers of population, what is copied the population of bigger fitness, to ensure the number of population is stable. In order to that the population should create new individuals to make the population evolve endlessly, two operators crossover operator and mutation operator are presented. Crossover operator imitates the hybridize theory of biology, interchange saome chars (gene) between two individual chromosomes, it's the main tool to create new individuals; Mutation operator is another method to create new individuals in GA, it's a complementation operation to the chars means that the mutation of certain gene in the chromosome, change 0 to 1,or 1 to 0. The GA is a searching method of reiterative iteration, it approaches optimal solution step by step through evolving repeatedlily, not equal to the optimal solution exactly, so it need to make sure termination conditions. For the termination conditions, some rule the evolution (iteration) times, the iteration should be stop when the iteration times was bigger than the specified value; another some estimate the optimal individuals, the iteration should be stop when the maximum fitness of the population should be invariable[12-14].

Genetic algorithm takes the methods of exchange, duplication, mutation and so on without calculating the derivate of function to get the global optimal solution of search. In a sense, it's a kind of black box problems which just considers the input and output of it that is suitable for dealing with all kinds of complicated problems. For its unique characteristic, the genetic algorithm has been widely used in every field.

## 3   Algorithm Analysis

In the complex virtual environment, objects are constantly moving, when objects were changing in space position, it need to make corresponding conversion for the object bounding box to real-time update K-DOPs tree. For rigid object speaking, it's movement is divided into two categories: translation and rotation. When the object translation moves and you do the same translation conversion for the bounding box, you will get the bounding box in a new position[15]. Occurred when the object rotation, the new position can't get through simple rotation transformation. If you recalculate the object bounding box ,it will spend a very long time. As for the K-DOPs tree of  the update, the traditional method is to use a kind of approximation method: calculate the bounding box of the object's when the object would rotated to get the current condition of K-DOPs object bounding box an approximate. Then the approximate form for the new K-DOPs bounding box tree, it need to use the current activity objects from the roots of a tree node to traverse other activities object tree. There would often be some repetitive traverse process that increase unnecessary spending to collision detection algorithm.

The Motion Paths of the kinetic object in virtual environment is consecutive: when one object collide with another object at a certain time point, they should still possibly collide at next time point, the point of colliding should be nearby the last[16]. According to the temporal-spatial coherence in virtual environment, this paper proposes that the GA is applied to update process of K-DOPs bounding box tree when the object would been athletic, it can reduce the cost when the collision detection object motion or deformation that coused the update of the bounding volume hierarchies tree, thus improve the speed of collision detection greatly. The specific solving process is as follows:

① Initialize the controls parameter of GA, such as: the scale of population N, the probability of mutation pm, the probability of crossover pc.
② Randomly engender the initial solution population p(t)={p0 p1 p2...pn}, the number of individuals is definite, every individual expressed as the gene coding of the chromosome.
③ Calculate the fitness of every individual in population. Search by utilizing the fitness of every individual. The solution is dependent on the fitness, the fitness larger means to the solution better.
④ Choose to copy the individual according to the fitness, the fitness larger means that the probability to copy should be larger.

The choosing process is a kind of select the superior and eliminate the inferior process that based on fitness, it means that select the superior and eliminate the inferior from the population on the basis of fitness, in order to make sure the group or intersectional individual and how many offspring should be copied from the individual had been chosen.

⑤ Do intersecting operation to the existing solution population to get new individual according to certain mutation probability and mutation method.
⑥ Do mutation operation to the intersected individual according to certain mutation probability and mutation method.
⑦ Get a new population by intersecting operation and mutation operation, end the evolutionaryprocess if it settles for the convergence prerequisite, else turn to step ③.

By using this algorithm, when the collision detection object motion or deformation result to update the K-DOPs bounding box tree, just need to traverse from the parent node of the current node in the active object tree, not must to traverse from the beginning of the root node just like the traditional approximate method. Such that we should avoid some repeating and same ergodic process, reduce the dispensable cost, and improve the speed of K-DOPs greatly.

## 4   Experimental Result and Performance Analysis

An emulational testing scene of the collision between two cars (figure 2、3 shows) is built to analyse the algorithm's performance and characteristic. The experiment uses a PC (Pentium(R)Dual-Core/CPU, E5300, 2.60GHz, 2.0GB), the operating system is Windows XP professional, the simulation program was developed using Microsoft Visual C++6.0 and OpenGL was used for 3D scene rendering and animation to simulates collision detection, self collision detection and collision response of cars. The simulation testing and verify that firstly the collision detection arithmetic improved in this paper is viable, secondly the real-time and the veracity of collision detection had been improved, in addition, the simulation realizes the interactivity in virtual environment preliminarily.

**Fig. 2.** The collision detection of cars  I

**Fig. 3.** The collision detection of cars  II

Figure 4 and figure 5 displayed the areal models of the cars front and back whether the collision happened by using anomalous polygons to indicate the plane projection of the two cars' model.

**Fig. 4.** The areal models of the cars before the collision happened

**Fig. 5.** The areal models of the cars after the collision happened

In order to test and verify the effect of the improved algorithm before, the cars' simulated-time of collision process had been contrasted in front and back of improved. The specific method n front and back of improved just as table 1 shows.

**Table 1.** The instruction for the methods in front and back of improved

|  | update policy of bounding box tree |
|---|---|
| the former algorithm | nearness algorithm |
| the improved algorithm | genetic algorithm |

Describe the complexity of the collision detection object in the number of geometric element (triangle facets), table 2 shows the average collision detection time of deal with one frame of patterning with the two methods of different complexity objects, for collision detection, self collision detection and collision response.

**Table 2.** The average collision detection time of deal with one frame of patterning

| Complexity (the number of triangle facets) | 1000 | 1400 | 1800 | 2200 | 3000 |
|---|---|---|---|---|---|
| The former algorithm | 15.823 | 18.572 | 19.341 | 20.457 | 21.690 |
| The improved algorithm | 15.535 | 18.164 | 18.761 | 19.896 | 20.974 |
| The percentum between the former algorithm and improved algorithm | 98.2% | 97.8% | 97.0% | 97.3% | 96.7% |

The two methods' change situation of average collision detection time ,with the complexity increasing in the emulational testing scene of the collision between cars, in front and back of improved algorithm, had been displayed in figure 4. Figure 5 had display that the contrast of the collision detection time between the algorithm was presented in this paper and the classic hill-climbing algorithm. The ascensional velocity of the algorithm was presented in this paper is slower, it means that the algorithm was presented in this paper, the improved K-DOPs collision detection algorithms based on genetic algorithms, has biggish increase, in the same complex scene.

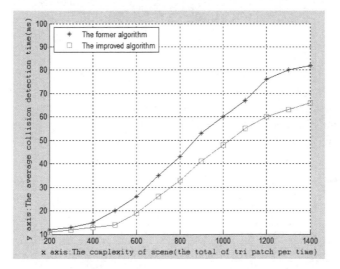

**Fig. 6.** the contrast of the collision detection time in front and back of improved algorithm. X axis: the complexity of scene (the total of tri patch per time); Y axis: the average collision detection time (ms).

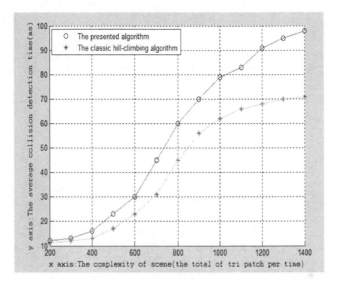

**Fig. 7.** the contrast between the algorithm that presented in this paper and the classic hill-climbing algorithm. X axis: the complexity of scene (the total of tri patch per time); Y axis: the average collision detection time (ms).

## 5  Peroration

The paper find illumination in the temporal-spatial coherence in virtual environment, using the genetic algorithm instead of traditional approximate method when the collision detection object motion or deformation that coused the update of the bounding volume hierarchies tree, thereby improve the speed of collision detection greatly. The experiment attests that this algorithm could handle arbitrary variform polyhedron efficaciously,  it should cut the collision detection time down by using the GA to update the bounding box tree, and it's suitable for dynamic, complex, interactive scene for real-time collision detection.

Of course, this algorithm still exist some disadvantages and await perfection further. The major future job is to improve the algorithm further aim at crossover rate and mutation rate, to get better balance between fast convergence and global optimum,  in order to settle the computational complexity problem of the collision detection and ameliorate the performance of the collision detection more effective in the virtual environment.

**Acknowledgement.** This paper supported by the Key Projects in Scientific and Technological Development Program of Jilin Province (20100214); the science and technology development planning of Jilin Province (20100155, 20100149, 201101113, 201101114, 201101115); the National Science Foundation of Jilin Province (20101521, 201115188); the Doctor Programs Foundation of Jilin Agricultural University (201022).

# References

[1] Wei, Y.-m., Wang, Y., Wei, Y.-m., Wang, Y., Wu, Q.-y., Shi, J.-y.: Research on Fixed Direction Hull Bounding Volume in Collision Detection. Journal of Software 12(7), 1056–1063 (2001)

[2] Ma, D.-w., Ye, W., Li, Y.: Survey of Box-based Algorithms for Collision Detection. Journal of System Simulation 18(4), 1058–1061 (2006)

[3] Shi, J.-y.: Virtual Reality Foundation and Applied Algorithm. Science Press, Beijing (2002)

[4] Wei, Y.-m.: Research on Collision Detection in Virtual Evironment. National University of Defense Technology, Changsha (2000)

[5] Zhao, W., He, Y.-s.: Rapid algorithm for parallel collision detection. Journal of Jilin University(Engineering and Technology Edition) 38(1), 152–157 (2008)

[6] Huang, H., et al.: Genetic algorithm principle, realization and their application research, prospect in mechanical engineering. Journal of Machine Design 17(3), 1–6 (2000)

[7] Li, W., Wang, Y., Hao, C.: Improved collision detection based on K-DOPs for cloth simulation system. Electronic Measurement Technology 30(8), 30–33 (2007)

[8] Liu, Z., Li, Z., Cao, B.: Collision Detection and Response of Dynamic Cloth Simulation in Virtual Environment. Journal of System Simulation 19(7), 1497–1499 (2007)

[9] Provot, X.: Collision and self-collision handling in cloth model dedicated to design garment. In: Proc. Of Graphic Interface 1997, Kelowna, Canada (1997)

[10] Li, K., Mannan, M.A., Xu, M., et al.: Electro-hydraulic proportional control of twin-cylinder hydraulic elevators. Control Engineering Practice (S0967-0661) 9, 367–373 (2001)

[11] Jiang, B.: A Mended Collision Detection Algorithm Based on k-DOPs. Journal of Yanshan University 32(4), 351–355 (2008)

[12] Zhao, W., Tan, R.-p., Li, Y.: Real Time Collision Detection Algorithm in Complex Virtual Environment. Journal of System Simulation 22(1), 125–129 (2010)

[13] Michalewicz, Z., Zhou, J.-j., He, X.-f.: Genetic Algorithms + Data Structures = Evolution Programs. Science Press, Beijing (2000)

[14] Bi, W., Ren, H., Wu, Q.: A new elitist strategy in genetic algorithms. Journal of Zhejiang University (Science Edition) 33(1), 32–35 (2006)

[15] Zhang, L., Zhang, B.: Research on the Mechanism of Genetic Algorithms. Journal of Software 11(7), 945–952 (2000)

[16] Zhou, Y.-b., Yan, Q.-d., Li, H.-c.: Collision Detection Algorithms Analysis in Virtual Environment. Journal of System Simulation 18(1), 103–107 (2006)

# Abstract Reporting and Reformation Schemes for Wireless Sensor Networks

Hock Guan Goh[1,2], Soung Yue Liew[2], Kae Hsiang Kwong[1,3],
Craig Michie[1], and Ivan Andonovic[1]

[1] Centre of Intelligent Dynamic Communications, Department of Electronic and Electrical Engineering, Faculty of Engineering, University of Strathclyde, Royal College Building, 204 George Street, Glasgow, G1 1XW, United Kingdom
[2] Department of Computer and Communication Technology, Faculty of Information and Communication Technology, University of Tunku Abdul Rahman, Jalan Universiti, Bandar Barat, 31900 Kampar, Perak, Malaysia
[3] MIMOS Berhad, Wireless Network and Protocol Research, Technology Park Malaysia, 57000 Bukit Jalil, Kuala Lumpur, Malaysia
{gohhg,syliew}@utar.edu.my,
{kwong,c.michie,i.andonovic}@eee.strath.ac.uk

**Abstract.** Energy resource constraints inherent in wireless sensor network deployments limit the amount of data that can be transported to a destination sink. An alternative strategy that could be invoked to address this issue is to only report the data sample when there is significant change in the sensed data from sensor nodes, and reconstruct the unreported data at the base station without compromising the needs of the application. It is shown that judicious reporting of data significantly reduces the number of packets that are transmitted. In this paper, a mechanism that adopts these principles, referred to as Abstract Reporting and Reformation (ARR), is proposed and demonstrated.

**Keywords:** Abstract Reporting and Reformation, Data Aggregation, Wireless Sensor Networks.

## 1 Introduction

The aggregation of physical sensing data poses significant challenges in the deployment of a Wireless Sensor Network (WSN) [1]. By its nature, a WSN comprises low cost, small form factor devices providing limited storage and processing resources and able to establish dynamic multi-hop routes. Since large scale deployments are typically battery powered, inefficient management of networked data will result in the rapid exhaust of that scant resource. Consequently the transportation of significant volumes of data is difficult, and this drives the development of efficient methods for data aggregation. Techniques such as the Tiny Aggregation (TAG) [2] and Data Aggregation and Dilution by Modulus Addressing (DADMA) [3] are used to reduce the number of packets transported through a network.

P. Sénac, M. Ott, and A. Seneviratne (Eds.): ICWCA 2011, LNICST 72, pp. 69–74, 2012.

In this paper, a mechanism that only reports the data sample when there is significant change in the sensed data from sensor nodes, and reforms the data at the destination sink is proposed and demonstrated. Such mechanism is referred to as Abstract Reporting and Reformation (ARR).

## 2  Data Filter and Data Recovery Schemes

In practice, configuring the sampling rate for data capture directly by the user control is non trivial. Thus to circumvent this, the approach adopted is to apply some intelligence at the sensor node that governs the reporting of a processed stream of original data without compromising the application. In this example, the amount of data to be reported is reduced by only transporting modified, abstracted samples only when the difference between the current and the previous reported data samples exceeds a pre-defined threshold. The threshold is set according to the equation below;

$$th_n = a + (n-1)s \tag{1}$$

where $a$ is a value assigned based on the degree of sensor sensitivity, $s$ is the sensor sensitivity value obtained from its datasheet and $n$ is a variable incremented by 1 after each threshold comparison until it reaches a maximum value of 10. After a data sample is reported, $n$ is reset to 0. Assume that the previous reported sample has a value of $x_0$ and after $i$-1 unreported sampling rounds, the current reading of the sensed data is $x_i$. The following algorithm is applied to determine whether or not to report this data sample;

```
increase i by 1
n ← min(i, n_max)
th_n ← a + (n - 1) × s
if |x_i - x_0| ≥ th_n, then
    report the values of i and x_i
    x_0 ← x_i
    i reset to 0
```

When the abstracted data reaches the sink, the unreported data is recovered using a simple recovery mechanism. This scheme fills the unreported data with the previous updated data until there is new reported data.

## 3 Results

A sensor network device, MICAz [4] with a temperature sensor was configured to sample sensor readings every second and report the sampled data to a base station at the same rate. The network was tested under three sensor data patterns designated as burst (from t = 1 to t = 200), slowly incremented and decremented (from t = 201 to t = 400) and random (from t = 401 to t = 600) (Fig. 1, Full sensor readings). Three types of ARR with threshold parameter a = 0.05, 0.1 and 0.2 were applied to full sensor readings. Since ARR only reports abstracted data, a significant reduction in the number of packets transported through the network is achieved (Fig. 1).

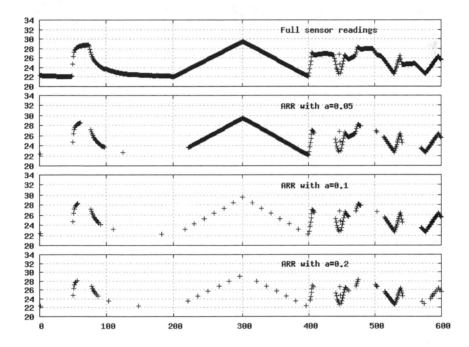

**Fig. 1.** Full sensor readings (1-200 burst data, 201-400 slowly incremented and decremented data, 401-600 random data), data reported using ARR with a = 0.05, data reported using ARR with a = 0.1 and data reported using ARR with a = 0.2. x-axis represents timeline and y-axis represents temperature in degree Celsius.

Fig. 2 shows the total number of transmitted packets with the assumption that one packet is required for each sensor reading. On average, ARR reduces the number of packet being transmitted by up to 50%.

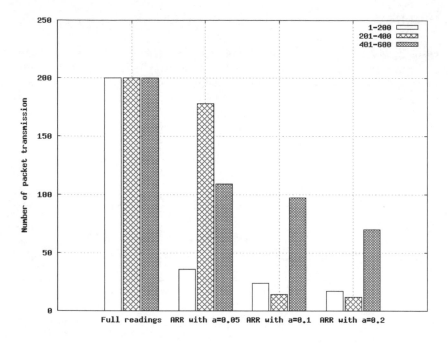

**Fig. 2.** Number of packets transmitted for full sensor readings and sensor data using ARR with a = 0.05, 0.1 and 0.2.

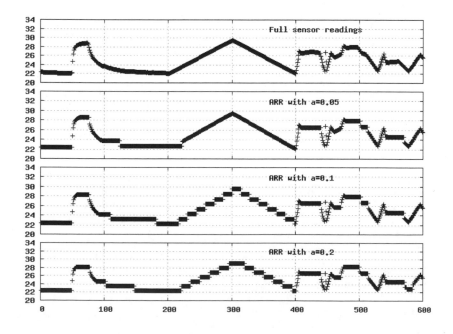

**Fig. 3.** Complete data after the data recovery scheme

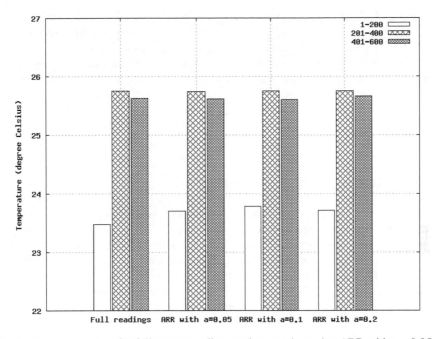

**Fig. 4.** Mean temperature for full sensor readings and sensor data using ARR with a = 0.05, 0.1 and 0.2

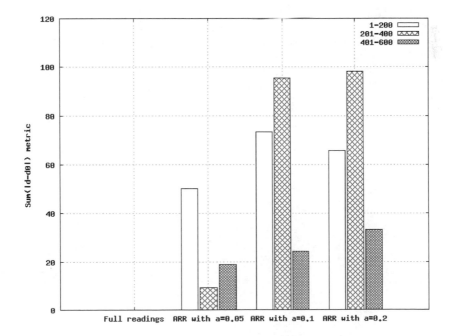

**Fig. 5.** The sum of differences for full sensor readings and sensor data using ARR with a = 0.05, 0.1 and 0.2.

At the sink, data were reformed using the data recovery scheme illustrated in Fig. 3. After the data is reformed, the means of the ARR recovered measurement data are less than 0.5 different compared to the means of the full sensor readings (Fig. 4).

In Fig. 5, the sum of differences for ARR recovered data and full sensor readings is on average <100. Equation 2 was used to evaluate the sum of differences where $d$ is the recovered data and $d_0$ is the data originated from the full sensor readings;

$$sum\_d = \sum |d - d_0| \qquad (2)$$

## 4 Conclusions

Abstract reporting and reformation schemes provide an alternative solution for data aggregation in wireless sensor networks. In situations where energy is a constraint, this proposed method allows certain data to be collected and reformed. Results show that the proposed solution is able to reduce the number of packets transported through the network by 50% without appreciable loss of information. Since the power required to transmit data is by far the greatest burden on the power source, this approach can yield significant increases in the lifetime of batteries.

## References

1. Akyildiz, I.F., et al.: A Survey on Sensor Networks. IEEE Communications Magazine 40(8), 102–114 (2002)
2. Madden, S., et al.: TAG: A Tiny Aggregation Service for Ad-hoc Sensor Networks. ACM SIGOPS Operating Systems Review 36, 131–146 (2002)
3. Cayirci, E.: Data Aggregation and Dilution by Modulus Addressing in Wireless Sensor Networks. IEEE Communications Letters 7(8), 355–357 (2003)
4. Crossbow Technology, http://www.xbow.com

# Research on Smart Substation Equipment Condition Monitoring System Based on Wireless Sensor Networks

Jie He, Xiaoqing Huang, and Yang Yang

College of electrical and information engineering, hunan university
Changsha, 410082 Hunan Province, China
hexie691@sohu.com

**Abstract.** Reference to characteristics of wireless sensor networks (WSNs) technology and the three-tier architecture of smart substation, the paper designs an on-line condition monitoring system of smart substation equipment based on WSNs. The system is designed as a hierarchical distributed structure and is divided into perception level, convergence level and application level. Then the paper proposed some of the key issues resolved in the design of monitoring system. These key issues include sensor node design, network topology, error handling, information management, network security, time-synchronized, integrating with substation communication network. It provides a new solution for improvement and optimization of substation equipment monitoring system and contributes to improving the running speed and flexibility.

**Keywords:** wireless sensor networks, smart substation, on-line condition monitoring, hierarchical distributed architecture, key issues.

## 1 Introduction

Currently, Smart grid [1-2] becomes an international hot point on the development of the future grid. As an integral part of power transformer link in smart grid, smart substation [3] has also been concerned and researched in the power industry. With the development of related technologies and smart devices in substation and with the growing capabilities of self-describing and self-diagnostic, the on-line condition monitoring system of power equipment in substation will better reflect these advantages. Collection of equipment condition information in substation is the basis of condition assessment, risk assessment, development of maintenance strategy and so on [4]. Traditional substation equipment monitoring system is typically realized through wired communication. However, the wired monitoring system requires expensive communication cables to be installed and regularly maintained, and thus, it is not widely implemented today because of its high cost [5]. Hence, there is an urgent need for cost-effective wireless monitoring system that improves system reliability and efficiency by optimizing the management of smart substation.

P. Sénac, M. Ott, and A. Seneviratne (Eds.): ICWCA 2011, LNICST 72, pp. 75–89, 2012.
© Institute for Computer Sciences, Social Informatics and Telecommunications Engineering 2012

Wireless Sensor Networks is a new type of information acquisition and processing system. It is the combination of computer technology, sensor technology, MEMS manufacturing technology and network communication technology, involves multidisciplinary fields such as micro-sensors and micro-machinery, communications, automatic control and artificial intelligence. With the development of WSNs technology, it can not only collect, transmit and process simple scalar data, but also can obtain sounds, images and other multimedia data containing massive information. Thus, WSNs realize fine-grained information monitoring and comprehensive monitoring of the perception area. The application of WSNs has been extended by the military to anti-terrorism, explosion prevention, environmental monitoring, health care, home dwelling, commercial, industrial and other fields [6-8].

Compared with the traditional substation equipment condition monitoring system, the advantages of using WSNs include followings:

(1) Nodes in WSNs highly integrated data acquisition, data processing and communications functions. It greatly simplifies equipments and achieves multi-parameters and comprehensive monitoring of smart substation equipment.

(2) Because wireless communication mode does not require complex circuit wiring, it makes WSNs more cost-effective.

(3) WSNs has self-organized, large-scale and dynamic characteristics. These make WSNs more suitable for distributed processing, increases the scalability of monitoring system and build the protection platform rapidly without the need to add more facilities.

(4) WSNs can quickly build an application platform based on different programs. It can be configured with appropriate sensor nodes and sensed multiple types of data for different substation environment.

Therefore, low-cost and low-power wireless sensor networks will likely become the solution of substation equipment on-line monitoring [9-11].

Combined with smart substation three-tier architecture and in the analysis of characteristics of WSNs, the paper proposes an on-line condition monitoring system of smart substation equipment based on WSNs and designs the hierarchical distributed architecture. Finally, some of the key issues that achieve reliable operation of the monitoring system are researched.

## 2   WSNs Characteristics and Communication Protocols

### 2.1   WSNs Technical Characteristics

WSNs are usually composed of nodes by self-organizing way. These nodes include embedded processors, sensors and wireless transmitters and receivers. WSNs use these nodes to work together to collect and process network coverage area of the target information. Figure 1 is often cited as a typical network deployment of WSNs [12].

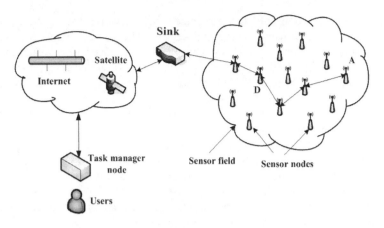

**Fig. 1.** WSNs network deployment

It can be seen from the WSNs deployment figure that it is a large-scale self-organization network centered with data and related to applications. It is a kind of specific Ad hoc network. Although WSNs and Ad hoc self-organizing networks have some similarities, there are also some different features between them [13]: ①The number of nodes in WSNs is much more and intensively deployed than Ad hoc. ② WSNs need higher requirement of fault-tolerance for it is often deployed in dangerous or unprotected area. ③WSNs nodes are generally relative static, while Ad hoc are strong mobility. The transforms of WSNs topology are mainly on account of electricity drained, parts fault, captured factors, but shift of node position. ④WSNs are also exposed to some limitation including processing power, storage and communication ability. The various solutions for WSNs are contented with as low complexity and power consumption as possible. ⑤Sensor nodes usually are not charging, and are fragile to failure for energy exhausted and environmental impact. The request of the quality of service (QoS) is not too high. In contract, improving the network service quality is its primary goal in Ad hoc; ⑥According to WSNs application characteristics, it often uses multicast or radio communication mode, and its data correlation is larger, so it is adapt to data-centric design; Rather, communication mode in Ad hoc is primarily point-to-point. It is suitable to the node centered design which can provide distributed applications with interconnection and processing power. ⑦WSNs often belong to an institution. Some global parameters or individual information in operation process can be pre-allocated before deployment.

As we know from the above, WSNs cannot effectively utilize in communication protocols which are suitable to conventional wireless networks and Ad hoc networks. Thus, WSNs need to formulate corresponding routing and MAC protocols.

## 2.2 Routing Protocol

The main objective of WSNs routing protocol is: seeking for power-efficient routing method and reliable data transmission method for WSNs, balancing the entire network power consumption to maximize the network life cycle. Thus the conventional wireless network routing protocols may be not suitable to WSNs.

Many different routing protocols have been proposed for different WSNs applications. According to different communication ways which nodes participate in, routing protocols can be divided into Location-based protocol, Flat-based routing and Hierarchical-based routing. From the specific application of WSNs, according to the different degree of sensitivity which applications of WSNs caused, routing protocols can be divided into energy-aware routing, query-driven routing, geographical aware routing, reliable routing and IP-based routing; According to the network topology structure, it can be divided into flat routing protocols and cluster-based routing protocols [14-15]. So far, there is no complete and clear routing protocol classification. To sum up, above classification of routing protocols have the characteristics of energy priority, local topology information-based, data-centric and application related. Therefore, when designing the routing mechanism in the specific application, it should satisfy the WSNs routing mechanism requirements that include energy efficient, expansibility, robustness, load balance and fast convergence.

## 2.3 MAC Protocol

WSNs MAC protocol is used to build the understratum infrastructure of sensor networks system and solve nodes using what kind of rules to share media in order to obtain satisfactory network performance. MAC protocol used in WSNs directly affects the network throughput, delay and other performance. In the design for MAC protocols, the following aspects need take into consideration: saving energy consumption, expansibility, network efficiency (fairness, real-time, throughput rate and bandwidth utilization ratio) and QoS The MAC protocol design should have the following attributes: energy efficiency, scalable to node density, frame synchronization, fairness, bandwidth utilization, flow control, and error control for data communication, especially considering saving energy consumption as a key factors.

The current MAC protocols for WSNs include four types. They are protocol based on scheduling algorithm, non-collision protocol, protocol based on competition and hybrid MAC protocol. In MAC protocol based on scheduling, the time interval which sensor nodes send data is decided by a scheduling algorithm. Such type of protocols contains SMACS [16], DE-MAC [17] and EMACS [18]. The non-collision MAC protocol has completely avoided the generation of confliction theoretically, including IP-MAC [19], TRAMA [20] and MMF-MAC [21], etc. MAC protocol based on competition is to acquire channel access in a competitive way when nodes need to send data. The typical protocols include S-MAC [22], T-MAC [23] and B-MAC [24]. The hybrid MAC Protocol combines multiple mechanisms to get a compromise between their strengths and weaknesses, such protocols include Physical Layer Driven Protocol [25], Hybrid TDM-FDM MAC [26] and CAT-MAC [27]. At present time, it is generally accepted that TDMA is more suitable for wireless sensor networks.

## 3  Monitoring System Design of Smart Substation Equipment Condition Based on WSNs

In general, equipment condition monitoring in smart substation has two different ways, on-line monitoring and off-line monitoring. The on-line monitoring uses the measurement system and technology which is installed directly on the equipment and record the characteristic quantity of equipment operating condition in real time. The off-line monitoring includes essential tests and technologies which can obtain the operation condition data through indirect contact with the equipment such as infrared monitoring. This way is an important complement of the on-line monitoring technology [28]. Nowadays, the most researches of condition monitoring are focused on the on-line monitoring. Its model is developing to hierarchical and distributed comprehensive on-line monitoring system. Based on the diversity of smart substation equipment and the complex characteristic of equipment condition information, the paper provides general hierarchical and distributed on-line monitoring system architecture based on WSNs.

### 3.1  Smart Substation Architecture

Deployment of WSNs must be designed according to the needs of the object. Like digital substation architecture, the architecture of smart substation is divided into three levels in State Grid Corporation of China's latest technology guidelines. They are process level, bay level and station level. As shown in Figure 2.

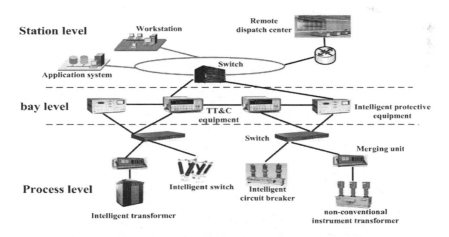

**Fig. 2.** Smart substation three-tier architecture

### 3.2  Monitoring Parameter of Smart Substation Equipment

As shown in figure 2, smart substation is a whole that requires harmonization work together of multiple equipments. Usually separated power equipments include intelligent transformer and circuit breaker, non-conventional instrument transformer, switchgear, reactor, type arrester and so on. Therefore, it needs to monitor more parameters including followings:

Intelligent transformer: partial discharge, grounded neutral current, dissolved gas analysis, moisture content, winging deformation, oil chromatogram, oil temperature

Intelligent circuit breaker: mechanical behavior, temperature, leakage current of exterior insulation, breaking time, current of opening and closing coil

GIS: partial discharge, air pressure, SF6 characteristic

Type arrester: phase current, capacitive current, resistive current, struck number

Capacitive equipment: dielectric loss, leakage current, equivalence condenser

Switchgear: temperature rise of bus contract points, partial discharge, temperature and humidity

In addition to these parameters, it also includes power quality on-line monitoring.

Sensors are the main equipments in distributed on-line monitoring system and there are many types, such as pulse current sensor, gas temperature and pressure sensor, hall sensor, photoelectric sensor. Here, the paper simply divides them into two types of data sensor and image sensor.

### 3.3  Monitoring System Design Requirements

(1) Flexibility in topology

According to the different design, the scale of smart substation is also different, and there are many intelligent electrical devices. In addition, line fault that may occur in the process of signal transmission must be considered. To ensure normal operation of equipment condition monitoring system, deployment of wireless sensor nodes need to be designed the net distribution and network architecture need to support flexible topology. So when happened a line fault, data can be transmitted from another line.

(2) Support multiple data types transmission

Based on the various reasons for equipment failure, monitoring data can be divided into two categories. One is scalar data type, such as operating voltages and load currents for transformer, GIS and circuit breaker, ambient temperatures. Another is image type, such as surface's texture images for transformer bushing and insulation situation of current transformer. Therefore, monitoring nodes must be required to have heterogeneity and include both traditional scalar sensor nodes and image sensor nodes. These nodes can also support a variety of data transmission and have higher transmission bandwidth.

With the development of WSNs technology, it can not only collect, transmit and process simple scalar data, but also can obtain sounds, images and other multimedia data containing massive information. Thus, WSNs realizes fine-grained information monitoring and comprehensive monitoring of the perception area.

### 3.4  Monitoring System Design

The on-line condition monitoring system of smart substation equipment adopts a distributed hierarchical architecture. It has been divided into substation-level monitoring system and dispatch center-level monitoring system as a whole. As shown in figure 3.

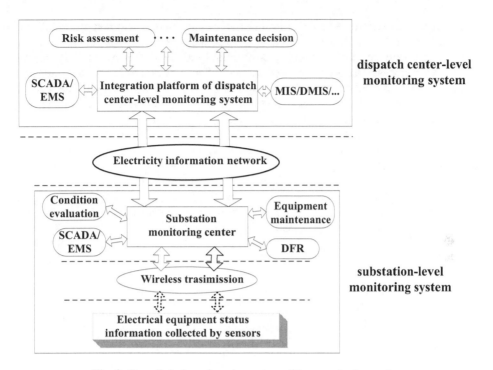

**Fig. 3.** Overall design of equipment condition monitoring system

Within smart substation, according to substation three-levels, the on-line condition monitoring system has been logically divided into three levels based on WSNs. The perception level is responsible for processing data and forming message. The convergence level is responsible for processing message and forming information. The application level is responsible for processing information and forming interaction. Clustered network topology and hierarchical routing protocol [29] is considered using in the monitoring system. As shown in figure 4.

Perception level mainly composed of sensor nodes that monitor a variety of electrical equipments. Besides traditional data sensors, it also adds image sensors that can realize equipment condition visualization. The first of deployment of sensor nodes logically divides substation equipments into different monitoring intervals according to different types. Inside the interval, sensor nodes have been divided into different cluster base on data sensors and image sensors. Each cluster is equivalent to a relatively fixed wireless network. So, the range of monitoring system is determined by actual situation of network coverage.

Convergence level's main task is to integrate these by cluster head node when equipment condition data and images through analog-to-digital conversion. Then the processed information is been sent to coordinator with GPRS modem. Through wireless gateway and GPRS network docking 100M/1000M Ethernet of station level, information arrives in substation monitoring center.

In order to ensure reliable transmission of substation equipment condition information, it has been considered node redundancy when cluster head node deployment. In each cluster, information is processed separately by data and image cluster head nodes. These cluster head nodes will fusion process collected data and image by sensor nodes under the jurisdiction of them, send information to the nearest coordination and can broadcast collected data packets from coordinator to jurisdiction of cluster at the same time. Cluster head node is located in a more central position where the cluster. It makes each node and cluster head node have the roughly same transmission distance and node power consumption of uniform distribution. Thus excessive energy consumption of some nodes has been avoided because of far transmission distance. Coordinator with GPRS modern is mainly responsible for cooperative building network. When designing the coordinator, because of taking in to account the possible connection failure between coordinator and wireless gateway, it can communicate between adjacent coordinators. Thus data and image of sensor nodes can be ensured the normal transmission through multi-hop path when a path failure.

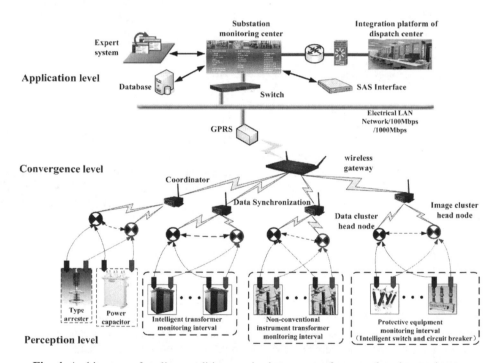

**Fig. 4.** Architecture of on-line condition monitoring system of smart substation equipment

Application level includes monitoring center, expert system, servers and so on. It is responsible for storage and analysis of equipment condition information. Then, monitoring center server completes the operation of general monitoring parameters with database and expert system, predicts the condition of equipment operation and finally provides the basis for maintenance decision system. Besides, equipment condition information can transmit to dispatch center-level monitoring system through the router via electricity information network.

## 4  Key Issues for WSNs Application in Smart Substation

The key issues for WSNs application in smart substation concerns sensor node, network topology, error handling, information management, network security, time-synchronized, integrating with substation communication network.

### 4.1  WSNs Node Design

Since the development of MEMS technology, low-power analog and digital circuit technology, low-power radio frequency technology and sensor technology, WSNs can consider the intelligent sensor in smart substation. As shown in figure 5. Processor unit, wireless transmission technology and chip are more important parts of node design.

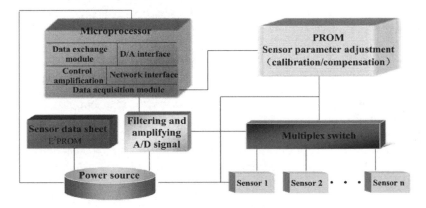

**Fig. 5.** Intelligent sensor structure

Sensor node processor that is responsible for collecting key equipment image and data can consider to using ARM processor. Because ARM processor has powerful processing capacity, it is suitable for application of high volume data services. Besides, it can also support energy saving policy such as DVS (Dynamic Voltage Scaling) or DFS (Dynamic Frequency Selection). Other sensor nodes can use low-performance microcontroller. Though processing power is week, energy consumption power is very small.

Commonly used in wireless communication technology typically include 802.11b, 802.15.4 (Zigbee), Bluetooth, UWB, RFID, IrDA and so on. Compared to other technologies, Zigbee technology is a short distance, low power, low-cost wireless communication technology [30] and its maximum bandwidth is 250kbit/s. It not only can meet temperature, sag and other needs of the scalar data transmission, but also can take into account image and other needs of mass data transmission in a small network area. It has a complete protocol stack only 32K and can be embedded in a variety of devises, while supporting geographic targeting. So it can consider using Zigbee in monitoring system based on the above characteristics. Alternatively, it can also choose an ordinary radio chip because the chip may customize MAC and routing protocols. In smart substation, wireless sensors are used to complete a variety of electrical quantities, digital, analog and other monitoring and testing. Therefore, it must fully consider the characteristics of substation in the design of monitoring system based on WSNs. Design of WSNs that is able to operate stable and reliable in substation environment is the key issue of custom communication protocols to be considered.

## 4.2  Network Topology

Network topology is one of the reasons for transmission reliability of sensor network. Access node adopts star structure in the traditional point to multipoint network. When a node fails, especially the central node fails, it will affect the normal operation of the entire work. The current improved point-to-point communication network has been adopted a number of protective measures in order to improve network reliability such as backup ling configuration. This method is simple, but requires each path to need equipped with two separate links and a protection switching. It greatly reduces the efficiency and improves the cost.

Thus, monitoring system design uses a net structure. It gives the function of each network node to automatically select the path. So each node may use multiple paths to connection and can be greatly increased with the number of link. If one out of a failure of a link, node can automatically link access to other optional link so that network reliability has been greatly improved. Arrangement of nodes in the network topology must also consider the impact of distance. Wireless signal transmission distance is affected by transmission power, receiving sensitivity, antenna gain and other factors. It can refer to the following formula to calculate.

$$20 \lg d = P_t + G_t + G_r - (L_t + L_r) - \Delta - 20 \lg f - 32.45 .$$

Here, $d$ is transmission distance. $P_t$ is transmission power. $G_t$ and $G_r$ are transmitting antenna and receiving antenna gain. $L_t$ and $L_r$ are transmitting antenna and receiving antenna loss. $\Delta$ is a wireless link power margin and usually takes 15~20. $f$ is frequency.

## 4.3  Error Handling and Information Management

WSNs spread signal through the air as a transmission medium. Wireless transmission signals will be affected by signal waveform reflection, diffraction and scattering, node movement, path loss, attenuation and obstacle. So bit error rate than conventional wired systems are usually several orders of magnitude higher. Through error control can guarantee error-free communication in WSNs. There are some measures to handling error including packet loss handling, excluding original error and forward error correction (FRC) [31]. Considering the energy loss factor and data features in

WSNs of substation monitoring system, it is able to use FEC coding control techniques for processing network error.

As large amount of monitoring data in the substation, different types of data requirements of different transmission quality and response time and the need to deal with different data, it requires the management of monitoring data and the use of hierarchical distributed processing mechanism. Only sensor combined with location information, its obtained information has practical meaning in substation. For example, only know exactly them specific location information, electrical quantum, switching value and other data can be effectively monitored and analyzed. Under the premise of satisfaction of substation positioning requirements, design a low overhead, low cost Distributed Location Algorithm is one of the key issues for WSNs applications in smart substation.

## 4.4 Security Problem

In the communication process, when the information of key equipments has been collected and transmitted in substation, it must guarantee their confidentiality, reliability and security to prevent data from being tapped or illegal user access. Network is vulnerable to tap and even to attack [32] because of characteristics of sensor node.

Security is determined by the openness of network deployment area and the broadcast nature of wireless networks in WSNs. It includes access control and confidentiality. Access control ensures that sensitive data is only accessed by authorized users. Confidentiality ensures that data transmitted is only received and processed by target. Therefore considered security threats must include conventional wire transmission with security threats and hidden troubles, transfer information without encryption or weak encryption, data theft and information tampered and inserted, which may lead to equipment malfunction and miss trip. The current measures to address security issues focuses on key management, identification, data encryption, attack detection and resist, secure routing and so on.

Now the main technology used in WSNs is symmetric encryption based on key pre-distribution and asymmetry encryption based on base station management key. But they have their own advantages and disadvantages, whereas using soft encryption is a feasible program.

Attack detection and resist is mainly to guarantee the normal operation of WSNs when sensor node has been hostile attacked such as interference service and node capture. "Method to find abnormal nodes by sending validation data to independent multi-path" is a solution [33]. This method proposed the "safe and flexible time-synchronized protocol".

Routing protocols in WSNs have many security weaknesses and are vulnerable to attack. If injecting malicious routing information to WSNs, the network will be paralyzed. For routing security issues, it has been proposed some methods such as "A defense method using certification against malicious injection" [34], "Broadcast encryption scheme" [35] and "a method that radio base station random tests node whether can receive its broadcast" [36].

## 4.5   Time-Synchronized and Substation Communication Network Access

WSNs application in substation must guarantee time-synchronized [37]. The main reasons are as follows. It needs collaboration between the sensor to comprehensive determine and analysis the monitoring electric quantum information. It will need synchronization mechanism to guarantee synchronization of each sensor data collected. Synchronization is beneficial to extend network lifetime and ensures that data will not lost because of mutual interference in the communication process. Smart substation currently includes three methods of time-synchronized. GPS has high precision and low cost characteristics and its related technology has matured [38-39]. The accuracy of Simple Network Time Protocol (SNTP) time synchronization can be achieved 1ms and the accuracy of IEEE1588 protocol network time synchronization may be achieved sub-microsecond [40]. How to use these three methods to realize WSNs time-synchronized is also one of the key issues to be resolved.

Electrical quantum, switching value, analog and other data of sensor nodes collected need to upload to monitoring center of the station level by monitoring network for analysis and monitoring. Smart substation communication network is the connecting link of a variety of intelligent electrical equipment. It uses a uniform standard IEC 61850 and is used to store and transmit events, quantity of electricity, operation, fault recording and other data. Therefore, it requires that WSNs accesses to smart substation communication network to achieve data sharing and complementation and avoid information isolated island.

## 5   Conclusion

WSNs application in various fields becomes increasingly widespread. Especially in difficult or adverse environmental conditions, it has unparalleled advantages compared with traditional monitoring techniques. Take into account characteristics of WSNs technology and the three-tier architecture of smart substation, the paper proposes an on-line hierarchical distributed monitoring system of smart substation equipment condition based on WSNs. Then some of key issues resolved in the design are discussed in detail such as sensor node design, network topology, error handling, information management, network security, time-synchronized, integrating with substation communication network. The monitoring system based on WSNs will not only help to improve the running speed and flexibility, but also is of great significance for comprehensive assessment of substation equipment health condition, as well as eliminate equipment potential failure and improve equipment reliability.

**Acknowledgments.** The authors would like to appreciate the financial support from the Grand Science and Technology Special Project of Hunan (No. 2009FJ1014) and Hunan Provincial Innovation Foundation For Postgraduate (No. CX2010B150).

# References

1. Xiao, s.: Consideration of Technology for Constructing Chinese Smart Grid. Automation of Electric Power System 32(9), 1–5 (2009)
2. Research Reports International. Understanding the smart grid, RRI00026 (2007)
3. Smart substation technical guide. State Grid Corporation of China (2009)
4. Zou, J.: Application of on-line monitoring technology on power grid. High Voltage Engineering 33(8), 203–206 (2007)
5. U.S. Department of Energy: Assessment study on sensor and automation in the industries of the future. Office of Energy and Renewable Energy Rep. (2004)
6. Ren, f.: Wireless Sensor Networks. Journal of Software 14(7), 1282–1291 (2003)
7. Akhondi, M.r., Talevski, A., Carlsen, S., Petersen, S.: Applications of Wireless Sensor Networks in the Oil, Gas and Resources Industries. In: The 24th IEEE International Conference on Advanced Information Networking and Applications, pp. 941–948 (2010)
8. Zhang, g., Pan, z.: The Application Research of Mobile Robots and Wireless Sensor Network in Laser Automatic Guided Vehicles. In: 2011 Third International Conference on Measuring Technology and Mechatronics Automation (ICMTMA), vol. 3, pp. 708–711 (2011)
9. Hainan, l., Leyang, z., Jiao, P., Caixia, L.: Design of substation temperature monitoring system based on wireless sensor networks. In: 2010 2nd International Conference on Advanced Computer Control (ICACC), vol. 1, pp. 127–130 (2010)
10. Nasipuri, A., Alasti, H., Puthran, P., Cox, R., Conrad, J.: Vibration sensing for equipment's health monitoring in power substation using wireless sensor. In: Proceedings of the IEEE SoutheastCon 2010 (SoutheastCon), pp. 268–271 (2010)
11. Gungor, V.C., Lu, B., Hancke, G.P.: Opportunities and Challenges of Wreless Sensor Network in Smart Grid. IEEE Transactions on Industrial Electronics 57(10), 3557–3564 (2010)
12. Akyildiz, I.F., Weilian, S., Sankarasubramaniam, Y., et al.: A Survey on Sensor Networks. IEEE Communications Magazine 40(8), 102–105 (2002)
13. Jing, q., Chen, z., et al.: Design and deployment of wireless sensor networks. Computer Engineering and Applications 43(27), 18–21 (2007)
14. Akkaya, K., Younis, M.: A survey on routing protocols in wireless sensor networks. Ad Hoc Nerwork 3(3), 325–349 (2005)
15. Farrukh, K.I., Younas, J.M.: A survey on routing protocols and challenge of holes in wireless sensor networks. In: 2008 International Conference on Wireless Communications, Networking and Mobile Computing, pp. 1–4. IEEE Inc., Dalian, China (2008)
16. Ma, z., Sun, y., Mei, t.: Survey on wireless sensor network. Journal of China Institute of Communications 25(4), 114–124 (2004)
17. Hill, J.L.: System Architecture for Wireless Sensor Networks. Ph. D Thesis, pp. 1-185, University of California at Berkeley, Department of Computer Science, Berkeley, California, USA (2003)
18. Mainwaring, A., Polastre, J., Szewczyk, R., Culler, D., Anderson, J.: Wireless Sensor Network for Habitat Monitoring. In: Proceedings of WSNA 2002, pp. 88–97 (2002)
19. Tsiatsis, V., Zimbeck, S., Srivastava, M.: Architecture Strategies for Energy-efficient Packet Forwarding in Wireless Sensor Networks. In: Proceedings of International Symposium on Low Power Electronics and Design, pp. 92–95 (2001)

20. Edgar, H.C.: Wireless Sensor Network: Architectures and Protocols, pp. 1–40. CRC Press LLC, Boca Raton (2004)
21. Weiser, M.: The Computer for the 21st Century. Scientific American 9, 265(3), 94–104 (1991)
22. Ye, W., Heidemann, J., Estrin, D.: An energy-efficient MAC protocol for wireless sensor networks. In: Proceedings of the 21st Annual Joint Conference of the IEEE Computer and Communications Societies (2002)
23. Dam, T., Langendoen, K.: An adaptive energy-efficient mac protocol for wireless sensor networks. In: Proceedings of the 1st International Conference on Embedded Network Sensor Systems (SenSys 2003) (November 2003)
24. Polastre, J., Hill, J., Culler, D.: Versatile low power media access for wireless sensor networks. In: Proceedings of the 2nd International Conference of Embedded Networked Sensor Systems (2004)
25. Rabaey, J.M., Ammer, J., da Silva Jr., J.L., Patel, D., Shad, R.: PicoRadio Supports Ad hoc Ultra-low Power Wireless Networking. IEEE Computer 33(7), 42–48 (2000)
26. Zhong, L.C., Shah, R., Guo, C., Rabaey, J.: An Ultra-Low Power and Distributed Access Protocol for Broadband Wireless Sensor Networks. In: IEEE Broadband Wireless Summit, Las Vegas, Nevada, 5 (2001)
27. Kahn, J.M., Katz, R.H., Pister, K.S.J.: Next Century Challenges: Mobile Networking for Smart Dust. In: Proceedings of MobiCom 1999, pp. 483–492 (1999)
28. Sun, c.: Present situation and development of condition on-line monitoring and diagnosis technology for power transmission and transformation equipment. Electric Power 38(2), 1–7 (2005)
29. He, x., Jia, z., Yang, g., et al.: Study on substation monitoring system based on Zigbee and IEC 61850. Telecommunication for Electric Power System 30(198), 25–29 (2009)
30. Han, b., Sheng, g., Jiang, x.: An Online Thermal Condition Monitoring System with Wireless Sensor Network Based on Zigbee Technology for Transmission Line Joints. Automation of Electric Power Systems 32(16), 72–77 (2008)
31. Wen, H., Lin, C., Ren, F., et al.: Retransmission or redundancy: transmission reliability in wireless sensor networks. In: Proceedings of the 2007 IEEE International Conference on Mobile Adhoc and Sensor Systems (2007)
32. Parnob, P.A., Glimgor, V.: Distributed detection of node replication attacks in sensor networks. In: Proceeding of the 2005 IEEE Symposium on Security and Privacy, Oakland, CA, USA, May 8-11, 2005, pp. 49–63. IEEE, New York (2005)
33. Deng, J., Han, R., Mishra, S.: A performance evaluation of intrusion tolerant routing in wireless sensor networks. In: The 2nd IEEE Int'l Workshop on Information Processing in Sensor Network (IPSN), California, USA (2003)
34. Hu, Y.-C., Perring, A., Johnson, D.: Packet leashes: A defense against wormhole attacks in wireless ad hoc networks. In: IEEE Int'l Conf. on Computer Communications (INFOCOM 2003), San Francisco, USA (2003)
35. Huang, S.C.-H., Ding-Zhu, D.: New constructions on broadcast encryption and key pre-distribution schemes. In: IEEE Int'l Conf on Computer Communications (INFOCOM 2005), New York, USA (2005)

36. McCune, J.M., Shi, E., Perrig, A., et al.: Detection of denial-of-message attacks on sensor network broadcasts. In: IEEE Symp. on Security and Privacy (S& P), California, USA (2006)
37. Huang, x., Liu, p., Miao, s.: Application of Wireless Sensor Networks in Power Monitoring System. Automation of Electric Power Systems 31(7), 99–103 (2007)
38. IEC 61850-5, Communication networks and systems in substation, part 5: Communication requirements for functions and device models (2003)
39. Zeng, x., Yin, x., Li, K.K., Chan, W.L.: Methods for Monitoring and Correcting GPS-clock. Proceedings of the Csee 22(12), 41–46 (2002)
40. IEC 61588, precision clock synchronization protocol for networked measurement and control systems (2004)

# Reducing Dependency on Middleware for Pull Based Active Services in LBS Systems

Saroj Kaushik[1], Shivendra Tiwari[2], and Priti Goplani[3]

[1,2] Dept. of Computer Science and Engineering
[3] Dept. of Mathematics, Indian Institute of Technology,
Delhi, Hauz Khas, New Delhi, India 110016
{saroj,shivendra}@cse.iitd.ac.in,
jca082084@maths.iitd.ac.in

**Abstract.** The middleware is the most commonly used solution to address the location privacy. But it becomes a bottleneck in terms of system performance and availability as the entire client's service transactions are routed through the middleware to the actual Location Based Service Providers (LSP). The proposed architecture mainly targets a variety of applications where the availability of the services is probably more important than the location security. In the new flexible middleware based architecture the client and the LSPs can communicate directly. Autonomy on the client-server communication increases the possibility of communication even in the scenarios where the middleware is not available. But it also introduces authentication and security challenges to be addressed. The trusted middleware is used to generate the authentication certificates containing the Proxy Identity (also called Pseudonyms) to fulfill the authentication requirements at the LSP servers. The rest of transactions among the clients and the LSPs are accomplished independently. Further, the level of anonymity can be tuned by altering pseudonyms generation techniques i.e. "One-to-One", "One-to-Many" and "Many-to-One" depending on the type of the service and security requirements. It also attempts to maintain almost the same level of security for the targeted services.

**Keywords:** Trusted Middleware, Location Based Services (LBS), LB Service providers, Authorization, Pseudonyms, Location Based Service Provider (LSP), Location Privacy.

## 1 Introduction

A Location Based Services (LBS) are entertainment, information and alert type services which are accessible through Over the Air (OTA) network on computers and mobile devices. The LBS services can be divided into various major categories – Pull vs Push services, Person vs Device oriented services, and Active vs Passive services. The push services need real-time location update to the LSP server, so that it can keep track of user's current location, i.e. security alerts, news updates, geo-fencing, and friend finder etc. However, the pull services don't require the continuous update of

P. Sénac, M. Ott, and A. Seneviratne (Eds.): ICWCA 2011, LNICST 72, pp. 90–106, 2012.

the user location, and hence user can send the location on-demand to LSP to get the services like point of interest (POI) Searches, Geocoding, and Reverse Geocoding etc. Person-oriented LBS comprises all of those applications where a service is user-based. Thus, the focus of application is to position a person or to use the position to enhance a service. Device-oriented LBS applications are external to the user, where instead of only a person, an object (e.g., a car, a bus) or a group of people (e.g., a fleet) could be located. In device-oriented applications, the person or object located is usually not controlling the service e.g., car tracking for theft recovery. In Active Services, the user initiates the service request; however in the Passive services a third party locates one user (locatee) at the request of another user (the locator). Typical Passive location services are friend finder services, location-based gaming, or fleet management [10].

In LBS systems, there are numerous actors such as content providers (LSP), operators, virtual operators and service administrators etc, all of which can be separate entities. A service provider (LSP) will have automatic access to a customer's location as the location is an essential input to provide the location aware services. Simultaneous observation of the three attributes such as "location" of the user, the "time" at which that location is observed and the "identity" of user creates a threat to user's privacy. The "identity" of the user has the highest importance from privacy point of view. The server has access to learn the location of the customer while the customer is using the service, but it should never know the customer's identity or a combination of it along with "location" and/or "time" attributes. Request trends or query pattern is also crucial for privacy model along with these attributes. Disclosure of the combination of user's identification and query pattern (it implicitly involves user's location) is dangerous. By analyzing the query pattern an adversary can determine the user's location [15, 16, 17, and 18]. Thus there is a need to protect the user's location from being misused. Currently, the middleware architecture is considered to be trusted approach which acts as a three way privacy mediator between the law, the users and the LSPs. The middleware manages a very large number of information providers and high volatility of users' interests (e.g., profile updates, insertion, and deletion etc). The whole subscription database also lies with middleware. The use of the middleware as a single window system ensures greater security as the entire request from the clients to the application service providers are routed through it. So the service providers have no clue of user identity and its location. It has to support high availability despite node failures (e.g., guarantee notification delivery), perform accounting, security and privacy functions etc.

In this paper, we have proposed a system architecture with the least use of trusted middleware and greater autonomy in client-LSP server communication. The proposed architecture is flexible in nature and uses middleware to get the user authentication, but achieve the actual services directly from the service providers (LSP) without middleware's intervention. The architecture is backward compatible and hence the old style of client-LSP communication through the middleware is still possible for the services other than pull based and/or the services requiring a very tight location security. Other than the introduction of the domain in this section, related research work and problem definition are described in section 2 and section 3 separately. The Proposed Solution is explained in sections 4. Section 5 contains possible LBS applications which could be handled by the proposed system. Advantages of the proposed system, limitation and future research possibilities are mentioned in sections 6 and 7. Finally, section 8 concludes the underlying research.

## 2   Related Work

Fig.1 depicts the architecture already in use for middleware based LBS services, showing mobile users, network operator, third-party service providers, and several of the aforesaid subsystems [10]. The client has to go through the middleware to reach the content providers (LSP) asking for any service.

Yingying Chen, et al [7] proposed both; a centralized architecture as well as a fully decentralized enforcement mechanism. They proposed a trusted middleware for facilitating the access control of the location information by enforcing that the mobile devices are only able to access the location information in a manner that conforms to their privileges. Apurva Mohan et al [5] proposed an interesting idea of access control by user profile. They proposed an implementation which can change the policies dynamically. A LBAC (Location Based Access Control) system is integrated with privacy-enhanced techniques based on location obfuscation [2]. Pseudonyms are used by Christian Hauser [6] for handling Identity Privacy. With pseudonyms there arise problems like non associate-ability, non-repudiation and accountability. As the disclosure of personal information in the context of a pseudonym is a monotonic process, the users should be enabled to use different pseudonyms. By this mechanism, users can tune their level of anonymity.

The ticket based service access scheme for the mobile users proposed by Hua Wang et al talks about the mobile databases accessed across multiple service domains anonymously [12]. However this research only talks about the anonymity while mobile roams among the multiple service providers. It doesn't consider the level of anonymity, and have to contact the credential center for the ticket clearance all the time. It also doesn't consider the ticket clearance scenarios where the Credential Center is not available due to any unforeseen reason. In the emergency applications a mobile client needs to access the services where user might not be much worried about the security of the data.

Pseudonyms are another useful research done by Christian Hauser [14] for handling Identity Privacy. As the disclosure of personal information in the context of a pseudonym is a monotonic process, the users should be enabled to use different pseudonyms. By this mechanism, users can tune their level of anonymity [13, 14]. They presented both a centralized architecture as well as a fully decentralized enforcement mechanism. But this work is related to location sharing and access control management in order to reveal location to different entities.

Fig-2 shows dependency of the Middleware in the whole architecture. The middleware is the entity which interacts with the content providers (LSP) to get various services for client. The logical working of the architecture depicted in the figure goes as– client forwards every request to middleware; middleware interacts with LSP for the requested service and passes back the response to client.

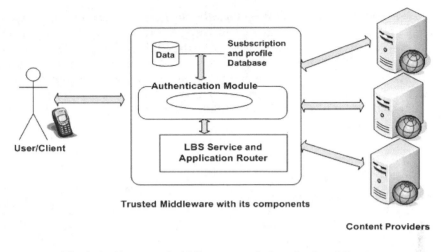

**Fig. 1.** Architecture of middleware centric Location based Services

# 3 Problem Definition

The key aspect of the problem is being middleware a bottleneck. The client-LSP communication is completely dependent on the middleware. It raises availability, speed, reliability, and response time etc issues in the location services. A user in a human-less jungle would need important services like Food Search, Pedestrian & Car Navigation services etc. At this point the user might not be worried about its location privacy or it might be willing to compromise with the privacy up to some extent for survival-critical services. Following are the key problematic points which will be addressed in the subsequent sections:

- *Minimize the Dependency on Middleware:* Availing the direct communication among client and content providers (LSP); minimizing the use of middleware are the major aspect we want to handle. Obviously, it creates other new issues which we have to handle in order to support this point.

- *Location Revelation to Un-trusted LBS Providers (LSP):* Due to direct communication among the clients and un-trusted LSPs, they could be potential privacy threats of misusing the location information of the user. Making the user's location queries and current location, time of the location observation (along with the identity) known to service providers could be dangerous. The transaction queries have to be anonymous.

- *Minimize Traceability of the Transaction Pattern:* Even after making the transactions anonymous using proxy identity (pseudonyms), getting service by the same identity every time gives a fair chance to the eavesdroppers to predict user's nature and day to day routine. This data can be misused in a variety of ways by adversaries.

- **Ensuring Authorization and Accountability in Location Servers:** Surely use of single or multiple Pseudonyms could be a potential solution to the problem discussed above. However the challenge to the LBS service providers is to keep the accountability of the usage of the services. They also need to filter out the users according to the authorization and access control they have allowed. In this way we need a standard mechanism to ensure the accountability of the users along with the access control even if they don't reveal their real identity while getting the services.

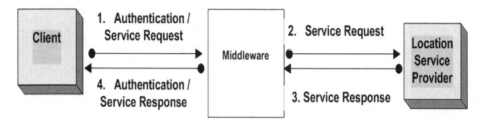

**Fig. 2.** Transaction Flow in Currently Prevalent Architecture

The main focus is to minimize the dependency on the middleware but the user should get the service without letting know its location to the LSPs – on the contrary, location is essential in order to get the Location Based Service. This problem can be tackled by disassociating user identity and its location. But the LSPs need identity to maintain access control and accountability. Following subsections describe a solution which is flexible in nature which allows using the old architecture for the high security requirement services; at the other hand it also allows to bypass the middleware and the clients directly communicate with the LSPs. There are assumptions for the proposed solution such as client is already registered with middleware and has taken the subscription of services of its choice; client has already determined its location and the subscription and profile database lies with the middleware only.

## 4   Proposed Solution

The block diagram of the proposed system is shown in Fig. 3. It mainly consists of three modules:

**a. The Client or User Application:** A client module refers to the end user application for the location services. It generally resides on mobile and PDA devices.

**b. Un-trusted Location Based Service Providers:** The un-trusted LSP servers are the real service providers. The key responsibilities of the LSPs are providing service to clients, credential verification, determining access control information.

**c. The Trusted Middleware:** It is a trusted component of the whole system for direct communication between client and LSP. The user Authentication and Subscription Management, pseudonym generation, service request routing, location determination and billing are the key responsibilities of the middleware.

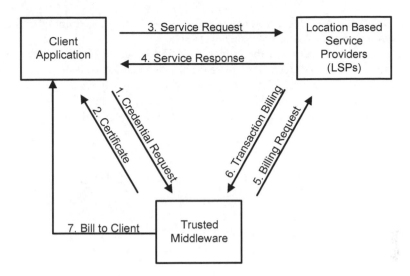

**Fig. 3.** Block diagram of the proposed architecture

## 4.1 Flexible Middleware Architecture

The middleware is mainly divided into three parts – Authentication, Service Routing, and the Billing Management module. The Authentication module takes care of the verification of the client's subscription and authenticity. The service request module routes the request to the desired LSP which is as per the old architecture. The Billing management module handles the transaction billing activities. The middleware generates a Pseudonym against a user to hide user's real identity. The applicability of the pseudonyms enables the user to make it anonymous. But on the other hand service provider needs to know if the client is an authenticated; client is authorized for the requested service and the period of service availability. The functioning of middleware modules are given as below:

**The User Authentication:** When the client wants to initiates the service session with the location server (LSP), it has to first contact middleware to get the Authentication Certificate; which will be used for the subsequent request to the location server (LSP). The middleware has to generate the pseudonym(s) according the user's requested level of anonymity (discussed in the later sections). The certificate should contain the pseudonym generated by the middleware. The certificate is digitally signed by middleware so as to ensure that the certificate is actually generated by middleware. It should also be encrypted by the LSP's public key so that the certificate is used by the targeted LSP only.

**Access Control to the Services (authorization):** We can easily anticipate the problem in the above discussion – authorization. How the LSPs decide if the underlying client is authorized for the requested service even if it is a registered user? The middleware should include all the required access control information into the certificate like services subscribed and temporal validity of the certificate. The access control information should be stored in the LSP server for the running session with the pseudonym for verifying subsequent requests.

The detailed architecture of the proposed system is shown in fig.4. It is flexible as it can also work as old system where each service request and response is routed through middleware which works as a transaction router. Alternatively, the proposed system can disassociate middleware after generating the certificate(s). Now actual service transactions take place between the client and LSP based on the certificate(s). In this mode middleware works as a certifying authority.

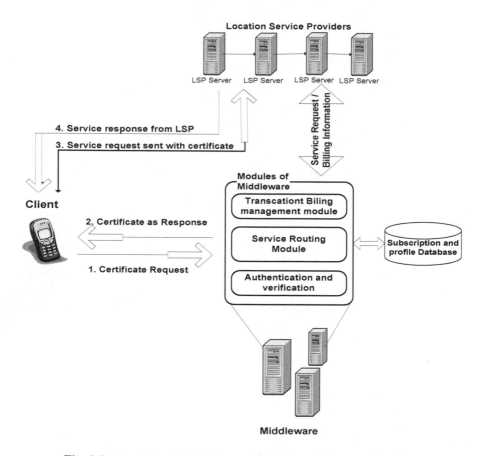

**Fig. 4.** Proposed Flexible Middleware Architecture with transaction flow

## 4.2  Transactional Flow

Following are the steps and the transaction flow of the proposed system architecture:

1.  Clients send request to Middleware
    - Middleware generates a Pseudonym against the user's requested level of anonymity.
    - It creates a complete package with the Pseudonym and Access control information as the part of certificate content.
    - It uses LSP's public key to encrypt the certificate content which can be further decrypted by its private key only.
    - The certificate will also be digitally signed by the middleware.

2.  Client application prepares and sends the service request to the LSP server
    - The session should be created into the LSP server so that the subsequent requests for the current session don't require further authentication.
    - The request should contain the certificate received from the middleware.

3.  LSP Server's Authentication and Session Creation
    - The location server decrypts the certificate by using its private key. It checks for temporal validity of the service and the certificate.
    - It saves the Pseudonym and the corresponding access control information in the newly created session database for the future use.
    - The service response is communicated back to the client.

4.  After completion of transaction and/ or expiry of temporal validity, middleware sends transaction accountability request to LSP. In response to this request LSP sends account and whole record of transactions for the users specified.

5.  Middleware then generates the bill for the specified pseudonym and sends it to the corresponding user.

## 4.3  Pseudonym Generation

Fig-5 shows the pseudonym generation and recovering the real identity from the given pseudonym. The pseudonym is generated corresponding to a user id with the help of a key available with middleware. The key is selected randomly by the "Key Selector" block on the basis of the "Encryption Key Index" that is generated by the "Random Key Generator" bolck. The key is further passed to the encryption module to perform encryption operation. The pseudonym can be directly generated by using standard symmetric encryption method i.e. Data Encryption Standard (DES)/ Advanced Encryption Standard (AES) given in [8]. The pseudonyms should be recoverable, efficiently computable and hard to decrypt without the key. The key index is suffixed with pseudonym in order to identify the corresponding key later at the time of recovering the user id by middleware. When recovering the user-id from a given pseudonym, the decryption method in the Fig 5 is used. The "Key Index Extract" block extracts the key index from the pseudonym that is passed to the "Key Selector" block. The "Key Selector" blocks fetches the appropriate key which is further used for the decryption by the "Decryption" block.

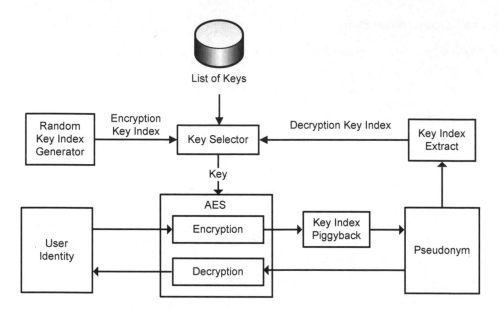

**Fig. 5.** Pseudonym Generation and Recovering User-id – Flow Diagram

In the proposed architecture, user can tune its level of anonymity. Different levels of anonymity can be achieved and their usage scenarios are described in the following subsections. In the algorithms mentioned in the following subsections the AES() procedure has been used as a standard procedure that encrypts the given input using AES cryptography algorithm. Also the notations $E_{ki}$ and $D_{ki}$ are used in the equations for an encryption and decryption operators respectively with the key $k_i$. .

### 4.3.1 One-to-One Pseudonym

It is simplest form of the anonymity denoting a user-id's mapping to a single pseudonym. Apply AES Encryption method [8] to generate Pseudonym by using the User-Id:ID and a key:k, such as P= $E_k$(ID). The pseudonym can be reversed by using the same key by middleware for billing purpose as ID = $D_k$(P). A user can opt for a single pseudonym for the entire session if his privacy requirements are low.

Creation of the pseudonym:

$$P= E_k(ID) \tag{4.3.1.1}$$

Recovering user-id from the pseudonym:

$$ID = D_k(P) \tag{4.3.1.2}$$

The procedure *GenPseud-OnetoOne(User-Id:ID, key:k)* generates the pseudonym corresponding to the given user-id. Here k is the key; ID is the user identity to be encrypted; and P is the pseudonym to be generated as an output.

```
GenPseud-OnetoOne(User-Id:ID,key:k)

    {

        P = AES(User-Id:ID,key:k);

        Return P;

    }
```

### 4.3.2  One-to-Many Group Pseudonyms

In this method the user itself requests multiple pseudonyms for a single user-id. The middleware generates 'n' number of pseudonyms and separate 'n' corresponding certificates but with the same access control information.  The same ID is supplied to the encryption procedure along with 'n' different randomly selected keys ($k_1 \ldots k_n$). As a result 'n' different pseudonyms ($P_1 \ldots P_n$) are generated. The pseudonyms can be generated and recovered as given below:

Creation of the pseudonym(s):

$$P_1 = E_{k1}(ID)$$
$$P_2 = E_{k2}(ID)$$
$$\ldots$$
$$P_n = E_{kn}(ID)$$

(4.3.2.2)

Recovering user-id from the pseudonym(s):

$$ID = D_{k1}(P_1)$$
$$ID = D_{k2}(P_2)$$
$$\ldots$$
$$ID = D_{kn}(P_n)$$

(4.3.2.2)

The  procedure  *GenPseud-OnetoMany(* `User-Id:ID`,  Keys:($k_1 \ldots k_n$), Anonymity_Degree:n*)* given below also calls the standard AES encryption method 'n' times separately to generate the pseudonyms ($P_1 \ldots P_n$) corresponding to the given user-id name and a list of different keys ($k_1 \ldots k_n$).

```
GenPseud-OnetoMany(User-Id:ID,Keys:(k₁...kₙ),Anonymity_Degree:n)
{
    Initialize i = 0;
    /*loop through all the keys to generate n pseudonyms*/
    While (i < n)
    {
        /*create pseudonyms for each key*/
        Pᵢ = GenPseud_One-to-One(User-Id, kᵢ);
        i++;
    }
    /*a list of n pseudonyms*/
    Return (P₁...Pₙ);
}
```

### 4.3.3  Many-to-One Group Pseudonyms

The "Many-to-One" pseudonym generation method assigns the same pseudonym to 'n' number of users. This scheme can be used for group subscription where a group of people are agreed to get billed with the same subscription account – a group ID i.e. GID. If we would like to know which user exactly used the service in the group, it can be achieved by piggybacking group user index information with the pseudonym itself; however the rest of the Pseudonym generation method remains the same.

Creation of the pseudonym:

$$P = E_k(GID) \qquad (4.3.3.3)$$

Recovering global user-id from the pseudonym:

$$GID = D_k(P) \qquad (4.3.3.2)$$

The procedure defined below generates a single pseudonym corresponding to the given user-id and a group key. It uses two functions namely *getGroupUserID()* that maps the User-Id to the GID and the *getGroupPseudonym()* that fetches already created group pseudonym to avoid the rework. We have not defined these procedures explicitly.

```
GenPseud-manytoOne(User-Id:ID, Key:k, Anonymity_Degree:n)
{
    /*a group of users are recognized by a Global ID*/
    GID = getGroupUserID(ID);
    /*Fetch the pre-generated pseudonym for the GID*/
    P =  getGroupPseudonym(GID);
    if (P == NULL)
    {
        /*generate the new pseudonym if it doesn't exist*/
        P = Gen Pseud_One-to-One(GID,  k);
    }
    Return P;
}
```

For a scenario with rigorous privacy requirements, one can opt for "Many-to-One" or "One-to-Many" pseudonym schemes. Use of these two schemes makes the chances of a user being tracked, very low. One can argue on the reliability of the different anonymity levels. As a drawback, while using the "One-to-Many" pseudonyms, samples of multiple transactions having the same control information and other attributes may lead to identify the pattern of the requests, in the worst case. Even if the multiple transactions are mapped to one pseudonym, the scenario boils down to a "One-to-One" pseudonym. It still doesn't reveal the user's real identity.

## 4.4  Certificate Generation

The authentication certificates are used to validate a client's subscriptions communicating directly to the LSP. The certificate is a digitally signed document by the middleware with its private key – it uses public key cryptography to encrypt the certificate. The LSP or the client can decrypt the certificate with the middleware's public key.

The authentication certificate contains access control attributes. The LSP can blindly serve the authorized services to the client as the certificate is generated by the middleware with the information available at the subscription database. The access control information along with the pseudonym, are stored in the LSPs so that during the further service requests, it can use the existing credentials. The certificate contains – Pseudonym, Access Control information (a list of services which are allowed to the user on service request) and certificate validity (the service should be provided to the user till the valid period only). Procedure for certificate generation is given as follows.

Generate_certificate() procedure produces is a high-level list of instructions in simple English. The *PrepareContent()* procedure only creates a well formatted attribute document using XML or any other document format, hence it has not been defined separately.

```
Generate_certificate(User-Id:ID,      Pseudonyms:P,      Access
Control:authm, LSP Public Key:LSPk, Middleware Private Key :
MDWk)

{

    /*  prepare  the  certificate  content  for  the  given
    pseudonym P */

    C  =  PrepareContent(User-Id:ID,  Pseudonyms:P,  Access
    Control:authm);


    /*encrypt the certificate with the public key of the LSP
    i.e. LSPk*/

    C1 = AES(LSP Public Key:LSPk, Certificate Content:C);


    /*Certificate Signing: Encrypt the certificate using with
    the private key of the middleware MDWk */

    Cert  =  AES(Middleware  Private  Key:MDWk,  Encrypted
    Certificate:C1);


    /*return the encrypted certificate*/

    Return Cert;

}
```

## 5  Applications with the Flexible Middleware

The applications requiring the user profile information for decision making need to follow middleware path to get the services. Following are some of the applications which can be handled efficiently by the proposed Flexible Middleware architecture with direct communication between client and LSP. By using the proposed architecture for these applications we can achieve high availability and scalability due to the direct communication to the LSPs. Also proposed architecture expects less response time even in the high number of transactions per minutes scenarios.

*1. Proximity Search:* It is one of the most popular LBS applications. It is a technology that let people search for information like nearest cinema/gas station in their area using mobile equipments.

*2. Turn by Turn Navigation:*  This application is about getting the navigation instructions to reach a particular place. For this application, when client sends the request along with the certificate to the LSP, LSP sends the response to the device / user at the location from which the request has arrived as LSP anyways knows the location but identity is hidden.

*3. Geocoding & Reverse Geocoding :* Geocoding is the process of finding associated geographic coordinates from other geographic data, such as street addresses, or zip codes (postal codes) and reverse Geocoding is opposite of this. This method makes use of data from street geographic information system.

*4. M-Commerce and Advertisement:* It is a new form of advertising and commerce that uses location-tracking technology in mobile networks to target consumers with location-specific advertising on their mobile devices. The proposed architecture works well for pull based advertisements in which user subscribes and then asks for the incoming ad alerts and LSP sends the advertisements to a specific pseudonym.

*5. Near-me Area Network (NAN):* It is a logical communication network that focuses on two way communication among wireless devices in close proximity [11]. For example, a user lost its child in the street, and wants to locate him/her with the help of passers-by in the proximity. This application can be handled by the proposed system as follows – it is assumed that a user has already subscribed for this type of service (or this can be accessed on an emergency basis also). Users sends a request with child's picture to LSP who broadcasts the picture to all those devices with whom the LSP is communicating and are in proximity of the area from which request has come. If any device wishes to respond this type of query, it can directly ping the LSP. The LSP server further informs to the victim user(s).

# 6  Advantages of the Proposed Solution

In this section, we highlight advantages of the proposed system. Table 1 has an intuitive comparison of the proposed architecture against the prevelent one and is based on the metrics taken from software architecture theory. The attribute values for the columns is based on the theratical knowledge of the corresponding architectures [19]. The "Good" means the sufficient attribute strength of the corresponding architecture; the "Average" value denotes that it is not sufficient and it can be further improved; however the "Poor" value indicates that the attribute is unaccepable for the real deployments, hence it must be improved further. The attribute value "NA" indicates that the value is either not available or insignificant.

*1. Threat Handling:* It doesn't require disclosing the real user identity to the LSP as the pseudonyms are used instead of user-id. The authentication and authorization are taken care by the use of authentication certificates. Randomized use of Pseudonym minimizes the risk of disclosure of request pattern analysis.

*2. Configurable Levels of Anonymity:* Through the use of One-to-One, "One-to-Many" and "Many-to-One" pseudonym(s) user is having control on its degree of anonymity. Depending upon its security requirements user can opt for one or group pseudonyms

*3. Distributed Architecture:* Middleware is no more a bottlenecked component. Apart from distributed transaction architecture, proposed solution also provides distributed transaction accountability.

*4. Recoverable Pseudonyms:* Pseudonyms are recovered easily with the help of keys lying with middleware. They can be recovered by the direct decryption methods using the corresponding key. The keys are stored in the middleware that can be identified with the associated key index in the pseudonyms. This is required for billing purposes or tracking the user incase of using the system for criminal activities.

5. *Dynamic and Easy Access Control:* The access control information is included in the certificates itself; hence LSPs don't have to look for authentication information anywhere else.

**Table 1.** Feature Comparisons

| Middleware Type(→), Middleware Key Features (↓) | Conventional Middleware Architecture [10] | Token Based Authentication System [12] | Flexible Middleware Architecture (Proposed) |
|---|---|---|---|
| Flexibility to LSP Selection | NA | Good | Good |
| Distributed Services | NA | Good | Good |
| Access Control Configurability | Good | Average | Good |
| Emergency Services in case of Middleware Failure | NA | NA | Good |
| Distributed Transaction Accountability | NA | Good | Good |
| Response Time | Poor | Good | Good |
| Service Transactions Autonomy | NA | Poor | Good |
| High Availability of services | Average | Average | Good |
| Transaction Accountability | Good | Good | Good |
| Location Privacy | Good | Average | Good |
| Extendability (adding more LSPs/features)/scalability | Poor | Good | Good |
| Flexibility (bypass middleware) | Poor | Poor | Good |
| Robustness | Average | Average | Good |
| Reliability | Good | Good | Good |

6. *Non Link-ability of Pseudonyms:* As the pseudonyms can be picked and changed randomly by the user for each of the service request, therefore it is difficult to link them to the user's real profile on the basis of footprint trace.

7. *Less Transaction Time:* Overall transaction time is reduced because of direct communication between client and LSP after certificate generation. Time of encryption and certificate generation is amortized as the certificates are valid for iterative service transactions.

8. *High Availability*: In the proposed architecture services are available all the time despite the possibility of middleware failure. After Authentication Certificate(s) are generated for a session, there is no dependency on the middleware for further transaction.

# 7 Limitations and Future Work

The proposed solution handles the access control and authorization issues efficiently in theory, but this is yet to be proved by the real statistics. The work is in progress to implement the complete system architecture so that we can evaluate the system with the real performance figures. This architecture is more suitable for the Pull-based Active Services. The new architecture is less suitable for the applications which need continuous tracking of the user such as child fencing. So an open issue is still to minimize the middleware usage for other kinds of location services (including push based services). In case of a session loss, certificate has to be sent again to location server and thus creates another computation overhead at LSP while decrypting the certificate. To prevent the misuse of certificate by the client itself by sharing them to other users, we can associate the generated certificate to the device id. Or the device foot prints can be used to ensure that the authentication certificates are used by only the targeted devices. But again this will raise an issue of only one device being used by a user for all transactions which is another constraint.

# 8 Conclusion

The proposed solution is a methodological way of minimizing the dependency on the middleware and enabling the direct client-LSP communication. It also handles the issue of access control based, temporal based, and transaction based accountability. The authentication happens through the middleware's trusted certificate without revealing the identity to the LSPs. The authorization and access control information get included into the certificate itself therefore the location servers don't have to bother about accountability of the users due to anonymity. Also, the clients can directly talk to the content providers, rather than sending each and every service request through the middleware as in prevalent architectures. The certificate encrypted with the location server's public key makes easy to handle the decryption by the location server using its private key. The anonymity again became blurred due by implementing anonymity in two ways i.e. "One-to-Many" and "Many-to-One" anonymity.

# References

1. Lioudakis, G.V., et al.: A Middleware architecture for privacy protection. The International Journal of Computer and Telecommunications Networking 51(16), 4679–4696 (2007)
2. Ardagna, C., Cremonini, M., Damiani, E., De Capitani di Vimercati, S., Samarati, P.: New Approaches for Security, Privacy and Trust in Complex Environments. In: Venter, H., Eloff, M., Lahuschagne, L., Eloff, J., von Solms, R. (eds.) IFIP International Federation for Information Processing, vol. 232, pp. 313–324. Springer, Boston (2007)
3. The European Opinion Research Group. European Union citizens' views about privacy: Special Eurobarometer 196 (December 2003)

4. Ardagna, C.A., Cremonini, M., De Capitani di Vimercati, S., Samarati, P.: Access Control in Location-Based Services. In: Bettini, C., Jajodia, S., Samarati, P., Wang, X.S. (eds.) Privacy in Location-Based Applications. LNCS, vol. 5599, pp. 106–126. Springer, Heidelberg (2009)
5. Mohan, A., Blough, D.M.: An attribute-based authorization policy framework with dynamic conflict resolution. In: Proceedings of the 9th Symposium on Identity and Trust on the Internet. ACM International Conference Proceeding Series, pp. 37–50 (2010)
6. Hauser, C., et al.: Privacy and Security in Location-Based Systems With Spatial Models. Institute of Communication Networks and Computer Engineering University of Stuttgart, Germany (2002)
7. Chen, Y., Yang, J., He, F.: A Trusted Infrastructure for Facilitating Access Control. IEEE, Los Alamitos (2008), 978-1-4244-2677-5/08/ 2008
8. Hohenberger, S., Weis, S.A.: Honest-verifier private disjointness testing without random oracles. In: Proceedings of the 6th Workshop on Privacy Enhancing Technologies, June 2006, pp. 265–284 (2006)
9. Hauser, C., Kabatnik, M.: Towards Privacy Support in a Global Location Service. In: Proceedings of the WATM/EUNICE (2001)
10. Schiller, J., et al.: Location-Based Services, pp. 16, 91–96. Morgan Kaufmann Publishers, San Francisco (2005), ISBN: 1-55860-929-6
11. Kin, Y.W.: NAN: Near-me Area Network. In: IEEE Internet Computing. IEEE computer Society Digital Library. IEEE Computer Society, Los Alamitos (2010)
12. Hua, W., et al.: Ticket-based Service Access scheme for Mobile Users. In: ACSC 2002 Proceedings of the Twenty-fifth Australasian Conference on Computer science, vol. 4 (2002), ISBN:0-909925-82-8
13. John, B., et al.: Method for Generating Digital Fingerprint Using Pseudo Random Number Code. International Patent WO 2008/094725 A1
14. Hauser, C., et al.: Privacy and Security in Location-Based Systems With Spatial Models. Institute of Communication Networks and Computer Engineering University of Stuttgart, Germany
15. Duckham, M., Kulik, L.: A Formal Model of Obfuscation and Negotiation for Location Privacy. In: Gellersen, H.-W., Want, R., Schmidt, A. (eds.) PERVASIVE 2005. LNCS, vol. 3468, pp. 152–170. Springer, Heidelberg (2005)
16. Gedik, B., Liu, L.: A Customizable k-Anonymity Model for Protecting Location Privacy. In: ICDCS 2005 (2005)
17. Magkos, E., et al.: A Distributed Privacy-Preserving Scheme for Location-Based Queries. In: Proceedings of the 2010 IEEE International Symposium on A World of Wireless, Mobile and Multimedia Networks, WoWMoM (2010)
18. Hengartner, U.: Hiding Location Information from Location-Based Services. IEEE, Los Alamitos (2007), 1-4244-1241-2/07
19. Quality Attributes,
   http://www.softwarearchitectures.com/go/Discipline/Designing Architecture/QualityAttributes/tabid/64/Default.aspx
   (last visited on April 27, 2011)

# Fault Location Scheme of Smart Grid Based on Wireless Sensor Networks

Tian-Bao Zhang, You-Ling Zhou, and Bao-Dan Chen

College of Information Science & Technology Hainan University, China

**Abstract.** The paper develops a fault location scheme for Smart Grid based on wireless sensor networks. Some fault location and detection principles are illustrated based on wireless sensor networks. The scheme is designed according to the requirements of end—to—end delay, reliability, and synchronization in power distribution system and simulation results indicate that it is feasible to implement the Smart Grid fault location based on wireless sensor networks.

**Keywords:** Smart Grid, Wireless Sensor Networks, Fault Location.

## 1 Introduction

Nowadays, the development of power sector is faced up with many challenges such as low investment efficiency and reliability of power supply, weak flexibility and adaptability, serious environmental damage and so on. The developed countries like USA and EU all believe that to construct a Smart Grid based on brand-new technological architecture is the best way to solve the problems. Once the Smart Grid is put forward, it immediately becomes popular and booms all around the world, which turns into the trend of the next generation power grid.

Smart Grid based on integrated and high-speed two-way communication networks performs well for the power grid. Through advanced sensor, measurement techniques, the control method and decision support system, it guarantees the power grid can operate in a reliable, safe, economic, efficient and economically friendly way.

With the rapid development of MEMS(Micro-Electro-Mechanism System), SOC(System on Chip), wireless communication and low-power embedded technologies, WSN (Wireless Sensor Networks) comes into being and brings a revolution of information perception owing to its low power consumption and cost, distributed and self-organizing features. WSN is a multi-hop and self-organized network formed from a large amount of cheap mini sensor nodes. It has a wide application in multiple targets, short distance communication, and also plays significant roles in the construction of Smart Grid.

Based on the fault handling automatic technology in power distribution system, the paper employs the signal injection method to locate the fault sector based on the wireless sensor network, thus offers a new idea for the construction of Smart Grid.

In order to have a systematic and clear understanding about the fault process of power distribution system, we divide the process into three stages [1].

P. Sénac, M. Ott, and A. Seneviratne (Eds.): ICWCA 2011, LNICST 72, pp. 107–115, 2012.

①Faults switch and remove when faults occur. The stage can finish in milliseconds using high voltage breaker combination with relay protection automatic device. If the relay protection quickly breaks, the duration is commonly 100ms around.

② Fault sector's isolation and normal sector's power restoration. The duration generally lasts seconds to minutes.

③Fault location and remove. It usually needs ten minutes to several hours

In the three stages above, problems concerned are not the same. The paper mainly considers the third stage, aims to improving the repairing efficiency and lowering the cost.

## 2  Current Research Situation

At present, most of the power distribution system can't carry out monitoring over all distribution circuits, even in main lines with a switch subsection. The system can only isolate limited segments, so it's inevitable to consume large manpower and material resources to locate the faults.

The power distribution network covers a wide range included the urban area, rural area and mountainous area, so it suffers from wind and rain all year ,plus the unpredictable man-made factors, which lead to the short-circuit accidents occur- red frequently.

Once the fault occurs, if it can't be rapidly located, the efficiency is very low. Especially when single-phase-to-ground fault occurs in the power distribution network with neutral point not grounded, the voltage is square root of three times the normal voltage although no large short-circuit current exists, so if we can't promptly remove the ground fault, it can trigger a new short-circuit fault. It's more difficult to locate the fault in the single-phase-to-ground system.

For a long time, it is a technical difficulty when it comes to single-phase-to-ground fault's line selection and location in the low current grounding system. Choosing grounding lines accurately and locating the single-phase-to-ground sector can avoid the unnecessary switching operation on non-fault lines so as to maintain the power continuity, therefore, researchers at home and abroad focus on the issue, and many corresponding products are already used in power grid.

The fundamental principle of single-phase-to-ground fault detection is the same as single-phase–to-ground line selection. Basically, the methods to detect single-phase-to-ground fault are as follows, five times harmonic method, current mutations hair method, the first half wave method, the zero sequence current method and signal injection method[2-4]. Except signal injection method, the rest detection methods are passive detections, which rely on the change of the parameters before and after single-phase-to-ground fault. Owing to the complexity of distribution network's topology structure and the varied operation mode, also plus the electromagnetic interference and harmonic pollution, the signal would be distorted when single-phase-to-ground fault occurs, therefore, the accuracy of the signal can't be guaranteed.

Considering the features of the low current grounding system, this paper employs signal injection method for fault location. When single-phase-to-ground fault occurs, the source from the transformer substation will spontaneously inject a special signal into the bus bar, which will pass around the loop circuit composed of the source and the ground point. Once the power sensor detects the signal, it sends the fault information.

Signal injection method is free from the effect of the system operating mode, topology structure, the method of grounding the neutrals, and random fault and so on. There is no need to set threshold for fault indicator. Moreover, the method of detecting single-phase-to-ground fault is far more accurate than other methods.

## 3   Principle

This system uses a signal injection method for fault location. Firstly, locate the fault sector through distribution terminal, and then improve the location accuracy by WSN.

The system employs three layers of wireless communication networks, which is composed of base stations, FTU (feedback terminal unit), CT (current sensor), PDA, source, GPRS networks and WSN,   as shown in Fig.1. between sensor nodes and PDA using without the routing protocol 470MHz short-range wireless communication; besides sensor nodes and between sensor nodes and FTU using ZigBee Pro protocol stack based on WSN communication, which is the 2.4GHz Mesh network; between FTU and base station using the GPRS network.

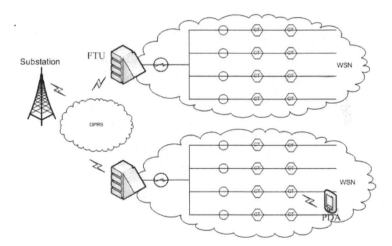

**Fig. 1.** the structure of system

There installs a dynamic-impedance load source device in the transformer substation, so when single-phase-to-ground fault occurs, in a period of time, offset voltage can be detected by the controller at neutral point, meanwhile the source device will automatically work for a few seconds and then exit. The system with extinction coil which has a delay for the source input is designed to let the ground-fault point automatically extinguish arc and eliminate the fault consequently. As is known, grounds points only exist in the fault lines, which can form a loop circuit combined with the source, it's no doubt that there is a current flow in the circuit. In order to detect the current of each phase-line, sensors for current detection are scattered around each phase-line in the transformer substation's coil out or the branch of the distribution circuit. If the indicator in some line can demodulate the current, it illustrates that the line is the fault line. The method can also be used to detect short-circuit fault, we can see clearly in Fig.2.

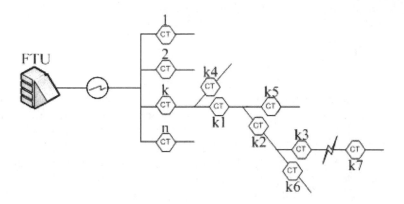

**Fig. 2.** The principle of system

(1) Single-phase ground fault occurs. Source substation operation automatic after a few seconds delay, stop running after 10s; The sensor node which is installed in the substation outlet indicates the fault outlet(k No sensor action); selecting device automatically display and record the fault outlet, and reported to the FTU by WSN, The sensor node k installed on the fault line sending fault information the it child node k1 and k4, the sensor node k4 installed on the normal line send back normal information, the sensor node k1 installed on the fault line send fault information back and send this message to it son node k2 and k5, Information will dissemination by this principle, until the sensor node k3 installed on the fault line receive feedback information by it child nodes are all normal message, it can be determined that a fault point is between the k3 and it's child node k7.

(2) Phase short circuit fault occurs. Signal source does not move, the other procedures were the same as (1).

## 4    Simulation

Electric power fault detection system has established rules for system communication [5]. Some crucial criteria are as follows. Transmission time for fault information is within 4ms and maximal transmission time for fault information between substations is commonly 8 ~ 12ms. For a breaker, its controlling signal's maximal transmission time is commonly 2 ~ 8ms, while sending a signal to the adjacent area needs 8 ~ 12ms. Also, time synchronization should be less than 1ms. In reliability, transmission error should be immune to environmental noise, and when a fault occurs, the system can detect and deliver the fault timely and accurately to regional management node unit for further processing.

## 4.1 Reliability

To ensure data information from low-layer sensor node can reliably transmit to regional management node, we model the system in the network simulation software OMNeT++ as seen in Fig.3. The degree of redundancy for each line is 1, data transmission rate is set to 150kb/s, packet transmission rate is 50 per second, packet length is 28 bytes. Besides every second intervals, the link error that is caused by environmental interference obeys **Poisson distribution which** parameters λ is 0.5.

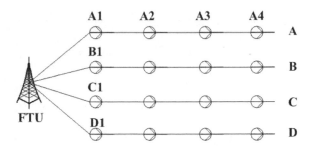

**Fig. 3.** Topology of a simulation network

MAC layer use CSMA/CA protocol. All communications employ ACK mechanism, if no ACK frame received, the system retransmit data. It can be seen in Fig.4, for regional management node, the probability for successfully receiving data from line nodes is 97.83% and 98.62%. When the maximal retransmission number is set to be R≥4, regional management nodes can successful receive all packets. A packet RTT (round-trip time) is defined as the time difference between the sending and receiving the corresponding confirmation, then RTO (retransmission timeout) can be evaluated as follows:

$$RTO=\beta \times RTT \tag{1}$$

Where β is larger than 1, so RTO should be slightly larger than RTT, namely, the much closer to 1, the timelier for retransmission. But if the packet is not lost, retransmission may even heavy network burden just for a slight time delay, so, in the simulation β is set to 1.5. According to the requirements, we have RTT bigger than 1.5ms, thus RTO is bigger than 2.25ms. Obviously, the delay of successfully sent is greatly increased with each retransmission. But the power protection system has a high demand for data transmission delay, usually less than 4ms[5]. Generally, the packet loss rate is high in wireless sensor networks so to ensure the reliability of data transmission more retransmissions are inevitable, which contradicts with the maximal delay. In order to solve this problem, this paper develops a kind of reliable transmission mechanism oriented to events.

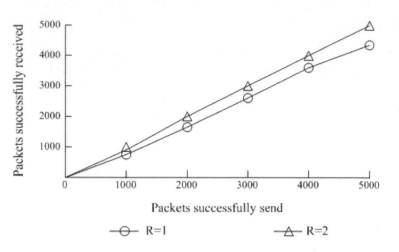

**Fig. 4.** Probability of packets successfully received

One important feature of wireless sensor networks is its node's redundancy which makes the system blessed with the ability of strong tolerance. Induced by the redundancy properties, event-oriented reliable transmission mechanism comes into being. We define event-oriented reliability as the packets set required in fault detection during a time interval t, denoted by P.

In our simulation network model, each perception object (A phase, B phase, C phase, D phase) has four wireless sensor nodes for data collection. Suppose in Fig.3, single-phase-to-ground fault happens at A phase, according to the fault detection model[6], the current data at A, B and C and D phase should be first obtained. Let Sa, Sb, Sc and Sd denote the current data at A, B and C and D phase, respectively, then we have:

$$P = \{Sa, Sb, Sc, Sd\} \tag{2}$$

Sa can not only be obtained by the node Node_A1, but also by A phase's other nodes. i.e., during t time, at least one node of A phase can successfully transmit its sampling data to regional management node. For Sb, Sc and Sd , it's the same case.

Event-oriented reliable transmission mechanism can be briefly described as follows:

(1) In each regional management node unit, save the transmission link-state of all the nodes involved in the unit, and each node's link-state can be seen as the transmission reliability of the nodes before it;

(2) Compared with redundant nodes, the node with a higher reliability possesses a better transmission priority;

(3) When a node send a request, regional management node inquires the information whether it has been received or not. If so, the node won't send the data information.

Fig.5 gives the number of transmission packets of different redundancy, based on event-oriented reliable mechanism under the same reliability condition. It can be seen in Fig.4 that the reliability of data collection is increased with the redundancy, but when redundancy exceeds 4, redundancy has little effect on the reliability. Moreover, the larger the redundancy, the higher the installation cost of wireless sensor network. So we should take comprehensive consideration of the node's redundancy.

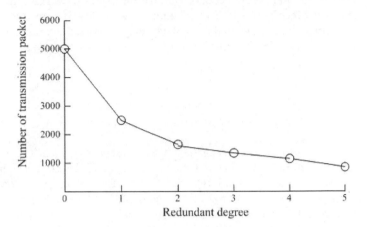

**Fig. 5.** Number of transmission packets versus redundant degree

## 4.2  Delay

Above, we have known that the power protection system has a high demand for data transmission delay, usually less than 4ms[5]. So the data gathering delay should be paid great attention when making the feasibility analysis.

### 1. Single-hop link data gathering delay
See in Fig.3. Gathering delay mainly investigates the average delay and the maximal delay of the multi-nodes sending data which are gathered at regional management node. Gathering delay mainly includes:

(1) Internal data processing delay Tp;
(2) Waiting for sending delay Tw;
(3) The transmission delay from the sending node to gathering node Tt;
(4) Processing data delay at regional management node Tr.

The delay simulation results based on the network structure in Fig.3.are shown in Table.1:

**Table 1.** Delay of the delivery packets

|  | communication traffic / Network capacity / (%) | | |
|---|---|---|---|
|  | 4% | 10% | 15% |
| average delay / ms | 1.46 | 1.62 | 1.87 |
| maximal delay / ms | 2.83 | 3.07 | 3.42 |

It can be seen that data gathering delay has a sharp increase along with the increased network communication.

**2. Multi-hop link data gathering delay**

In WSN the maximal delay for fault data determines the maximal coverage area for regional management node to collect data. Simulation results show that multi-hop link data gathering delay increases with the hop numbers. As in Fig.3, if the traffic/network capacity is 4%, then the average gathering delay is 3.72ms, and the maximal delay is 7.83ms, which is far more than allowed maximal transmission delay 4ms.

## 4.3 Synchronization

The fault monitoring system based on wireless sensor network is a typical distributed system that requires multi-nodes cooperation. And the cooperation work needs time synchronization.

The synchronization precision between the wireless sensor nodes is 0.05 ~ 0.1ms[5]. The network architecture in Fig.3 is based on the platform of Mica2 node[7], its clock is 7.3728 Mhz, which employs RBS (Reference Broadcast Synchronization)[8] and TPSN(Timing-sync Protocol for Sensor Networks)[9], where the synchronization precision of RBS is 0.027ms, TPSN's is 0.016ms. They all meet the requirements.

As the hop increases, the network synchronization precision increases. Take TPSN as an example, the simulation results is shown in Fig.6.

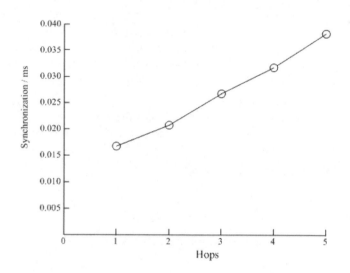

**Fig. 6.** Multi-hop synchronization analysis of TPSN

# 5   Conclusion

Through analysis, we can see that the fault detection for power system based on WSN meets the requirements in reliability, delay and synchronization precision.

As the processing capacity and distributed collaborative ability of WSN improve, WSN has laid the foundation of the new relay protection in power system.

For instance, Crossbow company launch an Imote2 wireless sensor node which has integrated PXA271 X Scale processor and 14 A/D conversions, compatible with IEEE802.15.4 RF chip. Its transmission rate reaches 250Kb/s and offers a variety of I/O interfaces.

Simulation results show that, for single-hop data gathering based on wireless sensor network, its maximal delay doesn't exceed 4ms, which satisfies power protection system's requirements on communication.

Especially for distributed bus bar protection and short-circuit protection, which has small coverage area of protection unit. Owing to its many outgoing lines, adopting conventional protection device will lead to complicated connection and high cost. In such an environment, it's more suitable and effective to use WSN to realize protection.

This paper is supported by key discipline construction project of Hainan province (No, xkxm0841-02), research projects of Hainan University (No, hd09xm88) and The 211 Project Central Special Fund of Hainan University.

# References

[1] Yuan, Q.-c.: Summary of Automation Technology for Fault Handing in Distribution System. Electrical Equipment 8(12), 1–5 (2007)
[2] Wang, H., Hu, K., Sang, Z.-z.: A S's signal injection method and special connection modes of voltage transformer. Relay 32(3), 26–28 (2004)
[3] Ma, J., Yu, W.-h., Che, W.-y., et al.: A novel fault localizer of tree form distribution networks based on an improved S injection method. Relay 30(10), 51–54 (2002)
[4] Cai, W., Zhang, X.-s., Liu, C.-z., et al.: Distribution network fault location method based on PT injecting signal and neural network fault diagnosis system tracking the character of wavelet transform modulus maxima. Relay 34(23), 44–53 (2006)
[5] IEEE.TRP1525, Draft IEEE Technical Report on Substation Integrated Protection, Control and Data Acquisition Communication Requirements (2003)
[6] Huang, X.-y., Liu, P., Miao, S., hong, et al.: Application of Wireless Sensor Networks in Power Monitoring System. Automation of Electric Power Systems 3l(7), 99–103 (2007)
[7] Online: [EB / OL], http://www.xbow.com
[8] Elson, J., Griod, L., Esrein, D.: Fine-grained Network Time Synchronization Using Reference Broadcast. In: Proc. 5th Symp. Operating Systems Design and Implementation, Boston (2002)
[9] Ganeriwal, S., Kumar, R., Srivastava, M.B.: Timing-syn Protocol for Sensor Networks. In: Proc. 1st Int'l Conf. on Embedded Networked Sensor Systems, LosAngles, pp. 138–149 (2003)

# Information-Analytical Systems of Thermo-Power Engineering

Yurzin Bogdanov and Valeri Chipulis

Institute of Automation and Control Processes FEB RAS
Radio str., 5, 690041, Vladivostok, Russia
{bogdanov,chipulis}@vira.dvo.ru

**Abstract.** One of the main activities of the Institute of Automation and Control Processes FEB RAS is development, implementation and support (together with the service company LLC "Infovira") of information and analytical monitoring for both heat-and-power engineering objects (HPEO): thermo-power generation companies and consumers in the Russian Far East. The report highlights recent developments in this direction.

**Keywords:** information-analytical system, heat-and-power engineering objects, data acquisition, database system, metering devices (heat meters).

## 1 Introduction

In 2000, information-analytical system (IAS) "SONA" [1] was completed and since then was applied used for monitoring and management of thermo-energy (including thermo energy meters) by Administration of Vladivostok on the objects of education.

Since 2001, IAS equipped the boiler room of All-Russian Children's Center "Ocean" for monitoring and analysis of operation modes of heat sources "ISMA-ocean" [2].

The intensive applications of SCADA-systems enabled new development of IAS "AIST" [3] for heat sources, implementing function of the technological process monitoring using SCADA system  Trace Mode 5, enriched by functions of retrospective data analysis. Requirement of analysis caused design of special subsystem with totally redesigned data structures and development of new processing modules for data visualization. System "AIST" designed and implemented in 2005 and operates in the boilers "Course" and "Southern", (both city of Arseniev). Further, in 2006, step-wise development of IAS with similar functions took place for  boiler LLC Teploenergo "Bolshoi Kamen".

Well-known model of hydraulic and thermal systems are based on parameters reflected in the project documentation. However, using these relationships for analysis of functioning might be not  possible due to difference between project and reality caused by the deviation from the project specifications during construction, aging of the object. That is why in vast majority of cases real information taken from measurement of the object becomes crucial and therefore essential to define technical

P. Sénac, M. Ott, and A. Seneviratne (Eds.): ICWCA 2011, LNICST 72, pp. 116–124, 2012.

state of the object and real dependencies, taking into account the actual technical state of the object. This information becomes useful for various real analysis. While volume of information is significant statistical methods including regression might be used. These methods became a foundation of information-analytical system "Scooter"

## 2 IAS "Scooter"

Stages of development associated with the introduction of a new technologies and measuring equipment. Monitoring functions in the system are implemented using SCADA platform Trace Mode 6 with built-in data analysis.

The next step in the development of this direction is associated with the new platform [4] (the universal framework) for creating systems to analyze modes of operation of HPEO.

The main pursued goals were:

- framework has to contain a database [5] and a reasonably complete set of software tools to analyze operations (using proposed database) and
- to allow efficient, with minimum time overheads assembling the system of analysis for specific applications.

The finalized version of the IAS Industrial "Scooter", was completed in 2006, mostly corresponding the mentioned above requirements. Figure 1 presents the structure of the standard IAS.

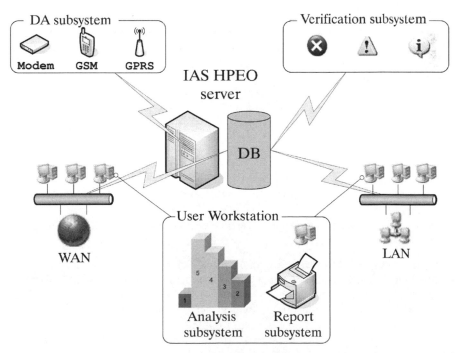

**Fig. 1** Structure of the IAS

The information base of the system uses results of measurements of HPEO, as a result of the monitoring process using SCADA-system (mainly for heat sources), or includes application of archived data previously accumulated from heat meters (mainly for the objects of consuming heat).

The system includes a set of independent software modules that focused on the required applications and performed special functions required.

The main modules of the system are: "Data Acquisition", "Graphics", "Tables", "Reports", "Temperature schedule", "Heat Mode", "Recommendations", "Defects", "Diagrams", "Dependencies", "Configurator". Independent modules are interconnected by a data structure (which may be edited, recorded, accumulated and used by different modules). Data structure is stored one database, supported by *Windows* protocols formats of standard data exchange. The system implements a client-server architecture, using single database, accessible for client applications (modules) through a local area data network with TCP / IP protocol stack.

Modules of the system can be used autonomously (with its local copy of the database), for example, using aggregating module for manual data acquisition, followed up by synchronization of data within data base.

Another example of the use of separate databases is collecting of data from metering devices in a regional data accumulation centers (for example, through cellular links), transmission and synchronization of data in the overall data center for high-speed lines (TCP / IP). [4] presents the functionality of the main modules of the system.

## 2.1  Data Acquisition

The primary objective of IAS is to obtain the results of measuring basic parameters of operation of HPEO. This task consists of collection of archived data from metering devices (heat meters), the primary processing and storing in the database of measurement results, including retrospective ability to retrieve and use information. The list of devices supported by the system includes a set of heat meters, widespread in use. Other types of meters can be added by writing the appropriate driver.

The module supports different modes:

- Direct poll;
- Manual survey modem
- Automatic dial-up fee schedule;
- Distributed data acquisition via GSM / GPRS modems with the help of technology M2M;
- Monitoring current measurement results when connected metering devices via RS-232 converters in Ethernet.

Mode of direct check of parameters collects data from the heat meter archives. Mode is implemented using laptop for direct connected via a serial port (RS-232 or RS-485) or the optical head.

Manual poll allows connecting devices via a modem, using public switched telephone network (PSTN) or a network of mobile operators (GSM).

Automatic mode is used for the mass survey group of devices on a schedule of informational and analytical center. Communication equipment and communication channels are the same as the manual survey. The advantage of a distributed way of collecting data (GPRS) is the use of innovative hardware and software that allows to move from standard technology of switched access to the heat meter (CSD) at a certain time (scheduled) to asinc-driven data acquisition with a large number of heat meters without the need to increase the switching equipment at the DA server.

In addition, this method is more flexible, addressing the organization of data acquisition network and, significantly reducing communication costs.

For scheduling and management of large real scale of thermo-consuming heat infrastructures and for the possibility of connecting the heat meter to a local area network (LAN) or wide area network (WAN) a special adapter or interface cards, are required, allowing monitoring of the pseudo-real time and manipulate these objects from any point network through the Internet.

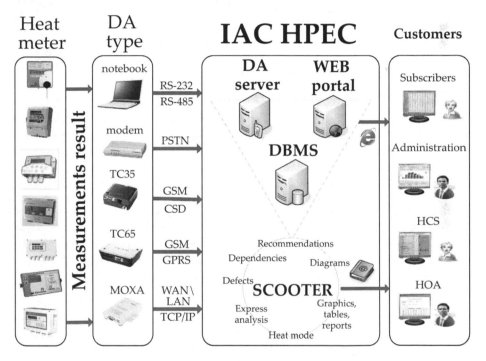

**Fig. 2.** Architecture of information-analytical center

Upon completion of reading data from the archives of the heat meter, the results of measurements are reduced to a unified structure and stored in the Database management system (DBMS) of thermal energy to heat facilities. Database process each item individually using service set static information (energy passport) and accumulated since the start of service retrospective information on the results of measurements. Currently, IAS "Scooter" services for more than five hundreds of consumers of thermal energy in Primorsky Krai, Russia. Among them individual subscribers, city administrations, housing and communal services (HCS), homeowners association (HOA).

In 2007-2009, IES "Scooter" adds on was performed by modules "Express-analysis" (verification of the results of measurements to determine their validity) and "Web-portal" (giving the user the results of measurements and data analysis in the Internet network). Below is a brief description of these modules.

## 2.2  Express-Analysis

To assess efficiency of the subsystem for data collection as an increasing number of serviced sites is impossible without the implementation of automated control and diagnostics at all stages of the process of data receiving: the connection with metering, reading of archive information, transfer data to server for accumulation, preliminary data processing and recording in the database.

Initially, the automatic collection of data provides journaling survey of storing a sequence of events occurring in the process of 24 hours date recording using substantial amount of meters. To display information from a journal of operation registration of thermal units a module plug-in "Express-analysis" [6] was developed. The module is displaying an operational data acquisition with heat meters for a group of objects heat supply for a given period of time.

Data acquisition also requires verification of data consistency and shows that it is important also to ensure adequate and reliable remote transmission of measurement results from the heat meters archives the database system. New data from metering devices need to be assessed in terms of reliability and validity of measurement results [7], as well as detection of abnormal situations on the thermal point and diagnosing defects measuring equipment [8].

Diagnostics tasks are performed by special module "Express-analysis". On the basis of the developed methods and algorithms for diagnosis [9] created a subsystem of automatic verification of results. The inputs to the subsystem verification are the results of measurements coming from the heat meters and passport details of the thermal points: thermal load, temperature schedule, equipment specifications, the metrological characteristics of measuring tools and other information about the object.

The results of processing the input data after performing the verification process (the information about detected violations, deviations from the normal operation mode, the detected abnormal situations, etc.) are entered into the database. Accumulated diagnostic information is used later in other modules of IAS for the solution of various tasks: informing about the unreliability of data for a specific time interval, the recommendation to eliminate the defects on the thermal site, signaling the emergence of critical or emergency situations, etc.

Example of visualization of detected violations is shown in Fig. 3. Detailed information about discrepancies detected for a particular object can be accessed through the dialog box by clicking the appropriate cell in the table. To improve the perception of information and simplify analysis special filter was introduced that allows to display the relevant class of deviations.

Typically, the duration of violations shows the seriousness of the problem and the need for intervention. Using data from express analysis, maintenance engineer can quickly conduct a more thorough analysis of the situation and make a final decision on the causes of violations with the help of more powerful systems "Scooter". For example, estimation of the magnitude of error can be published for the allowable range, additionally changes of parameter over time can be presented as a graph or in tabular form using a system module "Graphs, Tables, Reports" [10].

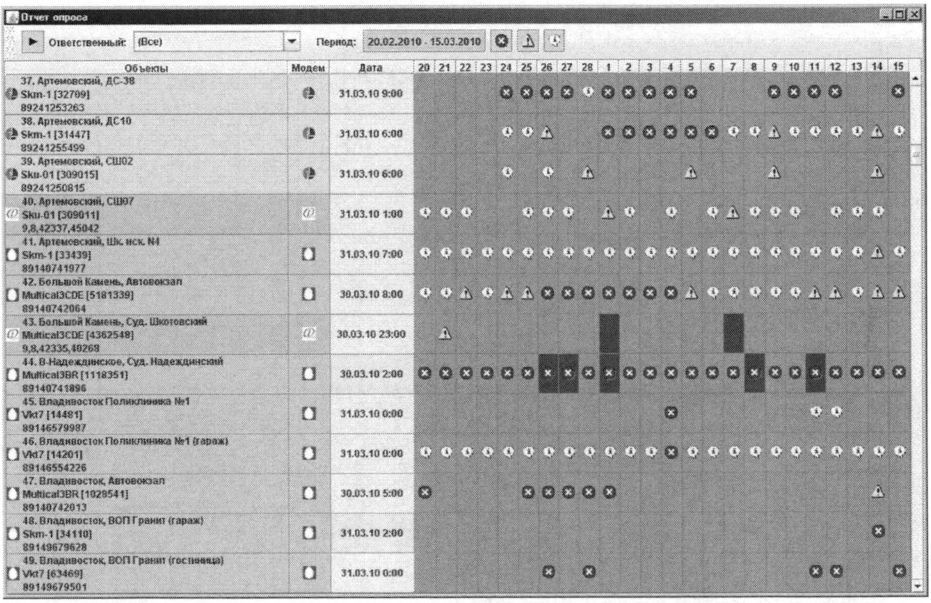

**Fig. 3.** Visualization of diagnostic information

## 2.3  Web-Portal

The development of new technologies in the IT field makes periodically review the approaches of software development. Distributed systems became the most popular in recent years, due to ability to support remote operation via web-portals (using Internet, for example). This software works on web-server for information service providers, and users can view and access the information on the server anywhere in the world. In this connection there is need for a transition to a new platform for software development with a view to rapid and creating programs that run as a traditional way (on the user's computer) and on the web-server as a distributed system.

Clients web-portal have the opportunity to request data (collected, for example, with their own heat meters) from the central database of information service providers in the form of graphs, tables. In addition, it is possible to generate the report for the heat supply organization.

Modern web-technologies allow output data in the form of static (graphs, charts, tables) or in a dynamic, interactive format. In the latter case, the user, for example, using the mouse to perform certain actions: scale, move, hide unnecessary graphics, etc. Currently, the web-portal www.infovira.ru enables to access available dynamic graphics, tables and reports, having  the core functionality as in the" Scooter " tool described above.

# 3  Implementation

The latest versions of IAS developed for the Radiopribor heating, Vladivostok (2008) and the MC Topolinaya Alley subscribers heating, Vladivostok (2010) are implemented with new functions of monitoring and analysis of process of control heating.

In 2006 there was a need in the development of IAS for the Radiopribor closed system of heating, Vladivostok (19 thermal units are installed on their meters and controls). In addition to traditional individual thermal units tasks of calculation and analysis were supplied by the customer other specific to the system object tasks: monitoring operating conditions (Fig. 4) with control of frequency and periods of reading of metering information, on request of the operation manager, analysis of cost balance and energy consumption for the whole factory, and its sectors, analysis of regulatory efficiency of thermal energy; control of butterfly valves with actuators on the thermal head node, determining the total heat consumption of the system.

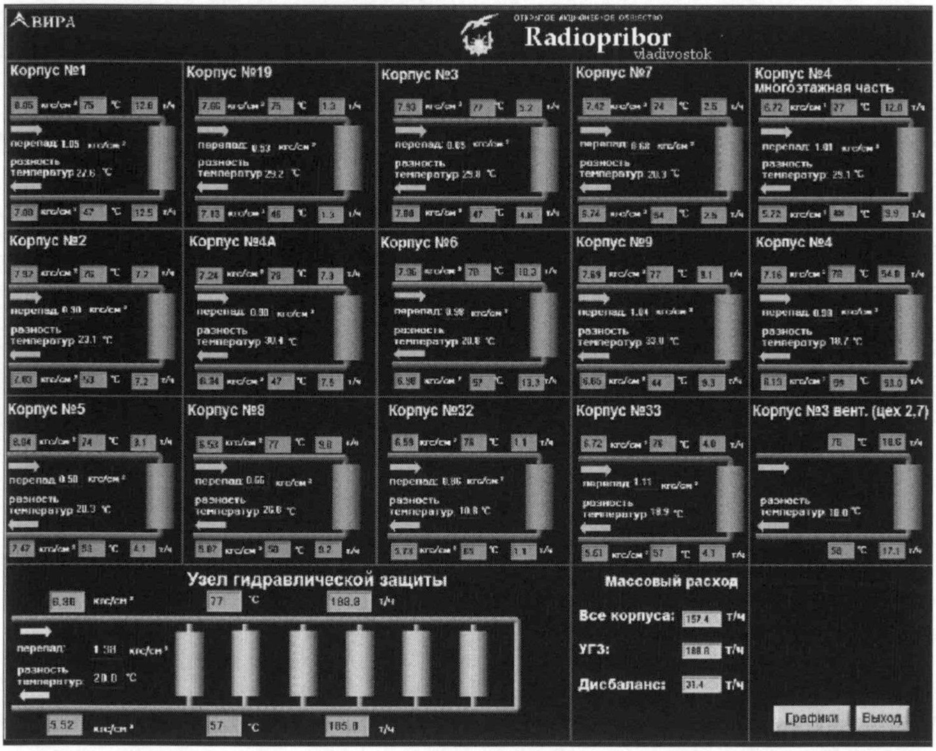

**Fig. 4.** The monitoring system of the Radiopribor heating

Valves are controlled electrically by AUMATIC AC 1.1. Made configuration of the control unit electrically improves regulation and de-risk hydraulic impact. For the organization of a remote control valve designed software and set up an individual communication channel with a control unit electrically independent from the existing data collection system with heat meters. Access to the control unit is performed using protocol MODBUS / RTU via converter ICP DAS RS232-RS485. The software allows monitoring the electric control unit and set the set point for opening / closing valves.

Recently, similar tasks of monitoring and analysis were initiated for the MC "Topolinaya alley" heating. Developed for this object IAS differs significantly from the previous in terms of implementation of the collection of measurement results. It also has a function of scheduling and remote management of the regulatory process for all thermal units of the system (Fig. 5)

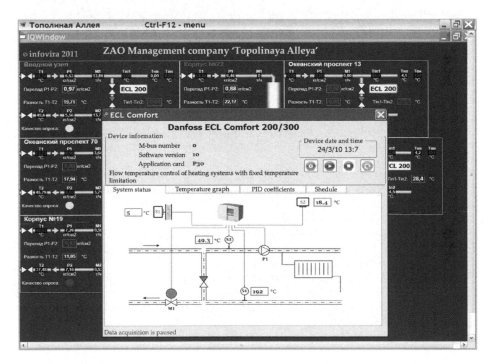

**Fig. 5.** The monitoring control system of the MC "Topolinaya alley" heating

The main effect of the introduction of emerging information and analytical systems defines new level of process control and monitoring of using of thermal resources: all supported by measuring equipment and a new generation of modern information technology.

Features of system ensure continuity and quality of heat supply, maintain optimal (energy efficient) operating conditions of objects, and achieve real economic effect and, consequently, control the growth of tariffs for heat and hot water.

# References

1. Malyshko, A.V., Chipulis, V.P.: Analysis of thermal modes of operation of heat consumers with the information - analytical system SONA. In: Proceedings of the 15 th International Scientific-Technical Conference "Commercial metering of energy", St. Petersburg, April 2002, pp. 23–25 (2002)
2. Malyshko, A.V., Mikhaltsov, A.S., Chipulis, V.P.: The system of monitoring and retrospective analysis of modes of operation of heat sources. In: Proceedings of the 18 th International Scientific Conference "Commercial metering of energy", St. Petersburg, December 2003, pp. 2–4 (2003)
3. Vinogradov, A.N., Gerbek, F.E., Razdobudbko, V.V., Kuznetsov, R.S., Chipulis, V.P.: Accounting for the parameters of technological processes of heat energy. In: Materials 23rd International Scientific and Practical Conference "Commercial metering of energy", St. Petersburg, May 2006, pp. 23–25 (2006)
4. Babenko, V.N., Danielyan, S.A., Kuznetsov, R.S., Razdobudko, V.V., Chipulis, V.P.: The platform for the design of information-analytical systems for monitoring and analysis of objects of power. In: Commercial metering of energy resources: proceedings of the 25 th International Scientific and Practical Conference, pp. 280–292. Borey Art, SPb (2007)
5. Babenko, V.N., Kuznetsov, R,S., Razdobudko, V.V.: Database account of thermal energy to heat the objects of Primorsky Territory. Federal Service for Intellectual Property, Patent and Trademark Office. Certificate on state registration databases № 2008620273, July 16 (2008)
6. Chipulis, V.P., Babenko, V.N.: Scooter - Express-analysis. The Federal Service for Intellectual Property, Patent and Trademark Office. Certificate on state registration of a computer program № 2009616498, November 24 (2009)
7. Chipulis, V.P.: Evaluation of reliability of measurement results in power / measurement equipment, vol. (5), pp. 53–58. Publishing house "Technology", Moscow (2005)
8. Chipulis, V.P.: Diagnostics of metrological defects in the problems of thermal energy accounting. J. Automation and Remote Control (11), 166–178 (2005)
9. Kuznetsov, R.S.: To analyze the reliability of measurement results in problems of thermal energy accounting. J. Sensors and Systems (7), 45–47 (2008)
10. Chipulis, V.P., Razdobudko, V.V.: Scooter - graphs, tables, reports. Federal Service for Intellectual Property, Patent and Trademark Office. Certificate on state registration of a computer program № 2009616500, November 24 (2009)

# A Node-Grouping Superframe-Division MAC Protocol for Smart Home Based on IEEE802.15.4 Protocol

Ganqing Ma, Chong Shen, and Baodan Chen

College of Information Science & Technology Hainan University, China
vitoshen@gmail.com, cbd@hainu.edu.cn

**Abstract.** As an application of Wireless Sensor Network (WSN), Smart Home obtained fast development in recent years, and the researches for the Media Access Control (MAC) protocol are mainly focused on energy efficiency and consumption, which pay little attention on the access control of urgent information about the security and guard. To introduce urgent information priorities and reduce the cost of independent security information overhead, this paper proposes a node-grouping superframe-division MAC protocol based on IEEE802.15.4 MAC protocol. This protocol is designed for Smart Home applications, and focused on priority facility in an emergency. This modified protocol has good network performance, especially to the node with transmission priority. The simulation result indicates that the new protocol is better than the traditional IEEE802.15.4 MAC protocol in terms of packet delivery ratio, transmission delay, network throughput, and energy efficiency.

**Keywords:** Smart Home, IEEE802.15.4 MAC protocol, Superframe-division, Priority.

## 1 Introduction

With the development of micro-electronic technology, wireless communication technology, and embedded technology, the WSN got rapid development, with the characteristics of low consumption, high efficiency, low complexity and short-distance communication. The IEEE802.15 series standard main applies to short-distance wireless communication network, in which IEEE802.15.4 is a set of early network service standard formulated for the Low-Rate Wireless Personal Area Network (LR-WPAN). Because of the energy efficiency, robustness and flexibility characteristic, IEEE802.15.4 standard is suitable for most WSN applications [1][2]. As an important application of WSN, Smart Home also adopts IEEE802.15.4 standard as one of its main communication protocols [3][4].

The MAC protocol is mainly used to manage and coordinate channel resources for multiple users. The MAC layer is in the bottom of the WSN protocol stack, which is the direct controller for the date message and control frame carrying on transmission and

P. Sénac, M. Ott, and A. Seneviratne (Eds.): ICWCA 2011, LNICST 72, pp. 125–136, 2012.

receiving on the wireless channel. The quality of the MAC protocol is one of the most essential factors direct related with other protocol track's service quality.

## 2   IEEE802.15.4 MAC Layer

IEEE802.15.4 standard defined the main functions of MAC layer including six aspects: constructs and maintains PAN (coordinator), supports the connection and separation between the equipment of network (coordinator), channel resource access, applies guaranteed time slot (GTS) for specific application, supports equipment's security, and provides reliable data link between the MAC entity.

The channel access is a major function of MAC, IEEE802.15.4 network accesses the channel in two ways: based on competitive or not. In competition-based channel access pattern, node take Carrier Sense Multiple Access with Collision Avoidance (CSMA/CA) algorithm to compete channel in the distributed method [5][6], while non-competition channel access is managed completely by the Pan Area Network (PAN) coordinator in the manner of GTS. GTS is similar with CDMA, but it can distribute specific time slot dynamically for the nodes which have sending and receiving requests.

IEEE802.15.4 support two kinds of network operating patterns: the beacon-enabled pattern and the nonbeacon-enabled pattern.

In the beacon-enabled pattern, the coordinator broadcasts beacon-frame which contains network synchronization information and a variety of control information to the entire network periodically. Terminal get synchronize with the coordinator through receiving the beacon frame periodically. The terminal compete the channel through slotted CAMA/CA algorithm.

### 2.1   Superframe Structure

In the beacon-enabled pattern, the coordinator defines the superframe structure, and MAC takes the superframe as the cycle to organize the communication between the network equipments. Each superframe begins with beacon which contains the superframe's duration, the assignment information and so on. Once equipment receives the beacon, it can act according to the content of the beacon to arrange its duty, such as competing to the channel and entering the inactive period.

The superframe structure main includes Active Period and the optional Inactive Period [7], as shown in Fig 1. In the Inactive Period, the device enters the sleep state to save energy. The Active Period which is divided into 16 equal-long time slots contains three phases that is Beacon, Contention Access Period (CAP), and Contention Free Period (CFP). The length of each slot time, the number of the time slot CAP and CFP contains, and other parameters are all set by the coordinator which broadcasting them to the network.

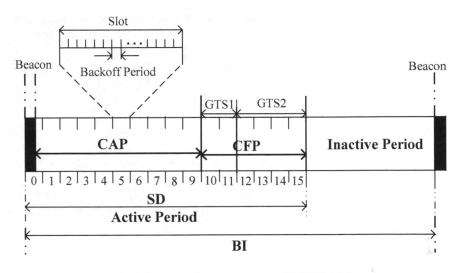

**Fig. 1.** The superframe structure of IEEE802.15.4

The superframe structure is described by the values of macBeaconOrder (BO) and macSuperframeOrder (SO). The value of Beacon Interval (BI) is given by: when $0 \leq BO \leq 14$, BI=aBaseSuperframeDuration*$2^{BO}$ symbols, if BO=15, there is no Beacon, the value of macSuperframeOrder is ignored. The value of Superframe Duration (SD) is given by: when $0 \leq SO \leq BO \leq 14$, SD=aBaseSuperframeDuration*$2^{SO}$ symbols, if SO=15, there is no Inactive Period.

In the Contention Access Period, MAC uses slotted CSMA/CA algorithm to compete channel resources. In the Contention Free Period, the coordinator divides this period into a number of GTS according to the application situation of devices in the last superframe. Each GTS is composed of certain time slots, which number is assigned by the coordinator when the device applying GTS. If the application of a device be approved, this device gets the number of time slots it wants. During this time, this device can monopolize channel resources in its GTS without competition.

Fig 2 has given a superframe example. In this example, CAP takes up 9 slots; CFP takes up 6 slots allocated to two devices, one takes up 2 slots, another takes up 4 slots.

## 2.2 CSMA/CA Algorithm

In the CAP, in order to sent data frames or command frame, devices need to use CSMA/CA mechanism, except that send data frames after the acknowledgement frame immediately. CSMA/CA cannot be used for sending frames in the CFP.

In the slotted CSMA/CA algorithm, the backoff time boundary of each PAN device is consistent with superframe slot boundary. Whenever a device needs to send data frame or command frame, it first locates the boundary of the next slot, and waits for a random number of time slots. After the waiting, the device begins to detect the channel state, if the channel is idle, the device begin to sent data packet at the beginning of the next slot; if channel is busy, the device needs to wait for random number of slots again, and then check the channel state, repeat this process until a idle channel appears. The sending of acknowledgment frame does not need to use CSMA/CA.

To realize the slotted CSMA/CA algorithm, each device needs to maintain three variables: CW, NB, and BE. CW (Contention Window) is the contention window size, which is the number of the continuous detecting channel idle before sending data packet. When the CSMA/CA algorithm starts or the channel is detected to be busy, CW is initialized to 2. CW is only used for the slotted CSMA/CA algorithm. NB (Number of Backoff) is the number of backoff for achieving the algorithm, which is initialized to 0. BE (Back off Exponent) is connected with the backoff period which the device needs to wait for before it sending information. Algorithm use backoff period as the implementation time unit. When macBattLifeExt is set to FALSE, BE is initialized to macMinBE; when macBattLifeExt is set to TRUE, BE is initialized to the lesser between 2 and macMinBE.

Backoff delay time= Random()*aUnitBackoffPeriod,
Where, Random()=[0, $2^{BE}$-1], aUnitBackoffPeriod=20 symbols.
We'll describe the slotted CSMA/CA algorithm refers to Fig 3 as follows.

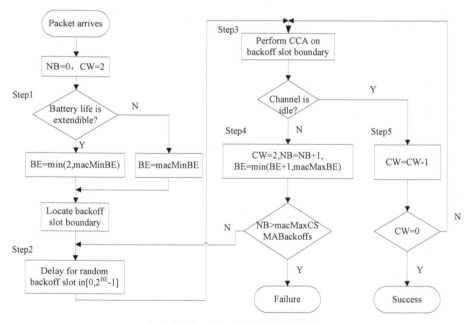

**Fig. 2.** Slotted CSMA/CA algorithm

Step1: When the device buffer has data frame waiting to be sent, MAC first initializes the algorithm parameters, including NB, CW and BE. After this, MAC positions the next slot boundary.

Step2: MAC selects a random backoff value in [0, $2^{BE}$-1], and waits for corresponding backoff slots to avoid collision.

Step3: After the waiting time, MAC sends a channel idle listening request to the physical layer. MAC determines the current channel state through the Clear Channel Assessment (CCA) of the physical layer.

Step4: If CCA demonstration channel condition for busy, MAC increases NB and BE value for 1, and CW value is reset to 2. If NB≤macMaxCSMAbackoffs, the algorithm will jump to Step2, else algorithm declares "Failure".

Step5: If CCA demonstration channel condition for idle, MAC reduces CW value for 1. If CW>0,  the algorithm will jump to Step3, else algorithm declares "Success".

### 2.3   The Application of IEEE802.15.4 MAC Protocol in Smart Home

Collision is the main factor affecting network performance, transmission data collision will cause many adverse effect, including energy loss, transmission delay, and data loss.

Generally speaking, IEEE802.15.4 LR-PAN has two kinds of collision, one of which is contention collision. Node A and B both contention channel successfully, and choice the same Unit Backoff Period (UBP), which will lead collision on the coordinator side as a result of simultaneous transmission. This kind of collision occurs in the beginning of the packet transmission. Another collision is caused by hidden node problem (HNP). Such collision may occur in any time spot during the packages transmission.

Because the network scale of WSN in Smart Home is small, and the general transmission range of IEEE802.15.4 is 0.1cm~10m, some may reach 100m, so the impact of collision caused by HNP is relative small.

The competition collision in the IEEE802.15.4 network is caused by node implementing CSMA/CA algorithm and accessing channel. When detected the channel is idle, all devices which have information to sent, produces a backoff delay time to reduce the probability of contention collision. BE decides a devices' waiting time before accessing channel. Obviously, the bigger the BE value, the bigger the probability of waiting time, which will increase the energy consumptions. Therefore, BE is general assigned range from 3 to 5 in the IEEE802.15.4 protocol. Although the BE value's small scope change may guarantee the device has shorter waiting time, the following transmission easy to cause collision.

In the Smart Home WSN, IEEE802.15.4 MAC protocol cannot reduce contention collision effectively.

## 3   A MAC Protocol Based on Priority and Superframe-Division

Due to collision or the failure of competition,  node need to contend for the channel again, once NB reach the biggest number, it will discard the packets. In order to ensure the nodes which collected urgent information could have priority to sending their information to coordinator successfully, and reduce the impact of collisions in certain emergencies--the invasion, gas leakage, creepage, and etc. This paper presents a MAC protocol based on priority and superframe-division: assign different priorities to different event monitoring sensor.

In this paper, node is classified into three groups according to priorities: the first group nodes (denoted as Priority-node1, P-node1) are designed for security & control system, such as gate control and gas leakage system; The second group nodes (P-node2) are embedded in high-power appliances such as electric heater, electric kettle or air conditioning; The third group nodes (P-node3) are embedded in low-power appliances such as illumination device, fan, and thermometer. For simulations, we take 400W as the boundary of the size power.

To ensure different nodes with different priorities are still take the superframe as the cycle to communicate with each other, and staggered communication from the time, the superframe structure must be adjusted appropriately.

The superframe structure which would be adjusted should maintain as far as possible consistent with the structure which IEEE802.15.4 protocol defines, that is they similar use BO and SO these two values to describe the active period and the inactive period. The active period contains 16 equilong time slots, which was still divided into three stages: beacon transmission period, the contention access period (CAP) and the contention-free period (CFP). The adjusted superframe structure may also support GTS mechanism, when a network selects GTS mechanism, it must guarantee that the CFP has the reservation time slot to assign to the nodes which have request in advance. Otherwise, the entire active period will be assigned completely as CAP to the nodes.

CAP still takes slot as time unit. The aim of slot distribution is then to form different node groups. One or more time slots are assigned to each group and we name these time as Priority-slot (P-slot). The allocation method for P-slots is similar with GTS, but the objects of assigned slots are different, the former is a collection of nodes need competition, while the latter is a collection of nodes don't need competition. Fig 3 describes proposed superframe structure which distributes three equal-long P-slots to different subfield wiht priority.

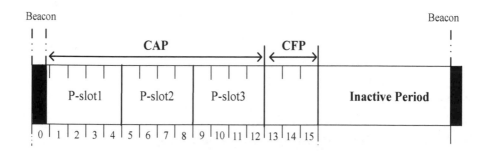

**Fig. 3.** Superframe division of IEEE802.15.4 based on priority

Based on the above description, this paper proposes two kinds of priority schemes.

Scheme one: The highest priority nodes are located at the P-slot1 to compete channel; the second-priority nodes are located at the P-slot2 to transmit information with competition; the lowest priority nodes are located at the P-slot3, as shown in Fig 3. In this scheme, because the higher priority nodes are in the preceding P-slot, this node can prior transmit their information to the coordinator. However, the same rank of priority nodes are set at a P-slot, which cannot reduce collision effectively. Then, we propose another scheme.

Scheme two: Assigns the different priority nodes mixed in different P-slots, that is, a P-slot contains different priority nodes. In the CSMA/CA algorithm, we set different BE value for different priority nodes, and increase the max backoff number of the higher priority nodes appropriately. The specific improvement measures of the algorithm are as follows:

(1) The BE's initial value is different for different priority node, e.g., 1 for P-node1, 2 for P-node, and 3 for P-node;

(2) In the fourth step of the original algorithm, every time backoff let the BE value (when BE<macMaxBE) add 1. In the new algorithm, BE value add 1 every three time backoff for P-node1, two time for P-node2, and three for P-node3 until BE equal to macMaxBE.

(3) For the purpose of guarantying the reliable transmission of the urgent information, and preventing those nodes from discarding the package, the NB value of P-node1 is increased suitably.

This improved algorithm enables the urgent information to get reliable transmission and priority treatment by the coordinator, and could reduce the transmission collision caused by the small scope change of BE.

## 4    Simulations and Analysis

The goal of the proposed scheme is to reduce the collision of the communication information, especially the urgent information, and then meets the goals of reducing the delivery delay, increasing the throughput of data transmission, and conserving energy. In order to evaluate the performance of the proposed schemes, this paper uses the OMNET++ discrete event simulator to simulate the wireless sensor network environment. Three slotted CSMA/CA based MAC protocols are evaluated in the simulation: IEEE802.15.4 MAC, scheme 1, and scheme 2 this paper designs.

### 4.1    Environment and Parameter Configuration

The simulations of this paper are all based on slotted CSMA/CA algorithm. The bandwidth is set to 250kb/s. The topology network we used is as shown in Fig 4, which is beacon-enabled star network with superframe structure. Nodes exchange messages using the wireless communication. We assume that there is no noise and no error model in wireless channel. In this network, seven nodes distributed in a 10m radius circular area, which contains a PAN coordinator (ID=0) and 6 fixed ordinary nodes (ID=1, 2… 6), the max sending distance is 15m. There is no CFP in a superframe, which is all consisting of CAP. All of the nodes need to competing channel using CSMA/CA algorithm.

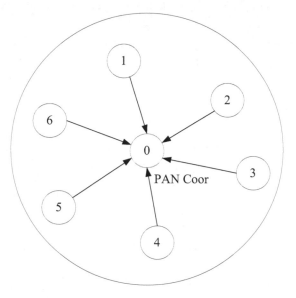

**Fig. 4.** Topology

There are some constant parameters need to use in the simulations as follows:

aNumSuperframeSlots = 16;
aBaseSlotDuration = 0.96ms;
aBaseSuperframeDuration = 15.36ms.

In our experiments, we set the transmitting power to 52.2mW, receiving power to 56.4mW, and in sleep mode to 0.06mW (referenced to the TI Chipcon2420 chipset data sheet) [8].By changing packet arrival interval, we can adjust the network load. The "Interval" parameter will use 0.1s as one unit and it increases from 0.1s to 1.0s. It represents that the network load changes from its upper-bond to its lower-bond.

## 4.2   Results and Analysis

Fig 5 describes the packet delivery ratio for nodes using different MAC protocols. For Scheme1 this paper proposed, the packet delivery ratio for the highest priority nodes (P-node1) is steady relatively, while the packet delivery ratio for other priority nodes is much lower than IEEE802.15.4 MAC', which is not good to improve the network performance. Scheme2 not only guarantee high packet delivery ratio for nodes with higher priorities, but also ensures most nodes deliver packets relatively stable. The result on the other hand proves that the proposed Scheme2 effectively avoids packet access collisions and reduces the packet loss probability.

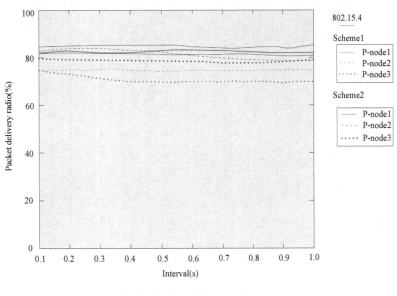

**Fig. 5.** Packet delivery ratio

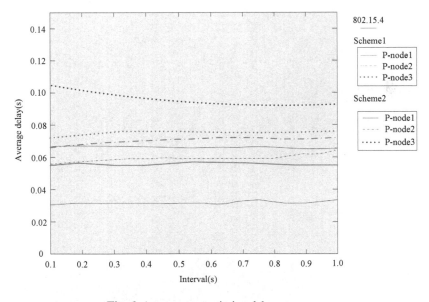

**Fig. 6.** Average transmission delay

Fig 6 presents average transmission delay using different MAC protocols. We can see from the results that the packet transmission delays of P-node1 using Scheme2 is very small, which has reached the design goal to transmit urgent information with priorities. However, the transmission delay of P-node2 and P-node3 are relative higher. Overall, the average transmission delay of the network is improved when compared to original 802.15.4 MAC.

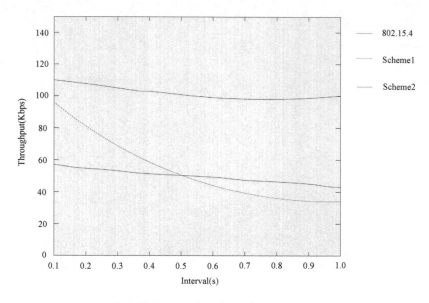

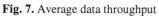

**Fig. 7.** Average data throughput

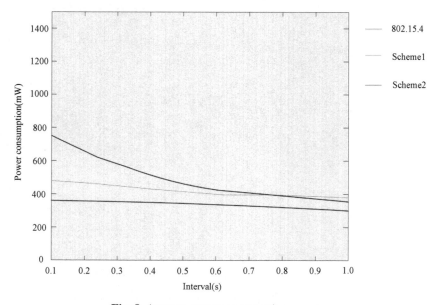

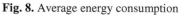

**Fig. 8.** Average energy consumption

Fig 7 shows the results of throughput with different network load. The x-axis denotes the network load and the y-axis denotes the average throughput. The higher the network load, the higher the throughput. It can be seen, Scheme1's throughput changes large, and Scheme2' throughput is ideal. With the increase of network load, competition collisions are happening with increasing frequency, and packet loss also increased, then network throughput has a slight fluctuation. However, the overall performance of Scheme2 is superior.

Fig 8 describes the average energy consumption for nodes with data transmission. We can see, in the low load, the energy consumption of three protocols is relative close. When the load increases ("Interval" value decreases), the energy consumption also increases. The average consumption of the proposed Scheme2 protocol is higher than two others' with high data generating rate. It is because that Scheme2 needs more energy to ensure that the higher priority nodes to prior competed channel successfully. In low network load, the Scheme2 protocol can also conserve energy without urgent information transport.

## 5  Conclusions

In this letter, we propose a node-grouping superframe-division MAC protocol based on IEEE802.15.4 MAC protocol. For different events monitoring tasks in smart home, nodes are classified into three classes with priorities. A group of nodes with priorities is assigned to a P-slot in CAP. Two algorithms for slot division are proposed to reduce delivery delay, increase throughput, and conserve energy consumption. The proposed Scheme2 improves urgent information delivery efficiency and facilitates it first to be transmitted. Using the protocol, we can prevent the occurrence of fires, gas leakage or other security incidents and create a safe environment. The protocol also reduces the cost of dedicated security & control systems for smart home sensor applications. The performance evaluation shows that the proposed Scheme2 has lower delivery delay than IEEE802.15.4 MAC and Scheme1. Meanwhile, Scheme2 can conserve energy and increase throughput in low network load. This thesis is supported by "The 211 Project Central Special Fund of Hainan University".

## References

1. Sun, L., Li, J., Chen, Y., et al.: Wireless sensor networks. Tsinghua University Press, Beijing (2005)
2. IEEE 802.15.4 Standard 2003. Part 15.4: Wireless medium access control (MAC) and physical layer (PHY) specifications for Low-Rate Wireless Personal Area Networks (LR-WPANs). IEEE Standard for Information Technology, IEEE-SA Standards Board (2003)
3. Xu, X.: Introduction to smart grid. China Electric Power Press, Beijing (2009)
4. Yu, Y., Luan, W.: Smart grid. Power System and Clean Energy 25(1), 7–11 (2009)

5. Pollin, S., Ergen, M., Ergen, S., Bougard, B.: Performance Analysis of Slotted Carrier Sense IEEE802.15.4 Medium Access Layer. IEEE Transaction on Wireless Communication 7(9), 3359–3371 (2008)
6. Kim, T.O., Park, J.S., Chong, H.J., Kim, K.J., Choi, B.D.: Performance analysis of IEEE 802.15.4 non-beacon mode with the unslotted CSMA/CA. IEEE Communications Letters 12(4), 238–240 (2008)
7. Fang, M.: Research of IEEE802.15.4 network performance with slot CSMA/CA. Hefei University of Technology (2009)
8. Data Sheet for CC2420 2.4 GHz IEEE802.15.4/ZigBee RF Transceive, http://www.chipcon.com/files/CC2420_Data_Sheet_1_3.pdf

# A Public Transport System Based Sensor Network for Fake Alcohol Detection

Maneesha V. Ramesh and Riji N. Das

Amrita Center for Wireless Networks and Application, AMRITA Vishwa
Vidyapeetham(Amrita University), Kollam, Kerala, India
maneesha@am.amrita.edu

**Abstract.** Illicit and spurious alcohol consumption is leading to numerous deaths in rural India. The aim of this paper is to reduce the death due to the consumption of spurious alcohol by reducing the production of spurious alcohol. A Vehicular Ad-Hoc Sensor Network, MovingNet, is used to detect the production of spurious alcohol. Multiple sensors capable to detect the presence of methanol content or diazepam in a wide geographical area, is incorporated on the available public transport system that traverse through the rural areas of India, where high rate of spurious alcohol production is observed. The data received from the wireless sensors will be transmitted using the delay tolerant, public transport vehicular ad-hoc network, and analyzed at the central data management center. The results of the data analysis will provide the details of geographic information, the amount of presence of methanol content or diazepam, and the warning degree. This will be sent to the excise department which will help them to locate the position and stop the production of spurious alcohol. Thus the implementation of MovingNet will reduce the production of spurious alcohol and contributes the reduction in hazards due to the consumption of spurious alcohol. MovingNet is a cost effective solution since it uses a very few sensors and the available public transport system for data collection and transmission.

**Keywords:** Alcohol Sensorl Fake Alcohol, GPS, MovingNet, Sub Stations.

## 1 Introduction

The production and consumption of spurious alcohol causes severe health problems or even leading to death in rural parts of India. Statistical studies proved that the rate of the casualties is increasing day by day. The objective of this paper is to control the production of spurious alcohol and thereby cut down the deaths due to the consumption of spurious alcohol. In order to control the production of spurious alcohol, a wide geographical area needs to be monitored in a periodical basis.

A Vehicular Ad-Hoc Sensor Network, MovingNet is used for the monitoring of geographical area to detect the production of spurious alcohol. In many countries, the public transport buses cover almost all areas of a territory[1]. In the MovingNet architecture, multiple sensors which are capable of sensing the presence of methanol or diazepam content in air is incorporated on the public transport system.

P. Sénac, M. Ott, and A. Seneviratne (Eds.): ICWCA 2011, LNICST 72, pp. 137–144, 2012.
© Institute for Computer Sciences, Social Informatics and Telecommunications Engineering 2012

In MovingNet, each vehicle can be considered as a mobile unit that consists of sensor node and external memory. Each sensor node consists of one or more sensors for the detection of alcohol content and the GPS for locating the coordinates of the place being monitored. The data collected by the sensor nodes is being aggregated in a central place, analyses it and issues warning whenever necessary. Depending upon the sensors used in the sensor nodes the MovingNet architecture can be used for variety of terrain monitoring applications that are delay tolerant in nature.

MovingNet alerts concerned authorities to the existence and location of spurious alcohol; thus, enabling the much needed reduction of the production, consumption and hazardous effects of spurious alcohol.

## 2  Related Works

The DakNet[3] provides digital communication services to remote villages using buses as a mechanical backhaul [4] for data transfer. The use of buses in DakNet is purely for data transfer between Internet access points and Internet kiosks in villages. In MovingNet the buses provide the means to sense, collect and transfer data necessary for reduction in alcohol hazards.

DataMULEs[5] architecture uses mobile entities, including buses, to collect data from sensors deployed in an environment and ferry them to access points. In contrast the buses in MovingNet are not simple ferries; they carry the sensors and they are the data collection source. DakNet and the Data MULEs are examples of delay tolerant networks [5]. They are proposed as solutions for the lack of better communication infrastructure. However, the MovingNet is proposed purely as a low cost solution, and uses the capability to reach most appropriate place data collection such as rural India.

Even if a good communication infrastructure exists, the data collection and transporting buses in the MovingNet are the most natural form of communication infrastructure for the road surface monitoring system. MovingNet provides physical security for the sensors, reduces the cost of deploying sensors, and also simplifies the management and maintenance of the sensors.

In ZebraNet [6] Zebras carry collars that contain sensors and the collected data are transferred to other Zebras and collection points opportunistically. ZebraNet is conceptually closest to the MovingNet. However, there is a crucial difference between ZebraNet and MovingNet. Whereas ZebraNet is an ad-hoc opportunistic network, in the MovingNet there is a stable fixed infrastructure for data transfer. The bus routes are regularly serviced by scheduled buses barring a major disaster which is an exception rather than the rule. Therefore, the MovingNet is a stable network and it has stable network routes. If not for the mobile buses it can even be called a fixed network.

Zhao et al.[7] also present a vehicle assisted data delivery system for vehicular ad-hoc networks. In that work the vehicles are used as data carriers and the route to the destination is set up based on the ad-hoc connectivity of the vehicles. In contrast, the MovingNet not only delivers data it also generates data and furthermore in MovingNet we use the stable transport infrastructure and does not rely on the ad-hoc connectivity between vehicles.

MovingNet, which implements a sensor network on top of the public transport network, is ideal for monitoring the road surface condition; the sensor mounted buses use the very roads that we want to monitor. We designed the road surface monitoring system based on the MovingNet. In this system one of the heavy users of the road system and hence a major contributor to the deterioration of the road surface helps in monitoring of the road system. A few hours of latency in MovingNet is not an obstacle to this application because the data gathered on road surface condition are not needed in real time.

## 3   System Design

MovingNet is designed for monitoring the presence of fake alcohol in a wide geographical area. Effective monitoring of wide geographical area requires large number of static sensor nodes spread over the monitoring location. Such a sensor system with large number of static sensors poses several problems. It would be quite expensive to develop a system with large number of static sensors when each sensor is expensive. Maintaining and managing a system that has large number of static sensors is quite difficult. The regular replacement of batteries and replacement of faulty sensors are costly and labor intensive tasks. In addition, locating faulty sensors to replace them is not an easy task. Protecting a large number of sensors scattered throughout a large terrain is a daunting task. Sensors can be damaged by animals, heavy rains, and there is also a possibility of vandalizing.

It is observed that most countries have a public transport system that spans the country. MovingNet makes use of the existing public transport system as the backbone of the proposed network architecture. MovingNet has several sensors mounted on the vehicles of the public transport system as a replacement for a network consisting of large number of static sensors. These vehicle mounted moving sensors gather data that covers a large geographical area. When the buses arrive at bus stations, which also function as data collection centers, gathered data are transferred over a wireless link to the collection point. Data gathered in regional collection points are transferred to buses traveling between the regional centers and the main collection center. In this scenario the public transport system functions as a data delivery network as well as a data collection network. It is assumed that the gathered data are not required in real time. The data collected by the alcohol sensors are not immediately transferred to the data processing unit. Therefore this network is delay tolerant.

### 3.1   MovingNet Architecture

Fig. 1 depicts the architecture of the MovingNet. The MovingNet has three main components; Sensor Units, Sub- stations, and Main Station.

*1) Sensor Unit:* The sensor unit consists of a Crossbow MICAz mote [2], and several sensor boards including a GPS sensor board. The sensor boards contain sensors to gather the information regarding methanol level, temperature, carbon monoxide level, location etc. This sensor unit will be mounted on top of a bus and is powered from the battery of the bus. The sensors gather the required data along the bus route. The sensed data together with the GPS coordinates will be stored in the memory of the sensor mote. Extra storage device, such as a flash drive, can be added to the sensor unit.

The sensor unit is capable to act as a sensing unit and also as a router. The buses that travel towards the sub-station will collect the data from the buses travelling in the opposite direction and delivers the data to the sub-station. This will reduce the delay in data transfer.

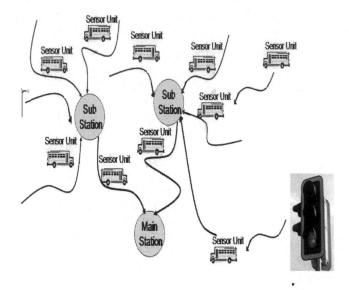

**Fig. 1.** MovingNet System Architecture

*2) Sub-station:* The sub-stations are the collection nodes located at the regional bus stations. Regional bus routes span out from the sub-stations. Buses going out and coming towards the sub-stations collect data about the alcohol content beyond the threshold level at regular intervals and store them together with the GPS coordinates. Once the buses reach the sub-station the data are transmitted over a wireless network to the data collection unit. The data analysis is done only at the main station. Therefore the sub- stations route these collected data to the main station over the bus network. This routing can be done by transferring the collected data from the sub-station to the sensor unit of buses heading to the main station.

*3) Main-Station :* The collected data from all sub stations reach the main station and it is stored in a central database at the main station. Further these data are analysed and issues an alarm whenever a coordinate with high methanol content is identified. The main station also has a list of coordinates where the licensed production of methanol is permitted. This will help in avoiding false alarms.

### 3.2 Data Transfer Protocol

When the bus reaches the sub-station or main station the data is transferred to the data collection unit through the wireless network. The main bottleneck associated with this data transfer is that, the buses may not wait at the station until the completion of the data transfer. To handle this problem a protocol which prioritizes the data transfer is designed. It transfers data collected at 1 kilometer intervals first and the bus stays in the station for longer time it transfers data collected at 500 meters interval and so on.

The protocol prioritizes the data based on the spatial coordinates so that the data collected over a large area is transferred first and only covers the points in between if the time permits. In addition to this, when there is more than one bus transferring data, the station must make sure that it collects data from all the buses in a round robin basis to ensure that it collects data from all the routes in a fair manner.

The proposed data transfer protocol does not stop to retransmit lost packets; that is, if a packet is lost its retransmission is delayed and retransmission starts only after the first attempt transmission of all the packets. Therefore, retransmission takes place only if the bus stays long enough to retransmit. Priority is given to the first attempt packets to ensure transmission of data to cover a large terrain as much as possible. The main station is similar to the sub-stations but it has a direct connection to the data processing centre and it does not have to route data to other stations. The data analysis and alarm issuing is done in the main station.

### 3.3 System Operations and Control Flows

Fig. 2 shows the control flows of the MovingNet system for alcohol detection. The sensor units, S1, S2,..........Sn, are fixed on top of n vehicles. Whenever the methanol or diazepam content in air crosses the threshold level the GPS associated with the sensor unit records the co-ordinate position and stores it in the memory. The data collected in the sensor unit can be transferred to the processing centre by the following methods:

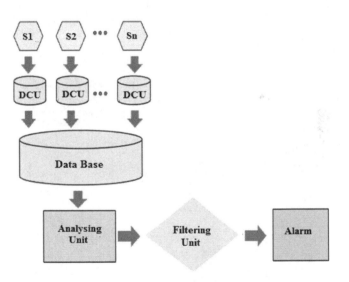

**Fig. 2.** MovingNet Flow Control Diagram

*1) Store and Forward*: The data stored in the sensor unit is transferred to the data collection unit placed in the substations, Fig 1. All data analysis is done in the main station. Therefore the data collected in all the sub-stations need to be transferred to the main station. In store and forward method, as on Fig 3, the sub-stations collect data from the vehicles, say V1,V2,V3 and V4, when they reach the station. The data analysis is done at the main station. Therefore the collected data are forwarded to the main station by sending it back to the vehicles that head to the main station.

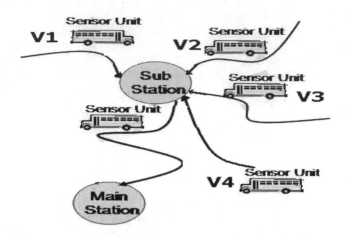

**Fig. 3.** Store and Forward Data Transfer

*2) Mobile Data Transfer:* In this method, as shown in Fig. 4., the data stored in the sensor unit associated with a vehicle, V1, is transferred to the sensor unit of another vehicle,V2, which crosses V1 and is expected to reach a sub-station before V1 reaches a sub-station.

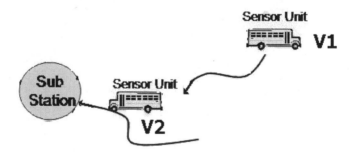

**Fig. 4.** Mobile Data Transfer

*3) Intermediate Store and Forward:* Intermediate store and forward method is a combination of the above mentioned methods. In this method, as shown in Fig 5, the data stored in a vehicle,V1 is transferred to the memory unit connected to stationary objects like street light, traffic light or mobile tower. These data can be transferred to vehicles, like V2, that cross the unit and is expected to reach a sub-station or main station before V1. In the main station the collected data are analysed and issues an alarm in the form of an emergency call or SMS. The comparison unit helps to avoid unnecessary alarms if the GPS coordinate value matches the flagged coordinate values of licensed production units of the ingredients of fake alcohol.

On receiving the alarm the concerned authority is expected to take the necessary action.

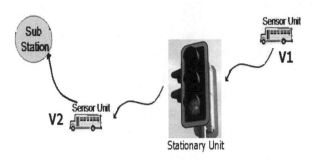

**Fig. 5.** Intermediate Store and Forward Data Transfer

## 4 Advantages of the System

MovingNet has several advantages over a traditional sensor network system and it solves the problems associated with a large number of sensors spread over a large terrain as follows.

The MovingNet uses only a few moving sensors instead of large number of static sensors. This brings down the cost of the monitoring system. Power management is the main problem as far as any Wireless Sensor Network(WSN) system is concerned. In MovingNet the sensor node takes power from the battery of the vehicle to which it is fixed. Therefore no periodical replacement of battery is needed. The GPS stores the coordinates of the location only when the sensor reading crosses the Minimum Resistance Limit(MRL). This will minimise the utilisation.

MovingNet architecture is flexible to change in accordance with the application requirement. The mobile units, carrier of the sensor node, can be a Public Transport Vehicle, a Military Vehicle or a Boat. Also the change in sensors used in sensor nodes makes the system useful for monitoring the terrain for different types of data.

Since the sensors eventually come to a Sub-station or the Main Station, maintenance work such as battery replacement, if needed, and the replacement or repairing of faulty sensors can be done at these stations. Buses are parked in secured areas when they are not in operation and this reduces the possible theft and damages to the sensors.

## 5 Challenges

The sensor should be able to withstand the tropical conditions – they are to be mounted on top of the buses. However, ruggedizing the sensor units is beyond the scope of this work and will not consider this for the prototype designing. A real world deployment certainly needs a robust sensor unit. In addition, the data gathered would be useless unless the authorities responsible for taking action establish a system to monitor the collected data and respond accordingly.

There may be situations in which similar ingredients should be present in the atmosphere when it is used for some other licensed purposes. In such cases the coordinates correspond to those places are marked and can be ignored during the analysis phase eventually avoiding from issuing alarms.

## 6  Conclusions

MovingNet, which implements a sensor network on top of the public transport network, is ideal for terrain monitoring. MovingNet is a novel approach in building vehicle based data network in the sense that the sensor system which collects the data and the data themselves travel in the vehicles. The intermediate collection of data in stationary sensors, such as traffic lights or electric posts, and data transfer while in motion, from vehicle to vehicle, increases the speed of data transfer. Even though the system is a delay tolerant one this can be used for applications like Urban-Rural data transfer in situations in which Internet connectivity is not available. The MovingNet reduces the cost of deploying a large number of static sensors by replacing them with a very few moving sensors. It also solves the management, maintenance, and the security problems associated with a sensor network deployed over a large terrain. MovingNet has got the flexibility to use in different applications only by changing the sensor(s) used in the sensor node. The basic architecture of MovingNet can also be modified by changing the mobile units, such as vehicles, related to the application.

**Acknowledgment.** We are grateful to Amrita University for providing an ambience where research and innovation are celebrated as a way of life. We are thankful to our Chancellor Mata Amritanandamayi Devi who taught us the importance of doing research in accordance with social needs.

## References

[1]  Zoysa, K.D., Keppitiyagama, C.: A Public Transport System Based Sensor Network for Road Surface Condition Monitoring
[2]  Crossbow Technology Inc. MPR-MIB user's manual (2006), http://www.xbow.com
[3]  Pentland, A.S., Fletcher, R., Hasson, A.: Daknet: Rethinking connectivity in developing nations. Computer 37(1), 78–83 (2004)
[4]  Seth, A., Kroeker, D., Zaharia, M., Guo, S., Keshav, S.: Low-cost communication for rural internet kiosks using mechanical backhaul. In: MobiCom 2006: Proceedings of the 12th annual international conference on Mobile computing and networking, pp. 334–345. ACM Press, New York (2006)
[5]  Shah, R., Roy, S., Jain, S., Brunette, W.: Data mules: Modeling a three-tier architecture for sparse sensor networks. In: Proc. of the IEEE International Workshop on Sensor Network Protocols and Applications. IEEE, Los Alamitos (2003)
[6]  Juang, P., Oki, H., Wang, Y., Martonosi, M., Peh, L.S., Rubenstein, D.: Energy-efficient computing for wildlife tracking: design tradeoffs and early experiences with zebranet. SIGOPS Oper. Syst. Rev. 36(5), 96–107 (2002)
[7]  Zhao, J., Cao, G.: VADD: Vehicle-assisted data delivery in vehicular ad hoc networks. Technical Report NAS-TR-0020-2005, Network and Security Research Center, Department of Computer Science and Engineering, Pennsylvania State University, University Park, PA, USA (July 2005)

# Performance of LDPC Coded SFH System with Partial-Band Interference

Gong Chao[*], Zhang YingXian, Zhang BangNing, and Guo DaoXing

Nanjing, China, Institute of Communications Engineering of PLAUST,
NO.2 in Biaoying Road, Street Yudao, Nanjing, Jiangsu
gongchao.089@163.com

**Abstract.** The application of Low Density Parity Check (LDPC) code in the anti-interference systems has drawn an increasing attention, due to its admiring performance which is very close to the theory limit. This paper focuses on a LDPC encoded slow frequency hopping (SFH) communication system with partial-band interference. Firstly, a modified soft-decision algorithm based on the utilization of interference information is proposed, and its performance is compared with some other soft-decision methods. Secondly, with numerical simulation, the influence of code rate, code length and the number of symbols per hops on the performance of the system with partial band noise interference is illustrated and examined in detail. Considering the great influence of hops per symbol on the performance, interleaver should be used and its influence on the performance is further examined by simulation. Finally, some constructive advices for the design of LDPC coded SFH system are given. Simulation results show that, with a reasonable design, the SFH system with LDPC code could achieve a desirable performance.

**Keywords:** LDPC, SFH, soft-decision, partial-band interference.

## 1 Introduction

Frequency hopping (FH) transmissions, whose carrier frequency hops under control of a pseudorandom pattern, is an attractive access method in wireless communication, due to its special ability to anti interference and provides continuous communication under a severe interference situation [1]. In the civil communication, FH is often used in the wireless communication system working in unlicensed industrial, scientific and medical (ISM) band, such as Bluetooth and ZigBee, to overcome the interference coming from other electronic equipment working in the same frequency band. While in the military communication, FH , which is almost to be a characteristic of military communication system, is widely used in the short-wave, microwave and satellite communication to overcome intentional interference.

---

[*] Main research interests are in the area of anti-jam communications,such as channel coding, interferenc detection and noncoherent iterative receiver techniques.

P. Sénac, M. Ott, and A. Seneviratne (Eds.): ICWCA 2011, LNICST 72, pp. 145–155, 2012.
© Institute for Computer Sciences, Social Informatics and Telecommunications Engineering 2012

For example, both of America's domain tactical wireless networks (JTIDS) and the Milstar satellite communication system base on frequency hopping transmission [3]. Apart from that, FH is also used in the cognitive radios due to the available frequency changes from time to time [4].

So far, researchers all along pay attention to the enhancement of FH systems' anti-interference performance, some useful methods, such as channel coded diversity, interleave, are widely used. As an excellent channel code method, LDPC, which is close to the theory limit, has drawn an increasingly attention of researchers from worldwide, especially its application in the FH communication. In [5], some diversity methods based on LDPC-FH system were examined. And the paper [6] focused on the technology of interference erasure in the LDPC-FH communication. The performance of LDPC encoded fast frequency hopping (FFH) system under partial-band noise interference was analyzed in paper [7], and the performance of LDPC encoded FFH system with partial band multitone interference was given by [8].In this paper, we are focused on the performance of LDPC-SFH system under partial-band noise interference.

There are some theory methods for the analysis of the performance of LDPC, some of which is illustrated in [9], such as *density evolution*, *Gaussian approximate*, *extrinsic information transfer (EXIT) charts*. All of those methods pay attention to the performance of certain kind of LDPC, rather than that of certain type of LDPC. However, in practice, the choice of LDPC is limited to the feasibility of hardware, code length, code rate and code structure and so on, which causes the real performance of LDPC has a large difference with the theory bound. In the interference environment, the channel is no longer to be an additive white Gaussian noise (AWGN) channel, which makes it even more difficult for the analysis of performance of LDPC. As the approximation and simplification have to be used for theory analysis, the result will be imprecise. In the practical system design, numerical simulation with certain type available code is a feasible and effective way for analysis. Based on above considerations, numerical simulation is exploited in this paper for analysis of application of LDPC on the SFH system, and some key points of designing anti-interference communication are analyzed further.

## 2   System Model

The system model in this paper is shown as Fig. 1. The transmitter consists of encoder, interleaver, and modulator and up frequency converter. By the number of '1' in every row and column of check matrix, LDPC can be divided into kinds: regular LDPC and irregular LDPC. Generally, performance of irregular LDPC is better than regular LDPC, which is at the cost of more complex realization of hardware. With a tradeoff between performance and complexity degree of hardware realization, this paper chooses quasi-cyclic regular binary LDPC [10] as channel code. In the SFH system, number of symbols per hop (SPH) is more than one, when the signal is jammed, it will bring about burst symbol errors. If number of burst symbol errors in a coded packet is larger than threshold number of decoding, decoding error will occur. In order to alleviate the burst errors influence and reduce frame error rate, in practice, the coded bit stream is interleaved in the transmitter, making burst errors decentralize into every packet equally. The following simulation will show that interleaving do improved the performance of system with short code length dramatically when the code length is short. While it comes to long code length, impact of interlacing is not obvious, so it can conclude that interleaver is unnecessary for the system, and it can be chosen depending on the length of code. In the SFH system, FSK, DPSK, PSK is widely used, PSK has a higher bandwidth efficiency, so BPSK is used in this paper. Under the control of FH pattern, the modulated signal is transmitted through the up frequency converter, as Fig. 1 shows. As the control methods of FH pattern isn't the content of this paper, we don't introduce it here. The transmitting signal is given by

$$x_{ij} = c_{ij} e^{j(2\pi f_i nT + \theta_i)}, \quad i = 1, 2, \cdots N \tag{1}$$

Where $c_{ij} = \pm 1$ is information sequence, $f_i$ is carrier frequency, $T$ is symbol interval, $\theta_i$ is initial phase per hop, $N$ is number of symbols per hop.

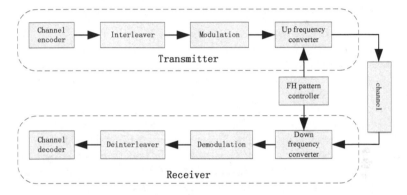

**Fig. 1.** Model of LDPC-SFH system

The channel model that we employ is an example of a block-interference channel, including additive white Gaussian noise (AWGN) and partial-band interference, which has been used in several previous investigations of FH communication [11]. Model of partial-band interference is given by bandwidth-limited white Gaussian noise with a $\rho$ band rate, here $\rho$ is the partial-band interference factor, and it is a constant but unknown number for both transmitter and receiver. We assume all the symbols in a FH time slot are jammed when the signal in certain moment of the slot is hit by the interference signal, and vice versa. The probability of FH signal jammed is $\rho$, power spectral density (PSD) of interference signal in the current time slot is $\rho^{-1} N_I$, and in other slot without interference, the PSD is 0. Power of the interference signal is in direct proportion to $N_I$ and irrelevant with $\rho$. AWGN diffuse during the transmitting, and PSD is $N_0$, rate of bit power to PSD of AWGN is given by $ENR = 10\log 10(\xi_b / N_0)$, rate of bit power to PSD of interference signal is given by $EIR = 10\log 10(\xi_b / N_I)$. The receive signal is given by

$$\tilde{x}_{ij} = c_{ij}e^{j(2\pi f_i nT + \theta_i)} + n_{ij} + w_{ij}, \quad i = 1, 2, \cdots N \tag{2}$$

Where $n_{ij}$ is wide-band white Gaussian noise, and $w_{ij}$ is partial-band interference.

As Fig. 1 shows, receiver consists of decoder, deinterleaver, demodulator and down frequency converter. With the same FH pattern, the receiver change the FH signal to lowpass or fixed band pass signal, and the demodulater estimate the carrier phase and symbol timing in order to realize carrier and symbol synchronization, and then the information sequence will be obtained by soft-decision method. Signal after carrier and symbol synchronization is given by (3),

$$y_{ij} = c_{ij} + \tilde{n}_{ij} + \tilde{w}_{ij}, \quad i = 1, 2, \cdots N \tag{3}$$

Where $\tilde{n}_{ij}$, $\tilde{w}_{ij}$ is wide-band white Gaussian noise and partial-band interference after carrier and symbol synchronization respectively.

In this paper, we don't focus on carrier and symbol synchronization, so we assume carrier phase and symbol timing are estimated correctly in the following. Soft-decision methods will be discussed in the following section detailedly. Deinterleaver reorder the receive sequence to make it same as the original sequence, and finally channel decoder decodes the sequence after soft-decision. Decoding methods of LDPC is sorted into two kinds: hard-decision and soft-decision. Generally speaking, performance of soft-decision methods is better than those of hard-decision. Considering the complexity of hardware realization, modifying-minimum-sum soft-decision method [12], which has low complexity for hardware realization and good performance close to the optimum method, is used in this paper.

## 3 Modifying Soft-Decision

The probability of transmitting signal should be proportional to the value of soft-decision for modifying-minimum-sum soft-decision method (MMSSD). Without interference, $y_{ij}$ maintain its probability statistic characteristic, which could give probability of transmitting signal directly, so the sequence can be decoded with direct-decision (DD). While there is interference with the received signal, the probability statistic characteristic of $y_{ij}$ with and without interference will be different, so it will represent different probability of transmitting signal in the two conditions. In this case, probability of signal can't archive from $y_{ij}$ directly, which lead to drastic deterioration of performance is DD method is used. As Fig. 2 shows, when $\rho = 1$, performance based on direct soft-decision is very close to that the method with perfect channel side information (PCSI). However, with the decreasing of $\rho$, the performance will deteriorate drastically. To solve above problem, we can estimate ENR of signal in every hop, and then modify the soft-decision value accordingly. In [12], a simple square signal to noise ratio estimator is introduced, where the estimator is given by (4)

$$\lambda_i = \frac{\left[\dfrac{1}{N}\displaystyle\sum_{i=0}^{N-1}|y_{ij}|\right]^2}{\dfrac{1}{N-1}\displaystyle\sum_{i=0}^{N-1}y_{ij}^{\,2} - \dfrac{1}{N(N-1)}\left[\displaystyle\sum_{i=0}^{N-1}|y_{ij}|\right]^2} \tag{4}$$

With the estimated value of ENR in $i$ th FH time slot, we can modify value of soft-decision with (5)

$$z_{ij} = y_{ij}\lambda_i \tag{5}$$

When the EIR is low, it is imprecise to estimate the EIR by above method, however, simulation suggests that the precision of the estimation can meet the need of LDPC-SFH system, and comparing with DD, we have got admirable performance improvement. Fig. 2 shows three soft-decision methods' performance, where the vertical axis is the required value of EIR to archive a packet error probability of 10-2. We found that the EIR increases no more than 0.2dB to reduce the packet error probability from 10-2 to 10-3. In general, most wireless networks, such as Ad hoc

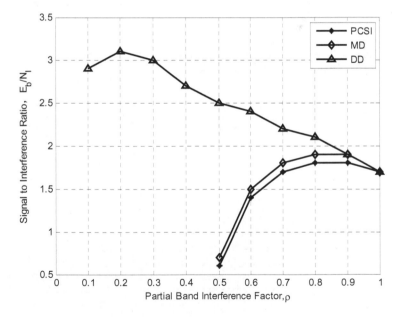

**Fig. 2.** Performances of different soft-decision methods

network, could work normally with a frame error rate of 10-2. The AWGN is considered in the following simulation, though PSD of partial-band interference signal is far higher than that of AWGN. In the simulation of this paper, we assume $ENR = 20dB$. $\lambda_i$ is a exact known number and the methods of modifying the soft-decision value are the same, when the interference signal is known. From the Fig. 2 we can see that the performance of modifying the value of soft-decision based on estimating ENR with square-ENR estimator is close to that of PCSI.

## 4  Performance of Anti-interference

The following numerical simulation bases on the system model and MMSSD introduced in above sections, which will give performance of LDPC-SFH system with different code rate, code length, SPH and way of interleaving. In the simulation, two cases are considered: the first is that, code length is fixed-8064, value of code rate getting from 1/2, 5/8 and 7/8; the second is code rate fixed-3/4, and code rate varying with 8064, 4032, 2016 and 1008. Performance of above cases with AWGN channel is shown in Fig. 3. In order to make a clear analysis, here, we introduce two basic conceptions: first is that the $\hat{\rho}$ corresponding to the highest value of EIR is represented as worst partial-band interference (WPBJ) factor, second is throughput, which is a key standard of a system, is given by ratio of number of available source sequences to that of encoded transmitting packet sequences. Besides, we also assume that it is a available packet only when the receiving sequences are all right, otherwise, the packet is un available.

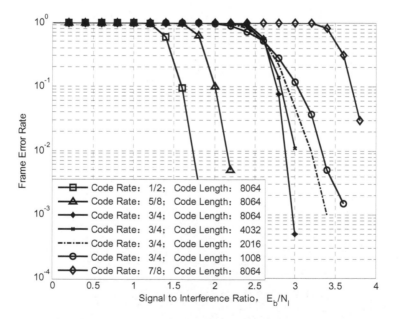

**Fig. 3.** Performances of different code rate and length

## 4.1  Influences of Code Rate

Code rate is a vital factor of the performance, when code length is fixed, with decreasing of code rate , performance is improving, which don't result in decreasing of system's throughput, as Fig. 4 shown, performance of system with 1/2、5/8、3/4 and 7/8 code rate and a fixed code length 8064 are given. When $\rho = 1$, difference of Interference-to-Signal (JNS) threshold of four code rate is about 2dB, which will enlarge with decreasing of $\rho$. When $\rho < 0.5$, JNS threshold of LDPC with a 1/2 code rate is lower than 0dB; when $\rho = 0.2$, JNS threshold of LDPC with a 7/8 code rate is larger than 7dB. Different code rate have different performance with the worst partial-band interference, and with increasing of code rate, $\hat{\rho}$ is decreasing, and so is the threshold of $\rho$.

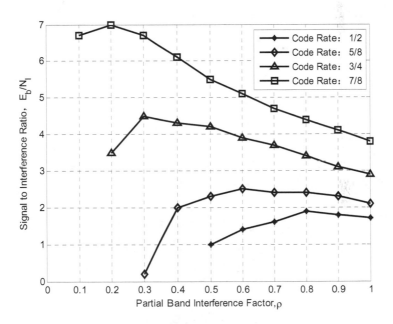

**Fig. 4.** Performances of different code rate with partial-band interference

In Fig. 5, throughput of different code rate is shown. We can see, low code rate has a stronger adaptability to drastic change of $\rho$, and there is an inconspicuous change of throughput, with $\rho$ changing from 0 to 0.7, when LDPC code rate is 1/2. However, when $\rho$ is very small, the throughput of code with low rate is lower comparatively, which leads to low transmission efficiency. Therefore, in practice, throughput could improve with a proper LDPC designed depending on $\rho$, and code length of a system could be designed depending on throughput and cost of hardware.

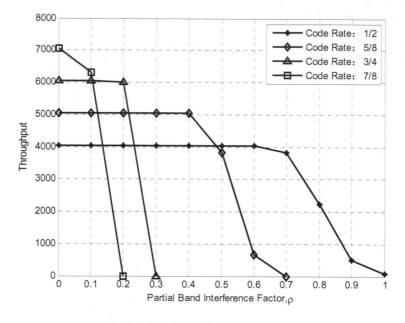

**Fig. 5.** Throughput of different code rate

## 4.2  Influences of Code Length

In Fig. 6, performance of LDPC with a 3/4 code rate under 8064,4032,2016,1008 code length are shown, while number of symbols is 336( $N = 336$ ). When $\rho = 1$,

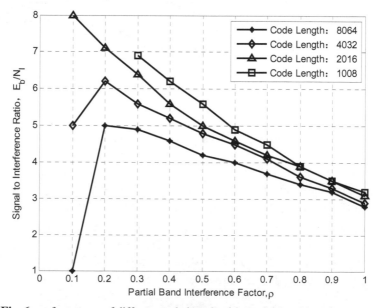

**Fig. 6.** performances of different code length with partial-band interference

performance of the four codes are very close, difference between maximum code length and minimum code length is only 0.5dB, however, which will enlarge with decreasing of $\rho$. After JNS of code 8064 and 4032 reach to the highest, it will decreasing along with the decreasing of $\rho$, and then JNS of 2018 and 1008 is in direct proportion to $\rho$. The main reason of that is, short code has a weak ability of anti-outburst-wrong, moreover, its performance also depend on the value of $N$.

### 4.3   Influences of Symbols Per Hop

Influence of symbols per hop on the performance is shown from two aspects: on one hand, a increasing $N$ will exaggerate the outburst wrong, and performance of system will also decrease, especially when $\rho$ is very small; on the other hand, amount of data processed by ENR estimator will also increase for $N$'s increasing, which lead to a more precise estimation and higher performance. As Fig. 7 shows, when code length is 1008, code rate is 3/4, and $N=12$, performance keeps good with most value of $\rho$, and when $\rho=0.1$, EIR reaches to the highest. From Fig. 7, we can conclude that number symbols $N$ is another factor which should be in a proper range during practical system design, and it is better design when value of $N$ is chosen depending on the change of $\rho$. In practice, there is a simpler and available method of choosing $N$, basing on interleaving, which makes outburst wrong sequence dispersing into all the transmitting packets, therefore, even with a large $N$, performance still keeps a good level.

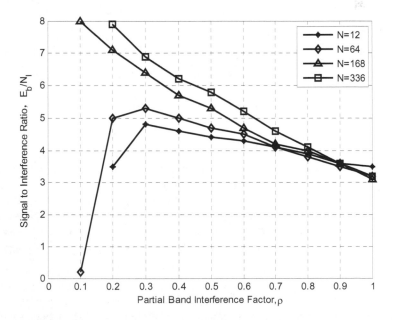

**Fig. 7.** Performances of different symbols per hop with partial-band interference and code rate 3/4

## 4.4 Influence of Interleaving

The key parameter of interleaver is the deep degree of interleaving ( $D$ ), in the simulation, different values of $D$, which is 4, 8, and 16, are considered, while code length is 1008 and code rate is 3/4. As Fig. 8 shows, with increasing of $D$, performance is also increasing. In general, a bigger $D$ makes random wrong sequences discrete further, which could improve the performance, however, a bigger $D$ will also means increasing of transmitting delay of the system. Therefore, both $D$ and transmitting delay should be taken into consideration. Meanwhile, a proper $D$ also depend on exact value of code length and methods of interleaving.

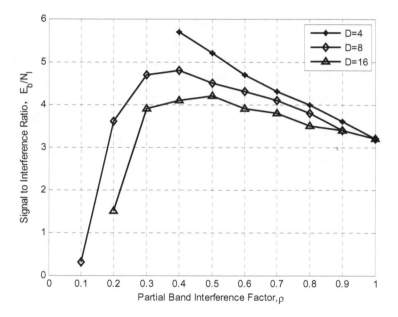

**Fig. 8.** Performances of different deep degree of interleaving with partial-band interference

## 5   Advices for System Design

When it comes to design a higher performance LDPC-SFH communication system, code rate, code length, symbols per hop and deep degree of interleaving are key parameters. Different code rate will result in different performance, it is better for a low code rate when throughput of system is not considered in the design. But a higher code rate can benefit for the throughput when $\rho$ is small, it is advised the system's code rate could adjust to the change of $\rho$. As is analyzed in above section, when $\rho$ is small, it will bring about a drastic difference of EIR with different code length, so a longer code will our best choice, however, which is only at cost of complexity of hardware. And of cause, considering the complexity of hardware, short will be better, when symbols per hop is small and sequences is interleaved, performance could also meet the need of design.

# 6  Conclusions

This paper focuses on the design and performance analyses of LDPC-SFH system in partial-band interference channel. A new soft-decision method based on the estimation of EIR hop by hop is proposed, performance could be improved drastically as illustrated by simulation. The Influences of code rate, code length, symbols per hop and deep degree of interleaving are also analyzed with numerical simulation. Further more, some constructive advises for practical system design are given based on the former work. The results of this paper will be benefit for the design of anti-jamming communication systems.

# References

[1] Torrieri, D., Cheng, S., Valenti, M.C.: Robust Frequency Hopping for Interference and Fading Channels. IEEE Transactions On Communications 56(8), 1343–1351 (2008)

[2] Popovski, P., Yomo, H., Prasad, R.: Strategies for Adaptive Frequency Hopping in the Unlicensed Bands. IEEE Wireless Communications, 60–67 (December 2006)

[3] Cook, K.L.B.: Current Wideband MILSATCOM Infrastructure and the Future of Bandwidth Availability. IEEE A&E Systems Magazine, 23–28 (December 2010)

[4] Hu, W., Willkomm, D., Chu, L., Abusubaih, M., Gross, J., Vlantis, G., Gerla, M., Wolisz, A.: Dynamic frequency hopping communities for efficient IEEE 802.22 operation. IEEE Commun. Mag., Special Issue:Cognitive Radios for Dynamic Spectrum Access 45(5), 80–87 (2007)

[5] Wu, X., Zhao, C., You, X., Li, S.: Robust Diversity-Combing Receivers for LDPC Coded FFH-SS with Partial-Band Interference. IEEE Communications Letters 11(7), 613–615 (2007)

[6] Kim, Y.H., Kim, K.S., Ahn, J.Y.: Erasure decoding for LDPC-coded FH-OFDMA system in downlink cellular environments. Electronics Letters 40(22) (October 28, 2004)

[7] Jeng, L.-D., Lee, S.-S., Wang, C.-H., Ueng, F.-B.: Low-Density Parity-Check Codes for FFH/BFSK Systems with Partial-Band Noise Interference. In: IWCMC 2006, Vancouver, British Columbia, Canada, July 3–6, pp. 1213–1217 (2006)

[8] Jeng, L.-D., Lee, S.-S., Wang, C.-H., Ueng, F.-B.: Performance of Low-Density Parity-Check Coded FFH/BFSK Systems under Band Multitone Interference. In: IWCMC 2007, Honolulu, Hawaii, USA, August 12–16, pp. 434–438 (2007)

[9] Ashikhmin, A., Kramer, G., ten Brink, S.: Extrinsic information transfer functions: Model and erasure channel properties. IEEE Trans. Inform. Theory 50, 2657–2673 (2004)

[10] Liva, G., Ryan, W.E., Chiani, M.: Quasi-Cyclic Generalized LDPC Codes with Low Error Floors. IEEE Transactions On Communications 56(1), 49–57 (2008)

[11] Pursley, M.B., Skinner, J.S.: Adaptive Coding for Frequency-Hop Transmission in Mobile Ad Hoc Networks with Partial-Band Interference. IEEE Transactions On Communications 57(3), 801–811 (2009)

[12] Pauluzzi, D.R., Beaulieu, N.C.: A Comparison of SNR Estimation Techniques for the AWGN Channel. IEEE Transactions On Communications 48(10), 1681–1691 (2000)

# Worm Nonlinear Model Optimization and Feature Detection Technology

Xiaojun Tong and Zhu Wang

School of Computer Science and Technology, Harbin Institute of Technology,
Weihai 264209, China
tong_xiaojun@163.com

**Abstract.** The static worm propagation model can not accurately describe the propagation of worm. This paper analyzes worm non-linear propagation models, draws out the worm propagation trend and proposes a new dynamic worm non-linear propagation model. Then the worm feature detection technology is designed based on the worm non-linear propagation models. The system uses rule-based detection method to monitor network worms, and gives alarms to server. Experimental results show that the scheme is a good solution to worm detection in multiple network environments and possess with higher detection rate and lower false alarm rate.

**Keywords:** IDS, Worm, Worm model optimization, Feature detection.

## 1 Introduction

As the computer and internet technology are continuously developing, the open resources and sharing of information have brought us great conveniences but also brought us the security problems. The network worm attacks are on the top of the list among varieties of network security threats.

The models research of worm propagation is hot fields. The ideal propagation model reflects the worms' propagation activities effectively and identifies the weaknesses of the worm propagation circle. At the same time, it can also forecast the potential threats brought by the worms and provides instructions for worm detecting.

The routing-worm propagation model in the IPv6 network has been proposed in Reference [1]. Based on the IPv6 network environment, it analyzed the scanning strategy of routing worm-IPv6 and simulated the propagation trends of Routing Worm-IPv6 via Two-Factor model. The model of anti-worms against malignant-worms[2] indicates that if the anti-worms adopts some control strategies, it can achieve a satisfactory effect in resisting malignant-worms, such as specifying the activity time, specifying the spread range, specifying the amount of copies and the slow-spreading mechanism.

There are many detection models in response to the large-scale and swift worm propagation[3-8]. A worm detection algorithm CWDMLN was proposed in Reference [3] , which makes use of the local network's cooperation and analyzes some worm's propagation features. The algorithm supplies alarms for worms' intrusion according to

P. Sénac, M. Ott, and A. Seneviratne (Eds.): ICWCA 2011, LNICST 72, pp. 156–169, 2012.

the worms' petal-like communication mode and invalid connections by deploying honey-pot in the LAN. Although it is feasible in the LAN, it is helpless in extensive detecting in multiple networks. In reference [3], the author comes up with some suggestions for the improvement but hasn't realized it yet. Reference [4] has brought up a distributed worm containment mechanism. Although the computational overhead is small and detection rate is high, but such detection mechanisms must be deployed on the router and does not apply to small and medium networks in general as the environmental requirements are too high.

In this paper, we analysed detail worm non-linear propagation model and proposed a new optimization model according to the adding of parameters, designed a distributed fusion-worm-detection system which has great practical significance on detecting large scale worm propagation and on limiting the damage to the network.

The paper is constructed as follows. First, we analyzed the worm features and work method of worms. Then, we did some researches on several classical non-linear worm propagation model, proposed the non-linear propagation optimization of worm and designed the distributed worm detection model . We did some experiments to verify it. Finally, we conclude the paper.

## 2 Analysis of Worm Non-linear Model

### 2.1 Feature of Worm

Network worm is usually a standalone program which runs without any user intervention. It spreads itself to other computers in the same LAN which has vulnerabilities. While the virus is a program or programming code that can graft its copying onto another program including the operating system. The virus can not run automatically, it needs to be activated by the host program [9]. Both the computer worm and virus can replicate and can spread themselves, which makes it's difficult to distinguish them. Especially, in recent years, more and more virus come to use worms' technology[10-11]. Meanwhile, worm adopts the virus technology too. So it is of great necessity to distinguish and to analyze their features (showed in Table 1).

**Table 1.** Differences between virus and worm

| Item | virus | worm |
|---|---|---|
| state of existence | parasitism | independent entity |
| replication form | insert into a file | replicate itself |
| transmission mechanism | activated by host program | system vulnerability |
| targets | local files | other hosts on the network |
| trigger | computer users | program itself |
| mainly influence | files , system | network and system performance |
| precautionary measures | remove from the host file | patch for the system,  firewall |

## 2.2  Work Flow of Worm

Worm is a kind of intelligent and automatic program [12-14]. Its working process is divided into four stages seen in Fig.1: scanning, penetration attack, on-site processing and replication. First, the infected hosts attempt to pick up the victims with vulnerabilities hosts for infection. Secondly, the worm sends packets to the victims to carry out the penetration attack. Thirdly, the worm does the on-site processing then hides itself and collects information, the aim is to make sure that the victims have no ware of being infected so that it is to cause more serious damage. Finally, during the self-replication stage, worm produce copies itself and repeats the steps above. The work flow of worm is seen in Fig.1.

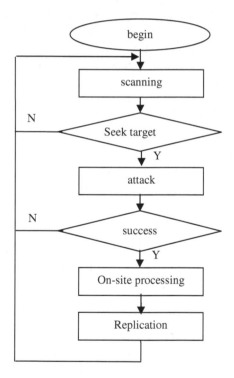

**Fig. 1.** Flow of worm work

## 2.3  Analysis of Worm Non-linear Propagation Model

Our research and analyses are based on several classical propagation models, which respectively are Simple Epidemic Model, Kermack-Mckendrick model, and the Two-Factor model.

**SEM Model.**   In the simple epidemic model we divide the hosts into two groups: susceptible hosts and infective hosts. The model assumes that once a host is infected by a worm, it will stay in its infectious state forever, which means that the state of a host must be either susceptible or infective. The simple epidemic model for a finite population is as follows:

$$\frac{dJ(t)}{dt} = \beta J(t)[N - J(t)] \tag{1}$$

where " $J(t)$ " is the number of the infective hosts at time $t$. "N " is the size of hosts. $\beta$ is the infection rate. At the beginning,

**Kermack-Mckendrick Model.** Different from the simple epidemic model, Kermack-Mckendrick model considers the removal process of infectious hosts. So there are totally three states of the vulnerable hosts: susceptible, infective and immune. Hosts in "immune" state can not infect other hosts forever.

Set $I(t)$ is the number of the infective hosts at time $t$. $R(t)$ is the number of immune hosts at time $t$. While $J(t)$ is the number of hosts which have been infected by time $t$.

So that we get the equation:

$$J(t) = I(t) + R(t) \tag{2}$$

The Kermack-Mckendrick model :

$$\begin{cases} dJ(t)/dt = \beta I(t)[N - J(t)] \\ dR(t)/dt = \gamma I(t) \\ J(t) = I(t) + R(t) = N - S(t) \end{cases} \tag{3}$$

Where $\beta$ is the infection rate. $\gamma$ is the immune hosts' removed rate from the hosts infected. $S(t)$ is the number of susceptible hosts at time $t$. $N$ is the total number of the vulnerable hosts.

**The Two-Factor Model.** There are several dynamic parameters to be assured: $\beta(t)$、$R(t)$ and $Q(t)$. $\beta(t)$ is the infection rate which changes with time. $R(t)$ is the number of removed hosts from infective ones at time $t$. $Q(t)$ matches the number of removed hosts from susceptible ones at time $t$. So between the time $t$ and $t + \Delta t$, the change of the number of susceptible hosts is:

$$S(t + \Delta t) - S(t) = -\beta(t)S(t)I(t)\Delta t - \frac{dQ(t)}{dt}\Delta t \tag{4}$$

where $s(t)$ is the number of susceptible hosts at time $t$. $I(t)$ is the number of infective hosts at time $t$.

The susceptible hosts' immunity process is described as follow in the Two-Factor model:

$$\frac{dQ(t)}{dt} = \mu S(t)J(t) \tag{5}$$

Based on the Two-Factor-Model's assume of the dynamic properties, the complete differential equations are as follows:

$$
\begin{cases}
dS(t)/dt = -\beta(t)S(t)I(t) - dQ(t)/dt \\
dR(t)/dt = \gamma I(t) \\
dQ(t)/dt = \mu S(t)J(t) \\
\beta(t) = \beta_0[1 - I(t)/N]^\eta \\
N = S(t) + R(t) + I(t) + Q(t) \\
I(0) = I_0 \ll N; S(0) = N - I_0; R(0) = Q(0) = 0;
\end{cases}
\tag{6}
$$

where $\gamma$ is the infective hosts' immunity, $J(t) = I(t) + R(t)$ describes the number of hosts which have been infected now or before. $\mu$ is a constant, $\mu J(t)$ is the immunity rate of susceptible hosts at time $t$.

$\beta_0$ is the initial value of infection rate. The exponent $\eta$ is used to adjust the infection rate sensitivity to the number of infective hosts $I(t)$.

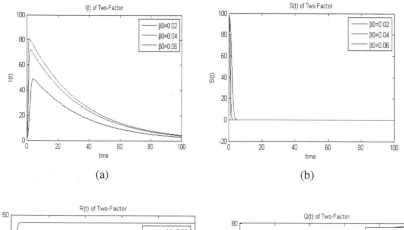

(a)                                           (b)

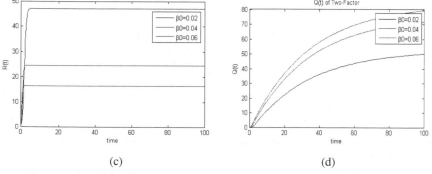

(c)                                           (d)

**Fig. 2.** $I(t), S(t), R(t), Q(t)$ of Two-Factor Model

If we set $\mu = 0$, $\eta = 0$ and $\gamma = 0$, we can get the SEM from the Two-Factor-Model. If we set $\mu = 0$, $\eta = 0$, and $\gamma \neq 0$, we get KM from the Two-Factor-model.

Set $\gamma = 0.03$, $N = 100$, $I(0) = 1$, $R(0) = 0$, $Q(0) = 0$, $\mu = 0.01$, $\sigma = 3$, and $\beta$ respectively are 0.02, 0.04, 0.06. According to the formula (9) and (11), we can get the function of $I(t)$, $S(t)$, $R(t)$, $Q(t)$ and $t$ as follows in Fig. 2

The Two-Factor-Model is the extension of the SEM and KM. It makes up for the shortage of the two models and is more suitable to describe the network worm's propagation model. But the Two-Factor-Model doesn't take the large-scale automatic patches or upgrades into consideration. Similarly, it also considers $\gamma$ as a constant. Since that the Two-Factor-Model believes that the immunity rate of the susceptible hosts is increasing with time, the immunity rate of the infective hosts also should be increasing with time. So it is not appropriate to take $\gamma$ as a constant.

## 2.4 Improved Two-Factor Model

The two-factor model already can describe the worms' propagation well. But there still are some flaws. Although the two-factor has brought the susceptible and infected hosts' immune into consideration, but the immune rate is constant here which is not in accordance with the actual network situation.

We can consider the problem from two aspects:

First, the infected hosts' immunity $\gamma$. The infected hosts can eliminate the worms by downloading patches, anti-virus software or network administrator's intervention. And at the same time, the infected host can get his immunity. Here $\gamma$ is exactly the parameter describing the ability of infected hosts' immunity. Parameter $\gamma$ is infected by many factors such as the total number of the immunity hosts, the official patches and corresponding anti-virus software and so on. So $\gamma$ must be a variable which changes with time. In the early period, $\gamma$ is quite low and later it begins to grow when there are more and more immunity hosts in the network or the official patches released. For that reason, we need to find a propitiate model to describe $\gamma$ dynamic features in order to explore the worms propagation in actual situation more accurately.

Secondly, the susceptible hosts' immunity $\mu$. Taking the susceptible hosts' immunity into consideration is a great improvement of two-factor model compared with the SEM. But two-factor only considers the perfect condition which $\mu$ is a constant through all the worm propagation process, which is obviously not according to the actual situation. In order to understand the dynamic features of $\mu$, let us propose a question first. How do the susceptible hosts get their immunity? We can explain the question from two aspects:

A, the susceptible host gets information about the worm or official patches or even anti-virus software from other immunity hosts in the same network. So it gets its immunity.

B, the susceptible host itself gets in touch with the network monitor center and gets the corresponding anti-virus software.

For the last two reasons, $\mu$ must be a variable and its evolution must be similar to $\gamma$'s. In the early time, $\mu$ is quite low as there are few immunity hosts in the network.

While with the time going, more and more immunity hosts emerge and $\mu$ begins to grow, meanwhile the ability of susceptible hosts' immunity grows too.

After a mount times of experiment, we conclude the math model of $\mu$ and $\gamma$ as Fig.3 and Fig.4.

$$\gamma = \gamma_0 (1 + R(t)/N)^\sigma \tag{7}$$

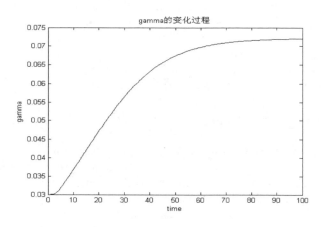

**Fig. 3.** The model of $\gamma$

$$\mu = \mu_0 (1 + Q(t)/N)^\sigma \tag{8}$$

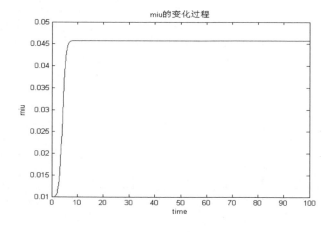

**Fig. 4.** The model of $\mu$

The worm propagation trend of the modified model is same to primary Two-Factor model. As shown in the fig.5 and in Fig.6.

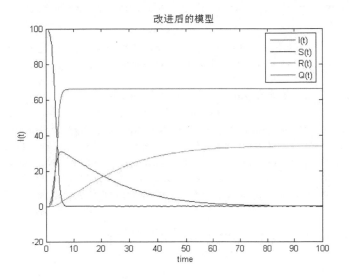

**Fig. 5.** Improved model of Two-Factor

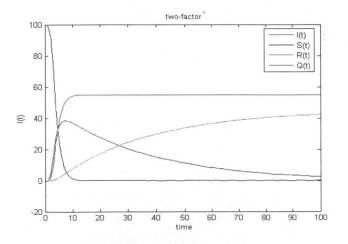

**Fig. 6.** The model of Two-Factor

After simulation by MATLAB, the improved two-factor model's overall trend is the same with the original model.

The difference is that the modified model can return to normal more quickly than the primary model, which is conform to the actual situation perfectly. Because after a certain worm breaks out, the network administrator and the clients will take all kinds of measures to restrain the worm's propagation as soon as possible, so that the network can recover to the normal situation.

We can conclude from the trend figure that there are two improvements of the improved model:

1. A certain worm breaks out in a network with 100 hosts. There are totally 38 hosts get infected in the original model while 30 hosts exist in the improved model. Compared with the original model, the total infected host is 8 percentages lower than the original ones, which is according with the actual situation well.

2. The improved model reaches its peak 6 seconds after the worm breaks out and then the infected hosts decrease sharply. The original model's peak is about 10 seconds after the worm break out and infected hosts decrease slowly. For that reason, the improved model can describe the worm propagation more accurately. With the improvement of the technology, quickly information communication and people's awareness of worms, the time taken to defeat worm must be shorter and shorter.

# 3    Worm Feature Detection Model of Worms

## 3.1    Common Intrusion Detection Framework

In recent years, the intrusion detection has been greatly developed. The Defense Advanced Research Projects Agency (DARPA) together with the Intrusion Detection Working Group of Internet Engineering Task Force (IERF) have set the standard criterion of IDS and bring up the Common Intrusion Detection Framework (CIDF) showed in Fig.7 as follows:

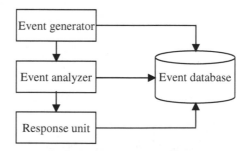

**Fig. 7.** Architecture of CIDF

The event generator picks information which interests it and transforms the information into the standard form so that other components in the system can use. The event analyzer analyses events and do core-intrusion-detection and then creates new GIDOS. The response unit decides the measures which should be taken according to the new GIDOS.

## 3.2  Design of Worm Rules

Through some researches on several common worms, we get the rules of them which have been detected in our detection system as follows.

（1） Rules of Ramen Worm

Alert tcp $HOME_NET any -> $EXTERNAL_NET 27374 (msg::"MISC ramen worm";flow:to_server    ,    established;    content:"GET    ";    depth:8; nocase;reference:arachnids , 461; classtype:bad-unknown; sid:514;rev:5;)

（2） Rules of CodeRed Worm

Alert tcp $EXTERNAL_NET any -> $HTTP_SERVERS $HTTP_PORTS (msg:"WEB-IIS CodeRed v2 root.exe access"; flow:to_server , established; uricontent:"/root.exe";    nocase;    reference:    url    , www.cert.org/advisories/CA-2001-19.html;    classtype:web-application-attack; sid:1256;rev:8;)

（3） Rules of Slapper Worm

Alert udp $EXTERNAL_NET 2002 -> $HTTP_SERVERS 2002 (msg:"MISC slapper worm admin traffic"; content:"|00  00|E|00  00|E|00    00|@|00"; depth:10; reference:url    ,    isc.incidents.org/analysis.html?id=167;    reference:url, www.cert.org/advisories/CA-2002-27.html;    classtype:Trojan-activity;    sid:1889; rev:5;)

（4） Rules of Slammer Worm

Alert udp $HOME_NET any -> $EXTERNAL_NET 1434 (msg:"MS-SQL Worm propagation attempt OUTBOUND"; content:"|04|"; depth:1; content:"|81 F1 03 01 04 9B 81 F1|"; content:"sock"; content:"send"; reference: bugtraq, 5310; reference:bugtraq, 5311; reference:cve, 2002-0649; reference:nessus , 11214; reference: url , vil.nai.com/vil/content/v_99992.htm; classtype:misc-attack; sid:2004;rev:7;)

（5） Rules of ACworm Worm

Alert tcp $EXTERNAL_NET any -> HTTP_SERVERS   $HTTP_PORTS (msg:"WEB-MISC Apache Chunked-Encoding worm attempt"; flow:to_server, established;    content:"CCCCCCC|3A|AAAAAAAAAAAAAAAAAAAA";    nocase; reference:bugtraq,    4474;    reference:bugtraq,    4485;    reference:bugtraq,    5033; reference:cve, 2002-0071; reference:cve, 2002-0079; reference:cve, 2002-0392; classtype:web-application-attack; sid:1809; rev:9;)

(6)  Rules of Sadmind Worm

Alert tcp $EXTERNAL_NET any -> $HTTP_SERVERS $HTTP_PORTS (msg:"WEB-MISC sadmind worm access"; flow: to_server, established; content:"GET x HTTP/1.0"; depth:15; reference:url, www.cert.org/advisories/CA-2001-11.html; classtype:attempted-recon; sid:1375; rev:6;)

(7)  Rules of Code Red II Worm

Alert tcp $external_net any -> $http_net $http_ports (msg:"Web-IIS ISAPI.ida attempt"; uricontent:".ida?"; nocase; dsize: 239; flags:A+;)

(8)  Rules of Nachi Worm

Alert icmp $HOME_NET any -> $ EXTERNAL_NET any (msg:"Nachi"; content:"laaaaaal"; dsize:64; itype:8; offset:1; depth:6; reference:arachnids, 154; sid:483; classtype:misc-activity; rev:2;)

(9)  Rules of Witty Worm

alert udp any 4000 -> any any (msg:"ISS PAM/Witty Worm Shellcode"; content:"|65 74 51 68 73 6f 63 6b 54 53|"; depth:246; classtype:misc-attack; reference:url,www.secureworks.com/research/threats/witty; sid:1000078; rev:1;)

(10)  Rules of Lion

①  BIND infoleak root uses follows rules :

Alert     udp     $EXTERNAL_NET     any     ->     $HOME_NET     53 (msg:"IDS482/named-exploit-infoleak-lsd";content:"|AB CD 09 80 00 00 00 01 00 00 00 00 00 00 01 00 01 20 20 20 20 02 61|"; sid:1000081;rev:1;)

②  BIND8 TSIG buffer overflow uses follows arachNIDS rules :

Alert     udp     $EXTERNAL_NET     any     ->     $HOME_NET     53 (msg:"IDS489/named-exploit-tsig-lsd";content:"|3F 90 90 90 EB 3B 31 DB 5F 83 EF 7C 8D 77 10 89 77 04 8D 4F 20|"; sid:1000082;rev:1;)

# 4  The Analysis of Experiment Results

Considering the security of system, the paper uses self-developed simulation program to send worms that meet specific characteristics of the worm packets. Here mainly to simulate the three kinds of worms: Witty worm, Slammer worm and Ramen worms. They represent the three kinds of worms of UDP and TCP protocols using two types of worm spread .

Slammer worm itself is packaged in a size of 376 bytes of UDP packets from any source port and is sent to any address on the network host port 1434 of UDP.

If the SQL Server Resolution Service of host opens and does not install the appropriate patch program, the worm will use the buffer overflow vulnerability to infect them. The first byte of Slammer worm packet is 0x04, in which has the contents of 0x810xF10x030x010x040x9B0x810xF1, 'sock' and 'send' content.

The processes of experiment are as follows:

(1) Start the console and set the state for waiting connection of the worm detection end.

(2) Start worm detection end and connect it to the console.

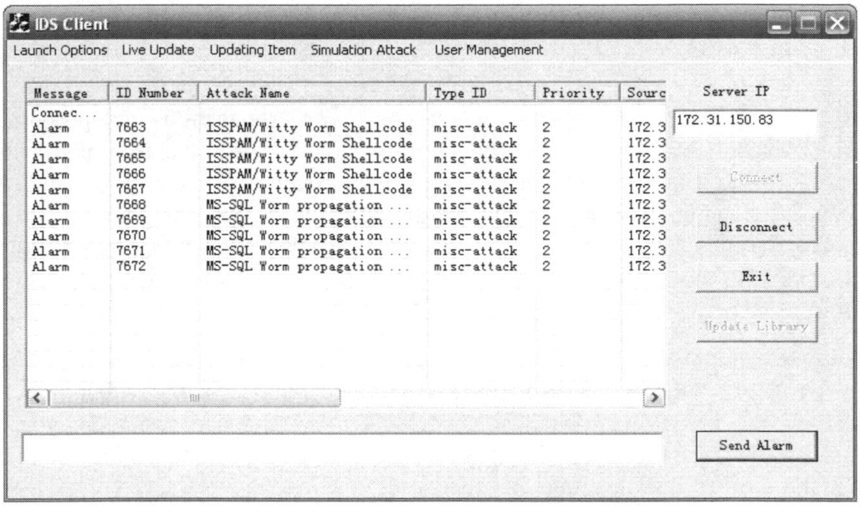

**Fig. 8.** Witty worm detected on client end

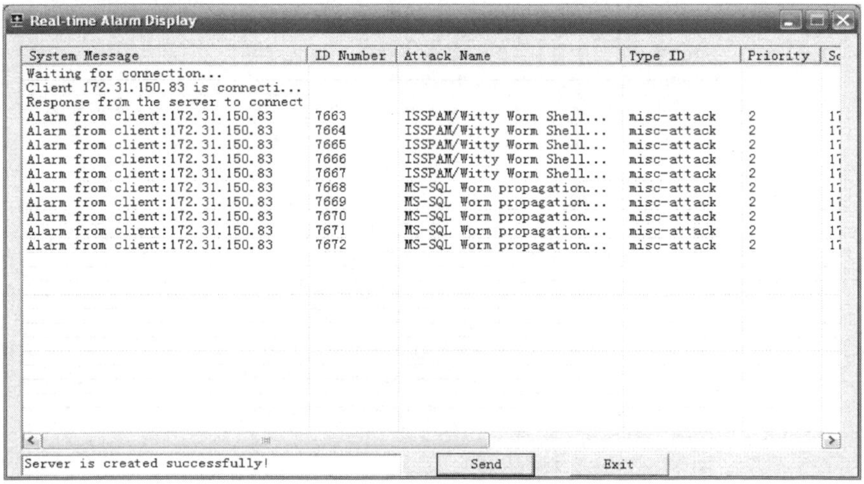

**Fig. 9.** Worm Alarm received on console end

(3 ) Start the host A and host B and run normal TCP and UCP applications on them.

(4) Run the worm simulation program on host A and host B. The program generates worm packets such as Slammer worm, Witty worm or Ramen worms. The detection side detected the corresponding worm data packets and generated alerts as shown in Fig. 8. At the same time the console receives the worm alert information, as shown in Fig. 9.

# 5 Conclusions

This paper analyzed the model of worm non-linear propagation, and proposed a nonlinear model optimization of worm and designed a distributed detection system of worm. Experiments have proven that the new model can accurately reflect the propagation trend of the worm, and the worm feature detection system not only is able to achieve a high detection rate, but also be able to carry out a wide range of network monitoring. The system has high detection rate and low false alarm rate can be applied to worm detection..

**Acknowledgements.** This work was supported by the National Natural Science Foundation of China (Grant No. 60973162), the Natural Science Foundation of Shandong Province (Grant No. ZR2009GM037), the Science and technology of Shandong Province of China (Grant No.2010GGX10132), the Scientific Research Foundation of Harbin Institute of Technology at Weihai (Grant No. HIT(WH) ZB200909).

# References

1. Xu, Y.-g., Qian, H.-y., Li, H.-f.: Routing worm propagation model in IPv6 networks. Application Research of Computers 3920 (2009)
2. Zhang, D.-x., Peng, J., Hong, H.E.: Research the Propagation Model of Internet Worm. Network Communication and Security, 1244–1246 (2007)
3. Zhang., X.-y., Qing, S.-h., Li, Q., Li, D.-z., He, C.-h.: A Coordinated Worm Detection Method Based on Local Nets. Journal of Software, 412–421 (2007)
4. Zhao, g., Zhang, t.: Design of the worm detection system Based on the worm propagation characteristics. Computer Security, 114–118 (2009)
5. Ram, D., Cangussu, W., Sudeep, P.: Fast Worm Containment Using Feedback Control. Dependable and Secure Computing 5(2), 119–136 (2007)
6. Kim, H.A., Karp, B.: Autograph. Toward Automated, Distributed Worm Signature Detection. In: Proceedings of the 13th USENIX Security Symposium, San Diego, CA, pp. 59–66 (2004)
7. Dagon, D., Qin, X., Gu, G., Lee, W., Grizzard, J.B., Levine, J.G., Owen, H.L.: HoneyStat: Local worm detection using honeypots. In: Jonsson, E., Valdes, A., Almgren, M. (eds.) RAID 2004. LNCS, vol. 3224, pp. 39–58. Springer, Heidelberg (2004)
8. Tang, Y., Chen, S.: Defending against internet worms: A signature-based approach. In: Proceedings of IEEE INFOCOM 2005, Hong Kong, pp. 13–23 (2005)
9. Eugene, H.: The Internet worm programs. ACM Computer 23(3), 17–57 (1989)

10. Wang, Y., Wang, C.X.: Modeling The Effects of Timing Parameters on Virus Propagation. In: Proceedings of the ACM CCS Workshop on Rapid Malcode (WORM 2003), pp. 61–66. ACM press, Washington (2003)
11. Dantu, R., Cangussu, J., Yelimeli, A.: Dynamic control of worm propagation. Information Technology 1(3), 419–423 (2004)
12. Streftaris, G., Gibson, G.J.: Statistical Inference for Stochastic Epidemic Models. In: Proceedings of the 17th International Workshop on Statistical Modeling, China, pp. 609–616 (2002)
13. Zou, C.C., Gong, W., Towsley, D.: Code Red Worm Propagation Modeling and Analysis. In: Proceedings of the 9th ACM Symp on Computer and Communication Security, pp. 138–147. ACM Press, Washington (2002)
14. Bishop, M.: A Model of Security Monitoring. In: Proceedings of Fifth AnnualComputer Security Applications Conference, New Orleans, pp. 249–251. IEEE Computer Society, Washington DC, USA (1989)

# Phase Measurement of Three-Phase Power Based on FPGA[*]

Xiyuan Zhang, Yonghui Zhang, and Xinning Lu

College of Information Science & Technology, Hainan University,
570228, Haikou, China
xiyuan5805931@126.com,
zhyhemail@163.com,
416443101@qq.com

**Abstract.** As the frequency of the three-phase power signal is instability and it contains multiple harmonics signal, the error can not be ignored when FFT algorithm applied to measure the phase directly. Although corrected by many correction methods such as ratio method, center of energy gravity method, etc. the precision of phase measurement is also severely influenced by harmonic signal. In order to solve these problems, the power phase measurement system is designed based on FPGA which embedded all-phase FFT algorithms. It realized the measurement of the phase with high accuracy, and the results indicate it almost immune to the harmonic and noise of power.

**Keywords:** Phase Measurement, All-phase FFT, FPGA.

## 1 Introduction

The phase of three-phase voltage and current signal is one of the most important measurement issues of the power test and control system. The research on the phase of voltage and current signal focuses on how to get the accurate measurement result rapidly. As the main method of digital signal processing, FFT is often used to measure the phase of power signal. For the frequency of the three-phase power signal is instability and it contains multiple harmonics signal, the error can not be ignored when FFT algorithm is applied to measure the phase directly. Although corrected by many correction methods such as ratio method, center of energy gravity method, etc. the precision of phase measurement is also severely influenced by harmonic signal. With the phase invariability, the all-phase FFT is suitable to solve this problem. Based on all-phase FFT, the phase of the three-phase voltage and current signal can be measured accurately, and it almost immune to the harmonic and noise of power. In this paper, the three-phase voltage and current phase measurement system based on FPGA is proposed to realize the phase accurate measure by using the all-phase FFT algorithm.

[*] Supported by Program of International S&T Cooperation[GJXM20100002], Hainan Province Natural Science Fund[808132], Scientific Research in Higher Education Department of Hainan Province [Hjkj2011-08] and 211 Project of Hainan University.

P. Sénac, M. Ott, and A. Seneviratne (Eds.): ICWCA 2011, LNICST 72, pp. 170–179, 2012.
© Institute for Computer Sciences, Social Informatics and Telecommunications Engineering 2012

## 2 System Design

This paper proposes utilizing FPGA to realize all phase FFT algorithm, and using the algorithm to accomplish phase and phase difference's measure of the three-phase electricity. Due to FPGA has characteristics of design flexibility and fast processing-speed, so the phase measurements based on FPGA can be realized conveniently and also make it meet the real-time measurement requirements. Using the signal regulate circuit to convert the three-phase voltage current signal to A/D conversion chip's required range, realize High voltage signal's isolation, expand 6 road 12 bits high-speed synchronous ADC and collect three-phase voltages and three current signal simultaneously, then process the collected multiple signals in FPGA chip and calculate some measured value such as the voltage and current phase and so on. The three-phase electricity phase measuring system overall charts based on FPGA are shown in Figure 1.

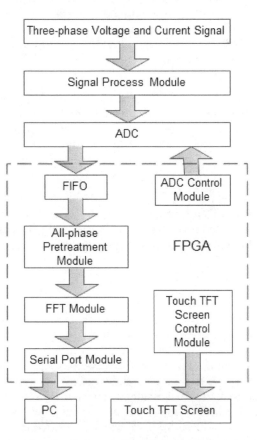

**Fig. 1.** The three-phase voltage and current phase measurement system framework based on FPGA (Dotted box is FPGA)

## 2.1  Hardware Circuit of Measurement System

(1)Voltage and current signal process module

No distortion test of three-phase electrical signals is the premise to realize phase signal's high precision measuring. Design signal regulate circuit can convert 380V ac voltage signal to the voltage signal within A/D conversion required range with no distortion, testing the input voltage to effect the A/D converter.

(2)ADC module

ADC module's sample quantization is a necessary step to realize digital signal processing. Design ADC sampling module to convert the three-phase voltage current analog signals into digital signals, and then send it to FPGA for digital signal processing.

(3) The FPGA function module

The FPGA function module is the core of the three-phase electricity phase measuring system that it not only deal with data, but also control the whole system's coordination. This module mainly responsible for collecting data on all phase pretreatment, FFT processing, cut transform and the control work of modules such as ADC, LCD, Flash Memory and so on.

(4) Touch Screen

In the design of three-phase electricity phase measuring system, touch screen realized the function of keys in order to facilitate future function expansion and upgrades. Because the touch screen coated in the upper part of the LCD display screen, so functions that can be realized in different area of the touch screen are provided by LCD modules, namely, touch screen and LCD display are used together with as buttons.

(5) PC Software

PC mainly accept the FFT frequency domain data coming from Serial, and then finish anyway, cutting operations and calculate the phase in Labview software. At last, show the user a visual interface with displaying measured results graphically.

## 2.2  The FPGA Function Modules

(1)Asynchronous FIFO module

Asynchronous FIFO module has two main roles, the first role is to complete ADC sampling data's receiving. ADC samples the three-phase signal under the control of FPGA, and then stores the sampled data into FPGA for processing. The second role is to complete speed matching between modules. Due to ADC chip's speed limits, the advantage of FPGA fast speed can't be fully exerted. In order to make the entire system treat operations as soon as possible, we must introduce asynchronous FIFO to solve this problem, which finishes reading and writing data operations through two separate clocks. As ADC's low speed, we can set low frequency clock to finish the writing operation of sampled data. And also because the preprocessing module needs large quantity, so we need to set higher frequency clock to finish the reading operation of data.

(2) All phase pretreatment module

All phase pretreatment module is the core of system algorithm. The phase spectrum invariability of Acquisition signal after transformed by FFT can be assured only after the signal has been all phase preprocessed. And the phase invariability is not only the premise of precision measuring, but also the suggested theoretical basis of this design. All phase pretreatment which based on FPGA is mainly use FPGA' owning eighteen bits on-time multiplier to complete the pretreatment work, thus getting the N preprocessing data. The on-time multiplier's multiplicand is the sampled data that coming from FIFO module, while the multiplier is the convolution coefficient stored in the procedure. Treat the 2N - 1 item data which get from the on-time multiplier as following: item 1 plus N + 1 item, the first 2 plus N + 2 item until the first N - 1 plus item 2N - 1 item, and then put N item before N-1 item. Finally get N point pretreatment data.

(3)FFT module

FFT module invokes Altera Company's Quartus II 9.1 software's bringing FFT IP core to finish the FFT processing. This IP nuclear processing precision can reach 24 bits in binary, and there are many structural frames to choose from. So we can be reasonable to use FPGA hardware resources to do FFT transformation quickly and efficiently. In this design, FFT used a flow pattern data structure with a fixed transform size. The input and output are continuous flow of data, and the output data format is mass index structure which is a compromise structure between designated structure and floating-point structure.

(4)Serial interface module

Serial interface module mainly be responsible for transmitting the specific FFT frequency-domain data to the PC, and also use anyway, cutting processing to find out the corresponding phase values in Labview software. The results of FFT transformation are plural, and then use its imaginary part to divide its real part. Next, this point phase value is the value of that number's arc tangent.

(5) Control module

Control module is responsible for coordinating the whole system, such as control the ADC initialization, control the data acquisition and transmission, control the touch screen initialization and control signal transmission and so on.

# 3   Hardware Design

The three-phase electric measuring system based on FPGA not only should ensure the phase measuring accuracy, but also should assure the real-time measuring requirements. So the chip selection and hardware circuit design were crucial.

## 3.1   Features of the Chip

(1) ADC chip

ADC uses the MAXIM's MAX1308 chip whose sampling accuracy can up to 12-bit and maximum sampling rate reaches 4Msps.Except that,it has 8 acquisition channels. Three-phase voltage and current signal data's acquisition requires 6 channels, so the sampling rate of each channel signal can up to 600ksps, it is easy to meet requirements of the three-phase electrical phase measurement. MAX1308 chip uses 12-bit parallel port to communicate with the FPGA, which can sent the 12 bits collected data to the FPGA for processing at the same time,and also can control the FPGA' work mode by received control word coming from FPGA to make it complete tne acquisition of three signal phase.within time sequence.

(2) FPGA chip

The project selected the Altera Cyclone II series FPGA chip EP2C35F672C8N which with a hardware multiplier inside. The chip is the core of the phase measurement system which not only processes the data, but also controls the entire system's work coordination. The main responsibility of this chip includes doing all preprocessing phase to the collected data, FFT processing, data operations,and ADC, LCD, Flash etc. chip's control work. Due to FPGA chip having the feature of thirty-five 18-bit multiplier that not only guarantees the speed of all preprocessing phase﹑ FFT processing and the arctangent computation, but also will not take up too much hardware resources.

(3) Touch screen and LCD display

TSC2046 of Texas Instruments Company is selected to be used in this project. This chip can test the press points on the two-dimensional screen, and it's highest detection accuracy can up to 12 bits. LCD display is a LCD color display with a size of 3.0 inches,and resolution of 400×240 pixel. Between the LCD display and FPGA chip is connected the control chip ILI9326of Technology Company which used to drive the LCD display and can show 65K colors (18 bits).

## 3.2  Design and Working Principle

(1) Regulate circuit design

The phase measuring systems based FPGA can not detecte the 380V three-phase electrical signals directly,while it is necessary to design the signal regulate circuit to convert the AC voltage with amplitude of 380V to the required range of ADC samples with no distortion. Secondly, in order to ensure detection of phase with no distortion and the original phase information not changed in the process of the regulate circuit convertion. We used the principle of resistance's partial voltage in the design for the resistance won't make the signal phase information lead or lag.

(2) Sample circuit design

In design of the phase measuring system ,the design of sample circuit is very critical and it's Stand or fall has a direct impact on the accuracy of the measuring results.As the Three-phase electricity has three-phase voltage and three-phase current ,so when measure it's phase value simultaneously,it required at least 6 ADC acquisition channels. MAX1308 chip of MAXIM company has 8 acquisition channels, and it's sampling accuracy can up to 12-bit ,maximum sampling rate reaches 4Msps The three-phase voltage and current signal's data acquisition requires 6 channels, so the sampling rate of each channel signal can up to 600ksps, it is easy to meet requirements of the three-phase electrical phase measurement. The MAX1308 chip uses dual power to supply and 12-bit parallel port to communicate with the FPGA,That is to say, we can sent 12 bits collected data to the FPGA for processing at the same time,and also, MAX1308 chip can control the FPGA's acquisition channels by the 8-bit control word of FPGA.

The input high voltage of MAX1308 chip's digital port neeeds at least 0.7 times the DVCC. When the DVCC selects 5V, the high voltage which FPGA output to the MAX1308 will not be recognized.So DVCC should choose 3.3V Digital Power. If selecting external clock, R3 is always be connected to it . On the contrary,R4 would be connected to it.

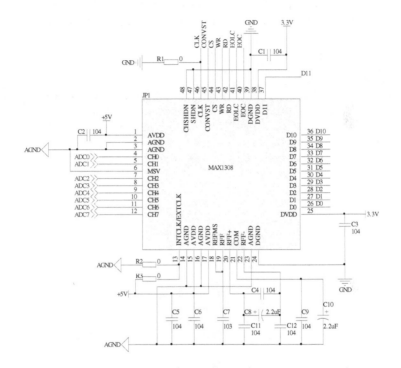

**Fig. 2.** Sampling circuit

# 4   Software Design

## 4.1   The Platform of Software Design

The software development platform of the design is used Quartus II. Quartus II is a comprehensive PLD developing software of Altera Company. It supports various design input forms such as Principle Diagram, VHDL, Verilog HDL, AHDL (Altera Hardware Description Language) and so on. What's more,it has embedded integrated device and emulator, and can complete the PLD design flow from design input to the hardware configuration. Quartus II supports Altera's IP Core which contains Macro function module base of LPM/Mega Function. So the users can use the mature module fully, simplify complexity of the design and accelerate it's speed. The good support for third-party EDA tools also allows the user to use the familiar third-party EDA tools in all stages of the design process.

The hardware design language is VHDL, which is a high-level language used in circuit design. VHDL is mainly used to describe digital system's structure ,behavior, function and interface. The design ideas based on the VHDL state machine is especially embodiment in this design. State machine can be thought as a special combination of portfolio logic and registers logic. Portfolio logic part can be divided into state machine decoder and output decoder, and state decoder determines the next state of the state machine. Output decoder determines the state machine's output.

## 4.2  Program Design

(1) Acquisition procedures

Acquisition procedures is the control program of MAX1308 chip. The key problem of the control program is to ensure the points of each acquisition from began gathering to end  integer times the FFT needed points, in order to ensure that each FFT have effectively output. In this design, state machine thought is adopted to complete the data acquisition control. Programming design flow chart as Figure 3 shows.

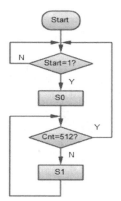

**Fig. 3.** Data acquisition flow chart

On the right flowcharting, S0 represents initialization state of MAX308,S1 represents a state of waveform sampling,Start represents start collecting signal, Cnt is collecting counter.

From reading the picture,we know even if the Start becomes 0 in sampling, the acquisition circulation won't be affected. And it will not stop until 512 data bits collected. When start collecting, the MAX1308 should be initialized and its acquisition channel number should be settled every time. The collection timing diagram of Quartus II simulation is as shown in Figure 4.

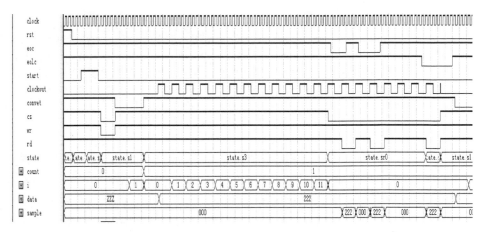

**Fig. 4.** Collection timing diagram

(2) FFT program

Because the Quartus II supports Altera's IP core,which curing various modules such as Adder module, Multiplication module, division module, FFT module, FIFO module and so on.So the design invokes the IP core's FFT module to reliaze it's own FFT. The FFT is taking advantage of the flow pattern data structure, transform size is 64 (take fewer points facilitate simulation and validate the results). The FFT results of Quartus II simulation is shown in Figure 5.

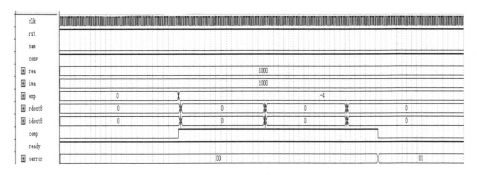

**Fig. 5.** Simulation timing diagram

As the above figure shows, if the real part and imaginary part input are 1000, the first item of FFT transformation result is 64000 and other items are 0.And rea, ima in the charts are Separately referred to the real part , imaginary input. Exp, rdout, idout are Separately referred to the quick exponential term, the real part ,imaginary part output. According to the handbook of FFT's IP core, we can get to know the final output is rdout*2(-exp) and idout*2(-exp).

(3) Touch screen control module procedure

The touch screen's control procedure mainly contains correct control of TSC2046 chip and ILI9326 chip. The TSC2046 chip must receive and transit data bidirectionally with the FPGA chip,while the ILI9326 chip only need to receive the control information and the data message correctly from the FPGA chip. In the design ,we discovered that as these two chips must transmis information with the main chip frequently and high-speedly,therefore the timing control becomes very important and we must eliminate the competition risk which possibly appears in the procedure as far as possible. This module's timing chart is as shown in Figure 6. DIN first outputs control word of the Y coordinate, and then outputs control word of the X coordinate.

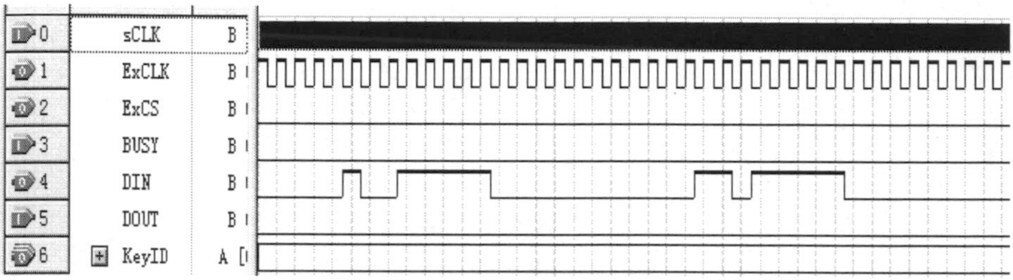

**Fig. 6.** Touch screen control timing diagram

## 5   System Commissioning

### 5.1  Hardware Circuit Debugging

This design is a extending system based on EP2C35F672C8N chip's teaching and multimedia development platform,and that the EP2C35F672C8N chip belongs to Altera company's Cyclone II series. In the three-phase electricity phase detection system, the first thing is to design special voltage regulate circuit, which can convert the three-phase 380V power distortionless into the range of high voltage signals,which ADC conversion required.As there are three voltage signal road in the three-phase electricity, So if we want to measure the instantaneous phase difference between each phase,there must have multiple acquisition channel in the acquisition circuit to ensure synchronous sampling and transform the three-phase voltage current analog signals into digital signals. Then, use a FPGA to make a full phase FFT processing to the transmited ssion digital signal.Finally,translate the data to PC through serial port and use Labview software to test and verify them.

### 5.2  Practical Measurement Based on Labview

Combining Labview with acquisition card can validate all phase FFT phase detection algorithm. Use the acquisition card which controlled by FPGA to collect and process three-phase electricity, and then send the data though serial data bus to PC and display them on the Labview software. Finally,   the measured results are shown in Figure 7.

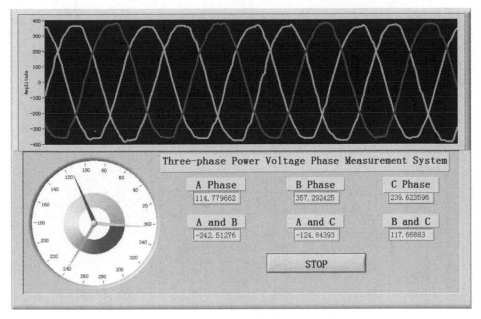

**Fig. 7.** Phase detection interface of Labview

## 6 Summary

This system design all phase FFT algorithm based on FPGA, which phase invariability makes it does not acquire any compensation algorithm correction to calculate three-phase electricity phase values. Realize the overall design of three-phase electricity phase detection system, and measured its phase value with a higher precision and practical value. All that laid a foundation for the further three-phase electricity phase measurement special chip (ASIC)'s research.

## References

1. Wang, Z., Huang, X.: All phase spectrum of digital signal analysis and filtering techniques. Electronic Industry Press, Beijing (2009)
2. Huang, X.: All phase digital signal processing [D]. Tianjin University doctorate paper (11) (2006)
3. Du, N., Guo, L., Fu, S.: The Fourier method of development measures the phase error analysis. Electronic Surveying and Instrument 21(1), 15–19 (2007)
4. Ma, L., Shen, L.: High accuracy power frequency phase meter's development. Electrical measurement and measuring appliance 12(1), 42–44 (2006)
5. Liu, H., Jing, F., Ning, F.: Three-phase multi-purpose volt-ampere phase system's development based on DSP portable. Machinery and electron (10), 18–20 (2006)
6. Jia, F., Tian, L., Hao, L., Wang, C.: Studies and realizes [J] based on the CPLD phase difference measuring technique. Tianjin Scientific and Technical University Journal 19(3), 59–61 (2004)
7. Wang, Z., Hou, Z., Su, F.: Entire phase digital filtering (19) (supplement), 1-4 (2003)

# Over-the-Sea Radio Propagation and Integrated Wireless Networking for Ocean Fishery Vessels

Yong Bai, Wencai Du, and Chong Shen

College of Information Science & Technology, Hainan University,
58 Renmin Ave., Haikou, Hainan 570228, China
{bai,wencai,chongshen}@hainu.edu.cn

**Abstract.** To facilitate the mobile users on ocean fishery vessels to communicate efficiently and cost-effectively in any sea areas, this paper analyzes the applicability of existing wireless technologies to over-the-sea communications, especially their over-the-sea radio propagation effects. To make their respective advantages complementary to each other, this paper proposes an integrated wireless networking system which is composed of mobile ad hoc network, cellular mobile network, and satellite mobile network. The system architecture of the proposed heterogeneous wireless networking system is described, and the access selection mechanism is proposed with always-best-connected (ABC) concept for the benefit of mobile users. Lastly, this paper reports a developed prototype system to evaluate the feasibility and validity of our proposals.

**Keywords:** radio propagation, mobile ad hoc network, mobile communications, maritime communications.

## 1 Introduction

With the development of ocean fishery, mobile users on fishery vessels need effective ship-to-ship and ship-to-shore communications methods at any sea area. In such a environment, the major user requirements on communications are cost-effectiveness and full coverage of fishing areas. We firstly surveyed and evaluated whether the existing communications networks can be the candidate networking technology. Actually, there are pros and cons of the existing communications technologies. Currently the communications methods can be used on fishery vessels at sea include single sideband (SSB) shortwave radio, VHF (Very High Frequency) radio, FM radio, cellular phone, and satellite equipments. Among them, the SSB shortwave transmission can be used for long-range communications with reflected signals by the ionosphere. However, blind zones exist in SSB radio manner when the receiver is located away from the bounced distance, and it often suffers from serious interference problems because of overcrowding on the wavebands and atmospheric disturbances. The transmission distance of VHF radio is about 20 nautical miles and the VHF radio transceiver is mainly used only for voice communications. The FM radio is mainly used for short-distance ship-to-ship voice communications with effective transmission

P. Sénac, M. Ott, and A. Seneviratne (Eds.): ICWCA 2011, LNICST 72, pp. 180–190, 2012.
© Institute for Computer Sciences, Social Informatics and Telecommunications Engineering 2012

distance of 8 nautical miles. Another option is cellular phone, such as WCDMA mobile phone with a global positioning system (GPS), whose advantages are low equipment cost and cheap calling fee. Nevertheless, its drawback is the limited coverage of cellular base station signal, which usually can only cover the tens of nautical miles offshore. The last option is satellite mobile communication by the Inmarsat (International Maritime Satellite) system [1], which is suitable for ships far away from shores. However, the mobile users (e.g. fishermen) can not always afford it due to the expensiveness of satellite terminal equipment, high cost of maintenance and replacement, and high communication fee. The above discussion on the current available communication technologies shows that the maritime mobile users are still lack of the cost-effective communication methods to be used at sea.

To further evaluate the wireless technologies for the ship-shore and ship-to-ship communications at sea, the radio propagation effects of existing wireless systems are analyzed. In the analysis, the phenomena of curvature of the earth, propagation over water, diffraction are taken into account. The coverage capabilities of different wireless systems for over-the-sea communications are compared. To meet the user requirements of ocean fishery vessels on communications, this paper proposes to utilize the approach of integrated wireless networking. The proposed integrated maritime communication system is composed of three heterogeneous wireless networks, i.e., MANET (mobile ad hoc network) between ships, cellular mobile network, and satellite mobile network. The proposed system takes advantage of the pros of each individual wireless network. A MANET is a self-configuring multi-hop network that does not rely on available fixed infrastructure. In this paper, we advocate to set up MANET between ships for ship-to-ship communications at sea. The benefit of using MANET is that the ship-to-ship communications within a ship fleet can be achieved without involving satellite mobile network. For ship-to-shore communications, there are two options depending on the locations of fishery vessels. When the mobile users are within the radio coverage of cellular network such as ports and costal areas, the cellular mobile network can be employed. The satellite mobile network gets involved in the ship-to-shore communications only when the mobile users are not covered by cellular mobile network. In the last scenario, mobile terminals on board first access the MANET and then access satellite mobile network via a satellite gateway. Since the proposed system can support multiple transmission paths with the integration of the MANET, the cellular mobile network, and satellite mobile network, automatic access selection method is discussed for the mobile users to choose an always-best-connected communication path. To further evaluate the feasibility and validity of the proposed system and the relevant technical solutions, we are developing a prototype system, and we give a report of the current progress of our development.

The rest of the paper is organized as follows. Section 2 investigates over-the-sea radio propagation of different wireless systems. In Section 3, we present the system architecture of integrated wireless networking system, and describe always-best-connected access selection method in the proposed system. The Section 4 reports our developed prototype system. The Section 5 makes the final conclusions.

## 2  Over-the-Sea Radio Propagation

Radio propagation describes how radio waves behave when they are transmitted from one point on the earth to another. During the transmission, radio waves can be affected by the phenomena of reflection, refraction, diffraction, absorption, polarization and scattering.

For over-the-sea transmission to and from fishery vessels, the effect of earth curvature on the radio propagation needs to be taken into account.

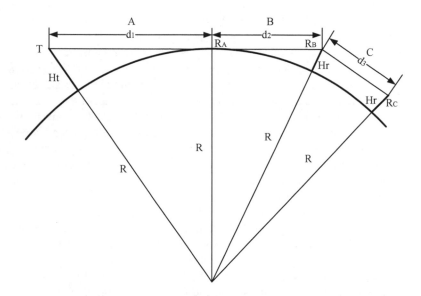

**Fig. 1.** Illustrative diagram of integrated maritime communication system

As shown in Fig. 1, the ship-to-shore radio propagation distance can be divided into three segments considering curvature of the earth: segment A, which is from $T$ (the point of the base station) to $R_A$ (the sightline of the base station) with length $d_1$ ; segment B, which is from $R_A$ to $R_B$ (the sightline of the terminal) with length $d_2$ ; and segment C, which is the shadow area beyond $R_B$ [4].

Assume that the antenna heights of base station and terminal are $H_t$ , and $H_r$ , respectively. From trigonometry we have

$$d_1^2 + R^2 = (H_t + R)^2 \tag{1}$$

$$d_2^2 + R^2 = (H_r + R)^2 \tag{2}$$

and we get

$$d_1 = \sqrt{2RH_t + H_t^2}, \quad d_2 = \sqrt{2RH_r + H_r^2} \tag{3}$$

Since $R \gg Ht, Hr$, $d_1$ and $d_2$ can be approximated by

$$d_1 = \sqrt{2RH_t}, \quad d_2 = \sqrt{2RH_r} \tag{4}$$

where $R$ is the earth radius and $R = 8500$ km.

Next, we analyze the path loss between transmitter and receiver. As we know, the free-space path loss is the loss in signal strength of an electromagnetic wave resulting from a line-of-sight path through free space, with no obstacles nearby to cause reflection or diffraction. It does not include factors such as the antenna gains at the transmitter and receiver, nor any loss associated with hardware imperfections. The equation for free-space path loss (PL) is given by $PL = \left(\dfrac{4\pi d}{\lambda}\right)^2 = \left(\dfrac{4\pi df}{c}\right)^2$

where $\lambda$ is the signal wavelength (in meters), f is the signal frequency (in Hz), d is the distance from the transmitter (in meters), c is the speed of light in a vacuum, $3 \times 10^8$ meters per second. A convenient way to express free-space path loss is in terms of dB as follows $L = 32.44 + 20 \lg f + 20 \lg d$ where $d$ is the path length (in km), $f$ is the frequency (in MHz).

When considering the effect of the earth surface, the expressions for the received signal become more complicated than that in case of free space propagation. The signals reflected off the earth surface need to be taken into account. For radio propagation over the land, the phase difference between the direct and the ground-reflected wave can be found from the two-ray approximation by considering only a line-of-sight and a ground reflection. The full path loss expression shows an interference pattern of the line-of-sight and the ground-reflected wave for relatively short ranges, and a rapid decay of the signal power beyond the turnover distance. For propagation distances substantially beyond the turnover point path loss tends to the fourth power distance law, i.e., 40dB/dec.

However, the propagation model would be different for land-to-mobile transmission over water. In this case, three-ray approximation can be employed for the radio propagation by considering only a line-of-sight and two water reflections. In addition to the direct wave, there are always two equal-strength reflected waves, one from the water and the other from the proximity of the mobile unit. The reflected wave, whose reflected point is on the water is counted because there are no surrounding objects near this point. The other reflected wave that has a reflection point proximal to the mobile unit also carries strong reflected energy to it. Therefore, the reflected power of the two reflected waves can reach the mobile unit without noticeable attenuation. The total received power at the mobile unit would be obtained by summing three components. It is deduced in [2] that the equation of radio propagation is the same as that expressing the power received from the free-space condition. Therefore, we may conclude that the path loss for land-to-mobile propagation over land, 40 dB/dec, is different for land-to-mobile propagation over water. In the case of propagation over water, the free-space path loss, 20 dB/dec, is applied.

Based on the above arguments, when the radio propagation path in the segment A, the path loss is expressed by

$$L_a = 32.44 + 20\lg f + 10\gamma_1 \lg d \tag{5}$$

where $\gamma_1$ is the path loss exponent, and $\gamma_1 = 2$. In the segment B, diffraction arises because of the curved way in which waves propagate. By the Huygens-Fresnel principle, the propagation of a wave can be visualized by considering every point on a wavefront as a point source for a secondary radial wave. Considering the earth as a half-infinite blocking panel to the propagation, the E-field strength at the receiver is half of that received from free space. Hence, the resulted path loss by diffraction is 6 dB.

Meanwhile, the propagation model of three-ray approximation over water is not perfect in the segment B. For simplicity, assuming that the additional path loss falls off with path loss exponent $\gamma_2$ with respect to distance in the segment B, the path loss when the receiver is in the segment B can be expressed by

$$\begin{aligned} L_b &= 32.44 + 20\lg f + 10\gamma_1 \lg d_1 + 10\gamma_2 \lg(d - d_1) \\ &= L_a + 10\gamma_2 \lg(d - d_1) \end{aligned} \tag{6}$$

where $\gamma_2 > 2$. The empirical value of $\gamma_2$ can be obtained by testing.

For diffraction in Segment C, the method given for diffraction over a spherical Earth specified by ITU can be used [3]. For simplicity, assuming that the additional path loss falls off with path loss exponent $\gamma_3$ with respect to distance in the segment C, the path loss when the receiver is in the segment C can be expressed by

$$\begin{aligned} L_c &= 32.44 + 20\lg f + 10\gamma_1 \lg d_1 + 10\gamma_2 \lg(d - d_1) + 10\gamma_3 \lg(d - d_1 - d_2) \\ &= L_b + 10\gamma_3 \lg(d - d_1 - d_2) \end{aligned} \tag{7}$$

where $\gamma_3 > \gamma_2 > 2$. The empirical value of $\gamma_3$ can be obtained by testing.

Next, we obtain the radio transmission distance for ship-to-shore and ship-to-ship communication cases by link budget analysis. A link budget is the accounting of all of the gains and losses from the transmitter, through the medium (free space, cable, etc.) to the receiver. Here, link budget analysis is employed to determine the coverage in the ship-to-shore and ship-to-ship radio transmissions.

For coastal cellular communications, UMTS WCDMA technology is assumed to be used for ship-to-shore radio coverage. UMTS WCDMA macro cell coverage is uplink limited because mobiles power level is limited to mobile terminal. The WCDMA link budget example is given in Table 1.

The ship-to-shore transmission distance by WCDMA cellular network $d_{max}$ can be estimated by using (5),(6), and (7) with the Total available path loss $L_T = 152.2$ dB.

The estimation of $d_{max}$ is given in Table 2. In Table 2, $H_t$ is the antenna height of WCDMA BS, and $H_t$ is set to 100m, 50m, 25m, 10m. $H_r$ is the antenna height of mobile terminal on fishery vessel, and $H_r$ is set to 10m. The frequency of WCDMA $f$ is set to 2100M. $L_a$ is calculated by (5), and $L_b = 10\gamma_2 \lg(d - d_1) = 10\gamma_2 \lg(d_2)$. In the calculation, $\gamma_2$ is set to 3. It is seen that $L_T = 152.2$ dB only supports the radio transmission of Segment A and Segment B for WCDMA system, i.e., $L_T = L_a + L_b$, and $d_3 = 0$.

**Table 1.** WCDMA Link Budget Example

| TX | |
|---|---|
| Mobile max power = 0.125W (dBm) | 21 |
| Body loss-Antenna gain (dB) | 2 |
| EIRP (dBm) | 19 |
| RX | |
| BTS noise density (dBm/Hz) | -168 |
| RX noise power (dBm)=-168+10*log(3840000) | -102.2 |
| Interference margin (dB) | 3 |
| RX interference power (dBm) | -102.2 |
| Noise and interference (dBm) | -99.2 |
| Processing gain (dB), 12.2k voice=10*log(3840/12.2) | 25.0 |
| Required $E_b/N_0$ for speech (dB) | 5 |
| Antenna gain (dBi) | 17 |
| Cable and connector losses (dB) | 3 |
| Rx sensitivity (dBm) | -133.2 |
| Total available path loss (dB) | 152.2 |

**Table 2.** Estimated Ship-to-Shore Transmission Distance $d$ of WCDMA Network

| $H_t$ (m) | $d_1$ (km) | $L_a$ (dB) | $L_b'$ (dB) | $d_2$ (km) | $d_{max}$ (km) |
|---|---|---|---|---|---|
| 100 | 41.23 | 131.18 | 21.02 | 5.01 | 46.24 |
| 50 | 29.16 | 128.17 | 24.03 | 6.31 | 34.46 |
| 25 | 20.62 | 125.16 | 27.04 | 7.96 | 28.58 |
| 10 | 13.04 | 121.19 | 31.01 | 10.81 | 23.85 |

**Table 3.** WLAN Link Budget Example

| TX | |
|---|---|
| Transmitter output power (dBm) | 27 |
| Antenna gain (dB) | 6 |
| Cable loss (dB) | -3 |
| EIRP (dBm) | 19 |
| RX | |
| Antenna gain (dBi) | 6 |
| Cable loss (dB) | -3 |
| Rx sensitivity (dBm) | -90 |
| Total available path loss (dB) | 124 |

For ship-to-ship communications, IEEE 802.11s mesh network is assumed to be employed. The WLAN link budget example is given in Table 3. It is assumed that APs used are outdoor APs with maximum output power 500mW (27dBm). In this case, the antenna heights of APs $H_t$ and $H_t$ are set to 10m. The frequency of IEEE 802.11s $f$ is set to 2.4GHz. By using(8), $L_a$ is calculated to be 121.2 dB with

$d_1 = 13.04$ km. and $L'_b = L_T - L_a = 10\gamma_2 \lg d_2 = 2.8$ dB. In the calculation, $\gamma_2$ is set to 3. Then, we can get $d_2 = 1{:}24$ km, $d_{max} = 13.24$ km. In this case, $L_T = 124$ dB supports the radio transmission of Segment A and Segment B for WCDMA system as well.

## 3  Integrated Wireless Networking for Ocean Fishery Vessels

### 3.1  Networking Architecture

The investigation in Section 2 reveals the coverage capabilities of different wireless systems for over-the-sea communications. Considering the user requirements of cost-effectiveness and full coverage on over-the-sea communications, this paper proposes to utilize the approach of integrated wireless networking. The proposed integrated communication system is composed of MANET, cellular mobile network, and satellite mobile network. The illustrative diagram of the proposed system is shown in Fig. 2. In the proposed system, MANET between ships plays two roles: it is the transmission network for ship-to-ship communications, and it also acts as the transit network for ship-to-shore communications. MANET connects with satellite network via shipborne satellite gateway (S-GW), and connects with cellular network via shipborne cellular gateway (C-GW) depending on the offshore distance. It is supposed that the satellite network connects with the cellular network via a terrestrial gateway. The implementation of MANET between ships can be implemented by using the IEEE 802.11s wireless mesh network [5] or IEEE 802.16 WiMAX mesh mode [6].

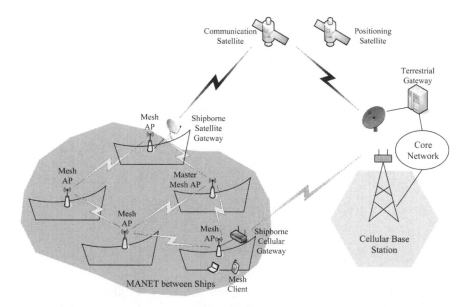

**Fig. 2.** Illustrative diagram of integrated maritime communication system

In an 802.11 mesh network, the network devices include mesh Mesh Access Points (Mesh APs) and Mesh Clients. The dual-mode phone with both cellular and WiFi interfaces and laptop computers with WiFi interface can be used as Mesh Clients to access the wireless mesh network. To establish a mesh network between ships, each ship firstly sets up a Mesh AP. One-hop wireless link is formed between neighboring ships, and then multi-hop wireless route via Mesh APs on the whole ship fleet can be established to support ship-to-ship communications. Shipborne cellular gateway (C-GW) enables those shipborne user devices without cellular interface (e.g., laptop PC) to access the cellular services. Shipborne satellite gateway (S-GW) enables those shipborne user devices without satellite interface (such as dual-mode phone, laptop PC) to access the satellite services when they are out of the cellular coverage. When using satellite mobile network alone without MANET at offshore areas, each ship needs to deploy satellite terminal. In the proposed system, MANET between ships operating with a satellite gateway deployed on one ship can finish the job. Thus, the proposed system helps to reduce the number of necessary satellite terminals and the deployment and maintenance costs caused by the satellite mobile network.

## 3.2   Always Best Connected Access Selection

The always best connected (ABC) concept allows a person connectivity to applications using the devices and access technologies that best suit his or her needs, thereby combining the features of access technologies to provide an enhanced user experience [8]. As shown in Fig. 2, the proposed system provides multiple wireless access options, i.e., the MANET between ships, cellular network, and satellite network, for the mobile users on board to select.

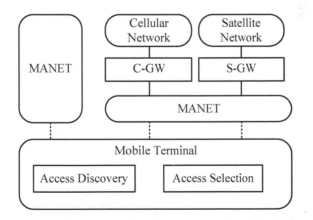

**Fig. 3.** Multiple access alternatives for mobile users

The mobile terminal first discover the multiple access network alternatives via the access discover module. To select the most desirable network from them, the mobile users can observe and analyze the attributes of networks and users such as price, bandwidth, coverage, and location of callee. After obtaining the relevant attributes, the next step for a mobile user is to capture the multiple conflicting attributes and make a proper decision on network selection. Some researchers directly design functions over the attributes and weights assigned on the attributes [9] [10]. As presented in [9], a cost function of a network is formulated in terms of the bandwidth, power consumption, and price. The network with the lowest value of cost function is selected. In [10], a consumer surplus function is defined as the difference of utility function and cost, and the consumer surplus function is used for the network selection. This problem of network selection can also be tackled with the Multiple Attribute Decision Making (MADM) technique [11] [12]. MADM is a process to make preference decisions over the available alternatives which are characterized by multiple (usually conflicting) attributes. In MADM, the attributes of alternatives are constructed as the decision matrix. The attributes in the decision matrix are aggregated with relative importance weights to yield a ranking order of alternatives for decision making. The selection of appropriate communication path in the proposed system can be based on service requirement (ship-to-ship or ship-to-shore), the network conditions, and the location of ships. The above-mentioned selection methods (e.g., MADM) can be used for the decision making. With the assumption of high cost of satellite networks, the following simplified decision-making can be employed. For ship-to-ship communications, the mobile users can use the MANET between ships only. For ship-to-shore communications, a ship-to-shore radio link can be established by only using the cellular network when the ships are within the coverage of cellular network. On the other hand, if the ships are out of the coverage of cellular network, a ship-to-shore communication path can be established by using MANET between ships, satellite gateway, and satellite system. Hence, the communication scenarios that the satellite system needs to be involved are reduced by using the proposed system.

## 4   Development of Prototype System

To further evaluate the feasibility of the proposed system and validity of the proposed technical solutions, we are developing a prototype system as shown in Fig. 4.

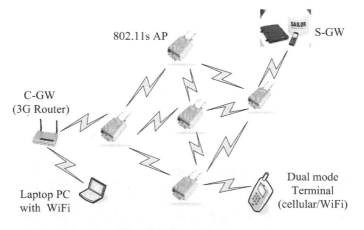

**Fig. 4.** Prototype system

The first step of establishing the prototype system is to construct the IEEE 802.11s wireless Mesh network. Multiple IEEE 802.11s outdoor APs are employed to form a multi-hop Mesh network. The mobile terminals used in the prototype system include the dual mode smart phone with both cellular and WiFi interfaces and the laptop PCs with WiFi interface. The mobile terminals act as the Mesh Clients to connect with the 802.11s Mesh network. Then, the cellular gateway (C-GW) and satellite gateway (S-GW) are developed for network integration. The C-GW can be implemented by using a commercial 3G router, which can route data between the 3G cellular network and WiFi network seamlessly. The S-GW can be developed based on a FBB satellite terminal, (e.g., FBB 150). Finally, the experimental prototype system is formed by integrating the 802.11s Mesh network, C-GW, S-GW, and mobile terminals. The access selection algorithm is implemented in the mobile terminal for mobile users to have always-best-connected access. The VoIP and video over IP applications are implemented via SIP protocol. The performance of the applications are to be tested in a few connection scenarios: connection with the 802.11s Mesh network, connection with remote mobile terminal via the C-GW, connection with remote terminal via the S-GW.

## 5 Conclusions

The mobile users on ocean fishery vessels need to be facilitated with effective communications technology in any sea areas. The over-the-sea radio propagation investigation in this paper reveals the radio coverage of existing wireless systems such as WCDMA and Wireless LAN. To support both ship-to-ship and ship-to-shore communications, this paper proposes an integrated wireless networking system composed of MANET (mobile ad hoc network), cellular mobile network, and satellite mobile network. The integrated wireless system takes advantage of the pros of each individual network. Hence, the ship-to-ship communications can be provided via the MANET between ships established, and the ship-to-shore communications can be accomplished via either shipborne cellular gateway or shipborne satellite gateway depending on the offshore distance. With the proposed system, the number of satellite terminals onboard within a ocean fishery fleet can be reduced, and always-best-connected communication path can be selected for the benefits of mobile users during their call setup according to their locations and radio coverage conditions. A prototype system has been under establishment at Hainan University to evaluate our proposals.

**Acknowledgments.** This paper was supported by the National Natural Science Foundation of China (Grant No. 61062006) and the Natural Science Foundation of Hainan Province, China (Grant No. 610215).

## References

1. Inmarsat web site, http://www.inmarsat.com/
2. Lee, W.C.Y.: Lee, Wireless & Cellular Communications. McGraw-Hill, New York (2006)

3. ITU-R P.526-11, Propagation by diffraction (October 2009)
4. He, W., Zhang, H.: Over-the-Sea Radio Propagation Model and Adjustment for 3G Network. Master Thesis, Northwestern Polytechnical University, China (March 2006)
5. IEEE, Draft amendment ESS mesh networking. IEEE P802.11s, Draft 4.0 (2009)
6. WiMAX Forum web site, http://www.wimaxforum.org/
7. Inmarsat FleetBroadband web site,
   http://www.inmarsat.com/Services/Maritime/FleetBroadband/
8. Gustafsson, E., Jonsson, A.: Always best connected. IEEE Wireless Communications 10(1), 49–55 (2003)
9. Wang, H.J., Katz, R.H., Giese, J.: Policy-enabled handoff across heterogeneous wireless networks. In: Proc. 2nd IEEE Workshops on Mobile Computing and Applications (WMCSA), pp. 51–60 (1999)
10. Ormond, O., Murphy, J., Muntean, G.-M.: Utility-based intelligent network selection in beyond 3G systems. In: Proc. IEEE International Conference on Communications (ICC), pp. 1831–1836 (2006)
11. Yu, Y., Bai, Y., Chen, L.: Utility-dependent network selection using MADM in heterogeneous wireless networks. In: Proc. IEEE International Symposium on Personal, Indoor and Mobile Radio Communications (PIMRC) (2007)
12. Zhang, W.: Handover decision using fuzzy MADM in heterogeneous networks. In: Proc. Wireless Communications and Networking Conference (WCNC), pp. 653–658 (2004)

# Design and Performance Analysis of Multiradio Multihop Network Using IEEE802.11n 2.4GHz Access and 5.8GHz Backhaul Radios

Kae Hsiang Kwong, Alvin Ting, David Chieng, and Mazlan Abbas

Wireless Communications, MIMOS Berhad
Technology Park Malaysia, Kuala Lumpur, Malaysia
{kh.kwong,kee.ting,ht.chieng,mazlan.abbas}@mimos.my

**Abstract.** This paper presents the design and performance insights of a multiradio multihop network using IEEE802.11n radios. The widely adopted architecture that uses 2.4GHz access and 5.8GHz multihop backhaul links is considered. More specifically, this study looks into the feasibility of such design to provide backhauling between two base stations while providing WiFi access along the multihop routers. The analysis covers the performance of different designs or configurations such as distance between hops, multihop chain distance, choice of Modulation and Coding scheme (MCS), backhaul link rate, channel bandwidth, number of spatial streams required to support certain capacity per AP and connection rate per user. The findings show that by ignoring the number of hops required, at least 3 MIMO spatial streams and 16QAM3/4 are required to support the basic 2Mbps connection rate per user per AP along the multihop chain. This is on top of 120Mbps raw physical data rate required to provide backhaul connectivity between the base stations.

**Keywords:** WiFi, IEEE802.11n, Wireless Multihop, Wireless Mesh.

## 1 Introduction

The needs to provide broadband wireless access coverage rapidly and cost effectively continue to fuel innovations in the area of wireless mesh or multihop networking (WMN). Over the years WMN technologies particularly the WiFi mesh, have evolved from single radio systems to multiradio systems involving heterogeneous radio interfaces such as IEEE802.11a,b,g and n. The most commonly known industrial practice adopts the architecture which consists of IEEE802.11a radio as backhaul and IEEE802.11g for the access. This is largely motivated by the fact that IEEE802.11a has more non overlapping channels and much less congested spectrum band therefore giving a better performance. IEEE 802.11n standard [1], which introduces Physical data rates up to 600Mbit/s using MIMO technology and increased tolerance to interference looks promising to push up the capacity limitation of WMN.

Many household mesh vendors have already included the IEEE 802.11n radio into their solutions and products design. Ruckus claims to provide more efficient indoor enterprise wireless mesh without using the new 5GHz band due to the use of directional beam forming technique [2]. Meraki offers 3-radio 802.11n outdoor mesh

P. Sénac, M. Ott, and A. Seneviratne (Eds.): ICWCA 2011, LNICST 72, pp. 191–200, 2012.

product that costs $500 per radio [3]. Tropos later joined the 11n-Mesh club by releasing the x6320 routers which start at $2,995 [4]. Motorola soon after that announced the high-performance, reliable and secure 802.11n outdoor mesh wide area network (MWAN) solution [5]. More recently Strix Systems released its new solution which supports up to six (6) radios in various design options including 11n MIMO, 4.9GHz, as well as a choice between licensed or unlicensed frequencies [6].

On related research works, [7] modified the existing IEEE 802.11n MAC to support aggregation of both unicast and broadcast frames, and analyzed the throughput performance of their design over 2 and 3-hop chain topologies. [8] characterizes the effective throughput of IEEE802.11n-based multihop network and analyzed the upper bound throughput at MAC layer as a function of bit error rate, frame aggregation level and path length. [9] investigates the effectiveness of different MAC (Medium Access Control) and transmission rate adaptation schemes on wireless mesh networks such as IEEE 802.11, 802.11e, and 802.11n MAC, and three rate adaptation schemes, i.e., ARF (Automatic Rate Fallback), RBAR (Receiver-Based Auto Rate), and 802.11n rate adaptation. However the scope of the works above is only limited to single radio system. Furthermore [7] and [8] mainly focus on improving TCP transmission.

Although there is a wide range of 11n-based wireless mesh/multihop network products and solutions, the performance of such network is not well understood especially from the capacity and range (coverage) point of view. Clearer insights are needed on the relationships between number of hops, multihop distance, backhaul link rate, modulation and coding scheme (MCS), number of MIMO spatial stream, channel bandwidth, and effective capacity per access point which can later be translated into connection rate per user, etc.

This paper is organized as follows: section 2 presents the assumptions required for this high level analysis. Section 3 introduces methodology, equations and related models used. General parameters and results are discussed in section 4. Finally, conclusions and future work are drawn in section 5.

## 2    Assumptions

### 2.1    Potential Application Scenario

Multiradio multihop network with separate access and backhaul radios offer a variety of application scenarios. Figure 1shows a potential application scenario where while providing alternative backhaul link to two base stations, the network can also provide wireless access to end users along the multihop chain.

Logically the backhaul radio will be using directional antenna and the typical omni-directional antenna for the access. Different access radio types can also be considered depending on coverage, capacity as well as user requirement. Such feature is particularly attractive in places where wired backhaul is expensive or not available. Also while providing alternative backhaul and access, such design also offers the benefit of offloading for the macro cells as illustrated in Figure 2.

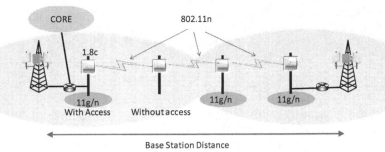

**Fig. 1.** Potenial scenario using multi-hop network between two macro base stations

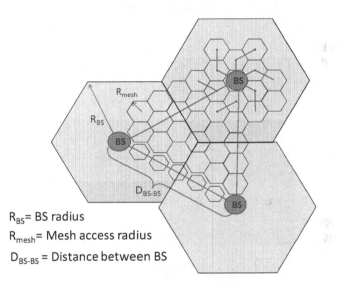

$R_{BS}$= BS radius

$R_{mesh}$= Mesh access radius

$D_{BS-BS}$ = Distance between BS

**Fig. 2.** Exempler topology based on scenario in Figure 1

## 2.2 Data Rate and Overbooking Factor

The target backhaul data rate for each Access Point (AP) is representative of the connection speed (or headline speed) typically sold by a network operator. The overbooking factor (OF) is the ratio of the potential maximum demand to the actual bandwidth consumed. A typical OF assumed for internet browsing is around 50:1 and for higher bandwidth applications such as video streaming or FTP, the OF is around 10 or 20:1 [10]. In other words, the lower the OF the higher the mean bandwidth or QoS demand for that service. This is subsequently translated to data rate per user which represents the maximum downlink rate that can be enjoyed by each end user.

## 2.3 Interference

Interference arising from co-channel, adjacent channel and foreign devices are assumed to be minimal and are represented as a margin increase. For the 5 GHz spectrum, this assumption is reasonable as there are 23 non-overlapping channels available (North America). Hence even with channel bonding there will be 11 non-overlapping 40MHz channels. For the access at 2.4GHz, since the access capacity is unlikely to exceed the backhaul, 3 non-overlapping 20MHz channels is sufficient to provide some degree of interference mitigation.

## 2.4 Fair Sharing of Bandwidth for AP

Within a cluster, bandwidth is fairly distributed across all APs so that nodes with more hops away from the gateway enjoy the same bandwidth as compared to those nodes nearer to it. This can be achieved by applying various well-known techniques described in existing literatures such as traffic admission control at the AP and fair bandwidth scheduling at the MRAR. It is also assumed that 100% traffic is flowing between users/APs and gateway hence base station [10] .

# 3   Model

This section describes the methodology, equations and related models used to develop our model.

**Table 1.** Notations

| Notation | Description |
|---|---|
| $PL$ | path loss in dB |
| $EIRP$ | effective isotropic radiated power |
| $G_{rx}$ | receiver antenna gain |
| $M_{total}$ | total margin such as shadow, interference, fading, etc. |
| $R_{sen}$ | receiver sensitivity |
| $C_{phy}$ | ideal data rate at the PHY layer |
| $C_{eff}^{\downarrow}$ | effective downlink data rate at IP layer |
| $\varphi$ | link efficiency measured at the IP layer |
| $DLUL$ | Downlink to uplink traffic ratio |
| $DR^{\downarrow}$ | designed data rate at the downlink |
| $\overline{DR}^{\downarrow}$ | statistical average data rate at the downlink |
| $N_{SS}$ | number of spatial stream |
| $R$ | coding rate |
| $N_{SD}$ | number of complex data numbers per spatial stream  per OFDM symbol |
| $T_{SYM}$ | symbol duration |
| $N_{hop}$ | Number of wireless hops |

Typical receiver sensitivity values per modulation and coding scheme (MCS), channel bandwidth and corresponding physical data rate for different number of spatial streams are tabulated in TABLE 2.

**Table 2.** IEEE802.11n Receiver Sensitivity, MCS, Channel Bandwidth and PHY Data Rate

| MCS | Receiver Sensitivity | | Physical Data Rate where ($N_{ss}$= 1/2/3/4) | |
|---|---|---|---|---|
| | 20MHz | 40MHz | 20MHz | 40MHz |
| BPSK 1/2 | -95.0 | -91.0 | 7.2 Mbps x $N_{ss}$ | 15 Mbps x $N_{ss}$ |
| QPSK 1/2 | -93.0 | -90.0 | 14.4 Mbps x $N_{ss}$ | 30 Mbps x $N_{ss}$ |
| QPSK 3/4 | -90.0 | -87.0 | 21.7 Mbps x $N_{ss}$ | 45 Mbps x $N_{ss}$ |
| 16-QAM 1/2 | -87.0 | -84.0 | 28.9 Mbps x $N_{ss}$ | 60 Mbps x $N_{ss}$ |
| 16-QAM 3/4 | -84.0 | -82.0 | 43.3 Mbps x $N_{ss}$ | 90 Mbps x $N_{ss}$ |
| 64-QAM 2/3 | -80.0 | -78.0 | 57.8 Mbps x $N_{ss}$ | 120 Mbps x $N_{ss}$ |
| 64-QAM 3/4 | -79.0 | -76.0 | 65.5 Mbps x $N_{ss}$ | 135 Mbps x $N_{ss}$ |
| 64-QAM 5/6 | -77.0 | -74.0 | 72.2 Mbps x $N_{ss}$ | 150 Mbps x $N_{ss}$ |

The general link budget used is:

$$PL = EIRP - R_{sen} + G_{rx} - M_{total} \tag{1}$$

For each MCS, the physical data rate of IEEE802.11n can be derived using the following equations:

$$C_{phy} = \frac{N_{SD}}{T_{SYM}} * R * N_{SS} \tag{2}$$

Consequently the effective downlink data rate at IP layer,

$$C^{\downarrow}_{eff} = C_{phy} * \varphi * DLUL \tag{3}$$

From (3) and by assuming simultaneous transmissions with multiradio support, the effective capacity per AP or per hop can be defined as:

$$C^{\downarrow}_{eff,AP} = \frac{C^{\downarrow}_{eff}}{N_{hop}} \tag{4}$$

The required statistical average data rate (per direction) per Mesh AP $\overline{DR}$, is given by [10]:

$$\overline{DR}^{\downarrow} = \frac{DR^{\downarrow}}{OF} \tag{5}$$

In this study we only focus on the downlink direction as the uplink can be easily deduced from equation (3). From (3) ,(4) and (5) we can get the maximum possible number of users supported by a mesh AP at data rate $DR$, $N^{DR\downarrow}_{user,max}$ with the condition that effective IP layer data rate per AP, $C^{\downarrow}_{eff,AP}$ must be larger than the designed data rate.

$$N^{DR\downarrow}_{user,max} = \begin{cases} \left\lfloor \frac{C^{\downarrow}_{eff,AP}}{\overline{DR}^{\downarrow}} \right\rfloor, & C^{\downarrow}_{eff,AP} \geq DR^{\downarrow} \\ 0, & otherwise \end{cases} \tag{6}$$

# 4  General Parameters and Results

## 4.1  General Parameters

Both access and backhaul radios are using IEEE802.11n with access at 2.4GHz and backhaul at 5.8GHz respectively. The Effective Isotropic Radiation Power (EIRP) for 2.4GHz and 5.8GHz are set at 27dBm and 30dBm respectively, which are the maximum EIRP allowable for these frequency bands in Malaysia. The TDD ratio is set at 3:1 assuming that the APs are predominantly serving downlink intensive applications such as Internet browsing. Overbooking factor of 50:1 is assumed to represent typical residential usage scenario. The link layer efficiency is assumed to be around 50% of physical layer data rate. This means only 50% of the physical layer raw data rate will be translated to IP layer's throughput [11]. Although there are some differences between TCP and UDP traffics in terms of link layer efficiency, the value 50% is believed to be appropriate for general representation.  The parameters and default values used for the subsequent experiments are summarized in 0.

**Table 4.** General parameters and values

|  | Units | WiFi |
|---|---|---|
| **RF** | | |
| Frequency band (access/backhaul) | GHz | 2.4/5.8 |
| EIRP (access/backhaul) | dBm | 27/30 |
| $G_{rx}$ (backhaul) | dBi | 15 |
| $G_{rx}$ (user terminal) | dBi | 0 |
| $\varphi$ | | 0.5 |
| Propagation model | | Modified Free Space Path Loss model (urban) |
| Path Loss Coefficient | | 3.5 (access), 2.0 (backhaul assuming LOS) |
| Interference | dB | 3 |
| **System and User requirements** | | |
| *DLUL* | | 3:1 |
| *OF* | | 50:1 |
| $DR^{\downarrow}$ | Mbps | 2, 5 |
| Distance between base stations | | |
| Reserved end to end data rate between base stations | Mbps | 120 (raw physical) for typical 4G base station |

## 4.2  Results

*A) Effective capacity per AP vs. MCS type vs. Number of spatial streams*

In Figure 3 the relationship between effective capacity per AP, MCS used and number of spatial streams at 20 and 40MHz channel can be deduced. As expected, effective capacity increases with higher order MCSs. It is also shown that to achieve at least 2Mbps per AP, 2 spatial streams of 40MHz channel is required. For 20MHz, at least 4 streams are required using 64QAM3/4 and 64QAM5/6. One interesting finding here is that the best capacity per AP (17Mbps) is found to be provided by 64QAM2/3 rather than higher order schemes such as 64QAM3/4 or 64QAM5/6. However, the result does not reveal the difference between the number of hops along the 3km distance required by each configuration.

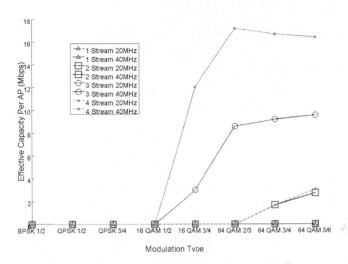

**Fig. 3.** Capacity per AP vs. type of MCS at backhaul vs. number of spatial streams at backhaul using 20MHz and 40 MHz channel. Multihop chain network distance is fixed at 3km with equidistance between hops and 120Mbps raw physical rate reserved for base stations.

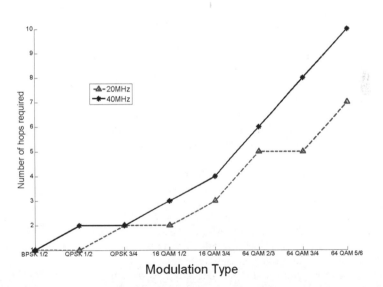

**Fig. 4.** Total number of hops required vs. MCS at backhaul with multihop chain network distance fixed at 3km and equidistance between hops

Figure 4 shows that the number of hops increases when higher order MCSs are used. This is expected as higher order MCS higher requires higher receiver sensitivity therefore lower distance between hops. It can also be deduced that highest order MCS such as 64QAM5/6 requires at least 10 hops using 40MHz channel while 20MHz only requires around 7 hops in order to cover a distance of 3km.

## B) Data rate per user

Next, the design requirements for supporting two typical data rates currently offered to wireless broadband customers 1) 2 Mbps and 2) 5Mbps are investigated.

### B.1) 2 Mbps connection rate per user

Figure 5 shows that 20MHz channel is unable to support 2Mbps connection rate per user even with overbooking factor of 50:1.

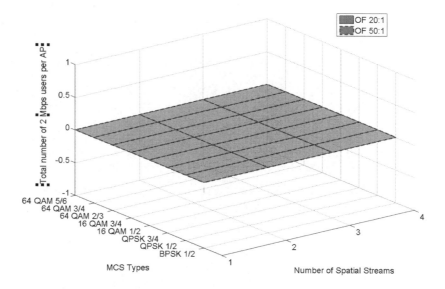

**Fig. 5.** Number of 2Mbps users supported per AP vs. type of MCS at vs. number of spatial streams over 20MHz Channel. Multihop chain network distance is fixed at 3km with equidistance between hops and 120Mbps raw physical rate reserved for base stations

As shown in Figure 6, using 40MHz channel over the same configuration, up to 200 simultaneous 2Mbps connections per AP with OF=50:1 can be supported using 4 spatial streams at 64QAM5/6. For more demanding applications which require OF of 20:1, only up to 80 users per AP can be supported. MCS with 16QAM1/2 and lower are unable to support any user with 2Mbps connection rate due to the limitation stated in equation 6. It can also be derived from the figure that at least 3 spatial streams are required to support 2Mbps connection rate per user.

As observed in Figure 7, using 40MHz channel over the same configuration, up to 50 simultaneous 5Mbps connections per AP with OF=50:1 can be supported using 4 spatial streams at 64QAM5/6. For more demanding applications requiring OF of 20:1, only up to 20 5Mbps users can be supported per AP. MCS with 16QAM3/4 and lower are unable to support any user with 5Mbps connection rate. It is also shown that at least 4 spatial streams are required to meet this requirement.

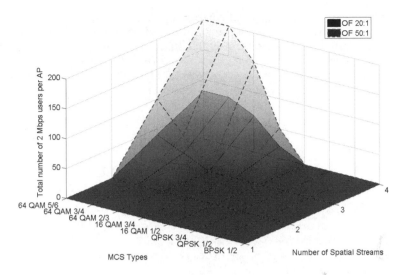

**Fig. 6.** Number of 2Mbps users supported per AP vs. type of MCS at vs. number of spatial streams over 20MHz Channel. Multihop chain network distance is fixed at 3km with equidistance between hops and 120Mbps raw physical rate reserved for base stations.

*B.1) 5 Mbps connection rate per user*

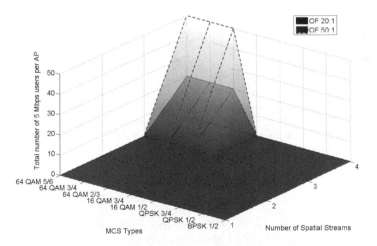

**Fig. 7.** Number of 5Mbps users supported per AP vs. type of MCS at vs. number of spatial streams over 40MHz Channel. Multihop chain network distance is fixed at 3km with equidistance between hops and 120Mbps raw physical rate reserved for base stations.

## 5   Conclusion and Future Work

In this paper, a high level design and analysis on the of multiradio multihop network using IEEE802.11n access radio at 2.4GHz and 5.8GHz for backhaul radio have been carried out. Various configurations such as MCS/distance between hops, backhaul link rate, multihop chain distance, channel bandwidth, number of spatial streams required to support certain capacity per AP and connection rate per user have been investigated. A general conclusion can be derived from this study is that by ignoring the number of hops required, at least 3 MIMO spatial streams and 16QAM3/4 are required to support the basic 2Mbps connection rate per user per AP along the multihop chain network. This is on top of 120Mbps raw physical data rate required to provide backhaul connectivity between base stations.

Future work shall take into consideration of the access coverage and degree offloading that can be provided by this design. There scenario will also be extended to include multihop tree or mesh topology.

## References

[1] IEEE 802.11n: Standard for Wireless LAN Medium Access Control (MAC) and Physical Layer (PHY) Specifications: Enhancements for Higher Throughput (2009)
[2] Judge, P.: Ruckus launches enterprise 802.11n mesh. Techworld (April 2008),
    http://news.techworld.com/mobile-wireless/12042/
    ruckus-launches-enterprise-80211n-mesh/
[3] Vos, E.: Meraki releases 802.11n outdoor mesh product, Municipal Wireless, February 24 (2009),
    http://www.muniwireless.com/2009/02/24/meraki-releases-
    80211n-mesh-product/
[4] Ngo, D.: Tropos joins 802.11n outdoor mesh router club. CNET News, April 7 (2009),
    http://news.cnet.com/8301-17938_105-10212296-1.html
[5] Motorola Press release, Motorola Takes 802.11n Technology Outdoor with Powerful Mesh Wide Area Network Solution, October 8 (2009),
    http://www.motorola.com/web/Business/Products/Wireless%20Net
    works/Wireless%20Broadband%20Networks/Mesh%20Networks/_Chann
    elDetails/MWAN_AP_7181/Documents/MWAN7181_pressrelease.pdf
[6] Press Release, Strix Systems® Announces MIMO based 802.11n for its Access/One® Network Family of Solutions, October 12 (2010),
    http://www.strixsystems.com/pr-2010-802.11n.aspx
[7] Kim, W., Wright, H., Nettles, S.: Improving the Performance of Multi-hop Wireless Networks Using Frame Aggregation and Broadcast for TCP ACKs. In: Proc. ACM CoNEXT, Madrid, Spain (2008)
[8] Frohn, S., Gubner, S., Lindemann, C.: Analyzing the effective throughput in multi-hop IEEE 802.1 in networks. In: IEEE International Symposium on A World of Wireless, Mobile and Multimedia Networks (WoWMoM), Montreal, Canada, June 14-17 (2010)
[9] Kim, S., Lee, S.-J., Choi, S.: The Impact of IEEE 802.11 MAC Strategies on Multi-Hop Wireless Mesh NetworksWireless Mesh Networks. In: 2nd IEEE Workshop on Wireless Mesh Networks, Reston, Virginia USA, September 25-28 (2006)
[10] Chieng, D., Von-Hugo, D., Banchs, A.: A Cost Sensitivity Analysis for Carrier Grade Wireless Mesh Networks with Tabu Optimization. In: Workshop of Carrier Grade Wireless Mesh Network, Proceeding of IEEE INFOCOM, San Diego, California, March 15-19 (2010)
[11] Fiehe, S., Riihijärvi, J., Mähönen, P.: Experimental study on performance of IEEE 802.11n and impact of interferers on the 2.4 GHz ISM band. In: Proceedings of the 6th International Wireless Communications and Mobile Computing Conference IWCMC 2010, Caen, France, June 28–July 2 (2010)

# Intelligent Monitoring System on Refrigerator Trucks Based on the Internet of Things*

Yonghui Zhang, Baodan Chen, and Xinning Lu

College of Information Science & Technology,
Hainan University, 570228, Haikou, China
zhyhemail@163.com,
cbd@hainu.edu.cn,
416443101@qq.com

**Abstract.** Refrigerator transportation is an important part of cold chain. Aimming at monitoring the temperature and humidity inside the refrigerator trucks,and managing information of the the refrigerator trucks internal. At the paper, there is a design of an intelligent monitoring system based on the Internet of thing, realized monitoring temperature and humidity inside the refrigerator trucks and the intelligent cargo identification, and tracking the location of refrigerator trucks real-time in the entire transportation process by using advanced RFID technology, the sensor technology and the wireless communication technology.

**Keywords:** Refrigerator Trucks, Internet of Things, Intelligent Monitoring, RFID.

## 1 Introduction

With the continuous development of society, people pay more and more attention on the food safety in daily life, especially fruit, dairy and meat food's preservation problem. In the food cold-chain process, the transport process of refrigerator trucks is an important segment to ensure food safety. In this segment, the temperature and humidity conditions within the refrigerator trucks, the state of door switch and the location of refrigerator trucks must be real-time monitored.

The Internet of things is a combination of the Internet and all kinds of information sensing devices such as radio frequency identification devices (RFID), infrared sensors, global positioning systems, laser scanners, etc. Meanwhile, it based on the simple RFID technology and combined the existing network technology, database technology and middleware technology to form a huge network including lots of networking reader and countless mobile labels. This technology is widely used in intelligent transportation, environmental protection, public security, peace household,

---

* Supported by Colleges and Universities Scientific Research Projects of Education Department of Hainan Province [Hjkj2011-08], Youth Foundation of Hainan University[qnjj1023] and 211 Project of Hainan University.

P. Sénac, M. Ott, and A. Seneviratne (Eds.): ICWCA 2011, LNICST 72, pp. 201–206, 2012.
© Institute for Computer Sciences, Social Informatics and Telecommunications Engineering 2012

intelligent fire, industrial monitoring, and many other areas, which greatly improved the social intelligence and automation level.

Appling the Internet of things technology in refrigerator trucks' transportation can track the position of refrigerator trucks and monitor the temperature and humidity etc real-time,and monitor the whole transport process Intelligently to improve transport efficiency.

The paper is based on the concept of thing networking, and used the advanced RFID technology, humidity sensor technology, door switch monitoring device, GPRS/GPS technology, wireless communication technology and the Internet to form a remote monitoring intelligent system for the refrigerator trucks. The remote intelligent monitoring system based on this networking technology can have a real-time monitoring of the temperature and humidity, gate switch state, cargo information and the location of refrigerator trucks,all that make the whole monitoring process reach informatization.

## 2   Intelligent Monitoring System Design Scheme

Because of the refrigerator trucks' wide transportation range and some are still in areas with bad environment, which causes management difficulties in the process of transportation. The transport goods are mostly fresh meat, fruit, vegetables and dairy products, cold drinks, health food, which need high requirement of environment. Combined with the characteristics of transportation process refrigerator trucks above, this paper puts forward refrigerator trucks remote intelligent monitoring system based on the Internet of things. The system adopts modular design, and be constituted by multi-point temperature and humidity acquisition module, the door switch monitoring device, RFID module, monitoring module in trucks , GPRS/GPS module, wireless network, remote monitoring center, and so on. The system composition diagram was as shown in Figure 1. This system relies on advanced content networking technologies and combines existing technology to achieve real-time and accurate monitoring purposes. The temperature and humidity acquisition module constituted by high performance temperature and humidity sensor can be used to read the temperature and humidity conditions data within the refrigerator trucks real-time. In order to measure more accurate temperature and humidity data, more temperature and humidity acquisition modules can be placed in the box according to actual needs. The door switch is used to monitor the monitoring device switch state in the process of goods transportion to avoid goods loss. Through advanced RFID technology, labeling goods with electronic tag, entrying relevant information on goods labels and putting RFID reade beside the the box, the RFID reader senses induction cargo information when the goods loading or unloading. The temperature and humidity data, the door switch state and the RFID information are all sent to the refrigerator cockpit monitoring module screen through the RS485 bus to accessory personnel check and management. And the refrigerator tracks position is located and tracked by the GPS satellite,and returns it's positioning information with temperature and humidity data, door switch state and cargo information to monitoring center through GPRS network and the Internet. Using intelligent analysis software on the remote monitoring center terminal to display refrigerator trucks temperature and humidity data, door switch state and cargo information real-time to locate and track the location refrigerator trucks to implement intelligent monitoring management and make the whole system constitute a real-time, intelligent thing networking[2].

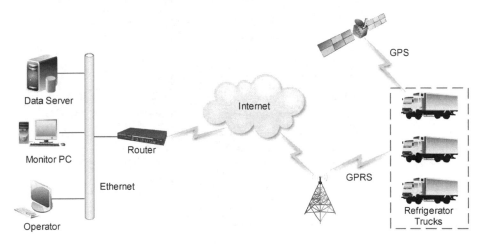

**Fig. 1.** Monitoring System Framework of Refrigerator Trucks

## 3   The Monitoring Center Inside the Refrigerator Trucks

The refrigerator temperature and humidity acquisition module, the door multi-points monitoring device and RFID reader switch, GPRS/GPS module and monitoring modules in trucks together can be regarded as the monitoring center inside the refrigerator trucks. System composition diagram is as shown in Figure 2. The temperature and humidity data, the door switch state and cargo information read in the box are sent to the cockpit monitoring module through the RS-485 bus. At the same time, returning positioning information to determine the location of refrigerator trucks, temperature and humidity data, door switch state and cargo information and refrigerator location information displayed real-time in monitoring module on the LCD panel through GPS satellite.And the alarm device on monitoring module automatic send out a warning message to accessory personnel and remote monitoring center to let the accessory personnel make corresponding processing when the trucks temperature and humidity data beyond the preset numerical cap or lower than lower limit. The refrigerator trucks also have installed SOS switch. When meeting special events, as long as people press emergency switch, the remote monitoring center will know that this refrigerator need assistance. While monitoring module intrucks read all information on the refrigerator trucks, the information also is sent to remote the monitoring center by GPRS module.

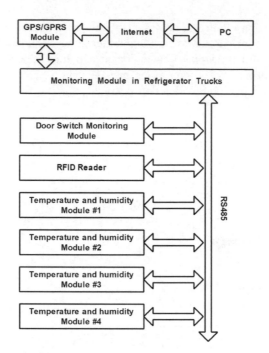

**Fig. 2.** Monitoring System of Refrigerator Trucks

## 3.1   Temperature and Humidity Acquisition Module

Temperature and humidity acquisition module is used to read the temperature and humidity in refrigerator. For the temperature and humidity acquisition module using STH10 High-performance and humidity sensor has characteristics of fast response time, high data collection precision and big acquisition range, all make it meet the trucks' testing environment condition requirements of refrigerator in the transport process. In order to measure more accurate data, we install multiple temperature and humidity acquisition module to collect multi-point temperature and humidity in the trucks, meanwhile. The data collected by each module is sent to the monitoring center inside refrigerator trucks by RS485 bus.

## 3.2   The Door Switch Monitoring Module

In order to avoid the goods loss caused by the door's abnormal switch in transport process, we need to do a real-time monitoring of the switch state of the trunk door. The door switch condition monitoring device uses hall sensor to probe refrigerator door's switch state, to record the related information of time and location when the trunk door switch every time ,and always transmit the key information to the remote monitoring center at any time .

### 3.3  RFID Module

The RFID commonly known as the electronic tag, is a simple wireless system. This system is consisted by a reader and a lot of tags, which is an important part of the Internet of things technology and widely used in information exchange, detecting and tracking on goods. Using the technique, the system posted tag in the cargo, and input the tag number, goods related information to the label. When loading or unloading goods, the goods will be recognized in the box by the RFID reader installed beside the door. The information read from the label would be sent to the remote monitoring center through the transmission control module on RS485 bus. So the people of remote monitoring center can understand the situation of the cargo inside the trucks by viewing the data at any time.

## 4  Remote Monitoring Center

The monitoring center inside refrigerator trucks can connect to the remote monitoring center through wireless communication network and Internet. The database server, the monitoring center and monitoring terminal together compose the remote monitoring center, which can monitor refrigerator trucks real-time. Using the intelligence analysis software to design humanized monitoring interface to output the data from monitor terminal and display every refrigerator trucks' data real-time,such as alarming, processing, recording, printing and determining the location of per refrigerator trucks. Meanwhile, the remote monitoring center monitor the cargo information of loading and unloading, record the loading, unloading time and cargo information to ensure cargo's safety conditions in transport process. If the refrigerator trucks have not in normal operation in the process of transportation, the remote monitoring center alarms prompt, which made the whole system accomplish intelligence, and information monitoring.

## 5  Conclusion

The refrigerator trucks intelligent monitoring system which put forward by this paper was based on content networking technology. And combined with advanced RFID technology, sensor technology and wireless communication technology, etc. to realize purposes such as monitoring the transport process intelligently, improving the refrigerator trucks' transport efficiency, preventing the deterioration of goods in transit, and avoiding the loss of goods during transportation, and so on.

## References

1. Jia, b., Xie, s., Xie, f.: The design based on the sensor network and RFID modern logistics monitoring system. Journal of Liaocheng University (natural science edition) (1) (2008)
2. Li, j., Wang, l., Gao, x.: Multi-spot temperature and humidity remote wireless monitoring system design. Micro Computer Information (25), 31–32 (2009)

3. Dai, l., Zhang, y.: The RFID and GPS technology in the integrated application of logistics industry. In: The first session of China the first China intelligent transportation conference intelligent transportation conference papers assembly (2005)
4. Zhang, x., Wang, x., Wen, p.: The wireless remote temperature and humidity control system based on TCP/IP protocol. Instrument technology and sensors 6, 44–46 (2008)
5. Hu, l., Zhou, s.: Reefer containers monitoring system present situation and the development tendency. Containerization (1), 43–46 (2006)

# An Effective Evolutionary Computational Approach for Routing Optimization in Networks with Shared Risk Link Groups

Xubin Luo and Qing Li

Southwestern University of Finance and Economics,
Chengdu, Sichuan, 610051, China
{xbluo,liqt}@swufe.edu.cn

**Abstract.** In this work, we study a routing optimization problem in networks with shared risk link groups (SRLGs). Specifically, a path between a source and a destination is determined such that the combined path cost and the weight of SRLGs to which the links of the path belong is minimized. We develop evolutionary computation based algorithms to solve the problem. The performance of the proposed algorithms is evaluated via extensive simulation and is compared with the solutions obtained by integer linear programming and the heuristic algorithm in [1].

**Keywords:** routing, shared risk link group (SRLG), evolutionary algorithm, combined cost.

## 1 Introduction

A shared risk link group (SRLG) is used to represent a set of links that are affected by a single failure (e.g., a failure in the physical layer such as a cable cut). The failure of any SRLG that a connection traverses will disrupt the service provided to the connection. A cost is also incurred on a link when it is used to provide the service to the connection. An link in a path introduces two component costs, one is the risk of an SRLG failure and the other is the link cost. The failure of an SRLG can be measured by a risk factor, e.g., the probability of failure. If the probability of failure of an SRLG $i$ is $p_i$, the probability of no SRLG failure along a path can be calculated as (with standard independence assumptions) $\Pi_i (1 - p_i)$ where $i$ is any SRLG that the path traverses, which can be expressed as a summation, $\sum_i \ln(1 - p_i)$ , on the logarithmic scale. When provisioning a connection service for a client, it is important for the network to minimize both the risk and cost of a route (where the cost can be monetary cost, delay, etc), i.e., the accumulative risk and cost on the route of the connection should be minimized. However, it may not be possible to minimize the two potentially conflicting objectives simultaneously. The problem is then to determine a path that minimizes a combined cost in a network with SRLGs and finds a tradeoff between the two objectives.

P. Sénac, M. Ott, and A. Seneviratne (Eds.): ICWCA 2011, LNICST 72, pp. 207–215, 2012.

The solution to this problem can be used to calculate a risk bounded and delay bounded path for a connection, or to design algorithms that find a pair of low-cost SRLG-diverse paths between a source and a destination for survivable service provisioning. In SRLG diverse routing, a demand requires two paths in the network, one working path and one protection path, so that the service to the demand can be honored in case of a single network failure, such as a fiber cut. The diverse routing problem in networks is to find a pair of paths between a source and a destination such that no single failure in the network may cause both paths to fail. The diverse routing problem in networks with generally defined SRLG failures has been proved to be $NP$-complete [2] where an SRLG may include an arbitrary group of links. In addition, finding a pair of least cost SRLG-diverse routes is also $NP$-complete [2]. This problem can be solved in polynomial time under some special definition of SRLGs [3, 4]. In many cases, it is desirable for service providers to make sure that both the working path and backup path are risk-bounded and cost bounded to provide certain degree of quality of service and protection.

In work [1], an ILP formulation and a heuristic algorithm for the minimum combined cost routing problem were presented. The heuristic is a Bellman-Ford style algorithm. Instead of keeping routing information of the optimal path alone, the algorithm maintains at each node the routing information for the best $k$ routes from the source to the node, where k is a tunable parameter. The reason to keep $k$ routing entries at each node is that, unlike the single-metric minimum cost routing, given an optimal path from the source node $src$ to the destination node $dest$, a subpath on the end-to-end optimal path may not be optimal for the two end nodes of the subpath when the combined path cost is considered. By maintaining multiple routing entries at a node, the algorithm has a better chance of obtaining the optimal path from the source.

In this work, we develop evolutionary computation based algorithms to solve the minimum combined cost routing problem that minimizes the combined link and SRLG cost. The performance is evaluated via extensive simulation and compared with existing solutions. A genetic algorithm (GA) is a type of evolutionary computation based search technique that finds true or sub-optimal solutions for optimization problems [5]. An individual solution is usually represented by a string, called a chromosome. The chromosome can be decoded to obtain a solution. A typical genetic algorithm imitates the evolutionary process of genetic population over generations. The objective of a genetic algorithm can be expressed as finding a string such that a function of the string is maximized or minimized. A fitness function is defined to evaluate how good the solution of each individual chromosome is with regard to our optimization objective. A GA starts by initializing a set of chromosomes which is called the initial population. Then the current population produces the next generation of population by mating, mutation, and survivor selection. It borrows from Darwin's Theory of Evolution, i.e., natural selection acts to preserve and accumulate minor advantageous genetic mutations. By preserving those individuals with higher fitness, a GA is expected to converge at optimal solutions or sub-optimal solutions. The flow of a typical genetic algorithm is shown in Figure 1.

---

**Algorithm 1.** *Flow of a Typical Genetic Algorithm*

1:    Initialize population: create an initial population and evaluate each individual's fitness w.r.t. the problem.
2:  **while** the stopping condition is not met **do**
3:      **while** the number of offsprings is not enough **do**
4:        Select a pair of parent chromosomes;
5:        Do mating between the parents (crossover) and produce offspring(s);
6:        Randomly select N chromosomes, mutate them, and add them into the new population;
7:    **end while**
8:    Evaluate all the individuals in the new population;
9:    Select the survivors based on their fitness and put them into the next generation. Those individuals that are not selected are discarded.
10:  **end while**
11:  **return** the solution represented by the best individual in the last generation.

---

Genetic algorithms are popular in solving graph theory problems such as travel salesman's problem (TSP) [6, 7, 8]. At the same time, GAs have also been applied to solve service provisioning problems in WDM optical networks. Reference [9] studies the traffic grooming problem in a ring network with a static traffic model and [10, 11, 12] extends the work to deal with dynamic traffic models. A genetic algorithm is also developed to solve the traffic problem in WDM optical mesh network in [13]. In [14, 15, 16], a genetic algorithm is applied to solve the optimal logical topology design problem in WDM optical networks. The routing and wavelength assignment problem (RWA) in WDM optical networks is studied in [17, 18, 19, 20]. The authors of [21, 22] study the problem of optimal placement of wavelength converters in WDM ring networks using genetic algorithms.

The rest of this paper is organized as follows. The formal definition of the problem under study is given in Section 2. Section 3 presents the details of our algorithm. Performance evaluation and results are reported in Section 4. Section 5 concludes the paper.

## 2  Problem Definition

We formally define the routing optimization problem as follows. Consider a network $E = (v, \varsigma)$ where $v$ is the set of vertices and $\varsigma$ is the set of links in the network, each of which is associated with a link cost $c(e)$. A set of SRLGs are given as $R = \{r_i \mid 1 < i < |R|\}$, where $r_i$ is the $i$-th shared risk link group. Each SRLG has a set of links that are included in this risk group, which can be represented as $r_i = \{l_1, l_2, ..., l_m\}$. A cost $c(r_i)$ that captures the group's risk factor is associated with each SRLG. A path P is represented as $P = \{v_1, v_2, v_3, ..., v_i, v_{i+1}..., v_{n-1}, v_n\}$ where $(v_i, v_{i+1})$ is a link on P (which is denoted as $(v_i, v_{i+1}) \in P$ or $l_i \in P$), and $v_1$ and $v_n$ are the source and destination, respectively. We say a path P travels through an SRLG $r_i$ (represented as $P \rightarrow r_i$) when there exists at least one link such that

$l \in r_i$ and $l \in P$. Given a source node *src* and a destination node *dest*, the objective of this route optimization problem is to find a path P from *src* to *dest*, such that the combined link cost and SRLG cost are minimized. More specifically, the objective is to find a path $P = (src, v_2, v_3, ..., v_i, v_{i+1}, v_{n-1}, dest)$ such that $C(P) = w \cdot \sum_{r_i : P \to r_i} c(r_i) + (1-w) \cdot \sum_{l \in P} c(l)$ is minimized where $0 \le w \le 1$.

## 3  Proposed Algorithm

One important aspect of genetic algorithms is to define the encoding and decoding rules for the chromosomes. Another important aspect is to define the fitness function or evaluation function. For our routing optimization problem, a chromosome is defined as a string of node identities. We choose to have each individual in the population representing a valid path for a connection request. That is, each chromosome should represent a connected path and this path should start from the source node (*src*) of the request and end at the destination node (*dest*). Therefore a chromosome is defined as follows:

$$C = src, n_1, n_2, ..., n_k, dest$$

and the fitness function is defined as:

$$f(C) = \alpha \cdot S_l + \beta \cdot S_{srlg} \qquad (1)$$

where $S_l$ is the total cost of the links on the path, $S_{srlg}$ is the total weight of SRLGs that the path is associated with, and $\alpha$ and beta determine how much weight the link cost and SRLG cost, respectively, take in the combined cost.

Using this fitness function, we penalize the path that has high total link cost and/or high total SRLG weight. In the survivor selection, we try to preserve the chromosomes with small fitness values. Thus in the evolutionary process the algorithm is more likely to converge to a solution that is optimal or is close to the optimal.

Yet another important issue in our genetic algorithm is the generation of offsprings. Since we require each chromosome to represent a valid solution, we can not simply do random mating and mutation as many other genetic algorithms do. Our approach is detailed as follows:

For mating we pick two chromosomes as the parents if the corresponding two paths share at least one common node (not including the source and destination nodes). For example

$$C^a = src, n_1^a, n_2^a, ..., n, ..., n_{k_a}^a, dest,$$

$$C^b = src, n_1^a, n_2^a, ***, n, ***, n_{k_b}^b, dest.$$

In addition to nodes *src* and *dest*, $C^a$ and $C^b$ share a common node $n$. Through mating we generate two offspring chromosomes, $C_c^1$ and $C_c^2$, by swapping the segments of the two chromosomes at the common node $n$:

$$C_c^1 = src, n_1^a, n_2^a, ..., n, ***, n_{k_b}^b, dest,$$

$$C_c^2 = src, n_1^b, n_2^b, ***, n, ..., n_{k_a}^a, dest.$$

If there is more than one common node between the two paths, the algorithm randomly picks one and the segment swapping is performed.

It is worth noting that it is possible to have loops in the paths corresponding to the generated chromosomes due to the crossover. As a result, some chromosomes may grow bigger and bigger in the long run. We can add an additional step to remove the loops in the path. We choose not to spend time on checking and removing those loops, but to let the selection scheme deal with the problem. Note that those big chromosomes are inferior to those short ones in surviving the selection process.

For the mutation of a chromosome, the algorithm randomly picks two nodes (suppose they are $n_i$ and $n_j$) on the path and replaces the sub-path between $n_i$ and $n_j$ with a detour route between these two nodes. A random path between these two nodes is generated as the detour route. To avoid producing loops in this process, this detour should exclude any node on the original path except the two end nodes ($n_i$ and $n_j$ in this case). The detailed algorithm for the mutation process is described in Algorithm 2, which calls Algorithm 3 to generate the random path.

---

**Algorithm 2.** *Mutation with Detour Routing* (C)

---

**Require:**  $C = src, n_1, ..., n_{i-1}, n_i, ..., n_j, n_{j+1}, ..., n_k, dest.$

1: Pick two nodes $n_i$ and $n_j$ randomly, such that the path is divided into three parts: $C' = P_{src, n_i}, P_{n_i, n_j}, P_{n_j, dest}$

2: Call subroutine $RandomPath(n_i, n_j, FN)$ , to route a random path $P_{n_i, n_j}$ between nodes $n_i$ and $n_j$ . This random path, should exclude the nodes in $P_{src, n_i}$ and $P_{n_j, dest}$ (except $n_i$ and $n_j$ )

3 Mutate $C$ to $C' = P_{src, n_i}, P_{n_i, n_j}, P_{n_j, dest}$

4 **return** $C'$

---

Subroutine $RandomPath(n_i, n_j, FN)$ (Algorithm 3) is designed to find a random path between a pair of nodes. Certain nodes in the graph can be excluded from this random path, by specifying those nodes in a *forbidden set FN* . The basic idea of this algorithm is, starting from the source node, to randomly select a next node to append to the path, until it reaches the destination node at a certain point. In this algorithm, the last node in the path is the current node (represented as *CurNode* in Algorithm 3), and we randomly select a *next* node (represented as *next* in Algorithm 3) to append to the path. We select from all the nodes that are reachable from the current node through a single link, but excluding the nodes in the forbidden set *FN* . In some cases, it is possible that there is no available node to select from, i.e., the path reach a deadend at the current node. In this case, we remove the last node from the path and set the immediate upstream node as the current node. Meanwhile, to avoid loops in the path, all the nodes that have already been visited are inserted into the forbidden set F N , so that no node will be visited more than once by the path. By *visited*, we mean that the node has (ever) been selected as a part of the path, although it is possible that the node is removed later from the path.

---

**Algorithm 3.** *RandomPath*($n_i, n_j, FN$)

---

**Require:**   *src* is the source node, *dest* is the destination node, and *FN* is a forbidden set that constains the nodes that should be excluded from the path.

1:   $CurNode \leftarrow src, path \leftarrow src$ .
2:   **while** the path has not reached the destination node *dest* **do**
3:      $FN \leftarrow FN \cup CurNode$ ;
4:      Set *next_node* $\leftarrow$ all the nodes that can be reached from *CurNode* through a single link;
5:      Remove from next nodes any node that belongs to *FN* ;
6:      **if** *next_node* $\neq$ *NULL* **then**
7:        Randomly pick a node *next* from *next_node* ;
8:        Append path by link $(CurNode, next)$ ;
9:      **else**
10:        Remove the last node from *path* ;
11:       If there is no more node in *path* ,terminate with failure;
12:        $CurNode \leftarrow$ the last node of path;
13:      **end if**
14: **end while**
15: **if** $CurNode$ is the destination node , return *path* ;
16: **else** return failure

---

Another key point in the genetic algorithm is the generation of the initial population. We can generate the k-shortest paths(KSP) or k random paths (KRP) from the source node to the destination node as the initial population.

Finally, for the stopping condition that determines when to stop the iterations of the evolutionary process in the main algorithm 1, one way is to set a fixed number for the iterations. But in the simulations we find that it is hard to set a proper value for this number. Instead, we deem the chance of further improvement is very slow and stop the iteration, if the best solution in the population is not improved over the last 3 generations. In this way the number of iterations can be automatically adapted with the progress of the evolutionary and the complexity of the problem. Still, we set a upper limit on the number of iterations. Once the number of iterations reaches that limit, we terminate the iteration no matter whether there is improvement on the solution or not.

# 4  Performance Evaluation

In this section, we evaluate the proposed algorithms using a topology with 100 nodes and 455 bidirectional links, which is generated by Waxman's random network topology generator [23]. Different options in this genetic algorithm are implemented and compared through extensive simulations. Specifically, we simulated the k-shortest paths as the initial population (KSPIP) and the k random paths as the initial population (KRPIP). The performance is compared with the ILP formulation (ILP) and the heuristic algorithm (k-Heuristic) with k set to be 3 in [1]. For the comparison, we relax the constraints of Eqns. (9-10) in the ILP formulation in [1] to consider the same minimum combined cost routing problem as the problem considered in this work. In the simulation, both $\alpha$ and $\beta$ in the combined cost are set to be 0.5 for all these four approaches considered in the simulation.

Two types of SRLGs (localized and non-localized SRLGs) are generated and studied. The first method randomly picks a node, and then randomly picks the links that are within N hops from the selected node to be included in an SRLG. If we want to generate an SRLG with certain number of link but there are not enough links within within N hops from the selected node, N will be automatically increased by 1 so that we get enough links. This method produces *N-hop* localized SRLGs. We set the N to be 5 in our simulation. The second method randomly picks links in the topology to be included in an SRLG. This method produces non-localized SRLGs. In both cases, the weight of an SRLG is proportional to its size, i.e., the number of links in the group multiplied by a constant (50 in our simulation). The size of an SRLG (number of links in a SRLG) is uniformly distributed in [8, 12]. For each case simulated, 10 SRLG sets of fixed size are generated. For each SRLG set,100 source-destination pairs are randomly generated. So the total number of simulation instances for a case is 1000. The proposed algorithms and ILP are then run to find the paths. The performance figures are based on the average performance of all the instances with the same settings.

For each case simulated, 10 SRLG sets of fixed size are generated. For each SRLG set, 100 source-destination pairs are randomly generated. Therefore the total number of simulation instances for a case is 1000. The performance figures are based on the average performance of all the instances with the same settings.

As we can see from Figure 1 for the localized SRLG case and 2 for the non-localized SRLG case, firstly, KSPIP and KRPIP are performing very closely, which means the initial population does not really have much influence on the final solution of the genetic approach in both cases. We also observe that, in the non-localized SRLG case (Figure 2), the solutions obtained by KSPIP and KRPIP are close to, but not as good as the solutions obtained by ILP and the k-heuristic. However, in the localized SRLG case the genetic approaches perform as well as the k-heuristic algorithm. Obviously the genetic algorithm works better in the localized SRLG case, which can be reasoned that the segment mutation and crossover on the chromosomes works better for the localized SRLGs. Meanwhile, Figure 3 shows that the time needed to obtain a solution with genetic algorithm, in localized SRLG case, does not grow as fast as ILP and k-heuristic. Both KSPIP and KRPIP take less time than ILP and k-heuristic when the number of SRLGs in the topology is 160, although the genetic algorithm consumes more time when the number of

SRLGs is 20. The reason behind this is, for the ILP approach the computation time usually grows exponentially as the complexity of the network is growing. As for the k-heuristic, one major component of the algorithm is to compare the SRLGs associated with the routing entries on a node, and the complexity compare two sets of SRLGs is $O(|R|^2)$ where n is the number of SRLGs in the topology. For the genetic algorithm the complexity to evaluate a chromosome is $O(|R|^2)$. Therefore the time consumed by both the ILP and k-heuristic grows faster than the genetic algorithm in this work as the number of SRLGs in the network increases. Thus, the genetic algorithm in our work can provide a tradeoff between the cost and the time when the complexity of the network is high. In the meantime, we can see that with k-shortest paths as the initial population, KSPIP consumes less time than KRPIP which uses the k random paths as the initial population. This is reasonable since generally the k-shortest paths are more close to the optimal solution region than the pure random paths, thus it take less time for KSPIP to converge.

## 5  Conclusions

In this work, we have studied a routing optimization problem in networks with shared risk link groups (SRLGs) to deter- mine a path between a source and a destination such that the combined path cost and the weight of SRLGs to which the links of the path belong is minimized. The path cost is measured as the sum of cost of links on the path while the weight of SRLGs is calculated as the sum of the weight of individual SRLGs along the path. We have developed evolutionary computation based algorithms to solve the problem and compared the performance with previous heuristic algorithm proposed in [1]. Our simulation studies showed that, when the complexity of the problem is high, the proposed algorithm consumes less time to obtain the solution than the heuristic algorithm. In the localized SRLG cases, the genetic algorithm can obtain solutions as good as the ones obtained by the integer linear programming and the heuristic algorithm in [1] but consumes less time when the number of SRLGs in the topology is large.

## References

1. Luo, X., Wang, B.: Multi-constrained routing in networks with shared risk link groups. In: IEEE Broadnets, 3rd International Conference on Broadband Communication, Networks and Systems, San Jose CA (October 2006)
2. Hu, J.Q.: Diverse Routing in Optical Mesh Networks. IEEE Transactions on Communications 51(3), 489–494 (2003)
3. Datta, P., Somani, A.K.: Diverse Routing for Shared Risk Resource Groups (SRRG) Failures in WDM OpticalNetworks. In: BROADNETS 2004, San Jose CA, October 2004, pp. 120–129 (2004)
4. Luo, X., Wang, B.: Diverse Routing in WDM Optical Networks with Shared Risk Link Group (SRLG) Failures. In: Proceedings of the 5th IEEE International Workshop on Design of Reliable Communication Networks (DRCN), Island of Ischia (Naples), Italy (October 2005)
5. Eiben, A.E., Smith, J.E.: Introduction to evolutionary computing. Springer, New York (2003)

6. Nagata, Y., Kobayashi, S.: Analyses of genetic algorithms for traveling salesman problems for effective searches. In: 32nd ISCIE International Symposium on Stochastic Systems Theory and Its Applications, pp. 44–45 (2000)
7. Nagata, Y., Kobayashi, S.: An analysis of edge assembly crossover for the traveling salesman problem. In: Proc. 1999 International Conference on Systems, Man and Cybernetics, pp. III-628–III-633 (1999)
8. Nagata, Y., Kobayashi, S.: Edge assembly crossover: High-power genetic algorithm for the traveling salesman problem. In: Proc. 7th International Conference on Genetic Algorithms, pp. 450–457 (1997)
9. Xu, S.C., Wu, B.X.: Traffic grooming in unidirectional WDM ring networks using genetic algorithms. Computer Communications 25(13), 1185–1194 (2002)
10. Xu, Y., Xu, S.C., Wu, B.X.: Strictly nonblocking grooming of dynamic traffic in unidirectional SONET/WDM rings using genetic algorithms. Computer Networks 41(2), 227–245 (February)
11. Liu, K.H., Xu, Y.: A new approach to improving the grooming performance with dynamic traffic in SONET rings. Computer Networks 46(2), 181–195 (2004)
12. Jiao, Y.G., Zhou, B.K., Zhang, H.Z., Guo, Y.L.: Heuristic Algorithms for Grooming of Arbitrary Traffic in WDM Ring Networks. Photonic Network Communications 8(3), 309–318 (2004)
13. Jiao, Y.G., Zhou, B.K., Zhang, H.Z., Guo, Y.L.: Grooming of Arbitrary Traffic in Optical WDM Mesh Networks Using a Genetic Algorithm. Photonic Network Communications 10(2), 193–198 (2005)
14. Gazen, C., Ersoy, C.: Genetic algorithms for designing multihop lightwave network topologies. Artificial Intelligence in Engineering 13(3), 211–221 (1999)
15. Borella, A., Cancellieri, G., Chiaraluce, F.: Design techniques of two-layer architectures for WDM optical networks. International Journal of Communication Systems 14(2), 171–188 (2001)
16. Zheng, J., Zhou, B., Mouftah, H.T.: Virtual Topology Design and Reconfiguration of Virtual Private Networks (VPNs) over All-Optical WDM Network. Photonic Network Communication 7(3), 255–266 (2004)
17. Banerjee, N., Mehta, V., Pandey, S.: A genetic algorithm approach for solving the routing and wavelength assignment problem in WDM networks. In: International Conference on Networks (ICN 2004), French Caribbean (2004)
18. Bisbal, D.: Dynamic routing and wavelength assignment in optical networks by means of genetic algorithms. Photonic Network Communications 7(1), 43–58 (2004)
19. Le, V.T., Ngo, S.H., Jiang, X., Horiguchi, S., Guo, M.: A genetic algorithm for dynamic routing and wavelength assignment in WDM networks. In: Proc. Inter. Symp. Parallel and Distributed Processing and Applications, HongKong (December 2004)
20. Ali, M., Ramamurthy, B., Deogun, J.S.: Routing and wavelength assignment with power considerations in optical networks. Computer Networks 32(5), 539–555 (2000)
21. Chan, T.M., Kwong, S., Man, K.F.: Solving the Converter Placement Problem in WDM Ring Networks using Genetic Algorithms. Computer Journal 46(4), 427–448 (2003)
22. Vijayanand, C., Kumar, M.S., Venugopal, K.R., Kumar, P.S.: Converter placement in all-optical networks using genetic algorithms. Computer Communications 23(13), 1223–1234 (2000)
23. Waxman, B.M.: Routing of multipoint connections. IEEE Journal on Selected Areas in Communications 6(9), 1617–1622 (1988)

# Design of Wireless Sensor Networks Considering the Robustness of the Topology

Yu-Dong Tan[*], Xiao-Qin Huang, Ye Cai, Yi Tan, and An-Gang Chen

College of Electrical and Information Engineering, Hunan University,
ChangSha, 410082 Hunan Province, China
yudongtan@126.com

**Abstract.** In wireless sensor networks, the sensor nodes are facing the random failure and the selective attacks all the time, which will cause partial or even entire network disintegrating. How to control the failures resulted from random failure or the selective attacks has become a hot topic in recent years. In this paper, we applied three matching models of capacity on three common kinds of wireless sensor network topology, and each model developed a profit function to defense cascading failures. Performances of the proposed matching models of capacity are evaluated using computer simulations. By studying the relationship between network investment and robustness, we find that NM model can defend against cascading failures better and requires a lower investment cost when higher robustness is required .The network performance analysis and the simulation results indicated that it can improve network robustness and invulnerability which are particularly important for the design of networks after applying this algorithm in the wireless sensor network.

**Keywords:** reliability, robustness, complex network, wireless sensor networks.

## 1 Introduction

In recent years, wireless sensor networks have attracted more and more related researchers for its advantages. Wireless sensor networks consist of large amounts of wireless sensor nodes to collect information from their sensing terrain, such as seismic and acoustic data [1-4]. People can spread the nodes in the high temperature, high humidity, harmful gases and other enemy controlled areas where our personnel can not reach, to achieve continuous real-time data acquisition in order to achieve unattended monitoring purposes. With the development of technology (system on a chip), integrating the sensor nodes into a micro-chip, like smart dust [5] and other micro-sensor networks will become the future trend of development. In the near future, it will be possible that hundreds or even thousands of sensor nodes form a network.

Different from traditional wireless networks, apart from the need for local information collection and data processing, the sensor nodes should also store and

---

[*] Corresponding author.

P. Sénac, M. Ott, and A. Seneviratne (Eds.): ICWCA 2011, LNICST 72, pp. 216–227, 2012.
© Institute for Computer Sciences, Social Informatics and Telecommunications Engineering 2012

forward integrate the data sent by other sensor nodes, and sensor nodes require mutual coordination and communication with each other and work together to complete complex work. Restricted by price and volume of the nodes, the wireless sensor network nodes have only a relatively limited signal processing capabilities, computing power and storage capacity. Sensor nodes of the network can be divided into different categories according to the sensing capability, computing power, energy, and etc. Thus the sensor networks can be divided into homogeneous sensor networks and heterogeneous sensor networks. Homogeneous sensor network is constituted by the same nodes (sensor nodes), and the heterogeneous sensor network is constituted by the different nodes including sensor nodes and sink nodes. The sensors monitor environmental variations then transmit observation results to a fusion center [6-9]. For example, seismic and acoustic datas are collected by several sensors and then transmitted to a sink node for joint processing to detect, classify, and track vehicles [6].Sink node also has the relatively strong processing power, storage capacity and communication capacity, for the use of connecting the wireless sensor network and the external networks. Sink nodes can be either an enhancement of the sensor nodes or only the particular gateway device with the wireless communication interface without monitoring functions to ensure the sink nodes have adequate energy and more memory and computing power. Regardless of sensor nodes or sink nodes, they only have relatively limited data processing and communication capabilities.The integrity of the original networks will be destroyed and other nodes will have more business burden for data transmission if some certain nodes fail. When the load of these nodes exceeds the capacity of their own or their operating environment deteriorate, these sensor nodes will also be out of service.

In the category of complex networks, the phenomenon has been abstracted into the two types of situations:(1) the breakdown of node is random, each node has the equal probability of breakdown; (2) selective attacks, with the purpose to attack the most connected nodes for destruction[10]. More processing and communication capabilities can be allocated to the nodes to avoid affecting the entire network connectivity due to breakdown of some nodes. Regardless of how much of the investment cost, the sensor network can reach a high robustness through allocating sufficient redundancy capacity to the nodes. But it is definitely improper in designing the network of reality. The designer must take robustness and economy of the sensor network into account simultaneously.

With the development of wireless sensor networks,  the key issue of sensor network research is to allocate more investment cost to some critical nodes to ensure them have a higher reliability, thus enhance the sensor network robustness when the total investment cost of the sensor network is fixed, which means finding a balance between economy and reliability[11].

## 2   Robustness of the Complex Networks

The complex network theory has been for some time since first proposed by Barabási and Albert in 1998, but complex network theory and analysis method applied to wireless sensor networks research are seriously rare and develop in slow progress. It is necessary to introduce a way of how to study wireless sensor network by complex network theory and analysis methods. The key of which lies in a successful modeling which is able to make complex network theory and analysis methods more suitable for the application of wireless sensor network in order to achieve the optimization of some certain network characteristics of wireless sensor network. The complex system theory study the large-scale network that exists in social system with the systemic perspective, such as internet, electricity networks, metabolic networks and protein networks, and etc. Watts and Strogatz revealed the small-world properties of complex network in 1998, and established a small world network model [12]. Barabási further revealed the complexity of many real-world networks with the degree distribution of power law form, called scale-free network [13], and established a scale-free network model. These pioneering works promote the complex networks research into a new era. Therefore, complex networks have recently attracted considerable attention in physics and other fields. Interestingly, many real-world networks share a certain number of common topological properties, such as small-world and scale-free properties [14-17] .

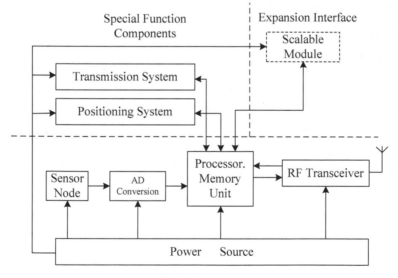

Fig. 1. Components of wireless sensor network node

Robustness refers to the malfunction avoiding ability of a network when a fraction of its constituents are damaged. The network robustness has been one of the most central topics in the complex network research [18]. In scale-free networks, the existence of hub nodes with high degrees has been shown to yield fragility to intentional attacks, while at the same time the network becomes robust to random failures due to the heterogeneous degree distribution [19–22]. Sensor network is a real network, must have the characteristics of complex network. Study the dynamic behavior and complex networks' characteristics of wireless sensor network will have special significance for the development of sensor network. In different applications, the compositions of the wireless sensor network nodes are different [23]. But generally the core of node consist of three parts: the processing unit (CPU, memory unit, Embedded Operating System), communication unit and power management unit. The type of sensor node is determined by the kinds of physical signals monitored by the node [24].

Fig. 1 is hardware schematic diagram of the sensor node, the sensor node is a miniaturized embedded system [25], it is typically composed of data acquisition module, data processing and control module, communication module and power modules. These units are hold in a matchbox-sized module, some even smaller [26-27]. Because limited by the volume, sensor nodes are usually battery-powered, this greatly limits the energy of sensor nodes. In addition, as constrainted by the energy and volume, the processing power and storage capacity of the sensor nodes is limited [28-29]. The operating environment of sensor nodes is harsh, as a result, the entire network may collapse due to the breakdown of some nodes, because nodes prone to be lack of processing capacity or the destruction of nature to the nodes. And the anti-investigation actions of enemy will carry out the purpose of destruction to our sensor networks. People must overcome these problems into account when they construct a wireless sensor network. The most effective way is to increase investment cost of the sensor networks. But how to spend less investment cost for a maximum robustness? The researchers of complex networks have made some significative works in the topology robustness.

Network robustness [30-34] subjects to random or intentional attacks has been one of the most central topics in network safety. Therefore, failures on complex networks have been highly concerned and widely investigated. The network robustness has been one of the most central topics in the complex network research.

Each node (sensor or fusion center) of the wireless sensor network, its load such as seismic and acoustic data is either produced or transferred to other nodes, and it is possible that for the limited processing power and storage capacity, node is overloaded beyond the given capacity, which is the maximum data that the node can handle. The breakdown of the heavily loaded single node will cause the redistribution of loads over its neighboring nodes, and load is reassigned to bypass malfunctioning nodes which can trigger breakdowns of newly overloaded nodes. This process will go on until all the loads of the remaining nodes are below their capacities.The damage caused by failures can be quantified by the relative size of the largest connected component $G$, defined as following

$$G = N' / N \tag{1}$$

Where $N$ and $N'$ are the numbers of nodes in the largest component before and after the failure, respectively. The integrity of a network is maintained if $G \approx 1$, while breakdown occurs if $G \approx 0$. The relative size $G$ also represents the robustness of wireless sensor network against intentional attacks or random failure.

For wireless sensor network, the breakdown of some nodes is sufficient to collapse partial even the entire system. In the research of the failures, the following two issues are closely related to each other and of significant interests: one is how to improve the network robustness to failures, and the other particularly important issue is how to design manmade networks at a less cost. In most circumstances, a high robustness and a low cost are difficult to achieve simultaneously. The failure can be prevented by assigning extra capacities (processing power and storage capacity) to sensor nodes. Since the extending of sensor network capacity will bring economic and technique pressure, it is important to explore how to rationally allocate the limited capacity onto sensor nodes or sink nodes, and efficiently improve the robustness of sensor network. In general, one can split, at least conceptually, the total cost for the sensor networks into two different types: on one hand, there should be the initial construction cost to build a sensor network structure, another type of the cost is required to allocate extra capacities to sensor nodes or sink nodes of the given sensor network. For the latter, we need to spend more to have bigger memory sizes and processing power and so on for the server of sensor node which it can handles more data packets. In the present letter, we assume that the sensor network structure is given, (accordingly the construction cost is fixed), and focus only how to efficiently allocate limited resources of capacity to make sensor network more robust, which should be spent in addition to the initial construction cost. Assume that in a sensor network, the load of sensor node is $l_i$, we expect the capacity $c_i$ of this sensor node should be an increasing function of $l_i$

$$c_i = \lambda_i \cdot l_i \tag{2}$$

Although it should be possible to find, via a kind of the variational approach, the optimal functional form of $\lambda_i$ ‹ that sensor networks can indeed be made more robust while spending less cost.

For a given sensor network structure, we aim to increase $G$ and decrease the cost, which will eventually provide us a way to achieve the high robustness and the low cost at the same time. In the present letter, for simplicity, we try to find a possible way of assigning the extra capacities. For the improvement of robustness of the network, based on the work [35], many models have been studied extensively. While for the design of manmade networks, Motter-Lai first proposed ML model, Wang et al, proposed a high-robustness and low-cost model (WK), H.J. Sun et al, also proposed a NM model to improve networks. In our research, we will apply ML,WK and NM model to the improvement of sensor networks' robustness[36]. Our results suggest that networks can indeed be made more robust while spending less cost.

## 3  Model

Among the previous works, ML model assumes the capacity $c_i$ of node i be proportional to the initial load $l_i$ as

$$c_i = \lambda_i \cdot l_i = (1+\alpha) \cdot l_i, i = 1, 2, ..., N, \tag{3}$$

Where $\alpha \geq 0$ is the control parameter representing the extra capacity. In WK model, Wang et al . set $\lambda(i)$ as

$$\lambda(i) = 1 + \alpha\theta(l_i / l_{max} - \beta) \tag{4}$$

Where $\theta(x) = 0(1)$ for $x_i 0 (\dot{\iota} 0)$ is the Heaviside step function, $l_{max} = \max(l_i)$ (i=1,2,3...N), and they use $\alpha \in [0, \infty)$ and $\beta \in [0,1]$ as two control parameters in the model. In ML model, $\lambda$ has been a constant, which corresponds to the limiting case of $\beta = 0$ with the identification $\lambda = 1 + \alpha$ in the WK model. ML model raises a linear correlation between extra capacity and initial load, while WK model prefers to protect the highest-load nodes.

In the research of how to design robust manmade network, there is another capacity allocation model proposed by H.J. Sun. This model considered the betweenness distribution, the flow generation rate and the network structure in the process of network designment at the same time, the failures will be alleviated effectively. In the model, it is assumed that, at each time step, on average, $\mu$ packets are generated and the flow is forwarded along the shortest path. The betweenness $B_i$ can be used to characterize the number of shortest paths between pairs of nodes that run through node i. The betweenness of node i can be defined as

$$B_i = \sum_{j,l \in N, j \neq l} \frac{n_{jl(i)}}{n_{jl}} \tag{5}$$

Where $n_{jl}$ is the number of shortest paths connecting j and l, while $n_{jl}(i)$ is the number of shortest paths connecting j and l and passing through i. The model assumes the capacity of a node as the maximum load that the node can handle and is proportional to its initial load. Thus, the capacity allocation model is given as follows

$$\lambda_i = 1 + \alpha \frac{B_i}{\mu ND + \mu} \tag{6}$$

Where the capacity $c_i$ of node i be proportional to its initial load $l_i$, $\alpha$ is a tolerance parameter, $\mu$ is the average flow generating rate, N is the size of network, D is the average shortest path length. As we know, in man-made networks, the capacity is severely limited by cost.

For convenience define the cost e as

$$e = \frac{1}{N} \sum_{i=1}^{N} (\lambda_i - 1) \tag{7}$$

In ML model, the cost is

$$e_{ML} = \frac{1}{N} \sum_{i=1}^{N} (\lambda_i - 1) = \alpha \tag{8}$$

In the WK model, the cost is

$$e_{WK} = \frac{1}{N} \sum_{i=1}^{N} (\lambda_i - 1) = \frac{1}{N} \sum_{i=1}^{N} \alpha \cdot \theta(\frac{l_i}{l_{max}} - \beta) = \alpha \cdot \frac{N''}{N} \tag{9}$$

Where $N''$ is the number of nodes with initial load larger than $\beta l_{max}$

In the NM model, the cost is

$$e_{NM} = \frac{1}{N} \sum_{i=1}^{N} (\alpha \frac{B_i}{\mu ND + \mu}) \tag{10}$$

Generally the number of nodes of a network is large, thus

$$e_{NM} = \frac{1}{N} \sum_{i=1}^{N} (\alpha \frac{B_i}{\mu ND}) \tag{11}$$

Because $\sum_{i=1}^{N} B_i = N(N-1)D$, the equation above can be simplified to

$$e_{NM} = \frac{1}{\mu N} \alpha \frac{\sum_{i=1}^{N} B_i}{ND + 1} \approx \frac{\alpha}{\mu} \tag{12}$$

Apparently, when $\mu = 1$, the cost of our model is equal to ML model.

## 4   Simulation and Application

There are three kinds of common network topology in the wireless sensor network: (1) line structure based on chains, and the sensor nodes are connected in series on one or more chains in this network topology, while, users are connected at the end of the chains; (2) planar structure based on network, the wireless sensor network is connected into a network and very robust, which has a good flexibility; (3) hierarchical structure based on cluster, and this network topology possesses the naturally distributed processing ability, meanwhile, cluster head is the distributed processing center, and sensor nodes deliver the data to the cluster head, accordingly, the processing and fusion of the data is finished in the cluster head, then the results will be delivered through multi-hop by other cluster heads or directly delivered to the users. In this letter, we will not only apply three matching models of capacity mentioned above, but also analyse the effect of the models on different network topology.

The final purpose of our research is to maximize the benefits within limited resources. The traditional method is to allocate larger capacity to the node with the largest degree or load, which may only obtain a tiny benefit even a negative one in some circumstance. Therefore, it is important to find the optimal strategy of capacity allocation in order to maximize the profit of the investment.

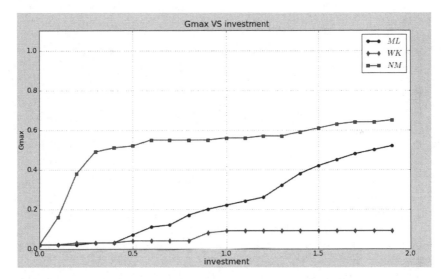

**Fig. 2.** The effects of ML,WK, NM on the topology of line structure based on chains

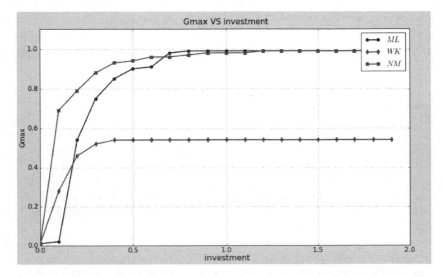

**Fig. 3.** The effects of ML,WK,NM on the topology of planar structure based on network

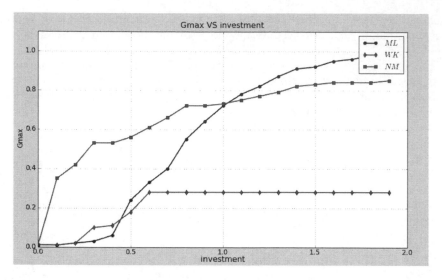

**Fig. 4.** The effects of ML,WK, NM on the topology of hierarchical structure based on cluster

In this paper, we call $G_{max}$ and cost e as the income and the cost functions respectively. we illustrate how the models work in practice by considering three sensor network topologies: (1) line structure based on chains; (2) planar structure based on network;(3) hierarchical structure based on cluster. The tested sensor network is created according to the BA mode with network size N=1000, average degree <k>=4.

Here we focus on failures triggered by the removal of a single node, which is among those with higher load.

Figure 2 describes the effect of the models applied on three different sensor network topologys, abscissa is the investment for the nodes of wireless sensor network, vertical axis is $G_{max}$ , indicating flexibility of the network confronts deliberately attacks and random failures. The larger $G_{max}$ is, the better the matching model of capacity is. Constructing a wireless sensor network according the strategy of this model can make the network get a higher robustness. In Figure 2, we can see that, applying ML, WK and NM to the construction of sensor network that is based on the topology of line structure based on chains. Therefore, the NM model get the highest profit, and the NM model has the best robustness against the failures. Figure 3 reveals that when the abscissa increase from 0 to 0.66, the effect of NM is better than ML and WK. However, when the abscissa increases from 0.66 to 1.2, the effect of ML is better than NM, and the effect of ML and NM is nearly the same lever at 1.0 when abscissa is larger than 1.2.This indicates that constructing wireless sensor network according to the topology of planar structure based on network can get a higher robustness.

Figure 4 reveals that when the abscissa increase from 0 to 1.02, the effect of NM is obviously better than ML and WK, but when the abscissa increase larger than 1.02, the effect of ML is better than WK and NM. To sum up the three figures above, we can find out that when allocating different investment on different topologys, the ML.

WK and NM can get different effects. But overall the effect of NM is better than ML and WK.

## 5  Conclusion

The main idea in our research is the same as in existing studies: in a highly heterogeneous wireless sensor network with a broad load distribution, nodes with large loads should be more protected by assigning large capacities such as processing power, storage capacity and communication capability. This study presents how to enhance robustness of the wireless sensor network by the way of allocating more capabilities to the important and hub nodes based on the concept of robustness of complex network. We proposed three matching models of capacity (ML, WK and NM) then applied these matching models of capacity on three common kinds of wireless sensor network topologies and compared the effects of these modes. Simulation results show that improves the robustness of the wireless sensor networks through allocating more processing and communication capabilities to the important and hub nodes is definitely feasible. Under the same network investment, applying the algorithm of NM model can get a higher robustness. we believe this work have its theoretical importance and potential application in designing wireless sensor networks from the point of economic view. It can also provide guidance in designing more robust artificial networks.

**Acknowledgments.** The authors would like to appreciate the financial support from the National Natural Science Foundation of China (No. 50977022) and Hunan Provincial Innovation Foundation For Postgraduate (No. CX2010B150).

## References

1. Li, D., Wong, K.D., Yu, H.H., Sayeed, A.M.: Detection, classification, and tracking of targets. IEEE Signal Process. Mag. 19(3), 17–29 (2002)
2. Madden, S.R., Franklin, M.J., Hellerstein, J.M., Hong, W.: The design of an acquisitional query processor for sensor networks. In: Proceedings of the SIGMOD Conference, pp. 491–502. ACM Press, New York (2003)
3. Ma, Z.C., Sun, Y.N., Mei, T.: Survey on wireless sensors network. Journal on Communications 25(4), 114–124 (2004)
4. Almomani, I., Al-Akaidi, M., Reynolds, P., Ivins, J.: Architectural framework for wireless mobile adhoc networks. Computer Communications 30(1), 178–191 (2006)
5. Smart Dust, http://robotics.eecs; Berkeley, Edu/~pister/SmartDust/
6. Aldosari, S.A., Moura, J.M.F.: Detection in decentralized sensor networks. In: Proc. ICASSP, Montreal, QC, Canada, May 2004, pp. 277–280 (2004)
7. Chamberland, J.-F., Veeravalli, V.V.: Asymptotic results for decentralized detection in power constrained wireless sensor networks. IEEE J. Sel. Areas Commun. 22(6), 1007–1015 (2004)
8. Tsitsiklis, J.N.: Decentralized detection by a large number of sensors. Math. Control Signals Syst. 1(2), 167–182 (1988)

9. D'Costa, A., Ramachandran, V., Sayeed, A.M.: Distributed classification of Gaussian space-time sources in wireless sensor networks. IEEE J. Sel. Areas Commun. 22(6), 1026–1036 (2004)
10. Paul, G., Tanizawa, T., Havlin, H., et al.: Optimization of robustness of complex networks. Eur. Phys. J B 38, 187–191 (2004)
11. Albert, R., Jeong, H., Barabási, A.-L.: Error and attack tolerance of complex networks. J. Nature 406, 378–382 (2000)
12. Watt, D.J., Strogtz, S.H.: Collective dynamics of small-world networks. J. Nature 393, 440–442 (1998)
13. Barabási, A.L., Albert, R.: Emergence of scaling in random networks. J. Science 286(5439), 509–512 (1999)
14. Newman, M.E.J.: Model of the small world. Journal of Statistical Physics 101, 819–841 (2000)
15. Strogatz, S.H.: Exploring complex networks. Nature 410, 268–276 (2001)
16. Albert, R., Barabási, A.L.: Statistical mechanics of complex networks. Reviews of Modern Physics 74, 47–97 (2002)
17. Dorogovtsev, S.N., Mendes, J.F.F.: Evolution of networks. Advances in Physics 51, 1079–1187 (2002)
18. Schafer, M., Scholz, J., Greiner, M.: Proactive Robustness Control of Heterogeneously Loaded Networks. Phys. Rev. Lett. 96, 108701 (2006)
19. Holme, P., Kim, B.J., Yoon, C.N., Han, S.K.: Attack vulnerability of complex networks. Phys. Rev. E 65, 056109 (2002)
20. Zhao, L., Park, K., Lai, Y.C.: Attack vulnerability of scale-free networks due to cascading breakdown. Phys. Rev. E 70, 035101(R) (2004)
21. Motter, A.E.: Cascade Control and Defense in Complex Networks. Phys. Rev. Lett. 93, 098701 (2004)
22. Crucitti, P., Latora, V., Marchiori, M.: Model for cascading failures in complex networks. Phys. Rev. E 69, 045104(R)(2004)
23. Pister, K., Hohlt, B., Jeong, J., Doherty, L., Vainio, J.P.: Ivy-A sensor network infrastructure (EB/OL) (2003),
   http://www-bsac.eecs.berkeley.edu/projects/ivy
24. Corson, S., Macker, J., Batsell, S.: Architectural considerations for mobile mesh networking. Internet Draft RFC Version 2 (1996)
25. Warneke, B., Last, M., Liebowitz, B., Pister, K.S.J.: Smart dust: Communicating with a Cubic-millimeter computer. IEEE Computer Magazine 34(1), 44–51 (2001)
26. Tilak, S., Abu-Ghazaleh, N.B., Heinzelman, W.: A taxonomy of wireless micro-sensor network models. J. Mobile Computing and Communication Review 1(2), 1–8 (2002)
27. Li, J.Z., Li, J.B., Shi, S.F.: Concepts, issues and advance of sensor networks and data management of sensor networks. J. Journal of Software 14(10), 1717–1727 (2003)
28. Peters, L., Moerman, I., Dhoedt, B., Demeester, P.: Q-WEHROM: Mobility support and resource reservations for mobile senders and receivers. J. Computer Networks 50(6), 1158–1175 (2006)
29. Bonnet, P., Gehrke, J., Seshadri, P.: Querying the physical world. IEEE Personal Communication 7(5), 10–15 (2000)
30. Tanizawa, T., Paul, G., Cohen, R., Havlin, S., Stanley, H.E.: Optimization of network robustness to waves of targeted and random attacks. J. Phys. Rev. E 71, 047101 (2005)
31. Cohen, R., Erez, K., ben-Avraham, D., Havlin, S.: Resilience of the internet to random breakdowns. J. Phys. Rev. Lett. 85, 4626 (2000)

32. Cohen, R., Erez, K., ben-Avraham, D., Havlin, S.: Breakdown of the internet under intentional attack. J. Phys. Rev. Lett. 86, 3682 (2001)
33. Motter, E.A.: Cascade control and defense in complex networks. Physical Review Letters 93(9), 98701 (2004)
34. Newman, M.E.J.: The structure and function of complex networks. SIAM Review 45(2), 167–256 (2003)
35. Motter, A.E., Lai, Y.-C.: Cascade-based attacks on complex networks. J. Phys. Rev. E 66, 065102 (2002)
36. Wang, B., Kim, B.J.: A High Robustness and Low Cost Model for Cascading Failures. J. Europhys. Lett. 78, 48001 (2007)

# A Model of Survivable Storage System Based on Information Hiding

Qingjie Zhang, Jianming Zhu, and Yiheng Wang

School of Information, Central University of Finance and Economics,
Beijing, P. R. China 100081
cufe_dbzy@163.com, tyzjm65@163.com,
wangyiheng722@163.com

**Abstract.** A new model of survivable storage system based on the information hiding, which is called SSSBIH, is presented in this paper, This SSSBIH model is derived from the PASIS model. SSSBIH model can make stored data more security than PASIS model. We design the information hiding function in client agent and describe its principle of work in this paper. Note that data tampering from internal intruders is difficult to be detected nowadays. The information hiding function can detect tampering whatever any user accesses the data. With threshold themes, our model can carry out effective recovery for tampered data. Our model also doesn't need the history pool of the old data versions. This can save the storage space of storage nodes. At last, we give out an information hiding algorithm based on the discrete cosine transformation and make a simulation. In short, our model can enhance data credibility, survivability and security of a storage system.

**Keywords:** survivable storage system, information hiding, intrusion diagnosis and recovery, discrete cosine transformation.

## 1 Introduction

As the society increasingly relies on digitally stored and accessed information, supporting the availability, integrity, and confidentiality of information is crucial. The system should securely store users' critical information and ensure that the data is kept confidential and continuously accessible and cannot be destroyed. A *survivable storage system* can provide these guarantees.

Paul Stanton [1] compared confidentiality, data integrity, reliability and performance of the eight existing security storage systems, which are NASD, PASIS, S4, CFS, SFS-RO, SNAD, PLUTUS and SiRiUS. All of these systems share a common goal: to protect stored data from malicious adversaries. However, the design approaches to reach this goal vary tremendously in each system.

P. Sénac, M. Ott, and A. Seneviratne (Eds.): ICWCA 2011, LNICST 72, pp. 228–240, 2012.
© Institute for Computer Sciences, Social Informatics and Telecommunications Engineering 2012

PASIS is a storage system that encodes information via threshold schemes so as to distribute trust amongst storage nodes in the system [4]. The PASIS architecture combines decentralized storage system technologies, data redundancy and encoding, and dynamic self-maintenance to create survivable information storage. It strives to prevent data by storing elements of a file in different locations so that a single compromised server cannot disclose the entire relevant information. PASIS increases data availability in the face of failed servers [1].

By using the technology of information hiding, we present a new model named SSSBIH (Survivable Storage System Based on Information Hiding). In the client sides, an agent is added for the management capabilities of information hiding, and its main function is to detect attacks from internal intruders. Thus, it can improve security and survivability of a storage system.

In section 2, we present the architecture of SSSBIH. In section 3, we describe the service properties of our model. In section 4, we describe the algorithms used in our model. In section 5, we evaluate the performance of SSSBIH via simulations. In section 6, we describe the advantage of SSSBIH model. Finally, we conclude our paper and discuss future directions in Section 7.

# 2  SSSBIH

Survivable systems operate from the fundamental design thesis that no individual service, node, or user can be fully trusted. Survivable storage systems must distribute data among many nodes. Individual storage node must not expose information to anyone.

Threshold schemes, also known as secret sharing or information dispersal algorithms [1], offer a method that provides both information confidentiality and availability in a single, flexible mechanism. These schemes encode, replicate, and divide information into multiple pieces, or shares that can be stored at different storage nodes. The system can only reconstruct the original information when enough shares are available.

This section presents an overview of the PASIS system and the SSSBIH system, and the difference of them. More details of the PASIS system can be found in [4] and [5].

## 2.1  SSSBIH Architecture

The SSSBIH architecture, shown in Figure 1, combines decentralized storage systems, data redundancy and encoding, and dynamic self-maintenance to achieve survivable information storage. It is similar with the PASIS architecture. Most of decentralized storage systems are the similar architecture.

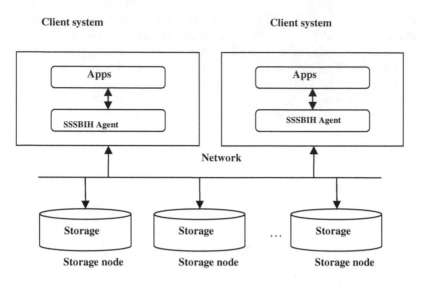

**Fig. 1.** SSSBIH architecture

## 2.2 SSSBIH System Components and Operation

Figure 3 presents the design of the SSSBIH Agent, which is derived from the PASIS Agent in figure 2.

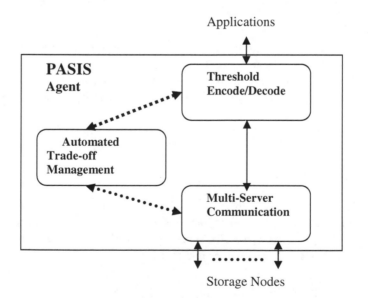

**Fig. 2.** PASIS agent

A SSSBIH system includes clients and servers. The servers, or storage nodes, provide persistent storage of shares; the clients provide all other aspects of SSSBIH functionality. Specifically, SSSBIH agents communicate with collections of SSSBIH servers to collect necessary shares and combine them using threshold schemes. A SSSBIH system uses threshold schemes to spread information across a decentralized collection of storage nodes. Client-side agents communicate with the collection of storage nodes to read and write information. The information hiding component is implemented in SSSBIH agents.

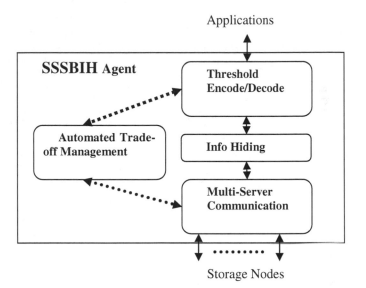

**Fig. 3.** SSSBIH agent

As with any distributed storage system, SSSBIH requires a mechanism that translates object names-for example, file names-to storage locations. A directory service shows the names of information objects stored in a SSSBIH system to the names of the shares. A share's name has two parts: the name of the storage node on which the share is located and the local name of the share on that storage node. A SSSBIH file system can embed the information needed for this translation in directory entries.

## 2.3   Automatic Trade-Off Management

For the SSSBIH architecture to be as effective as possible, it must make the full flexibility of threshold schemes available to clients. We believe this option requires automated selection of appropriate threshold schemes on a per-object basis. This selection should combine object characteristics and observations about the current system environment. For example, a SSSBIH client could use short secret sharing to store an object larger than a particular size, and conventional secret sharing to store smaller objects. The size that determines which threshold scheme to use could be a function of the object type, current system performance, or both. As another example, an object marked as archival for which availability and integrity are the most important storage characteristics-should use an extra-large n. For read write objects, increased write overhead makes large n values less desirable. Moreover, if the archival object is also marked as public-such as a Web page-the client should ignore confidentiality guarantees when selecting the threshold scheme.

System performance observations can also be used to dynamically improve per-request performance. For example, clients can request shares from the m storage nodes that have responded most quickly to their recent requests. Storage nodes can also help clients make these decisions by providing load information or by asking them to look elsewhere when long response times are expected.

## 3  Service Properties

Secure storage servers sometimes face undesirable requests from legitimate user accounts. These requests can originate from malicious users, rogue programs e.g., e-mail viruses run by unsuspecting users, intruders exploiting compromised user accounts, or even normal legitimate user. Real users may abuse their access to data on the implementation of intentional or unintentional tampering.

In particular, they can modify or delete their accessible data. Even after an intrusion has been detected and terminated, system administrators still face two difficult tasks: determining the damage caused by the intrusion and restoring the system to the state before the intrusion. Especially, the restoration often requires a significant amount of time, reduces the availability of the system, and may cause data losses. SSSBIH offers a solution to these problems.

This section describes the problems of client-side intrusion diagnosis and recovery, and designs storage method based on information hiding.

### 3.1  Intrusion Diagnosis and Recovery

After gaining access to a system, an intruder has several ways to attack it. Most intruders attempt to destroy evidence of their presence by erasing or modifying system log files. Many intruders also install back doors in the system, allowing them to gain access at will in the future. They may also install malicious software, read and modify sensitive files, or use the system as a platform for launching additional attacks and so on. Once an intrusion has been detected and terminated, the system administrator is left with two difficult tasks: diagnosis and recovery[8].

Diagnosis is challenging because intruders sometimes can compromise the "administrator" account on most operating systems, giving them full control over all resources. In particular, they can manipulate audit logs, file modification times, and tamper detection utilities. Recovery is difficult. In this section we will discuss intrusion diagnosis and recovery in detail, and in the next section we will describe how SSSBIH deals with them.

### 3.1.1  Diagnosis

If an intruder tampers a data segment on a storage node, then the information hiding management component will discover that the data segment has encountered distortion, similarly, if the corresponding information hidden on the client agent is tampered, the information hiding management component will also discover it. But, its restoration is the lag, only when some data object accessed then to this object carries on the detection.

Intrusion diagnosis consists of three phases: firstly, take out hidden information from a data segment. Then compare the hidden information with the one preserved on the client-side agent. Finally, according to the comparison result, determines whether the data segment is tampered and credible.

If the data segment is credible, we enter the normal data access stage. When we verify that all  data segments of a file are credible, we can combine them and form the whole file.  If it is incredible, we enter the data recovery stage.

### 3.1.2  Recovery

Recovery aims at restoring incredible data. Recovery data come from the redundant data which are saved on some storage nodes. In general, we update the incredible data segment by its credible backup. At first we should check whether this backup is credible using the method in Section 3.1.1, and we do the following recovery if it is.

If the hidden information of the data segment's backup is identical to that preserved in the client agent, we update the original data segment by the backup. Otherwise, it indicates that the hidden information of the original data segment is tampered, and we update it by the hidden information of the backup. In this way, we enhance security and survivability of a storage system.

### 3.2  SSSBIH Design

SSSBIH have two advantages: it safeguards secure data storage by information hiding technology, and it realizes data recovery using threshold schemes.

The following is the detailed explanation on it.

### 3.2.1  SSSBIH Agent Info Hiding Component

Figure 4 shows the work flow of the tamper detection and data recovery of SSSBIH agent Info Hiding component.

**Data pieces** refer to data segments after being processed by threshold schemes.
**Hiding Info** refers to performing the information hiding operation.
**Pieces in node** refer to storing the data segments in the storage node.
**Hidden info** in c refers to storing the hidden information on the client.
**Comp Hidden info** refers to comparing the hidden information which is from the data segment with the one preserved on the client.
**Credible pieces** refer to reconstructing the data object with all of its credible data segments.
**Data recovery** refers to the process in Section 3.1.2

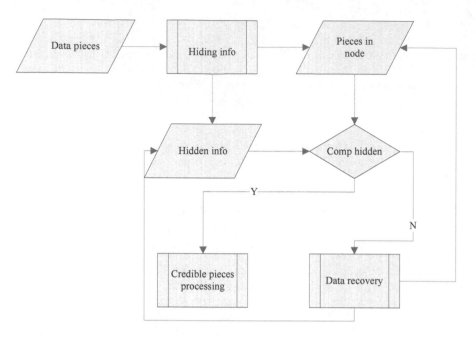

**Fig. 4.** SSSBIH agent Info Hiding elements

### 3.2.2  System Survivability

We assume a Byzantine fault model for servers, where a compromised node can behave arbitrarily.

In SSSBIH agent, Info Hiding component can enhance the survivability and the security of a storage system. This kind of safeguard stems from its mechanism to detect intrusion and to recover data. No matter an intruder modifies data segments or hidden information preserved in clients, the system can detect them and recover them by using redundant data.

This kind of recovery ability especially refers to the recovery of data segments distorted by malicious intruders.

If there is no hidden information in data segment, the above distortion is not easy to be detected.

### 3.3  Based on Information Hiding Storage Summary

Based on the information hiding function implemented in client agents, SSSBIH enhances survivability, security and credibility of a storage system.

For a data segment in many nodes redundancy storage with information hiding in it, can carry on the restoration effectively data. It can detect attacks to the data segment, and can carry on effective restoration to the attacked data segment.

Intrusion diagnosis consists of three phases: extract information which hidden in the original data, compare the hidden information with the one preserved on client agent, and determine whether the data segment is credible according to comparison result.

Incredible data segments can be recovered if its credible backups can be found.

The approach can solve the problem as the size and complexity of the data grows which history pool of old data versions method brings. To save the storage space in the storage node is the strongpoint. Another strongpoint is to omit the maintenance about using history the pool method to the old versions.

# 4  Algorithms

We denote the set of replicas by R and identify each replica using an integer in 0, 1 ...(R-1). For simplicity, we assume $|R|=3f+1$, where $f$ is the maximum number of replica that may be faulty. [7]

### Algorithm 1: Write hidden information

**Step1:** divide the data object into $|R|$ data segments using threshold schemes;

**Step2:** carry on the information hiding operation to each data segment, and hide a bit sequence $h$ in the data segment ($h$ can be time stamp, file name or serial number of the data segment);

**Step3:** save and manage the hidden information in client agent.

### Algorithm 2: Read and compare hidden information

**Step1:** for each data segment of the data object, the hidden information $h$ is extracted.

**Step2:** compare $h$ with the corresponding hidden information $h'$ preserved in client agent.

**Step3:** judge whether this data segment is credible based on the comparison result, i.e.,

> **If** $h$ and $h'$ are identical
> **Then** marking the data segment as credible
> **Else** recover the data segment
> **End If**
>  Reconstructing the data object by all of its credible data segments
> **End**

### Algorithm 3: Recover data

For the data segment which needs to be recovered,

**Step1:** get the backup of the data segment from other nodes

**Step2:** extract the hidden information ($h_1$) from the backup

**Step3:** compare the hidden information $h_1$ with the corresponding hidden information $h_1'$ preserved in client agent

**Step4:** judge this data segment to be credible

> **If** the hidden information $h_1$ and the corresponding one in client agent are consistent
> **Then** replace the data segment in the faulty node with the one that just read

**Else If** the hidden information $h_l$ and the corresponding one in client agent are inconsistent

**Then If** the hidden information $h_l$ is equal to $h$ that the hidden information to be gotten before

**Then** replace corresponding hidden information $h'$ that saved in client agent of $h$ or $h_l$ **Else** read the corresponding data segment in next node. Go to step2

**End If**

**Else** with the backup to rewrite this data object

**End If**

**End If**

**End**

In the following, we give an algorithm using DCT (discrete cosine transformation) to extract hidden information from a data segment.

**Algorithm 4: Extract hidden information**

Write the hidden bit $h_k$, k=1... J (m)

**Step1:** Divide the data segment into 8*8*8 size (512-byte) blocks.

**Step2:** Observe the relations between the two selected DCT coefficients (e.g., (a12) k and (a21) k) of a block and the next hidden bit. When need to invert the bit in hidden bit sequence, make the bit sequence can implicitly saved in a client agent, and make the bit and the selected coefficient constitutes one kind of specific relations. Said in detail, to all hidden bit $h_k$, k=1... J (m), makes following operation:

If ($h_k$ =1 and $(a_{12})$ $_k$ > $(a_{21})$ $_k$) or ($h_k$ =0 and $(a_{12})$ $_k$ < $(a_{21})$ $_k$, then the relations already satisfied, does not make any change to the bit of the bit sequence's. Otherwise, must invert the bit of the bit sequences. Generate a new bit sequence $h'$.

**Step3:** save the new bit sequence h' in client agent.

We can obtain the implicit hidden information by compares the two DCT coefficients in each block. Reading hidden information is similar to writing hidden information. And we omit the details here.

# 5   Simulation and Evaluation

In this section, we evaluate the performance and the capacity of SSSBIH via simulations, in comparison with the history pool of old data versions method [8].)

## 5.1   Simulation Settings

We carry out SSSBIH simulation experiments by the MALAB software, focusing on its effectiveness, performance, and the space size occupied.

### 5.1.1   Experimental Setup

Hardware Environment: CPU 2GHz AMD Athlon (tm) 64 Processor 3200 +, 512M memory, 64G hard drive.

Software Environment:
Operating System: Windows XP professional version 2002 service pack 2.
Simulation software: MALAB Version 7.4.0.287 (R2007a)
Experimental data: 6 data files, and file sizes are as follows:
43Kb, 142Kb, 1134Kb, 2243Kb, 3330Kb, 4442Kb.

### 5.1.2  Experimental Content

a. We divide each file into three data segments and write hidden information in it.

b. We verify the credibility of data segments of a file according to Section 3.1, and assemble them.

c. We deliberately tamper data segments or the hidden information preserved at client agents for testing the system detection and recovery functions.

## 5.2  Evaluation

### 5.2.1  Validity

The experiments prove that SSSBIH model is valid. First, the simulations show the system can successfully divide a file and write hidden information. Secondly, Assembling of data segments can be completed successfully. Last but not the least, when the data segments stored on storage nodes or the hidden information stored on client agents are tampered, the system can successfully detect them.

### 5.2.2  Performance

Table 1 shows the file size and the processing time of the experiments, including the time of file division and the time of file assembly.

**Table 1.** Experimental files size and processing time (seconds)

| Experiment number | File size | The time of file division | The time of file assembling |
|---|---|---|---|
| 1 | 43Kb | 0.0887 | 0.1017 |
| 2 | 142Kb | 0.1286 | 0.1190 |
| 3 | 1134Kb | 0.8626 | 0.7386 |
| 4 | 2243Kb | 1.5177 | 1.4028 |
| 5 | 3330Kb | 2.3773 | 2.0603 |
| 6 | 4442Kb | 2.8417 | 2.7149 |

Figure 5 shows visual display the relationships of the file size and processing time. It can be seen from the figure: split file processing time is slightly higher than the combination of the file, and between the file size and processing time are the basic linear.

As the hardware configuration increases and the program to be compiled, the model fully meets performance requirements.

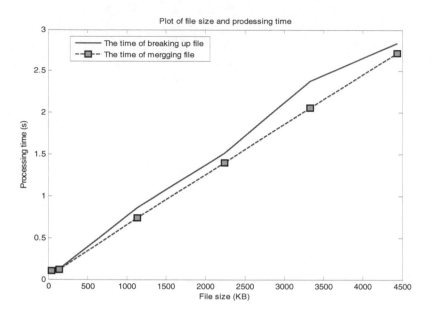

**Fig. 5.** SSSBIH Performance

### 5.2.3 Capacity

In comparison with the history pool method, SSSBIH can greatly save storage space because it does not allocate space for old-version data and it only use a small amount of space for hidden information at client agents. The storage space of hidden information is not more than 1/4096 of that of the data.

The size of hidden information is:

Hsize = (data segment size) / 4096. This is because according to Algorithm 4 each block (512 bytes) corresponds to one bit of hidden information.

Applying history pool method, a 10GB history pool can provide a detection window of between 50 and 470 days [8].

However, our method does not need to save historical data, and can save 20% of storage space in each storage node at least.

Therefore, if the amount of data stored does not exceed disk space limit, the detection window that our method provides, is unlimited.

## 6 The Advantage of SSSBIH Model

### 6.1 To Compare with PASIS Model

In PASIS model, even if operating systems and communication are totally normal, intruders also can tamper data segments without affecting the data reconstruction. This is one of faults of PASIS model. Data reconstructed by tampered segments will send wrong information. And wrong information often causes significant loss.

SSSBIH model can solve this problem with the combination of threshold schemes and information hiding. Using information hiding technology, we can detect data segments tampering. No matter invaders modify data in storage nodes or hidden information in client agent, the SSSBIH system can discover tampering with data.

In addition, hidden information implicitly stored in client, can effectively reduce the possibility that intruders maliciously tamper with hidden information and matched data segments at the same time. This also improves system's survivability.

## 6.2  To Compare with S4: Self-Securing Storage System

S4: self-securing storage system model adopts the history pool of old data versions method. It monitors tampering with data then uses the old data to recover the tampered data.

The history pool of old data versions method of S4 will produce large amounts of redundant data. And a lot of storage space will be occupied. However, the more amount of data increase, the more complex the maintenance for the old version is. That will make the system easily be intruded.

By using the information hiding method of SSSBIH model, we can prompt detect tampering with data. So the maintenance of the old versions will be eliminated, and storage nodes of storage space will be saved. Thus, it improves the security and survivability of system. On the other hand, S4 model's recovery is lagging behind the tamper with the data was found, while perhaps tampered data has been read by some users. In SSSBIH model, at the first stage of users' accessing, tampered data is found and recovered. So it can guarantee the read data is correct.

## 7  Summary

This paper proposes a survival storage system model based on the unification of threshold schemes and information hiding. It describes the client agent information hiding part's composition and the principle of work in detail and gives an information hiding algorithm based on the discrete cosine transformation for credible storage system.

This model has the merits of detecting tampering from internal intruders and saving storage space.

This paper mentioned the data storage can save more space of a storage node than the Self-securing storage. In this paper, we only present non-compression data storage and we will study compressed data storage in the future.

**Acknowledgment.** This research is supported by National Natural Science Foundation of China (Grant No. 60573035, 60743005).

This research is supported by The National Natural Science Foundation of China (No.60970143)

This research is also supported by the Key Project of Chinese Ministry of Education. (No.109016)

This research is supported by the third stage of "Project 211" of Central University of Finance and Economics.

# References

1. Stanton, P.: Securing Data in Storage: A Review of Current Research,
   `http://www.projects.ncassr.org/`
   `storage-ec/papers/stantontechnicalreport2004.pdf`
2. Chockler, G., Lynch, N.: Fault-Tolerant Distributed Storage. MIT Computer Science and Artificial Intelligence Laboratory (2004)
3. Suhail, M.A., Obaidat, M.S.: Digital Watermarking-Based DCT and JPEG Model. IEEE Transactions on Instrumentation and Measurement 52(5) (October 2003)
4. Gregory, R., et al.: Survivable Storage Systems. In: DARPA Information Survivability Conference and Exposition, Anaheim, CA, June 12-14, vol. 2, pp. 184–195. IEEE, Los Alamitos (2001)
5. Wylie, J.J., Bigrigg, M.W., Strunk, J.D., Ganger, G.R., Kılıççöte, H., Khosla, P.K.: Information Storage Systems, Computer, Carnegie Mellon University (August 2000)
6. Hayashi, D., Miyamoto, T., Doi, S., Kumagai, S.: Agents for Autonomous Distributed Secret Sharing Storage System. In: Proc. 2002 International Conference on Circuit/Systems Computers and Communications (2002),
   `http://www.kmutt.ac.th/itc2002/CD/pdf/17_07_45/WP1_PJ/6.pdf`
7. Goodson, G.R., Wylie, J.J., Ganger, G.R., Reiter, M.K.: Efficient Byzantine-tolerant erasure-coded storage. Appears in the Proceedings of the International Conference on Dependable Systems and Networks, Carnegie Mellon University (June 2004)
8. Strunk, J.D., Goodson, G.R., Scheinholtz, M.L., Soules, C.A.N., Ganger, G.R.: Self-Securing Storage:Protecting Data in Compromised Systems. In: Proceedings of the Foundations of Intrusion Tolerant Systems (OASIS 2003), Carnegie Mellon University. IEEE, Los Alamitos (2003)
9. Maheshwari, U., Vingralek, R., Shapiro, W.: How to Build a Trusted Database System on Untrusted Storage,
   `http://www.usenix.org/events/osdi00/full_papers/`
   `maheshwari/maheshwari.pdf`
10. Riedel, E., Kallahalla, M., Swaminathan, R.: A framework for evaluating storage system security. Appears in the Proceedings of the 1st Conference on File and Storage Technologies (FAST), Hewlett-Packard Laboratories, Palo Alto, California, Monterey, CA (January 2002)
11. Xu, L.: Hydra: A Platform for Survivable and Secure Data Storage Systems. In: Proceedings of the 2005 ACM workshop on Storage security and survivability, Virginia, USA, November 11 (2005)
12. Lakshmanan, S., Ahamad, M., Venkateswaran, H.: Responsive Security for Stored Data. IEEE Transactions On Parallel And Distributed Systems 14(9) (September 2003)
13. Zhu, J., Wang, C., Ma, J.: Intrusion-Tolerant Based Survivable Model of Database System. Chinese Journal of Electronics 14(3) (July 2005)

# Novel Communication System Selection Applying the AHP Algorithm in Heterogeneous Wireless Networks

Misato Sasaki, Akira Yamaguchi, Yuichi Imagaki,
Kosuke Yamazaki, and Toshinori Suzuki

KDDI R&D Laboratories Inc.
2-1-15 Ohara, Fujimino-shi, Saitama, 356-8502 Japan
{m-sasaki,yama,yu-imagaki,ko-yamazaki,suzu}@kddilabs.jp

**Abstract.** In this paper, we propose a novel selection policy for a communication system in heterogeneous wireless networks, which applies the analytic hierarchy process (AHP) algorithm by taking into account the mobility of the user terminals. In particular, the AHP algorithm has excellent characteristics of improving overall performance within the existing wireless systems. We certify the performance improvement by applying the AHP through software simulations under the conditions where Wi-Fi and WiMAX are used in the heterogeneous wireless networks.

**Keywords:** system selection policy, analytic hierarchy process (AHP), heterogeneous wireless networks, performance improvement.

## 1 Introduction

Considering the lack of frequency resources in wireless networks, it is quite important to efficiently use exiting wireless systems. One solution is to apply multiple systems and adequately select one system, which is generally called a heterogeneous wireless network. Cellular networks, such as WiMAX and cdma2000, support bandwidths over a wide geographical area. On the other hand, the Wi-Fi based on IEEE 802.11 provides bandwidths in a small coverage area of a few thousand square meters around a single access point. In heterogeneous wireless networks, a dynamic network selection mechanism must be developed to determine the appropriate radio access technology for specific situations.

This paper proposes a novel selection policy for a communication system in heterogeneous wireless networks, which applies the analytic hierarchy process (AHP) algorithm by taking into account the mobility of user terminals. In particular, the AHP algorithm offers the excellent characteristics of improving the overall performance within existing wireless systems. We certify the performance improvement by applying the AHP through software simulations under conditions where Wi-Fi and WiMAX are used for the heterogeneous wireless network.

Some related works have been reported on the selection of radio access in heterogeneous wireless networks. Multimode terminal measures the signal to interference noise ratio (SINR) of each radio access and converts them to effective SINR. Then, the

P. Sénac, M. Ott, and A. Seneviratne (Eds.): ICWCA 2011, LNICST 72, pp. 241–249, 2012.
© Institute for Computer Sciences, Social Informatics and Telecommunications Engineering 2012

radio access with maximum effective SINR is selected in [1]. However, the quality of the radio signal like SINR does not always present application quality. Position information can be used for radio selection in [2]. However, when a short distance radio access is included in the heterogeneous wireless network, it is difficult to determine the coverage area from the position. These are classified into single attribute decision making. Another approach is multi attribute decision making (MADM), which uses some parameters simultaneously. Various parameters such as receive signal strength Indication (RSSI), throughput, delay, pricing rules, and user preferences can be treated as input parameters for MADM in [3]. Fuzzy logic and neural networks are proposed for radio selection in [4]. One vital approach is the AHP proposed in [5] [6]. In such work, the effect of AHP is evaluated for only one terminal environment. From a realistic viewpoint, in order to accurately evaluate the selection algorithm, an area simulation with multiple terminals is mandatory. We focus on this point and introduce the area simulation results in this paper.

The rest of the paper is organized as follows: the system selection policy is introduced in Section 2. The AHP-based system selection policy and the simulation model, condition, and results are described in Section 3. Finally, Section 4 concludes this paper.

## 2   System Selection Policy in Heterogeneous Wireless Networks

### 2.1   Outline of System Selection Policy

The outline of the system selection policy is shown in Figure 1. The proposed system selection policy works by considering multiple user terminals, which move around the Wi-Fi and WiMAX areas. To select a wireless system, the user terminal's mobility and the result of AHP calculation are used. One of the branches uses AHP calculation to select the communication system. The processes surrounded by the dotted line are described in Section 2.2 and Section 3, respectively.

To realize the proposed system selection policy for actual networks, we decided that the system architecture would consist of a user terminal, sensing node, and location service server as shown in Figure 2. The proposed policy is installed on the user terminal, and this cooperates with the location service server to efficiently search the wireless network. This works on a heterogeneous wireless network where each WiMAX BS (base station) cell overlays several Wi-Fi hot-spot APs (access points).

The sensing node with a GPS module scans the quality information of the Wi-Fi and periodically uploads the information with location information to the location service server. The location service server stores the quality information of the sensing node with location information and holds the table of the Wi-Fi AP location. By using this information, the location service server estimates the position of the AP. The positioning information of the user terminal acquired by the GPS module will be uploaded to the location service server. Then, the location service server will query the database for the corresponding area and reply to the user terminal with the AP allocation information. By receiving the information, the user terminal discovers the potential reachable wireless networks. After discovering the potential reachable wireless networks, the user terminal searches for an appropriate Wi-Fi AP.

**Section 2.2**

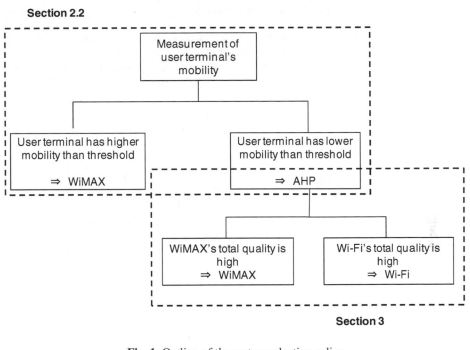

Measurement of
user terminal's
mobility

User terminal has higher
mobility than threshold

⇒ WiMAX

User terminal has lower
mobility than threshold

⇒ AHP

WiMAX's total quality is
high
⇒ WiMAX

Wi-Fi's total quality is
high
⇒ Wi-Fi

**Section 3**

**Fig. 1.** Outline of the system selection policy

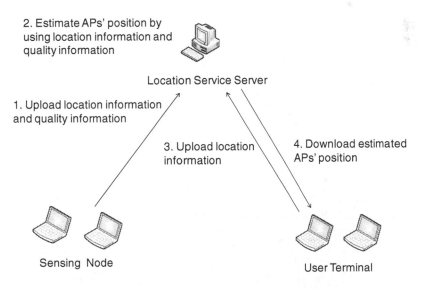

2. Estimate APs' position by
using location information and
quality information

Location Service Server

1. Upload location information
and quality information

3. Upload location
information

4. Download estimated
APs' position

Sensing Node

User Terminal

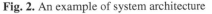

**Fig. 2.** An example of system architecture

## 2.2  Consideration of User Terminal's Mobility

In the selection policy we propose, the user terminal with a global positioning system (GPS) module measures mobility. To determine the access communication system, the user's mobility is considered. When the user terminal has higher mobility than the threshold for a certain period, WiMAX is selected because WiMAX coverage is usually broader than Wi-Fi. When the user terminal has lower mobility than the threshold during a certain period, the access communication system will be determined by the calculation of the AHP. The mobility threshold of the user terminal is considered higher than walking speed.

# 3  Application of AHP Algorithm

## 3.1  Principle of AHP and Its Feature

This section introduces the AHP-based approach to provide a more efficient system selection solution for user terminals that connect to WiMAX and Wi-Fi networks.

AHP solves complicated tasks by decomposing into a hierarchy of simpler sub-portions. The sub-portions are usually called decision factors and weighted according to relative importance. The solution is given as the bottom decision. AHP selects the solution with the greatest synthesized weight.

Structuring a task as a hierarchy of multiple criteria is the first step in implementing AHP. The task is placed at the top of the hierarchy. The decision factors of the task are identified within the hierarchy. The solution will be placed at the bottom of the hierarchy. In this paper, the task requiring a solution is to make the decision to use Wi-Fi or WiMAX. The decision factors are uplink data rate, round-trip time (RTT), RSSI, and power consumption. The hierarchy for the selection of the wireless system is established as shown in Figure 3.

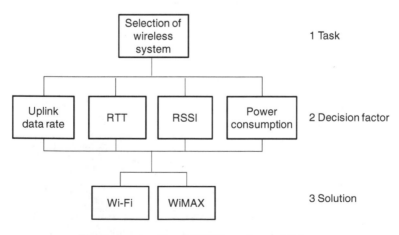

**Fig. 3.** An example of AHP hierarchy establishment

An example of the AHP matrices is shown in Table 1. The comparison scale uses a range of 1 to 9, each representing entries as follows: 1: Equally important, 3: Moderately more important, 5: Strongly more important, 7: Very strongly more important, 9: Extremely more important. The elements of the AHP matrices might equal 1, 3, 5, 7, 9, 1/3, 1/5, 1/7, 1/9. The elements in Table 1 represent that any delay is considered *very strongly more important* than others with regard to traffic. Each pair in the comparison matrix is solved using the geometric mean method. The weights determined using the geometric mean method and the resulting weights are shown in Table 1. The overall score of an alternative network selection is determined by the score measured in an actual network environment, and the score is computed as the weighted sum of the attribute values.

**Table 1.** Example of AHP matrices for each traffic class

|  | UL data rate | RTT | RSSI | Power consumption | Geometric Mean | Importance weights |
|---|---|---|---|---|---|---|
| UL data rate | 1 | 1/9 | 1 | 1 | 0.5773 | 0.0833 |
| RTT | 9 | 1 | 9 | 9 | 5.1962 | 0.7500 |
| RSSI | 1 | 1/9 | 1 | 1 | 0.5773 | 0.0833 |
| Power consumption | 1 | 1/9 | 1 | 1 | 0.5773 | 0.0833 |

Different applications may assign different weights to a particular factor. For example, the importance of RTT is different in real time applications compared to non-real time applications, so the applications may assign different weights. The AHP calculation runs periodically to detect changes in the wireless conditions. When the user terminal discovers a wireless network with higher utility than the current network, the user terminal will change the network.

## 3.2 Simulation for AHP Algorithm

### 3.2.1 Simulation Model

In this section, we investigate the sensitivity of using quality information in the calculation of AHP for system selection. To see the superiority of selecting the system via AHP, we conducted a simulation. In the simulation, we considered an area where there were three Wi-Fi APs and a WiMAX BS, as shown in Figure 4. The WiMAX BS was placed in the center, and the Wi-Fi APs were placed at distances of 100 m from the WiMAX BS at 120 degrees. In the simulation scenario, dual mode terminals, which were transferring a file, were located at random within a distance of 400 m from the WiMAX BS. The numbers of dual mode terminals were 50, and they were all settled as static.

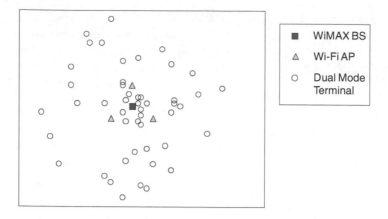

**Fig. 4.** Example of node's allocation in simulation

### 3.2.2 Simulation Condition

The condition of the simulation is shown in Table 2. The Wi-Fi and WiMAX frequencies were 2.4 GHz and 2.6 GHz, respectively. The channels of the three Wi-Fi APs were the same. To imitate the movement of the user terminals, the propagation condition for WiMAX, shadowing effect of 4 dB, and the Rayleigh fading effect of 3.6 km/h were given as the fading characteristics as shown in Table 2. The Wi-Fi radio only influenced the distance characteristics. The dual mode user terminal transferred data on average of 2 MB with a maximum of 5 MB. The simulation time was 40 seconds, and the data were taken 10 times. This was done by changing the position of the dual mode terminal.

The AHP matrices used in the simulation are shown in Table 3. The decision factors were uplink throughput and RTT. The importance weights for the uplink throughput and RTT were 0.5, respectively. The uplink throughput and RTT of the simulation were taken every 10 seconds and used for the calculation to select the wireless system.

To investigate the effect of using quality information with AHP, we compared the average application throughput. To compare throughput, four modes were tested as shown in Table 4. The conventional mode is a conventional policy used in smartphones.

**Table 2.** Simulation conditions

| Condition | Wi-Fi | WiMAX |
|---|---|---|
| Frequency | 2.4GHz | 2.6GHz |
| Shadowing | Not considered | 4 dB |
| Rayleigh | Not considered | 3.6km/h |

**Table 3.** The AHP matrices used in the simulation

|  | Uplink throughput | RTT | Geometric mean | Importance weights |
|---|---|---|---|---|
| Uplink throughput | 1 | 1 | 1 | 0.5 |
| RTT | 1 | 1 | 1 | 0.5 |

**Table 4.** Four types of system selection modes

| Mode | System selection policy |
|---|---|
| Conventional | Select Wi-Fi whenever it is available for use |
| AHP | Select wireless system by AHP calculation |
| Wi-Fi | Select Wi-Fi which is only available |
| WiMAX | Select WiMAX which is only available |

This mode selects Wi-Fi as the wireless system whenever it is available for use. The AHP mode selects wireless systems using AHP. The Wi-Fi mode selects Wi-Fi only, which is the only available system. The WiMAX mode selects WiMAX only, which is the only available system.

### 3.2.3 Simulation Results

Figure 5 shows the average cumulative distribution function (CDF) application throughput rate of 10%, 50%, and 90% under four different system selection modes. Conventional and Wi-Fi modes take almost the same rate. In conventional mode, it is assumed that all dual mode user terminals selected Wi-Fi. The WiMAX mode shows a rate 1.64 times higher, in a CDF of 90%, compared to the conventional mode. The AHP mode shows a rate 1.33 times higher in a CDF of 50% compared to the conventional mode. And in a CDF of 90%, the AHP mode shows rates 2.37 times higher compared to the conventional mode and 1.4 times higher compared to the WiMAX mode. This shows that the AHP mode, which selects wireless systems using AHP, enables higher throughput than the conventional, Wi-Fi, and WiMAX modes.

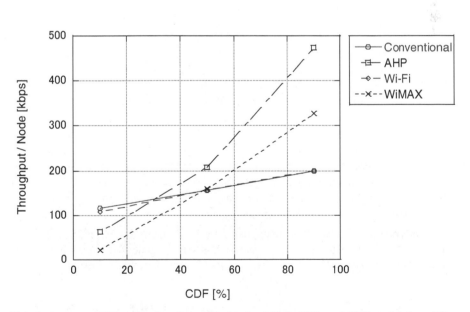

**Fig. 5.** Average CDF application throughput rate of 10%, 50%, and 90% under four different system selection modes

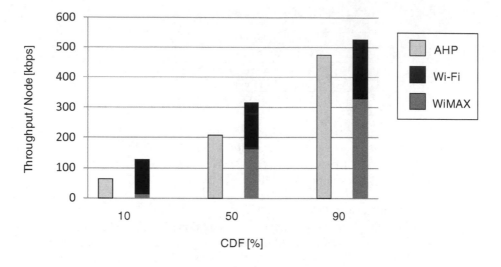

**Fig. 6.** Comparison of the total application throughput of Wi-Fi and WiMAX modes with AHP mode

Figure 6 shows the comparison of the total application throughput of Wi-Fi and WiMAX modes with the AHP mode. The AHP mode's CDF of 90% average rates is almost 90 percent, compared to the total rate of Wi-Fi and WiMAX modes. The AHP mode's simulation throughput rate is only slightly lower than the simply added rate of Wi-Fi and WiMAX. This shows that the proposed communication system selection policy using AHP is effective.

## 4   Conclusions

In this paper, we proposed an AHP-based system selection policy for heterogeneous wireless networks that hold Wi-Fi and WiMAX. The proposed system selection policy used AHP by calculating the weights of the various traffic quality parameters. We conducted a software simulation that used uplink throughput and RTT as attributes. The simulation results showed that the proposed policy using AHP provided higher throughput than the conventional policy that chose Wi-Fi when available. For future work, we will conduct a software simulation using other quality information for AHP calculation under various models and conditions.

**Acknowledgments.** This work was supported by funds from the Ministry of Internal Affairs and Communications. This research has been conducted under a research contract organized by the Ministry of Internal Affairs and Communications, Japan.

# References

1. Yang, K., Gondal, I., Qui, B., Dooley, L.S.: Combined SINR Based Vertical Handoff Algorithm for Next Generation Heterogeneous Wireless Networks. In: Global Telecommunications Conference, pp. 4483–4487 (2007)
2. He, F., Wang, F.: Position aware vertical handoff decision algorithm in heterogeneous wireless networks. In: International Conference on Wireless Communications, pp. 1–5 (2008)
3. Sur, A., Sicker, D.C.: Multi Layer Rules Based Framework for Vertical Handoff. In: International Conference on Broadband Networks, vol. 1, pp. 571–580 (2005)
4. Stoyanova, M., Mahonen, P.: Algorithmic Approaches for Vertical Handoff in Heterogeneous Wireless Environment. In: Wireless Communications and Networking Conference, pp. 3780–3785 (2007)
5. Song, Q., Jamalipour, A.: A Network Selection Mechanism for Next Generation Networks. In: International Conference on Communications, vol. 2, pp. 1418–1422 (2005)
6. Guan, X., Tang, R., Bai, S., Yoon, D.: Enhanced Application-Driven Vertical Handoff Decision Scheme for 4G Wireless Networks. In: International Conference on Wireless Communications, pp. 1771–1774 (2007)

# Modeling and Analysis of MU-CoMP HARQ in 3GPP LTE System Level Simulation

Yuan Gao[1], Yi Li[1], HongYi Yu[2], and ShiHai Gao[2]

[1] State Key Laboratory on Microwave and Digital Communications
National Laboratory for Information Science and Technology,
Tsinghua University, Beijing, China
[2] Department of Communication Engineering
Information Science and Technology Institute, Zhengzhou, China
{yuangao08,lyi09}@mails.tsinghua.edu.cn

**Abstract.** In modern wireless mobile networks such as LTE and LTE-Advanced, performance of cell-edge users is in greet need to be improved. Coordinated multipoint transmission/reception is raised to solve the problem in 3GPP # bis 53meeting. In this paper, we present our design of (Multi-User) MU-HARQ transmission scheme in CoMP where previous studies on (Single-User) SU-CoMP HARQ have already been submitted to ChinaCom 2011. In our design, a newly MU-HARQ transmission method is presented which will help improve target user throughput and total cell throughput under some conditions. This result is significant for 3GPP proposals.

**Keywords:** multi-user, CoMP, HARQ, LTE System Level Simulation.

## 1 Introduction

Coordinated multipoint transmission/reception (CoMP) is raised to increase cell-edge user performance and spectrum efficiency in common cellular networks [1].There is two different types of CoMP: Joint Processing (JP) and Coordinated Beamforming/ Scheduling (CB/CS). However, study and standardization of CoMP are freezed by 3GPP in around 2009 [2], further studies about physical features and performance evaluations have nearly stopped. In 3GPP specifications and proposals of release 10, conclusions and simulation results about CoMP-JP and CoMP-CB/CS have been accepted by 3GPP members [3].

In this paper, we studied and designed the HARQ scheme in CoMP transmission which has not reached any conclusions in 3GPP discussions. As we all know that HARQ is mentioned firstly in wired communications to ensure the reliability of transmission [4]. Same in wireless communications, HARQ is still important for the wireless fading channel makes the reliable transmission harder to achieve. In CoMP scenario, HARQ is more complex than non-CoMP scenario and the design of CoMP-HARQ is very important to keep the integrality of CoMP system. We mainly focus on CoMP-JP in this paper.

P. Sénac, M. Ott, and A. Seneviratne (Eds.): ICWCA 2011, LNICST 72, pp. 250–264, 2012.
© Institute for Computer Sciences, Social Informatics and Telecommunications Engineering 2012

This paper is organized as follows. In part 2, we introduce the system model of MU-CoMP. In part 3, our design of CoMP –HARQ process is presented and analyzed. In part 4, we present the simulation result under our Matlab-based 3GPP LTE system level simulator, brief introduction of the simulator is also introduced in this part. Conclusions are drawn in part 5.

## 2  System Model

In this part, system model of CoMP-JP is presented. We consider each user may have a service cell which is determined by physical attach, and other cooperative cells by system decision. Different from CoMP-JP, CoMP-CB/CS mode only allow one service link between user and target eNodeBs. This type of CoMP will reduce interference from adjacent cells using beamforming or coordinated scheduling to allocate time-frequency blocks.

At user side, CoMP-JP mode allows packets from both service cell and cooperative cells. Fig 1 shows a typical scenario of CoMP-JP and different colors indicate different cells. In original research of intra-site CoMP-JP, cooperative areas are limited to same cell, just like the same color area in figure 1. In 3GPP release 10, cooperative area has been extended to inter-site [5] just like the dotted area in figure 1.

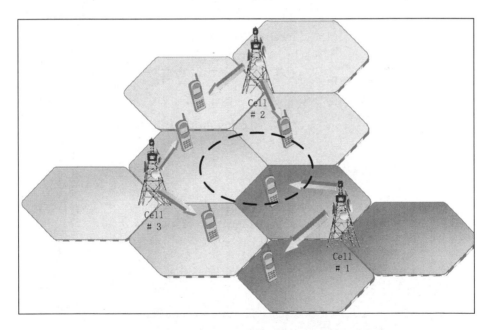

**Fig. 1.** A Typical System Scenario of CoMP

Sorted by coherence of the received signal, we will discuss coherent and non-coherent CoMP-JP. In coherent mode, we consider global codebook is used and same data packet is send through service cell and cooperative cell at the same time. The receiving vector can be described as follows:

$$r(k,l) = H(k,l)Us(k,l) + n(k,l).$$ (1)

Where $k$ the index of OFDM [7] is symbol in resource blocks and $l$ is the index of OFDM symbols. Consider there are $M$ transmit antennas and $N$ receive antennas, $H$ is the $N \times M$ channel matrix, $U$ is the $M \times 1$ precoding matrix and $n$ is the $N \times 1$ Additive White Gaussian Noise.

## 2.1  Coherent CoMP-JP

First we talk about the single user scenario. In this mode, both service cell and cooperative cell can evaluate service channel and cooperative channels and data packet is transmitted through both service and cooperative cells. This scenario is shown in the full line area shown in fig 2.

Received signal of target user is:

$$r(k,l) = (H_0(k,l)\ H_1(k,l))\binom{U_0}{U_1}s(k,l) + n(k,l).$$ (2)

After the commonly used MMSE receiver [7], the prediction of the received signal is:

$$\hat{r}(k,l) = W(k,l) \times (H_0(k,l)\ H_1(k,l))\binom{U_0}{U_1} \times s(k,l) + W(k,l) \times n(k,l)$$ (3)

The MMSE detector $W(k,l)$ is calculated using the equation below:

$$W(k,l) = \binom{U_0}{U_1}^H (H_0(k,l)\ H_1(k,l))^H (k,l) \times$$

$$\left\{ (H_0(k,l)\ H_1(k,l))(k,l)\binom{U_0}{U_1}\binom{U_0}{U_1}^H (H_0(k,l)\ H_1(k,l))^H (k,l) + \frac{R_n}{\sigma^2} \right\}^{-1}$$ (4)

The self-correlation matrix of Gaussian noise $R_n$ is calculated below:

$$R_n = E[n(k,l)n^H(k,l)]$$ (5)

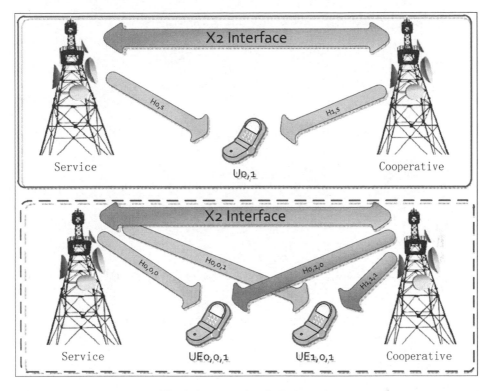

**Fig. 2.** Coherent CoMP-JP Scenario

The Signal to interface plus noise ratio (SINR) of the received signal is given in formula (6).

$$SINR(k,l) = \frac{\sigma^2 \, |W(k,l)(H_0(k,l) \; H_1(k,l))(\begin{smallmatrix} U_0 \\ U_1 \end{smallmatrix})|^2}{W(k,l)R_n W^H(k,l)} \tag{6}$$

Expanded to multi-user scenario of coherent CoMP-JP signal model as shown in dashed line area in fig 2, users are served by both service cells and cooperative cells. Both UE0 and UE1 can estimate service channels and cooperative channels and the global precoding scheme is determined by cells. For the $i$-th (i=0, 1) user, the received signal can be described as:

$$r(k,l) = (H_{i,0}(k,l) \quad H_{i,1}(k,l)) \times (\begin{smallmatrix} U_{0,0} \\ U_{0,1} \end{smallmatrix}) \times s_0(k,l) + $$
$$(H_{i,0}(k,l) \quad H_{i,1}(k,l)) \times (\begin{smallmatrix} U_{1,0} \\ U_{1,1} \end{smallmatrix}) \times s_1(k,l) + n(k,l) \tag{7}$$

After the MMSE detector, the prediction of the signal is:

$$\hat{r}_i(k,l) = W_{i,0,1}(k,l) \times$$

$$[(H_{i,0}(k,l) \quad H_{i,1}(k,l)) \times (\begin{matrix} U_{0,0} \\ U_{0,1} \end{matrix}) \times s_0(k,l) +$$

$$(H_{i,0}(k,l) \quad H_{i,1}(k,l)) \times (\begin{matrix} U_{1,0} \\ U_{1,1} \end{matrix}) \times s_1(k,l) + n(k,l)] \tag{8}$$

The MMSE detector $W_{i,0,1}(k,l)$ is calculated in formula (9):

$$W_1(k,l) = (\begin{matrix} U_{i,0} \\ U_{i,1} \end{matrix})^H (H_{i,0}(k,l) \quad H_{i,1}(k,l))^H \times$$

$$\left\{ \begin{matrix} (H_{i,0}(k,l) \quad H_{i,1}(k,l))(\begin{matrix} U_{0,0} \\ U_{0,1} \end{matrix})(\begin{matrix} U_{0,0} \\ U_{0,1} \end{matrix})^H (H_{i,0}(k,l) \quad H_{i,1}(k,l))^H + \\ (H_{i,0}(k,l) \quad H_{i,1}(k,l))(\begin{matrix} U_{1,0} \\ U_{1,1} \end{matrix})(\begin{matrix} U_{1,0} \\ U_{1,1} \end{matrix})^H (H_{i,0}(k,l) \quad H_{i,1}(k,l))^H + \dfrac{R_n}{\sigma^2} \end{matrix} \right\}^{-1} \tag{9}$$

The received SINR is:

$$SINR_i(k,l) =$$

$$\frac{\sigma^2 \mid W_{i,0,1}(k,l)H_{i,0,1}(k,l)(\begin{matrix} U_{i,0} \\ U_{i,1} \end{matrix}) \mid^2}{\sigma^2 \mid W_{i,0,1}(k,l)H_{i,0,1}(k,l)(\begin{matrix} U_{1-i,0} \\ U_{1-i,1} \end{matrix}) \mid^2 + W_{i,0,1}(k,l)R_n W_{i,0,1}{}^H(k,l)} \tag{10}$$

From previous analysis of coherent CoMP-JP, we can infer that the macro diversity gain will help improve throughput of cell-edge user, and HARQ design may help reduce retransmission times to improve user performance. If delay in X2 interface [8] is introduced, these set of method may have problem in transmitting both control signal and data packets.

## 2.2 Non-coherent CoMP-JP

The main difference between coherent and non-coherent is that data packets from service cell and cooperative cells are different at the same time. In non-coherent mode, data packet, codebook and precoding matrix are different from service cells and cooperative cells and in coherent mode, precoding matrix is designed jointly in transmit terminals.

Same in coherent mode, we will show this problem from single user to multi-user. The scenario is shown in fig 3. Single user mode is shown in full line area of fig 3.

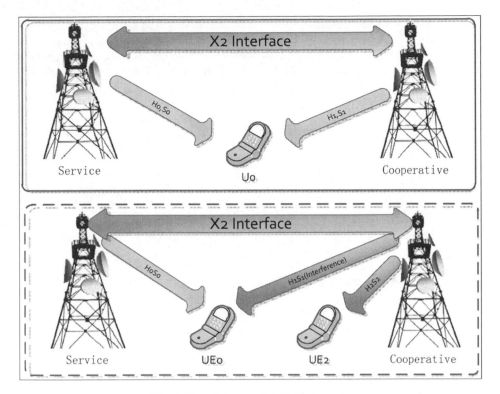

**Fig. 3.** Non-Coherent CoMP-JP Scenario

The received signal after MMSE detector can be described as:

$$\hat{r}_i(k,l) = W_i(k,l) \times \{H_0(k,l) \times U_0 \times s_0(k,l) + \\ H_1(k,l) \times U_1 \times s_1(k,l) + n(k,l)\} \tag{11}$$

Where $W_i(k,l)$ is the MMSE detector and can be described as:

$$W_i(k,l) = U_i^H H_i^H(k,l) \times \\ \begin{Bmatrix} H_0(k,l)U_0 U_0^H H_0^H(k,l) + \\ H_1(k,l)U_1 U_1^H H_1^H(k,l) + \dfrac{R_n}{\sigma^2} \end{Bmatrix}^{-1} \tag{12}$$

So the SINR of data packet $s_i$ is calculated using formula (13):

$$r_i(k,l) = \frac{\sigma^2 \mid W_i(k,l)H_i(k,l)U_i \mid^2}{\sigma^2 \mid W_i(k,l)H_{1-i}(k,l)U_{1-i} \mid^2 + W_i(k,l)R_n W_i^H(k,l)} \tag{13}$$

Expand the scenario to multi-user shown in dashed line area of fig 3, we consider that service cell and cooperative cells serves different users and send different data packet using their own codebook. UE0 can estimate service channel and cooperative channel but UE2 in cooperative cell can only get its own channel. In this mode, the estimation of received signal is given in formula (14).

$$\hat{r}(k,l) = W_0(k,l) \times$$
$$\{H_0(k,l) \times U_0 \times s_0(k,l) + H_1(k,l) \times U_1 \times s_1(k,l) + n(k,l)\}$$
(14)

The MMSE detector $W_0(k,l)$ can be described as:

$$W_1(k,l) = U_0{}^H H_0{}^H(k,l) \times \left\{ \begin{array}{l} H_0(k,l)U_0U_0{}^H H_0{}^H(k,l) + \\ H_1(k,l)U_1U_1{}^H H_1{}^H(k,l) + \dfrac{R_n}{\sigma^2} \end{array} \right\}^{-1}$$
(15)

Easily we can get the SINR of the data which is shown in formula (16).

$$SINR(k,l) = \frac{\sigma^2 |W_0(k,l)H_0(k,l)U_0|^2}{\sigma^2 |W_0(k,l)H_1(k,l)U_1|^2 + W_0(k,l)R_n W_0{}^H(k,l)}$$
(16)

After the detailed analysis of CoMP-JP scenario, we can infer that cooperative transmission in both coherent and non-coherent mode will have diversity gain and improvement of throughput. The difference is that data transmitted in X2 interface. In this paper, we do not consider delays and capacity of X2 interface.

## 3   Design of Multi-user CoMP-HARQ

Received SINR of data packets is always used to design link transmission scheme, the received SINR is also the infrastructure of our MU CoMP-HARQ. In previous work of 3GPP release 10 [9], design for HARQ process hasn't reached any conclusions. In standardization of 3GPP release 11, influence of CoMP-HARQ and design of HARQ will be studied. We raised our design of MU CoMP-HARQ in this paper, the design will help improve performance and reduce Block Error Rate (BLER).

Previous work of SU CoMP-HARQ shows that the retransmission link selection scheme can improve average throughput and reduce retransmission times, this part of work has been submitted to ChinaCom 2011 conference [10]. In this paper, we extend the scenario to multi-user.

In 3GPP LTE transmission system, HARQ packet is scheduled before data packet. Commonly, HARQ packet is not treated specially. Consider that HARQ packet contains redundant information for previous error packet which needs to be demodulated immediately, so the less retransmission times it takes the better performance user will get.

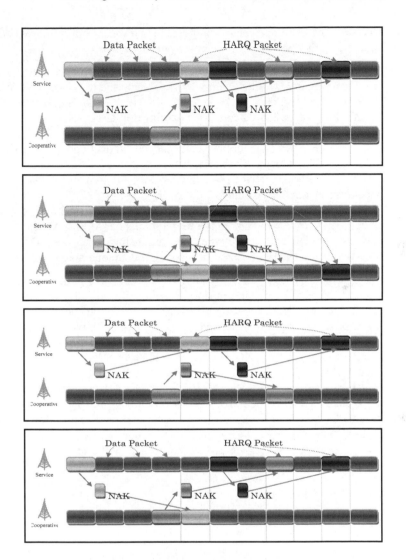

**Fig. 4.** Scenarios of CoMP-HARQ

Figure 4 shows four different policies of CoMP-HARQ. From top to bottom, they are:

1. Retransmission from only service cell
2. Retransmission from only cooperative cells
3. Retransmission from where error packet from
4. Retransmission from best link (e.g. best receive SINR)

Theoretically, HARQ is an auxiliary transmission function used to ensure probability of success and reduce BLER. The four different policies cause different performance in 3GPP LTE system level simulation. Referring to commonly dynamic cell selection (DCS) scheme in CoMP-JP, we expand the use of DCS in CoMP-HARQ.

After deep study of CoMP-JP related proposals [11], we introduce our MU-CoMP process. The process of CoMP-HARQ is shown below:

1.  Target cell-edge user measure Reference Signal Receiving Power( RSRP) or Reference Signal Receiving Quality (RSRQ) and send to service eNodeB;
2.  According to RSRP/RSRQ and CQI/PMI, eNodeB decide CoMP transmission points and calculate scheduling for target user and decide the best retransmission link for HARQ packet;
3.  Service eNodeB send scheduling, data packet, HARQ and control signal to cooperative cells through X2 interface;
4.  In given TTI, servicing eNodeB send downlink assignment to CoMP UE and cooperative eNodeB send data to CoMP UE;
5.  After getting all required information from servicing eNodeB and cooperative eNodeB, CoMP UE will demodulate signal to decide ACK/NACK;
6.  Servicing eNodeB will decide whether a retransmission is needed, if needed, go to step 2 and decide a best retransmission link among all existed links

Note that the downlink HARQ is a nonsynchronous process, so both data packet and retransmission packet have similar scheduling policy. In step 2, we mention that eNodeB will decide the best transmission link for retransmission packet. In this paper, the best link is chosen using uplink feedback of target user. In part 2, both coherent and non-coherent scenario, user will be able to calculate received SINR according to formula (6) (10) (13) (16), and eNodeB will scheduler CoMP UE using the 'out-of-date' information.

In a very short time interval such as a timeslot in LTE system, the large scale information of channel such as path loss and shadow fading nearly remain stationary [12] and the small scale information such as Doppler and multi path information will change fast. In a statistical result show in next part, dynamic link selection for HARQ packet is a delay-sensitive process, delay of X2 interface will affect the performance. There may also some other policies of HARQ design that will work better than DCS-HARQ.

## 4  Simulation and Analysis

Under the widely used 3GPP LTE system level simulation [13], we performed our DCS HARQ design in MU-CoMP. In this part, we mainly performed two parts of work. Firstly, we make a comparison of DCS-HARQ and non DCS-HARQ; secondly, we studied the influence of delay in X2 interface.

### 4.1  Brief Introduction of Our Matlab-Based LTE System Level Simulator

In order to verify and evaluate physical concepts and new methods in 3GPP LTE system, 3GPP has established a set of standards and simulation scenarios to ensure the comparability of the simulation. In most 3GPP members, the LTE system and link level simulator are secured as commercial secrets. In our Matlab-based simulator [15], there are three basic functional parts. In initialize part, parameters of eNodeBs, UEs and channel matrix are generated; in transmission part, abstract of system level transmission is performed, eNodeBs will schedule each attached users. In CoMP mode, the cycle control sub function decides CoMP points of current TTI and performs link transmission; in evaluation part, output of all results is gathered.

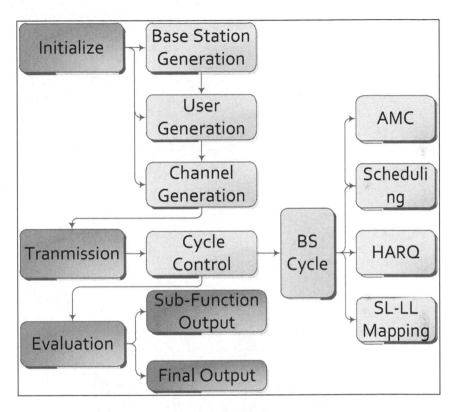

**Fig. 5.** Process of our LTE System Level Simulation

## 4.2  Compare of DCS-HARQ and Non DCS-HARQ

In this part, we compare the average retransmission times and average throughput of target users and CoMP cells. Simulation assumptions and parameters are listed in table 1.

In each simulation cycle, we consider the 10% users who have the worst SINR working in CoMP mode. Statistically, these set of users always located at the edge of the cell. We will trace one of them that will represent the performance of these set of users. In order to get a statistical result, we repeated the simulation for 1000 times and get the average performance. Note that the random seed to generate the channel changed in every Monte Carlo simulation.

**Table 1.** Simulation Assumptions and Parameters

| Name | Value |
| --- | --- |
| Channel Model | SCME, urban macro |
| Carrier Frequency | 2GHz |
| Tx Antenna | 2 |
| Rx Antenna | 2 |
| Transmit Power | 46dBm |
| BS Number | 19 |
| Sectors per BS | 3 |
| Users in Simulation | dynamic |
| Bandwidth | 10MHz |
| SL to LL Mapping | EESM |
| Inter-site distance | 500m |
| Pathloss Model | $L = 128.1+37.6\log10(R)$ |
| Shadowing Std | 4dB |
| HARQ Scheme | CC |
| AMC Table | QPSK(R ={1/8, 1/7, 1/6, 1/5, 1/4, 1/3, 2/5, 1/2, 3/5, 2/3, 3/4, 4/5}) 16QAM(R = {1/2, 3/5, 2/3, 3/4, 4/5}) |
| UE Sig Processing | MMSE |
| Max Re-trans times | 4 |
| UE Speed | 3KM/h |
| Channel Estimation | Ideal |
| Simulation TTIs | 1000 |

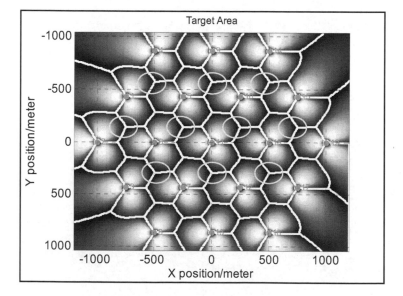

**Fig. 6.** Simulation Target Area [10]

Figure 6 represents the simulation scenario of our assumption. Different in 3GPP release 10, we mainly focus on inter-site CoMP which may be discussed in 3GPP release 11 [15].The green dots with different number indicate center of eNodeBs, yellow circle represents our target areas. Users located in the yellow area will receive low SINR in very high probability. In this part, we consider that there is no delay in X2 interface.

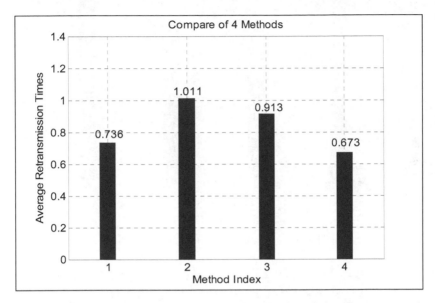

**Fig. 7.** Compare of Target User Average Retransmission Times

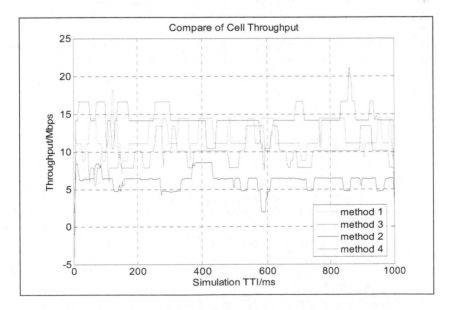

**Fig. 8.** Compare of Total CoMP Cell Throughput of One Simulation

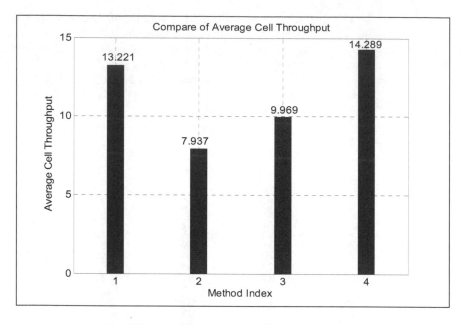

**Fig. 9.** Compare of Total Cell Throughput

Figure 7~9 shows the simulation result under our Matlab-based simulator. The four different method of CoMP-HARQ are described in figure 4. In figure 7, we compare the average retransmission times of target CoMP user. In one complete simulation, we average the retransmission times of all 1000 timeslots and repeat the same experiment 1000 times to get the final average result. It is obvious that our DCS-HARQ method can reduce retransmission times than other three methods. Figure 8 and 9 are the total CoMP cell throughput. Corroborating to figure 7, we can see that the DCS-HARQ will increase total cell throughput. The gain is from chase combine of HARQ process. These set of simulation results proved that our DCS-HARQ method can increase cell throughput in statistical point of view with merely no other costs. This is a very meaningful result for 3GPP release 11 proposals.

## 4.3   Analysis of Delay in X2 Interface

In this part, we present our simulation result in consideration of delays in X2 interface. The existed result of delays in X2 interface shows that delays will affect performance of CoMP. The simulation assumptions and parameters are the same in part 4.2.

We compare the influence delays using our DCS-HARQ method in MU-CoMP HARQ. In non-CoMP mode, delay tolerance of successfully receive a packet is set to 3ms [16], and in CoMP mode, the tolerance will be longer. In our simulation, we take 0ms, 3ms, 5ms ,10ms and 18ms as an example [17].

Figure 10 shows the simulation result of delays in X2 interface. We can infer that when delay is less than 5ms, the influence is little. When delay is larger than 10ms, it will encumber the system performance. So new design of X2 interface is needed in CoMP-JP where there is much information need to be exchanged using X2 interface.

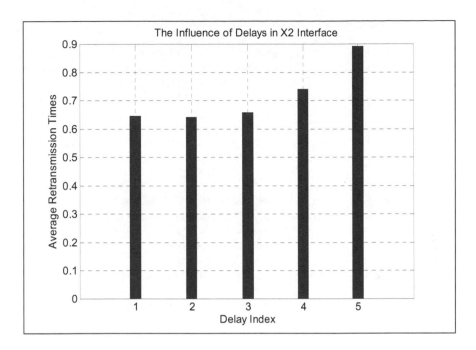

**Fig. 10.** The Influence of Delays in X2 Interface

## 5   Conclusion

In this paper, we studied the MU HARQ process in CoMP-JP scenario and raised our own DCS-HARQ method which is proved effective to improve system performance and reduce system retransmission times with little system costs. Analysis of delays in X2 interface is also given in this paper. We strongly recommend that in CoMP-JP mode, capacity and delay features need to be improved to satisfy the need of CoMP. This is a meaningful method for 3GPP LTE standardization of release 11.

**Acknowledgment.** This work is funded as part of the National Basic Research Program of China (2007CB310608), National Natural Science Foundation of China (60872063), China's 863 Project (2009AA011501), National S&T Major Project (2008ZX03O03-004) and PCSIRT, whose funding support is gratefully acknowledgment.

## References

1. NTT DoCoMo, Chair Presentation: LTE Rel 9 and LTE-Advanced in 3GPP, May 19 (2009)
2. 3GPP.TSG-RAN1 WG1#43, R1-051422,
   http://www.communications.org.tw/upfiles/%E5%B7%A5%E6%A5%AD%
   E5%B1%80%E9%9B%BB%E5%AD%90%E5%A0%B13GPP_Aug_Richard.pdf2009
3. R2-093728, Impact of DL CoMP on User Plane, CATT

4. R2-093925 HARQ operation in UL CoMP Huawei
5. R2-093727 Impact of CoMP on Control Plane CATT
6. Robertson, P., Kaiser, S.: The effects of Doppler spreads in OFDM(A) mobile radio systems. In: Vehicular Technology Conference, VTC 1999 - Fall, IEEE VTS (1999)
7. Kay, S.M.: Fundamentals of Statistical Signal Processing: Estimation Theory, pp. 344–350. Prentice Hall, Englewood Cliffs (1993), ISBN 0-13-042268-1
8. 3GPP LTE presentation, Kyoto, May 22 (2007), Alcatel Lucent,
   `http://www.google.com.hk/url?sa=t&source=web&cd=1&ved=0CBgQF`
   `jAA&url=http%3A%2F%2Fwww.3gpp.org%2Fftp%2Finformation%2Fpres`
   `entations%2FPresentations_3GPP-`
   `LTEv2.ppt&ei=XzWOTYOiFI_JcY_12ZkK&usg=AFQjCNHlGy-`
   `mCuknbxZxNBVysK3Z40_IqA`
9. Nakamura, T.: Proposal for Candidate Radio Interface Technologies for IMT-Advanced Based on LTE Release 10 and Beyond(LTE‐Advanced),
   `http://www.3gpp.org/IMG/pdf/2009_10_3gpp_IMT.pdf`
10. Gao, Y., Li, Y., Yu, H., Gao, S.: Modeling and Analysis of SU-CoMP HARQ in 3GPP LTE System Level Simulation (Submitted to ChinaCom) (2011)
11. 3GPP TSG RAN WG1 Meeting #56, Sharp, Considerations on precoding scheme for DL joint processing CoMP
12. Gao, Y., Yu, H.: An Enhanced System Level to Link Level Mapping Method for 3GPP LTE System Level Simulation, CSIE 2011 (accepted 2011)
13. 3GPP TSG-RAN-1 Meeting #37,OFDM-HSDPA System level simulator calibration (R1-040500)
14. Gao, Y., Sun, Y., Zhou, C., Su, X., Xu, X., Zhou, S.: Accelerating the 3GPP LTE System Level Simulation with NVidia CUDA, ICITMS 2011 (accepted 2011)
15. Overview of 3GPP Release 11 V0.0.5 (February 2011),
   `http://www.3gpp.org/ftp/Information/WORK_PLAN/Description_Re`
   `leases/`
16. R1-073027, On the number of hybrid ARQ processes in LTE, Ericsson
17. R3-070593 X2 Interference delay, Motorola

# On Timing Offset and Frequency Offset Estimation in LTE Uplink[*]

Juan Liu, Bin Wu, and Pingan Li

School of Information Engineering, Wuhan University of Technology, No.122 Luoshi Road,
Hongshan District,Wuhan, Hubei, China, 430070
Liujuan10010@126.com, wubin146011@hotmail.com,
pingan_liwhut@yahoo.com.cn

**Abstract.** In this paper, the timing offset and frequency offset estimation in LTE uplink is studied. The approaches proposed are based on the demodulation reference signals (DMRS) in PUSCH for FDD mode. With the channel estimation in the frequency domain at the receiver by using the two DMRS, i.e., DMRS located in two OFDM symbols, within one sub-frame, timing offset estimation is conducted by exploring the phase shift between different sub-carriers for each DMRS, while the frequency shift estimation is implemented by studying the phase rotation between the two DMRS for each sub-carrier. Statistical average is used to enhance the performance of estimation. Simulation results demonstrate that the proposed algorithms can offer satisfactory performance even at relatively low signal to noise ratios in the additive whiten Gaussian noise environments.

**Keywords:** Channel estimation, timing offset, frequency offset, LTE.

## 1 Introduction

By the end of 2004, the third Generation Partnership Project (3GPP) started the 3G long term evolution (LTE) project to ensure its long-term comparative advantage of wireless standards. In LTE systems, the uplink transmission scheme is based on single-carrier frequency division multiple access (SC-FDMA) transmission with cyclic prefix[1,2].Compared with orthogonal frequency division multiple access (OFDM) scheme, a prominent advantage of SC-FDMA over OFDM is that its transmitted signal has a lower peak-to-average power ratio (PAPR)[3]. Nominally SC-FDMA leads to a single-carrier transmit signal, in fact, the signal is based on multiple frequency bins for every symbol and is under the influence of frequency offset and timing errors. This is because that imperfect synchronization can generate inter-carrier interference (ICI) and inter-symbol interference (ISI), thus will induce both co-channel and inter-channel interference[4]-[6] . Moreover, carrier frequency synchronization for the uplink of SC-FDMA system is more difficult, since the frequency recovery for one user may result in the misalignment of the other synchronized users [7]-[9].

---

[*] This work is supported by the National Special and Important Project under Grant: No. 2009ZX03002-009.

P. Sénac, M. Ott, and A. Seneviratne (Eds.): ICWCA 2011, LNICST 72, pp. 265–274, 2012.
© Institute for Computer Sciences, Social Informatics and Telecommunications Engineering 2012

Until now, several timing and frequency synchronization techniques for LTE uplink system have been studied [10]-[12]. [10] has proposed an accurate timing and frequency offsets estimation algorithm for SC-FDMA uplink, however, the work only considers the timing and frequency offsets of a new user entering the system and assume all the other users have already been perfectly synchronized. In our work, we should consider the timing and frequency offsets of all active users. In [11], a maximum-likelihood (ML) based joint channel and frequency offset estimation algorithm for SC-FDMA system is proposed using one training block. The algorithm has good estimation performance and fast convergence rate. However, the computational complexity is prohibitively high due to too much matrix inversion calculation, particularly when the number of sub-carrier is large. The timing synchronization method proposed in [12] is based on a raw channel estimation using the sounding reference signal (SRS) of the respective channels for each antenna and time slot in PUCCH, PUSCH. First the phase deviation between neighboring sub-carriers is calculated, then a weighted averaging in MAC layer is carried out to convert the phase into a time offset estimation value. This algorithm has good estimation performance over a large number of samples. However, it just considers the phase deviation between adjacent sub-carriers, while we will explore in this paper all the phase deviations between a sub-carrier couple with m (m is an integer larger or equal to 1) sub-carrier interspacing to achieve a more accurate time offset value by averaging the estimates corresponding to different and possible m values. The method to present in the following sections is based on channel estimation by using DMRS in PUSCH in LTE uplink. With efficiency in computation, the approach shows high accuracy in estimation even at a relatively low SNR.

## 2   System Model

### 2.1   DMRS Sequence in LTE Uplink

The DMRS positions in a sub-frame of a LTE system in the frequency division duplex (FDD) is given in Fig.1. In LTE FDD, each radio frame of 10ms consists of 20 slots of length 0.5ms, numbered from 0 to 19[13]-[14].A sub-frame is defined as two consecutive slots each consisting 12 or 14 OFDM symbols, depending on whether normal or extended cyclic prefix is used. In PUSCH, the pilot occupies the fourth SC-FDMA symbol in each slot of a sub-frame with normal cyclic prefix. The two pilot sequences in a sub-frame are the same.

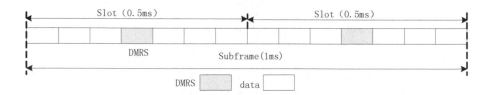

**Fig. 1.** DMRS in LTE uplink

The DMRS for PUSCH in the frequency domain will be mapped to the same set of physical resource blocks (PRB) used for the corresponding PUSCH transmission with the same length expressed by the number of sub-carriers.

## 2.2 Structure of Our Proposed Algorithm

The simplified block diagram of our proposed algorithm in LTE SC-FDMA system is illustrated in Fig.2. At the transmitter in base-band, the binary information bits are firstly grouped and mapped to the 16QAM symbol before the SC-FDMA modulation. To generate a SC-FDMA symbol, an M-point DFT is applied to a group of 16QAM symbols before mapping to consecutive M sub-carriers at the input of an N-point IFFT operator. Furthermore, Cyclic Prefix (CP) with a length larger than channel maximum delay is added.

At the receiver, the CP is removed from received symbol first. After N-point FFT and sub-carrier de-mapping, channel estimation is carried out to estimate time offset and frequency offset.

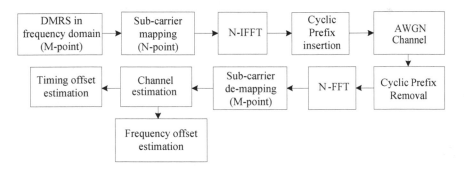

**Fig. 2.** System model of our proposed algorithm in base-band

## 3   Timing Offset Estimation

From Fig. 1, we can see that these are two DMRS symbols in each sub-frame. In the time-domain, each DMRS can be denoted by a $N_{RS}$-dimensional sampling vector

$$x_i(n) = [x_i(1),...,x_i(N_{RS})]^T, i = 1, 2,$$ where $N_{RS}$ is the length of the demodulation reference signal. If there is a timing offset $\tau_T$, then the corresponding reference signal in the frequency-domain at the receiver can be written as

$$Y_i(k) = \exp(-j2\pi\tau_T k / N)H_i(k)X_i(k) + W_i(k), i = 1, 2 , k = 0, \cdots, M-1 \quad (1)$$

where $H_i(k)$ is the channel frequency response of the $i$th DMRS without time offset, $W_i(k) = FFT(w_i(n))$, $w_i(n)$ denotes the additive whiten Gaussian noise (AWGN). In

(1), $\tau_T$ is the normalized timing offset, i.e., $\tau_T = \tau / T$ with $T$ being the sampling period.

From (1), the least square channel estimation based on DMRS can be implemented by

$$H^{TO}_{\ i}(k) = \frac{Y_i(k)}{X_i(k)} \ , \ k = 0,...,M-1 \tag{2}$$

To present the proposed approach more explicitly, let us consider the received signal without AWGN. In this case, the received signal in the frequency-domain can be rewritten as

$$Y_i(k) = \exp(-j2\pi\tau_T k / N)H_i(k)X_i(k), i = 1,2 \tag{3}$$

For the signal model (3), we have

$$H^{TO}_i(k) = \exp(-j2\pi\tau_T k / N)H_i(k)$$

$$= A_i \exp(-j2\pi\tau_T k / N)\exp(j\theta_i), i = 1,2 \tag{4}$$

where $A_i$ and $\theta_i$ denote the amplitude and phase of $H_i(k)$. Without AWGN, the frequency response of channels will be an accurate evaluation by using (4).

Let us define

$$R_i(k_1, k_2) = (H^{TO}_i(k_1))^* (H^{TO}_i(k_2))$$

$$= A_i \exp(j2\pi\tau_T m / N), i = 1,2 \tag{5}$$

And

$$\varphi_{m,i} = 2\pi\tau_T m / N, i = 1,2 \tag{6}$$

where $m = k_1 - k_2$ is the interspacing between sub-carrier $k_1$ and sub-carrier $k_2$. Then, we can get

$$\phi_{m,i} = a\tan 2(\frac{\sum \text{Im}\{R_i(k_1, k_2)\}}{\sum \text{Re}\{R_i(k_1, k_2)\}}) = 2\pi\tau_T m / N, i = 1,2 \tag{7}$$

where the function atan2(*) is defined by

$$a \tan 2(y, x) = \begin{cases} \arctan(\dfrac{y}{x}) & x > 0 \\[2mm] \pi - \arctan(\dfrac{y}{x}) & y \geq 0, x < 0 \\[2mm] -\pi + \arctan(\dfrac{y}{x}) & y < 0. x < 0 \\[2mm] \dfrac{\pi}{2} & y > 0, x = 0 \\[2mm] -\dfrac{\pi}{2} & y < 0, x = 0 \\[2mm] undefined & y = 0, x = 0 \end{cases} \tag{8}$$

The normalized time offset can be calculated as

$$\tau_T = \frac{\phi_{m,i} N}{2\pi m} \tag{9}$$

The actual time offset is given by

$$\tau = \tau_T T = \frac{\phi_{m,i} NT}{2\pi m} = \frac{\phi_{m,i}}{2\pi m \Delta} \tag{10}$$

where $\Delta$ represents the interspacing between each two neighboring SC-FDMA sub-carriers in the frequency domain. For a system with 20MHZ bandwidth, $\Delta$ has a value of 15KHZ defined by 3GPP LTE specifications [1].

The timing offset calculated by using (10) for model (3) is an accurate evaluation value. In practice, however, AWGN should be considered and (10) is an estimate for corresponding channel estimates by using (2). In this case, a second average can be further used over different $m$ to acquire a more precise timing offset estimate.

## 4 Fractional Frequency Offset Estimation

In this section, a channel estimation based fractional frequency offset estimation approach in PUSCH is presented. It is well known that a frequency shift is equivalent to a phase rotation in time domain by assuming that the channel during a sub-frame is fixed. This assumption is ideal but is reasonable for the very short sub-frame duration in LTE. In ideal AWGN environments, the received signals in time-domain corresponding to the two DMRS in PUSCH, $x_1(n)$ and $x_2(n)$, can be expressed by

$$y_1^{FO}(n) = \exp\{-j2\pi\delta n / N\}x_1(n) + v_1(n) \tag{11}$$

$$y_2^{FO}(n) = \exp\{-j2\pi\delta(n+Q) / N\}x_2(n) + v_2(n) \tag{12}$$

Where $n = 0, \cdots, N_{RS} - 1$, $\delta$ is a fractional frequency offset normalized by the sub-frame interspacing $\Delta$, $v_1(n)$ and $v_2(n)$ denote AWGN introduced in the received signals.

To present the proposed approach fractional frequency offset estimation, let us ignore the AWGN component for an ideal wireless channel with no any noise. In this case, the received signal corresponding to the two DMRS in a sub-frame can be expressed, respectively, by (13) and (14).

$$x_1^{FO}(n) = \exp\{-j2\pi\delta n / N\}x_1(n) \tag{13}$$

$$x_2^{FO}(n) = \exp\{-j2\pi\delta(n+Q) / N\}x_2(n), n = 1, 2, ..., N_{RS} \tag{14}$$

In (14), $Q$ denotes the integral sampling point deviation between the first sampling points of the two reference signals. The value of $Q$ is decided by the bandwidth of LTE system. For bandwidths of 5MHz, 10MHz and 20MHz, $Q$ are 3840, 7680 and 15360, respectively.

After $N$-point FFT operation at the receiver, the output of the reference signal in frequency-domain corresponding to (13) and (14) can be written as

$$X_1^{FO}(k) = \sum_{n=0}^{N-1} \exp\{-j2\pi(k+\delta)n / N\}x_1(n)$$

$$= X_1(k+\delta) \tag{15}$$

And

$$X_2^{FO}(k) = \exp\{-j2\pi\delta Q / N\}X_2(k+\delta) \tag{16}$$

In practice, the received signals will suffer from the influence of the multipath propagation. Hence, the received signal components in the frequency-domain corresponding to (15) and (16) after the FFT conversion can be further expressed as

$$X_1^{FO}(k) = H_1(k)X_1(k+\delta) \tag{17}$$

$$X_2^{FO}(k) = \exp\{-j2\pi\delta Q / N\}H_2(k)X_2(k+\delta) \tag{18}$$

Since the transmitted two DRMS are the same in one sub-frame, and we can also assume that the channel during a sub-frame is fixed, the fractional frequency offset value can be obtained by calculating

$$\delta = a \tan 2([\frac{1}{N_1} \sum_{k=0}^{N_1-1} [H_2^{FO}(k)]^* H_1^{FO}(k)]) \bullet \frac{N}{2\pi Q}$$ (19)

$$df = \delta\Delta = \frac{\Delta N}{2\pi Q} \bullet a \tan 2([\frac{1}{N_1} \sum_{k=0}^{N_1-1} [H_2^{FO}(k)]^* H_1^{FO}(k)])$$ (20)

Where

$$H_i^{FO} = \frac{X_i^{FO}(k)}{X_i(k+\delta)}, \quad i = 1,2$$ (21)

In practice, we do not know $X_i(k+\delta)$ for each DMRS. In addition we have to consider the effects of AWGN. Therefore, we use the following estimates in (20) to get the fractional frequency offset estimates, i.e.

$$\hat{H}_i^{FO} = \frac{Y_i^{FO}(k)}{X_i(k)}, \quad i = 1,2$$ (22)

For a system with a bandwidth of 20MHZ, $\Delta = 15 KHz$. The range of fractional frequency offset estimation algorithm can reach $[-\frac{1}{15}, \frac{1}{15}]$ and the corresponding range of the actual frequency offset is $[-1KHz, 1KHz]$.

## 5  Numerical Examples

In this section, performance of the proposed timing-offset and frequency offset estimation algorithms for LTE system is evaluated through simulations. The ideal AWGN channel is assumed. A 16QAM-SC-FDMA system with a sampling frequency of 30.72MHZ is considered. 2048-point FFT/IFFT with sub-carrier interspacing 15KHz is used. The lengths of CP are 160 samples in the first SC-FDMA symbol and 140 samples in the rest six symbols, respectively. During the simulations, 12 SC_FDMA symbols and 2 reference signals in each sub-frame are generated. 100 resource blocks (RB) are adopted for PUSCH data transmission. That means that during the 2048 sub-carriers, 1200 sub-carriers are used for pilots and data transmission.

In Fig.3, a timing offset of length 100 sampling periods are set, the root mean square error (RMSE) of the SC-FDMA symbol timing offset estimation measured in samples is plotted against the signal to noise ratio (SNR). As for the low SNR case the estimation is very accurate too, the estimation error is as low as 0.043 sampling periods in SNR of 0dB. Then in a high SNR of 30dB, the error is reduced to 0.001 sampling periods, almost to zero. This means that proposed timing offset estimation algorithm can offer a very excellent performance in AWGN channel.

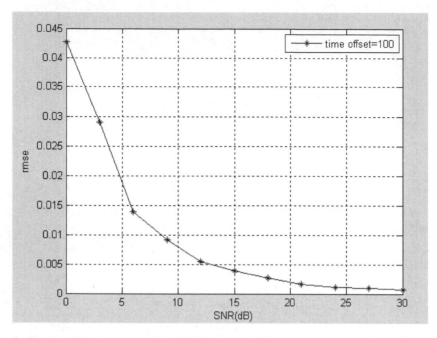

**Fig. 3.** Timing offset in terms of the RMSE vs. the SNR, measured in numbers of sampling periods

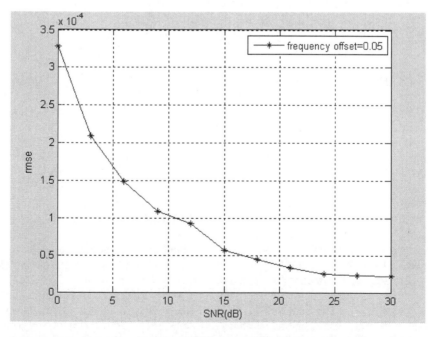

**Fig. 4.** Frequency offset in terms of the RMSE vs. the SNR, measured in numbers of sub-carrier spacing

In Fig.4, a frequency offset of 0.05 sub-carrier spacings are set in this simulation example. The RMSE of the SC-FDMA symbol frequency offset estimation measured in sub-carrier spacing is plotted against the SNR. It can be seen that the proposed fractional frequency offset estimation approach also demonstrates satisfied performance in AWGN even at relatively low SNR values.

## 6  Conclusion Remarks

The paper deal with the timing and frequency offset estimation in PUSCH of LTE systems. A timing offset algorithm and a frequency offset estimation approach are presented. Both the approaches are based on the channel estimation in the frequency-domain and exhibit low costs in computation. The proposed algorithm show excellent performance in ideal AWGN. In addition, the approaches can be also applied to the sounding channel and PUCCH channel for timing error estimation and frequency offset estimation.

## References

1. 3GPP TS 36.211 V8.8.0: Evolved Universal Terrestrial Radio ACCES (E-UTRA); Phycical Channel and modulation (September 2009)
2. R1-063057.EUTRA SC-FDMA Uplink Pilot/Reference Signal Design. 3GPP RAN WG1 meeting 47, November 6-10 (2006)
3. Myung, H.G., Lin, J., Goodman, D.J.: Singal Carrier FDMA for Uplink Wireless Transmission. IEEE Vehicular Tech. Magazine (September 2008)
4. Wang, Y., Zheng, A., Zhang, J., Yang, D.: A Novel Channel Estimation Algorithm for Sounding Reference Signal in LTE uplink Transmission, December 7 (2009)
5. Khalwati, M., Reza Soleymani, M.: Enhanced Uplink Frequency Synchronization Algorithm for OFDM Systems in a Multi-Path Fading Environment. In: IEEE Conference on Electrical and Computer Engineering, November 15, pp. 1766–1770 (2007)
6. Tsai, Y., Zhang, G.: Time and Frequency Synchronization for 3GPP LTE Long Term Evolution Systems. In: IEEE Vehicular Technology Conference, 65th VTC 2007-Spring (April 2007)
7. Lee, J.-H., Kim, S.-C.: Time and Frequency Synchronization for OFDM Uplink System using the SAG Algorithm. IEEE Trans. Commun. 6(4) (April 2007)
8. Sun, P., Zhang, L.: Low Complexity Pilot Aided Frequency Synchronization for OFDMA Uplink Transmissio. IEEE Trans. Commun. 8(7) (July 2009)
9. Hoeher, P., Kaiser, S., Robertson, P.: Pilot symbol aided channel estimation in time and frequency. In: Proc. of Communication Theory Mini-Conference within IEEE Global Telecommunications Conference, pp. 90–96 (1997)
10. Morelli, M.: Timing and frequency synchronization for the uplink of an OFDMA system. IEEE Trans. Commun. 52(2), 296–306 (2004)

11. Pun, M., Morelli, M., Kuo, C.: Maximum-likelihood synchronization and channel estimation for OFDMA uplink transmissions. IEEE Trans.Commun. 54(4), 726–736 (2006)
12. Tack, J., Kratzert, A.: UL Timing Alignment based on PUCCH, PUSCH and SRS, August 25 (2009)
13. Wang, Y., Zheng, A., Zhang, J., Yang, D.: A Novel Channel Estimation Algorithm for Sounding Reference Signal in LTE uplink Transmission. In: IEEE Conference on Communications Technology and Applications, December 7, pp. 412–415 (2009)
14. Hou, X., Zhang, Z., Kayama, H.: DMRS Design and Channel Estimation for LTE_Advanced MIMO uplink, July 25 (2010)

# Multichannel Opportunistic Spectrum Access in Fading Environment Using Optimal Stopping Rule

Yuhua Xu, Zhan Gao, Jinlong Wang, and Qihui Wu

Institute of Communications Engineering,
PLA University of Science and Technology, Nanjing 21007, China
yuhuaenator@gmail.com

**Abstract.** This paper studies the tradeoff between throughput and multichannel diversity in multichannel opportunistic spectrum access (OSA) systems. We explicitly consider channel condition as well as the activities of the primary users. We assume that the primary users use the licensed channel in a slotted fashion and the secondary users can only explore one licensed channel at a time. The secondary users then sequentially explore multiple channels to find the best channel for transmission. However, channel exploration is time-consumed, which decreases effective transmission time in a slot. For single secondary user OSA systems, we formulate the channel exploration problem as an optimal stopping problem with recall, and propose a myopic but optimal approach. For multiple secondary user OSA systems, we propose an adaptive stochastic recall algorithm (ASRA) to capture the collision among multiple secondary users. It is shown that the proposed solutions in this paper achieve increased throughput both the scenario of both single secondary user as well as multiple secondary suers.

**Keywords:** opportunistic spectrum access, multichannel diversity, optimal stopping rule.

## 1 Introduction

Recently, opportunistic spectrum access (OSA) has drawn great attention [1-4], for it has been regarded as a promising solution to the problem of spectrum shortage that wireless communication systems are facing today. In OSA, there are two types of users. One is the primary user (PU) which is the licensed owner of the spectrum, and the other is the secondary user (SU) which is allowed to transmit on the licensed spectrum at a particular time and location when and where the PUs are not active [5].

We consider an OSA system consisting multiple licensed channels and multiple SUs. Due to hardware limitation, the SUs can only sense one channel at a time. The key concern in such a system is designing a spectrum decision rule with which the SUs use the licensed channels. An intuitive approach is that the SUs sense the licensed channels according to the decent order of channel idle

P. Sénac, M. Ott, and A. Seneviratne (Eds.): ICWCA 2011, LNICST 72, pp. 275–286, 2012.

probabilities [6]. However, only considering the presence of the primary users is not enough in practical systems. The reason is that different channels always have different quality, which eventually results in different transmission rate. To capture the variation in channel conditions, a more reasonable approach is considering channel condition as well as the activities of PUs when designing spectrum decision rule in OSA systems. To achieve this, the SUs are required to detect the activities of PUs and estimate channel conditions. For simplicity, we use the term channel exploration to indicate the tasks of detecting the activities of the PUs and estimating channel conditions.

In this paper, the SUs are assumed to have slotted transmission structure, and can explore multiple licensed channels according to a particular order in a slot. Specifically, the SUs have to spend time to perform efficient and reliable channel exploration before they transmit data. Obviously, as the number of explored channels increases, the multichannel gain increases. However, since channel exploration is time-consumed, the effective transmission time in a slot decreases. Thus, there is a fundamental tradeoff between multichannel diversity and throughput. To address this tradeoff, we formulate the channel exploration problem as an optimal stopping problem with recall. The key idea of our approach can be described as follows. After exploring each licensed channel, each secondary user decides (1) to continue to explore the residual licensed channels or (2) to stop channel exploration and choose one previous explored idle channel with the highest channel condition to transmit. The goal of SUs is to choose a time to stop to maximize their expected throughput.

It should be mentioned that optimal stopping rule has been widely applied to OSA systems. For instance, in [7], the authors formulated the spectrum sensing as an optimal stopping problem by taking the hardware constraint into consideration. In [8], the authors presented a sequential spectrum sensing algorithm, which explicitly takes into account the sensing overhead. The considered problem can be solved by the method of optimal stopping rule. In [9], optimal strategies for determining which channels to probe, in what sequence and which channel to use for transmission have been investigated. In addition, they considered both constant access time (CAT) and constant data time (CDT) policy. Most of existing approaches have assumed that the SUs are not allowed use the previous explored channels. The given reason is that recalling a previous explored channel may leads to collision since the channel may be occupied by other secondary users. However, this consideration is limited. In an OSA system with multiple SUs, the unexplored channels may also be occupied by other secondary users. In this sense, both recalling a previous explored channel and exploring a residual channel may result in collision. Thus, the optimal design for multichannel multiuser OSA systems is not achieved in most existing work.

In summary, we make the following contributions in this paper:

- For single user OSA systems, we formulate the channel exploration problem as an optimal stopping problem with recall and propose a myopic but optimal approach. It is shown that the proposed approach achieves an increased thought.

- For multiuser OSA systems, we propose an adaptive stochastic recall algorithm (ASRA). It is also shown that the proposed ASRA achieves higher throughput.

The rest of this paper is organized as follows. In section II, we present the system model and define the channel exploration problem. In section III, we develop an optimal stopping problem with recall for the channel exploration problem, and propose efficient approaches for single secondary user and multiple secondary users. In section IV, simulation results and discussions were presented. Finally, we make conclusion in section V.

## 2   System Model and Problem Formulation

### 2.1   System Model

We consider an OSA system involving $M$ SUs and $N$ licensed channels. The PUs are assumed to use the licensed channels in a slotted fashion. We assume that the activities of the primary users are independent from channel to channel and from slot to slot. Furthermore, we assume that each licensed channel is not occupied with probability $\theta_n$ in each slot. We denote the state of each channel in a slot as $S_n, n \in \mathcal{N}$, where $\mathcal{N} = \{1, 2, ..., N\}$ is the set of licensed channels. Specifically, $S_n = 1$ indicates that licensed channel $n$ is idle while $S_n = 0$ indicates that it is occupied. For simplicity of analysis, we assume that the spectrum sensing is perfect in this paper[1].

We consider Rayleigh fading environment in this paper; moreover, each channel undergoes block-fading in each slot. That is, the channel gain of each channel is fixed in a slot and changes randomly in the next slot. Thus, the channel gain of the $n$th SU, $G_n, \forall n \in \mathcal{N}$, is identical independent distributed (i.i.d.) exponential random variables with mean unit. Namely, the common probability density function for all $G_n, \forall n \in \mathcal{N}$ is given by $f_g(x) = e^{-x}, x \geq 0$.

### 2.2   Problem Formulation

The SUs are assumed to employ constant transmitting power policy. Thus, the instantaneous received signal-to-noise-ratio (SNR) on channel $n$ is given by $\gamma_n = Pg_n/\sigma^2$, where $P$ represents the peak power of the SU, $\sigma^2$ represents the variance of white Gaussian noise which is set to be one for simplicity of analysis, and $g_n$ represents the instantaneous channel gain.

The transmission process of the SUs is shown in Fig. 1. Let $T$ and $\tau$ denote the length of the slot and the length of required time for reliable channel exploration respectively. Suppose that a SU stops channel-exploration after exploring the first $n$ licensed channels, and chooses one of the explored idle channels for transmission. Then the obtained throughput for this SU is given by:

---

[1] Although the analysis in this paper is mainly for the scenario of perfect sensing, it can easily be extended to the scenario of imperfect sensing.

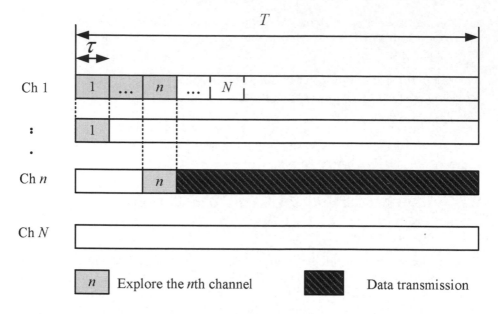

**Fig. 1.** The diagram of the transmission of the secondary users in a slot

$$R_n = c_n F\big((s_1, g_1), ...(s_n, g_n)\big) \tag{1}$$

where $c_n = T - n\tau$ represents the effective transmission time in a slot, $(s_n, g_n)$ represent the realizations of random variables $(S_n, G_n)$ and $F$ represents the capacity function which is determined by specific transmission policy.

After exploring the first $n$ channels, the US observes the sequence $\{o\}_{n=1}^N$, where $o_n = (s_n, g_n)$. Based on the observations and the achieved throughput $R_n$ specified by (1), the SU decides whether to stop channel exploration with receiving the throughput given by $R_n$ or to proceed to explore the remaining channels.

The goal of the each SU is to choose a time to stop to maximize the expected throughput. Our problem belongs to the optimal stopping problem with finite horizon [11], since the SU must stop at the last channel. Generally, we can define the following function at each stage $n$:

$$V_n^{(N)} = \begin{cases} R_n(o_1, ..., o_n), & n = N \\ \max\{R_n(o_1, ..., o_n), E[V_{n+1}^{(N)}|o_1, ..., o_n]\}, & 1 \le n < N \end{cases} \tag{2}$$

where $E[V_{n+1}^{(N)}|o_1, ..., o_n]$ represents the expected throughput that the SU can achieve starting from stage $n$ having observed the sequence of $\mathbf{O}_n = (o_1, ..., o_n)$. Thus, the optimal stopping time for the channel exploration problem is given by:

$$N^* = \min\{n \ge 1 : R_n(o_1, ..., o_n) \ge E[V_{n+1}^{(N)}|o_1, ..., o_n]\} \tag{3}$$

In other words, it is optimal to stop if the current obtained throughput is no less than the expected throughput of stopping at a future channel.

## 2.3   Optimal Stopping Rule without Recall

In [10], the channel exploration problem was formulated as the problem of optimal stopping without recall. Specifically, the SU is one allowed to use the current channel and is not allowed to use a previously explored channel, which leads to the following defined reward function:

$$R_n^{norec}(o_1, ..., o_n) = R_n^{norec}(o_n) = c_n \log(1 + s_n g_n P) \tag{4}$$

It is seen that the reward in each stage is only a function of current observation, then the expected throughput of proceeding exploration can be reduced to $E[V_{n+1}^{(N)}|o_n]$. Moreover, by the method of of backward induction, it is given by:

$$E[V_n^{(N)}] = \begin{cases} c_n \theta_n E_x[\log(1 + xP)], n = N \\ \left(1 - \theta_n + \theta_n E[V_{n+1}^{(N)}]\right) E_x\left[1| \log(1 + xP) < E[V_{n+1}^{(N)}]\right]+ \\ c_n \theta_n E_x\left[\log(1 + xP)| \log(1 + xP) \geq E[V_{n+1}^{(N)}]\right], 1 \leq n < N \end{cases} \tag{5}$$

where $E_x[\,]$ represents taking expectation over $x$.

Based on (4) and (5), the optimal stopping rule for channel exploration problem can be easily described as follows. After exploring each channel, the SU compares the current obtained throughput specified by (4) and the expected throughput of proceeding exploration specified by (5). The SU stops channel exploration if the former is no less than the later, otherwise proceeds exploring residual channels.

# 3   Optimal Stopping Rule with Recall for Channel Exploration

Since we do not focus on designing optimal sensing order in this paper, we assume that all licensed channels have the same idle probability, i.e., $\theta_n = \theta, \forall n \in \mathcal{N}$. As a result, the SUs explore the licensed channels in a random order.

It is known that the SUs in existing work is not allowed to use a previously explored channel, which leads to a conservative design. To improve the throughput performance, the SUs should be allowed to use the previous explored idle channels. First, for single user OSA systems, we formulate the channel exploration problem as an optimal stopping problem with recall and propose a myopic but optimal rule. Secondly, for multiuser OSA systems, we investigate the impact of interactions among users and propose an adaptive stochastic recall algorithm.

## 3.1   Single SU Scenario

Unlike existing work, we assume that the SU is allowed to use a previously explored channel for transmission, which motivates us to define the current obtained throughput as follows:

$$R_n^{rec}(o_1, ..., o_n) = c_n \log(1 + \eta_n^{max} P) \tag{6}$$

where $\eta_n^{\max} = \max_{1 \le i \le n} \{s_i g_i\}$ is defined as the maximum effective channel gain among the first $n$ explored channels.

Under the framework of optimal stopping with recall, it is noted from (2) that at each stage $n$, we have to calculate $E[V_{k+1}^{(N)} | \mathbf{O}_k]$ backward from stage $N$ to stage $n+1$. However, such a backward induction solution is a type of dynamic programming, which has exponential complexity. Furthermore, each $g_n, n \in \mathcal{N}$, is a continuous random variable which results in an un-trackable calculating space for the backward induction solution. Thus, such a backward induction approach is not feasible in practice.

A feasible approach is considering a truncated version of the problem. The simplest version of such truncation is the 1-stage ahead rule (1-SLA), with which the stopping time is determined by:

$$N_1 = \min\{n \ge 1 : R_n^{rec}(o_1, ..., o_n) \ge E[V_{n+1}^{(1)} | o_1, ..., o_n]\} \tag{7}$$

In other words, 1-SLA calls for stopping at the first $n$ channels for which the throughput for stopping is at least as great as the expected throughput of continuing one stage and then stopping. In this sense, the 1-SLA rule is also called as myopic rule. In our problem, we have

$$E[V_{n+1}^{(1)} | o_1, ..., o_n] = c_{n+1} \int_0^\infty \log(1 + \max\{\eta_n^{\max}, x\}P)h_g(x)dx \tag{8}$$

where $h_g(x)$ is the auxiliary probability distribution function defined as follows:

$$h_g(x) = (1 - \theta)\delta(x) + \theta f_g(x) \tag{9}$$

where $\delta(x)$ is the impulse function specified $\delta(x) = 0, x \ne 0$ by and $\int_{-\infty}^\infty \delta(x)dx = 1$.

## 3.2     The Optimality of 1-SLA Rule

In general, 1-SLA is not optimal. However, when the following condition is satisfied, the 1-SLA rule is optimal.

**Definition1[11]:** Let $A_n$ denote the events $\{R_n(\mathbf{O}_n) \ge E[V_{n+1}^{(1)} | \mathbf{O}_n]\}$ . We say that the stopping problem is monotone if

$$A_1 \subset A_2 \subset ... \subset A_N \tag{10}$$

Namely, if the 1-SLA rule calls for stopping at stage $n$, then it will call for stopping at all future stages no matter what the future observations turn out to be.

**Theorem 1.** *In a finite horizon monotone stopping rule problem, the 1-SLA rule is optimal.*

*Proof.* Refer to [11].

**Theorem 2.** *The 1-SLA rule is optimal to the channel exploration problem.*

*Proof.* We define the following function:

$$
\begin{aligned}
F_n(\eta_n^{\max}) &= R_n^{rec} - E(V_{n+1}^{(1)}|\mathbf{O}_n) \\
&= c_n \log(1 + \eta_n^{\max} P) - c_{n+1} \int_0^\infty \log(1 + \max\{\eta_n^{\max}, x\} P) h_g(x) dx
\end{aligned}
\tag{11}
$$

and the following auxiliary function:

$$
\begin{aligned}
G_n(\eta_n^{\max}) &= \tau \int_0^\infty \log(1 + \max\{\eta_n^{\max}, x\} P) h_g(x) dx \\
&- (T - n\tau) \int_0^\infty [\log(1 + \max\{\eta_n^{\max}, x\}) - \log(1 + \eta_n^{\max})] h_g(x) dx
\end{aligned}
\tag{12}
$$

It is noted that $G_n(\eta_n^{\max})$ is a transformation of $F_n(\eta_n^{\max})$, and they exhibit the following properties:

$$
\begin{cases}
G_n(\eta_n^{\max}) = 0 \Leftrightarrow F_n(\eta_n^{\max}) = 0 \\
G_n(\eta_n^{\max}) > 0 \Leftrightarrow F_n(\eta_n^{\max}) > 0
\end{cases}
\tag{13}
$$

We then compare $G_{n+1}(\eta_{n+1}^{\max})$ and $G_n(\eta_n^{\max})$ as follows:

$$
\begin{aligned}
&G_{n+1}(\eta_{n+1}^{\max}) - G_n(\eta_n^{\max}) \\
=& \tau \int_0^\infty \log(1 + \max\{\eta_{n+1}^{\max}, x\} P) h_g(x) dx - \tau \int_0^\infty \log(1 + \max\{\eta_n^{\max}, x\} P) h_g(x) dx \\
&+ c_n \int_0^\infty [\log(1 + \max\{\eta_n^{\max}, x\} P) - \log(1 + \eta_n^{\max} P)] h_g(x) dx \\
&- c_{n+1} \int_0^\infty [\log(1 + \max\{\eta_{n+1}^{\max}, x\} P) - \log(1 + \eta_{n+1}^{\max} P)] h_g(x) dx
\end{aligned}
\tag{14}
$$

It is seen that $\int_0^\infty \log(1 + \max\{\eta_n^{\max}, x\} P) h_g(x) dx$ is a strictly monotone increasing function of $\eta_n^{\max}$, $c_n \int_0^\infty [\log(1 + \max\{\eta_n^{\max}, x\} P) - \log(1 + \eta_n^{\max} P)] h_g(x) dx\}$ is a strictly monotone decreasing function of $\eta_n^{\max}$ and $c_n > c_{n+1}$ is always true for all $n \in \mathcal{N}$. Moreover, recall the transmission policy of the secondary users, we have $\eta_{n+1}^{\max} = \max\{\eta_n^{\max}, s_{n+1} g_{n+1}\} \geq \eta_n^{\max}$. Thus, the following inequality can be obtained immediately:

$$
G_{n+1}(\eta_{n+1}^{\max}) - G_n(\eta_n^{\max}) > 0
\tag{15}
$$

Let us re-write $A_n$ as follows:

$$
A_n = \{\eta_n^{\max} : F_n(\eta_n^{\max}) \geq 0\} = \{\eta_n^{\max} : G_n(\eta_n^{\max}) \geq 0\}
\tag{16}
$$

Using (16) and (14), we have:

$$
F_{n+1}(\eta_{n+1}^{\max}) > 0, \eta_n^{\max} \in A_n
\tag{17}
$$

which is equivalent to $A_n \subset A_{n+1}$. Finally, the following can be inductively obtained:

$$
A_1 \subset A_2 \subset \dots \subset A_N
\tag{18}
$$

By definition 1 and Theorem 1, Theorem 2 follows.

Theorem 2 characterizes the optimality of 1-SLA rule for the channel exploration problem. In the following, we investigate the structure of the 1-SLA rule.

**Lemma 1.** *Denote $a_n$ as the solution of the following equation,*

$$F_n(\eta_n^{\max}) = 0 \qquad (19)$$

*Then $a_n$ is unique for each $n \in \mathcal{N}$ and $a_{n+1} < a_n$.*

*Proof.* It is known that $G_n(\eta_n^{\max})$ is a strict monotone increasing function of $\eta_n^{\max}$. In addition, the following always holds:

$$\begin{cases} G_n(0) = -c_{n+1} \int_0^\infty \log(1 + xP)h_g(x)dx < 0 \\ \lim_{\eta_n^{\max} \to \infty} G_n(\eta_n^{\max}) = \tau \lim_{\eta_n^{\max} \to \infty} \log (1 + \eta_n^{\max} P)dx > 0 \end{cases}, \forall n \in \mathcal{N} \qquad (20)$$

Hence, $G(\eta_n^{\max}) = 0$ has unique root, which means that $F_n(\eta_n^{\max}) = 0$ also has unique root. Now, suppose $F_n(a_n) = 0$ and $F_{n+1}(a_{n+1}) = 0$, then the following equation can be obtained from (13) and (15):

$$G_{n+1}(a_n) > G_n(a_n) = G_{n+1}(a_{n+1}) = 0 \qquad (21)$$

We then have $a_{n+1} < a_n, \forall n \in \mathcal{N}$, where we use the fact that $G_{n+1}$ is a monotone increasing function. Therefore, Lemma 1 is proved.

**Lemma 2.** *The optimal stopping rule for the channel exploration problem is described as follows:*

$$N^* = \min\{n \geq 1 : \eta_n^{\max} \geq a_n\} \qquad (22)$$

*Proof.* Straightforward obtained from Theorem 2 and Lemma 1.

**Remark 1:** $a_n$ can be regarded as the threshold of each stage. A closed-form expression of $a_n$ is unavailable and we can resort to numeric method.

**Remark 2:** According to Lemma 2, the optimal stopping rule for the channel exploration problem is simple and can be described as follows. After exploring each channel, the SU compares $\eta_n^{\max}$ with the threshold $a_n$. It stops exploration and chooses the explored idle channel with the highest channel gain for transmission if $\eta_n^{\max}$ is no less than the threshold; otherwise, it proceeds to explore residual channels.

**Remark 3:** $a_{n+1} < a_n$ can be interpreted as follows. At the early stage, the probability of obtaining a higher throughput in a future stage is high since there are a number of unexplored channels. However, as $n$ increases, the number of unexplored channels decreases and the exploration overhead increases. Thus, the SU may perform more aggressively in the early stage while more conservatively in the later stage.

### 3.3    Multiple SUs Scenario

In the last subsection, we formulated the channel exploration problem for single SU scenario as an optimal stopping problem with recall. In this section, we

---

*Adaptive stochastic recall algorithm (ASRA)*

---

**Step 1:** 1. After exploring the first $n$ licensed channels, the SUs recall with probability $p_{recall}(n, M)$. Thus, the maximum effective channel gain is calculated in a stochastic manner, i.e.,

$$\Pr(\eta_n^{\max} = \max_{1 \leq i \leq n} \{s_i g_i\}) = 1 - \Pr(\eta_n^{\max} = s_n g_n) = p_{recall}(n, M) \tag{23}$$

where $p_{recall}(n, M) = (\frac{1}{N-n+1})^{M-1}$.
**Step 2:** After obtaining $\eta_n^{\max}$, the SUs perform channel decision according to Lemma 2.

---

consider the multiple SUs scenario. It is seen that in an OSA systems with multiple SUs, a collision occurs when more than one SU access the same channel at the same time. Thus, traditional optimal stopping rule will not lead to optimal design in the scenario of multiple SUs. To address this problem, new methods that consider the interactions among SUs is needed.

Normally, the optimal design for multiple SUs scenario is hard to obtain. We then seek for a heuristic method with which the SUs stochastically recall a previously explored channel. Specifically, in stage $n$, the SUs stochastically do not always recall the explored channels; instead, it recall with probability $p_{recall}(n, M)$. Instinctively, the probability $p_{recall}(n, M)$ should have the following properties:

1. Increases when $n$ increases while decreases when $M$ increases. In other words, the SUs are encouraged not to recall in the early stage while are encouraged to recall in the last stage.
2. $p_{recall}(n, 1) = 1, \forall n$. That is, if there is only one SU then it always recalls.

Based on the above, we propose an adaptive stochastic recall algorithm (ASRA) as described at the top of this page, for multiple SU OSA systems. We choose a simple $p_{recall}(n, M)$ in this paper, but other expressions can also be used.

## 4   Simulation Results and Discussion

In the simulation study, the common simulation parameters are as follows: $T = 100ms, \tau = 5ms, \theta = 0.5, P = 10dB$.

First, we evaluate the throughput performance of single SU OSA systems. Fig. 2 shows the expected throughput versus the number of licensed channels, for recall approach and no recall approach respectively. It is shown that the expected throughput of recall approach is higher than that of no recall approach. Furthermore, it is shown that the expected throughput of both approaches grows as the number of licensed channels increases, but it is saturated when the number of licensed channels becomes sufficiently large.

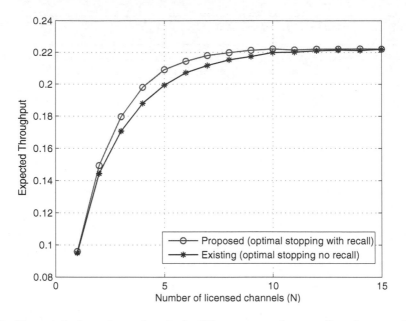

**Fig. 2.** Expected throughput for single SU systems using recall and no-recall approaches respectively

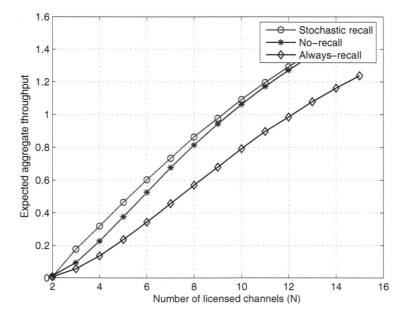

**Fig. 3.** Expected throughput versus the number of licensed channels for multiple SU systems (The number of SUs is set to $M = 10$)

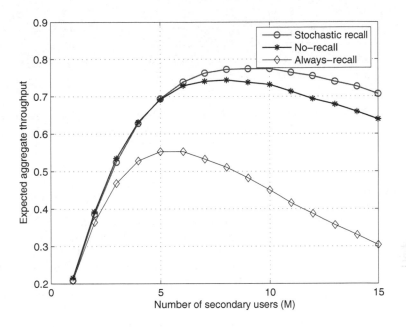

**Fig. 4.** Expected throughput versus the number of secondary users for multiple SU systems (The number of licensed channel is set to $N = 8$)

Second, we evaluate the throughput performance for multiple SU OSA systems. Specifically, we compare the obtained throughput of stochastic recall, always recall and no recall in multiple user scenario. Fig. 3 shows the expected throughput versus the number of licensed channels, for the above three approaches respectively. It is shown that the expected throughput of stochastic recall approach is always higher than those of no recall and always recall.

Third, we evaluate the throughput performance of three approaches when varying the number of SUs. Fig. 4 shows the expected throughput versus the number of SUs. It is noted from the figures that the expected throughput of stochastic recall outperforms other two approaches. In addition, the expected throughput grows as the number of secondary users increases for the scenario with small number of secondary users, but it decreases as the number of secondary users increases for the scenario with large number of secondary users.

## 5    Conclusion

We investigated the tradeoff of throughput and multichannel diversity for opportunistic spectrum access in fading environment. We considered the presence of primary users as well as the channel conditions when optimizing the expected throughput of secondary users. For single user systems, we formulated the channel exploration problem as an optimal stopping problem with recall and proposed a myopic but optimal approach. However, the approach presented for single secondary user is not fit for that of multiple secondary users, since the secondary users will collide multiple secondary users transmit on the same channel at the same time. Thus, we presented a stochastic recall approach for multiple users systems. Further work including re-establishing an optimal stopping framework for the multiple users systems is ongoing.

**Acknowledgement.** This work was supported by the national basic research program of China (grant No. 2009CB320400), and the national science foundation of China (grant No. 60932002).

# References

1. Haykin, S.: Cognitive radio: brain-empowered wireless communi-cations. IEEE Journal on Selected Areas in Communications 23, 201–220 (2005)
2. Suraweera, H.A., Smith, P.J., Shafi, M.: Capacity limits and performance analysis of cognitive radio with imperfect channel knowledge. IEEE Transactions on Vehicular Technology 59, 1811–1822 (2010)
3. Chou, C.T., Kim, S., Shin, K.G.: What and how much to gain by spectrum agility? IEEE Journal on Selected Areas in Communications 25, 576–588 (2007)
4. Srinivasa, S., Jafar, S.A.: How much spectrum sharing is optimal in cognitive radio networks? IEEE Transactions on Wireless Communications 7, 4010–4018 (2008)
5. Zhao, Y.P., Mao, S.W., Neel, J.O., Reed, J.H.: Performance evaluation of cognitive radios: metrics, utility functions, and methodology. Proceedings of the IEEE 97, 642–659 (2009)
6. Zhao, Q., Tong, L., Swami, A., Chen, Y.X.: Decentralized cognitive MAC for opportunistic spectrum access in ad hoc networks: A POMDP framework. IEEE Journal on Selected Areas in Communications 25, 589–600 (2007)
7. Juncheng, J., Qian, Z., Xuemin, S.: HC-MAC: a hardware-constrained cognitive MAC for efficient spectrum management. IEEE Journal on Selected Areas in Communications, 106–117 (2008)
8. Jun, K.S., Giannakis, G.B.: Sequential and Cooperative Sensing for Multi-channel Cognitive Radios. IEEE Transactions on Signal Processing, 4239–4253 (2010)
9. Chang, N.B., Liu, M.Y.: Optimal Channel Probing and Transmission Scheduling for Opportunistic Spectrum Access. IEEE-ACM Transactions on Networking 17, 1805–1818 (2009)
10. Hai, J., feng, L.L., fei, F.R., Poor, H.V.: Optimal selection of channel sensing order in cognitive radio. IEEE Transactions on Wireless Communications 8, 297–307 (2009)
11. Ferguson, T.S.: Optimal stopping and applications, http://www.math.ucla.edu.tom/Stopping/Contents.html

# The Design of Shaped-Beam Bifilar Helix Antenna with Conical Pattern

Xiao-Yun Qu[1], Wei-Hua Zong[2], Zhi-Qun Yang[1], and Jian-Ming Mu[1]

[1] China Aerospace Science and Technology Corporation No.513 Institute,
Yantai, Shandong Province, China 264003
[2] Shandong Provincial Key Laboratory of Industrial Control Technology, School of Automation
Engineering, Qingdao University, Qingdao, Shandong Province, China 266071
selina.qu@163.com, weihuazong@126.com

**Abstract.** A shaped-beam antenna is proposed using bifilar helix antenna. The antenna is fed by a notched balancer. The radiation pattern and the axial ratio changing with the helix pitch distance are simulated in the paper. The measured gain and |S11| are also given. The antenna has a wide bandwidth of more than 40% with conical radiation pattern and circular polarization. It can be used in outer space communications due to its low profile and high reliability.

**Keywords:** helix antenna, bifilar helix antenna, shaped-beam, impedance match.

## 1 Introduction

The circular polarization antenna has been widely used for its inherent performance with the development of wireless communication, measurements and electronic reconnaissance. A number of novel circular polarization antennas have been invented in these years [1-6]. Among these antennas, helix antennas with double or quad filar are of the most popular ones used in satellite measurement and control system [1-4].

There are mainly two types of radiation pattern of helix antennas, axial mode and normal mode. The axial mode helix antenna has a heart-shaped pattern and is the most widely used one. The normal mode helix antenna has a radiation pattern vertical to its axis as dipole antenna.

In this paper, a bifilar helix antenna with circular polarization is proposed. The beam of the proposed antenna can be shaped with conical pattern. The radiation energy of the antenna is concentrated into a cone. Therefore, the radiation pattern can be shaped for particular use in the out space. The proposed antenna is of fast-wave mode type.

The shaped-beam antenna is becoming more and more favorite in the application of the satellite-to-satellite and satellite-to-earth communications. By use of this kind of antenna, the amplitude of the signal can be kept relatively stable for the needed radiation range, and the coverage range of the antenna can be enlarged efficiently.

P. Sénac, M. Ott, and A. Seneviratne (Eds.): ICWCA 2011, LNICST 72, pp. 287–292, 2012.
© Institute for Computer Sciences, Social Informatics and Telecommunications Engineering 2012

## 2 Antenna Design

### 2.1 Design of the Bifilar Helix Antenna

The main parameters of the helix are defined as following :

$D$: diameter of the helix,
$p$: pitch distance of the helix,
$n$: number of the turns,
$l=n\times p$: length along the axis.
$\theta_m$: the maximum radiation direction of the pattern.

The antenna presented in this paper is a fast-wave mode helix antenna. The radiation beam of the antenna is opposite to the direction of the feeding current. The radiation pattern of the bifilar helix antenna is mainly determined by the ratios of D/λ and p/λ. By tuning the parameters of helix pitch distance and diameter, the maximum radiation angle can change from the axial direction to the normal direction. Therefore the radiation pattern can be shaped as conical shape. The conical pattern of bifilar helix antenna is introduced by the complex propagation constant which can be written as [7]:

$$\beta = \beta_r + \beta_i \tag{1}$$

where $\beta_r$ is the real part of the propagation constant. And the propagation factor is:

$$e^{-j\beta z} = e^{-j\beta_i z} e^{-j\beta_r z} \tag{2}$$

When this kind of wave is excited, the angle of the maximum radiation direction is approximated as

$$\theta_m = \cos^{-1}(\beta_r / k) \tag{3}$$

The eigen value equation can be obtained from the boundary conditions. And the propagation constant and radiation field can be solved from the equation. It is not so easy to get the antenna's pattern from the equation. After all, some simulation software can help us to optimize the antenna to satisfy the required radiation performance.

### 2.2 Feeding of the Bifilar Helix Antenna

Compared with the quadrifilar helix antenna, the bifilar helix antenna is more compact in size, and easier to feed [4]. The feeding point is at the top, the two arm of the antenna is feed out of phase.

A balancer is adopted when using coaxial cable to feed the antenna. As shown in Fig. 1, a slot is cut along the outer conductor of the coaxial transmission line. One arm of the helix is connected with the inner conductor, and the other is connected with the outer conductor. Compared with the typical balancer, the outer conductor is turned about 45 degree around the axial to get better impedance match and wider bandwidth.

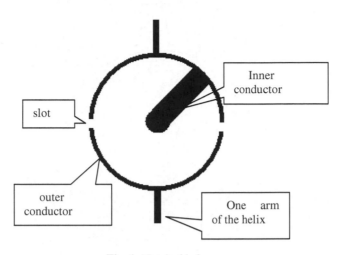

**Fig. 1.** Notched balancer

## 3  Simulation and Measurement

Considering the special environment in the outer space, the selection of the material of the bifilar helix antenna is quite important during the design. The radiation part of the antenna is supported by a kind of insulated material with permittivity of 3 or so. The thickness of the support can be as thin as possible if it is strong enough. The feeding point is located at the top of the antenna. The terminals of the two helixes can be released as free or connected together with the ground due to less current flowing along the terminal of the radiation part.

The antenna has a conical pattern. Its gain and beam shape is decided by the turn numbers of the helixes. It is easier to get shaped beam with more helix turns, whereas the reliability of the structure need be considered with more turns. The turn number of each helix is chosen as 4 in this case.

The antenna is omni-directional in the azimuth plane and is shaped with conical pattern in the elevation plane. Fig. 2 shows the radiation patterns in the elevation plane with the variation of pitch distance of p when D=0.16λ. It is shown that the maximum direction of $\theta_m$ changes from 0° to 90° with the increase of p, and the beam width becomes narrower with the increase of the p. For the case of p=0.224λ, the antenna has a typical heart shape radiation pattern with $\theta_m$=0°, and its 3dB beam-width covers -30°~+30°. For the case of p=0.425λ, $\theta_m$ =64°, its 3dB beam-width covers 45°~81°. For the case of p=0.62λ, $\theta_m$=84°, its 3dB beam-width covers 74°~94°. The radiation pattern is close to the circularity radiation pattern.

Fig. 3 shows the simulated axial ratio of the antenna. It is shown that the axial ratio is better than 5dB within the 3dB beam width. The antenna has perfect circular polarization performance.

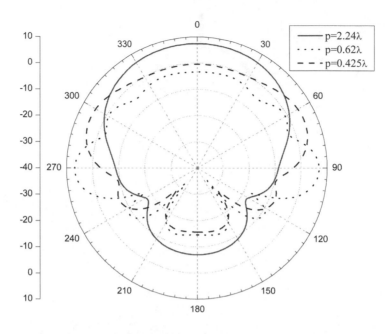

**Fig. 2.** Simulated radiation pattern of the bifilar helix antenna

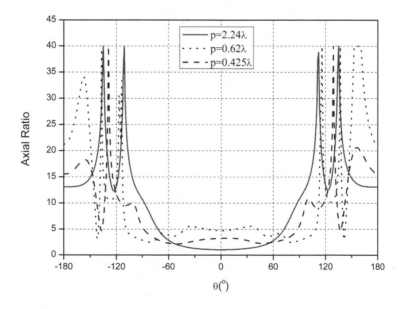

**Fig. 3.** Simulated axial ratio

With the notched balancer, the bandwidth is increased to more than 10 percent. This kind of back-fire antenna is less influenced by the mounting carrier, which act as the ground of the antenna, especially the main lobe. The back lobe will be decreased if the mounting carrier is made of metal material.

Fig. 4 shows the measured $|S_{11}|$. By tuning the feeding part of the helix antenna we can get a perfect match with the bandwidth of more than 40% of the center frequency.

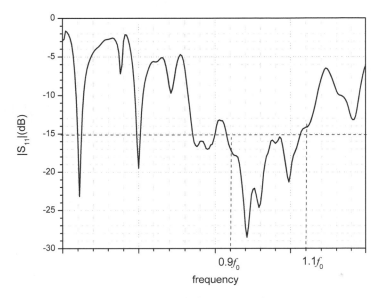

**Fig. 4.** Measured $|S_{11}|$ of the proposed antenna

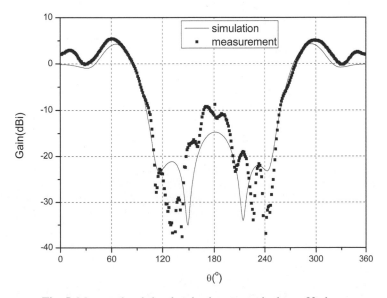

**Fig. 5.** Measured and simulated gain patterns in the $\varphi=0°$ plane

Fig. 5 shows the measured and simulated gain patterns in the φ=0° plane. The 3dB beam width of the antenna covers 45°~78°. It is shown that the measurement agrees well with the simulation, especially in the main beam area. The maximum radiation direction is 58° from simulation result and 60° from the measurement result. This small disagreement may come from the error of permittivity of the supported material adopted in production compared with the simulation one. This kind of error can not be avoided in the first design and is easy to be corrected during the re-design procedure. The small ripples in side lobe and back lobes may come from the measurement error or the system error.

# 4  Conclusion

The bifilar helix antenna with conical pattern has many excellent performances, such as compact structure, easy beam shaping and high reliability. By optimizing the parameters of the helix, different radiation pattern can be obtained meeting special requirement. This kind of antenna has already found its application in the measurement and control communication between satellite and earth.

**Acknowledgment.** The work of Wei-hua Zong was supported in part by Shandong Provincial Education Department, P. R. China under the International Cooperation Program for Excellent Lectures of 2009.

# References

1. Bhuma, N., Himabindh, C.: Right hand circular polarization of a quadrifilar helicalantenna for satellite and mobile communication systems. In: Recent Advances in Space Technology Services and Climate Change (RSTSCC), pp. 307–310 (2010)
2. Sharaiha, A., Letestu, Y.: Quadrifilar helical antennas: Wideband and multiband behavior for GPS applications. In: 2010 International Conference on Electromagnetics in Advanced Applications (ICEAA), pp. 620–623 (2010)
3. Keen, K.M.: Bandwidth dependence of resonant quadrifilar helix antennas. Electronics Letters 46, 550–552 (2010)
4. Chair, R., Yang, S.L.S., Kishk, A.A., Lee, K.F., Luk, K.M.: Aperture Fed Wideband Circularly Polarized Rectangular Stair Shaped Dielectric Resonator Antenna. IEEE Trans., Antennas and Propagat 54(4), 1350–1352 (2006)
5. Zainud-Deen, S.H.: Characteristics of Two-arm Wire Conical Spiral Antennas. In: NRSC (2004)
6. Chen, H.-D., Chen, W.-S.: Probe Feed Compact Circular Microstrip Antennaa for Circular Polarization. Microwave Opt., Technol. Lett. 29(1), 52–54 (2001)
7. Mittra, R.: Propagation and Radiation Characteristics of Taper Helix with a Conducting Core and Dielectric. IEEE Trans. Antennas Propag. 38, 578–584 (1990)

# A Precoding Scheme to Improve Performances of MIMO Systems

Zhenchuan Zhang[1], Bo Chen[1], and Ting Luo[2]

[1] School of Information Science & Engineering, Northeastern University
Shenyang 110004, China
[2] Shenyang Radio and Television University
Shenyang 110003, China
zhangzhenchuan@ise.neu.edu.cn, chenbo201@126.com

**Abstract.** MIMO technology can be divided into two ways: based on the spatial multiplexing technique, such as VBLAST, and based on the launch diversity technology, such as STBC. This paper proposes a structure which mixes the two ways, that is STBC-VBLAST structure. In principle of minimizing pair-error probability, we design the precoding matrix of this system using the features beam molding algorithm. This proposal is suitable for TDD mode. It takes advantage of CSI to reduce error rate and increase capacity. Simulation results show that this algorithm could achieve remarkable effects, especially in low constellation dimension.

**Keywords:** MIMO, Precoding, Features beam shaping.

## 1 Introduction

MIMO (multi-input multi-output)[1]system which is good at channel capacity and diversitygain, is regarded as the development direction of the future wireless communication system. In 1990s based on the multiple antenna channel sending principle, there is a new technology—Space-time codes. According to the different designing methods it can be divided into two ways: based on the spatial multiplexing technique, such as VBLAST (vertical bell layered space-time code), and based on the launch diversity technology, such as STBC (space-time block codes).

This paper proposes a STBC-VBLAST mixing system [2], and design the precode of sending signal.

## 2 STBC-VBLAST System Precoding Model

In Ref. [3] Lan Zhao etc. come up with the STBC-VBLAST composite structure, that is, multiple STBC code block reuse in space, and transmit at the same time, the receiver detect by group and decode the multiple STBC code block one by one. Tianyu Mao etc. propose a new STBC-VBLAST mixing scheme in Ref. [4]. They use VBLAST transmission scheme in some antennas, while in the remaining antennas

P. Sénac, M. Ott, and A. Seneviratne (Eds.): ICWCA 2011, LNICST 72, pp. 293–298, 2012.
© Institute for Computer Sciences, Social Informatics and Telecommunications Engineering 2012

reuse the multiple STBC code blocks together to transmit, the receiver use sorting continuous interference eliminate QR assay to decode. In Ref. [5] proposed a precoding transmission scheme based on the structure of Ref. [4], it improves the original system considerably both in the flat decline and frequency selective fading channel.

This paper using the known CSI (channel status information) of transmitter propose a precoding transmission scheme based on the STBC-VBLAST mixing structure in Ref. [3],.This scheme referencing the features beam molding algorithm of the monolayer STBC system in Ref. [6], process the each STBC layer's independent feature beam molding on STBC-VBLAST mixing structure.

The precoding system scheme of STBC-VBLAST composite structure is shown as Fig.1.

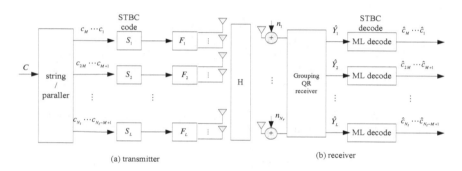

(a) transmitter                    (b) receiver

**Fig. 1.** STBC-VBLAST precoding system scheme

We suppose that the number of transmitting and receiving antenna is $N_t$ and $N_r$ ($N_r \geq N_t$). The original sending signal is $C = \begin{bmatrix} c_1 & c_2 & \cdots & c_{N_t} \end{bmatrix}$. The number of STBC code blocks reuse layer is $L$. Every layer using its code elements to STBC code, form $S_u$ ($1 \leq u \leq L$) which is $M \times T$ dimension matrix, standing for sending $M$ code element symbols in $T$ time piece. Each STBC layer process by linear precoding matrix, finally reuse the signal on $N_t$ antennas to transmit. The value of $M$ is decided by the STBC code scheme we taken, e.g. if we take G2 (Alamouti) code [7] scheme, $M=2$, $L=N_t/2$, as Fig.2 shown.

$$S = \begin{bmatrix} c_1 & -c_2^* \\ c_2 & c_1^* \\ c_3 & -c_4^* \\ c_4 & c_3^* \\ \vdots & \vdots \\ c_{N_t-1} & -c_{N_t}^* \\ c_{N_t} & c_{N_t-1}^* \end{bmatrix} \begin{matrix} \left.\vphantom{\begin{matrix}c\\c\end{matrix}}\right\} \text{Layer 1 STBC code block } S_1 \\ \left.\vphantom{\begin{matrix}c\\c\end{matrix}}\right\} \text{Layer 2 STBC code block } S_2 \\ \\ \left.\vphantom{\begin{matrix}c\\c\end{matrix}}\right\} \text{Layer } L \text{ STBC code block } S_L \end{matrix}$$

The first The second
moment    moment

**Fig. 2.** Piece layered schemes in G2 code scheme

Transmitting signals across a quasi-static flat Rayleigh fading channel $H$, arrive at the receiver.

The received signal is $Y = HFS + n$, $F$ is the precoding matrix whose designing method is expressed in part **3**. $n$ is the $N_r \times T$ dimensional complex Gaussian white noise, in which each element obeys the mean for 0, variance for $\delta^2 / 2$ Gaussian distribution independently. Then the receiver divides the equivalent matrix $HF$ by QR to gain the sufficient statistics $\hat{Y} = Q^H Y = RS + \hat{n}$. It processes $R$ by the layers of the transmitter, to draw the equivalent son channel which is corresponded each layer's signal coded by STBC matrix $R_{uu}$.

Signal $\hat{Y}$ and noise $\hat{n}$ also take the block process, so after the STBC coded signal of layer $u$ $S_u$ transmitted to the receiver, the received signal is expressed as (1).

$$\hat{y}_u = R_{u,u} S_u + \sum_{l=u+1}^{L} R_{u,l} S_l + \hat{n}_u, 1 \leq u \leq L \tag{1}$$

The receiver decodes from layer $L$ layer by layer. When STBC decode in each layer, we use ML (maximum likelihood) decode [8], gaining code element of the signal of layer $u$ is $\hat{c}_{(u-1)M+1} \cdots \hat{c}_{uM}$.

## 3 The Design of Precoding Based on the Composite Structure

According to the transmitting antenna corresponding different STBC code block, we make every adjacent $M$ line of the channel matrix $H = \begin{bmatrix} H_1 & H_2 & \cdots & H_L \end{bmatrix}$. $H_u$ is the $N_r \times M$ dimensional channel son matrix composed by the $(u-1)M+1$ line and the $uM$ line. To reduce the interference between each layer effectively, we need precode each layer independently. Its structure is as (2) shown.

$$F = \begin{bmatrix} F_1 & 0 & \cdots & 0 \\ 0 & F_2 & \ddots & \vdots \\ \vdots & \ddots & \ddots & 0 \\ 0 & \cdots & 0 & F_L \end{bmatrix} \tag{2}$$

In (2), $F_u$ is $M \times M$ dimensional matrix, represent the precoding matrix which is corresponding with the STBC code block of layer $u$. We can design $F_u$ according to the principle of making paired mistake rate of layer $u$. The paired error probability of layer $u$ STBC boundary meets (3).

$$P(S_u \to \hat{S}_u) \leq [\det(I + H_u F_u (S_u - \hat{S}_u)(S_u - \hat{S}_u)^H F_u^H H_u^H)]^{-N_r} \tag{3}$$

In order to make (3) minimum, $F_u$ in meeting energy constraint conditions, need to make (4) maximum.

$$\max_{tr(F_u F_u^H) < E_s} \det(I + H_u F_u (S_u - \hat{S}_u)(S_u - \hat{S}_u)^H F_u^H H_u^H) \tag{4}$$

If the code words differential matrix is $W_u = (S_u - \hat{S}_u)(S_u - \hat{S}_u)^H$, the transmitter divides $H_u$ by QR matrix $H_u = Q_{u,u}^{'} R_{u,u}^{'}$, we can gain $\max_{tr(F_u F_u^H) < E_s} \det[I_M + R_{u,u}^{'} F_u W_{ss,u} (F_u^{'})^H (R_{u,u}^{'})^H / \delta_n^2]$. Make singular value decomposition to $R_{u,u}^{'}$, $R_{u,u}^{'} = U_u \Lambda_u V_u^H$. Diagonal matrix $\Lambda_u = diag\left[ \lambda_{R_u,u,1} \quad \lambda_{R_u,u,2} \quad \cdots \quad \lambda_{R_u,u,M} \right]$, each non-zero elements is in descending order. We gain (5).

$$
\max_{tr(F_u F_u^H) < E_s} \det\left( I_M + \frac{1}{\delta_n^2} U_u \Lambda_u V_u^H F_u W_{ss,u} F_u^H V_u \Lambda_u U_u^H \right)
$$
$$
= \max_{tr(F_u F_u^H) < E_s} \det\left( I_M + \frac{1}{\delta_n^2} \Lambda_u V_u^H F_u W_{ss,u} F_u^H V_u \Lambda_u \right)
$$
(5)

In terms of Hadamard inequality, arbitrary phalanx $B$ meets: $\det(B) \le \prod_i B_{i,i}$, '=' is obtained when the $B$ for diagonal matrix. So if (5) is maximum, we must assure the matrix in det(.) is diagonal matrix. Due to using orthogonal STBC code, $W_{ss,u} = \alpha I$, α is decided by different modulation dimension and STBC code scheme. (5) can be written into (6).

$$
\max_{tr(F_u F_u^H) < E_s} \det\left( I_M + \frac{\alpha}{\delta_n^2} \Lambda_u V_u^H F_u F_u^H V_u \Lambda_u \right)
$$
(6)

When the eigenmatrix of $F_u F_u^H$ match $V_u$, just meeting $F_u F_u^H = V_u P V_u^H$, and the matrix in det(.) is diagonal matrix, (6) can gain the maximum. At this moment the precoding matrix of layer $u$ is $F_u = V_u P^{1/2}$. $V_u$ is features beam forming direction, $P_u$ is diagonal matrix, representing the energy distribution of each beam direction, each element on diagonal line obeys the water-filling distribute.

Making each STBC code block of layer $1 \cdots L$ diagonalization according to the above method, finally we can gain the precoding matrix $F$, just as (2) shown. If analyzing the design of precoding matrix by making the channel ergodic capacity biggest, we gain that the channel capacity of layer $u$ is described as (7).

$$
C_u = \max_{tr(F_u F_u^H) < E_s} \log_2 \det(I_{N_r} + H_u F_u S_u S_u^H F_u^H H_u^H / \delta_n^2)
$$
(7)

Seeking for the question of making (7) maximization is equivalent with the question of making (4) maximization. So the STBC-VBLAST precoding system based on the above features beam shaping method can make the BER (bit error rate) lower effectively and improve the channel capacity.

## 4  Simulations

Flat Rayleigh fading channel model is used in simulations. $H$ is the $N_r \times N$ dimensional matrix in which each element obeys the mean for 0, variance for 1 Gaussian distribution. The system has four transmitting antennas and four receiving antennas. Ready to send signal is divided into 2 layers. Each layer adopts G2 code scheme to STBC code, just Alamouti code.

We first use common STBC-VBLAST structure to send signals, getting the curve expressed by "-o-"; then we use the precoding STBC-VBLAST structure proposed by this paper to transmit, getting the curve expressed by "-*-".

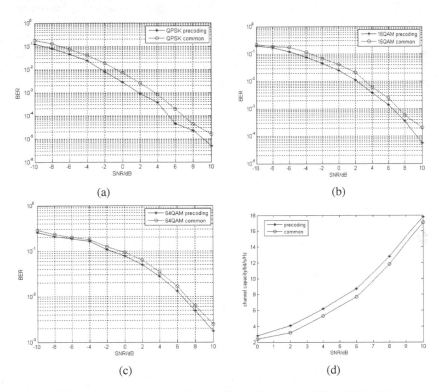

(a)

(b)

(c)

(d)

**Fig. 3.** BER and channel capacity of precoding and common STBC-VBLAST system

In Fig.3 (a)(b)(c), horizontal ordinate is SNR (signal to noise ratio) whose unit is dB. Vertical axis is BER. We compare the BER of the two methods under QPSK, 16QAM and 64QAM signal modulation. According them, we can make the blow conclusion. In Fig.3(a) QPSK modulation, the algorithm of feature beam molding proposed in this paper can make the system precoding gain reach about 2dB; In Fig.3(b) 16QAM modulation, the gain can reach about  0.5 dB; In Fig.3(c) 64QAM modulation, the precoding gain is about 0.1~0.2 dB. So, by comparing we can obtain that at the same SNR condition feature beam molding precoding algorithm can improve the system BER, but along with the increasing of modulation dimension, the performance of BER improving has reduced.

Fig.3 (d) simulates the traversal channel capacity of low SNR in QPSK modulation. The channel capacity of the precoding STBC-VBLAST system is improved to some extent than the common system, but increment is limited.

## 5 Conclusions

In this paper we propose a precoding scheme for STBC-VBLAST mixing structure. This method designs the precoding matrix on the principle of making the paired error probability of the system smallest or the channel capacity maximum by the feature beam molding algorithm.

The simulation use Matlab shows that in the same condition of SNR, the method proposed in this paper can make the utmost of the CSI, effectively reduce the BER of STBC-VBLAST system and improve the channel capacity. In the flat Rayleigh fading channel, using low dimension signal modulation the effect is more apparent. In the paper we only discussed the flat Rayleigh fading channel. Making the MIMO-OFDM system self-adapting transmission according to the different channel conditions is an important way in future.

## References

1. Liu, X., Shen, J.: Challenges of MIMO Technology and Testing in LTE. J. Modern Telecommunication Technology 32, 24–27 (2009)
2. Li, Y.: The Research of Precoding Technology for Multi-antenna System. Master Degree Theses. CAAC, Tianjin (2009)
3. Zhao, L., Dubey, V.K.: Detection Schemes for Space-time Block Code and Spatial Multiplexing Combined System. J. IEEE Communication Letters, 49–51 (2005)
4. Mao, T., Motani, M.: STBC-VBLAST for MIMO Wireless Communication Systems. In: IEEE International Conference on Communications, pp. 2266–2270 (2005)
5. Meng, C., Tuqan, J.: Precoded STBC-VBLAST for MIMO Wireless Communication Systems. In: IEEE International Conference on Acoustics, Speech and Signal Processing, pp. 337–340 (2007)
6. Zhao, Y., Adve, R., Lim, T.J.: Optimal STBC Precoding with Channel Covariance Feedback for Minimum Error Probability. In: 15th IEEE International Symposium on Personal, Indoor and Mobile Radio Communications, pp. 503–507 (2004)
7. Li, Y.: Precoding For Transmit Diversity in LTE. J. Electronic Test, 26–29 (2009)
8. Tarokh, V., Hafarkhani, H., Robert Calderbank, A.: Space-time Block Coding for Wireless Communications: Performance Results. J. IEEE Journal on selected areas in communications 17, 451–460 (1999)

# A New Dynamic Spectrum Access Technology Based on the Multi-features Model Clustering in the Cognitive Network

Jupeng Li*, Zhenhui Tan, Houjin Chen, and Cheng Tao

School of Electronics and Information Engineering, Beijing Jiaotong University,
Haidian District ShangYuanCun 3. Beijing, China
{jpli1,zhhtan,hjchen,chtao}@bjtu.edu.cn

**Abstract.** In order to fully utilize the scarce spectrum resources, with the development of cognitive radio technologies, dynamic spectrum access becomes a promising approach to increase the efficiency of spectrum usage. In this paper, we consider the spectrum access in wireless networks with multiple selfish legacy spectrum holders and unlicensed users. In order to improve transmission quality for different cognitive users with various services in the cognitive network, a novel dynamic spectrum access technology based on multi-features model clustering is presented. After the model of the sub-channels extracted, these channels are clustered into different spectrum pools using multi-objective clustering algorithm. These channels in white pools are priority to be accessed for cognitive users. Analysis and simulation results show that the access efficiency of channels can be improved for cognitive users.

**Keywords:** Cognitive radio, multi-features model, spectrum pooling clustering, dynamic spectrum access.

## 1 Introduction

Recently, regulatory bodies like the Federal Communications Commission (FCC) in the United States are recognizing that current static spectrum allocation can be very inefficient considering the bandwidth demands may vary highly along the time dimension or the space dimension [1]. The spectrum shortage is not scarce physically, but the frequency management policy leads to this misunderstanding.

Cognitive Radio (CR) is a kind of intelligent radio which can constantly senses surrounding environment and changes own situation. According to the external environment change for making decisions, cognitive user adjusts its own communication mechanism (carrier frequency, modulation patterns, transmission power, etc). The biggest advantage is that cognitive users can access network without

---

* Supported by the Important National Science & Technology Specific Projects (2009ZX03003-007-03), the National High Technology Development 863 Program of China with Grant (2009AA011805), and the Fundamental Research Funds for the Central Universities (2009JBM010).

P. Sénac, M. Ott, and A. Seneviratne (Eds.): ICWCA 2011, LNICST 72, pp. 299–309, 2012.

a special authorization by frequency management department and interfering the authorized users. They dynamically access spectrum of the Primary Users (PU) which has been authorized and use the so-called idle spectrum resources by opportunity. This greatly enhances the efficiency of radio resource. As a result, it can not only improve the efficiency of spectrum resource utilization but also enhance the link stability, network coverage and system capacity, obviously.

At present, Dynamic Spectrum Access (DSA) technology has been widely researched which based on the spectrum pooling clustering strategy. DSA permits the cognitive users accessing the band without authorization [2-5].

Spectrum pooling, first presented by Mitola J., allows primary user to lease its band to cognitive users during the time when don't occupy spectrum in order to realize spectrum sharing [3]. When there are many idle channels can be used for cognitive users, how to select channels to obtain better access ability and achieve a better transmission quality is a difficult problem in the current research of cognitive radio. The basic idea of spectrum pooling strategy [3] is to distribute the spectrum outside the special frequency spectrum to different types and  then merged into several public spectrum pools, according to ultralow frequency, low frequency, intermediate frequency and high frequency. Spectrum pooling can be divided into several sub-channels. Dr Seidel divided spectrum into excluded space, gray space, and white space. Cognitive users determine their own spectrum access strategies [6] according to the result of spectrum perception. Luwen Z. integrates ideas about how to set up spectrum pools, divide certain areas of spectrum into white spectrum pooling, gray spectrum pooling and black spectrum pooling on the basis of energy detection. Cognitive users mainly access the white channels for better transmission [7]. According to the current research, these methods do not consider cognitive user's various transmission types of channel requirements, but rather  doing some simplification assumptions. Comparing to the actual diversity application of network transmission, more attention should be paid on to solve cognitive user's access strategies of dynamic spectrum well.

To satisfy the different needs of channel performance along with different transmission, this paper presents a novel dynamic spectrum access technical based on multi-features model clustering. Once the spectrum pooling is established, cognitive users with different needs can choose these suitable channels to access dynamically, according to the characters of bearing services. The reminder of this paper is organized as follows: The system model of spectrum pooling is described in Section II. In Section III, we formulate dynamic spectrum access strategy based on the multi-features model clustering. The simulation studies are provided in Section IV. Finally, Section VI concludes this paper.

## 2   System Model

### 2.1   Spectrum Pool Model

Based on the channel performance requirements of different transmission types, cognitive users can improve own multimedia services flexibility and the utilization rate of the spectrum by renting channels in the spectrum pooling by opportunity.

Reference [8] shows that current spectrum allocation policy leads to different frequencies at the same time (place), or the same frequency at different time (place) occupied degree uniform. Considering hardware restrictions of the terminals and cost constraint, cognitive users should focus on some specific frequencies according to transmission services types. In the following analysis, we assume that cognitive users only focus on $n$ sub-channels $F = \{ f_i \mid i = 1, 2, \cdots, n \}$ generally. According to certain classification rules, the sub-channels are divided into spectrum pooling $P = \{ p_i \mid i = 1, 2, \cdots, k \}$, here $k \leq n$, and each channel in spectrum pooling has an approximate performance to satisfy current cognitive user's transmission needs. The model of this spectrum pooling shows in Fig 1.

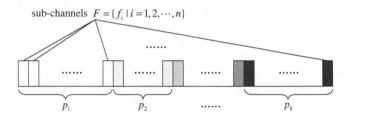

**Fig. 1.** This shows a model of the spectrum pooling, which includes $n$ sub-channels $F = \{ f_i \mid i = 1, 2, \cdots, n \}$. According to certain classification rules, the sub-channels are divided into spectrum pooling $P = \{ p_i \mid i = 1, 2, \cdots, k \}$, here $k \leq n$, and each channel in spectrum pooling has an approximate performance to satisfy current cognitive user's transmission needs.

The bearer ability of spectrum pooling for different cognitive users' transmission needs declined accordingly. (1) Spectrum pooling (white space) is suitable for the current needs of cognitive users' transmission. (2) Spectrum pooling $p_b$ ($b = 2, 3, \cdots, k-1$, gray space) partly meet the needs, due to the low energy authorized users and interference occupation. And (3) Spectrum pooling $p_k$ (black space) cannot be used in cognitive users' services transmission, because of the high energy of and interference occupation to authorized users.

Using various spectrum senses, estimation and analysis technologies, cognitive users realize the observation to the available channel performance. Once the establishment of spectrum pooling, they formulate the spectrum access strategies to choose sub-channels of white spectrum pool, so that a better services transmission performance can be gotten.

## 2.2  Multi-features Model

To describe the dynamic characters of the cognitive network, features of each sub-channel should defined according to time variation and environment changes, including activity of primary user, frequency band and bandwidth, etc. Therefore, features such as interference grade, channel error ratio, path loss, link layer delay and holding time are introduced to explain the performance of certain channels. Reference [9] gives these common features to character channel performances.

(1) *Interference threshold H* : the superior limit of signal power that cognitive users are allowed to transmit, which is determined by the interference degree of the main user's receiving end.

(2) *Path loss L* : the amount of loss caused by propagation environment introduction between transmitters and receivers. Path loss increases following the working spectrum location. Similarly, increment of transmission power can decrease path loss, but will cause greater interference to other users.

(3) *Error ratio E* : index that is measured data transmission accuracy within the time specified. According to different modulation modes and interference levels, channel error ratio would be different.

(4) *Link layer delay D* : To address different path loss, wireless link error, and interference, different types of link layer protocols are required at different spectrum bands. This results in different link layer packet transmission delay.

(5) *Holding time T* : Holding time refers to the expected time duration that the CR user can occupy a licensed band before getting interrupted. Obviously, the longer the holding time, the better the quality would be.

Owing to the diversity of cognitive user transmission services, features of sub-channel are required to synthesized to evaluate its performance and to guide the cognitive users to create dynamic access strategies of channels. To character the transmission features of available channels dynamically, here a multi-features model $M(f)$ of sub-channel $f$ is established.

$$M(f) = \left[ I^1, I^2, \cdots, I^j, \cdots, I^m \right], 1 \le j \le m. \tag{1}$$

The multi-features model includes $m$ features, $I^j$ refers to the first $j$ feature of the channel. Here, both $I^j$ and $m$ are variables, and the combination includes these features that characterize the sub-channels mostly to services be transmitted. For the $n$ sub-channels $F = \{ f_i \mid i = 1, 2, \cdots, n \}$, the multi-features model can be expressed as a matrix by size of $n \times m$, $M_{n \times m}(F) = [I_i^j]_{n \times m}$, $1 \le i \le n$, $1 \le j \le m$,

$$M_{n \times m}(F) = \begin{bmatrix} I_1^1 & I_1^2 & \cdots & I_1^m \\ I_2^1 & I_2^2 & \cdots & I_2^m \\ \vdots & \vdots & \ddots & \vdots \\ I_n^1 & I_n^2 & \cdots & I_n^m \end{bmatrix}. \tag{2}$$

Where, $I_i^j$ refers to the first $j$ feature of the sub-channel. As a matter of convenience to describe below, the row vector $M_{i\bullet} = [I_i^1, I_i^2, \cdots, I_i^j, \cdots I_i^m]$ can be seen as one sample of the model $M$ , column vector $M_{\bullet j} = [I_1^j, I_2^j, \cdots, I_i^j, \cdots I_n^j]^{\mathrm{T}}$ as a characteristic or quality.

# 3 Dynamic Spectrum Access Strategy Based on the Multi-features Model Clustering

## 3.1 Multi-objective Clustering Algorithm

The objective of cluster analysis is the classification of objects according to similarities among them, and organizing of data into several groups. Clustering techniques are among the unsupervised methods, they do not use prior class identifiers.. The main potential of clustering is to detect the underlying structure in data for classification and pattern recognition. The data are typically observations of some physical process. Each observation consists of n measured variables, grouped into an m-dimensional row vector $\mathbf{x}_i = [x_{i1}, x_{i2}, \cdots, x_{im}]^{\mathrm{T}}$, $\mathbf{x}_i \in \mathbf{R}^n$. n observations is denoted by $\mathbf{X} = \{\mathbf{x}_i \mid i = 1, 2, \cdots, n\}$, and is represented as an $n \times m$ matrix:

$$\mathbf{X} = \begin{bmatrix} x_{11} & x_{12} & \cdots & x_{m1} \\ x_{21} & x_{22} & \cdots & x_{m2} \\ \vdots & \vdots & \ddots & \vdots \\ x_{n1} & x_{n2} & \cdots & x_{nm} \end{bmatrix}. \tag{3}$$

The clustered data $\mathbf{X}$ can be described as $\mathbf{U} = [\mu_{ij}]_{n \times k}$, meeting the condition in (4):

$$C_k = \{\mathbf{U} \in \mathbf{R}^{n \times k} \mid \mu_{ij} \in 0, 1, \forall i, j; \sum_{j=1}^{k} \mu_{ij} = 1, \forall i; 0 < \sum_{i=1}^{n} \mu_{ij} < n, \forall j\}. \tag{4}$$

Contrast with multi-features model $M_{n \times m}(F)$, the row vector $\mathbf{x}_i = [x_{i1}, x_{i2}, \cdots, x_{im}]^{\mathrm{T}}$ of $\mathbf{X}$ corresponds to features model of sub-channel $i$, and the column vector (property) corresponds to a feature of the channel $F = \{f_i \mid i = 1, 2, \cdots, n\}$. Multi-objective clustering algorithm are used to establish spectrum pooling, based on the multi-features model of the channel that was paid attention by cognitive user according to certain rules.

## 3.2 Dynamic Spectrum Access Based on the Multi-features Model Clustering

The multi-objective clustering algorithms, each method has its own properties and scopes of application. To achieve the target that cognitive users get a high speed of communication, K- Means Clustering method can be used here that is widely used for massive dataset with fast convergence rate. However, this method is limited to sensitiveness initial clustering center and will produce uncertain results, due to selecting initial clustering center randomly in the most common applications. This paper proposed a feature space partition method to calculate an optimized initial clustering center for K-Means clustering algorithm and achieved spectrum pooling rapidly with multi-features model.

Taking the multi-features model $M_{n \times m}(F) = [I_i^j]_{n \times m}$ and number of spectrum pooling $k$ of $F = \{f_i \mid i = 1, 2, \cdots, n\}$ as input, the spectrum pooling access strategy algorithm based on improved K-Means clustering algorithm is as follows.

(1) *Partition of Feature Space*

Multi-features model of channel $F$ is given, features space $W^j$ of $F$ can be calculated by features space $M_{\bullet j}$ ( $j = 1, 2, \cdots, m$ ),

$$W = \prod_{j=1}^{m} W^j = \prod_{j=1}^{m} [I_{\min}^j, I_{\max}^j]. \tag{5}$$

Here, $I_{\min}^j$ and $I_{\max}^j$ are the minimum and maximum characteristics values respectively. According to the classification number $k$, the features space of $I^j$ can be divided into $k$ subinterval $W_b^j$ without crossing,

$$W_b^j = (I_{\min}^j + \frac{(b-1)(I_{\max}^j - I_{\min}^j)}{k}, \ I_{\min}^j + \frac{b(I_{\max}^j - I_{\min}^j)}{k}], \ b = 2, 3, \cdots, k. \tag{6}$$

Especially, the left side of $W_1^j$ is closed interval when $b = 1$ to maintain the integrity of the parameters space.

(2) *Multi-Features Model Coding*

The model $M(f_i) = \left[ I_i^1, I_i^2, \cdots, I_i^j, \cdots, I_i^m \right]$ of channel responds to one sequence of binary $(b_i^1, b_i^2, \cdots, b_i^m)$, meeting $M(f_i) \in \prod_{j=1}^{m} W_{b_i^j}^j$, and,

$$I_i^j \in W_{b_i^j}^j, \ j = 1, 2, \cdots, m. \tag{7}$$

Here, this vector can be named code of multi-features model, shown as,

$$B(f_i) = (b_i^1, b_i^2, \cdots, b_i^m). \tag{8}$$

(3) *Calculate the Initial Clustering Centers*

By grouping the multi-features model with same model code into one group $G_b^0$, the average method are used to calculate the initial clustering center $C_b^0$ for each set,

$$C_b^0 = \frac{1}{n_b} \sum_{i=1}^{n_b} M(f_i), \ b = 1, 2, \cdots, k. \tag{9}$$

Here, $n_b$ is the number of channel contained in $G_b^0$.

(4) *Spectrum Pooling Clustering*

The distance between channel model $M(f_i)$, $1 \le i \le n$ and clustering centers is calculated in (10),

$$d(M(f_i), C_b^t) = \sum_{j=1}^{m} \left\| I_i^j - c_b^j \right\|^2 . \tag{10}$$

Parameter $t$ is iteration of clustering centers, the closest clustering center is classified into group $G_b^t$.

(5) *Clustering Centers Update*

Calculate new data clustering center through $G_b^t$ obtained by the time $t$.

$$C_b^{t+1} = \frac{1}{n_b} \sum_{i=1}^{n_b} M(f_i), \ b = 1, 2, \cdots, k . \tag{11}$$

Here, $n_b$ is the number of sub-channel. If $C_b^{t+1} = C_b^t$, $b = 1, 2, \cdots, k$, clustering ends and enters spectrum dynamic access strategies stage (6), or turn to (4) and set $t = t + 1$.

(6) *Dynamic Spectrum Access Strategies*

Once spectrum pooling clustering $p_b = G_b^t$, $b = 1, 2, \cdots, k$, is established, cognitive users formulate channel access strategies to access white spectrum pool to get better transmission performance.

Based on requirements of different services transmission, the cognitive users establish spectrum pooling clustering and access strategy process dynamically.

# 4 Simulations and Performance Analysis

## 4.1 Simulations and Experiments

To testify that the proposed adapting multi-features model clustering algorithm can improve the performance of accessing authorized channel for the cognitive users, the following assumptions can be adapted to simulations.

(1) The sub-channels can be accessed for the cognitive users is $F = \{f_i \mid i = 1, 2, \cdots, n\}$, in other words, $n = 9$;

(2) Assume the channel features are many different combinations including interface threshold ($H$), path loss ($L$), error ration ($E$), link layer delay ($D$), and holding time ($T$) and so on. For a complete analysis of spectrum pooling clustering performance, three simulations with different combination of the features were designed, shown in table 1-3. Meanwhile the forth simulation were used to test dynamic performance of our algorithm.

(3) To simplify the simulation analysis, the number of spectrum pooling clustering was set $k = 3$, respectively corresponding to the white spectrum pooling $p_1$, gray spectrum pooling $p_2$ and black spectrum pooling $p_3$.

*The first simulation*: Holding time is the key feature to measure channel quality which is also the most concerned channel feature to cognitive users.. The longer the channel holding time is, the better the channel quality can be achieved for cognitive users. Channel holding time is used as the single feature of the first simulation experiment. The channel situation was shown in table 1.

**Table 1.** Sub-channels utilization for the first simulation

|   | Sub-channels | | | | | | | | |
|---|------|------|------|------|------|------|------|------|------|
|   | $f_1$ | $f_2$ | $f_3$ | $f_4$ | $f_5$ | $f_6$ | $f_7$ | $f_8$ | $f_9$ |
| $T$ | 16 | 32 | 22 | 45 | 2 | 18 | 21 | 5 | 38 |

*The second simulation*: Except channel holding time, the channel interference threshold was added. To find the effect of two features on the spectrum clustering result, the specific channel features are shown in table 2.

**Table 2.** Sub-channels utilization for the second simulation

|   | Sub-channels | | | | | | | | |
|---|------|------|------|------|------|------|------|------|------|
|   | $f_1$ | $f_2$ | $f_3$ | $f_4$ | $f_5$ | $f_6$ | $f_7$ | $f_8$ | $f_9$ |
| $T$ | 16 | 32 | 22 | 45 | 2 | 18 | 21 | 5 | 38 |
| $D$ | 0.8 | 0.9 | 0.4 | 10 | 0.4 | 0.5 | 0.5 | 0.1 | 0.9 |

*The third simulation*: The third simulation experiment designed contained five kinds of common channel features, including holding time and interference threshold used in the first and the second simulation. The result was shown in table 3.

**Table 3.** Sub-channels utilization for the third simulation

|   | Sub-channels | | | | | | | | |
|---|------|------|------|------|------|------|------|------|------|
|   | $f_1$ | $f_2$ | $f_3$ | $f_4$ | $f_5$ | $f_6$ | $f_7$ | $f_8$ | $f_9$ |
| $T$ | 16 | 32 | 22 | 45 | 2 | 18 | 21 | 5 | 38 |
| $D$ | 0.8 | 0.9 | 0.4 | 10 | 0.4 | 0.5 | 0.5 | 0.1 | 0.9 |
| $L$ | 0.02 | 0.08 | 0.5 | 0.01 | 0.3 | 0.1 | 0.01 | 0.3 | 0.04 |
| $E$ | 1 | 1 | 10 | 2 | 6 | 8 | 12 | 4 | 2 |
| $H$ | 1.0 | 0.2 | 2.3 | 0.02 | 0.7 | 0.4 | 0.08 | 1.2 | 0.1 |

*The fourth simulation*: In order to inspect effectiveness of the algorithm further, channel usable time obeys the uniform distribution with the parameters of $(T_{\min} = 0, T_{\max} = 5)$. The spectrum pooling cluster was simulated 1024 times and the channel holding time was re-generated each simulation. Here the average holding time of all the spectrum pool is presented.

## 4.2   Simulation Results and Performance Analysis

In the environment given in 4.1, four experiments are simulated for $F = \{f_i \mid i = 1, 2, \cdots, 9\}$ using Matlab R2006. The results of spectrum pooling clustering were obtained.

The spectrum pooling clustering result for the first experiment is:

$$P_1 = \{f_2, f_4, f_9\}, \quad P_2 = \{f_1, f_3, f_6, f_7\}, \quad P_3 = \{f_5, f_8\}.$$

The average holding time of white spectrum pooling $p_1$ is 38.33, is bigger than the gray and black spectrum pooling of 19.25 and 3.5. Then, cognitive users formulated the accessing strategy according to the generating spectrum pooling. The available sub-channels in white spectrum pool $p_1$ will be chosen firstly as the high-performance transmission channels. The first simulation experiment can get similar results using the spectrum pooling clustering method referred in document [4]. But the multi-characteristic parameters spectrum pooling, such as the second and third simulation experiment designed here, cannot be achieved.

The spectrum pooling results for the second simulation experiment is:

$$P_2 = \{f_1, f_2, f_3, f_6, f_7, f_9\}, \quad P_1 = \{f_4\}, \quad P_3 = \{f_5, f_8\}.$$

And the clustering result for the third simulation is:

$$P_1 = \{f_2, f_9\}, \quad P_2 = \{f_4\}, \quad P_3 = \{f_1, f_3, f_5, f_6, f_7, f_8\}.$$

Contrasting results among these three simulations, more channel features have greater effects on the spectrum pooling clustering. The comparison of average holding time between three simulations is shown in Fig 2. After clustering, the average holding time has greater changes. Due to increasing the number of features, the average holding time of spectrum pooling $p_1$ was decreased. Because the link layer delay of channel $f_4$ is big enough, this channel was grouped into other spectrum pooling. Though the average holding time of white spectrum pooling was shorter, it is longer than the time of black spectrum pooling.

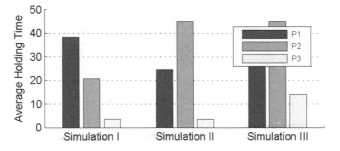

**Fig. 2.** This shows Average Holding Time of the three experiments, in which blue bars are the first simulation results, green bars are the second results and red bars are the third results

Spectrum pooling clustering of dynamic spectrum was given in the forth simulation. The front 64 times simulation results of average holding time are plotted in Fig 3. The average holding time of white spectrum pooling is longer than other spectrum pools.

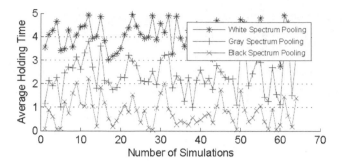

**Fig. 3.** This shows dynamic simulation results of spectrum spooling clustering. The average holding time of white spectrum pooling is longer than other spectrum pools.

## 5 Conclusion

To present an universal and accuracy dynamic accessing dynamic technology based on spectrum pooling, the multi-feature model and K-Means clustering are used in this paper. Combining the efficient primary users detection technologies, such as circle-steady detection and joint detection the spectrum features was characterized comprehensively using the multi-features model of sub-channels. Thus the spectrum pooling clustering provides a more accurate and reliable criteria for cognitive users when accessing channels. Also a new idea of the spectrum assigning is given: the sub-channels can be clustered according to the different demands of different cognitive users. According to the demands of services quality, cognitive users choose a more suitable sub-channel to access dynamically and the transmission performance of the whole system can be improved greatly.

The different channel features have the same effect to the spectrum pooling clustering. But actually, they have different influence coefficients to different services of cognitive users. Using an influence coefficient in the channel multi-features model in our future research, the accuracy of the spectrum clustering can be improved. And a more accurate and reliable basis is given for cognitive users to access sub-channels.

## References

1. Federal Communications Commission, Notice of proposed rule making and order. ET Docket No 03-222. FCC, USA (2003)
2. Cabric, D., Mishra, S., Willkomm, D., Brodersen, R., Wolisz, A.: A cognitive radio approach for usage of virtual unlicensed spectrum. IST Mobile Summit (2005)
3. Mitola, J.: Cognitive radio for flexible mobile multimedia communication. Mobile Multimedia Communication 11(1), 3–10 (1999)
4. Weiss, T., Jondral, F.: Spectrum Pooling - An Innovative Strategy for the Enhancement of Spectrum Efficiency. IEEE Communications Magazine 42(3), 8–14 (2004)
5. Friedrich, K.: Cognitive Radio – A Necessity for Spectrum Pooling. Universität Karlsruhe Communications Engineering Lab (2006)

6. Seidel, S.: IEEE 802 Tutorial: Cognitive Radio (2010),
   http://www.ieee80-2.org/802tutorial/-
   july05/IEEE/20802/20CR/20Tutorial/207-18-05/
   20se-idel/20input.pdf
7. Luwen, Z., Zhimin, M., Zhijie, Z., Hao, Z.: Dynamic spectrum access technical base on
   K-means clustering. Signal Processing 25(12), 1825–1829 (2009)
8. Beibei, W., Ji, Z., et al.: Primary-prioritized Markov approach for dynamic spectrum
   allocation. IEEE Transactions on Wireless Communications 8, 1854–1865 (2009)
9. Akyildiz, F., Won-Yeol, L., Mehmet, C., Shantidev, M.: Next generation /Dynamic
   spectrum access/Cognitive radio wireless networks: A survey. Computer Networks
   Journal 50, 2127–2159 (2006)

# Hardware Design of Aquaculture Water Quality Wireless Monitoring System

Ding Wen[1], Ma Yinchi[1,*], and Xi Weichao[2]

[1] Beijing Fisheries Research Institute, Beijing, 100068, China
[2] Xi'an Yuan Zhi System Technology Co., Ltd., Xian, 710077, China
{Dingwen,mayinchi}@bjfishery.com,
wangluo@bjfishery.com

**Abstract.** Environmental monitoring of aquaculture for the current means of monitoring equipment and a weak infrastructure, relatively backward status quo, using wireless sensor technology, embedded computing technology, MEMS technology (MEMS), distributed information processing technology and wireless communication technology in one of the wireless network Sensor network environments for aquaculture digital, networked, intelligent real-time dynamic monitoring system. The system not only can the principal detection of aquaculture environment indicators (temperature, PH, dissolved oxygen, turbidity, ammonia, etc.) in real-time monitoring, but also able to detect indicators of data fusion and data mining to establish a history of aquaculture environmental monitoring indicators Database, monitoring data to achieve a local or remote, real-time, dynamic display and analysis, in order to improve the process of aquaculture, water resources utilization, improve the quality of the culture environment and reduce emissions of pollutants provides an important technical means and scientific basis . The hardware architecture design is the core technology of this system. We will detail this part in the article.

**Keywords:** wireless sensor network, node, gateway, hardware platforms, aquaculture applications.

## 1 Introduction

Wireless sensor network is a kind of wireless network without infrastructure. It integrates the sensor technology, the embedded computing technology, the modern network technology, the wireless communication technology and the distributed intelligent information processing technology. The system can work under a state of long-term unattended[1]. It can detect, perceive and gather the information of the monitoring or environmental objects within the networks distribution region in real-time. It receives and sends messages through wireless and self-organization multi-hop routing [2]. Merging the logical information world and the real physical world together

---

* Ma Yinchi (1982 -), male, Beijing Fisheries Research Institute, Engineer, Master, graduated from Beijing Normal University, State Key Laboratory of Remote Sensing Science, mainly engaged in research of agriculture remote sensing and fisheries information technology.

P. Sénac, M. Ott, and A. Seneviratne (Eds.): ICWCA 2011, LNICST 72, pp. 310–315, 2012.
© Institute for Computer Sciences, Social Informatics and Telecommunications Engineering 2012

will change the interaction way between people and nature. The technology has good prospects in many areas, especially in agriculture area. Wireless sensor networks will be able to play a significant role in environmental monitoring, precision agriculture, section irrigation and livestock breeding [3~5].

This study is using the wireless sensor network technology to build an intelligent, network-based wireless monitoring system for aquaculture environment. The technology can be quickly applied to the field of aquaculture environmental monitoring, and promote the research and application of the wireless sensor networks technology. So as to improve the current traditional farming methods and aquaculture environmental monitoring instruments in the field of aquaculture in China. In this paper, we propose a set of practical hardware architecture design for the application of aquaculture.

## 2  System Design

The system mainly consists of the multi-parameter water quality sensors, the digital-analog transmission module, the wireless sensor network, the GPRS transmission unit, the data query and messaging real-time analysis of early warning system, and several other components. As shown in Figure 1, a set of wireless real-time water quality monitoring system includes the data acquisition node, the relay node and the gateway node.

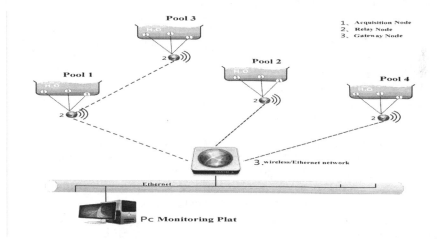

**Fig. 1.** Hardware architecture

## 3  Hardware Implementation

### 3.1  Acquisition Node

Monitoring can be arbitrarily placed in the desired area. Real-time collection includes water temperature, PH, dissolved oxygen, turbidity, ammonia, etc., and transmit the collected data to a wireless repeater or wireless gateway by wireless way.

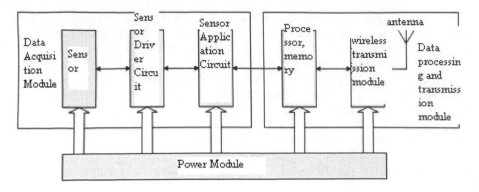

**Fig. 2.** Data Acquisition Node

As the figure 2 shows, the data acquisition node is an integrated structure. And it mainly contains the data acquisition module and the data transmission module, including the following several units divided by function:

● Sensor module

Sensor module contains the sensors, the sensor drive circuit and the sensors applied circuit. Sensors including the water temperature sensor, the PH value sensor, the oxygen sensor, the turbidity sensor, the ammonia nitrogen sensor for the water environment monitoring of the aquaculture water.

● Data processing and transmission module

I. Processor and memory unit: including the processor, the memory and the I/O. Among them, the processor is the low-energy micro controller.

II. Wireless transmitting/receiving module unit: the unit is composed of the wireless communication module according with IEEE802.15.4 / Zigbee. And this unit is used for the data wireless transmission and communication.

● Power module

Power supply unit is the power and control section of the system. The most important characteristic of the sensor node is that it will work under the condition of no lasting permanent power supply. This feature requires the work energy necessary of the sensor node is very low, and the sustainable power supply time of its own power must be long. According to the different application, appropriately adjusting the sleep time of sensor is the main task of the power control. Usually, the AA batteries and lithium battery can maintain a sensor node survival several months to 2 years. And adopting new technologies, such as solar energy, or using air micro vibration to produce electric power can make a sensor node survive longer. In the system, the scheme adopts the rechargeable efficient lithium battery.

### 3.2 Relay Node

The main function of relay nodes are forwarding sampling data from sensor node, and transmitting to gateway or other relay through wireless self-organization network. It can realize the transmission with a much longer distance. Relay node completely realized self-organizing network routing algorithms, within the wireless communication region, the relay nodes can immediately join in the network after powering, and establish the route of the data transmission.

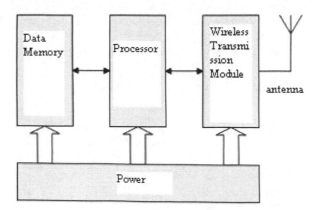

**Fig. 3.** Relay Node

As the figure 3 shows, the relay node mainly contains the data processing and wireless transmission modules with the same function as the data acquisition node. Among them according to their function, including the following several units divided by function:

● Data processing and transmission module
I. Processor and memory unit: including the processor, the memory and the I/O. Among them, the processor is the low-energy micro controller.
II. Wireless transmitting/receiving module unit: the unit is composed of the wireless communication module according with IEEE802.15.4 / Zigbee. And this unit is used for the data wireless transmission and communication.

● Data storage module
Data storage module is mainly composed of RAM or FLASH memory unit, and its main function is to store all kinds of sensor data and preserve the routing information of the whole network.

### 3.3 Gateway Node

The acquisition data by sensor node is transmitted to PC monitoring platform through Ethernet gateway. The wireless network/Ethernet gateway has wireless sensor networks, IEEE802.3 Ethernet and GPRS communication function. It can transfer the wireless communication data to the Ethernet protocol and the GPRS data. It can put any wireless input data transparent transmission to a server with designated IP address, and the maximum data throughput can achieve 22.5 Kbytes/s. The RFIC adopt CC1100 of Chipcon Company. The processor adopts Mega128L of Atmel Company. The maximum visual transmission distance can be more than 800m. The transmission distance of a typical aquaculture site is more than 300m, and it supports

IEEE802.3 Ethernet networks, GPRS wireless transmission, and TCP/IP, UDP protocol transparent data transmission.

Data communication can be set up through the Ethernet gateway, wireless networks and any other PC in Ethernet. Gateway IP address, address masking and communication port can be online set through gateway set software. PC monitoring software exchanges data with gateway according to IP address and communication port. Gateway will sent sensor network data to with conventional format.

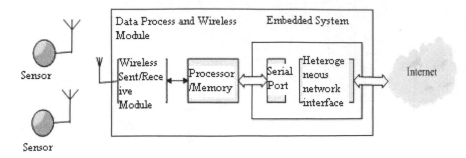

**Fig. 4.** Gateway Node

As the Figure 4 shows, the gateway node contains the data processing and wireless transmission module with the same function as the data acquisition node, and the embedded system connected with the heterogeneous network. As a IEEE802.15.4 and sensor network communication agent, the sensor node function modules must be equipped with a external I/O communication unit, used to communicate with the agency application server (Ethernet, RS232, USB, GPRS and satellite communication, etc.). The data from the sensor network accepted by the gateway node will be processed by the application server with stronger calculating function, but without power limit.

## 4   Conclusion

This study constructs an intelligent, networked aquaculture environment monitoring system using wireless sensor network technology. And the system is applied in the aquaculture environment monitoring field. It promotes the level of our wireless sensor network technology development and application. Ant it provides a new technical solution for improving the backward traditional breeding way and aquaculture environment monitoring method of the Chinese aquaculture field.

The low power consumption, low cost, and high reliability characteristics of the wireless sensor network make it have a broad application prospect in the wireless remote environment testing field [6~8]. We put forward the aquaculture water quality monitoring system construction program based on the study of Zigbee protocol of the wireless sensor network technology. And the water quality parameters collection and analysis was finished on this platform.

The results show that the development of the all-weather "wireless intelligent network real-time monitoring and warning system for aquaculture environment " can realize the real-time automatic monitoring, remote wireless transmission , automatic data processing and analysis, multi-platform control, intelligent warning, and SMS alarm for the water temperature, dissolved oxygen, PH, turbidity, ammonia and other indicator parameters of aquaculture environmental. So as to improve the utilization of aquaculture water maximum, provide the appropriate environmental condition for aquaculture objects, and control and ensure the quality security of aquatic products effectively. The system can realize automatic monitoring and scientific management for the aquaculture environment during the whole process. It will play a important role for protecting high-yield, efficient, safe, health of intensive aquaculture, improving aquatic product quality and safety in our city, and promoting the intensive, industrialization, refinement of aquaculture, and realizing the sustainable development of Beijing urban agriculture.

# References

1. Wu, J.: Design of Wireless Sensor Network Node for Water Quality Monitoring. Computer Measurement & Control 12 (2009)
2. Du, Z.: Design of water quality monitoring wireless sensor network system based on wireless sensor. Computer Engineering and Design 17 (2008)
3. Liu, X.: Aquaculture security guarantee system based on water quality monitoring and its application. Transactions of the Chinese Society of Agricultural Engineering 6 (2009)
4. Ma, C., Ni, W.: The design of a factory aquiculture monitor system based on PLC. Industrial Instrumentation & Automation 02 (2005)
5. Zhu, W., Ran, G.: Research of aquaculture environment parameter automatic monitoring and controlling system. Freshwater Fisheries 01 (2001)
6. Guo, S., Ma, S., Wu, P.: The application research of remote monitoring system based on Zigbee technology of wireless sensor network in family. Application of Electronic Technique 6, 28–30 (2006)
7. Ren, X., Yu, H.: The wireless sensor network safety analysis based on ZigBee technology. Computer Science 6(10), 111–113 (2001)
8. Zhang, H., Li, W.: Study of a Wireless Sensor Network Based on ZigBee Technology. Journal of Wuhan University of Technology (Information & Management Engineering) 8, 12–15 (2006)

# Best Effort Traffic Uplink Transmission Performance Evaluation of an Integrated EPON/IPACT and WiMAX (OFDMA) Architecture

Hammad Yaqoob[1], Craig Michie[1], Ivan Andonovic[1], Kae Hsiang Kwong[2], David Chieng[2], and Mazlan Abbas[2]

[1] Department of Electronic and Electrical Engineering
University of Strathclyde Glasgow, United Kingdom
hammad.yaqoob@strath.ac.uk
[2] Wireless Communications Cluster MIMOS Berhad
Kuala Lumpur, Malaysia

**Abstract.** A performance analysis has been undertaken for best effort uplink traffic within an integrated EPON and WiMAX OFDMA architecture. Although studies into this type of integration have been reported, a rigorous analysis has not been carried out in integrating EPON with WiMAX with mobility. The paper describes the last mile problem, EPON and WiMAX. Also an integration approach will be presented and analysed in the paper in the form of average delay, throughput and packet loss.

**Keywords:** Ethernet Passive Optical Network, WiMax, OFDMA, MAC, Dynamic Bandwidth Allocation.

## 1 Introduction

The last mile has been the focus of much development. Bandwidth intensive services such as VoIP, VoD, IPTV and Video teleconferencing are becoming increasingly popular with end users; however the current infrastructure exhibits limited evolution in terms of provisioning a rich mix of real-time services to a growing number of users.

One future proof approach centres on the deployment of optical fibre to end user's premises as it provides a virtually unbounded bandwidth capability. However this type of deployment represents a significant cost to the service providers [1]. Therefore to lower the cost of provisioning services an alternative strategy is to extend the reach – the 'last drop' - of the optical fibre through the use of appropriate wireless broadband technologies.

A route to implementing this strategy is to integrate Ethernet Passive Optical Networks (EPON) and technologies defined by the Worldwide Interoperability for Microwave Access (WiMAX) standards into a single architecture. Although a number of possible integration approaches have been reported [1][2], this paper highlights the issues and undertakes an initial performance evaluation of the integration in the WiMAX OFDMA mode for mobile users. Before detailing the potential integration option and its analysis, in order to provide a foundation to bring clarity to the results, a brief overview of EPON and WiMAX are presented.

P. Sénac, M. Ott, and A. Seneviratne (Eds.): ICWCA 2011, LNICST 72, pp. 316–326, 2012.
© Institute for Computer Sciences, Social Informatics and Telecommunications Engineering 2012

## 2   Technologies Review

### 2.1   EPON Overview

Ethernet Passive Optical Network (EPON) is a passive optical technology which consists of three components, the OLT, the ONU and the passive splitter [3] [4]. OLT (Optical line termination) is the interface between the service providers and the users and resides at the central office. The passive splitter/combiner is a device that requires no electrical supply and therefore lowers the cost of deployment. The functionality of the passive splitter/combiner is to split the signal to every user in the network and to combine signals from the user to the OLT. The ONU (Optical Network Unit) resides near the end user. The ONU can be either located near the end user or be an interface between the optical network and a copper or wireless network. The ONU receives packets from the users and stores them in the appropriate queue according to their type. The data rate between the ONU and OLT is 1GB\s symmetric. The topology of the network that the paper is focused on is the tree topology as shown below:

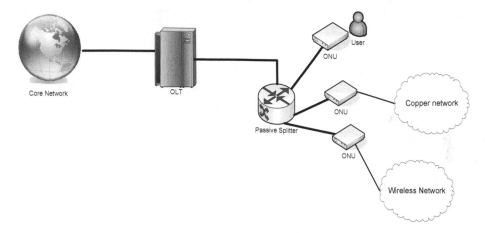

**Fig. 1.** The above network shows the topology of an EPON network. The network consists of an OLT which is connected to the core network, a passive splitter which is located between the OLT and ONUs and an ONU which is located near the end user or connected to another network.

At the packet level, in the downlink (OLT to ONU), packets are broadcast to all ONUs (at a wavelength of 1550nm) via the passive splitter [3]. Once each ONU receives the packets, it filters out the data designated for it and discards the rest. In the uplink, packets are transmitted (at a wavelength of 1330nm) again via the passive splitter; however since the fibre is a shared medium, time slots are normally allocated to each ONU so that they can transmit data without collisions. Time slots are allocated by the OLT and the amount granted is dependent on a bandwidth allocation process. Once the ONU receives a grant, scheduling is performed to allow queues inside the ONU to send data and requests.

## 2.2  WiMAX Overview

WiMAX (Worldwide Interoperability for Microwave Access) is a mobile broadband wireless access technology which operates between the bandwidth of 1.25MHz and 20 MHz [5][6]. The WiMAX network consists of two components the Base station (BS) and the Subscriber station (SS). In a WiMAX deployed network the BS like the OLT is the interface between the service providers and the users and resides at the central office. The SS resides at the user's home and collects packets from the user and stores them into appropriates queues. The transmit rate is dependent on the frame size, the DL to UL ratio, the modulation and coding rate assigned to the SS and the number of sub channels and slots assigned to the SS. A high level schematic of a typical deployment topology is shown in Fig. 2.

The BS functionality is similar to that of the OLT, receiving packets from the core network and broadcasting them to all SSs. When the SS receives the packets it filters out the intended data using a connection ID and discards the rest. For the uplink, the medium is again shared and therefore the BS needs to allocate resources to the SS. The resources allocated in the OFDMA mode are both in time and frequency and are referred to as slots. Once the SS receives a grant, scheduling is performed to allow queues or connections to send data and requests. Each connection has its own request mechanism [5] [6].

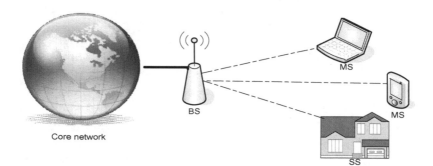

Core network

BS

MS

MS

SS

**Fig. 2.** The above network shows the topology of a WiMax network. The network consists of a BS which is connected to the core network, and an SS/MS which is located near the end user or connected to another network.

WiMAX supports five types of connections [5, 6]:

- Unsolicited Grant Service (UGS). It is used for services such as T1/E1 traffic and VOIP without silence suppression. WiMAX supports this service by allocating it fixed size grants on a real time periodic basis
- Extended Real Time Polling Service (ERTPS); used for VOIP with silent suppression. The BS supports this service by allocating grants to the SS on a periodic basis which the SS can use to send data or requests.
- Real Time Polling Service. (RTPS); used for video (MPEG) services. The BS supports this service by sending unicast polls to the SS at periodic intervals

- Non Real Time Polling Service (NRTPS). It is commonly used for FTP and other best effort traffic. The BS supports this service by either sending unicast polls at less frequent intervals than the RTPS service or by allowing the SS to send a bandwidth request in the collision region of the uplink frame
- Best Effort Service (BE); used for traffic such as http. This service is supported in the same way as the NRTPS service, however polling would occur at less frequent intervals.

## 3  Benefits of Integration

The integration of EPON and WiMAX will look similar to Figure 3, where EPON is used as a backhaul to WiMAX. The technologies are combined at the ONUs and the Base Stations to create the ONU-BSs.

The first benefit is that the extension of the reach of the broadband connectivity can be achieved without the deployment of optical fibre to end-user's premises which lowers the cost of the network deployment.

Secondly, WiMAX at close range can provide the user with high bandwidth connections; however when the user is relatively far, the connection bandwidth available will lower in proportion to the signal degradation. With EPON as a backhaul, many more BSs can be established closer to end premises resulting in an increase of end users enjoying enhanced quality mobile broadband connections.

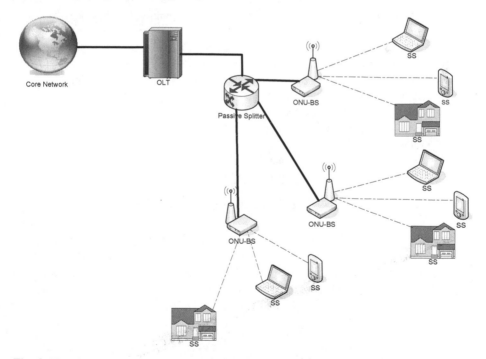

**Fig. 3.** The above diagram shows the schematic of the proposed integration where the EPON network is used as a backhaul to the WiMAX network. The two networks will integrate at the ONU and the BS to create the ONU-BS

The third benefit is that OFDMA distributes subcarriers among users; thus all users can transmit at the same time. Sub-channels can be matched to user needs taking into account location and propagation characteristics, in doing so provisioning optimum connection quality.

Previous studies [1] have proposed the integration of EPON and WiMAX OFDM and have shown that when the OLT is given the responsibility to allocate resource to the SS, the performance is better than alternatives. However none have explored the integration in the OFDMA domain for mobility.

# 4   Integration Approach

There are two options for integration. Either the systems bandwidth allocation can be fully controlled by the OLT or jointly controlled by the OLT and the BS. The paper will focus on the jointly controlled scheme, which is called the hybrid scheme.

The hybrid scheme was introduced in the paper [1] which we have adapted to the OFDMA domain. This scheme is jointly controlled by the OLT and BS, where the EPON and WiMAX run their own bandwidth allocation process. The following processes occur starting from the arrival of the packet to the SS:

1. Packets arrive from the user to the SS.
2. The SS waits for a grant to be received from the BS. Assuming it is a RTPS connection, when the grant arrives at the SS a bandwidth request will be sent to the BS.
3. The BS will receive the request and use it as an input for the bandwidth allocation algorithm. The grant will be sent out at the next frame.
4. When the SS receives the uplink grant, it waits till the next uplink section of the frame to use the grant.
5. When the SS applies the grant, it will divide the bandwidth among the various connections using a scheduling algorithm. Once the packet is selected it is sent to the BS.
6. Once the BS receives the message it will forward it to the ONU.
7. The ONU will store the packet into the appropriate queue and wait for a grant from the OLT.
8. Once a grant is received from the OLT the ONU will send a request to the OLT.
9. The OLT will receive the request and use it as an input for resource allocation in the next cycle. The OLT will send the grant to the ONU.
10. Once receiving the grant, the ONU will apply a scheduling algorithm and assign the bandwidth to the different queues.
11. The data will be sent from the ONU to the OLT.

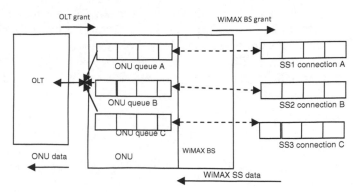

**Fig. 4.** The above diagram shows the resource allocation strategy of the hybrid scheme

# 5 Simulations

The parameters under which the hybrid integration scheme has been analysed are summarised in the following sections.

## 5.1 WiMAX MAC Parameters

- 8 http request applications per SS (362 bits/s each) [8]
- 3 email applications per SS (62123 bits/s each) [9].
- 2 ftp applications per SS (2920 bits/s each) [10].
- 1 http page application per SS (19511 bits/s each) [11].
- 214616 bit / s / SS.
- Email and HTTP pages inserted into BE connection
- FTP and HTTP requests inserted in NTRPS connection
- BE connection uses bandwidth stealing and collision area to send requests
- NRTPS uses polling opportunities and collision area to send requests
- 10 collision request opportunities per frame
- Polling interval 0.5s
- Frame size 5ms
- Sequential Bandwidth allocation and priority scheduling (NRTPS, BE)
- Max NRTPS and BE delay, 5s and 8s respectively.

## 5.2 WiMAX PHY Parameters [5][6]

- 92.4e-6s per symbol
- 70 uplink sub-channels per column
- Minimum uplink allocation slot is 3 symbols and 1 sub-channel
- Each uplink allocation slot contains 48 data carriers
- Modulation and coding scheme 64 ¾ QAM fixed. Therefore 216 bits per slot.
- 5ms frame (51 symbols + guard)

- Downlink to Uplink ratio 1:1. Uplink section begins at 27$^{th}$ symbol.
- Therefore there are 24 symbols (51 – 27) symbols available in the uplink.
- Per sub-channel there are 8 slots available (24 / 3 symbols)
- Therefore there are ((8 * 70) – 10 contention slots) slots available
- Therefore 118800 bits / frame (550 * 216 bits) which translates into 23.76 Mb/s (118800 bits * (1 / 0.05s))

### 5.3   EPON Parameters

- 1 Gb/s uplink capacity
- Priority scheduling in the ONU same as SS where NRTPS data is given priority over BE data.
- OLT uses the Limited IPACT bandwidth allocation process [3] with max requests 120000 bits and guard 5e-6.

## 6   Results

Fig. 5, Fig. 6 and Fig. 7 show the hybrid simulation's throughput, percentage packet loss and average packet delay with respect to increasing SS and increasing ONUs respectively.

From the throughput behaviour (Fig. 5), as the number of SS increase, so does the number of bits received at the OLT per second. The result is expected because the greater the number of SS inserted into the network the greater the incoming number of bits per second. Therefore the throughput increases. However there is no saturation of the throughput regardless of the increase in SS or ONU. This means that in the hybrid scheme the packet loss of 5 and 8 seconds does not have a major impact in the system as the number of SS increase or as the number of ONU increase.

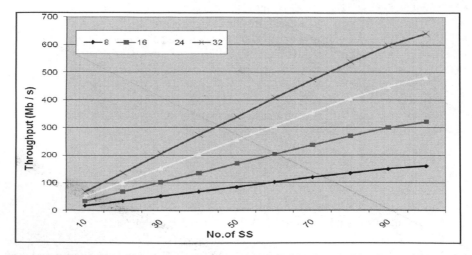

**Fig. 5.** The above graph shows the throughput of the hybrid scheme with respect to increasing SS and increasing ONU

From the packet loss graph below (Fig. 6), you can see why the throughput consistently increases as the number of SS increase. The average delay of 5s and 8s does not cause a significant impact on the packets at the SS until the 80 to 100 SS mark and at that mark the network has a packet loss of 6%. Therefore as the numbers of SS increase so does the throughput. The reason for such a low packet loss even at 100 SS is because even at this level the number of incoming bits per second does not exceed the number of bits WiMAX can support in a 5ms frame. Also from the graph below, the increase in the number of ONUs does not affect the packet loss. The same reasoning can be applied and is discussed later in the paper.

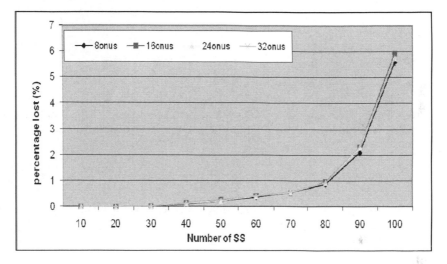

**Fig. 6.** Percentage packet loss as a function of increasing SSs and ONUs for the hybrid integration approach

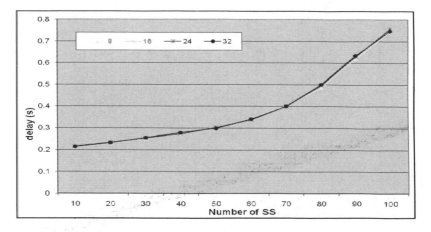

**Fig. 7.** Average packet delay as a function of increasing SSs and ONUs for the hybrid integration approach

The average packet delay increases as the number of SS per ONUBS increases. This is as expected because as more SS are introduced into an ONUBS network, an increasing number of SSs will have to wait longer to be allocated bandwidth as it is allocated sequentially. Therefore the packets will have to wait longer.

Also an increase in the number of ONUs does not affect the average delay. The reason for this is as follows. The limited schemes worst case cycle time for the ONUs is calculated using the following:

$$CT = ((\frac{(MD + R)}{DR}) + GT) * TO \tag{1}$$

Where,
  CT = Cycle time
  MD = Max Data sent = 119968 bits
  R = Request size = 32 bits
  GT = Guard Time = 5e-6s
  TO = total onus = 8 – 32.

The number of bits sent by the WiMAX frame can be calculated using the following method. Firstly a calculation of how many time slots are available within the polling cycle time has to be made.

$$Timeslots = Rounddown \quad (\frac{CT}{(92.4e^{-6} * 3)}) \tag{2}$$

The amount of bits transferred in that time can now be calculated by using the following:

$$UBS = Timeslots * BPS * 70 \tag{3}$$

Where,
  UBS = Uplinks bits sent
  Time slots = the amount of slots that will be received in the cycle time.
  Round down = Round down number
  BPS = Bits per slot = 216

Table 1 shows the cycle time of the ONUs in the worst case scenario and the number of bits that can be sent in that time.

**Table 1.** Worst case cycle time for the ONUs in the limited scheme

| ONUs | Polling time | WiMAX bits received |
|------|--------------|---------------------|
| 8    | 0.001        | 45360               |
| 16   | 0.002        | 105840              |
| 24   | 0.003        | 118800              |
| 32   | 0.004        | 118800              |

The values for 24 and 32 ONUs are the same since the polling cycle intervals leak into the next frame's downlink section where no data is transmitted in the uplink.

The maximum amount of bits that can be transferred from the ONU to the OLT one cycle is 120000 bits. The bits received from the WiMAX station are less than that maximum, consequently all the data can be sent in one cycle. That is why there is a slight but not noticeable difference in the packet delay for the different number of ONUs. The throughput increases as extra ONUs are added, as expected since additional ONUs means more SSs which results in more bits incoming per second and since the delay is not affected significantly as the number of ONUs increase, no extra packets are lost. Therefore the throughput rises.

## 7 Summary and Conclusions

The paper has introduced and evaluated the performance of a jointly controlled EPON and WiMAX OFDMA integration approach as a potential solution to the last mile problem; referred to as the Hybrid scheme. The performance of the scheme has been analysed as a function of the number of SSs and ONUs for best effort traffic and the results analysed in the form of throughput, packet loss and average packet delay..

In conclusion the results show that the Hybrid scheme, which relies on a joint OLT and BS control strategy, can be a viable solution to the last mile problem. In the Hybrid scheme, the BS can poll the SSs irrespective of the state of EPON resources, which translates into more frequent polling of the SS and therefore low delay and loss and high throughput. Also the hybrid scheme allows for the network to be flexible as from 8 to 32 ONUs, the increase in ONUs does not have an effect on the average delay or packet loss.

In practical network scenarios, channel conditions vary from SS to SS and the bandwidth allocation scheme is smarter in that it takes into account channel conditions, QoS conditions of a SS and ONU and the request made. In addition, any scheduling scheme at the SS and ONU would take into account packet delays and fairness as well as the end user accessing different services. Therefore the analysis of the Hybrid scheme will need to be executed for different traffic scenarios.

## References

[1] Shen, G., Tucker, R.S., Chae, C.-J.: Fixed Mobile Convergence Architectures for Broadband Access: Integration of EPON and WiMAX. IEEE Commun. Mag. 45(8), 44–50 (2007)

[2] Tang, T., Shou, G., Hu, Y., Guo, Z.: Performance Analysis of Bandwidth Allocation of Convergence of WiMAX and EPON. In: 2009 International Conference on Networks Security, Wireless Communications and Trusted Computing (2009)

[3] Kwong, K.H., Yaqoob, H., Michie, C., Andonovic, I.: WDM Dynamic Bandwidth Allocation Schemes for Ethernet PONs. In: Access Nets 2009. Springer, Heidelberg (2009)

[4] Kramer, G., Mukherjee, B., Perwento, G.: IPACT: A Dynamic Protocol for an Ethernet PON (EPON). IEEF Commun. Mag. 40(2), 74–80 (2002)

[5] Andrews, J.G., Ghosh, A., Muhamed, R.: Fundamentals of WiMAX. Prentice Hall, Englewood Cliffs (2007)

[6] IEEE 802.16 –, IEEE Standard for Local and metropolitan area networks. Part 16: Air Interface for Broadband Wireless Access Systems (2009)

[7] WiMAX General Information about the standard 802.16 Application note, Rhode& Schwarz (2006)

[8] Lee, J.J., Gupta, M.: White Paper: A New Traffic Model for Current User Web Browsing Behavior. Intel Research White Paper (September 2007)

[9] Gomes, L.H., Cazita, C., Almeida, J.M., Almeida, V., Meira Jr., W.: Workload models of spam and legitimate e-mails. Science Direct 64, 690–714 (2006)

[10] Multi-hop Relay System Evaluation Methodology (Channel Model and Performance Metric). IEEE 802.16 Broadband Wireless Access Working Group, IEEE 802.16j-06/013r3, 02/19/2007

[11] Staehle, D., Leibnitz, K., Tran-Gia, P.: Source Traffic Modeling of Wireless Applications, University of Würzburg, Technical Report No. 261 (2000)

# Research on the Interferometer Direction-Finding and Positioning Improved Algorithm under the Influence of Ground-to-Air Channel

Jianbo Yang[1], Yan Wang[1], and Hu Mao[2]

[1] Aviation Information Countermeasure Department,
Aviation University of Airforce, Changchun, China
[2] Telecommunication Engineering Academy Navigation Engineering,
Air Force Engineering University, Xian, China
jianbo_yang@yahoo.com,
wy_z@163.com,
mh_1987@163.com

**Abstract.** Based on analyses multipath fading of ground-to-air channel under different elevation angle circumstances, according to the characteristic and change range of ground-to-air channel Rice factor determining Weighted value, the direction-finding and positioning algorithm which airborne interferometer and spaceborne interferometer usually adopting is improved under the influence of different elevation angle ground-to-air channel, the simulation results have verified improvement algorithm validity in advancing positioning precision.

**Keywords:** Ground-to-air channel, Direction-finding and positioning, Weighed value.

## 1 Introduction

In the interferometer direction-finding and positioning system, the ground-to-air channel transmission usually cause the parameter measure error of receiving signal, but [1][2] studied interferometer direction-finding and positioning based on the perfect electromagnetic wave transmission circumstances, it did not accord with the actual application, [3][4]proposed the method of join weighted value in order to improve positioning precision, but how to determine weighted value is not presented, [5][6]mentioned the weighted value determining method, but the concretely applied occasion is not distinguished.

In this paper, according to transmitting signal actual fading degree in the different elevation angle ground-to-air channel transmission process sorting channel type, aiming at specific circumstances of different interferometer carrier propose weighted value determining method, airborne interferometer and spaceborne interferometer direction-finding and positioning algorithm have improved under the influence of different elevation angle ground-to-air channel through parameter measure is affected by different Rice factor.

P. Sénac, M. Ott, and A. Seneviratne (Eds.): ICWCA 2011, LNICST 72, pp. 327–339, 2012.
© Institute for Computer Sciences, Social Informatics and Telecommunications Engineering 2012

## 2   Characteristics of Multipath Fading in Ground-to-Air Communications

In ground-to-air communications, the causes of multipath mainly from three aspects: ① scattering from the surface feature and topography near the ground station; ②aerial carrier reflection or scattering; ③ remote ground barrier reflection. Usually, the degree of multipath fading in ground-to-air communications has involved with relative elevation angle of the aerial carrier and ground station, according to the different elevation angle, ground-to-air channel can be described by four types, such as Fig. 1.

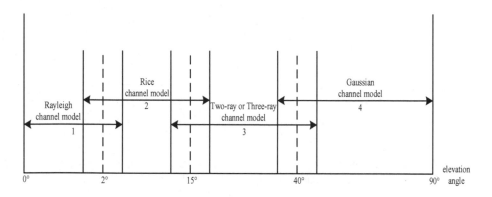

**Fig. 1.** Types of ground-to-air channel in different elevation angle

For the airborne interferometer, elevation angle of target radiation relative to aircraft will not be big in order to ensure enough distance of reconnaissance direction-finding and avoid the enemy fire. In Fig. 1, the ground-to-air channel is called Rice channel while the elevation angle is small. (Rayleigh channel is a special case of Rice channel), Rice factor $K$ is defined as the ratio between the direct component power and all scattering wave power, which completely determines the degree of multipath fading. The direct component power and all scattering wave power can express respectively

$$2\sigma^2 = P\frac{1}{K+1} \; , \; |\rho|^2 = P\frac{K}{K+1} \tag{1}$$

Where $P$ is total power of receiving signal.

Rice factor of ground-to-air channel under the low elevation is usually in the interval of 2-15dB[7]. For the spaceborne interferometer, the elevation angle of target radiation relative to satellite is observable, Rice factor $K$ is big, and ground-to-air channel will tend to Gaussian channel from the Rice channel.

The Power Spectrum of Angle of Arriving $\varphi$ (AOA) submit to three special distribution: even distributing, Gauss distribution and Laplace distribution. Due to the von Mises distribution can approach else distribution, so expression of von Mises distribution is

$$P_A(\varphi) = \frac{1}{2\pi I_0(u)} e^{u\cos(\varphi - \bar{\varphi})}, \quad \varphi \in [-\pi, \pi] \tag{2}$$

where $I_0$ is the zero-order modified Bessel function, parameter $u \geq 0$ control the

shape of Power Spectrum of Angle. When $u = 0$, $P_A(\varphi) = \frac{1}{2\pi}$; When $u = \infty$,

$P_A(\varphi) = \delta(\varphi)$, where $\delta(\varphi)$ is Dirac function; when $u$ is small, von Mises distribution approach cosine distribution; when $u$ is large, von Mises distributing

approach the Gauss distribution of mean $\bar{\varphi}$ and variance $\frac{1}{u}$.

## 3   Improved Direction-Finding Positioning Algorithm Used in Airborne Interferometer

Under the low elevation, the height of aircraft can be ignored, Namely that the aircraft and ground target radiation are horizontal, aircraft will measure the azimuth of the target radiation in different locations, and achieve positioning using the intersection of azimuth line[1].

### 3.1   Weighted Least Squares Estimates (WLSE) for Positioning

In order to improve the positioning accuracy, usually Least Squares Estimates (LSE) is used to process azimuth measure data, however, the error variance of azimuth measure is different in diverse channel state, so the location of target radiation can be estimated by Weighted Least Squares Estimates (WLSE). On the assumption that the actual position coordinates of target radiation is $(x, y)$, Coordinates of $i$th observation point of aircraft is $(x_i, y_i)$, measure azimuth is $\alpha_i$, then $\alpha_i$ can be calculated as follow,

$$\alpha_i = h_i(x, y) + v_i \tag{3}$$

where

$$h_i(x, y) = \arctan\left(\frac{y - y_i}{x - x_i}\right),$$

$v_i$ is $i$th measure error. The initial estimate point $(x_0, y_0)$ of formula (3) in the target position $(x, y)$ is linearized by Taylor series expansion, and retain the first and second items, then formula（3） can be changed into formula (4),

$$\alpha_i - h_i(x_0, y_0) = \begin{bmatrix} \dfrac{\partial h_i}{\partial x} & \dfrac{\partial h_i}{\partial y} \end{bmatrix}_{(x,y)=(x_0,y_0)} \times \begin{bmatrix} \Delta x \\ \Delta y \end{bmatrix} + v_i \tag{4}$$

where $\left.\dfrac{\partial h_i}{\partial x}\right|_{(x,y)=(x_0,y_0)} = -\dfrac{y_0 - y_i}{r_{0i}^2}$ , $\left.\dfrac{\partial h_i}{\partial y}\right|_{(x,y)=(x_0,y_0)} = \dfrac{x_0 - x_i}{r_{0i}^2}$ ,

$r_{0i}^2 = (x_0 - x_i)^2 + (y_0 - y_i)^2$ 。

All observation points are put into a matrix, observation equation can be obtained

$$Z = H \cdot W + V \tag{5}$$

where

$$Z = \begin{bmatrix} \alpha_1 - h_1 \\ \alpha_2 - h_2 \\ \vdots \\ \alpha_n - h_n \end{bmatrix}_{(x,y)=(x_0,y_0)}$$

$$H = \begin{bmatrix} \dfrac{\partial h_1}{\partial x} & \dfrac{\partial h_1}{\partial y} \\[2mm] \dfrac{\partial h_2}{\partial x} & \dfrac{\partial h_2}{\partial y} \\[2mm] \vdots & \vdots \\[2mm] \dfrac{\partial h_n}{\partial x} & \dfrac{\partial h_n}{\partial x} \end{bmatrix}_{(x,y)=(x_0,y_0)}$$

$$W = \begin{bmatrix} \Delta x \\ \Delta y \end{bmatrix}$$

$$V = \begin{bmatrix} v_1 \\ v_2 \\ \vdots \\ v_n \end{bmatrix}$$

Cost function of WLSE can be obtained as

$$\varepsilon = \mathbf{V}^T \mathbf{P} \mathbf{V} \tag{6}$$

where $\mathbf{P}$ is weighted matrix. （6）can also express

$$\varepsilon = \left[\mathbf{Z} - \mathbf{H} \cdot \mathbf{W}\right]^T \mathbf{P} \left[\mathbf{Z} - \mathbf{H} \cdot \mathbf{W}\right] \tag{7}$$

Order $\dfrac{\partial \varepsilon}{\partial \mathbf{W}} = 0$, so

$$\hat{\mathbf{W}} = \left(\mathbf{H}^T \mathbf{P} \mathbf{H}\right)^{-1} \mathbf{H}^T \mathbf{P} \mathbf{Z} \tag{8}$$

On the assumption that measure error of each observation point is independent and mean is null, variance is $\sigma_i^2$ $(i = 1, 2, ..., n)$ , then the matrix $\mathbf{P}$ meet the following condition,

$$\mathbf{P} = \mathbf{J}^{-1} \tag{9}$$

where

$$\mathbf{J} = diag\left[\sigma_1^2 \quad \sigma_2^2 \quad \cdots \quad \sigma_n^2\right], (i = 1, 2, ..., n)$$

On the assumption that the actual position coordinates and estimation position coordinates of target radiation is $\mathbf{X} = [x, y]^T$ and $\tilde{\mathbf{X}} = [\tilde{x}, \tilde{y}]^T$ respectively, so

$$\mathrm{E}\left[\hat{\mathbf{X}} - \mathbf{X}\right] = \mathrm{E}\left[\hat{\mathbf{W}} - \mathbf{W}\right] = \mathrm{E}\left[\left(\mathbf{H}^T \mathbf{J}^{-1} \mathbf{H}\right)^{-1} \mathbf{H}^T \mathbf{J}^{-1} \mathbf{V}\right] = \mathbf{H}^{-1} \mathrm{E}[\mathbf{V}] = 0 \tag{10}$$

The expression （10）prove that WLSE is agonic estimation algorithm when the mean of measure error equal to zero.

### 3.2    Weighted Value Determination under the Influence of the Ground-to-Air Channel

Measure error under the influence of Rice channel exist CRAMER-RAO bound, for the uniform linear array, The CRAMER-RAO bound is[8]

$$var(\alpha) \geq \cfrac{12}{(2\pi)^2 K \times \dfrac{M+1}{M-1} (\dfrac{L}{\lambda})^2 \sin^2 \alpha} \tag{11}$$

Where $K$ is Rice factor; $M$ is the number of antenna array elements; $L$ is the total length of the line array; $\lambda$ is the wavelength of the received wave; $\alpha$ is the azimuth of the received wave (the angle between the received wave and the direction–finding baseline). If using two mutual vertical linear arrays, the lesser one can be selected as the CRAMER-RAO bound of the actual direction–finding system. In formula (11), the weighted value of WLSE for positioning under the influence of the ground-to-air channel can be obtained by estimating the Rice factor $K$ .

The Rice factor $K$ can be estimated by the lookup table of the first and second-order moment information, not only the estimation precision is well, but also real time can be met. The expressions of Rice distribution random order moment is[9]

$$\mu_n = E[r^n] = (2\sigma^2)^{n/2} \exp(-K)\Gamma(1+n/2)\,_1F_1(1+n/2;1;K) \tag{12}$$

where $\Gamma(\bullet)$ is Gamma function, $_1F_1(\bullet)$ is Confluent hypergeometric function. The following formula can be obtained according to first and second-order moment information

$$\frac{\mu_1^2}{\mu_2} = \frac{\pi e^{-K}}{4(K+1)}[(K+1)I_0(\frac{K}{2})+K\,I_1(\frac{K}{2})]^2 \tag{13}$$

where $I_0(\bullet)$ and $I_1(\bullet)$ are the first and the zero-order modified Bessel function respectively.

Because the Rice factor $K$ of ground-to-air channel under the low elevation is usually in a certain range, it is easier to obtain the value of $K$ by lookup table than by equation (13), namely that $\mu_1$ and $\mu_2$ are obtained by calculating the formula (13) with the value of $K$ in a certain range, and compare them with the measured $\mu_1$ and $\mu_2$, then take the most similar value of $K$ in the table as estimation result.

## 4    Improved Positioning Algorithm Used in Spaceborne Interferometer

For the spaceborne interferometer, positioning can be achieved by measuring the azimuth and the elevation of target radiation on the ground. The positioning geometry model is shown in Fig. 2.

In Fig. 2, $r$ is the line of sight(connection between the receiving antenna O and the target radiation T on the ground)distance, $\beta_x$ and $\beta_y$ is the angle between the line of sight with the X-axis and Y-axis respectively, $h$ is the height of the satellite, $(x, y)$ is the coordinates of the target radiation on the ground, and the length of the two direction-finding baselines $d_x = d_y = d$ , then

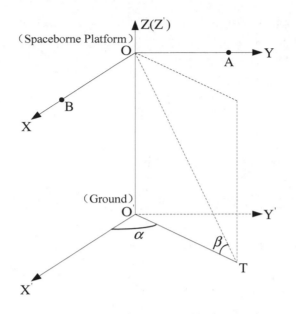

**Fig. 2.** Spaceborne interferometer positioning sketch map

$$\begin{cases} \varphi_x = 2\pi d \cos \beta_x / \lambda \\ \varphi_y = 2\pi d \cos \beta_y / \lambda \\ x = r \cos \beta_x \\ y = r \cos \beta_y \\ r = \sqrt{x^2 + y^2 + h^2} \end{cases} \quad (14)$$

The target radiation can obtain from formula (14)

$$\begin{cases} x = \left[ \dfrac{h^2 k_x^2}{1 - k_x^2 - k_y^2} \right]^{1/2} \\ y = \left[ \dfrac{h^2 k_y^2}{1 - k_x^2 - k_y^2} \right]^{1/2} \end{cases} \quad (15)$$

where

$$k_x = \cos \beta_x = \lambda \varphi_x / 2\pi d \, , k_y = \cos \beta_y = \lambda \varphi_y / 2\pi d$$

On the assumption that the satellite gets n positioning points $(x_i, y_i)$ $(i = 1, 2, ..., n)$ during the move, generally the n positioning points are fused by the average method [2], that is,

$$\begin{bmatrix} \tilde{x} \\ \tilde{y} \end{bmatrix} = \frac{1}{n} \sum_{i=1}^{n} \begin{bmatrix} x_i \\ y_i \end{bmatrix} \tag{16}$$

### 4.1    The Influence of Ground-to-Air Channel on the Average Fusion Method of the Positioning Points

When fusing the positioning points by the average method, if the distribution of the positioning point $(x_i, y_i)$ is agonic, the positioning point estimation $(\tilde{x}, \tilde{y})$ is agonic too, the estimation result is optimal, whereas, if the distribution of the positioning point is biased, a great error will exist in the fusion of the several positioning points by the formula (16). The demonstration about biased distribution of the positioning point under the influence of the ground-to-air channel is present as following.

For simplicity, only show demonstration that whether $x$ is biased, and the demonstration of $y$ biased result is similar. Set $f_x(k_x, k_y) = x$, which is in second order Taylor series expansion, then

$$f_x(k_x, k_y) = f_x(k_{x_0}, k_{y_0}) + \left. \frac{\partial f_x(k_x, k_y)}{\partial k_x} \right|_{(k_x, k_y) = (k_{x_0}, k_{y_0})} (k_x - k_{x_0}) + \left. \frac{\partial f_x(k_x, k_y)}{\partial k_y} \right|_{(k_x, k_y) = (k_{x_0}, k_{y_0})} (k_y - k_{y_0})$$

$$\left. \frac{\partial^2 f_x(k_x, k_y)}{2 \cdot \partial k_x^2} \right|_{(k_x, k_y) = (k_{x_0}, k_{y_0})} (k_x - k_{x_0})^2 + \left. \frac{\partial^2 f_x(k_x, k_y)}{2 \cdot \partial k_y^2} \right|_{(k_x, k_y) = (k_{x_0}, k_{y_0})} (k_y - k_{y_0})^2 \tag{17}$$

In the case of the large line of sight component, the phase difference $\varphi_x \sim N(\varphi_{x_0}, \sigma_{\varphi_x}^2)$ and $k_x \sim N(k_{x_0}, \sigma_{k_x}^2)$ gain mean by formula (17) is

$$\mathrm{E}(x) = f_x(k_{x_0}, k_{y_0}) + a\mathrm{E}[(k_x - k_{x_0})^2] + b\mathrm{E}[(k_y - k_{y_0})^2] \tag{18}$$

In formula (18), $a$ and $b$ is the second-order item coefficient respectively, because the mean of first-order item is zero and the mean of second-order item is biased, so the distribution of $x$ is biased.

### 4.2    Improved Fusion Algorithm of the Positioning Points

Due to the measured position points distribution is biased under the influence of ground-to-air channel, therefore, two issues need to be solved when fusing the positioning points in order to improve positioning accuracy: ① How to select the appropriate positioning point in fusion; ② How to determine the effective ways to fuse.

Due to the satellite during the move would not gain too many positioning points of target, in the case of the positioning points distribution is biased, it is not the more positioning points are involved in fusion, the error variance is smaller after fusion, if there is a positioning point with great error variance(maybe the biased degree is much larger than the variance value), the total positioning accuracy will be worse after fusion. So the positioning points should be filtered according to the criterion that "the muster of the points whose total positioning error variance are minimum", the "total error variance" formula which contain m positioning points can be expressed as:

$$T_m = \frac{1}{m^2}\sum_{i=1}^{m}\sigma_i^2, \quad m = 1, 2, ..., n \tag{19}$$

where n is the total number of the positioning points, $\sigma_i^2$ is the variance of the $ith$ positioning point in the muster. In the calculation process, all positioning points can be sorted according to error variance from small to large, then calculate $T_m$ of the former m positioning points, the positioning points involved in fusion can be obtained through n times calculation only. For the fixed target radiation in the ground, $\sigma_i$ can be substituted for the square root of the positioning error summation in horizontal and vertical direction(namely $GDOP = (\sigma_{xi}^2 + \sigma_{yi}^2)^{1/2}$), the positioning points which are involved in fusion can be obtained by gaining the muster which have the minimum value of $T_m$.

After obtaining positioning points involved in fusion, for each positioning point $(x_i, y_i)$, the positioning errors in the direction of $x$ and $y$ axis are composed of two parts respectively, one is the variance $(\sigma_{1i}^2, \sigma_{2i}^2)$ formed by the systematic bias between estimate and true values, the other is the variance $(\sigma_{xi}^2, \sigma_{yi}^2)$ formed by the spreading positioning points, therefore, the positioning error in the direction of two axis is $\tilde{\sigma}_{xi}^2 = \sigma_{1i}^2 + \sigma_{xi}^2$ and $\tilde{\sigma}_{yi}^2 = \sigma_{2i}^2 + \sigma_{yi}^2$ respectively. The positioning error variance after weighted fusion is minimum, through the determining method for optimized weighted value which based on the distribution of the positioning error variance, the method of weighted value determination is:

$$\omega_i = \frac{1}{(\tilde{\sigma}_{xi}^2 + \tilde{\sigma}_{yi}^2) \cdot \sum_{j=1}^{n} 1/(\tilde{\sigma}_{xj}^2 + \tilde{\sigma}_{yj}^2)} \tag{20}$$

Therefore, the result after fusion is:

$$Loc = \sum_{i=1}^{l} \omega_i \begin{bmatrix} x_i' \\ y_i' \end{bmatrix} \tag{21}$$

where $l$ is the number of the positioning points after filter, $\begin{bmatrix} x_i' \\ y_i' \end{bmatrix}$ is the $ith$ positioning point after filter.

# 5    Simulation Results

## 5.1    Power Spectrum of Angle of von Mises Distributing

When $\overline{\varphi} = 0°$ , $v = 200m/s$ , carrier wave frequency $f_c = 450\text{MHz}$ , Power Spectrum of Angle of von Mises distribution with different $u$ is shown in Fig.3.

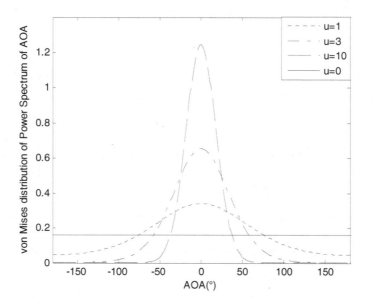

**Fig. 3.** von Mises distribution of Power Spectrum of AOA in Ground-to-Air communications

It can be seen from Fig.3 that, the AOA is changing more and more centralized with the $u$ increasing.

## 5.2    Comparison of Simulation Results for Different Direction-Finding Positioning Algorithm Used in Airborne Interferometer

Taking the starting point of the aircraft as origin and the direction of aircraft flight as $x$ axis, the rectangular coordinates can be established. The real position for target radiation has a coordinate of (150km, 150km), the aircraft flies along the horizontal direction, same as the positive direction of $x$ coordinate axis, and performs direction-finding and localization for the target radiation. One dimension uniform linear array is employed in the airborne interferometer direction-finding system and the ratio between the interval distance $d$ of linear array and the wavelength $\lambda$ of the received wave is 0.5. The Rice factor $K$ in measurement of the azimuth angle for the observation point submits to a random distribution in the interval of [10, 20]. The position of the target radiation is estimated by 200 iteration computation using the WLSE and LSE respectively. The simulation results are shown in Fig.3.

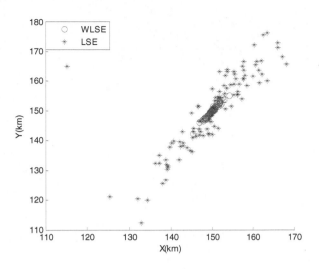

**Fig. 4.** Simulation results for position of the target radiation using the WLSE and the LSE

It can be seen from Fig.4 that, compared to the estimation results when using the LSE algorithm, a faster convergence speed and a smaller variance can be obtained when using the method of WLSE algorithm which determining the weighted value based on the estimation of channel Rican factor $K$.

## 5.3   Comparison of Simulation Results for Different Direction-Finding Positioning Algorithm Used in Spaceborne Interferometer

Assuming that the Rican factor $K$ submits to a random distribution in the interval of [50,100], and the height of the satellite is 150km, the coordinate can be established as shown in Fig 2. The satellite move along the positive direction of Y coordinate axis, and generates a positioning point every 1000m. The total number of positioning point is 20. The azimuth angle of target radiation relative to the starting point of satellite $\alpha = 30°$, and the elevation angle $\beta = 45°$ (that is to say the real position of target is (130000m, 75000m)). 100 iteration Monte Carlo experiments are performed on the average fusion and weighted fusion, and the simulation results are shown in Fig. 4.

It can be seen from Fig.4 that, the positioning precision of weighted fusion method when taking the influences of different Rican factor is better than that of average fusion method, and the weighted fusion method is validated. Table 1 lists the average positioning error when positioning different target points using the average fusion method and the weighted fusion method respectively, and it can be seen from Table 1 that the larger the distance of target position correspond the larger the average positioning error, and the advantages of weighted fusion method is more significant.

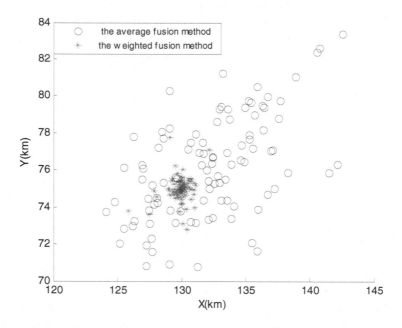

**Fig. 4.** Estimation results of target point using the average fusion method and the weighted fusion method

**Table 1.** The different target location points average position error using the average fusion method and the weighted fusion method respectively

| Real Position of Target ( m) | Position Error of Average Fusion Method ( m) | Position Error of Weighted Fusion Method ( m) |
|---|---|---|
| $T_1$( 130000, 75000) | ( 4503.4, 3159.8) | ( 998.5, 774.8) |
| $T_2$( 100000, 50000) | ( 3195.6, 2408.7) | ( 732.8, 646.5) |
| $T_3$( 100000, 50000) | ( 5643.8, 4625.9) | ( 1117.2, 864.7) |
| $T_4$( 100000, 50000) | ( 7986.2, 6699.1) | ( 1266.1, 965.6) |

# 6    Conclusion

Aiming at parameter measure is affected by different channel type, this paper adopts Weighted Least Squares Estimates and Weighted positioning points fusion algorithm through Rice factor of different type channel determining weighted value in order to improve interferometer direction-finding positioning precision, the simulation results show that weighted algorithm of considering channel influence advance the position precision effectively.

# References

1. Gavish, M., Weiss, A.J.: Performance Analysis of Bearing-only Target Location Algorithms. J. IEEE Trans. on Aerospace and Electronic Systems 28(3), 817–828 (1992)
2. Torrieri, D.J.: Statistical theory of passive location systems. J. IEEE Trans. on Aerospace and Electronic Systems 20(2), 183–198 (1984)
3. Friedlander, B.: A Passive Location Algorithm and Its Accuracy Analysis. J. IEEE Journal Oceanic Engineer 12(1), 234–245 (1987)
4. Becker, K.: An Efficient Method of Passive Emitter Location. J. IEEE Transon AES 28(4), 1091–1104 (1992)
5. Savarese, C., Rabay, J., Langendoen, K.: Robust Positioning Algorithms for Distributed Ad hoc Wireless Sensor Networks. A. Carla Schlatter Ellis. In: Ellis, A.C.S. (ed.) Proceedings of the USENIX Technical Annual Conference, pp. 317–327. USENIX Press, C. Monterey (1992)
6. Fowler, M.: Analysis of single-platform passive emitter location with terrain data. J. IEEE Trans. on Aerospace and Electronic Systems 37(2), 495–507 (2001)
7. Haas, E.: Aeronautical Channel Modeling. IEEE Transactions on Vehicular Technology 51, 254–264 (2002)
8. van Harry, L.: Trees. Optimum Array Processing, pp. 917–1138. M. Wiley-Interscience, Hoboken (2002)
9. Stuber, G.L.: Principles of mobile communication. Kluwer, M. Norwell (1996)

# Optimal Algorithm for Connected Dominating Sets

Nannan Zhao and Muqing Wu

Beijing University of Posts and Telecommunications,
Xitucheng str. 10, 100876 Beijing, China
znn812@gmail.com,
wumuqing@bupt.edu.cn

**Abstract.** There is no infrastructure in most energy constrained networks, such as WSN. Connected Dominating Set (CDS) has been proposed as virtual backbone. The CDS pays the way for routing, data aggregation and activity scheduling. In order to reduce the backbone size and prolong the lifetime of networks, it is desirable to construct a Minimum CDS (MCDS). Unfortunately, it is a NP-hard problem with a distribute manner. In this paper, a distributive algorithm for MESH CDS is introduced. Theoretical analysis and simulation results are also presented to verify the efficiency of our algorithm.

**Keywords:** WSN, Connected Dominating Sets, MESH CDS, Localized distributive algorithm.

## 1 Introduction

Wireless Sensor Networks (WSN) has attached more and more attention recently [1] [2] [3]. It revolutionizes information gathering and processing in both urban environments and inhospitable terrain. The nodes in WSN communicate with each other through multi-hop without physical infrastructure. Therefore a Connected Dominating Sets has been adopted in order to construct a virtual backbone.

The topology related problem in wireless sensor network usually has been modeled in Unit Disk Graph (UDG) [4], in which each node has the same transmission rage and there is an edge between two nodes if and only if their distance is within the transmission range. A Dominating Set (DS) is a subset of nodes so that each node is the UDG graph is either in it or adjacent to at least one node in it. If the DS is connected, it is a Connected Dominating Set (CDS).

The CDS plays a major role in routing, broadcasting, coverage and activity scheduling. To reduce the communication overhead, to simplify the network management, and to make more nodes stay in radio-sleep state which prolong the network life time, it is desirable to find a Minimum Connected Dominating Set (MCDS). Unfortunately, computing a MCDS for a given UDG has been proved to be NP-hard. Thus, only distributed approximation algorithms in polynomial time are practical for wireless sensor networks.

There are many distributed CDS algorithms which use a Maximal Independent Set (MIS) to build a Dominating Set (DS) [5] [6] [7]. An Independent Set (IS) is a subset of nodes which there is no edges between any two nodes in the subset. An MIS of a

P. Sénac, M. Ott, and A. Seneviratne (Eds.): ICWCA 2011, LNICST 72, pp. 340–350, 2012.

UDG is an IS that any other node is adjacent to some node in this IS. Later, the DS will be connected according to different criterion [8] [9].

In this paper, we proposed an algorithm to construct an Optimal CDS. It is a MESH CDS is size-and-energy optimized which has less number of nodes in the backbone we built, since the MIS node of CDS in qualified by degree. The energy cost of construction is lower than the previous CDS algorithms, because we do not use ACK messages in the CDS construction step. We choose MESH structure instead of tree structure, which make the virtual backbone have better robustness against nodes failure.

The remainder of the paper is organized as follows:

In section 2, we provide related research works on CDS and MCDS. Our MESH CDS algorithm is proposed in section 3, which also contains the performance analysis. The simulation results using OMNeT++ will be shown in section 4. At last, in section5, we conclude the paper.

## 2   Related Works

In WSN, most nodes have no need for global network information. Since MCDS problem is NP-hard in distributive manner, there are lots of approximation algorithms have been proposed. These approaches can be classified into two types. One type is to form a DS at first, for example, using MIS to construct a DS [8] [9]. At the second step, they try to find some connectors according to certain optimal principle, so that the DS in transformed to a CDS. Wan et al. proposed a distributed algorithm based on quasi-global information (Spanning Tree) with approximation ratio of 8, $v_i$ time complexity and $O(n \log n)$ message complexity. Another type is to find a CDS at the initial stage and then prune some redundant nodes or links to archive final CDS. Wu et al. proposed in [10], a distributed algorithm with message complexity, $\theta(m)$ time complexity and $O(\Delta^3)$ the approximation ratio at most $O(n)$, where $\Delta$ and $m$ are the maximum degree in graph and number of edges respectively.

As mentioned in [11], each of these two types has their own advantages and drawbacks. CDS built by the first type of algorithms have smaller size which means there would be fewer nodes whose radio state must be active. It seems that the energy efficiency of network is surely better than the CDS of the other type, however, we could not make this conclusion simply. The reason is that the latter type of algorithms has much lower energy cost due to its lower complexity. They do not have to send so many messages to achieve the CDS. What was worse, the network lifetime will be shorter using first type of CDS, because when the nodes in the CDS is fewer, the robustness will be weaker, so there will be much more times of CDS reorganization considering the nodes failure. This problem has been studied in [12]. The Second type of algorithms usually create a CDS which is obviously larger compared with the CDS produced by the first type of algorithm. In this situation, there must be a great number of nodes which could not close their communication module to save energy. As a result, the energy of nodes will not be used efficiently, since there will be a long time when most nodes in the CDS have no messages to send and receive but these nodes still wait to do that, spending lots of energy on communication module.

At last the time complexity and message complexity is also important. None of solutions mentioned above has $O(1)$ time complexity and $O(n)$ message complexity.

# 3 Our Proposal

## 3.1 Assumption

First, we assume that all the nodes in WSN are deployed in the 2-dimentional plane. Second, all the nodes have the same transmission range. So the network topology is modeled as a UDG. Each node $v_i$ has a unique id $ID_i$. The number of links which is connected to $v_i$ is represented as $D_i$. The maximum timeout for each node is noted $T_{max}$. For each node $v_i$, the timeout is $T_i$ set by:

$$T_i = \frac{T_{max}}{D_i}.$$

So the node which has larger $D_i$ has faster timeout.

We use colors to indicate the nodes' states. Each node has one of the four colors which represent its state: White, Black, Grey, Green and Blue. White color stands for the initial state which indicates that the node has not decided its role in MIS and joined the CDS neither. Black (Grey) color means the node has joined (or not) the MIS, but has not joined the CDS. The Blue node is the CDS node. At last, Green color represent a temporary state which tells that the node has already started the MIS/CDS processing but still not decided its final role .

## 3.2 Initial Process

Initially, each node is in White which means its role is not decided yet and all nodes' degree $D_i$ is initialized as 0. At first, each node broadcasts its $ID_i$. When the node received the broadcast, it adds the $ID_i$ to its neighbor table and $D_i$ is increased by 1.

---

**Algorithm 1:** Initial process

1. Each node $v_i$ set its color to white, set $D_i$ to 0.

2. Each node broadcast message including its own id $ID_i$.

3. When received the id broadcast message, it adds the received $ID_i$ to its neighbor table and increase the $D_i$ by 1.

---

## 3.3 MIS Construction

There are many MIS calculation proposals, such as [5] [6] [10] [13]. In fact, almost all the MIS protocols have the common algorithm:

- Initially, each node is in White which means its role is not decided yet;
- Each node broadcasts its weight (ID, degree or level in a tree);
- Each node collects neighbors' information and sorts the neighbors according to the weight;
- If a node has the highest weight among its neighbors, the node declares it is IN the MIS and set its color to Black;
- When a node receives the declaration of a Black node, it declares it is OUT the MIS and set its color to Grey;
- If the node with lower weight did not receive any Black declarations, it should wait the decisions of all the higher weight nodes until it becomes the highest weight node among the nodes whose roles are still not decided;
- The neighbor table will be kept updating during this period according to the declaration messages;
- When all the nodes are either Black or Grey, the algorithm is terminated.

The scheme quite simple and effective to make a MIS, however, this kind of algorithms will bring unnecessary time delay. The reason is that some node which is not the largest-ID node within its neighbors must wait for its neighbors' messages to decide its own color. There is no constrains for this time delay, what was worse, the neighbors messages may not be received successfully every time in fact. As a result, there may be some nodes waiting perpetually. In another word, these nodes will not be colored and stay white. Finally, it causes the failure of MIS construction because these white nodes are not covered by any nodes in the independent set.

So our algorithms give some modifications.

- We choose ID to be the measurement of weight;
- When a White node receives the declaration of a Black node, it set its color to Grey and broadcast a Grey declaration to inform its neighbors;
- When a White node receives a declaration of a Grey node, it set its color to Green, decrease $D_i$ by 1 and set timeout to $T_i = \dfrac{T_{max}}{D_i}$. This means the color of node need to be decided through competition;
- When a Green node receives a declaration of a Black node, it means the competition fails. Then the node set its color to Grey and broadcast a Grey declaration to inform its neighbors;
- When a Green node's timeout expires, it means the node win the competition, it set its color to Black and broadcast a Black declaration to inform its neighbors;
- When a Black node receives a declaration of a Black node which has larger node ID, it means there is a neighbor which has higher priority to be MIS node than itself. Then the node set its color to Grey and broadcast a Grey declaration to inform its neighbors;
- Finally, all the Black nodes form the MIS.

---

**Algorithm 2:** MIS construction

1.    Each node lookup its own neighbor table. If a node $v_i$ has the largest ID among its neighbors, it set its own color to Black and broadcast a message which indicates its own color and ID. We note this Black Message for short. Similarly, there will be Grey Message later.
2.    When a White node received a Black Message, it set its own color to Grey and broadcast a Grey Message.
3.    When a White node received a Grey Message, it set its color to Green, decrease $D_i$ by 1 and set a timer to $T_i = \dfrac{T_{max}}{D_i}$.
4.    When a Green node received a Black Message, the node set its color to Grey and broadcast a Grey Message.
5.    When a Green or Grey node received a Grey Message, decrease $D_i$ by 1.
6.    When a Green node's timer expires, the Green node set its color to Black and broadcast a Black Message.
7.    When a Black node receives a declaration of a Black node which has larger node ID, the node set its color to Grey and broadcast a Grey declaration to inform its neighbors.

---

Theorem 1: The set of black nodes computed the MIS construction algorithm is a MIS.

Proof: First, all the black nodes forms a Independent Set (IS). The reason is that any two black nodes are not neighbors. If they are, one of them must be colored grey according to the modification next to last.

Second, we say there is not any node which is independent form the black nodes set. For the contradiction, we assume there is one node $v_i$ which neither belongs to black nodes set nor covered by any black nodes. So node $v_i$ will never receive any declarations of Black node, and then it must be colored into Black. So node $v_i$ is a member of black nodes set and contradiction is made.

So we proved our black nodes set is a MIS.#

Theorem 2: If the size of MIS is no less than 2, for each MIS node calculated, it always has a non-MIS neighbor that connects it to at least another MIS node.

Proof: In order to make contradiction, we assume that there is a MIS node $u$ which has not any neighbors that connect $u$ to another MIS node.

We note all the neighbors of $u$ forms a set $N_u^1$. All the neighbors of nodes in $N_u^1$ forms a set $N_u^2$. Because there is not any node which connects $u$ and another MIS node, $N_u^2$ must be constitute of non-MIS node. Referring to the Algorithm2, there will not be another MIS node. This make contradiction to the precondition that the size of MIS is no less than 2.#

Apparently, after the MIS construction, the $D_i$ of Grey nodes is the number of Black nodes it connects with.

### 3.4  CDS Formation

The second step is making a CDS. Since an MIS is also a DS, a CDS can be constructed by connecting the nodes in an MIS with some nodes not in the MIS which we call connectors.

In the second step, a tree is usually formed in most of the backbone formation proposals. The tree is formed from one selected node and then the formation process spreads over the network until all Black nodes are in the tree backbone. Tree formation is a sequential process. In a WSN of large scale, the failure and adding of nodes may take place all the time. As a result, the tree backbone has to be reorganized frequently. So compared with tree backbone, we consider that MESH backbone which has additional links is more applicable to WSN. Many algorithms use ack messages to make the backbone constructed successfully and collect the parents-and-children information, however, we think it is not necessary. Topology control only make decisions that which node/link exists in the network. The parents-and-children information is used for routing which is the successive problem of topology control. So we only need to form a CDS as well as determine which nodes belong to CDS. Whatever their parents and children should be, it is not important. Our proposal only gives out the nodes in CDS without parents-and-children information.

The CDS formation is started from the initiator which is assigned at first. The initiator set its color to Blue and then broadcast a Blue message. When a Grey node receives the Blue message, it changes its own color to Green and then enters a waiting period which has Ti seconds. During this period, Green node does not handle any Blue messages. Once the green node timeout, it set its color to Blue and broadcasts a CLR message and a Blue message. When a green node receives a CLR message, it timeout immediately and set its color back to Grey. When a BLACK node receives the Blue message, it set its color to Blue and then broadcast a Blue message. When a node turns into Blue, it discards any messages it receives.

---

**Algorithm 3:** CDS construction

1. One Black node which was assigned to be initiator set its own color to Blue and broadcast a Blue Message.
2. When a Black node received a Blue Message, it set its own color to Blue and broadcast a Blue Message.
3. When a Grey node received a Blue Message, it set its own color to Green and set a timer to $T_i = \dfrac{T_{max}}{D_i}$. Then the Green node broadcast a Blue message.
4. Each Green node does not handle any Blue messages.
5. Once a Green node timeout, it broadcasts a CLR message
6. When a Green node receives a CLR message, its timer is cancelled immediately and set its color back to Grey.
7. When a Blue node received a message, the message will be ignored.

---

Theorem 3: The set of Blue nodes computed by the algorithm 3 is a CDS the network.

Proof: First we assume there is only one MIS node $u$ which is not blue. According to theorem 2, there is at least one non-MIS node which connect to another MIS node $v$. Then $v$ must be blue and has sent a Blue message. So the connector of $u$ and $v$ must have send a Blue message, which indicates that the node $u$ must be blue. There is contradiction. If there is other non-Blue MIS node we can make the contradiction similarly one by one. Now we can say that all the MIS node must be Blue.

Second we assume there is one Blue MIS node $u$ which is not connected to another part of MIS node. Then node $u$ has not received any Blue message, so it would not be a Blue node. There is contradiction.

Finally, we can say that all the Blue node forms a CDS of the network in conclusion.

## 4   Simulation Resluts

In this section, we verify our algorithm by test its performance with the simulation software OMNeT++ in different network size. We have made the comparison between our proposal , K. M. Alzoubi et. al.'s algorithm in [5] and a MESH CDS algorithm in [14]. We will show the result in 2 aspects, that is CDS size and energy cost.

The number of nodes is from 10 to 500. Node density is $1/10000 \, node/m^2$. Nodes are distributed randomly. Mobility model is set to be static. CSMA MAC is used. The energy model parameters is shown in TABLE 1.

**Table 1.** Energy model parameters

| Radio state | Energy cost (mW) |
|-------------|------------------|
| Tx          | 78               |
| Rx          | 78               |
| IDEL        | 0                |
| SLEEP       | 0                |

The CDS of algorithm in [5] is shown if Fig. 1 while the result of our proposal is shown in Fig. 2. All of them have the same network size, 50 nodes. The black node is the MIS nodes as well as the cyan nodes is the connectors. The Gray node stands for the non-CDS nodes. The dash line in Fig.1 show us the parent-child links of nodes'. We can see that the number of MIS nodes in Fig. 2 is than that in Fig. 1. Furthermore, the MIS nodes emerge at the area where nodes are distributed more densely. In another word, one MIS node computed by our algorithms covers more nodes. The reason is that when the nodes with larger degree have less time to wait in algorithm 2, which means they have larger probability to be selected as MIS node.

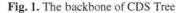

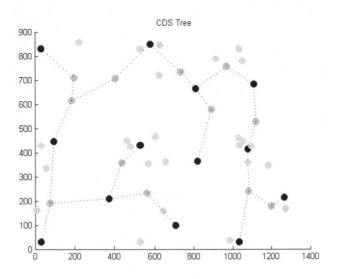

**Fig. 1.** The backbone of CDS Tree

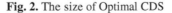

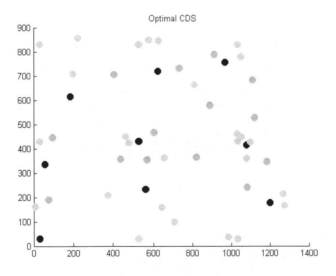

**Fig. 2.** The size of Optimal CDS

The size of MIS in different network scale is shown in Fig. 3. The number of nodes in MIS computed by the Optimal CDS is less than those computed by the other two algorithms. As we explained before, MIS nodes in our algorithm emerges at where the nodes are deployed more densely. While the network's scale increasing, the difference is growing larger. The fewer MIS nodes lead to the fewer connectors, so we can infer that the size of CDS constructed by our algorithm will be smaller than the MESH CDS in [14]. The results of CDS size is shown in Fig. 4. The CDS Tree in [5] has the least number of CDS, because the tree structure has less number of links.

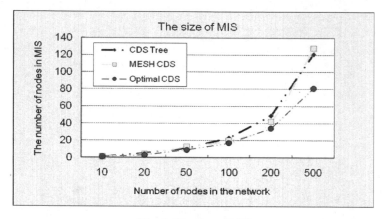

**Fig. 3.** The size of MIS

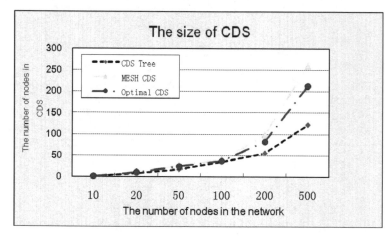

**Fig. 4.** The size of CDS

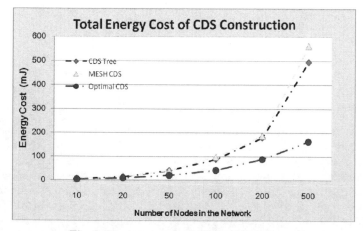

**Fig. 5.** The energy cost of CDS construction

The energy cost of CDS construction is shown in Fig. 5. It is clear to see that Optimal CDS saves a lot of energy than the other 2 algorithm. The reason is that there is no ACK message in our proposal, which reduces a great amount of messages in the CDS forming step. Though Optimal CDS has more connectors than those of CDS Tree, its energy cost is the least among the three.

## 5  Conclusion

In a random deployed network Connected Dominating Set plays an important role such as routing, broadcasting, coverage and activity scheduling in WSN. Our Optimal CDS is a CDS uses a time compete mechanism with the nodes' degree to make each MIS node covers other non-MIS nodes as many as possible. In order to enhance the energy efficiency of each node, we also removed the ACK messages and parent-child information which is unnecessary for topology control. The simulation results show us that the Optimal CDS has greatly reduced the number of MIS nodes and the energy cost of CDS construction.

## References

1. Pottie, G.J.: Wireless sensor networks. In: Information Theory Workshop, June 22-26, pp. 139–140 (1998)
2. Sohrabi, K., Gao, J., Ailawadhi, V., Pottie, G.J.: Protocols for self-organization of a wireless sensor network. IEEE Personal Communications 7(5), 16–27 (2000)
3. Ahmed, A.A., Shi, H., Shang, Y.: A survey on network protocols for wireless sensor networks. In: Proceedings. International Conference on Information Technology: Research and Education, ITRE2003, August 11-13, pp. 301–305 (2003)
4. Clark, B.N., Colbourn, C.J., Johnson, D.S.: Unit disk graphs. Discrete Mathematics 86, 165–177 (1990)
5. Alzoubi, K.M., Wan, P.-J., Frieder, O.: Distributed Heuristics for Connected Dominating Sets in Wireless Ad Hoc Networks. Journal of Communications And Networks 4(1) (2002)
6. Alzoubi, K.M., Wan, P.-J., Frieder, O.: Weakly-connected dominating sets and sparse spanners in wireless ad hoc networks. In: Proceedings. 23rd International Conference on Distributed Computing Systems (2003)
7. Raei, H., Sarram, M., Adibniya, F., Tashtarian, F.: Optimal distributed algorithm for minimum connected dominating sets in Wireless Sensor Networks. In: 5th IEEE International Conference on Mobile Ad Hoc and Sensor Systems, MASS 2008 (2008)
8. Wan, P.-J., Alzoubi, K.M., Frieder, O.: Distributed Construction of Connected Dominating Set in Wireless Ad Hoc Networks. Mobile Networks and Applications 9, 141–149 (2004)
9. Wang, F., Thai, M.T., Du, D.-Z.: On the construction of 2-connected virtual backbone in wireless networks. Wireless Communications (March 2009)
10. Wu, J., Li, H.: On calculating connected dominating set for efficient routing in ad hoc wireless networks. In: DIALM 1999: Proceedings of the 3rd International Workshop on Discrete Algorithms and Methods for Mobile Computing and Communications (1999)

11. Basagni, S., Mastrogiovanni, M., Petrioli, C.: A performance comparison of protocols for clustering and backbone formation in large scale ad hoc networks. In: IEEE International Conference Mobile Ad-hoc and Sensor Systems (2004)
12. Zhao, N., Zhang, Y.: The Relation between Organized Structure and Maintaining Cost in WSN. In: 5th International Conference on Wireless Communications, Networking and Mobile Computing, WiCom 2009, September 24-26, pp. 1–4 (2009)
13. Basagni, S., Petrioli, C., Petroccia, R.: Efficiently reconfigureureurable backbones for wireless sensor networks. Computer Communications 31(4), 668–698 (2008)
14. Zhao, N., Wu, M., Zhang, Y.: A Localized MESH-CDS Structure and Maintenance for Wireless Sensor Networks. In: 2010 6th International Conference on Wireless and Mobile Communications (ICWMC), September 20-25, pp. 262–267 (2010)

# FOMR: Fair Opportunistic Multicast Routing Scheme for Wireless Mesh Networks

S.R.N. Reddy, Neha Singh, Riya Verma, and Vandana Upreti

Indira Gandhi Institute of Technology
Department of Computer Science
Guru Gobind Singh Indraprastha University- Delhi
rammallik@yahoo.com, neha8.igit@gmail.com,
riyaverma08@rediffmail.com, vandana.upreti@gmail.com

**Abstract.** Opportunistic routing has recently attracted much attention as it is considered to be a promising direction for improving the performance of wireless adhoc and sensor networks. It exploits the broadcast nature of the wireless network. Multicast is an important communication paradigm in wireless networks. The availability of multiple destinations in a multicast tree can make the selection of forwarder candidates, distributed coordination among them and related prioritization complicated. Thus far, little work has been done in this area. Selection of an appropriate metric is very important for designing the opportunistic routing scheme.In this paper, we propose an efficient multicast scheme based on opportunistic routing and network coding that uses STR as a metric. The mathematical analysis shows that STR based FOMR scheme always outperforms ETX based OM.

**Keywords:** Opportunistic routing, multicast, network coding, metric.

## 1 Introduction

Wireless Mesh Networks (WMNs) are designed to provide resilient, robust and high-throughput data delivery to wireless subscribers. They are widely deployed in many scenarios such as campus networking, community networking and so on. Previous works on traditional routing protocols mainly focus on providing robust routing by selecting the best route according to different routing metrics. In such protocols the approach to routing traffic is to select a best path for each source- destination pair(according to some metric) and send the traffic along the predetermined path. Most of the existing protocols such as DSR[11], AODV[12], DSDV[14], and ZRP[10] fall into this category. Recent studies have shown that this strategy doesn't adapt well to the dynamic wireless environment where transmission failures occur frequently, which would trigger excessive link level retransmissions, waste of network resources or even system breakdown.

Opportunistic Routing (OR) is a new class of wireless technology that exploits the broadcast nature of the wireless medium and defers route selection after packet transmission. Here any node overhearing a transmission is allowed to participate in the packet forwarding thereby increasing the reliability of the transmission. It is able

P. Sénac, M. Ott, and A. Seneviratne (Eds.): ICWCA 2011, LNICST 72, pp. 351–361, 2012.
© Institute for Computer Sciences, Social Informatics and Telecommunications Engineering 2012

to combine multiple weak links into a stronger link. A forwarder set is maintained for each flow. Any packet in the flow may use all the nodes in the forwarding list and the nodes in the list are prioritized with some metric.

Each node only forwards the packets which have not been received by any high priority node. So this needs multiple forwarding nodes to coordinate among themselves when only one of them actually forwards the packets. Network coding seminally proposed by Ahlswede et al[3] can fully utilize the opportunistic listening and creates an encoded packet, so it is complementary to OR.

Multicasting is a method of communication by which an identical message is sent to multiple receivers. Its main applications are videoconferencing, teleconferencing, content distribution, remote teaching and so on. Till date, the protocols proposed for opportunistic multicasting such as Opportunistic Multicast (OM) protocol have used ETX as their metric[8]. ETX being an unfair metric doesn't consider multiple links information for each forwarder so it doesn't always make good decision. This results in non-optimal forwarder set selection that directly causes many duplicate transmissions. On the contrary, STR exploits multiple links and is calculated from the destination to the source node so it offers an optimal forwarder set that minimizes the average number of transmissions required to send a packet and the number of duplicate packets received by the destination thus increasing the throughput.

The rest of the paper is organized as follows. In section 2, we survey the related work and motivate opportunistic routing. Section 3 presents our proposed FOMR scheme. In section 4 we have given the mathematical proof to support our proposed work. Finally we conclude our work in section 5.

## 2     Related Work

Opportunistic routing was introduced by Biswas and Morris, whose paper explains the potential throughput increase and proposes the Ex-OR protocol as a means to achieve it[1]. Since then several protocols have been proposed that exploits the concept of OR for communication in wireless networks [2, 6, 9, 15, 16]. For opportunistic multicasting, researchers have already adopted an approach in which network coding is combined with opportunistic routing to support multicast traffic. But since the metric they have used is an unfair metric, it increases duplication and thus reduces throughput. Our work builds on this foundation but adopts a fundamentally different approach. It uses a fair metric Successful Transmission Rate (STR) instead of an unfair metric Expected Transmission Rate(ETX) to increase the throughput of the transmission. The resulting protocol is practical, allows spatial reuse and supports both unicast and multicast traffic.

Unfair OR scheme builds a candidate forwarder set in which many forwarders are prioritized with order. The higher priority indicates that the node is closer to destination. The higher prioritized node is entitled to send the packets it received and the rest of the nodes have to wait and listen to it. So that every node only forwards the packets that have not been received by any higher priority node. Fair OR scheme also builds a candidate forwarder set but all the nodes in it are fair without any priority. The set just includes some nodes closer to the destination than the source.

OR differs from traditional routing in that it exploits the broadcast nature of wireless medium and defers route selection after packet transmission. This can cope well with unreliable and unpredictable wireless links. There are two major benefits in OR. Firstly it doesn't compromise the reliability factor over the progress made in a transmission.

$$A \longrightarrow B \longrightarrow C \longrightarrow D \longrightarrow E$$

If A sends a packet to E via B, C, D then reliability is high but the progress made is less in each step. Instead if it sends packet directly to C then progress is high but reliability goes low. However in OR the packet is broadcasted to all nodes. All the nodes coordinate among themselves to decide which node is closer to E and the rest of the nodes will then drop the packet.

Secondly it takes advantage of the multiple links. It combines multiple weak links to form a stronger link.

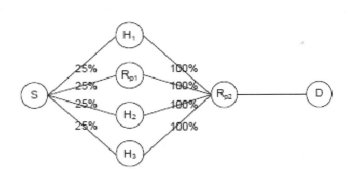

**Fig. 1.** Probability of sending data frames from source to Rp2

As shown in fig1 the probability of successfully delivering packets between S and the relay nodes is 0.25 and between the relay nodes and the node Rp is 1. In this case the expected number of transmissions required to send a packet from node S to Rp is equal to 5. However in OR all the four relay nodes will coordinate to deliver the packet. So the number of transmissions will reduce to $(1/(1-(1-0.25)4))+1$ i.e. 2.5 transmissions.

Work on network coding started with a pioneering paper by Ahlswede et al that established the value of coding in the routers and provided theoretical bounds on the capacity of such networks[3]. Besides the metric that we shall be using is STR proposed in 2009[7].It has shown that STR is a better metric when used with a fair scheme like MORE [15] or OM [8]. The paper has given that one can achieve 30% more throughput by using STR as a metric.

## 3   FOMR : Fair Opportunistic Multicast Routing Protocol

In this section, we will introduce a new multicasting protocol based on opportunistic routing and network coding based on STR.

## 3.1    Overview

FOMR scheme is based on proactive link state routing. Every node periodically measures and disseminates link quality in terms of STR. Based on this information, a multicast source selects the default multicast routing path employing the existing Steiner Tree algorithm [4,5] and a list of forwarding nodes that are eligible for forwarding the data packets. It then uses network coding to make coded packets and broadcasts them.

## 3.2    Steiner Tree Construction

To support opportunistic multicast routing, each node maintains a routing table consisting of three fields: multicast group, default path and the forwarder set where the default path is the average shortest cost path from the sender to the corresponding sub-group in terms of STR and forwarding list includes a list of next hop nodes that are eligible to forward the packet. We now explain how STR is computed for each node and the default multicast routing tree construction.

### 3.2.1    Computation of STR

STR denotes the expected Successful Transmission Rate between a certain node and the destination. Each node calculates its STR to the destination and chooses some of the neighbours with the higher STR values into its forwarder set.

The exact approach used to calculate STR is:
If the node X and the destination are within one hop, the STR of node X is

$$STRX = PXD$$

If there are two hops between node X and the destination, the STR of node X is

$$STRX = PX1P1D + i=1\sum N \quad PXiPiD \quad j=1\pi i\text{-}1\ (1\text{-}PXj)$$

If there are more than two hops between node X and the destination then the STR of node X is

$$STRX = PX1\ STR1D \quad + \quad i=1\sum N \quad PXi \quad STRiD \quad j=1\pi i\text{-}1\ (1\text{-} PXj)$$
(the corresponding figures are shown below)

so a node needs to know its one-hop forwarder's STR values to calculate its own STR value.

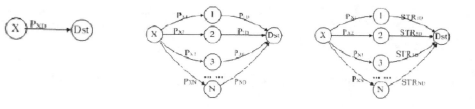

### 3.2.2 Default Multicast Path

To construct the Steiner tree and to get the default multicast path, every node calculates STR values of the links using the formulae given in the section 3.2.1. After computing the STR values of each link of the network, a Steiner tree denoting the multicast default routing path is obtained by applying the existing Steiner tree algorithm [4]. The Steiner tree algorithm is used to find the shortest interconnect for a given set of nodes. It is similar to minimum spanning tree except that in Steiner tree, extra intermediate vertices and edges may be added to the graph in order to reduce the length of the spanning tree. The Steiner tree helps the source to know the number of number of packets it needs to multicast via the existing default delivery tree to multiple forwarding set.

## 3.3 Forwarder Set Selection

Forwarding node selection is critical to the performance of FOMR protocol just like other unicast opportunistic routing protocol such as ExOR, MORE and SOAR and so on. In order to leverage path diversity while avoiding duplicate transmissions, FOMR protocol relaxes the actual route that data traverses to be along or near the default delivery tree. FOMR protocol constrains the nodes involved in routing a packet to be near the default multicast distribution tree. This prevents routes from diverging and minimizes duplicate transmissions. Moreover, this forwarding node selection also simplifies coordination since all the nodes involved are close to nodes on the default delivery tree and can hear each other with a reasonably high probability. Therefore, we can use overheard transmissions to coordinate between forwarding nodes in a cheap and distributed way.

Forwarding set selection algorithm consists of two steps. First, a sender selects an initial forwarding list based on the default multicast delivery path. Then, it further limits the number of forwarding nodes to minimize duplicate transmissions. These steps are taken by a sender on each packet, allowing for the forwarding set to quickly adapt to network conditions.

When node $i$ is on the default multicast delivery path, $i$ selects the forwarding nodes that satisfy the following conditions:

• The forwarding node's STR to the multicast sub-group is higher than $i$'s STR to the Multicast sub-group.
• The forwarding node's STR to $i$ is within a threshold.

The first constraint ensures that the packet makes progress. The second constraint ensures that $i$ hears the forwarding node's transmissions with a high probability to avoid duplicate retransmissions.

Since not only should we ensure that forwarding nodes make progress and have sufficiently good link quality from node $i$, but also we want the selected forwarding nodes to be adjacent to the default multicast delivery path and every pair of forwarding nodes has sufficiently good luck quality between them to avoid diverging paths. This results in the following two additional constraints in selecting forwarding nodes.

• Each forwarding node is close to at least one node on the default multicast delivery tree branch representing some multicast sub-group.

• The STR of a link between any pair of forwarding nodes in the same forwarding list is within a threshold.

These constraints ensure that forwarding nodes have good connectivity among themselves and to nodes on the default multicast delivery tree branch.

## 3.4    The Operation of FOMR Protocol

In this section we shall explain the working of FOMR protocol.

### 3.4.1    Packet Coding and Multicasting

The source breaks up the file into batches of K packets, where $K$ may vary from one batch to another. These K uncoded packets are called native packets. When the 802.11 MAC is ready to send, the source creates a random linear combination of the K native packets in the current batch. A coded packet is $p_j^{'} = \sum i \, c_{ji} \, p_i$ , where the $c_{ji}$ 's are random coefficients picked by the node, and the $p_i$ 's are native packets from the same batch.

We call $c_j = (c_{j1},\ldots,c_{ji}\ldots,c_{jk})$ the code vector of packet $p_j^{'}$ . Thus, the code vector describes how to generate the coded packet from the native packets. After the creating of encoded packet, the source multicasts the coded packet via the existing default multicast delivery tree to multiple forwarding set determined by the degree of the source. The sender keeps transmitting coded packets from the current batch until the batch is acknowledged by the farthest destination of the multicast group, at which time, the sender proceeds to the next batch.

### 3.4.2    Multicast Forwarding

Nodes listen to all transmissions. When a node hears a packet, it checks whether it is in the packet's forwarder list. If so, the node checks whether the packets contains new information, in which case it is called an innovative packet. Technically speaking, a packet is innovative if it is linearly independent from the packets the node has previously received from this batch. The node ignores non-innovative packets, and stores the innovative packets it receives from the the current batch. If the node is in the forwarder list, the arrival of this new packet triggers the node to broadcast a coded packet. To do so the node creates a random linear combination of the coded packets it has heard from the same batch and broadcasts it. Note that a liner combination of coded packets is also a linear combination of the corresponding native packets. Similar to the source, the forwarder forwards the multicast packet to multiple different forwarding set according to the degree of the forwarder locating at the current passion of the multicast delivery tree. That is the number of different forwarding set is determined by the number of branch of leaving the forwarder. The construction of forwarding set is formulated by the above mentioned forwarding set selection rules.

### 3.4.3    Acknowledgement

For each packet it receives, each destination of the multicast group checks whether the packet is innovative, i.e. it is linearly independent from previously received packets. The destination discards non-innovative packets. Once the destination receives K innovative packets, it decodes the whole batch using simple matrix inversion:

$$\begin{pmatrix} p_1 \\ \dots \\ p_k \end{pmatrix} = \begin{pmatrix} c_{11} \dots c_{1k} \\ \dots\dots\dots \\ c_{k1} \dots c_{kk} \end{pmatrix}^{-1} \begin{pmatrix} p_1' \\ \dots \\ p_k' \end{pmatrix}$$

where, $p_i$ is a native packet, and $p_i'$ is a coded packet whose code vector is $c_i$ $=(c_{i1},\dots,c_{ik})$. As soon as the farthest destination decodes the batch, it sends an acknowledgment to the source to allow it to move to the next batch. ACKs are sent using best unicast path routing and also given priority over data packets at every node.

## 4    Mathematical Proof

In this section we shall show the performance of STR over ETX using two different approaches.

**4.1**   In the first approach, we will take a network topology to show that STR based FOMRS outperform ETX based OM protocol. The parameters that we shall consider for comparison are the average number of transmissions required to send a packet from the source to the destination and the number of distinguished packets received by the destination in each case.

Consider the network topology given in fig2 where delivery probability of every link and the corresponding ETX values of the nodes are marked. S denotes the source and Dst refers to the destination. Rest of the nodes are the relay nodes that will coordinate in the transmission of a packet from S to Dst.

Let us first compute the ETX and STR values of all the nodes and figure out the forwarder set in each case.

**a)      Using ETX**
ETX value is calculated using the delivery probability of the link :

| Node | S    | A    | B    | C    | D    | E    | F    | G    | Dst |
|------|------|------|------|------|------|------|------|------|-----|
| ETX  | 3.75 | 2.58 | 2.58 | 2.50 | 1.25 | 1.33 | 1.25 | 1.25 | 1   |

Now since ETX is an unfair metric, it will prioritize the nodes based on their ETX values. The node with lower ETX value will get priority over one with higher ETX value as ETX denotes the expected number of total transmissions required to send a packet. So the source will select its forwarder set as {C, A, B} or {C, B, A}. This means most of the packets will be transferred through C.

**b)      Using STR**
STR denotes the total number of successful transmissions out of total transmissions in a packet transmission. So node with  higher value of STR will get priority over the node with lower STR value.

STR values can be computed using the formulae given in section 3.2.1 so

| node | S | A | B | C | D | E | F | G |
|------|-----|-----|-----|-----|-----|-----|-----|-----|
| STR(%) | 70.84 | 74 | 60 | 64 | 80 | 75 | 80 | 80 |

So using the algorithm of forwarder set selection with STR metric[7] , the forwarder set of S comes out to be {A, B, C}.

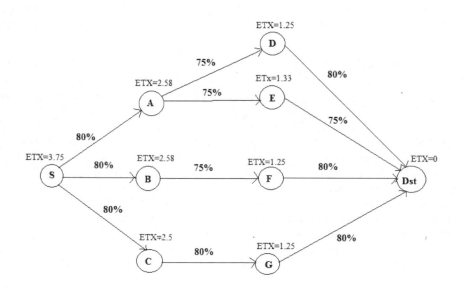

**Fig. 2.** Network topology with ETX values marked

**Analysis:**
We will now compare the two forwarder set selected on the basis of:

**a)     Distinguished packets**
Using the STR concept, we found that the number of distinguished packets received by the destination through A are 74 while the number of distinguished packets received through C are 64 only. This gives an increment of about 10.68%.

This means A can forward more packets (Distinguished) than C. So our STR based FOMRS will have more throughput than ETX based OM protocol.

**b)     Average number of transmissions required**
# Average number of transmissions required to send a packet from source to destination through A will be 3.368.

# Average number of transmissions required to send a packet from source to destination through C will be 3.75.

As is clear from the values above the average number of transmissions required to send a packet using STR is less than ETX based forwarder set.

**4.2**   In the second approach, we consider a set V of $n = |V|$ wireless nodes deployed in a given area. Each node has a unique identifier $vi \in \{v1, v2, \ldots, vn\}$ and has an omnidirectional antenna. We model the network with a probabilistic direct graph: $G = (V,L,D)$ in which a vertex $vi \in V$ denotes a node and an edge $li,j \in L$ represents a communication link from node $vi$ to node $vj$ Each link $li,j$ is characterized by a delivery ratio $di,j \in D$, which measures the probability that a packet is correctly received in a single transmission along such a link. Clearly, we have that $di,i = 1$.

Let $s, d \in V$ be the source and the destination of a packet transmission respectively, and let $f : V \times V \to R$ be the priority function2, i.e. the function that measures the routing progress of a packet toward the destination. We define the ordered set of the allowed relays $r_i \in V$ for the packet sent by $s$ toward $d$ as:

$\mathbf{R_{s,d}} = \{S=r_0,r_1,\ldots\ldots r_N,r_{N+1=d} \}$                              for all $i <= j$

$P_{ri,rj} = \{d_{ri,rj} \prod_{k=j+1}^{N+1} (1-d_{ri,rj}) \ \}$                for all $i<=j$      ... .(A)

$P_{ri,rj}=0$                                                                                          for all $i>j$      .....(B)

R is the relay node set    and $P_{ri,rj}$   represents the probability with which node j will receive the packet from I to forward it further.

Now, average number of transmissions is given by equation:

$$n_{s,d}=1/1-p_{s,s} \ [ \ 1+ \sum_{k=1}^{N} \ p_{s,rk} \ n_{rk,d} \ ] \tag{1}$$

and,

$$n_{rk,d}= 1/1-p_{rk,rk} [1+ \sum_{l=k+1}^{N} \ p_{rk,rl} \ n_{rl,d}] \tag{2}$$

**Analysis:**
We will now derive an expression for average number of transmissions in both cases

**a)    For ETX**
Average number of transmission can be derived using equations (1) and (2) as:
For ETX, delivery ratio between any two nodes is given by the expression
$d_{rk,d} = \quad 1/1-p_{rk,d}$  where
$p_{s,s}= d_{s,s} (1-d_{s,r1}) (1-d_{s,r2})\ldots\ldots (1-d_{s,rd})$
$\quad = 1. (1-1/p_{s,r1}) (1-(1/p_{s,r1} . 1/p_{r1,r2}))\ldots\ldots (1-ETX_{s,d})$
$\quad = K_1(1-ETX_{s,d}) \qquad\qquad$ where K1 is a constant
$$\quad = K_1 - K_1 \ ETX_{s,d} \tag{3}$$
Similarly,
$$P_{s,rk}= K_2 - K_2 \ ETX_{s,d} \tag{4}$$
and similarly we have $P_{rk,rk} = K_3$
Now, substituiting the values found in eq. (3)and (4)  in eq. (1) and (2), we get,
$$n_{s,d} =[ \ 1/1-(K_1-k_1ETX_{s,d})][\{1+\sum_{k=1}^{N} \ (K_2-k_2ETX_{s,d})\} \{(1/1-k_3)(1+ \sum_{l=k+1}^{N} \ k_3 \ n_{rl,d}) \}] \tag{5}$$

$n_{rl,d}= [1/1-p_{rl,d}] \ [1+ \sum_{k=1}^{N} \ p_{rl,k} \ n_{rk,d}]$
$$\quad = \ [1/1-(k_1 - k_1 \ ETX_{s,d})] \ [1+ \sum_{k=1}^{N} \ p_{rl,rk} \ n_{rk,d}] \tag{6}$$

On solving, we get

$$n_{s,d} = [1/1-(k_1-k_2 ETX_{s,d})][\{1++\sum_{k=1}^{N}(K_2-k_2ETX_{s,d})\}\{(1/1-k_3)(1+\sum_{l=k+1}^{N}k_3$$
$$[1/1-(k_1'-k_1'ETX_{s,d})] \qquad [1+\sum_{k=1}^{N}p_{rl,rk}\,n_{rk,d}]\}]  \qquad (7)$$

**b)   For STR**

Equation (7) can be modified by considering formulae of STR as given in the section 3.2.1.Putting these values in equation (1) and (A) for each ETX in it, we get

$$P_{s,s} = 1.\ (P_{s,r1})(P_{r1,r2})\ldots\ldots(P_{r(n-1),rm}) = C \qquad\qquad \text{where } C = \text{constant integer} <= 1$$

Using above value, we get

$$n_{s,d} = C'[1+\sum_{K=1}^{N}P_{s,rk}\,n_{rk,d}]$$

Where $C' = 1/1-C$

$$n_{s,d}=C'[1+\sum_{K=1}^{N}P_{s,rk}\{STR_{x-x1,\ldots..xn,d}\}] \qquad\qquad (8)$$

As can be concluded by considering equation (7) and (8) average number of transmissions is more in ETX than that required by STR.

# 5   Conclusion

In this paper, we proposed an efficient multicast protocol based on the opportunistic routing and network coding that uses STR as a metric Mathematical analysis reveals that the performance of the STR based FOMR protocol outperforms the conventional multicast protocols based on ETX in wireless mesh networks. It can improve the network performances, in terms of throughputs and the packet transmission cost. In the future work, we will continue to investigate the opportunistic multicast routing protocols . We will try to improve upon the acknowledgement scheme and the default path selection algorithm that will increase the reliability of FOMR protocol.

# References

1. Biswas, S., Morris, R.: ExOR: Opportunistic Multi-Hop Routing for Wireless Networks. In: Proc. ACM SIGCOM (August 2005)
2. Rozner, E., Seshadri, J., Mehta, Y.A., Qiu, L.: SOAR: Simple Opportunistic Adaptive Routing Protocol for Wireless Mesh Networks. IEEE Transactions on Mobile Computing 8(12), 1622–1635 (2009)
3. Ahlswede, R., Cai, N., Li, S.-Y., Yeung, R.W.: Network information flow. IEEE Trans. Information Theory IT-46(4),1204–1216 (2000)
4. wang, F.K.H.: Steiner Tree Problems. Networks 15(1), 55–89 (1992)
5. Kou, L., Markowsky, G., Berman, L.: A Fast Algorithm for Steiner Trees. Acta Informatica 15(2), 141–145 (1981)
6. Westphal, C.: Opportunistic Routing in Dynamic Ad Hoc Networks: The OPRAH protocol. In: Proc. IEEE MASS 2006, pp. 570–573 (2006)
7. Li, Y., Liu, Y.-a., Luo, P.: Link Probability Based Opportunistic Routing Metric in Wireless Network. In: International Conference on Communications and Mobile Computing (2009)

8. Yang, W.Z., Huang, C.H., Wang, B., Zhang, Z.Y., Wang, T.: OM: Opportunistic Multicast Routing for Wireless Mesh Networks. In: Fifth International Conference on Frontier of Computer Science and Technology (2010)
9. Plymoth, A.N., Bhorkar, A., Johansson, P.: Common Opportunistic Routing and Forwarding. In: IEEE conference (2010)
10. Beijar, N.: Zone Routing Protocol (ZRP), Networking Laboratory, Helsinki University of Technology
11. Johnson, D.B., Maltz, D.A., Broch, J.: DSR: The dynamic source routing protocol for multihop wireless ad hoc networks. In: Ad Hoc Networking (2001)
12. Perkins, C.E., Royer, E.M.: Ad hoc on-demand distance vector routing. In: Proc. of the 2nd IEEE Workshop on Mobile Computing Systems and Applications (February 1999)
13. Liu, H., Zhang, B., Mouftah, H.T., Shen, X., Ma, J.: Opportunistic Routing for Wireless Ad Hoc and Sensor Networks: Present and Future Directions. IEEE Communications Magazine (December 2009)
14. Perkins, Bhagwat: Highly Dynamic Destination- Sequenced Distance Vector Routing (DSDV) for mobile computers. Networking Laboratory, Helsinki University of Technology (2002)
15. Chachulski, S., Jennings, M., Katti, S., Katabi, D.: Trading Structure for Randomness in Wireless Opportunistic. In: SIGCOMM (2007)
16. Laufer, R., Ferrere, H., Kleinrock, L.: Multirate anypath routing in wireless mesh networks. In: Proc. IEEE INFOCOM (2009)

# The Design of Multi-channel Token Assignment Protocol Based on Received Signal Strength Indication*

Wei Cao**, Caixing Liu, and Wenbin Zeng

College of Informatics, South China Agricultural University
Guangzhou 510642, China
Weiweicao7016@163.com, liu@scau.edu.cn,
baggio23232@hotmail.com

**Abstract.** This paper presents the multi-channel token assignment protocol for the wireless sensor network based on received signal strength indication. Communication cycle is divided into several specific functional windows to received signal strength indication as the terminal node credentials for channel reservation and to reduce the overall network access competition and data collisions. At the same time it extends the node sleeping time, so the energy will be saved and prolong the life of the network will be obtained. Making use of dynamic channel assignment methods can improve the utilization of multi-channel, avoid packet collision and improve the network throughput.

**Keywords:** WSN, Token, Multi-channel.

## 1 Introduction

Wireless sensor network is self-organizing communication networks composed by a large number of wireless sensor nodes. The important function of wireless sensor networks is transmitted the physical data collected to receive points through the wireless network to facilitate data analysis and monitoring. Because of the vulnerability and interference of wireless sensor networks, when a large number of sensor nodes send data to the receiving node, it will inevitably lead to mutual interference, sending conflict, large number of network packet loss, data distortion, additional overhead and so on. Many studies show that the energy consumption used in the wireless sensor network for communication is much higher than using the CPU and other circuit energy[1]. Additional retransmission burden reduces the life cycle of wireless sensor network node, thus affecting the normal operation of the network and even cause network paralysis.

In our long-term monitoring study for cows estrus, wireless sensor networks is applied nodes deployed densely and data transmission volume environment. Therefore, to design an efficient multi-channel communication protocol is extremely important. It can minimize energy consumption of wireless sensor nodes under the

---

* This paper is supported by National 863 Fund under grant 2006AA10Z246.
** Female, Technician.

P. Sénac, M. Ott, and A. Seneviratne (Eds.): ICWCA 2011, LNICST 72, pp. 362–376, 2012.
© Institute for Computer Sciences, Social Informatics and Telecommunications Engineering 2012

premise of supporting the network normal communication. Therefore it can prolong the wireless sensor nodes' working time and entire network using life[2].

## 2 Technical Background

Multi-channel communication technology for wireless sensor networks is one of research focus in the current. Through separating communication channels between various nodes can effectively prevent crosstalk and data collision problems under a single channel. So that it increases network capacity and extends the network lifetime[2].The key for achieving Multi-channel communication technology in wireless sensor network is the design of MAC layer protocol. To promote the standardization and industrialization process of sensor networks, the industry developed the IEEE802.15.4[3], Zigbee[4] and other protocol specialized applications for wireless sensor network. In the current existing network protocols, the other MAC protocols have been using CSMA / CA method of single-channel communication mode in addition to IEEE802.15.4 protocol to support multi-channel communication,. Through monitoring the channel energy and RTS / CTS packet exchanged avoids packet collision in channel. Different nodes achieve control power of the channel through competition[5].

There are several keys for achieving multi-channel MAC protocol in wireless sensor network. As follows:

(1) Channel assignment and switch mode.

In the wireless sensor networks which support the multi-channel, efficiently assignment of channel resources, maximize efficiency and communication capacity of the network, is an important research topic. At present the models of channel assignment are as follows: fixed channel assignment, the assignment of same frequency hopping, phase channel hopping assignment and dynamic channel assignment based on coloration problem[6].

(2) Channel access mode.

The same as single channel network, after obtaining access to communication channel at the node, you need to follow certain access rules to access the network. At present channel access mode are as follows:

The mode based on channel Carrier Sense and competition access has the advantages like simple, without time synchronization and scalability well. But more energy will be needed

The mode based on TDMA which avoids the collision and carrier sense under competitive access mode. But it is difficult to ensure that each node can be assigned to a non-collision time slot.

The mixed-mode based on CSMA / CA and TDMA seeks to combine their advantages and avoid their shortcomings. But design complexity is higher[5]

(3)Node Coordination and found technology.

Node Coordination and foundd technology belongs to supporting technology for multi-channel MAC layer protocol. Control node's main task is unity the space of all common nodes, accepts applications for channel access, and distributed communication channel according to certain rules. The main node found means have active and passive. The active found is waking up the sleep node periodically and actively send a confirmation signal to the control node to justify their existence. The network control channel can be omitted under this mode. The passive found mainly refers that common control node reports own status after receives wake-up signal from control node. This mode generally requires a dedicated control channel to send control frames.

# 3    The Design Framework of the Multi-channel Token Protocol

This paper presents a multi-channel token assignment protocol based on receiving signal strength (RSSI), and it improves the node energy utilization and network throughput in the communication process. At the same time it can also reduce the energy consumption and prolong the life of the node and network.

## 3.1    Protocol Objects Description

(1) Terminal node. It is node concrete realization network function with sensor, in order to realize the wireless network inherent perception function. In our protocol terminal node is sensor node installed on the bulls' body. It has dormancy, detection, and activity three states These three states switching among each other under the interference of the internal timer and control node. Terminal node controlled by control node, according to its information, sends communication channel using request to control node. And then it will obtain transfer data token under a unified dispatch by the control node. After accessed token, terminal node will be switched to the corresponding communication channel and transmit data to communication node. This protocol allows exist multiple terminal node and they are battery-powered.

   (2) Control node. Control node acts as an intermediary in the protocol. It works in control frequency and its main job is synchronization time of communication nodes and every terminal node within the scope of communication range and controlling terminal node into channel application process. It also monitors communication node state, records communications channel's situation like free or busy, accept terminal node channel application and execute the corresponding algorithm to transmit communications channel token to terminal node. Last it assigns and activates corresponding free communication node. Control node works only in control frequencies. This protocol only allows one control node exists. The control node are battery-powered

   (3) Communication node. Each communication node works in two channels. One is controlled channel, and when there is no transmission data the communication node reports itself to control node through control channel. Another is data communication channel. Each communication node has a unique data communication channel. Control node can obtain Status like busy or free of the corresponding communication channel according to communication node. Communications nodes at receiving control node's activation information, it will switch to own communication channel and communicate to the terminal node with token. This protocol allows many communications nodes and communications nodes uses battery-powered.

## 3.2 Achieving Basis

The design and implementation of communication protocol is based on existing hardware and practical conditions. They are as follow:

(1)   wireless transceiver module has the ability of half-duplex multi-channel wireless communications. Wireless network nodes in the protocol include the wireless transceiver module used by terminal node, communication node and control nodes. All of them need to have half-duplex multi-channel communications capabilities so that they can switch from one working channel to another and switching between the various working channels does not overlap. Meanwhile in every working channel, the wireless transceiver module works under half duplex mode. The CC2500 wireless transceiver module used in this system has this capability.

(2)Wireless transceiver module has the ability of detection the strength of RSSI. Under the receiving state, the wireless transceiver module of the node can detect the wireless signal strength of the current environment and expressed that in units of dBm. In this protocol, the terminal node estimates little distance between itself and the control node by RSSI value. The CC2500 wireless transceiver module used in this system has this capability.

(3) The timing accuracy of built-in clock in the Wireless network is less than 1 ms. To coordinate the pace of each terminal node, a timer is necessary and the timing accuracy should be less than 1 millisecond. In this system, the node's MCU uses MSP430 series processor, which has the highest speed up 400KHz internal timer and the minimum period 2.5 microseconds.

(4) Channel switching time of wireless network nodes is less than 100 microseconds. Channel switching time is the guideline of wireless module hardware delay and will directly affect the protocol performance and network capacity. Channel switching time less than 100 microseconds can better ensure the needs of protocol performance.

(5) Multi-channel is divided into a number of communication channels and a control channel. Communication channel only transmits data packets and control channel only transmits control packets.

(6)Between the terminal node and control node is called single-hop communication. Under this application scenario, the cattle get into the access point communications area only needs a short time, so that the node should give priority to transmit its own data rather than as a relay node in the routing of other nodes. Nodes may withdraw at any time control node's communication area. If as the routing, it will easily lead to communication failure. This protocol requires the node assess the distance to the access point. If multiple routes is used, distance estimates will be too complex and difficult to manage.

## 3.3 Condition of Hypothesis

Before the multi-channel token assignment protocol is proposed, some assumed conditions in wireless sensor network realistic environment should be given in this section.

(1)The communication mode between terminal nodes and control nodes is single hop. The wireless communication signals which takes the control node as the center can cover the whole monitoring area. As long as the terminal node enter the communication region, it will monitor the data packets from the control nodes and the RSSI value can be get

(2)AS the distance between communication nodes and control nodes is short, the RSSI value between terminal nodes and control nodes can be considered equaling to the RSSI value between terminal nodes and communication nodes. It can use the RSSI value which is drawn from monitoring the control nodes to substitute the RSSI value which is from the communication nodes, and further acquisition is not needed.

(3)Terminal nodes enter the communication region to transfer signals, and the whole monitoring region is under the non-interference communication environment. The control packets and data packets can be transferred reliably.

## 3.4   Protocol Framework

Wireless sensor network nodes enter the communications monitoring area randomly, breaking the traditional cluster structure and transfer form. Free dynamic access network can realize efficient and fair acquisition to the channel token, stable and reliable data communication. According to the traditional access protocol based on TDMA and the access protocol on Multi-Channel, we design a communication model. Taking the control node as the center of a circle, it divides the communication region into some concentric intervals, as shown in figure 1. Each interval respectively represent period of communication signal strength band segment. The control nodes can be seen as the coordinate node of the Multi-channel token assignment protocol to manage the communication of the nodes in the monitoring region. After a terminal node obtain the communication token, it occupies a communication channel exclusively to transfer data reliably and credibly. This control node can be called gateway node.

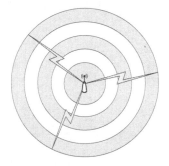

**Fig. 1.** communication region division

Energy consumption is undoubtedly the first considerable question in wireless sensor network. In communication region, it borrows ideas from TDMA to realize intermittent work cycle, reducing the loss and waste of the terminal node energy. Each terminal node works according to certain cycle, and the work cycle divides into dormancy period and activity cycles. In the communication monitoring region, the control node which is power-supply, radioes synchronous signal frame repeatedly, starts channel assignment scheduling cycle, not considering the energy loss. Through this framework, it can extend the dormancy and network lifetime goal of the node. As shown in figure 2, the assignment scheduling cycle divides into communication period and scheduling period. Each communication period is composed of four windows, synchronized signal window, detecting window, reservation window and assignment scheduling window. The scheduling period is after the channel detecting window and the channel reservation window. According to the obtained channel information and reservation information ,it dose the scheduling calculation and radioes the result in the next channel assignment scheduling window.

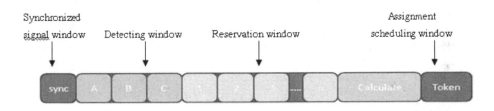

**Fig. 2.** Assignment scheduling cycle

(1)In synchronized signal window, control node broadcasts synchronous signals to the communication nodes and terminal nodes, noticing a new channel assignment cycle;

(2)In channel detecting window, free communication nodes report the current state to control node;

(3)In channel reservation window, terminal nodes can detect the RSSI value from itself to the control node by the signal synchronous data packets so that it can obtains its signal strength frequency band. It issues a reservation request in the corresponding reservation window.

(4)In channel assignment scheduling window, control node broadcast the scheduling result to all the nodes of the network. It specifies a terminal node to obtain the communication token. The node combines the corresponding communication nodes, switches to the corresponding channel together and transfers data.

After the network is divided into several non-overlapping signal strength interval, each terminal node locates the corresponding reservation period in channel reservation window according its signal strength interval, and calculate the dormancy cycle and activity cycle. In the activity cycle, it realize the efficient data communication, avoiding unnecessary network request and waiting and reducing the mutual interference. Once the terminal node obtains channel token, it switches to a specific channel exclusively, avoiding the outside interference and reducing the extra expenses which are brought by unnecessary packet loss and retransmission. Communication period defines as the period that the nodes communicate in synchronous information and control information. It is also called meeting time for nodes. The communication between the nodes should be finished on control channels.

# 4  Protocol Description

After the communication region which takes the control node as center is established, the whole wireless communication region repeats channel assignment scheduling cycle, started by the control node. Synchronous signal issued by the controlling node, is seen as a logo which starts a scheduling cycle. Synchronous signal covers the whole communication region. The states of terminal node states include dormancy, detection, activity. In order to save the energy consumption, terminal nodes are general dormant, start into detecting state periodically. In detecting state, terminal nodes open wireless transceiver and adjust to the controlling channel, detecting the synchronous information of the controlling channel. If it has not received any synchronous signal, it indicates that there is no terminal nodes in the communication region, and re-enter the sleep state. If synchronous signal is received, it indicates that terminal nodes have entered the communication region, and become active immediately. According to the RSSI value, it locates the period corresponding to the channel reservation window, defines the schedules in this assignment scheduling, sets the start time to coordinate the switching of the controlling node states.

## 4.1  Signal Synchronous

After terminal node detects the synchronized signal the first time, it considers the synchronized signal as a switching signal, and transforms into active state. Terminal node does not participate in the channel assignment scheduling cycle. According to the content of this synchronized signal, it identifies the start time of the next channel assignment scheduling cycle, sets the wake-up clock, and is dormant again. It wakes before the next synchronized signal, participates channel assignment scheduling cycle formally. Terminal node schedule is strict to the dormancy cycle and activity cycles of this protocol, ill the communication token is obtained and the communication finishes. And after terminal node converts to active state, it records the current time of the terminal node, and takes it as start time. In the later calculation process, it calculates out the waiting time of requesting communication token according to the start time.

   Channel assignment scheduling cycle begins with synchronized signal window. The active nodes wakes under the control of inner start time, open the wireless transceiver adjusting to control channel, and detects the synchronized information of the controlling channel. Meanwhile, control node in this window time broadcasts synchronized signal packets through the controlling channel. Synchronized signal is composed of {[packet type], [the number of communication nodes],[the number of RSSI band], [the number of time gaps],[checksum]}. Since each communication nodes shares a communication gap in the channel detecting window, it reports its state of corresponding channel to the control node. Therefore, the number of the communication nodes equals to the time gaps in the channel detecting window, terminal nodes can obtains the specific time width of the channel detecting window according to the number of the communication nodes. In addition, each RSSI band occupies a period in channel reservation window. Terminal node can calculate out the specific time width of the channel reservation window, according to the number of communication nodes, RSSI band, and time gaps in the synchronized signal packet.

Each terminal node can also define the RSSI value according to the synchronized signal strength. It can also define its reservation period in the channel reservation window according to the band of the RSSI value. Thus, it can set the start time of the next communication cycle accurate. Communication nodes who receive the synchronized signal just need to wake up according to the channel detecting window provided by the protocol, and report its state to the control node. It obtains the RSSI value to the controlling node, according to the strength of the received synchronous signal.

## 4.2  Channel Detection

In the window of channel detection, control node monitors the data packets from communication channel by transferring to receive status. This protocol divides the window into sever time slots, the number of which is equal to that of communication nodes. The time width of time slot is standardized by the practical situation of communication area. Every communication node has its own time slot on the basis of its ID. The smallest ID will be distributed the first time slot, conversely, the biggest one will be distributed the last time slot.

Because the communication nodes are fixed around the control node, and the quantity of communication nodes is artificially controlled, so there is not much change. Every communication node can conjecture its distributed time slot by means of obtaining the initialized information at the time of setting up the communication area. At the same time, the time width can be determined on the basis of the practical energy consumption and the performance parameter of specific transceiver. In order to reduce the overhead of the control information, the sequence of time slot every communication node obtained is regarded as its identification code in the communication area. Every communication node keeps one list, while the form of all records in this list is {node ID, time slot number}, realizing the mapping between communication node ID and time slot number.

All the communication nodes work in one of the control channel or communication channel. If the communication node is distributed to communicate with some terminal node by control node, the communication node will transfer into communication channel.

Communication node can not monitor the synchronizing signal of control node, and also can not send data to control node in the window of channel detection when communicating. Only the unoccupied communication node can transfer to control channel, and send the channel information to control node through the control channel in its time slot. While the terminal nodes don't participate the works of channel detection, closing the whole channel detection window and maintaining the wireless transmitter in sleep state can similarly reduce the energy consumption.

Because in the channel detection window, the reported data packets only indicate the communication node and its corresponding communication channel are in idle condition, the communication nodes which don't report data packets are regard as in busy state, the contents of data packet only need several bit status information.

Similarly, because the communication node IDs and the time slots of channel detection have the one to one relationship, control node can also conjecture the ID of communication node and don't send node ID any more by the means of the time slot due to the reported data packet, which reduces the sent amount of information by leaps and bounds, and alleviates the load of wireless network.

## 4.3   Channel Reservation

Enter into channel reservation window after channel detection window. Set up buffer mechanism in the control node, and record all the terminal node IDs and waiting time, the terminal nodes which have sent reservation requesting don't participate in this channel reservation and keep sleeping mode, in order to refrain from repeatedly applying and causing channel jams, this kind of terminal node only need to be awakening in the dispatching window and waiting for dispatching. While control node keeps accepting state to monitor the data packets from other terminal nodes in communication channel.

The same as channel detection window, this protocol divides the window into several reservation time intervals, the number of which is equal to the number of RSSI frequency band. Every terminal node determines the corresponding reservation time interval on the basis of frequency band its RSSI located in. Every time interval of channel reservation window has some time slots, in order to solve the access conflict of terminal in the same time interval. While the number of reservation time interval time slots and the time width should be determined on the basis of the practical energy consumption, the performance parameter of specific transceiver and the network capacity.

In the channel reservation window, the number of reservation time intervals is equal to the number of RSSI frequency band. There are several strategies of dividing the RSSI frequency band in communication area. In this protocol, control node is regarded as the centre of communication, the RSSI frequency band is divided into some concentric circles, the length of every interval is equal to the body length of a grown cattle, Fig.03 shows. While the value of RSSI of every interval is integrated into the same RSSI frequency band. The number of channel reservation window time intervals n=the length of radius of communication region/ the body length of a normal cattle.

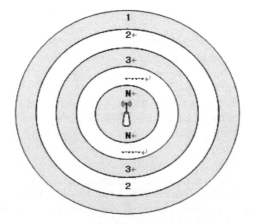

**Fig. 3.** Partition of concentric circles intervals in communication area

Because at the same time of receiving the signal synchronization packets, terminal node is monitoring the RSSI value which itself leaves from the control node, the number of communication nodes and the number of RSSI frequency band. So, terminal node can accurately figure out the time interval in which it should be awakened.

The terminal node transfers into control channel after being awakened, and sends the reservation requesting packets at the first time slot in the reservation time intervals. Because all the terminal nodes in the same concentric circles interval are in the same RSSI frequency band, while the RSSI frequency band and the reservation time interval have the one to one relationship. Therefore, in the same reservation time interval, there can be multiple terminal nodes send reservation requesting packets to control node and cause access conflict.

For the sake of access fairness, this protocol is based on the thinking of CSMA backoff algorithm, when the first time slot in reservation time intervals takes place access conflict, every terminal node will have a certain extent time delay in the following reservation time intervals. The terminal nodes which have delayed should send reservation requesting packets again, in order to avoid conflict risks. While after receiving the requesting packet, the control node return to terminal node a ACK acknowledge signal, confirming the reservation successful. The terminal nodes which don't receive the ACK acknowledge signal are deemed to be interfering with other terminal nodes, and requesting is failed, if it is still be failed after backoff access, then the terminal node should quit this dispatching cycle and enter into sleeping state again. If this terminal node is awakened before the next synchronizing signal is coming, it still can participate in channel dispatching cycle.

Channel reservation requesting packet is comprised of {[packet type],[symbol information],[terminal node information],[check sum]}. Terminal node information includes the ID of terminal node, terminal node records the start time when receiving the first synchronizing packet. The terminal nodes which have sent the reservation requesting packet enter into sleeping state again, and awaken in the channel dispatching window ,receiving the token applying result of control node broadcast.

After the channel detection window and the channel reservation window, control node has received the information of idle channel in the communication area and the reservation requesting information of all the terminal nodes, and starts to dispatch the channel and resource, calculate the channel dispatching, and broadcast the results in the communication though the channel dispatching window.

## 4.4   Channel Dispatching Calculation

After the channel detection window and the channel reservation window, the following step is dispatching period, control node starts to conduct the  channel dispatching calculation by the receiving idle channel information and the reservation requesting information. If the number of reservation requesting is smaller than the number of available channel, dispatching channel is simple, control node can select randomly idle channel for the terminal nodes which have sent the reservation requesting information. However, when the number of reservation requesting is larger than the number of available channel, it needs to dispatch and calculate the reservation requesting information, and get results of dispatching. Because dispatch calculation needs to be completed under limit time, so the time complexity of this algorithm can not be too high.

Because of the start time of every terminal node in the requesting packet, this start time is the system time that recorded by terminal node when entering into the communication area and transferring to active state. Control node can calculate the waiting time of communication token of various terminal nodes. At the same time maintaining a priority buffer queue by the means of the length of waiting time. Control node will allocate preferentially channel recourse to the requesting node who has high-priority, and render the requesting nodes who has not obtained channel recourse to keep in the buffer queue. For the following reservation requesting, control node place it into suitable location in the buffer queue by the waiting time of the terminal node.

The whole channel dispatching calculation figure out the waiting time of requesting communication token of all the terminal nodes, by the means of which, control node maintains a priority buffer queue for the token dispatching use.

## 4.5  Token Assignment

When scheduling calculation ended, it enter the channel assignment scheduling window, all nodes wake up under the control of their inner timing clock and still work on the controlling channel, monitoring and preparing to receive the channel scheduling packets which are sent by controlling nodes.

According to the priority scheduling buffer queue which is obtained by channel assignment scheduling calculations, controlling node selects the team head node. It sends probing packets to terminal node to enquire the current state. When the terminal node receives the probing packet, it feedbacks its current state to the controlling node. Feedback data packet is composed of {[Packet type], [Flags], [Current RSSI band], [Checksum]}. Current RSSI band refers to the RSSI value which is detected from the synchronous signal packet. The packet begins with the current channel assignment scheduling cycle. Flags are used to describe whether terminal nodes are quitting from communication region. After the RSSI value is detected, terminal nodes map it to the corresponding RSSI band. When a terminal node goes through the communication region and the RSSI band experience from weak to strong, from strong to weak. When terminal node detects the current RSSI band is weaker than the last record, it indicates that the node is quitting from the communication region and the flag is set to "1",otherwise set to"0".

Controlling node determine whether to distribute the communication token according to the state from the feedback of the terminal node. If the communication node is quitting the region and the RSSI band is too weak, its assignment qualification will be cancelled. It takes out the head node from the priority scheduling buffer queue to continue the inquiry. Until the terminal node which meets the requirements is find, it broadcast signal scheduling controlling packets. Channel scheduling controlling packet is composed of {[packet type], [communication node ID], [terminal node ID], [communication channel ID], [additional information], [Checksum]}. When the terminal node and the communication node receive the  scheduling controlling packets ,it switches the wireless transceiver to a specific communication channel according the channel assignment information of the scheduling packets, starting to communicate. As there is a certain time limit in channel assignment scheduling window, this method exist certain risk. Therefore, channel assignment scheduling window ends in strict accordance with the provision of the protocol. Even when the window ends, idle channel has not been distributed out, it will be reserved for the next channel assignment scheduling cycle.

### 4.6 Data Communication

Terminal node allocated communication token quits the channel assignment scheduling cycle, and exchange data with the designated communication node in designated channel directly. After the terminal node completes the exchange, it closes the wireless transceiver immediately and back to dormancy, while the communication node switches to controlling channel, and enters the channel assignment scheduling cycle. If the terminal node can't allocate the channel resource, it continues to wait.

The node has no fixed channel resource in this protocol and it allocates channel resource dynamically according to the reservation information of the terminal node. It not only improves the channel utilization, but also protects the data communication from the interference of other nodes, realizing the data transmission reliably and efficiently.

## 5   Simulation and Discussion

To study the protocol performance, we coded some program to simulate the protocol and have an emulation of the property. The initial parameters are set the default value according to the Table 1.

**Table 1.** Simulation parameter

| parameter | value |
|---|---|
| Regional area | 200 meters radius of the circle |
| The number of terminal nodes | 100 |
| Mode of entry | Random access communication area |
| The number of communication nodes | 5 |
| The number of RSSI bands | 10 |
| The amount of communication data | 256 byte |
| The rate of the cow | 0.2 meter per second |

In this experiment, we regard the number of the conflict as one of the most important indicator of assessment about the network communication. This value describes the risk the terminal node may encounter when they are sending an appointment request packet in the channel reservation window. If some terminal nodes are in the same RSSI frequency band, they will locate in the same booking period of the channel reservation window. As a result, the nodes are easy to make conflicts when sending request packets. In this study, we designed an appointment that request packet length is fixed at 100 bytes. The experimental results shown in Figure 4, with the increase of terminal nodes, the network increased the number of conflicts.

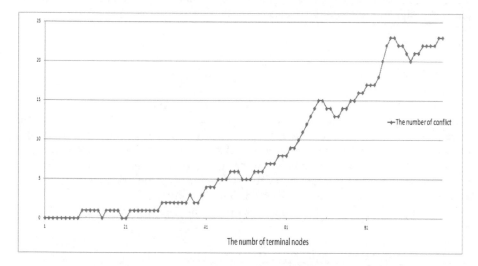

**Fig. 4.** Relationship between the terminal nodes and the frequency of network conflict

Here the conflict, including all the number of conflicts within the communicated region, some nodes may be encounter more than one conflict. The worst case is when the first appointment is conflicted, and the second appoint after avoidance is conflicted again, the node quits this scheduling cycle. The next scheduling cycle also be continue to meet the conflict. The nodes keep the conflict until they exit the communicated area. It can be seen from Figure 4, the network can't avoid the conflict, and the number of conflict is still at a relatively high frequency range. However, we found when the number of terminal nodes increases to a certain extent, with further increase in the number of terminal nodes, the number of conflicts is rising slowly. Because we use the Backoff algorithm to try to avoid the second conflict, make the total number of conflicts reduction and control it in a certain range. From the curve of the number of conflicts, we can see that after the number of terminal nodes reach a certain number, the increasing of the conflict is less obvious.

In this study, we assume that the number of the channel is 5 and the length of the packet is 256-byte. Under this condition, we study the relationship between the number of starvation and the number of terminal nodes. The simulation results shown in Figure 5, with the increase of the terminal nodes, increasing the number of starvation. The protocol uses the control node to coordinate the communication. However, network conflicts, lack of communication nodes, can also cause the starvation in the booking period. We can increase the number of communication nodes appropriately to reduce the number of starvation.

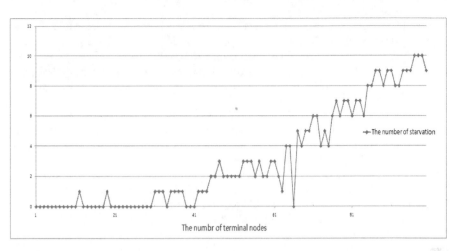

**Fig. 5.** Relationship between the terminal nodes and the frequency of network starvation

## 6 Conclusion

In this paper, we presents a multi-channel token assignment protocol in wireless sensor network. The efficiency of energy and stability of transmission is main factor in the design of this protocol. It divides the communication cycle into several windows with special function, and takes RSSI as the channel reservation credential of the terminal node. It reduces the competition of the network access and data collision, extends the dormancy of nodes, saving the energy greatly and extending the life of the network. The protocol uses dynamic channel assignment to improve the utilization of multichannel and the throughput of the network. Simulation results show that it can reach a better energy efficiency and higher throughput. We will study multi-channel token assignment protocol to support the QS and high-level protocol, improving the performance and lifetime of the wireless sensor network further.
hould be treated as a 3$^{rd}$ level heading and should not be assigned a number.

## References

1. Akyildiz, I.F., Su, W., Sankarasubramaniam, Y., Cayirci, E.: Wireless sensor networks: a survey. J. Computer Networks 38, 393–422 (2002)
2. Chen, X., Chen, W.-j., Han, P., Tu, S.-l., Chen, Z.-l.: Multi-channel Media Access Control Protocol for Wireless Sensor Networks. Journal of Chinese Computer Systems 28, 1729–1734 (2007)
3. IEEE Computer Society. IEEE 802. 15. 4: Wireless MediumAccess Control (MAC) and Physical Layer (PHY) Specifications for Low Rate Wireless Personal Area Networks (LRWPANs) (CPOL) (S. l.). IEEE Press, Los Alamitos (2003)
4. ZigBee Alliance. Zigbee Specification (CPOL). ZigBeeAuiance, Calif. (2007)
5. Chen, D.: Multi channel MAC protocols for wireless sensor networks: a survey. Journal of Shandong University (Engineering Science) 39, 41–49 (2009)

6. Zhang, L., Wang, X., Liu, C.: Channel Assignment in Multi-Radio Multi-Channel Wireless Mesh Network by Topology Approach. In: 2009 International Conference on Communications and Mobile Computing, pp. 358–362 (2009)
7. Kodialam, M., Nandagopal, T.: Characterizing achievable rates in multi-hop wireless mesh networks with orthogonal channels. IEEE/ACM Transaction on Networking 13(4), 868–880 (2005)
8. Wu, S.L., Lin, C.Y., Tseng, Y.C., Sheu, J.-P.: A new multi-channel MAC protocol with on-demand channel assignment for multi-hop mobile ad hoc networks. In: Proceedings of the International Symposium on Parallel Architectures, Algorithms and Networks, pp. 232–237 (2000)
9. Nasipuri, A., Zhuang, J., Das, S.: A multichannel csma macprotocol for multihop wireless networks. In: WCNC 1999, New Orleans, USA, September 21-24 (1999)
10. Polastrb, J., Hill, J., Culler, D.: Versatile low power median access for wireless sensor networks. In: ACM SenSys, Baltimore, USA (2004)
11. Yew Heidemann, J., Estrin, D.: An energy_efficient MAC protocol for wireless sensor networks. In: IEEE INFOCOM 156701576 (2002)

# Network Layer Challenges of IEEE 802.11n Wireless Ad Hoc Networks

Mehdi EffatParvar[1], Nasser Yazdani[2], MohammadReza EffatParvar[3],
Peyman Teymoori[4], and Ali Movaghar[5]

[1] Department of Computer and Electrical Engineering,
Ardabil Branch, Islamic Azad University, Ardabil, Iran
[2,3,4] Router Lab, Electrical & Computer Engineering Department,
University of Tehran, Tehran, Iran
[5] Computer Engineering Faculty,
Sharif University of Technology, Tehran, Iran
mehdi@effatparavr.co,
effatparvar@ut.ac.ir,
{p.teymoori,yazdani}@ut.ac.ir, movaghar@sharif.edu

**Abstract.** Recent demands toward high-speed wireless networks are growing. IEEE 802.11n, as the latest standard toward achieving higher speeds, aims to enhance IEEE 802.11 for higher throughputs. There are few works which analyze performance of this protocol in single-hop networks in terms of MAC layer-based parameters. Most of these works suggest disabling the RTS/CTS handshake to reduce MAC layer overheads. However, the effects of this protocol on the upper layers, especially the network layer, are still unknown. This paper deals with investigating performance of the network layer over IEEE 802.11n. Through extensive simulations performed in NS-2 we show that although network throughput is improved using IEEE 802.11n, it suffers from the problem of fairness among receivers. We also show that enabling RTS/CTS improves fairness but may lead to bandwidth inefficiency. In addition, it is shown that even at high physical rates, the end-to-end delay does not meet delay requirements of these networks.

**Keywords:** IEEE 802.11n, Routing, Network Layer, High-Speed Wireless Ad hoc Networks.

## 1 Introduction

IEEE 802.11n is the next generation wireless LAN technology that promises higher data rates, longer range and more reliable coverage than 802.11 a/b/g networks. In order to provide such gains, it introduces a variety of mechanisms such as physical layer diversity (using Multiple Input Multiple Output (MIMO) technology), channel bonding, and frame aggregation [1]. It also defines two modes of operation: *Distributed Coordination Function* (DCF) which is ad hoc and based on CSMA/CA, and *Point Coordination Function* (PCF) which is centralized.

P. Sénac, M. Ott, and A. Seneviratne (Eds.): ICWCA 2011, LNICST 72, pp. 377–388, 2012.
© Institute for Computer Sciences, Social Informatics and Telecommunications Engineering 2012

An ad hoc network is a dynamically reconfigurable wireless network with no fixed wired infrastructure. Ad hoc networks have numerous practical applications such as military applications, emergency operations, and wireless sensor networks. In many applications, ad hoc networks carry diverse multimedia applications such as voice, video and data. In order for delay sensitive applications such as voice and video to provide quality of delivery, it is imperative that protocols of ad hoc networks provide quality of service (QoS) support [3]. Due to the dynamic nature of ad hoc networks, traditional fixed network routing protocols are not viable. For this reason, several proposals for routing protocols have been presented.

On-demand routing is one of the most popular routing approaches in ad hoc networks. Instead of periodically exchanging routing messages in proactive routing protocols that results in excessive routing overheads [16] [17], on-demand routing algorithms discover routes only when a node needs to send data packet to a destination and does not have any route to it. Most of the existing on-demand routing protocols, e.g., Dynamic Source Routing (DSR) and Ad hoc On-demand Distance Vector (AODV), build and rely on single path for each data session. Therefore, route recovery process is required after each route failure that causes loss of transmitted data packets in such protocols. Multipath routing allows the establishment of multiple paths between a single source and single destination node. It is typically proposed in order to increase the reliability of data transmission (i.e., fault tolerance) or to provide load balancing [18], [19], [20], and [21].

In a data transmission flow from a sender to a receiver, MAC layer overheads affect network throughput; hence most of researches on IEEE 802.11n suggest disabling the RTS/CTS handshake to increase throughput [10, 4]. These works analyze the performance of this protocol in single-hop networks in terms of MAC layer-based parameters. Although disabling RTS/CTS may lead to more efficiency at the MAC layer, due to the ad hoc and multi-hop nature of theses networks, its effects are still unknown on upper layers, especially the network layer. The main issue of this paper is to investigate performance of the network layer over IEEE 802.11n.

Owing to the significance of routing protocols in communications of an ad hoc network, in this paper, we investigate performance of routing protocols such as Destination Sequenced Distance Vector (DSDV) [15], as a table driven protocol, and Ad hoc On demand Distance Vector (AODV), as an on demand protocol, at the network layer over IEEE 802.11n. We simulated various scenarios on the IEEE 802.11n MAC layer which were executed on NS-2 [22].

In our simulations, we investigate the two different modes of operations: the RTS/CTS handshake and basic access which disables RTS/CTS control packets. Results show that although network throughput is improved using IEEE 802.11n while RTS/CTS is disabled, it suffers from the problem of fairness among receivers. We also show that enabling RTS/CTS improves fairness. In addition, several working scenarios under which each of the handshake methods performs better are introduced.

In addition, we study the performance of DSDV at high physical rates. It is shown that even at high physical rates, the end-to-end delay does not meet the delay requirements [7] of these networks.

Section 2 reviews related works. In Section 3, we discuss network layer issues over the IEEE 802.11n MAC layer. Simulation results are presented in Section 4, and finally, we conclude the paper in Section 5.

## 2   Related Works

Approaches such as Burst and Block acknowledgements are proposed to improve efficiency at the MAC layer [6] [8] [9] [12] [13] [1]. In Burst ACK, the backoff process is performed once for a series of data packets and ACK frames. Block ACK uses a single ACK frame for multiple data frames, thus reducing the number of ACKs and SIFS. Aggregation schemes such as [1] [4] transmit multiple data frames together to reduce overheads. This is achieved by aggregating packets in a single large frame at the physical layer.

In [5] the authors present a theoretical model to evaluate the saturation throughput for the burst transmission and acknowledgment (BTA) scheme under error channel conditions in the ad-hoc mode show some advantages of BTA over the legacy MAC. The author in [11] proposes two enhancement mechanisms to reduce the overhead, concatenation (CM) and piggyback (PM). CM concatenates multiple frames into a single transmission. By PM a receiver station is allowed to piggyback a data frame to the sender station once if the receiver station has a frame to send to the sender.

In the AFR scheme [4], multiple packets are aggregated into and transmitted in a single large frame. If errors occur during transmission, only the corrupted fragments of the frame are retransmitted.

The aforementioned works consider a single-hop network to analyze their proposed methods. Network layer problems, however, are more crucial in the presence of mobile nodes as one the main characteristics of these networks. Since all of the works on high-speed wireless ad hoc networks concentrate on improving MAC efficiency in terms of throughput, performance of the network layer has not been investigated in these networks. This paper deals with this problem.

## 3   Network Layer Issues of IEEE 802.11n

The IEEE 802.11n protocol supports appropriate bandwidth and supplies suitable throughput for most of the applications in wireless communications. Unfortunately, because of its wireless infrastructure and resultant inherent problems, we cannot utilize the whole bandwidth efficiently in this protocol. Therefore, providing a reliable connection between a pair of source and destination in wireless networks is difficult because of many problems such as bandwidth limitation, energy consumption, hidden and exposed terminal problems and etc. There are many algorithms proposed for network routing and solving the above problems. They also use control packets to find stable routes.

During transmission of control packets, network bandwidth will be wasted and nodes cannot receive data packets. Moreover, higher priority of control packets may cause increasing delay in sending actual data packets; therefore, we lose bandwidth capacity. Sending control packet is one of the principle steps in routing algorithms; therefore, we cannot eliminate these packets. In addition, increasing raw bandwidth at the physical layer will not solve the inefficiency problem and the performance will not increase accordingly.

When the routing algorithm uses more control packets over the IEEE 802.11n MAC layer, due to node movements, route recovery or new path detection; the efficiency of IEEE 802.11n may decrease. Results presented in the next section confirm this problem.

In the next session, we show simulation results of DSDV routing protocol on the MAC layers of IEEE 802.11 and IEEE 802.11n, and discuss more regarding the characteristics of IEEE 802.11n which may affect routing protocols.

# 4   Simulation Results

In this section, we show performance results of DSDV and AODV in IEEE 802.11n networks using NS-2 simulator. In the simulation, we modeled a network of 50 mobile hosts which are placed uniformly in a 1000*1000 m$^2$ area. Radio propagation range for each node is 225 meters. Each simulation scenario runs for 300 seconds of simulated time. Also we use other conventional parameters of NS-2 in our simulations. Result of each scenario is averaged over 10 different runs with confidence level of 95% lower than 0.02.

Network improvement is calculated by the following metrics which are used by [4]:

- Throughput: is equal to the total amount of data, in bits, transmitted in the network over the simulation time. It represents the maximum rate at which the MAC layer can forward packets from senders to receivers. It can be seen as the rate achieved by the whole system rather than by a single station (STA).
- Average delay: This metric represents the delay a packet experiences in average until it is successfully received by the destination.
- Efficiency: is equal to the achieved throughput of the channel over the physical rate.
- Fairness: To measure fairness for all the STAs, we use Jain's fairness index. In particular, given $n$ STAs in the system, Jain's fairness index, $I$, is defined as

$$I = \frac{\left( \sum_{i=1}^{n} S_i \right)^2}{n \sum_{i=1}^{n} S_i^2} \qquad (1)$$

where $n$ stands for the number of STAs and $S_i$ is the throughput of the STA $i$. When every STA achieves exactly the same throughput, $I$ is equal to 1. If only one STA happens to dominate the channel entirely, $I$ approaches 1/n.

## 4.1   Mobility Effects on IEEE 802.11 and IEEE 802.11n

In this section, we compare performance results of the two MAC protocols IEEE 802.11 and IEEE 802.11n for different node speeds. We modeled a network of 50 mobile hosts which are placed randomly in a 1000*1000 m$^2$ area. Radio propagation range for each node is 225 meters. Each simulation scenario runs for 300 seconds of the simulation time. Data packet sizes, number of data flows, routing protocols, data rate and control rate  are 2048 bytes, 15, AODV and DSDV, 54Mbps, and 8Mbps, respectively. We use random waypoint movement model with 10 seconds paused time. Queue size is 70, and the maximum aggregation size is 40000 bytes. We use block ACK mechanism while using IEEE 802.11n, and packet rate is 200 packets per second like the scenario used in [14].

Throughput of AODV and DSDV routing protocols are shown in Fig. 1 for IEEE 802.11 and IEEE 802.11n. This figure indicates that IEEE 802.11n has better performance results in contrast to IEEE 802.11. In addition, any increase in the speed results in throughput decrease due to increase in the number of links failures.

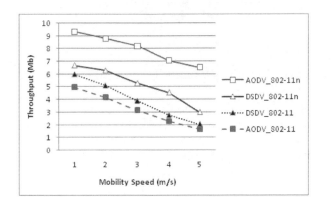

**Fig. 1.** Throughputs of IEEE 802.11 and IEEE 802.11n vs. mobility speed

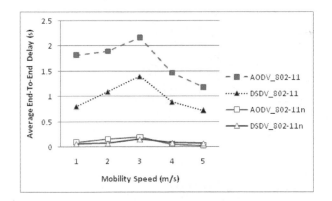

**Fig. 2.** End-to-end delays of IEEE 802.11 and IEEE 802.11n vs. mobility speed

Referring to Fig. 2, the end-to-end delay of IEEE 802.11n is shorter than that of IEEE 802.11 due to the use of aggregation in IEEE 802.11n. This confirms the idea of packet aggregation to decrease channel access overhead.

From Fig. 1 and Fig. 2, it can be observed that IEEE 802.11n increases throughput while it also decreases delay in contrast to IEEE 802.11. After careful log investigation, it is found that the other reason of these improvements is due to unfairness channel allocation to traffic flows. This means that IEEE 802.11n is not able to allow all flows to deliver their packets to their corresponding receivers.

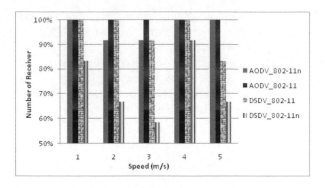

**Fig. 3.** Receiving percentage of IEEE 802.11 and IEEE 802.11n for various speeds

Fig. 3 shows the percentage of the flows were able to deliver their packets for each scenario. Since the aggregation scheme of IEEE 802.11n results in larger packets sizes and longer transmission durations in comparison with IEEE 802.11, and due to more failures in the network that happen when the speed increases, some receivers do not receive any packets; therefore, the average end-to-end delay of delivered packets decreases in IEEE 802.11n.

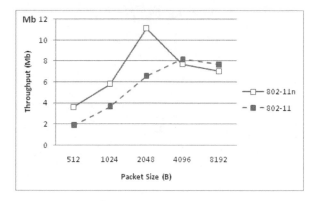

**Fig. 4.** Throughput of IEEE 802.11 and IEEE 802.11n for various packet sizes

## 4.2   Packet Size Effects on IEEE 802.11 and IEEE 802.11n

In this section, we compare IEEE 802.11 and IEEE 802.11n protocols using the AODV routing algorithm. The mobility speed is 1 meter per second and the other simulation parameters are the same as before.

Fig. 4 shows throughputs of IEEE 802.11 and IEEE 802.11n. It can be observed that the IEEE 802.11n protocol has a better throughput than IEEE 802.11 for small and medium packet sizes.

Fig. 5 shows that by increasing the packet size, the number of receivers decreases due to the same reason for the previous scenario. Referring to Fig. 6, the end-to-end delay of IEEE 802.11n is shorter than that of IEEE 802.11 because the number of receivers decreases.

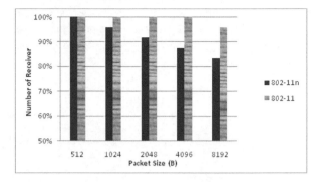

**Fig. 5.** Receiving percentage in IEEE 802.11 and IEEE 802.11n for various packet sizes

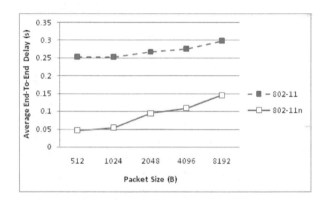

**Fig. 6.** End-to-end delay of 802.11 and 802.11n for various packet sizes

### 4.3  DSDV Performance in High-Speed Physical Rates

In order to compare performance of IEEE 802.11 and IEEE 802.11n in the previous sections, we used physical rates of up to 54Mbps. In this section, we only evaluate performance of DSDV on IEEE 802.11n for higher speeds than 54Mbps. The aforementioned metrics are also utilized to investigate the performance.

The simulation scenario used in this part is the same as that of the previous part. The major difference is that physical rate and aggregation size are increased up to 648Mbps and 64KB, respectively.

Fig. 7 shows the achieved throughput for various aggregation sizes. As it indicates, increasing the aggregation size improves throughput, especially for higher physical rates. If the physical rate increases, control packet durations dominate data packet transmission times that lead to lower throughput and losing efficiency. A compensation method is to aggregate more data and generate a larger frame. Results of the figure imply that for higher physical rates, more packets should be aggregated to improve throughput.

Efficiency of the protocol for various aggregation sizes is shown in Fig. 8. It shows that IEEE 802.11n performs less efficiently in higher speeds due to protocol overheads although increasing the aggregation size helps improve the efficiency. The best achievable efficiency is approximately 40% for 648Mbps, and this value will definitely degrade more as the number of nodes increases.

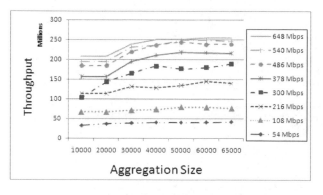

**Fig. 7.** Throughput of 802.11n for various aggregation sizes

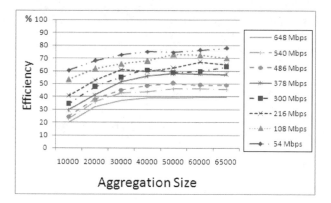

**Fig. 8.** Efficiency of 802.11n for various aggregation sizes

Fairness and delay values of the above simulated scenario are shown in Table 1 for different physical rates. As the rate increases, delay decreases due to shortened transmission durations, and fairness increases as well. It can be seen that the end-to-end delay is longer than the value specified in [7] for traffics such as HDTV, even at the rate 648Mbps. The fairness is still a problem although it is improved by increasing the physical rate.

**Table 1.** Fairness and delay for various physical rates

| Physical rate (Mbps) | Fairness (%) | Delay (s) |
|---|---|---|
| 54 | 80.85 | 0.7779 |
| 108 | 82.53 | 0.6363 |
| 216 | 83.52 | 0.5371 |
| 300 | 83.68 | 0.4817 |
| 378 | 84.88 | 0.4445 |
| 486 | 85.92 | 0.3913 |
| 540 | 86.53 | 0.3832 |
| 648 | 87.33 | 0.3801 |

### 4.4  Handshake Effects on IEEE 802.11n

It is obvious that control packets have significant roles in wireless network operations although they may waste the bandwidth. During transmission from a sender to a receiver, MAC layer overheads adversely affect the network throughput; hence most of researches on IEEE 802.11n such as [10, 4] consider disabling the RTS/CTS handshake during data transmission to increase network throughput.

In the following simulation scenario, we evaluate performance of IEEE 802.11n in two different handshake modes: RTS/CTS handshake and basic mode that disables RTS/CTS control packets. Simulation parameters are similar to the previous section. The RTS/CTS threshold is 300 bytes that allows RTS/CTS handshake before each data transmission.

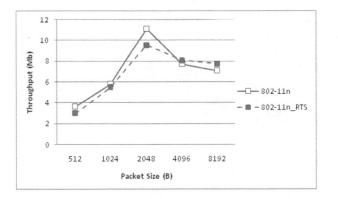

**Fig. 9.** Network throughput in RTS/CTS handshake and basic access for various packet sizes

Fig. 9 shows throughput variation in the two modes. Referring to this figure, when the packet size is small, sending RTS decreases throughput. In other words, when the packet size increases, sending RTS results in increase in throughput.

Referring to Fig. 10, when the RTS/CTS handshake is disabled, the number of receivers increases due to small data packet sizes and shorter transmission durations. When the RTS/CTS handshake is enabled, it wastes the bandwidth by RTS and CTS frames to transmit small data packets that results in lower receiver percentage. By increasing the packet size, the RTS/CTS handshake causes that more receivers receive data packets.

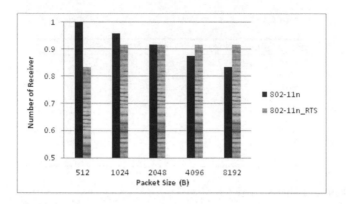

**Fig. 10.** Receiving percentage in the two handshake modes of IEEE 802.11n

Fig. 11 shows the end-to-end delay in the two access modes. The figure indicates that by using RTS, when we have small packet sizes, the end-to-end delay is shorter than that of Basic access because in this case, fewer receivers are able to receive data packets and their corresponding traffic flows dominate the channel. By increasing the packet size, the end-to-end delay increases too because more traffic flows can deliver their packets and fairness improves. It is worth noting that only delivered packets are considered for delay and throughput calculations.

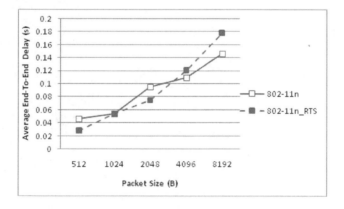

**Fig. 11.** Average end-to-end delay for various packet sizes

Some works such as [10, 4] claim that RTS/CTS handshake is not suitable in high speed networks due to its adverse effect on network throughput. On the contrary, as we showed in our simulation results, when packet size increases and because of inherent problems of wireless networks such as collision, hidden stations, and limited buffer size of receivers, throughput decreases without using the RTS/CTS handshake.

It can be seen that using the RTS/CTS handshake we can overcome some of the problems discussed above such as fairness. As a result, it can be inferred that the RTS/CTS handshake is not always useful, especially for smaller packet sizes. On the contrary, disabling RTS/CTS may cause problems such as throughput decrease for large packet sizes, and unfairness for smaller sizes. Therefore, the above result necessitates a revision in the RTS/CTS handshake which is out of the scope of this paper.

# 5 Conclusion

As technology trends toward multimedia applications over wireless LANs, it is very important that we have reliable and delay-sensitive wireless networks. With the increasing use of high-speed wireless networks, need to further improvement of these networks has been raised. Although IEEE 802.11n is suitable for broadband wireless applications, due to the intrinsic overheads of the protocol, we cannot utilize bandwidth effectively in data transfer. This protocol is also backward compatible with it pervious protocol, IEEE 802.11, because of the extensive use of Wi-Fi tools all over the world.

Simulation results show that IEEE 802.11n improves throughput and delay in comparison with IEEE 802.11 due to the aggregation method, but the in some cases such as small packet sizes, it suffers from fairness problems. Moreover, using the RTS/CTS handshake improves fairness although it imposes overhead at the MAC layer.

Performance study of DSDV for high-speed physical rates shows that delay decreases due to shortened transmission durations, and fairness increases as well, but the end-to-end delay is longer than HDTV requirements, even at the highest rate.

**Acknowledgments.** Our thanks to C. Wang and H. Wei, the authors of [10], for permitting us to use their NS-2 simulation source codes of IEEE 802.11n and also their help which allowed us to extend it for our purpose. This work is supported by Iran Telecommunication Research Center (ITRC).

# References

1. IEEE. Part 11: wireless LAN medium access control (MAC) and physical layer (PHY) specifications: Enhancements for High Throughput, IEEE 802.11n (October 2009)
2. IEEE. Part 11: wireless LAN medium access control (MAC) and physical layer (PHY) specifications: Medium Access Control (MAC) Quality of Service (QoS) Enhancements, IEEE 802.11e (February 2005)
3. Xue, Q., Ganz, A.: ad hoc QOS on-demand routing (AQOR) in mobile ad hoc networks. Journal of parallel and distributed computing, 154–165 (2003)
4. Li, T., Ni, Q., Malone, D., Leith, D., Xiao, Y., Turletti, T.: Aggregation with Fragment Retransmission for Very High-Speed WLANs. IEEE/ACM Transactions on Networking 17(2), 591–604 (2009)
5. Li, T., Ni, Q., Xiao, Y.: Investigation of the block ACK scheme in wireless ad hoc networks. Wireless Communications and Mobile Computing 6(6), 877–888 (2006)
6. Sadeghi, B., Kanodia, V., Sabharwal, A., Knightly, E.: Opportunistic media access for multirate ad hoc networks. In: Proceedings of the 8th Annual international Conference on Mobile Computing and Networking, MobiCom 2002, pp. 24-35. ACM, New York (2002)

7. Stephens, A.P.: IEEE P802.11 Wireless LANs: Usage Models. IEEE 802.11-03/802r23 (May 2004)
8. Tourrilhes, J.: Packet frame grouping: improving IP multimedia performance over CSMA/CA. In: ICUPC 1998, IEEE 1998 International Conference on Universal Personal Communications. Conference Proceedings (Cat. No.98TH8384), pp. 1345–1349. IEEE, Los Alamitos (1998)
9. Vitsas, V., Chatzimisios, P.: Enhancing performance of the IEEE 802.11 distributed coordination function via packet bursting. In: IEEE Global Telecommunications Conference Workshops, GlobeCom Workshops, pp. 245–252. IEEE, Los Alamitos (2004)
10. Wang, C., Wei, H.: IEEE 802.11n MAC Enhancement and Performance Evaluation. Mobile Networks and Applications 14(6), 760–771 (2009)
11. Xiao, Y.: IEEE 802.11 performance enhancement via concatenation and piggyback mechanisms. IEEE Transactions on Wireless Communications 4(5), 2182–2192 (2005)
12. Xiao, Y.: IEEE 802.11n: enhancements for higher throughput in wireless LANs. IEEE Wireless Communications 12(6), 82–91 (2005)
13. Xiao, Y., Rosdahl, J.: Performance analysis and enhancement for the current and future IEEE 802.11 MAC protocols. ACM SIGMOBILE Mobile Computing and Communications Review 7(2), 6 (2003)
14. EffatParvar, M.R., Teymoori, P., Yazdani, N., Movaghar, A., EffatParvar, M.: Evaluating Effectiveness of DSDV Routing Protocol on IEEE 802.11n Wireless LANs. International Journal of Electrical & Computer Sciences (IJECS) 10(3), 41–47 (2010)
15. Perkins, C.E., Bhagwat, P.: Highly Dynamic Destination-Sequenced Distance-Vector Routing (DSDV) for Mobile Computers. Comp. Comm. Rev., 234–244 (October 1994)
16. Broch, J., Maltz, D.A., Johnson, D.B., Hu, Y.C., Jetcheva, J.: A Performance Comparison of Multi-Hop Wireless Ad Hoc Network Routing Protocols. In: Proceedings of ACM/IEEE MOBICOM 1998, Dallas, TX, October 1998, pp. 85–97 (1998)
17. Johansson, P., Larsson, T., Hedman, N., Mielczarek, B., Degermark, M.: Scenario-based Performance Analysis of Routing Protocols for Mobile Ad hoc Networks. In: Proceedings of ACM/IEEE MOBICOM 1999, Seattle, WA, August 1999, pp. 195–206 (1999)
18. Cho, H.K., Kim, E.S., Kang, D.W.: A load-balancing routing considering power conservation in wireless ad hoc networks. In: Proc. of 16th International Workshop on Database and Expert Systems Applications, pp. 128–132 (2005)
19. Lee, S.J., Gerla, M.: AODV-BR: Backup Routing in Ad hoc Networks. In: Proceedings of IEEE WCNC 2000, Chicago, IL (September 2000)
20. Nasipuri, A., Das, S.R.: On-Demand Multipath Routing for Mobile Ad Hoc Networks. In: Proceedings of IEEE ICCCN 1999, Boston, MA, October 1999, pp. 64–70 (1999)
21. Park, V.D., Corson, M.S.: A Highly Adaptive Distributed Routing Algorithm for Mobile Wireless Networks. In: Proceedings of IEEE INFOCOM 1997, Kobe, Japan, April 1997, pp. 1405–1413 (1997)
22. Network Simulator (NS), http://www.isi.edu/nsnam/ns/

# Delay-Constrained Optimized Packet Aggregation in High-Speed Wireless Ad Hoc Networks

Peyman Teymoori, Nasser Yazdani, and Ali Sehati

Router Lab., Electrical & Computer Engineering Department,
University of Tehran, Tehran, Iran
{p.teymoori,yazdani}@ut.ac.ir, a.sehati@ece.ut.ac.ir

**Abstract.** In recent years, high-speed WLANs are introduced to service growing demand of delay-sensitive and multimedia applications. To improve efficiency at the MAC layer of high-speed WLANs, few researches have tried to utilize approaches such as Aggregation in which a number of packets concatenated into a larger frame to reduce protocol overheads. Since transmitting larger frames causes increases in delay and jitter which are crucial, especially in delay-sensitive and multimedia applications, selecting the best aggregated frame size is significant. In this paper, we propose an analytical model for optimized packet aggregation (OPA) that finds the optimized aggregation size with regard to delay constraints of nodes. OPA enhances one of the aggregation methods, aggregation with fragment retransmission (AFR) scheme, and models aggregation by a constrained convex optimization problem to maximize network throughput while constraining the delay. Simulation results show that OPA increases throughput and decreases the average delay as well.

**Keywords:** High-speed wireless networks, IEEE 802.11n, Aggregation, Convex optimization.

## 1 Introduction

Increasing the number of users of wireless technologies has raised the demand for real-time and delay-sensitive applications, and higher bandwidth [1]. For real-time applications and delay-sensitive traffic, constraining and preserving predictable delay is of significant importance [2]. Real-time applications over WLANs require that packets arrive at their destinations in a timely manner, and many applications require high throughput. Toward meeting this demand, IEEE 802.11n has emerged that supports physical rates of up to 600 Mbps and inherent QoS [3].

It has been shown that the inefficient protocol overhead of IEEE 802.11 distributed coordination Function (DCF) results in a theoretical throughput upper limit and delay lower limit for the IEEE 802.11 based protocols, even the wireless data rate goes to infinity [4]. Frame aggregation is one of the efficiency improvement methods at the MAC layer. It not only reduces the transmission time for preamble and frame headers, but also reduces the waiting time during random backoff period for successive frame transmissions [5]. IEEE 802.11n supports aggregated data frame sizes of up to 64KB at the MAC layer [3].

P. Sénac, M. Ott, and A. Seneviratne (Eds.): ICWCA 2011, LNICST 72, pp. 389–400, 2012.
© Institute for Computer Sciences, Social Informatics and Telecommunications Engineering 2012

Although frame aggregation can increase throughput at the MAC layer under ideal channel conditions, a larger aggregated frame will cause each station to wait longer before its next chance for channel access and makes channel access unpredictable [5]. Therefore, there is a tradeoff between throughput and delay for frame aggregation at the MAC layer. Moreover, under error-prone channels, corruption in a large aggregated frame may waste a long period of channel time and lead to a lower MAC efficiency [5], and also increase in delay.

In this paper, due to the importance of limiting delay in delay-sensitive applications in high-speed WLANs [6], in order to constrain delay at the MAC layer of wireless ad hoc networks as well as preserving the performance gain of frame aggregation, we propose an analytical model for wireless the MAC layer of high-speed wireless networks, called optimized packet aggregation (OPA). OPA finds the maximum aggregation size for nodes that does not increase nodes' delays. In other words, as the main parameter of optimization, OPA considers delay requirements of nodes and permits them to transmit a particular amount of data through determining the aggregation size at the MAC layer.

The main approach of increasing throughput is to aggregate more packets. Since increasing aggregation size results in more transmission time and increasing delays of nodes, the tradeoff between throughput and delay is calculated using an accurate analytical model by OPA. It optimizes throughput using a convex optimization method [7] while prevents delay increase through optimization constraints.

The rest of the paper is organized as follows. Section 2 reviews similar works. We introduce the analytical model of OPA in Section 3, and discuss in Section 4 the implementation issues. Section 5 explains algorithmic issues of our model while Section 6 presents detailed simulation results. Finally, we summarize our conclusions in Section 7.

## 2   Related Works

There are some approaches to improve the efficiency of high-speed wireless networks such as burst acknowledge (Burst ACK) proposed by [8], and block acknowledgement (Block ACK), e.g., [9], which try to reduce the protocol overhead. Approaches such as [9], [10] and [11] aggregate several packets to compensate overhead by increasing data length. In addition, in [11], through PM, the receiver station is allowed to piggyback a data frame to the sender station once if the receiver station has a frame to send to the sender. IEEE 802.11e [12] MAC mechanism also introduces transmission opportunity (TXOP) through which a station is allowed to transmit multiple data frames without entering backoff procedure.

With increasing demand for real-time and multimedia applications over wireless, the IEEE 802.11n Working Group standardized a new Medium Access Control (MAC) and Physical Layer (PHY) specification [3]. The throughput performance at the MAC layer of IEEE 802.11n is improved by aggregating several frames of at most 64KB before transmission. Although simulation results of [13] demonstrates the effectiveness of 802.11n MAC layer enhancement, the standard does not specify exactly how many packets should be aggregated and how delay requirements are treated.

In [5] authors study the performance of IEEE 802.11n under unidirectional and bi-directional data transfer. They also numerically propose an optimal frame size adaptation algorithm with A-MSDU under error-prone channels. Authors in [14] try to solve the performance anomaly of IEEE 802.11 multi-rate wireless networks. They introduce a transmission time which is similar to transmission opportunity (TXOP) proposed by IEEE 802.11e.

Convex optimization has been used in many engineering applications in order to reach an optimum situation. As an instance, the authors in [15] address the problem of rate assignment to sources of transmitting data and solve it through its dual problem using gradient projection algorithm.

These works only concentrate on how to concatenate packets into a larger frame to reduce protocol overhead. Since most of the works in the literature such as [9] only focus on proposing effective aggregation schemes, the effect of aggregation on delay and bounding such delay are paid no attention. To the best of our knowledge, this is the first work on analyzing and bounding delay caused by aggregation which is crucial to high-speed WLANs, especially for multimedia applications that are one the requirements of these networks [16], [17], and [18].

# 3 Optimized Packet Aggregation (OPA)

## 3.1 Network Model

We assume that there are $n$ nodes belonging to the set of nodes $\mathcal{N} = \{1,...,n\}$ which are contending for the wireless channel. Physical transmission rate is $r_i$ for node $i$ and the goal is to maximize the channel throughput by considering delay constraints of nodes. Upon accessing channel, we assume that the node $i$ aggregates a number of $x_i$ packets each of which is of the average length $l_{avg}$. This assumption can be utilized as the underlying aggregation mechanism in all methods.

MAC overhead is usually caused by specific headers and frame checksums. In addition, there is an extra overhead imposed by the physical layer to transmit a packet such as SIFS and DIFS, control frames such as RTS and CTS, physical layer preambles, etc. We denote overhead of the protocol by $P^{OH}$ meaning that summation of all overhead durations, in seconds, in which no data packet is transmitted.

By these assumptions, now, we can define the node utility function which indicates how much a situation is preferable for a node. In the context of wireless channel access, the more a node accesses the channel, the more this situation is profitable for the node. Throughput of a node has a direct relation with its number of aggregated packets [9]. Because of the use of BlockACK, the more packets a node aggregates, the more utility it achieves and, accordingly, the more throughput increase it has [9]. In other words, the utility function of a node $i$ is an increasing function of its number of aggregated packets $x_i$. We used a logarithmic function which is strictly increasing as the utility function and for node $i$, it is defined as

$$U_i(x_i) = \log x_i \quad , \quad x_i > 1 . \tag{1}$$

The behavior of a logarithmic function to its input is closer to a real throughput function of the number of packets, and also, simulation results of [9] approve this. The logarithmic function (1) is strictly concave and gives us some interesting properties as discussed in Section 5. With the goal of maximizing the network utility

$$U(\mathbf{x}) = \sum_{i=1}^{n} U_i(x_i)$$

(2)

which is the summation of utilities of nodes and $\mathbf{x}$ means a vector whose elements are $x_i$, $i \in \mathcal{N}$. This function has an optimum point which maximizes the function $U$, and we require finding the optimum point in order to maximize the network utility.

We define delay constraint of a node as the maximum duration the node can postpone sending and let the other nodes transmit their packets. In other words, this duration specifies how much the node can wait to access the channel, and it is usually specified by traffic characteristics of the node. Since access to the channel of a wireless ad hoc network is stochastic, nodes may access the channel differently but we assume that the channel access mechanism is fair and the expected values of the number of node accesses to the channel are the same. Moreover, we assume fair access to the channel meaning that if node $i$ finishes transmitting, all other nodes can have access to the channel if they have packets to send. IEEE 802.11-based protocols provide such fairness in a long-term basis [19]. Using the delay calculation of [5], by $d_i$, we denote how long it takes that node $i$ is able to transmit. Analytically, for each node $i$ we should have $B_i(\mathbf{x}) \leq d_i$ where

$$B_i(\mathbf{x}) = (n-1)P^{OH} + l_{avg} \sum_{j \neq i} (x_j / r_j).$$

(3)

This equation means that the time required for the other nodes to transmit their packets should be less than or equal to $d_i$. This time comprises the time of transmitting the number of packets that each node sends and the protocol overhead.

## 3.2 Optimization Problem

**Primal Problem.** We model the aggregation problem as a solution to the following optimization problem which is formulated as:

*Maximize* U($\mathbf{x}$)

(4)

*Subject to* $B_i(\mathbf{x}) \leq d_i$ for all $i \in \mathcal{N}$

(5)

This means that we try to find a vector $\mathbf{x}$ which specifies how many packets should be aggregated by each node in order to achieve the maximum utility in the network. This is performed by considering constraints (5).

**Dual Problem.** Although the problem (4) can be separated among nodes, its constraints will remain coupled over the network. The coupled nature of the problem necessitates using a centralized method which imposes great computational overhead to the system. In order to have a distributed solution and for the sake of simplicity in designing the channel access protocol, we solve the problem through its dual. First, by defining the Lagrangian problem, we take the constraints into account which leads to

$$L(\mathbf{x},\lambda) = U(\mathbf{x}) - \sum_{i=1}^{n} \lambda_i (B_i(\mathbf{x}) - d_i).$$

(6)

where $\lambda_i$ is the Lagrange multiplier associated with the $i^{th}$ inequality constraint and the vector $\lambda$ is called the dual variables of the problem (4) where $\lambda = (\lambda_i, i \in \mathcal{N})$. Then, the Lagrangian dual function is defined as

$$g(\lambda) = \sup_{\mathbf{x}} L(\mathbf{x},\lambda).$$

(7)

which is the maximum value of the Lagrangian over $\mathbf{x}$. The dual function yields upper bounds on the optimal value of the problem (4) and (5) [7]. In order to solve (7), we should find $x_i$ such that

$$\frac{\partial L(\mathbf{x},\lambda)}{\partial x_i} = 0.$$

(8)

Solving the above equation results in

$$x_i = \frac{r_i}{l_{avg} \sum_{j \neq i} \lambda_j}$$

(9)

Substituting (9) in (7) yields

$$
\begin{aligned}
g(\lambda) &= \log \frac{r_1}{l_{avg}(\lambda_2 + \lambda_3 + \dots + \lambda_n)} + \log \frac{r_2}{l_{avg}(\lambda_1 + \lambda_3 + \dots + \lambda_n)} + \dots + \log \frac{r_n}{l_{avg}(\lambda_1 + \lambda_2 + \dots + \lambda_{n-1})} \\
&\quad - \lambda_1(n-1)P^{OH} + \lambda_1 d_1 - \lambda_2(n-1)P^{OH} + \lambda_2 d_2 - \dots - \lambda_n(n-1)P^{OH} + \lambda_n d_n \\
&\quad - \frac{\lambda_1}{(\lambda_1 + \lambda_3 + \dots + \lambda_n)} - \frac{\lambda_1}{(\lambda_1 + \lambda_2 + \lambda_4 + \dots + \lambda_n)} - \dots - \frac{\lambda_1}{(\lambda_1 + \lambda_2 + \dots + \lambda_{n-1})} \\
&\quad - \frac{\lambda_2}{(\lambda_2 + \lambda_3 + \dots + \lambda_n)} - \frac{\lambda_2}{(\lambda_1 + \lambda_2 + \lambda_4 + \dots + \lambda_n)} - \dots - \frac{\lambda_2}{(\lambda_1 + \lambda_2 + \dots + \lambda_{n-1})} \\
&\quad \dots \\
&\quad - \frac{\lambda_n}{(\lambda_2 + \lambda_3 + \dots + \lambda_n)} - \frac{\lambda_n}{(\lambda_1 + \lambda_3 + \dots + \lambda_n)} - \dots - \frac{\lambda_n}{(\lambda_1 + \dots + \lambda_{n-2} + \lambda_n)}
\end{aligned}
$$

(10)

The Lagrangian dual problem is expressed as:

*Minimize* $g(\lambda)$

(11)

*Subject to* $\lambda \succeq 0$.

(12)

The Lagrange dual problem (11) is a convex optimization problem, since objective to be maximized is concave and constraint is convex. Due to the duality theory, a dual problem is always convex, and due to the strong convexity of the primal problem (4), it is guarantees that solving the dual problem will result in optimal solution for the primal problem. The above problem can be solved by differentiating $g(\lambda)$ of $\lambda_i$ which leads to

$$\frac{\partial g}{\partial \lambda_i} = -(n-1)P^{OH} + d_i - \sum_{j \neq i} \frac{1}{\sum_{k \neq j} \lambda_k} . \tag{13}$$

As an example, the above equation for $i = 1$ is as follows:

$$\frac{\partial g}{\partial \lambda_1} = -(n-1)P^{OH} + d_1 - \frac{1}{(\lambda_2 + \lambda_3 + \ldots + \lambda_n)} - \frac{1}{(\lambda_1 + \lambda_3 + \lambda_4 + \ldots + \lambda_n)} - \ldots - \frac{1}{(\lambda_1 + \lambda_2 + \ldots + \lambda_{n-1})} \tag{14}$$

Solving the equation $\partial g / (\partial \lambda_i) = 0$ computes the optimum $\lambda_i$ but because of the complexity of the (10), we cannot represent a closed-form solution. Then, the optimum point is calculated iteratively.

In order to obtain a distributed solution with low computational complexity, we solve the dual problem using gradient projection method [7] which iteratively steps toward the opposite direction of the gradient of the objective function of the problem. Using the following iterative equations, the optimum values of $\lambda_i$ for each node $i$ is calculated. Therefore, for the dual problem (11), we get

$$\lambda_i^{(k+1)} = \left[ \lambda_i^{(k)} - \gamma^{(k)} \frac{\partial g}{\partial \lambda_i^{(k)}} \right]^+ \tag{15}$$

$$\gamma^{(k+1)} = \frac{1}{\sqrt{k}} \tag{16}$$

where $\lambda_i^{(k)}$ is the value of $\lambda_i$ at iteration k and $[z]^+ = \max(z,0)$. This means that at iteration $k$, $\lambda_i$ is updated and improved. Equation (16) shows the step length of that round. Equation (15) is the descent method which produces a minimizing sequence to solve an optimization problem [20]. By this equation we mean an algorithm that computes a sequence of points $\lambda_i^{(0)}$, $\lambda_i^{(1)}$, ... $\in dom\ g$ with $g(\lambda_i^{(k)}) \to p^*$ as $k \to \infty$ where $p^*$ is the optimum point. The algorithm is terminated when $p^* - g\left(\lambda_i^{(k)}\right) \leq \varepsilon$, and $\varepsilon > 0$ is some specified tolerance.

## 4    Implementation

In the absence of a centralized coordinator in an ad hoc network, nodes should follow a distributed approach to compute how many packets they should aggregate to reach the optimal situation. Each node only knows its delay requirement ($d_i$), physical rate ($r_i$), and protocol overhead ($P^{OH}$). From (13) it is inferred that each node also requires $\lambda$ and the number of nodes, $n$, in order to solve (15).

The nodes can infer the number of nodes contending for the channel by listening to transmissions in the channel. In addition, the nodes should have $\lambda_i$ for all $i$. For this reason, a particular field is considered in the MAC header of the protocol which is called *LM* (Lagrange Multiplier). Each transmitting node $i$, calculates the latest value of its $\lambda_i$ and puts this value in this field. The receiving node and the other listening nodes extract this value, and update their local information.

Local information of $\lambda$ values of the other nodes is organized as a list, called *LM_list*. As communication proceeds and data packets are transmitted, nodes extract values of the LM field of transmitting packets and update their local list. This process continues until all nodes reach an optimized value for $\lambda$.

**Table 1.** Optimized Packet Aggregation (OPA) pseudo code for each node *i*

| Initialization | On sending | On listening/receiving |
|---|---|---|
| $\lambda_i = 1$ ; <br> $k = 1$ ; <br> LM_List = Empty; | p = output_packet; <br> if( p.type = data_packet ) { <br><br> $\lambda_i^{(k+1)} = \left[ \lambda_i^{(k)} + \gamma^{(k)} \dfrac{\partial g}{\partial \lambda_i^{(k)}} \right]^{+}$ ; <br><br> $\gamma^{(k+1)} = \dfrac{1}{\sqrt{k}}$ ; <br><br> $x_i = \dfrac{r_i}{l_{avg} \sum_{j \neq i} \lambda_j}$ ; <br><br> $x_i = \min(\max(x_i, \begin{smallmatrix} Min\_Frame\_Len \\ Max\_Frame\_Len \end{smallmatrix}))$ ; <br><br> update_LM_list(node$_i$.ID, $\lambda_i^{(k+1)}$ ); <br><br> p.LM = $\lambda_i^{(k+1)}$ ; <br><br> $k = k + 1$ ; <br><br> aggregate(p, $\lfloor x_i \rfloor$ ); // aggregates at <br><br> most $\lfloor x_i \rfloor$ packets into p <br><br> } | p = input_packet; <br> if( p.type = data_packet ) <br> update_LM_list( <br> extract_ID(p), <br> extract_LM(p)); |

The only value that should be transmitted is $\lambda$ which is carried by the LM field of the MAC header. This value implicitly consists of all information required to find an optimal solution like node physical rate and delay requirement. Therefore, transmitting entire parameters of nodes is not required. In Table 1, pseudo code of this process is presented. The parameters *Min_Frame_Len* and *Max_Frame_Len* represent the minimum and maximum allowed frame lengths. Nodes also assume zero-waiting meaning that if there are fewer packets than $x_i$ in their queues, they just aggregate available packets and do not wait for further packets.

# 5   Evaluation

## 5.1   Algorithm Analysis

Time complexity of OPA is $O(n^2)$. Each node *i* should compute the value of (15) in order to update its $\lambda_i$ value. The only time-consuming part of this formula is calculating $\partial g / (\partial \lambda_i)$. Equation (13) shows how many calculation steps are required to find this value for node $i$.

OPA does not impose any message complexity since each node informs other nodes of its $\lambda$ only through the LM field in the MAC header. Since $\lambda$ values are in a small fixed range of real numbers, the LM field that encodes $\lambda$ also imposes a very insignificant overhead.

Since time complexity of OPA is not high, and also, OPA does not impose any message complexity, the overhead of OPA, especially on energy consumption, is insignificant. This means it not required that nodes worry about energy issues.

One important issue regarding OPA is whether it can find the optimum point, i.e., the aggregation size leading to maximum throughput. If a function is concave/convex, it has a unique maximum/minimum point.

The primal problem stated by (4) is strictly convex and admits a unique maximizer because $(\partial^2 U_i(x_i))/(\partial x_i^2) < 0$ which indicates that the entire utility functions are concave, and since according to (2), $U(\mathbf{x})$ is a nonnegative and non-zero weighted sum of strictly concave functions, it is strictly concave.

## 5.2   Algorithm Stability

The main concern regarding the proposed algorithm is its stability under erroneous and dynamic conditions of a WLAN under which nodes may join or leave the network. We analyzed the algorithm in the presence of error in estimating the number of nodes. Referring to Table 2, error percent means that how much the number of nodes estimated by a node may deviate from what it actually is. For example, if there are 20 nodes in the network, 20% error may cause that a node estimates the number of nodes to a value in the range of [16, 24]. Results show that if, for example, there are 50 nodes in the network, and all nodes may have 20% deviate in their estimations, their average delay may increase or decrease to at most 25% of their optimum value.

Although the above results show that the delay may increase/decrease during these conditions, the fact is the algorithm should quickly converge to the new optimum point after any changes in the network. Referring to Table 2, convergence time shows how long, in seconds, it takes to reach the new optimum point in average. Evaluations for an extensive amount of input data show that the algorithm can converge to the optimum point after 100 iterations on average. This means that in real network scenario, each node can converge to the optimum point after receiving nearly 100 MAC data frames that according to Table 2, it takes less than 1 second which is fast enough to track changes such as node movement and sleep in WLANs.

**Table 2.** Delay deviation in the presence of error

| Number of nodes | 10% | 20% | 30% | Convergence time (s) |
|---|---|---|---|---|
| 6 | 10% | 20% | 35% | 0.29 |
| 10 | 9% | 22% | 36% | 0.42 |
| 20 | 11% | 25% | 35% | 0.65 |
| 50 | 11% | 25% | 39% | 0.89 |

# 6 Simulation Results

We used the AFR implementation as the base aggregation method and enhanced it by our proposed approach. AFR is one of the best schemes proposed for high-speed wireless networks. The implementation is performed in *NS-2* [21]. We used implementation and simulation scenarios of [22]. This code represents AFR implementation which is published by the authors of [9]. In the network topology, STA *i* sends packets to STA *i*+1. Results are reported for two different types of traffic, CBR and HDTV which are requirements of high-speed WLANs. In addition, improvement in the network utilization is computed by *Throughput* and *Average delay* which are introduced by [9].

HDTV is one of the requirements of high-speed wireless LAN protocols such as IEEE 802.11n [6]. It has a constant packet size of 1500 bytes, a sending rate of 19.2-24Mbps, and a 200ms peak delay requirement. We investigate OPA and AFR HDTV performance with a 128Mbps PHY data rate.

In addition, the simulation time is 10 seconds, that is, the nodes keep transmitting packets for 10 seconds. Results are averaged over all nodes and over 15 different runs with 95% confidence level. Fig. 1 shows the throughput and delay performance of these schemes for different number of STAs. In all of the following scenarios, AFR is executed with the frame size to which it responds well, i.e. 32KB. On the contrary, OPA follows a dynamic packet aggregation scheme and the frame size may vary. It equals to the optimized packet length that the algorithm proposed for that situation.

From Fig. 1, it can be observed that OPA results in shorter delays than AFR and, approximately, this value is half of the AFR average delay. Moreover, in the cases where BER is $10^{-5}$ and $10^{-6}$, OPA improves throughput and where BER is $10^{-4}$, these two approaches reach the same throughput although OPA decreases the average delay for all different BER values. When the number of nodes is small, both approaches cause short delay. As more nodes are added to the network, satisfying delay constraints becomes more critical since the number of contending nodes for the channel increases.

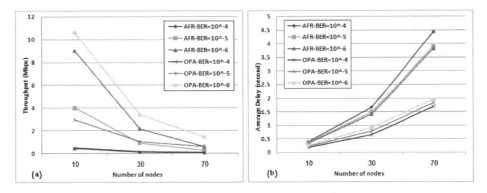

**Fig. 1.** HDTV traffic for various numbers of nodes

Other type of traffic which is used as test traffic is CBR which generates UDP packets at a constant rate. Two different scenarios which utilize CBR traffic are implemented. In the first one, each node constantly generates packets and sends them to a particular destination. The network is saturated and nodes transmit CBR streams at the physical rate. The number of stations varies from 10 to 90 and results are extracted for different BERs. The simulation duration is also 10 seconds, and results are depicted in Fig. 2. Results show that OPA method outperforms AFR especially where the network is heavily overloaded, i.e., the number of stations increases.

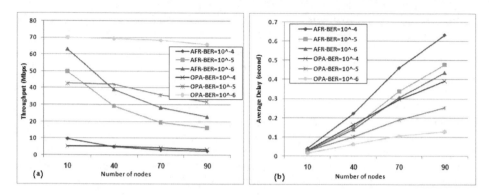

**Fig. 2.** CBR traffic for various numbers of nodes

From Fig. 2(a), it can be observed that OPA is not very sensitive to increase in the number of nodes in terms of throughput and decreasing slope of the lines are smaller in OPA. This means that the throughput decreases slower as the number of nodes increases in OPA than that of AFR. Fig. 2(b) shows the average delay of the above network scenario. Referring to this Figure, results indicate that OPA is more successful is decreasing delay under different BERs.

In the second scenario of using CBR traffics, the number of nodes is fixed and the physical rate varies from 54 to 432Mbps. There are 40 nodes sending CBR streams to one another. In Fig. 3, performance results of this scenario are presented for BERs $10^{-5}$ and $10^{-6}$.

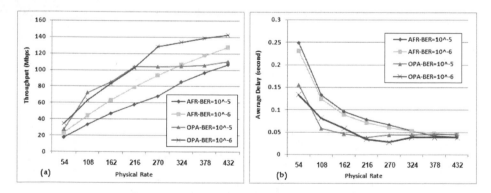

**Fig. 3.** CBR traffic for various physical rates

Fig. 3 shows that when the physical rate is low, OPA outperforms AFR. This consequence is obvious because OPA optimizes network access and the optimization process, in general, performs well when there is lack of resources. Therefore, in this situation, access to the channel should be accomplished wisely, and OPA handles this situation well. Delay constraints of OPA impose restrictions on access durations to the channel and as a result, delay in not increased. As the physical rate increases, and the network becomes less saturated, the average delay of both methods converges to a particular value although the OPA throughput is larger. Delay values of both approaches converges to 0.05 for the physical rate 432Mbps in which the network becomes unsaturated, and the same result is also held for throughputs.

## 7 Conclusion

One of the requirements of wireless networks is providing high-speed transmission of data, especially, multimedia traffics. There are few approaches that increase efficiency of the medium access control (MAC) layer through aggregating packets and reducing the protocol overhead. In this paper, in order to achieve high efficiency at the MAC layer of these networks as well as constraining resultant delay of large aggregation sizes, we proposed an analytical model of the wireless medium access, optimized packet aggregation (OPA), that finds the optimized aggregated size. This model, as the main parameter of optimizing, considers delay requirements, and permits nodes to transmit a particular amount of data as an aggregated data frame at the MAC layer to bound channel access delay. To evaluate the proposed model, we extended the AFR implementation in *NS*-2. Simulation results indicate that our method, OPA, decreases the average delay while increasing throughput, especially in saturated situations where the number of nodes and the traffic rate are large. As future work, we will try to extend the analytical model to consider different aspects such as the error rate.

## References

1. Marcelo, M., Carvalho, J.J., Garcia-Luna-Aceves: Delay Analysis of IEEE 802.11 in Single-Hop Networks. In: 11th IEEE International Conference on Network Protocols (2003)
2. Raptis, P., Vitsas, V., Paparrizos, K.: Packet Delay Metrics for IEEE 802.11 Distributed Coordination Function. Mobile Networks 14, 772–781 (2009)
3. IEEE, IEEE 802.11n-2009—Amendment 5: Enhancements for Higher Throughput (2009)
4. Xiao, Y., Rosdahl, J.: Performance analysis and enhancement for the current and future IEEE 802.11 MAC protocols. ACM SIGMOBILE Mobile Computing and Communications Review 7, 6 (2003)
5. Lin, Y., Wong, V.W.: Frame Aggregation and Optimal Frame Size Adaptation for IEEE 802.11n WLANs. In: IEEE Globecom 2006, pp. 1–6 (2006)
6. IEEE: IEEE 802.11n TGn Sync proposal technical specification (May 2005)
7. Boyd, S., Vandenberghe, L.: Convex optimization. Cambridge Univ Pr, Cambridge (2004)
8. Vitsas, V., Chatzimisios, P.: Enhancing performance of the IEEE 802.11 distributed coordination function via packet bursting. In: IEEE Global Telecommunications Conference Workshops, GlobeCom Workshops 2004, pp. 245–252. IEEE, Los Alamitos (2004)

9. Li, T., Ni, Q., Malone, D., Leith, D., Xiao, Y., Turletti, T.: Aggregation With Fragment Retransmission for Very High-Speed WLANs. IEEE/ACM Transactions on Networking 17, 591–604 (2009)
10. Li, T., Ni, Q., Xiao, Y.: Investigation of the block ACK scheme in wireless ad hoc networks. Wireless Communications and Mobile Computing 6, 877–888 (2006)
11. Xiao, Y.: IEEE 802.11 performance enhancement via concatenation and piggyback mechanisms. IEEE Transactions on Wireless Communications 4, 2182–2192 (2005)
12. IEEE, IEEE 802.11e, Part 11: Wireless LAN Medium Access Control (MAC) and Physical Layer (PHY) specifications Amendment 8: Medium Access Control (MAC) Quality of Service Enhancements (2005)
13. Wang, C., Wei, H.: IEEE 802.11n MAC Enhancement and Performance Evaluation. Mobile Networks and Applications 14, 760–771 (2009)
14. Razafindralambo, T., Lassous, I.G., Iannone, L., Fdida, S.: Dynamic packet aggregation to solve performance anomaly in 802.11 wireless networks. In: Proceedings of the 9th ACM international symposium on Modeling analysis and simulation of wireless and mobile systems - MSWiM 2006, p. 247. ACM Press, New York (2006)
15. Low, S., Lapsely, D.: Optimization flow control. I. Basic algorithm and convergence. IEEE/ACM Transactions on Networking 7, 861–874 (1999)
16. Ketchum, J., Al, E.: System Description and Operating Principles for High Throughput Enhancements to 802.11. 11, vol. 802, pp. 11–14. IEEE, Los Alamitos
17. Mujtaba, S.A., Al, E.: TGn sync proposal technical specification. TGn Sync Technical Proposal R 802, 11-04/889 (2004)
18. Xiao, Y.: IEEE 802.11n: enhancements for higher throughput in wireless LANs. IEEE Wireless Communications 12, 82–91 (2005)
19. Li, Z., Nandi, S., Gupta, A.K.: Modeling the Short-term Unfairness of IEEE 802.11 in Presence of Hidden Terminals. Performance Evaluation 63, 441–462 (2006)
20. Zhu, H., Chlamtac, I.: Performance analysis for IEEE 802.11e EDCF service differentiation. IEEE Transactions on Wireless Communications 4, 1779–1788 (2005)
21. Hindi, H.: A Tutorial on Convex Optimization II: Duality and Interior Point Methods. In: American Control Conference, pp. 686–696 (2006)
22. Network Simulator (NS), http://www.isi.edu/nsnam/ns/
23. AFR Implementation, http://www.hamilton.ie/tianjili/afr.html

# Algorithm Research of Top-Down Mining Maximal Frequent SubGraph Based on Tree Structure

Xiao Chen[1], Chunying Zhang[2,3], Fengchun Liu[1,2], and Jingfeng Guo[3]

[1] Qian'an College, Hebei United University,
5096 Yanshan Road, 064400 Qian'an, Hebei, China
chenxiao0604@163.com
[2] College of Science, Hebei United University,
46 Xinhua Road, 063009 Tang Shan, Hebei, China
{zchunying,lnobliu}@heut.edu.cn
[3] College of Information Science and Engineering, Yanshan University,
438 Hebei Ave, 066004 Qinhuangdao, Hebei, China
jfguo@ysu.edu.cn

**Abstract.** For the existence of problems with mining frequent subgraph by the traditional way, a new algorithm of top-down mining maximal frequent subgraph based on tree structure is proposed in this paper. In the mining process, the symmetry of graph is used to identify the symmetry vertex; determining graph isomorphism based on the attributed information of graph, the tree structure is top-down constructed and completed the calculation of support. Which is reduced the unnecessary operation and the redundant storage of graphs, and the efficiency of algorithm is improved. Experiments show that the algorithm is superior to the existing maximal frequent subgraph mining algorithms, without losing any patterns and useful information.

**Keywords:** Maximal Frequent Subgraph, Top-Down, Graph Isomorphism, Tree Structure.

## 1 Introduction

With the appearance of the large amounts of structured data, and the increasing demand on analysis, graph mining has become an active and important theme in data mining [1]. Among the various kinds of graph mining, the frequent subgraph mining is the most basic patterns and bottleneck; in order to improve the mining efficiency and reduce the number of the result set, we can convert mining frequent subgraph to mining maximal frequent subgraph. The existing methods of maximal frequent subgraph mining [2-4], which whether based on BFS or based on FP-growth are used the mining thinking of bottom-up, there are some problems, such as: (1) Need to through multiple iterations and the determine of subgraph isomorphism in the mining processing (to determine subgraph isomorphism is NP complete problems [5]). (2) Only reduced the number of results sets by pattern growth approach to mining maximal frequent subgraph sets, compared with the frequent subgraph sets, and does not reduced the mining difficult.

P. Sénac, M. Ott, and A. Seneviratne (Eds.): ICWCA 2011, LNICST 72, pp. 401–411, 2012.
© Institute for Computer Sciences, Social Informatics and Telecommunications Engineering 2012

In addition to the bottom-up mining methods, the top-down mining strategy is referred in [6], which using this search order, the itemsets are traversed and checked from big to small. It's the outstanding advantages as follows. (1) Reduced the number of calculate subgraph support by the property that if the supersets is frequent then its subsets must be frequent; (2) The maximal frequent itemsets to facilitate fast discovery by the top-down mining approach, reduced the difficulty of mining and storage redundancy. Therefore, it is can be applied to graph mining areas that the top-down mining strategy, however, due to the complex graph structure, which can not be directly applied to mining maximal frequent subgraph, and need to improve their algorithm.

In this paper, we propose a new algorithm of maximal frequent subgraph based on top-down mining strategy. The apache is top-down construct tree structure, calculated the support using the determining of graph isomorphism tree structure, which to improve the algorithm efficiency through avoid to determine subgraph isomorphism. And considering the symmetry structure and the attribute information of graph reduced the unnecessary operation and the storage redundant of graphs in reduced graphs scale. Experiment shows that the algorithm is superior to the previous algorithms.

The rest of this paper is organized as follows. In Section 2 the preliminary concepts are introduced. Section 3 presents the related properties and algorithm description. An experimental study is presented in Section 4 and we conclude in Section 5.

## 2   Preliminaries

There are some preliminary concepts contributions in [1, 5], such as Labeled Graph, SubGraph, SupperGraph, Support, etc. In order to facilitate understanding, only a few of the more important concept are given in the following.

**Definition 1.** Given grahpsets D = {$G_1$, $G_2$,..., $G_n$} and the user-specified *min_Sup* $\in$ (0,1], $G_i$ is a maximal frequent subgraph iff there isn't existing Sup($G' = G_i \Diamond e$) $\geq$*min_Sup* in D [4].

**Definition 2.** Given a pair of labeled graphs G={V,E,$\Sigma$V,$\Sigma$E,L} and G'={V', E', $\Sigma$V', $\Sigma$E', L'}, G is isomorphic to G' *iff* there exists a mapping $f$ : V(G) $\leftrightarrow$ V(G') such that:

$\forall u \in V$, $L(u) = L'(f(u))$, $\forall u,v \in V$, $V((u,u) \in E) \Leftrightarrow$, $(f(u), f(v)) \in E)$ $\forall (u,v)$ $\in V$, $L(u,v) = L'(f(u), f(v))$.

**Property 1.** If Graph G is isomorphic to G', then the vertices number of Graph G and G' is same, that is |V(G)| = |V(G')| [7].

**Property 2.** If Graph G is isomorphic to G', then the edges number of Graph G and G' is same, that is |E(G)| = |E(G')| [7].

**Property 3.** If Graph G is isomorphic to G', then the vertices number of same degrees in Graph G and G' is same [7].

The above three properties is the necessary conditions for graph isomorphism, but not sufficient. That is, the above three properties establish in the conditions of graph isomorphism, so graphs isomorphic is uncertain when only meeting the above three properties. For example, Given graph G and G', as shown in Figure 1, then, (1) |V(G)| = |V(G')| = 7 ; (2) |E(G)| = |E(G')| = 12 ; (3) The degrees of vertex a and 1 are 6, the other vertices degrees are 3. Obviously, the graph G and graph G' satisfies the above three properties, but the graph G and graph G' is non-isomorphic, this proved that the properties of the non-sufficiency.

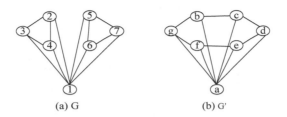

(a) G                    (b) G'

**Fig. 1.** An example of Non-isomorphic

**Definition 3.** A labeled graph G is subgraph isomorphic to a labeled graph G', denoted by $G \subseteq G'$, *iff* there exists a subgraph G'' of G' such that G is isomorphic to G'' [2].

However, in determining the subgraph isomorphism, because do not know in advance which the subgraph of G' isomorphism with G, need to match several times, reducing the algorithm efficiency. Therefore, it can be seen, subgraph isomorphism is more complex than isomorphism in computationally, so in the process of top-down mining, only determined graph isomorphism, to avoid the comparison of subgraph isomorphism, to improve the algorithm efficiency.

**Definition 4.** The graph G is Non-Unique Labeled Undirected Simple Graph iff the graph structure is described as following.

(1) A graph is simple graph, if the graph does not existing ring and the multiple edges between any two vertices;

(2) A graph is undirected, if the graph contains only undirected edges, such as (u, v);

(3) A graph is non-unique labeled graph, if exist the same vertex label or edge label in graph, which the label is the inherent information of the vertex or edge.

There are many non-unique identifier graphs in reality, such as benzene ring containing many carbon atoms of the same labels, the undirected graph of Non-unique identity are the study objects in this paper. In order to further simplify the determine graphs isomorphism, as the necessary conditions for determining isomorphic of non-unique identity graphs, attributed information of graph is defined as follows, which is storied by the form of single linked list.

**Definition 5.** An attributed information of labeled graph G is a four element-tuples $GAI = \{|V|; |E|; |C^{\Sigma V}_i|; C^{\Sigma V}_i[|V(C^{\Sigma V}_i)|\text{-MaxD}(C^V_i)])\}$ (order by the lexicographic order of vertex labeling). Where |V| is the number of vertices; $D(V_i)$ is degree of the vertices; $|E| = \sum D(V_i) / 2$ is the size of graph (that is the number of edges); $C^{\Sigma V}_i$ is the vertex labels types; $|C^{\Sigma V}_i|$ the number of vertex labels types; $|V(C^{\Sigma V}_i)|$ that the number of same labeling vertices; $\text{MaxD}(C^{\Sigma V}_i)$ that the maximum degree of vertex types.

**Example 1.** According to the method of reference [8] relabeled graph dataset $D = \{G_1, G_2, G_3\}$, as shown in Figure 2, the attributed information of graphs are as follows. $GAI(G_1) = (4; 6; 2; X[2\text{-}3], Z[2\text{-}2])$, that is, there are 4 vertices and 6 edges, which two types vertex labels are X and Z, the number of vertices with same labeled X is 2, the maximum degree of vertices X is 3, the other the same way available; $GAI(G_2) = (4; 5; 2; X[3\text{-}3], Z[1\text{-}3])$; $GAI(G_3) = (4; 5; 1; X[4\text{-}3])$.

Based on the traditional graph isomorphism property and the definition of attribute information of graph, the extended property as follows (the property of 1, 2 still valid).

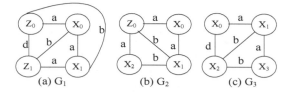

**Fig. 2.** Relabeled graph dataset

**Property 4.** If Graph G is isomorphic to G', then the number of vertex labels types is same in Graph G and G', that is $|C^{\Sigma V}_i(G)| = |C^{\Sigma V}_i(G')|$.

**Proof:** According to the definition graph isomorphism and labeled graph, when Graph G is isomorphic to G', $|V(G)| = |V(G')|$ and $|E(G)| = |E(G')|$, and $\forall u \in V(G)$, $L(G(u)) = L(G'(f(u)))$; $\forall L(G(u,v)) = L(G'(f(u), f(v)))$; then, then the number of vertex labels types is same in Graph G and G', that is $|C^{\Sigma V}_i(G)| = |C^{\Sigma V}_i(G')|$.

**Property 5.** If Graph G is isomorphic to G', then the number of same types vertex labeled and the maximum degree are same in Graph G and G', that is $C^{\Sigma V}_i[|V(C^{\Sigma V}_i)|\text{-}MaxD(C^V_i)](G) = C^{\Sigma V}_i[|V(C^{\Sigma V}_i)|\text{-}MaxD(C^V_i)](G')$.

**Proof:** According to the definition of graph isomorphism and the properties 1 and 4, when graph G is isomorphic to G', then $|V(G)| = |V(G')|$, and $\forall u \in V(G)$, $L(G(u)) = L(G'(f(u))) \Rightarrow |C^{\Sigma V}_i(G)| = |C^{\Sigma V}_i(G')|$, so $|V(C^{\Sigma V}_i(G))| = |V(C^{\Sigma V}_i(G'))|$; according to the properties 3, $MaxD(C^V_i(G)) = MaxD(C^V_i(G'))$; to sum up, when graph G is isomorphic to G', then $C^{\Sigma V}_i[|V(C^{\Sigma V}_i)|\text{-}MaxD(C^V_i)](G) = C^{\Sigma V}_i[|V(C^{\Sigma V}_i)|\text{-}MaxD(C^V_i)](G')$.

Similarly, the properties 1, 2, 4 and 5 are necessary conditions for determine graph isomorphism, that is, these are established in the conditions of graph isomorphism; the graph must be non-isomorphic when not meet any one of the above four properties. Therefore, the above four properties can be as a precondition for determine isomorphism, based on graph attribute information, the method as follows.

**Algorithm 1:** To determine the graph G and G' whether isomorphic

Input: Graph G and G', $GAI(G) = \{|V|; |E|; |C^{\Sigma V}_i|; C^{\Sigma V}_i[|V(C^{\Sigma V}_i)|\text{-}MaxD(C^V_i)])\}$,
$GAI(G') = \{|V|; |E|; |C^{\Sigma V}_i|; C^{\Sigma V}_i[|V(C^{\Sigma V}_i)|\text{-}MaxD(C^V_i)])\}$;

Output: True (isomorphic) or Flash (non-isomorphic).

Begin

(1)    If $|V(G)| \neq |V(G')|$, then the graph G and G' is non-isomorphic;

(2)    Else if $|E(G)| \neq |E(G')|$, then the graph G and G' is non-isomorphic;

(3)    Else if $|C^{\Sigma V}_i(G)| \neq |C^{\Sigma V}_i(G')|$, then the graph G and G' is non-isomorphic;

(4)    Else if $C^{\Sigma V}_i[|V(C^{\Sigma V}_i)|\text{-}MaxD(C^V_i)](G) \neq C^{\Sigma V}_i[|V(C^{\Sigma V}_i)|\text{-}MaxD(C^V_i)](G')$,
       then the graph G and G' is non-isomorphic;

(5)        Else, using DFS Cord or determinant judgments graph isomorphic

(6)    Return True or Flash

End

**Example 2.** To determine isomorphism of graph $G_2$ and $G_3$, based on the attributed information of graph, firstly, compare to the number of vertices: $|V(G_2)| = |V(G_3)| = 4$, to downward compare to the sizes of graphs: $|E(G_2)| = |E(G_3)| = 5$, and continue to compare to the vertex labels types: $(|C^{\Sigma V}_i(G_2)| = 2) \neq (|C^{\Sigma V}_i(G_3)| = 1)$, then graph $G_2$ and $G_3$ have the different numbers of vertex labels types, that is graph $G_2$ is non-isomorphic to $G_3$, which reduces the number of comparisons graph isomorphism and improve the efficiency of the algorithm.

**Definition 6.** An isomorphism from a graph G to itself is called an automorphism.

**Definition 7.** A graph G is symmetric if, given any two pairs of linked vertices $u_1$-$v_1$ and $u_2$-$v_2$ of G, there is an automorphism $f: V(G) \rightarrow V(G)$ such that $f(u_1) = u_2$ and $f(v_1) = v_2$[7]. Given automorphism graph G and its subgraph G' (G' $\subset$ G), if G' is symmetric, then G is locally symmetric graph.

**Property 7.** Symmetric graph G must be automorphism, automorphism graph G not necessarily symmetry [7].

Therefore, the symmetric vertex of symmetric graph must be a pair corresponding point in automorphism graph, as shown in Figure 2(a), $(X_0, X_1)$ and $(Z_0, Z_1)$ are symmetric vertices in $G_1$; the symmetric edge form by the symmetric vertices, that is a pair corresponding edge in automorphism graph, $(Z_0, a, X_0)$ and $(Z_1, a, X_1)$ are symmetric edges in $G_1$; graph $G_2$ is called a locally symmetric graph in Figure 2(b), because it contains symmetric subgraph $(X_2, a, Z_0, a, X_0)$.

**Definition 8.** Given a labeled graphset D= $\{G_1, G_2,..., Gn\}$, the frequency of g in D is the sum of the inner frequent of g in Gi, denoted by $f(g, D) = \sum_{i=1}^{i=|D|} in\_f(g, G_i)$ [8].

# 3   The Related Properties and Algorithm Description

## 3.1   The Unique Labeled Method Based on the Graph Symmetry

Usually, the unique labeled of graph is to distinguish different vertex with same label, which can simplify the problem of determining subgraph isomorphism, but this method can't reflect on the structure and other properties of graph. Therefore, we propose a new apache of unique labeled graph based on the graph symmetry and the storage table of frequent graph.

**Example 3.** Given graphset D= {$G_1$, G2, G3}, as shown in Figure 2, the frequency 1-edge sets is {(X, a, X), (X, a, Z), (X, b, Z)}. When the extension connected the subgraphs (X, a ,Z) and (X ,b, Z) of G1, because need to consider a variety of different connections between the same label vertices, it will produce 4 super-graph, respectively, ($Z_1$, b, $X_0$, a, $Z_0$), ($X_0$, a, $Z_0$, b, $X_1$), ($X_1$, a, $Z_1$, b, $X_0$) and ($Z_0$, b, $X_1$, a, $Z_1$), where ($Z_1$, b, $X_0$, a, $Z_0$) and ($Z_0$, b, $X_1$, a, $Z_1$), ($X_0$, a, $Z_0$, b, $X_1$) and ($X_1$, a, $Z_1$, b, $X_0$) are isomorphic, then appear to redundant storage. Although the algorithm can enhancethe space complexity to improve time efficiency, but still should pay attention to reduce the unnecessary waste of space, It is precisely because there is symmetry edge ($X_0$, a, $Z_0$) and ($X_1$, a, $Z_1$) in graph $G_1$ which leads to redundant storage. Therefore, to reduce redundancy, this paper relabeled graph G under assumes known the symmetry of graph (This paper only considering the rules of axial symmetry graph\locally symmetric graph, center symmetry graph and other symmetry graph for the further research). For example, the symmetric vertices ($X_0$, $X_1$) of graph $G_1$ is relabeled to ($X_{01}$, $X_{10}$) in Figure 2(a), it is example $X_{01}$ that 0 represents the original vertex label and 1 represents its symmetrical label, Similarly, other vertices can be relabeled, as shown in Figure 3, that is, the new unique labeled graph based on the graph symmetry is proposed in this paper. Then, $G_1$'s subgraph (X, b, Z, a, X) is stored as ($X_{01}$, b, $Z_{10}$, a, $X_{10}$) can be said a variety of forms, the storage table of G1 frequent 1-edge graph as shows in Table 1, each subgraph and it's in_frequency is stored within the table. Due to consider the graph symmetry, reducing the storage redundant of subgraph, and improves the efficiency of calculate the support.

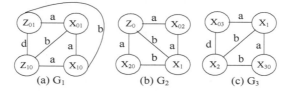

**Fig. 3.** Labeled GraphSets Based on Symmetrical Structure

**Table 1.** The new table of frequency graphs

| Egde | $in\_f(g_i,G_1)$ | | $in\_f(g_i,G_2)$ | | $in\_f(g_i,G_3)$ | | Sup |
|---|---|---|---|---|---|---|---|
| ($g_i$) | $G_1$ | $in\_f$ | $G_2$ | $in\_f$ | $G_3$ | $in\_f$ | |
| (X,a,X) | ($X_0$,a,$X_1$) | 1 | ($X_0$,a,$X_1$) | 1 | ($X_{03}$,a,$X_1$) | 2 | 3 |
| (X,a,Z) | ($X_{01}$,a,$Z_{01}$) | 2 | ($X_{02}$,a,$Z_0$) | 2 | | 0 | 2 |
| (X,b,Z) | ($X_{01}$,b,$Z_{10}$) | 2 | ($X_0$,b,$Z_0$) | 1 | | 0 | 2 |

## 3.2 Pruning Strategy

There are some properties in mining frequent subgraphs are as follows [1].

**Property 8.** Sup(g) ≥ Sup($g' = g \Diamond e$), which g' is a supergraph.

**Property 9.** If the subgraph g is infrequent, then any supergraph g' of g are infrequent.

In this paper, the top-down approach for mining maximal frequency subgraph sets, because includes some non-frequent edge in graphsets, so need to pre-operation graphsets by these two properties, which can delete all infrequent edge and the local frequent edge, when there is non-connected graph can be regarded as more graphs. Pretreated the graph set D to D' = {$G_1'$, $G_2'$, $G_3'$}, as shown in Figure 4.

**Property 10.** Give g and *min_Sup*, if g is a maximal frequency subgraph, so all subgrahp of g is frequency, then, can stop the operation to reduce the scale of g.

**Proof:** Due to using the top-down mining strategy, when g is a maximal frequency subgraph, Sup(g) ≥ *min_Sup*, then, Sup( $g' = g \Diamond e$ ) ≤ *min_Sup*, and Sup(g-e) ≥Sup(g) > Sup( $g' = g \Diamond e$ ). According to the concept of maximal frequency subgraph, g-e is frequent and not maximal, so completed a task of mining maximum frequent son figure, it can stop the operation of reduced graph scale.

**Example 4.** Using the traditional top-down approach to reduce the scale of $G_1'$ in Figure 4(a) as follows: First, remove the 1-edge of $G_1'$, as the graph G scale is 5, you need to 5 times delete operation and obtain 5 sub-graph that its scale is 4, as shown in Figure 5, but (b) and (c), (d) and (e) are isomorphic in Figure 5, in order to reduce storage redundancy needs to be judged isomorphic. But, if we consider t $G_1'$ is symmetric graph, that delete the symmetric edge ($X_{01}$, a, $Z_{01}$) or ($X_{10}$, a, $Z_{10}$) will be the same composition, thereby to reduce the unnecessary operation and to improve algorithm efficiency. At the same time, it is also necessary that identify the local symmetry vertices in the graph, such as the symmetric vertex of $X_{02}$ and $X_{20}$ in Figure 3(b), as graph G2' reduced to the symmetric graph ($X_{02}$, a, $Z_0$, a, $X_{20}$), and then delete the edge (X, a, Z) can be reflected on the value of the symmetry vertex. So we proposed a property based on the symmetry as follows.

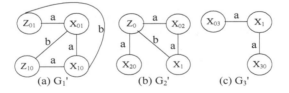

(a) $G_1'$        (b) $G_2'$        (c) $G_3'$

**Fig. 4.** Graph Dataset D'

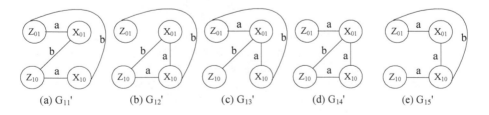

(a) $G_{11}'$        (b) $G_{12}'$        (c) $G_{13}'$        (d) $G_{14}'$        (e) $G_{15}'$

**Fig. 5.** K-1 Sub-graph Sets of Graph $G_1'$

**Property 11.** Given rule symmetric graph G(V,E), $e_1$, $e_2 \in E(G)$, if G' = G-$e_1$, G" = G-$e_2$, and $e_1$ and $e_2$ is a pair symmetric edge, then G' $\cong$ G".

**Proof:** According to the property 6 and the definition of graph isomorphism, we know that the symmetric graph must be auto-orphism, and exiting the corresponding symmetric edges. So, when remove the symmetry edge $e_1$, $e_2$ in rule symmetric graph G, can be obtained with the isomorphic graph G' and G". That is the property 11 is right.

Thus, in the case of known symmetric graph, the property of 10 and 11 simplifies the operation, which remove edge and the number of determine isomorphism, and then improved the algorithm efficiency without losing any result set.

### 3.3 Top-Down Mining Maximal Frequency Subgraph Based on Tree Structure

This paper, graph sets will be constructed to a two-way tree, calculate the support through the tree structure, and broken down the larger graph into a small graph, which each child node are obtained by removed an edge of his father node in the tree.

**Algorithm 2:** Top-Down mining maximal frequency subgraph (TD-MG)
    Input: Graphset D = {$G_1$, $G_2$, $G_3$} and *min_Sup* = 2;
    Output: The Maximal Frequency Subgraph Sets.
    Begin
    (1) Scanning graphset D and labeled it, record the attributed information of graphs and calculate the support of 1-edge;
    (2) Remove infrequent edges and local frequent edges by the property 8 and 9, obtain the storage table of frequent 1-edge, as show in Table 1, relabeled D into D' (Figure 3) using the symmetric, and the attribute information of graph as follows: GAI($G_1'$) = (4; 5; 2; X[2-3], Z[2-2]), GAI($G_2'$) = (4; 4; 2; X[3-2], Z[1-3]), GAI($G_3'$) = (3; 2; 1; X[3-2]);
    (3) Removed frequent 1-edge using the top-down method based on the property 10 and 11, establish tree and calculate the support, as shown in Figure 6.
      a) The root of tree is pretreatment graph set D'={G1', G2', G3'};
      b) The first layer nodes of the tree is graph Gi' which is the largest scale graph in D', D' = D' - $G_i'$, and record the support of $G_i'$ (for the first time, Sup($G_i'$) = 1), if there is more than the same scale graph, order by the order in graph set. For example, there is only one largest graph $G_1'$ in D , its scale is 5, and which is the first layer node in tree, $Sup(G_1')$ = 1, and then D' = {$G_2'$, $G_3'$};
      c) In reducing scale of G1' by removing 1-edge, reduce the operator number of deleted edge, determine isomorphic and the storage redundancy according to the property 11, and exclude non-composition using Algorithm 1, obtain G1' three sub-graphs of G1' that the scale is 4, as the second layer nodes, and calculate the support;
      d) Followed recursively, until finding all maximal frequent subgraphs of G1' so far, then established tree structure of graph G1';
      e) Continue to find the largest graph Gi' in the remaining sets D', and find to the corresponding layer of the tree. First of all, to determine isomorphism with graphs of the same layer, if existing isomorphism , with the pointer point to the graph  and add the attribute information of graph, support

cumulative; else, it as the last node in this layer, Sup(G1') = 1. For example, the largest graph is G2' in D' , which scale is 4 corresponds to the second layer node of the tree, first, determine to isomorphism comparison G2' with the second layer graphs, due to non-isomorphism, then it as the last node in this layer with other node together;

f) Due to Sup(Gi') ≤ min_Sup, reduce the graph Gi' scale and find to the maximal frequent subgraph of Gi', continue to construct the tree

g) Followed by recursion, Until D' = Φ.

Note: In order to express simple, link between the tree nodes is used double-way pointer, Node in the tree only shows he attribute information of graph, In the tree, the black point as a bifurcation point, that's it would be more than one sub-graphs when removed the edge of internal frequency is not 1, In the recursive process, labeled the layer and order of sub-graph, such as the $G_{11}'$, $G_{21}''$, etc.. $G_{11}'$ is the first K-1 sub-graph of $G_1'$, $G_{21}'$ is the first K-1 sub-graph of $G_2'$; the subscript of all sub-graphs of $G_1'$ are beginning with 1, the subscript of all sub-graphs of $G_2'$ are beginning with 2, similarly, can be get other label. So, we can calculation the number of super graph as long as find the different label of graph.

(4) Consture Tree T, as show in Figure 6, Shaded part of T for all frequently, to avoid output of non-maximal frequent subgraph, and need to verify it.

(5) Output the maximal frequent subgraphs sets.

End

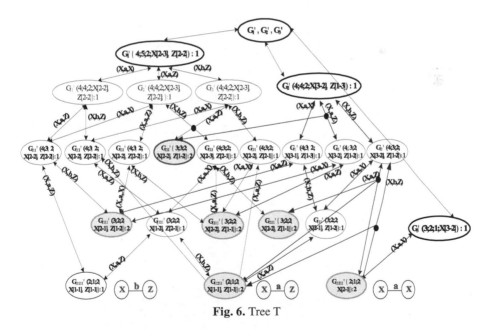

**Fig. 6.** Tree T

## 4  Experimental

Experimental environment: 2.26GHZ Intel Core i3 PC with 2G main memory, running Windows XP Professional SP3.

A comprehensive performance study has been conducted in our experiment on synthetic databases. We use a synthetic data *D10kT16V5E5* generator provided by Kuramochi and Karypis. In order to facilitate comparison with previous experiments, select *min_Sup* from 3% to 9% of the running time, the run time and the effect of maximal frequent subgraph's average size are shown in Figure7. Figure 7(a) shows the runtime with *min_Sup* varying form 10% to 3% on the synthetic dataset. Effect ofmaximal frequent subgraph's average size on running time is shown in Figure 7(b). As we can see through the data curve of coordinate, (1) the difference of run time is small when the support is high; (2) with the increasing of the support, the running time of sharp decline, the efficiency of the DT-CM algorithm to only show a slight increase in the data sets; (3) the result set of mining is the same basically, meanwhile, which is also verified the correctness of the algorithm. Experiments show that the DT-M algorithm is superior to Top-Down and MARGIN algorithm.

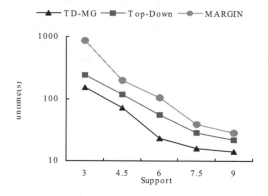

(a) The effect of support on runtime

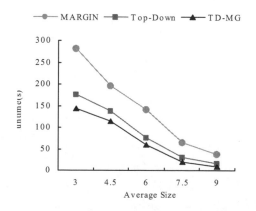

(b) Effect of maximal frequent subgraph's average size on running time

**Fig. 7.** The Experimental Result of Simulated Data Set

# 5 Conclusion

In this paper, we propose a new algorithm of top-down mining maximal frequent subgraph. We propose a new unique labeled apache by the graph symmetry, which is reduce the redundant storage and sacrificing space complexity; and reduced the number of determining graph isomorphism by the attribute information of graph. Our study shows that the algorithm outperforms other mining algorithms. However, we conduct the study on the premise of the symmetric of graph. Further researches are needed regarding how to judge the symmetric of graph, how to improve the accuracy and the efficiency of algorithm by the other structure and nature of graph.

**Acknowledgment.** This work is supported by the National Science Foundation of China, (No.60673136) Nation Science Program of Hebei Education Department (No.2009101) and Major Basic Research of Hebei Applied Basic Research Projects (No.10963527D). The authors also gratefully acknowledge the helpful comments and suggestions of the reviewers, which have improved the presentation.

# References

1. Han, J., Kamber, M.: Data Mining: Concepts and Techniques, pp. 79–165. Mechanical Industry Publishing, Beijing (2007), Translate by Fan, M., Men, X.f.
2. Thomas, L.T., Valluri, S.R., Karlapalem, K.: MARGIN: Maximal Frequent Subgraph Mining. In: Proc of ICMD 2006, Hong Kong, pp. 1097–1101 (2006)
3. Wang, Y.-l., Yang, B.-r., Song, Z.-f., Chen, Z., Li, L.-n.: New Algorithm for Mining Maximal Frequent Subgraphs. Journal of System Simulation 20(18), 4872–4877 (2008)
4. Guo, J., Chai, R., Li, J.: Top-Down Algorithm for Mining Maximal Frequent Subgraph. Advanced Materials Research 204 - 210, 1472–1476 (2011)
5. Chakrabarti, D., Flaoutsos, C.: Graph mining: laws, generators, and algorithms. ACM Computing Surveys 38(1), 1–69 (2006)
6. Gouda, K., Zaki, M.J.: Efficiently Mining Maximal Frequent Itemsets, pp. 101–108. Springer Press, New York (2002)
7. Chen, X.: How to Confirm Isomorphic of Graph, http://www.paper.edu.cn
8. Zou, X., Chen, X., Guo, J., Zhao, L.: An improved algorithm for mining CloseGraph. ICIC Express Letters Journal of Research and Surveys 4(4), 1135–1140 (2010)

# Dynamic ID-Based Password Authentication Protocol with Strong Security against Smart Card Lost Attacks

Qi Xie

School of Information Science and Engineering,
Hangzhou Normal University Hangzhou 310036, China
qixie68@yahoo.com.cn

**Abstract.** Seeing that the existing dynamic ID-based password authentication protocols are vulnerable to various attacks, a novel dynamic ID-based password authentication protocol using smart card is proposed. Compared to the existing protocols, the proposed protocol can protect the user's anonymity, can resist the password guessing attacks and smart card lost attacks. On the other hand, our protocol has many advantages, such as perfect forward security, no verification tables, no server's public key and timestamp. To the best of my knowledge, this is the first secure dynamic ID-based password authentication protocol.

**Keywords:** password authentication protocol, dynamic ID, smart card, anonymity.

## 1 Introduction

In order to access any resource of the remote server, the user and the server should pass through the mutual authentication in public networks. Password authentication is one of the simplest and the most widely used strategies, because the user only needs to use the short password. However, one of the major challenges of designing password authentication protocols is how to resist the password guessing attacks, as password is supposed to be easy-to-remember, and the password space is small.

In 1981, Lamport [1] proposed the first password authentication protocol with verification table, but this protocol is insecure if the verification table was modified or stolen. Therefore, how to design smart card based password authentication protocols without verification table is an important research topic. In 1993, Chang-Wu [2] introduced password authentication scheme with smart cards using public-key cryptography, but it requires high computation cost for implementation and public key directory for maintain and protection. Thus, many researchers dedicated to design password authentication schemes with smart cards without server's public key, and proposed many schemes [3-8]. However, most of them have been broken shortly after they were proposed [5-8]. Especially, most of the existing schemes are vulnerable to the off-line password guessing attacks if all the secret numbers stored in the smart card are disclosure.

In most of the proposed user authentication protocols the user's identity was static. Thus, it will leak partial information about the user to the adversary over an insecure channel, and cannot protect the user's privacy. Therefore, Das et al.[9] proposed a

P. Sénac, M. Ott, and A. Seneviratne (Eds.): ICWCA 2011, LNICST 72, pp. 412–418, 2012.
© Institute for Computer Sciences, Social Informatics and Telecommunications Engineering 2012

dynamic ID-based remote user authentication scheme using smart cards in 2004. Though their scheme has many advantages, Awashti [10] showed that their scheme is insecure, because no password is required to authenticate the user. Chien-Chen [11], Ku-Chang [12] and Liao et al.[13] also pointed out that Das et al.'s scheme cannot protect the user's anonymity, suffers from impersonation attack and guessing attacks, respectively. Moreover, Liao et al. proposed an improved scheme, but Misbahuddin et al. [14] showed that their scheme cannot resist impersonation attack and reflection attack. Recently, Wang et al. [15] proposed another improved dynamic ID-based remote user authentication scheme and claimed that their scheme is more efficient and secure than Das et al.'s scheme. However, Khan et al. [16] showed that their scheme has four weaknesses and proposed an improved scheme. In 2010, He et al. [17] pointed out that Khan et al.'s scheme still suffers from three weaknesses. Thus, Das et al. and all the improved schemes are insecure.

In this paper, we proposed a novel dynamic ID-based password authentication protocol using smart card. Compared to the existing protocols, the proposed protocol can protect the user's anonymity, can resist the password guessing attacks and smart card lost attacks. On the other hand, our protocol has many advantages, such as perfect forward security, no verification tables, no server's public key and timestamp.

## 2 The Proposed Protocol

In this section, we propose a novel dynamic ID-based user authentication protocol, which consists of three phases: user registration, authentication and session key generation, password change.

The following notations are used throughout this paper:

- $p, q$ : two large prime numbers, such as $q \mid p-1$ .
- $g$ : a primitive element for $GF(p)$ with order $q$ .
- $U_i$ : the user.
- $S$ : the server.
- $ID_i$ : $U_i$ 's identity.
- $SC$ : smart card.
- $PW_i$ : $U_i$ 's password.
- $x$ : $S$ 's secret number.
- $SK$ : a session key between $U_i$ and $S$ .
- $h()$ : a secure one-way hash function.

### 2.1 User Registration

$U_i$ and $S$ carry out the following steps during the user registration phase

Step 1: $U_i$ chooses his password $PW_i$ and identity $ID_i$, and sends $ID_i$ to $S$ .

Step 2: After receiving $ID_i$ from $U_i$ , $S$ computes

$$N_0 = h(ID_i)^x \bmod p , \tag{1}$$

where $x$ is the secret number of $S$. $S$ stores $ID_i$, one-way hash function $h()$ and $N_0$ into a smart card ($SC$ for short) and issues this smart card to $U_i$ via secure communication channel.

Step 3: When $SC$ is available, $U_i$ inserts $SC$ into a terminal device, keys his password $PW_i$, then $SC$ computes

$$N_i = N_0 \oplus h(PW_i) = h(ID_i)^x \oplus h(PW_i) \bmod p , \tag{2}$$

and replaces $N_0$ with $N_i$.

## 2.2  Authentication and Session Key Generation

When $U_i$ is about to logon to the server $S$, $U_i$ and $S$ carry out the following protocol. Figure 1 illustrates this phase.

Step 1: $U_i$ inserts smart card into a terminal device, keys his password $PW_i$, $SC$ generates random nonce $b$ and $k$, computes

$$N_s = g^k \bmod p , \tag{3}$$

$$CID = h(ID_i)^b \bmod p , \tag{4}$$

$$C_0 = (N_i \oplus h(PW_i))^b = h(ID_i)^{xb} \bmod p , \tag{5}$$

$$C_1 = C_0 \oplus N_s = h(ID_i)^{xb} \oplus N_s \bmod p , \tag{6}$$

Then $U_i$ sends $(C_1, CID)$ to $S$.

Step 2: After receiving $(C_1, CID)$, $S$ generates a random nonce $d$, computes

$$N_u = g^d \bmod p , \tag{7}$$

$$N_s = C_1 \oplus CID^x \bmod p , \tag{8}$$

$$h(N_s^d) , \tag{9}$$

and sends $(h(N_s^d), N_u)$ to $U_i$.

Step 3: When $h(N_s^d)$ and $N_u$ are available, $U_i$ computes $h(N_u^k)$, and checks if

$$h(N_s^d) = h(N_u^k) . \tag{10}$$

If so, then $S$ is authenticated, $U_i$ computes and sends $h(N_u^k + 1)$ to $S$. Otherwise, abort.

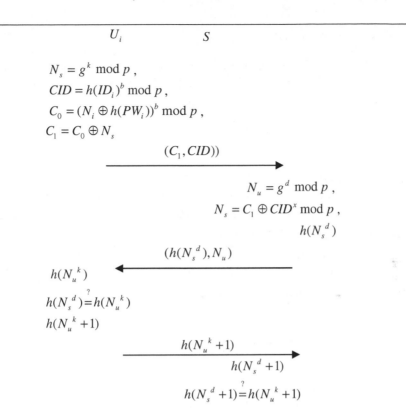

$$N_s = g^k \bmod p \,,$$
$$CID = h(ID_i)^b \bmod p \,,$$
$$C_0 = (N_i \oplus h(PW_i))^b \bmod p \,,$$
$$C_1 = C_0 \oplus N_s$$

$$(C_1, CID))$$

$$N_u = g^d \bmod p \,,$$
$$N_s = C_1 \oplus CID^x \bmod p \,,$$
$$h(N_s^d)$$

$$(h(N_s^d), N_u)$$

$$h(N_u^k)$$
$$h(N_s^d) \overset{?}{=} h(N_u^k)$$
$$h(N_u^k + 1)$$

$$h(N_u^k + 1)$$
$$h(N_s^d + 1)$$
$$h(N_s^d + 1) \overset{?}{=} h(N_u^k + 1)$$

Session key: $SK = h(N_u^k + 2) = h(N_s^d + 2)$

**Fig. 1.** Authentication and session key generation phase

Step 4: After receiving $h(N_u^k + 1)$, $S$ computes $h(N_s^d + 1)$ and checks if

$$h(N_s^d + 1) = h(N_u^k + 1) \tag{11}$$

If so, then $U_i$ is authenticated.

The session key shared between $U_i$ and $S$ is

$$SK = h(N_u^k + 2) = h(N_s^d + 2) \,. \tag{12}$$

## 2.3  Password Change

When $U_i$ wants to change his password, he inserts smart card into a terminal device, keys his old password $PW_i$ and the new password $PW_{new}$, the $SC$ computes

$$N_{new} = h(PW_i) \oplus N_i \oplus h(PW_{new}) \,, \tag{13}$$

and replaces $N_i$ with $N_{new}$.

# 3  Security Analysis

In this section, we show that the proposed scheme can resist all sorts of the existing attacks. To the best of my knowledge, this is the first secure dynamic ID-based password authentication protocol.

## 3.1  Password Guessing Attack and Smart Card Lost Attack

If an attacker obtains $N_i = h(ID_i)^x \oplus h(PW_i) \bmod p$ stored in the user $U_i$'s smart card, and wants to guess the password $PW_i$ by the following two cases.

Case 1: Attacker does off-line password guessing attack by eavesdropping the interactive messages between $U_i$ and $S$. Obviously, the attacker can get all interactive messages $(C_1, CID))$, $(h(N_s^d), N_u)$ and $h(N_u^k + 1)$, where $N_s = g^k \bmod p$ and $N_u = g^d \bmod p$, $N_u^k$ and $N_s^d$ are the Diffie-Hellman values of $N_u$ and $N_s$, which include the random nonce $k$ and $d$. However, the attacker cannot find the relationship between $h(ID_i)^x$ and interactive messages $(C_1, CID))$ without knowing $x$ and $b$. Therefore, an attacker cannot verify whether his guessed password is right or not.

Case 2: If an attacker does on-line password guessing attack, it is still impossible. Since the attacker can guess the password $PW_i'$ and compute

$$C_0' = (N_i \oplus PW_i')^e, \tag{14}$$

$$C_1' = C_0' \oplus g^f, \tag{15}$$

$$CID' = h(ID_i)^e \tag{16}$$

for randomly chosen $e$ and $f$, and sends $(C_1', CID'))$ to $S$, but he cannot generate the right $h(N_u^e + 1)$ for $S$. Therefore, $S$ can detect the attacker.

## 3.2  Replay Attack

If an attacker replay user $U_i$'s login message $CID = h(ID_i)^b \bmod p$ and $C_1 = C_0 \oplus N_s = h(ID_i)^{xb} \oplus N_s \bmod p$, $S$ can retrieve $N_s$ but the attacker cannot. $S$ can return the authentication message $h(N_s^d)$ and $N_u$, which include the random nonce $d$ and Diffie-Hellman value $N_s^d$, but the attacker cannot verify whether the authentication message $h(N_s^d)$ is right or not. On the other hand, the attacker cannot generate the authentication message $h(N_u^k + 1)$ and pass through the authentication of $S$. Therefore, the proposed protocol can resist the replay attack.

### 3.3  Impersonation Attack and Forgery Attack

If a legal user $U_v$ wants to impersonate $U_i$ to pass through the authentication of $S$, but it is impossible. The reason is that $U_v$ cannot generate the correct authentication message $h(N_u^{\ k} + 1)$ and pass through the authentication of $S$ without knowing the $U_i$'s password.

### 3.4  Perfect Forward Security

In proposed protocol, the session key is forward security. Since an attacker cannot obtain all the random nonce $k$ and $d$, even if he knows the user's password $PW_i$, $S$'s secret number $x$, $N_i$, $N_u$ and $N_s$. So he cannot get the Diffie-Hellman values $N_u^{\ k}$ or $N_s^{\ d}$ between the server and the user. Therefore, an attacker cannot compute

$$SK = h(N_u^{\ k} + 2) = h(N_s^{\ d} + 2). \qquad (17)$$

### 3.5  Known Key Security

In proposed protocol, because the session key $SK = h(N_u^{\ k} + 2) = h(N_s^{\ d} + 2)$ is dependent to the random nonce $k$ and $d$, which are different to other sessions. Therefore, an attacker cannot know the previous or the future session keys when he gets one session key.

### 3.6  The User's Anonymity and Untraceability

In proposed protocol, the user $U_i$'s $ID_i$ is hidden in the authentication messages $CID = h(ID_i)^b \bmod p$ and $C_1 = C_0 \oplus N_s = h(ID_i)^{xb} \oplus N_s \bmod p$, which include the one-time-used random nonce $b$. Therefore, our protocol keeps user's anonymity and untraceability.

## 4  Conclusions

In this paper, we proposed the first secure dynamic ID-based password authentication protocol. Compared to the existing protocols, the proposed protocol has many advantages, for example, it can protect the user's anonymity; can resist the password guessing attacks and smart card lost attacks.

**Acknowledgments.** This research was supported by National Natural Science Foundation of China (No.61070153).

# References

1. Lamport, L.: Password Authentication with Insecure Communication. Communications of the ACM 24, 770–772 (1981)
2. Chang, C.C., Wu, T.C.: Remote Password Authentication with Smart Cards. IEE Proceedings-E Computers and Digital Techniques 138, 165–168 (1993)
3. Hsiang, H.C., Shih, W.K.: Weaknesses and Improvements of the Yoon–Ryu–Yoo Remote User Authentication Scheme using Smart Cards. Computer Communications 32, 649–652 (2009)
4. Kim, S.K., Chung, M.G.: More Secure Remote User Authentication Scheme. Computer Communications 32, 1018–1021 (2009)
5. Munilla, J., Peinado, A.: Off-line Password-guessing Attack to Peyravian-Jeffries's Remote User Authentication Protocol. Computer Communications 30, 52–54 (2006)
6. Shim, K.A.: Security Flaws of Remote User Access over Insecure Networks. Computer Communications 30, 117–121 (2006)
7. Hölbl, M., Welzer, T., Brumen, B.: Improvement of the Peyravian-Jeffries's User Authentication Protocol and Password Change Protocol. Computer Communications 31, 1945–1951 (2008)
8. Munilla, J., Peinado, A.: Security Flaw of Hölblet et al.'s Protocol. Computer Communications 32, 736–739 (2009)
9. Das, M.L., Saxena, A., Gulati, V.P.: A dynamic ID-based Remote User Authentication Scheme. IEEE Transactions on Consumer Electronics 50, 629–631 (2004)
10. Awashti, A.K.: Comment on a Dynamic ID-based Remote User Authentication Scheme. Transactions on Cryptology 1, 15–16 (2004)
11. Chien, H.Y., Chen, C.H.: A Remote Authentication Scheme Preserving User Anonymity. In: International Conference on AINA 2005, vol. 2, pp. 245–248 (2005)
12. Ku, W.C., Chang, S.T.: Impersonation Attack on a Dynamic ID-based Remote User Authentication Scheme using Smart Cards. IEICE Transactions on Communications, E88-B, 2165–2167 (2005)
13. Liao, I.E., Lee, C.C., Hwang, M.S.: Security Enhancement for a Dynamic ID-based Remote User Authentication Scheme. In: International Conference on Next Generation Web Services Practices (2005)
14. Misbahuddin, M., Bindu, C.S.: Cryptanalysis of Liao–Lee–Hwang's Dynamic ID Scheme. International Journal of Network Security 6, 211–213 (2008)
15. Wang, Y.Y., Kiu, J.Y., Xiao, F.X., Dan, J.: A More Efficient and Secure Dynamic ID-based Remote User Authentication Scheme. Computer Communications 32, 583–585 (2009)
16. Khan, M.K., Kim, S.K., Alghathbar, K.: Cryptanalysis and Security Enhancement of a 'more efficient & secure dynamic ID-based remote user authentication scheme'. Computer Communications 34, 305–309 (2011)
17. He, D.B., Chen, J.H., Hu, J.: Weaknesses of a Dynamic ID-based Remote User Authentication Scheme, http://eprint.iacr.org/2010/240

# Two Attacks on Dutta's Dynamic Group Key Agreement Protocol

Hui Zhang, Chunxiang Xu, Chengbang Li[*], and Abdur Rashid Sangi

School of Computer Science and Engineering,
University of Electronic Science and Technology of China,
Chengdu, 61173, China
zzhui@yahoo.com.cn, chxxu@uestc.edu.cn, jeriffe@163.com

**Abstract.** Ratna Dutta and Rana Barua proposed a dynamic group key agreement protocol with constant round referred to as DGKA protocol. They claimed that the DGKA protocol is dynamic, efficient and provably secure under DDH assumption. In this paper, we analyze the security of the DGKA protocol and discovered its vulnerable nature towards two attacks. The first attack relates to the fact that this protocol does not satisfy the key independence property which is crucial for dynamic group key agreement protocol. The second one is an impersonation attack which demonstrates that the DGKA protocol is vulnerable to replay attacks.

## 1 Introduction

A group key agreement protocol allows a group of users to communicate over an untrusted, public network to share a common secret value called a session key. The session key can be later used in other security services providing communication privacy and integrity. Therefore the group key agreement protocol is fundamental for the other security mechanisms in group applications and received particular attention. Based on public key infrastructure, a group key agreement with authentication mechanism [3, 7, 1, 8, 2, 11, 12, 17], allows group users to agree upon a common secret key even in the presence of active adversaries. In a dynamic group key agreement, users can join or leave the group at any time. Such schemes should ensure the freshness of session key while any membership changes, hence the subsequent sessions remain protected from the members who left and the previous sessions remain protected from newly joining members. In recent years, quite a number of dynamic group key agreement protocols [4, 5, 6, 15, 13, 14, 17] have been proposed. In ISC 2005, Dutta et al. [9, 10] proposed a constant round authenticated group key agreement protocol (referred to as DGKA protocol) in dynamic scenario. They claimed that the DGKA protocol is dynamic and efficient. Compared with the authenticated group key agreement [12] the DGKA protocol requires less communication rounds.

---

[*] This research was sponsored by the National High Technology Research and Devel-opment Program (863 Program) of China(2009AA01Z415).

P. Sénac, M. Ott, and A. Seneviratne (Eds.): ICWCA 2011, LNICST 72, pp. 419–425, 2012.
© Institute for Computer Sciences, Social Informatics and Telecommunications Engineering 2012

In this paper, however, we discovered that this protocol is vulnerable to two attacks. The first attack relates to the fact that this protocol does not satisfy the key independence property which is crucial for dynamic group key agreement protocol. The second one is an impersonation attack which demonstrates that the authentication of the DGKA protocol is vulnerable to replay attacks.

This paper is organized as follows: In Section 2, we briefly review the DGKA protocol. Two attacks on DGKA protocol are described in Section 3. Finally, our conclusions are given in Section 4.

# 2   Review of DGKA Protocol

This section briefly reviews the DGKA group key agreement protocol [10].

All group members $\{U_1, \cdots, U_n\}$ which will establish a common session key among themselves are logically ordered into a cycle, i.e., the indices are taken modulo n so that user $U_0$ is $U_n$ and user $U_{n+1}$ is $U_1$. All mathematical operations are performed in a cyclic group $G$ of some large prime order $q$ with $g$ as a generator. It is assumed that the description of $G$ is implicitly known to all users. The protocol also uses a standard digital signature scheme $DSig = (K, S, V)$ for authentication. $K$ is the key generation algorithm which generates a signing key $sk_i$ and a verification key $pk_i$ for each user $U_i$, $S$ is the signature generation algorithm and $V$ is the signature verification algorithm. The protocol proceeds as follows.

## 2.1   Key Agreement Procedure

Round 1:   Each user $U_i$ randomly chooses a secret value $x_i \in Z_q^*$, computes $X_i = g^{x_i}$ and $\sigma_i = S_{sk_i}(M_i)$ where $M_i = U_i \| 1 \| X_i$, then sends $M_i | \sigma_i$ to $U_{i-1}$ and $U_{i+1}$ (note that $U_0 = U_n$ and $U_{n+1} = U_1$)

Round 2: Each user $U_i$, on receiving $M_{i-1} | \sigma_{i-1}$ from $U_{i-1}$ and $M_{i+1} | \sigma_{i+1}$ from $U_{i+1}$, verifies $\sigma_{i-1}$ on $M_{i-1}$ and $\sigma_{i+1}$ on $M_{i+1}$ using the verification algorithm $V$ and the respective verification keys $pk_{i-1}$, $pk_{i+1}$; if verification fails, aborts; else $U_i$ computes the left key $K_i^L = X_{i-1}^{x_i}$, the right key $K_i^R = X_{i+1}^{x_i}$, $Y_i = K_i^R / K_i^L$ and signature $\bar{\sigma}_i = S_{sk_i}(\overline{M}_i)$ where $\overline{M}_i = U_i \| 2 \| Y_i \| d_i$ ( $d_i$ is the instance number generated by counter); then sends $\overline{M}_i | \bar{\sigma}_i$ to the rest of the users.

(Note that $K_i^R = K_{i+1}^L$ for $1 \le i \le n-1$, $K_n^R = K_1^L$ and $K_{i+(n-1)}^R = K_i^L$.)

Key Computation: Each user $U_i$, on receiving $\overline{M}_j | \bar{\sigma}_j$ from $U_j$ verifies $\bar{\sigma}_j$ on $\overline{M}_j$ using the verification algorithm $V$ and the verification key $pk_j$; if verification fails, abort; else, $U_i$ computes $\overline{K}_{i+j}^R = Y_{i+j} \overline{K}_{i+(j-1)}^R$; $U_i$ verifies if $K_{i+(n-1)}^R = \overline{K}_{i+(n-1)}^R$; if verification fails, aborts; else, $U_i$ computes the session key $sk_{U_i}^{d_i} = \overline{K}_1^R \overline{K}_2^R \cdots \overline{K}_n^R$, the seed $x = H(sk_{U_i}^{d_i})$ and stores $K_i^L$, $K_i^R$. ($H$ is a hash function $H : \{0,1\}^* \rightarrow Z_q^*$.)

The session key $sk = g^{x_1 x_2 + x_2 x_3 + \cdots + x_n x_1}$.

## 2.2 Join Procedure

Suppose a set of $\{U_{n+1}, \cdots, U_{n+m}\}$ with secret values $x_{n+1}, \cdots, x_{n+m}$ want to join the group $\{U_1, \cdots, U_n\}$. It is assumed that after the $m$ users $U_{n+1}, \cdots, U_{n+m}$ joined the group, the new cycle is $U_1, \cdots U_n, U_{n+1}, \cdots, U_{n+m}$, $U_{n+m} = U_0$ and $U_{n+m+1} = U_1$. During the join procedure, users $U_2, \cdots, U_{n-1}$ are considered to be one user $U$ with the secret value $x$, and then the new group $\{U_1, U, U_n, U_{n+1}, \cdots, U_{n+m}\}$ executes the Key Agreement Procedure. Let $U_2$ computes and sends the message on behalf of $U$ and the remaining users $U_3, \cdots, U_{n-1}$ just receive the messages sent to $U$. At the end of the procedure, all the $n+m$ users are able to reach the new session key $sk' = g^{x_1 x + x x_n + x_n x_{n+1} + \cdots + x_{n+m} x_1}$.

## 2.3 Leave Procedure

Suppose $\{U_1, \cdots, U_n\}$ is a set of users with secret values $x_1, \cdots, x_n$ and an execution of Key Agreement Procedure has already been done. Let $K_i^L$, $K_i^R$, $1 \le i \le n$ be left and right keys respectively of $U_i$ computed and stored in this session. And suppose the users $U_{l_1}, \cdots, U_{l_m} \in \{U_1, \cdots, U_n\}$ want to leave the group. Then the new user set would be $\{U_1, \cdots, U_{l_1-L}\} \cup \{U_{l_1+R}, \cdots, U_{l_2-L}\} \cup \cdots \cup \{U_{l_m+R}, \cdots, U_n\}$ where $U_{l_i-L}$ and $U_{l_i+R}$ are respectively the closest remaining left and right neighbors of $U_{l_i}, 1 \le i \le m$.

Round 1: For each leaving user $U_{l_i}$, let $j_1 = l_i - L$, $j_2 = l_i + R$;

$U_{j_1}$, $U_{j_2}$ respectively choose the secrets randomly $x_{j_1}$, $x_{j_2} \in Z_q^*$, compute $X_{j_1} = g^{x_{j_1}}$, $X_{j_2} = g^{x_{j_2}}$ and $\sigma_{j_1} = S_{sk_{j_1}}(M_{j_1})$, $\sigma_{j_2} = S_{sk_{j_2}}(M_{j_2})$ where $M_{j_1} = U_{j_1} \| 1 \| X_{j_1} \| d_{j_1}$, $M_{j_2} = U_{j_2} \| 1 \| X_{j_2} \| d_{j_2}$

$U_{j_1}$ sends $M_{j_1} \| \sigma_{j_1}$ to $U_{j_1-1}$ and $U_{j_2}$;

$U_{j_2}$ sends $M_{j_2} \| \sigma_{j_2}$ to $U_{j_1}$ and $U_{j_2+1}$;

Round 2: For each leaving user $U_{l_i}$, let $j_1 = l_i - L$, $j_2 = l_i + R$;

$U_{j_1-1}$ and $U_{j_2}$ on receiving $M_{j_1} \| \sigma_{j_1}$ form $U_{j_1}$ verifies $\sigma_{j_1}$ on $M_{j_1}$ using the verification key $pk_{j_1}$;

$U_{j_1}$ and $U_{j_2+1}$ on receiving $M_{j_2} \| \sigma_{j_2}$ form $U_{j_2}$ verifies $\sigma_{j_2}$ on $M_{j_2}$ using the verification key $pk_{j_2}$;

If any of these verifications fails, aborts, otherwise $U_{j_1}$ modifies its left key $K_{j_1}^L = X_{j_1-1}^{x_{j_1}}$ and right key $K_{j_1}^R = X_{j_2}^{x_{j_1}}$;

$U_{j_2}$ modifies its left key $K_{j_2}^L = X_{j_1}^{x_{j_2}}$ and right key $K_{j_2}^R = X_{j_2+1}^{x_{j_2}}$;

$U_{j_1-1}$ modifies its right key $K_{j_1-1}^R = X_{j_1}^{x_{j_1-1}}$ ;

$U_{j_2+1}$ modifies its left key $K_{j_2+1}^L = X_{j_2}^{x_{j_2+1}}$

Then, re-index the $n-m$ users by $V_1, \cdots, V_{n-m}$ and $\{\hat{K}_1^L, \cdots, \hat{K}_{n-m}^L\}$, $\{\hat{K}_1^R, \cdots, \hat{K}_{n-m}^R\}$ respectively be the set of corresponding left and right keys.

Each user $V_i$ computes $Y_i = \hat{K}_i^R / \hat{K}_i^L$ and signature $\hat{\sigma}_i = S_{sk_i}(\hat{M}_i)$ where $\hat{M}_i = V_i | 2 | Y_i | d_i$ ;

$V_i$ sends $\hat{M}_i | \hat{\sigma}_i$ to the rest of the users in $\{V_1, \cdots, V_{n-m}\}$ ;

Key Computation: Each user $V_i$ on receiving $\overline{M}_j | \overline{\sigma}_j$ from $V_j$ ( $1 \le j \le n-m$, $j \ne i$ ), verifies $\overline{\sigma}_j$ on $\overline{M}_j$ using the verification algorithm $V$ and the verification key $pk_j$ ;

If verification fails, aborts, otherwise $V_i$ computes $\overline{K}_{i+1}^R = Y_{i+1} \overline{K}_i^R$ ;

For each $j$, $2 \le j \le n-m-1$, $V_i$ computes $\overline{K}_{i+j}^R = Y_{i+j} \overline{K}_{i+(j-1)}^R$ ;

$V_i$ verifies if $\hat{K}_{i+(n-m-1)}^R = \overline{K}_{i+(n-m-1)}^R$, if verification fails, then aborts, else $V_i$ computes the session key $sk = \overline{K}_1^R \overline{K}_2^R \cdots \overline{K}_{n-m}^R$, the seed $x = H(sk)$ and stores $\hat{K}_i^L$, $\hat{K}_i^R$.

# 3  The Attacks on DGKA Protocol

## 3.1  Attack Mounted by Leaving Users

The DGKA protocol is a dynamic group key agreement protocol and provides mechanisms to process member addition and deletion. However, there are some problems in the leaving mechanism. This attack shows that the DGKA protocol doesn't satisfy the key independence property [16] which encompasses the following requirements:

(1) Old, previously used group keys can not be discovered by new group member(s). In other words, a group member can not have knowledge of the keys used before it joins the group.

(2) New keys are required to remain out of reach from former group members.

Precisely, we find that the DGKA protocol does not meet the second requirement. That is, the leaving user can compute the newly generated group key after the remaining users execute the Leave Procedure.

We firstly choose the simplest scenario to demonstrate this attack. Suppose $P = \{U_1, \cdots, U_n\}$ be the set of $n$ users. They have executed the protocol for group key agreement and obtained the session key $sk$. $U_j$ is a malicious user, whose goal is to compute the new session key $sk'$ after it leaves the group. To be concise, we suppose $U_j$ is the only user who leaves the group and we do not re-index the users during the execution of the leave procedure.

As a malicious user, $U_j$ makes the following preparations for computing the new session key $sk'$. During the key agreement procedure, $U_j$ stored all the right keys $\overline{K}_1^R, \overline{K}_2^R, \cdots, \overline{K}_n^R$ it computed. After $U_j$ leaves the group, the rest $n-1$ users $P/\{U_j\}$ execute the leave procedure to obtain a new session key. At this moment, $U_j$

eavesdrops the session among $P/\{U_j\}$ and obtains all the information $\hat{M}_i \mid \hat{\sigma}_i$ which will be sent out by $U_i$ during Round 2 of the leave procedure ($U_i \in P/\{U_j\}$).

Up to now, $U_j$ has the following information: all the right keys of the key agreement procedure before $U_j$ leaves: $\overline{K}_1^R, \overline{K}_2^R, \cdots, \overline{K}_n^R$; all the $Y_i$, $Y_i = \hat{K}_i^R / \hat{K}_i^L$, which can be extracted from $\hat{M}_i$ ($1 \le i \le n, i \ne j$, $\hat{K}_i^L$, $\hat{K}_i^R$ are the left keys and right keys corresponding to the leave procedure). According to the DGKA protocol, during the leave procedure only three users $(U_{j-2}, U_{j-1}, U_{j+1})$ have to change their right keys and three users $(U_{j-1}, U_{j+1}, U_{j+2})$ have to change their left keys. Therefore, we have $\overline{K}_i^R = \hat{K}_i^R$ ($i \ne j-2, j-1, j, j+1$;). $U_j$ can compute the right keys of $U_{j-2}, U_{j-1}, U_{j+1}$ in following ways: $\hat{K}_{j-2}^L = \hat{K}_{j-3}^R = \overline{R}_{j-3}^R$, $\hat{K}_{j-2}^R = Y_{j-2} \cdot \hat{K}_{j-2}^L = \hat{K}_{j-1}^L$, $\hat{K}_{j-1}^R = Y_{j-1} \cdot \hat{K}_{j-1}^L = \hat{K}_{j+1}^L$, $\hat{K}_{j+1}^R = Y_{j+1} \cdot \hat{K}_{j+1}^L$. Then $U_j$ can get all the right keys of the new group users and compute the new session key $sk' = \hat{K}_1^R \hat{K}_2^R \cdots \hat{K}_{j-1}^R \hat{K}_{j+1}^R \cdots \hat{K}_n^R$.

In the illustration above, we assume there is only one user which leaves the group. Actually, if there are more users leaving at the same time, any malicious user can mount an attack and obtain the new session key successfully as long as there are more than two adjacent users which keep their secret values unchanged in the leave procedure. So, let more users change their secret values besides the neighbors of the leaving users and make sure that there are no two or more adjacent users whose secret values keep unchanged. Only in this way, this attack can be avoided.

### 3.2 Replay Attack by Two Malicious Users

In [10], the authors said they modified the Katz-Yung [12] technique to achieve authentication in the DGKA protocol. Compared with Katz and Yung's technique, the DGKA protocol does not use nonces as part of the signed message and that's why the DGKA protocol requires only 2 rounds. However, nonces (used in KY authentication technique) are essential to resist replay attacks. Without the nonces in the signed message, the users can not judge whether the message it received is a fresh or a replay one.

After analyzing the DGKA protocol, we find that any two malicious users whose logic indexes are not adjacent in the former execution of the protocol may mount a replay attack in new protocol executions. Through the attack, these two malicious users can make the other honest users believe that they have already gained a session key among the group. However, some of the users actually did not participate in the execution of the protocol but were impersonated by these two malicious users replaying some messages.

Suppose $P = \{U_1, \cdots, U_n\}$ be a set of $n$ users who have executed the protocol for group key agreement and obtained the session key. $U_i$ and $U_j$ are two malicious users and $j > i+1$. In addition to normal actions, following preparations should be made by $U_i$ and $U_j$ for the replay attack during the execution of the protocol.

Round 1: Store the secret value $x_i$ and $x_j$ they selected.
Round 2: $U_i$ stores its right key $K_i^R$, $U_j$ stores its left key $K_j^L$, one of them stores all the messages $\overline{M}_k \mid \overline{\sigma}_k$ they receive, $i < k < j$

After finishing a regular key agreement, user $U_i$ and $U_j$ can mount a new one in which $U_k$ $(i < k < j)$ are impersonated by some malicious users. These malicious users are in collusion with $U_i$ and $U_j$ or even may be $U_i$ and $U_j$ themselves.

The actions of $U_i$, $U_j$ and the malicious users are as following during the new group key agreement:

$U_i$ acts as follow:

Round 1: Reads the stored secret value $x_i$, computes $X_i = g^{x_i}$ and $\sigma_i = S_{sk_i}(M_i)$ where $M_i = U_i \| 1 \| X_i$, then sends $M_i \mid \sigma_i$ to $U_{i-1}$.

Round 2: On receiving $M_{i-1} \mid \sigma_{i-1}$ from $U_{i-1}$, verifies $\sigma_{i-1}$ on $M_{i-1}$ using the verification algorithm $V$ and the respective verification keys $pk_{i-1}$; if verification fails, aborts; else $U_i$ computes the left key $K_i^L = X_{i-1}^{x_i}$, read the stored right key $K_i^R$, computes $Y_i = K_i^R / K_i^L$ and signature $\overline{\sigma}_i = S_{sk_i}(\overline{M}_i)$ where $\overline{M}_i = U_i \| 2 \| Y_i \| d_i$; then sends $\overline{M}_i \mid \overline{\sigma}_i$ to the rest of the users.

Key Computation: Acts as normal.

$U_j$ acts as follow:

Round 1: Reads the stored secret value $x_j$, computes $X_j = g^{x_j}$ and $\sigma_j = S_{sk_j}(M_j)$ where $M_j = U_j \| 1 \| X_j$, then sends $M_j \mid \sigma_j$ to $U_{j+1}$.

Round 2: On receiving $M_{j+1} \mid \sigma_{j+1}$ from $U_{j+1}$, verifies $\sigma_{j+1}$ on $M_{j+1}$ using the verification algorithm $V$ and the respective verification keys $pk_{j+1}$; if verification fails, aborts; else $U_i$ computes the right key $K_j^R = X_{j+1}^{x_j}$, read the stored left key $K_j^L$, computes $Y_j = K_j^R / K_j^L$ and signature $\overline{\sigma}_j = S_{sk_j}(\overline{M}_j)$ where $\overline{M}_j = U_j \| 2 \| Y_j \| d_j$; then sends $\overline{M}_j \mid \overline{\sigma}_j$ to the rest of the users.

Key Computation: Acts as normal.

The $j$-$i$-1 malicious users who impersonate $U_{i+1}, \cdots U_{j-1}$:

    Round 1: Do nothing.

    Round 2: Each fake $U_k$ $(i < k < j)$ who have already gotten the message $\overline{M}_k \mid \overline{\sigma}_k$ from $U_i$ or $U_j$ sends $\overline{M}_k \mid \overline{\sigma}_k$ to the rest of the users.

Key Computation: Act as a normal legitimate user.

The remaining legitimate users cannot distinguish a replay attack from a normal key agreement. The only messages they receive from these fake users are $\overline{M}_k \mid \overline{\sigma}_k$ $(i < k < j)$, each $\overline{\sigma}_k$ is definitely a valid signature for $\overline{M}_k$ which is signed by user $U_k$. However, as the message $\overline{M}_k = U_k \| 2 \| Y_k \| d_k$ does not contain any information to keep it fresh, the honest users can't judge whether $\overline{M}_k$ a replayed message is. To avoid this attack, in our opinions, the mechanism of nonces [12] should be adopted in the protocol.

# 4 Conclusions

In this paper, we analyzed the security of the dynamic group key agreement protocol proposed by Dutta et al. in ISC 2005 and later published in IEEE Transactions on Information Theory in 2008. We gave two attacks on this protocol and demonstrated the serious flaw in its leave procedure and its vulnerability to replay attack and we also provided some suggestions for revision.

# References

1. Barua, R., Dutta, R., Sarkar, P.: Extending joux's protocol to multi party key agreement. In: Johansson, T., Maitra, S. (eds.) INDOCRYPT 2003. LNCS, vol. 2904, pp. 205–217. Springer, Heidelberg (2003)
2. Boyd, C., Nieto, J.M.G.: Round-Optimal Contributory Conference Key Agreement. In: Desmedt, Y.G. (ed.) PKC 2003. LNCS, vol. 2567, pp. 161–174. Springer, Heidelberg (2002)
3. Bresson, E., Catalano, D.: Constant Round Authenticated Group Key Agreement via Distributed Computation. In: Bao, F., Deng, R., Zhou, J. (eds.) PKC 2004. LNCS, vol. 2947, pp. 115–129. Springer, Heidelberg (2004)
4. Bresson, E., Chevassut, O., Pointcheval, D.: Provably Authenticated Group Diffie-Hellman Key Exchange - The Dynamic Case. In: Boyd, C. (ed.) ASIACRYPT 2001. LNCS, vol. 2248, pp. 290–309. Springer, Heidelberg (2001)
5. Bresson, E., Chevassut, O., Pointcheval, D.: Dynamic Group Diffie-Hellman Key Exchange under Standard Assumptions. In: Knudsen, L.R. (ed.) EUROCRYPT 2002. LNCS, vol. 2332, pp. 321–336. Springer, Heidelberg (2002)
6. Bresson, E., Chevassut, O., Essiari, A., Pointcheva, D.: Mutual Authentication and Group Key Agreement for low-power Mobile Devices. Computer Communication 27(17), 1730–1737 (2004); A preliminary version appeared in Proceedings of the 5th IFIP-TC6/IEEE, MWCN 2003
7. Bresson, E., Chevassut, O., Pointcheval, D., Quisquater, J.J.: Provably Authenticated Group Diffie-Hellman Key Exchange. In: Proc. 8th Annual ACM Conference on Computer and Communications Security, pp. 255–264. ACM, New York (2001)
8. Burmester, M., Desmedt, Y.G.: A Secure and Efficient Conference Key Distribution System. In: De Santis, A. (ed.) EUROCRYPT 1994. LNCS, vol. 950, pp. 275–286. Springer, Heidelberg (1995)
9. Dutta, R., Barua, R.: Constant Round Dynamic Group Key Agreement. In: Zhou, J., López, J., Deng, R.H., Bao, F. (eds.) ISC 2005. LNCS, vol. 3650, pp. 74–88. Springer, Heidelberg (2005)
10. Dutta, R., Barua, R.: Provably Secure Constant Round Contributory Group Key Agreement in Dynamic Setting. IEEE Transactions on Information Theory (TIT) 54(5), 2007–2025 (2008)
11. Dutta, R., Barua, R., Sarkar, P.: Pairing Based Cryptographic Protocols. A Survey. Cryptology ePrint Archive, Report 2004/064 (2004)
12. Katz, J., Yung, M.: Scalable Protocols for Authenticated Group Key Exchange. In: Boneh, D. (ed.) CRYPTO 2003. LNCS, vol. 2729, pp. 110–125. Springer, Heidelberg (2003)
13. Kim, Y., Perrig, A., Tsudik, G.: Simple and Fault-tolerant Key Agreement for Dynamic Collaborative Groups. In: Jajodia, S. (ed.) 7th ACM Conference on Computation and Communication Security, Athens, Greece, pp. 235–244 (2000)
14. Kim, Y., Perrig, A., Tsudik, G.: Tree based Group Key Agreement. Report 2002/009 (2002), http://eprint.iacr.org
15. Kim, H.-J., Lee, S.-M., Lee, D.-H.: Constant-Round Authenticated Group Key Exchange for Dynamic Groups. In: Lee, P.J. (ed.) ASIACRYPT 2004. LNCS, vol. 3329, pp. 245–259. Springer, Heidelberg (2004)
16. Steiner, M., Tsudik, G., Waidner, M.: Key Agreement in Dynamic Peer Groups. IEEE Trans. Parallel Distrib. Syst (TPDS) 11(8), 769–780 (2000)
17. Steiner, M., Tsudik, G., Waidner, M.: Diffie-Hellman Key Distribution Extended to Group Communication. In: ACM Conference on Computation and Communication Security (1996)

# Modified Authentication Protocol Using Elliptic Curve Cryptosystem for Virtual Subnets on Mobile Adhoc Networks

Ankush A. Vilhekar and C.D. Jaidhar

ABV-Indian Institute of Information Technology and Management, Gwalior
Morena Link Road, Gwalior India-474010
mtis_200904@students.iiitm.ac.in, cdjaidhar@rediffmail.com

**Abstract.** In 2010, an efficient authentication protocol has been proposed for virtual subnets on Mobile Adhoc Networks (MANET). It uses virtual subnet and each node in the subnet is authenticated using certificate. Further, it is claimed that protocol is robust, more efficient and practical. However, it is not suitable for devices have low computation power like mobile, PDAs, smart cards because number of computations are more in RSA based cryptosystem. In order to reduce the number of computation with same level of security, this paper proposes the same scheme using Elliptic Curve Cryptography (ECC) (modified scheme). Our scheme uses ECC in place of RSA to reduce number of computations with shorter key size.

**Keywords:** Mutual authentication, Mobile Ad-hoc Networks, Elliptic Curve Cryptography.

## 1 Introduction

A Mobile Ad-hoc Network (MANET)[1,6] is infrastructure-less communication network which is created on demand without support from central servers. It is an autonomous system of mobile nodes connected by wireless links. Each mobile node communicates with other nodes within its transmission range by radio waves and relays on other nodes to communicate with mobile nodes outside its transmission range. MANETs have some special characteristic such as topology changes dynamically, open medium, absence of fixed central structure, constrained capability, limited bandwidth, battery, lifetime and computation power of nodes etc. Due these characteristics, MANETs are vulnerable to various types of attacks such as impersonation, denial-of-service, passive and active attacks. Mobile phones, palm computers etc., got vide popularity in today's world because they are portable in nature. People can uses these portable devices at anytime and anywhere to do business over an Internet such as Internet banking, pay TV channel (dish TV, big TV), on-line shopping etc. Security is utmost important when user secrete information is transmitted over insecure communication channel. MANET needs to divide into sub domains or groups in order to provide security services and efficient

P. Sénac, M. Ott, and A. Seneviratne (Eds.): ICWCA 2011, LNICST 72, pp. 426–432, 2012.
© Institute for Computer Sciences, Social Informatics and Telecommunications Engineering 2012

communication. MANET architecture for single subnet is as shown in figure 1. Due to this, only legitimate node can access information and it also reduces redundant transmission. Despite the fact that there is no centralized device in MANET to construct the groups or virtual subnet [2, 3]. To provide secure group communication in virtual subnet to resist possible attacks from malicious nodes, authentication is the primary requirement. Public Key Cryptosystem (PKC) based authentication scheme has been proposed [4,5, 10,11]. Number of computations is more in PKC because of discrete logarithm problem. Mobile nodes in MANET have constraints on bandwidth, processor, memory and power. As the number of computation increases power consumption also increases. Hence, PKC is not suitable for MANET. In order to reduce the number of computations with same level of security, this paper propose modified scheme using Elliptic Curve Cryptosystem. Security of the ECC is based upon difficulty of Elliptic Curve Discrete Logarithm Problem (ECDLP) and Elliptic Curve Deffie-Hellman problem (ECDHP)[7,8,9]. Compared with PKC, ECC offers a better performance because it achieves the same security with smaller key size.

The rest of our paper is organized as follows. Section 2 provides review of the authentication protocol for virtual subnets on MANET. Proposed authentication scheme described in section 3. Security analysis discussed in section 4. Finally, conclusion given in section 5.

## 2  Review of Authentication Protocol for Virtual Subnet on Mobile Ad-Hoc Networks (MANET)[13]

Node authentication for virtual subnet has been proposed [13]. It consists of three phases named as Key Generation phase, Certificate Generation phase and Certificate Authentication phase. The process of assigning the key pair before deployment is as follows. All the nodes in virtual subnet elect a node called a leader node whose sole responsibility is to generate common shared key and individual private key for every node.

This section is providing the details of previous scheme [13] including three phases and they are as follows.

### 2.1  Key Generation

**Step 1.** Leader node generates two large prime number 'p' and 'q', then computes $N = p*q$: randomly selects $g$ such that $g \in Z_N^*$ where $Z_N^* = \{g \mid 1 \leq g \leq N\text{-}1, gcd(g, N) = 1\}$.

**Step 2.** Leader node generates $a_1, a_2, \ldots\ldots, a_k$. $k$ is number of nodes in virtual subnet, where $gcd(a_i, a_j) = 1$, $gcd(a_i, \phi(N)) = 1$, , $1 \leq i, j \leq k$ and $i \neq j$.

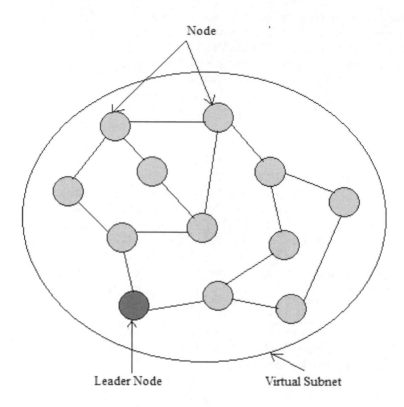

**Fig. 1.** MANET Architecture of single subnet

***Step 3.*** Leader node calculate private key $s_i = {_g}\Pi^k_{j=1,\,j\neq I}\ a_j\ mod\ N\ for\ node\ I,\ 1\leq i \leq k.$

***Step 4.*** Leader node calculate common shared key $v = 1\ /\ {_g}\ \Pi^k_{j=1,\,j\neq I}\ a_j\ mod\ N.$

***Step 5.*** Leader node sends $(s_i,\ a_i)$ to node i, where $1 \leq i \leq k.$
Leader node is no longer valid after the completion of key generation.

## 2.2 Certificate Generation

***Step 1.*** Node i randomly select $r$ such that $r \in Z^*_N$ where $1 \leq i \leq k.$

***Step 2.*** Node i generate $x = r^{ai}\ mod\ N.$

***Step 3.*** Node i calculates $\alpha = h(a_i,\ x)$, and $y = r * s_i^{\alpha}\ mod\ N$, certificate of node i is $cert\ i = (ID_i,\ a_i,\ \alpha,\ y)\ where\ ID_i$ is identity of node i and $h()$ is strong oneway hash function.

The source node broadcasts a virtual subnet join request packet as an advertisement which includes certificate.

## 2.3  Certificate Authentication

**Step 1.**  Any node in a subnet can authenticate the other nodes in the same subnet using certificate of node i.  Using public key $v$ *and cert* $i = (ID_i,\ a_i,\ \alpha,\ y)$ node in the subnet computes $x' = y^{ai} * v^{\alpha}\ mod\ N$.

**Step 2.**  $x'$ is used to generate $\alpha' = h(a_i,\ x')$.  If $\alpha = \alpha'$, then the node is legitimate one and belongs to the same group otherwise, discard certificated node.

# 3  Proposed Authentication Protocol Using Elliptic Curve Cryptosystem

Authentication scheme proposed in this paper is based on ECC and it is a modified version of scheme [13].  Elliptic Curve is cubic equation of basic form

$$y^2 + axy + by = x^3 + cx^2 + dx + e$$

where $a$, $b$, $c$, $d$ and $e$ are real numbers.  In ECC over prime finite field $F_p$, the Elliptic Curve equation is standardized in the form of

$$y^2 = ( x^3 + ax + b)\ mod\ p$$

and equation is denoted as $E_p(a, b)$. where $a$, $b \in F_p$, $p > 3$ and $4a^3 = 27b^2 \neq 0$ *(mod p)*.  Given an integer $s \in F_p^{\ *}$ and a point $B \in E_p(a, b$, the point multiplication $s \cdot B$ over $E_p(a, b)$ can be defined as $s \cdot B = (B + B + \ldots\ldots + B)_{s\ times}$.  Security of the ECC totally depends on the difficulties of following problems as defined in [8].

**Problem 1-** Given two points $A$ and $B$ over $E_p(a, b)$, the Elliptic Curve Discrete Logarithm Problem(ECDLP) is to find an integer $s \in F_p^{\ *}$ such that $B = s \cdot A$.

**Problem 2-** Given three points A, $s \cdot A$ and $t \cdot A$ over $E_p(a, b)$ for $s, t \in F_p^{\ *}$, Elliptic Curve Diffie- Hellman Problem (ECDHP) is to find the point $(s \cdot t) \cdot A$ over $E_p(a, b)$.

**Problem 3-** Given two points $A$ and $B = s \cdot A + t \cdot A$ over $E_p(a, b)$ for $s, t \in F_p^{\ *}$, Elliptic Curve Factorization Problem (ECFP) is to find two points $s \cdot A$ and $t \cdot A$ over $E_p(a, b)$.

Proposed scheme consists of three phases namely Key Generation phase, Certificate Generation phase and Node Authentication phase.  Prior to key generation, all nodes elect a node called as leader node.  Its function is to generate and distribute common shared key and individual private key for all the nodes.  The key generation steps are as follows.

## 3.1    Key Generation

**Step 1.** Leader node chooses Elliptic Curve $E_p(a, b)$ in which p is prime number used for modulo operation and a, b are the values of coefficient in equation $y^2 = x^3 + ax + b$.

**Step 2.** Leader node generates $a_1, a_2, \ldots\ldots\ldots, a_i$. k is number of nodes in the group where $1 \leq i \leq k$.

**Step 3.** Then leader node calculates private key $X_i$ for node i, $1 \leq i \leq k$, $X_i = B . \Pi^k_{j=1}$ $a_j \bmod p$ where B is base point on elliptic curve.

**Step 4.** Leader node computes common shared key $s = ( B. \Pi^k_{j=1} a_j \bmod p )^{-1}$

**Step 5.** Finally, leader node sends the parameters $(X_i, s, a_i)$ to node i where $1 \leq i \leq k$.

After the generation and distribution of private key and common shared key, leader node no longer valid in other words leader node is temporary. This is to ensure that a leader node does not maintain private key and common shared key of other nodes. Key generation phase is executed whenever there is a change in the subnet. Therefore, private key and common shared key are refreshed to provide forward secrecy and backward secrecy.

After the distribution of parameter to all the nodes of virtual subnet, they deploy over specified region and communication can be initiated randomly. Each node needs to generate its own certificate to provide authentication in virtual subnet. Certificate generation steps are as follows.

## 3.2    Certificate Generation

**Step 1.** Node i randomly selects r, r belongs to $Z_p^*$ where $1 \leq i \leq k$.

**Step 2.** Node i generates $q = r . a_i \bmod p$.

**Step 3.** Then node i calculates $C = h(a_i, q)$, $g = r . x_i . C \bmod p$. Certificate of node i is Cert i= (ID, $a_i$, C, g) where *IDi* is the identity of node i, h() is a strong one way hash function.

The source node broadcasts a virtual subnet join request packet as an advertisement in which certificate parameters are included. All other nodes in the same virtual subnet receive the join request packet and process them to authenticate the node in the subnet. The authentication procedure is as follows

## 3.3    Certificate Authentication

**Step 1.** Any node in a virtual subnet can to authenticate the other node i in the same subnet using public key s and node 'i' certificate parameters $Cert_i = (ID, a_i, C, g)$ to calculate $q' = g . a_i . s . C^{-1} \bmod p$.

$$q' = r \cdot x_i \cdot C \cdot a_i \cdot x_i^{-1} \cdot C^{-1} \bmod p$$
$$q' = r \cdot a_i \bmod p$$
$$q' = q$$

**Step 2.** Then it uses $q'$ to compute $C' = h(a_i, q')$ to verify whether $C = C'$, If they are equal then node is authenticated else drop the received certificate.

## 4 Security Analysis

### 4.1 Replay Attack

In the proposed scheme, the replay attack fails because the private key and shared key is refreshed whenever there is a change in the membership. Role of leader node is only for short span of time and no longer exists once the key generation and distribution phase is completes. This is to ensure that node cannot obtain private key of other nodes.

### 4.2 Outsider Attack

Attacker is unable to derive private key of the node 'i' from the intercepted certificate $Cert\ i = (ID, a_i, C, g)$. To obtain private key $X_i$ of node 'i' generated by leader node, attacker needs to compute $x_i$ and $r$. This is infeasible because of ECDLP and ECFP. As per the previous research, still there is no algorithm is able to solve these problems. Hence, proposed scheme withstands outsider attack.

### 4.3 Stolen Verifier Attack

Nodes in virtual subnet do not store any verification table. Hence, proposed scheme resists stolen-verifier attacks. When a new node is added in the virtual subnet, other nodes need not to keep private or shared secrete in the storage space. Whenever there is a change in change in the membership both the keys are refreshed which ensure the Therefore, the proposed scheme can resist stolen-verifier attacks and provides high scalability for the user addition such that it is very practical for the applications with large number of users.

## 5 Conclusion

Authentication protocol for virtual subnets on Mobile Adhoc Networks has been proposed using RSA based Public Key Cryptosystem. It has more computation cost because of RSA Public Key Crypto system. In order to reduce the number of computations with same level of security, this paper proposes the same scheme using Elliptic Curve Cryptosystem. Our scheme provides the same level of security with shorter key size. Further, security analysis shows that proposed scheme is highly secure.

# References

1. Aziz, B., Nourdine, E., Mohamed, E.-K.: A Recent Survey on Key Management Schemes in MANET. In: ICTTA 2008, pp. 1–6 (2008)
2. Perkins, C.: Ad Hoc Networks. Addison-Wesley, Reading (2001)
3. Rajaravivarma, V.: Virtual Local area Network Technology and Applications. In: Proceeding of the Twenty-Ninth Southeastern Symposium, March 9-11, pp. 49–52 (1997)
4. wieselthier, J.E., Nguyen, G.D., Ephremides, A.: Algorithms for Energy-Efficient Multicasting in Static Ad Hoc Wireless Network. In: Mobile Networks and Applications (MONET), June 2001, 6-3, pp. 251–263 (2001)
5. Li, F., Xin, X., Hu, Y.: Identity Based Broadcast Signcryption. Computer Standard and Interfaces 30, 89–94 (2008)
6. Capkum, S., Buttya, L., Hubaux, P.: Self-Organized Public Key Management for Mobile Ad Hoc Networks. IEEE Trans. Mobile Computing 2(1), 52–64 (2003)
7. Miller, V.S.: Use of Elliptic Curves in Cryptography. In: Williams, H.C. (ed.) CRYPTO 1985. LNCS, vol. 218, pp. 417–426. Springer, Heidelberg (1986)
8. Koblitz, N.: Elliptic Curve Cryptosystem. Mathematics of Computation 48, 203–209 (1987)
9. Forouzan, B.A.: Cryptography and Network Security, special Indian edition. Tata McGraw Hill (2007)
10. Chiang, T.-C., Yeh, C.-H., Huang, Y.M.: A Virtual Subnet Protocol for Mobile Ad Hoc Networks Using Forwarding Cache Scheme. International Journal of Computer Science and Network Security 6(1), 108–115 (2006)
11. Huang, Y.M., Yeh, C.H., Wang, T.I., Chao, H.C.: Constructing Secure Group Communication over Wireless Ad Hoc Networks based on a Virtual Subnet Model. IEEE Wireless Communications 14(5), 70–75 (2007)
12. Guillou, L.C., Quisquater, J.-J.: A "Paradoxical" Identity-Based Signature Scheme Resulting from Zero-Knowledge. In: Goldwasser, S. (ed.) CRYPTO 1988. LNCS, vol. 403, pp. 216–231. Springer, Heidelberg (1990)
13. Chang, C.-W., Yeh, C.-H., Tsai, C.-D.: An Efficient Authentication Protocol for Virtual Subnets on Mobile Ad Hoc Networks. In: International Symposium on Computer, Communication, Control and Automation, 3CA2010, pp. 67–70 (2010)
14. Kavak, N.: Data Communications in ATM Networks. IEEE Network 9(3) (May/June 1995)

# 3D-DCT Based Zero-Watermarking for Medical Volume Data Robust to Geometrical Attacks

Jingbing Li[1], Wencai Du[1], Yong Bai[1], and Yen-wei Chen[2]

[1] College of Information Science and Technology, Hainan University,
Haikou 570228, China
[2] College of Information Science and Engineering, Ritsumeikan University,
Kasatsu-shi 525-8577, Japan
Jingbingli2008@hotmail.com, wencai@hainu.edu.cn,
bai@hainu.edu.cn, chen@is.ritsumei.ac.jp

**Abstract.** This paper presents a method for robust watermarking of medical volume data using 3D-DCT. A feature vector of the volume data is utilized to enhance the robustness against rotation, scaling, translation, and cropping changes. The proposed algorithm utilizes the volume data's feature, Hash function, the third party authentication. We describe how to obtain the feature vector of medical volume data and embed and extract the watermarking. Simulation results demonstrate the proposed algorithm's robustness against rotation up to 30°, against scaling down to 20% of the image's original size, and against translation transform up to 10%.

**Keywords:** 3D-DCT, Digital watermarking, Medical volume data, Robust, Geometrical attacks.

## 1 Introduction

With the advancing of the multimedia and internet technology, telediagnosis, telesurgery and cooperative working session have been undergoing rapid development. However, when Electronic Patient Records(EPR) and medical images are transmitted on the Internet, there may be the risk of disclosure of personal privacy[1][2]. Medical image watermarking can be a effective technology to solve this problem[3][4]. Traditionally Digital watermarking technology is used in the copyright protection of digital media first. Using watermark's properties of invisibility and robustness, patient information, doctor diagnosis and Electronic Patient Records can be used as the watermarking hidden in the CT, MRI (Magnetic Resonance Imaging) and other medical images[5].

Medical image watermarking is usually divided into three types [4].

1) RONI(Region of non-interest)-based medical image watermarking. The content of medical images can not tolerate significant changes when watermarking is embedded. Hence, the watermarking information is embedded in the RONI of the medical images[6][7]. However, the capacity of hidden information is limited because most of the RONI area of the image is the black background.

P. Sénac, M. Ott, and A. Seneviratne (Eds.): ICWCA 2011, LNICST 72, pp. 433–444, 2012.

2) Reversible watermarking. Using reversible watermarking, once the embedded content is read, the watermarking can be removed from the image allowing retrieval of the original image[8]. Unfortunately, most of the reversible watermarking is fragile. Its robustness is poor and the capacity is still way below the embedding capacity of non-reversible watermarking technique.

3) Classical watermarking. In this method, watermarking is often embedded in the least significant bit (LSB) [9], or in the low or middle frequency coefficients in the frequency domain(DCT,DFT or DWT) [10]. However, compared to the previous two methods, the capacity of the embedded watermark affects the content of Region of Interest. It is necessary to control the amount of the embedded watermarking to avoid the doctors make the wrong diagnosis. In addition, the classical watermarking has low robustness especially against geometric attacks.

## 2   Three Dimension Cosine Transform(3D-DCT) and Inverse Discrete Cosine Transform(3D-IDCT)

### 2.1   Three Dimension Cosine Transform(3D-DCT)

Three dimension cosine transform is a signal analysis theory[12][13]. The $M \times N \times P$ volume data's 3D-DCT is defined by :

$$F(u,v,w)=c(u)c(v)c(w)\cdot[\sum_{x=0}^{M-1}\sum_{y=0}^{N-1}\sum_{p=0}^{P-1}f(x,y,z)\cdot\cos\frac{(2x+1)u\pi}{2M}\cos\frac{(2y+1)v\pi}{2N}\cos\frac{(2z+1)w\pi}{2P}]$$

(1)

where   $u = 0,1,...,M-1;\ \ v=0,1,...,N-1;\ w=0,1,...,P-1;$

$$c(u)=\begin{cases}\sqrt{1/M} & u=0 \\ \sqrt{2/M} & u=1,2,...,M-1\end{cases} , \qquad c(v)=\begin{cases}\sqrt{1/N} & v=0 \\ \sqrt{2/N} & v=1,2,...,N-1\end{cases}$$

$$c(w)=\begin{cases}\sqrt{1/P} & w=0 \\ \sqrt{2/P} & w=1,2,...,P-1\end{cases}$$

$f(x,y,z)$ are the voxel values of volume data V at the point( $x,y,z$ ) and $F(u,v,w)$ corresponds to the 3D-DCT coefficients.

### 2.2   Three Dimension Inverse Cosine Transform(3D-IDCT)

The $M \times N \times P$ volume data's 3D-IDCT is defined by :

$$f(x,y,z)=\sum_{u=0}^{M-1}\sum_{v=0}^{N-1}\sum_{w=0}^{P-1}c(u)c(v)c(w)F(u,v,w)\cos\frac{(2x+1)u\pi}{2M}\cos\frac{\pi(2y+1)v\pi}{2N}\cos\frac{\pi(2y+1)w\pi}{2N}]$$

(2)

where   $x=0,1,...,M-1;\ \ y=0,1,...,N-1;\ z=0,1,...,P-1$   and   $c(u),c(v),c(w)$   are the same as that in the formula (1).

# 3   3D-DCT Based Watermarking for Medical Volume Data

## 3.1   A Method to Obtain the Feature Vector of Medical Volume Data

The original volume data is computed using 3D-DCT. We choose 8 low-frequency coefficients (F(1,1,1), F(1,2,1) F(2,1,1)...F(2,2,2)), shown in Table 1. We find that the value of the low-frequent coefficients may change after the image has undergone an attack, particularly geometric attacks such as rotation, scaling, and transformation. However, the signs of the coefficients remain unchanged even with strong geometric attacks, as is also shown in Table 1. The different attacked images are shown in Fig. 1(b)-(h). If "1" represents a positive coefficient, and "0" represents a negative or zero coefficient, we can then obtain the sign sequence of low-frequency coefficients, as is shown in the column "Sequence of coefficient signs" in Table 1. After attacks, the sign sequence is unchanged, and the normalized cross-correlation (NC) is equal to 1.0.

**Table 1.** Change of 3D-DCT low-frequency coefficients with respect to different attacks

| Image Process | F(1,1,1) $(10^2)$ | F(1,2,1) $(10^2)$ | F(2,1,1) $(10^2)$ | F(2,2,1) $(10^2)$ | F(1,1,2) $(10^2)$ | F1,2,2) $(10^2)$ | F(2,1,2) $(10^2)$ | F(2,2,2) $(10^2)$ | Sequence of coefficient signs | NC |
|---|---|---|---|---|---|---|---|---|---|---|
| Original image | 145.11 | 5.32 | -36.2 | -1.53 | 9.81 | -3.33 | 4.23 | 1.52 | 1100 1011 | 1.0 |
| Gausian noise (3%) | 225.02 | 4.30 | -26.60 | -1.45 | 7.24 | -2.03 | 3.04 | 1.03 | 1100 1011 | 1.0 |
| JPEG (4%); | 154.70 | 4.76 | -32.54 | -1.50 | 10.04 | -3.13 | 4.88 | 1.76 | 1100 1011 | 1.0 |
| Median filter [3x3] | 146.06 | 5.35 | -36.47 | -1.61 | 9.67 | -3.42 | 4.62 | 1.54 | 1100 1011 | 1.0 |
| Rotation (20°) | 145.10 | 18.13 | -32.66 | -16.94 | 9.81 | -4.21 | 2.81 | 0.01 | 1100 1011 | 1.0 |
| Scaling (x0.5) | 72.67 | 2.67 | -18.12 | -0.76 | 4.93 | -1.67 | 2.12 | 0.76 | 1100 1011 | 1.0 |
| Translation (8%) | 141.71 | 5.21 | -69.74 | -2.76 | 8.97 | -3.32 | 3.04 | 2.39 | 1100 1011 | 1.0 |
| Cropping (10%,from z ) | 142.54 | 4.72 | -34.22 | -1.24 | 0.73 | -3.34 | 5.07 | 1.40 | 1100 1011 | 1.0 |

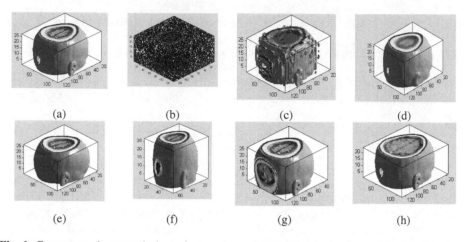

**Fig. 1.** Common and geometrical attacks to volume data: (a) Original volume data; (b) Gaussian noise(3%); (c) JPEG compression(4%); (d) Median filter[3x3]; (e) Rotation(20 ° clockwise); (f) Scaling(0.5times); (g) Translation(8%,down); (h) Cropping(10%,from z direction).

To prove that these sequences of coefficient signs can serve as the feature vector of medical volume data, we choose several common volume data, as shown in Fig. 2(a)-(e). After 3D-DCT, we choose 64 low-frequency coefficients--(F(1,1,1), F(1,2,1) F(2,1,1)...F(4,4,4). The 64-bit sequence of signs is then obtained and the NC is calculated. The values of NC between sequence of signs are shown in Table 2. We find that the NC values are very small (less than 0.28). This means that the sequence of signs can be regarded as the feature vector of the volume data.

**Fig. 2.** 3D images of different volume data ; (a) volume data_1; (b) volume data_2; (c) volume data_3; (d) volume data_4; (e) volume data_5

**Table 2.** The NC values between 64-bit feature vectors of volume data

|  | V1.V2 | V1.V3 | V1.V4 | V1.V5 | V2.V3 | V2.V4 | V2.V5 | V3.V4 | V3.V5 | V4.V5 |
|---|---|---|---|---|---|---|---|---|---|---|
| NC | -0.31 | -0.21 | 0.21 | -0.15 | 0.28 | -0.15 | -0.09 | -0.25 | -0.12 | 0.06 |

### 3.2  Watermarking Algorithm That Uses Feature Vectors

A group of independent binary pseudomorph sequences is generated for the watermarking. The group of sequences is described as: $W = \{w_{(j)} | w_{(j)} = 0,1; \quad 1 \le j \le L\}$. A volume data of size of 128×128x27 is selected as the original volume data. It is described as: $F=\{f_{(i,j,k)}|f_{(i,j,k)}\in R; \quad 1\le i\le M,1\le j\le N,1\le k\le P\}$, where $f_{(i,j,k)}$ denotes the voxel values of volume data V at the point (i,j,k).

## 1) Embed the watermarking into the volume data

*Step 1*: Acquire the feature vector of the volume data using 3D-DCT

DCT of the whole F(i,j,k) is computed, and the 3D-DCT coefficient matrix, FD (i,j,k), is acquired. Then, the frequency sequence $Y(j)$ –from low to high frequency– can be obtained. Finally, The feature vector $V=\{v(j)|v(j)=0,1; 1\le j\le J\}$, consists of the sequence of signs of the low-frequency 3D-DCT coefficients, where the value of J can tune the robustness and capability of the embedded watermarking (in this paper we set J = 125=5x5x5 bits). Procedure is described as:

$$FD(i, j,k) = DCT3(F(i, j,k));\tag{3}$$

$$V(j) = Sign(FD(i, j,k));\tag{4}$$

*Step 2* : Utilizing the watermarking W and volume data V, we can generate the logical sequence, *Key(j)*

$$Key(j) = V(j) \oplus W(j) ;\tag{5}$$

where $V(j)$ denotes the feature vector of volume data, $W(j)$ denotes the watermarking to be embedded, and "$\oplus$" is the exclusive-OR operator. The binary logical sequence, *Key (j)*, can be computed. The *Key(j)* should be stored, as it is necessary to extract the watermarking. Furthermore, *Key(j)* can be regarded as a secret key and registered to the third part to preserve the ownership of the original image [14].

## 2) Extract the watermarking from the tested Volume data

*Step 3*: Using the 3D-DCT of the whole tested Volume data F'(i,j,k) and acquire the feature vector V'(j)

This process of acquiring the feature vector V' is similar to step 1 of the above algorithm for embedding the watermarking. The obtained feature vector is $V'=\{v'(j)|v'(j)=0,1; 1\le j\le J\}$, which consists of the sequence of signs of the 3D-DCT coefficients and where J has the same meaning as previously.

Procedure is described as follows :

$$FD'(i, j,k) = DCT3(F'(i, j,k));\tag{6}$$

$$V'(j) = Sign(FD'(i, j,k));\tag{7}$$

*Step 4*: Extracting W'(j)

$$W'(j) = V'(j) \oplus Key(j);\tag{8}$$

where W'(j) is the extracted watermarking, V' (j) is the feature vector of the tested volume data, and Key(j) was obtained from the above process of embedding watermarking. The NC between W and W' is then computed. Finally, we can extract the hidden information from the volume data.

Furthermore, the hidden information(watermarking) can be extracted without the original data, which is advantageous to protect the safety of the medical volume data.

## 4 Experiments

In our experiments, 1000 groups of independent binary pseudomorph sequences are used. Every sequence consists of 125 bits. One group is selected at random from the 1000 groups as the embedded watermarking (in this paper, the 500th group is selected). Fig. 4(a) shows the original medical volume data of size 128×128x27. In order to measure the quantitative similarity, the normalized cross-correlation (*NC*) is used in this paper, defined as:

$$NC = \sum_i \sum_j [W(i, j) \cdot W'(i, j)] \Big/ \sum_i \sum_j [W(i, j)]^2 \qquad (9)$$

where *W* denotes the embedded watermarking and *W'* denotes extracted watermarking.

The higher the *NC* value, the more similarity there is between the embedded and extracted watermarking. In this paper, we use the peak signal to noise ratio (PSNR) to measure the distortion of the watermarked image, defined as:

$$PSNR = 10 \log_{10} \left[ \frac{\sum v_{max}^2}{\sum (v_i - v_i')^2} \right] \qquad (10)$$

Where $v_i$ and $v_i'$ denote the ith-voxel(or ith-pixel) values of the original volume V and watermarked V' ,respectively.

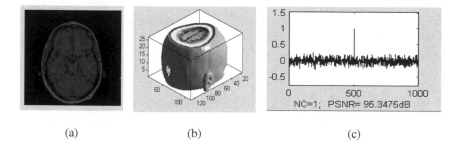

(a)                              (b)                              (c)

**Fig. 3.** The watermarked medicine volume data without attacks: (a) a slice of medicine volume data; (b)The corresponding 3D medical image ; (c) watermarking detector.

Fig. 3(a) shows a slice of medicine volume data without attacks. In this paper, the default is to select the tenth slice. Fig. 3(b) shows the watermarked medicine volume data (Three-dimensional)  without attacks. Fig. 3(c) gives the response of the watermarking detector. The only group of binary pseudomorph sequences that responds is the one that is watermarked. The value of NC is up to 1.0, so the watermarking is obviously detected.

## 4.1  Common Attacks

### (1) Adding Gaussian noise

The slice data under Gaussian attacks (20%) is shown in Fig. 4(a); The corresponding volume data with PSNR of 0.79 dB and NC of 0.61 is shown in Fig. 4(b). The watermarking can be detected, as shown in Fig. 4(c). Table 3 gives the PSNR and NC when the volume data have been added noise by different parameters. The result shows that the NC is 0.58 when the noise parameter is up to 25%. The watermarking can still be detected.

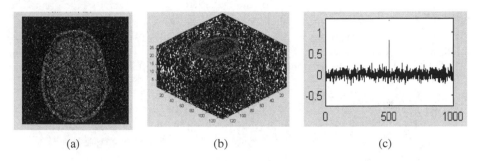

(a)                              (b)                              (c)

**Fig. 4.** Under noise attack(20%): (a) a slice under noise attack; (b) the corresponding 3D medical image; (c) watermarking detector

**Table 3.** The PSNR and NC under noise attack

| Noise parameters (%) | 1 | 3 | 5 | 10 | 15 | 20 | 25 |
|---|---|---|---|---|---|---|---|
| PSNR(dB) | 12.50 | 8.02 | 6.01 | 3.31 | 1.79 | 0.79 | 0.09 |
| NC | 0.86 | 0.81 | 0.79 | 0.77 | 0.71 | 0.61 | 0.58 |

### (2) Filter Processing

The slice data under median filter attacks[5x5] is shown in Fig. 5(a); The corresponding volume data with PSNR of 18.68 dB and NC of 0.90 is shown in Fig. 5(b). The watermarking can be detected, as shown in Fig. 5(c). Table 4 gives the PSNR and NC under different median filter parameters. The results show that the watermarking algorithm is robust to median filter.

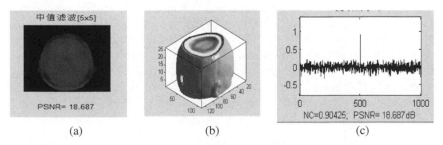

(a)                              (b)                              (c)

**Fig. 5.** Under filter attacks[5x5]: (a) a slice with filter attack; (b) the corresponding 3D medical image; (c) watermarking detector

**Table 4.** The PSNR and NC under median filtering

| Repeat times | Media filter[3x3] | | | Media filter [5x5] | | | Media filter [7x7] | | |
|---|---|---|---|---|---|---|---|---|---|
| | 1 | 10 | 20 | 1 | 10 | 20 | 1 | 2 | 10 |
| PSNR(dB) | 24.64 | 22.45 | 21.97 | 21.14 | 18.67 | 18.07 | 18.91 | 18.32 | 16.97 |
| NC | 0.93 | 0.93 | 0.93 | 0.89 | 0.90 | 0.88 | 0.92 | 0.93 | 0.87 |

**(3) JPEG attacks**

The slice data under JPEG attacks (4%) is shown in Fig. 6(a). The corresponding volume data with PSNR of 17.82 dB and NC of 0.83 is shown in Fig. 6(b). The watermarking can be detected, as shown in Fig. 6(c). Table 5 gives the PSNR and NC under different compression quality. The result shows that the NC is 0.84 when the compression quality is down to 2%. The watermarking can still be detected. The results show that the watermarking algorithm is robust to JPEG attacks.

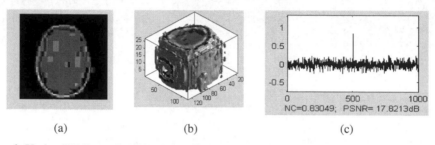

(a)                          (b)                          (c)

**Fig. 6.** Under JPEG attacks(4%): (a) a slice under JPEG attacks; (b) the corresponding 3D medical image; (c) watermarking detector

**Table 5.** The PSNR and NC under JPEG attacks

| Compression Quality(%) | 2 | 4 | 8 | 10 | 20 | 40 | 60 | 80 |
|---|---|---|---|---|---|---|---|---|
| PSNR(dB) | 16.57 | 17.82 | 20.21 | 21.19 | 23.10 | 25.06 | 26.61 | 29.30 |
| NC | 0.84 | 0.83 | 0.90 | 0.91 | 0.91 | 0.96 | 0.96 | 0.93 |

## 4.2  Geometrical Attacks

**(1) Rotation attacks**

Fig. 7(a) and Fig. 7(b) show the slice and volume data rotated clockwise by 20°, respectively. PSNR and NC are 12.44dB and 0.66, respectively. The watermarking can be detected, as shown in Fig. 7(c). Table 6 gives the PSNR and NC when the volume data has been rotated by different angles. The results show that the NC is 0.53 when the angle of rotation is up to 30°. The watermarking can still be detected. In [15] a watermarking was embedded in DFT domain, however, the maximum angle of rotation is not greater than 3°. Therefore we can conclude that our scheme is robust against rotation attacks.

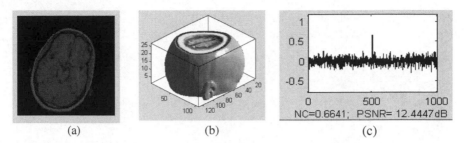

(a)                           (b)                           (c)

**Fig. 7.** Rotation attack (angle is 20°): (a) a slice with rotation attack; (b) the corresponding 3D medical image; (c) watermarking detector.

**Table 6.** The PSNR and NC under rotation attacks

| Rotation | 0° | 5° | 10° | 15° | 20° | 25° | 30° | 35° |
|---|---|---|---|---|---|---|---|---|
| PSNR(dB) | | 16.53 | 13.96 | 12.97 | 12.44 | 12.04 | 11.67 | 11.33 |
| NC | 1.00 | 0.79 | 0.76 | 0.69 | 0.66 | 0.56 | 0.53 | 0.45 |

**(2) Scaling attacks**

Fig. 8(a) and Fig. 8(b) show the slice and the corresponding 3D medical image shrunk with a scale factor of 0.5, respectively.

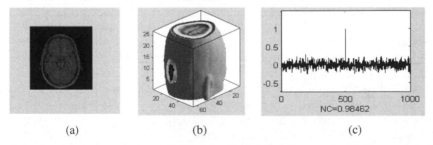

(a)                           (b)                           (c)

**Fig. 8.** Scaling attack (scaling factor 50%): (a) a slice with scaling attack; (b) the corresponding 3D medical image; (c) watermarking detector

Fig. 8(c) shows that the watermarking with a NC of 0.84 can be detected. Table 7 contains the NC value when the image has been scaled. If the scale factor drops to 0.2, then the NC value is 0.82. Therefore, our algorithm is robust to scaling attacks.

**Table 7.** The NC under scaling

| Scaling factor | 0.2 | 0.5 | 0.8 | 1.0 | 1.2 | 2.0 | 4.0 |
|---|---|---|---|---|---|---|---|
| NC | 0.82 | 0.98 | 0.90 | 1.0 | 0.96 | 0.98 | 0.98 |

**(3) Translation attacks**

Fig. 9(a) and Fig. 9(b) show the slice and the corresponding 3D medical image translated by 10 % vertical translation down, respectively. The PSNR and NC are 10.84dB and 0.56, respectively. Fig. 9(c) shows that the watermarking can be detected. Table 8 contains the values of PSNR and NC when the image has been translated. The results show that the scheme is robust against translation.

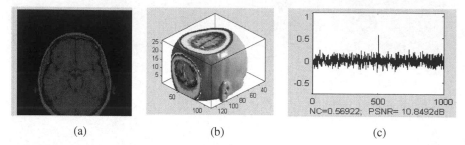

(a)                              (b)                              (c)

**Fig. 9.** Translation transforms (translation 10%): (a) a slice with translation attack; (b) the corresponding 3D medical image; (c) watermarking detector.

**Table 8.** The PSNR and NC under translation

|  | Horizontal translation(Left) | | | Vertical translation(Down ) | | |
|---|---|---|---|---|---|---|
| Distance (pixels) | 6 | 8 | 10 | 6 | 8 | 10 |
| PSNR (dB) | 11.13 | 10.43 | 9.99 | 11.65 | 11.09 | 10.84 |
| NC | 0.61 | 0.58 | 0.55 | 0.82 | 0.68 | 0.56 |

## (4) Cropping attacks

Fig. 10(a) and Fig. 10(b) show the slice and the corresponding medical volume data cropping from z axis at the ratio of 10 %, respectively. The NC is 0.77. Fig. 10(c) shows that the watermarking can be detected. Table 9 contains the values of NC when the image has been cropped. The results show that if the watermarked volume data is cropped by 14 % from z axis, then we can obtain NC of 0.71. Therefore, the watermarking is still detected. The results show that the proposed algorithm is robust against cropping attacks.

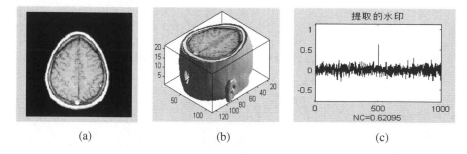

(a)                              (b)                              (c)

**Fig. 10.** Cropping (From the Z axis,10%): (a) the first slice after cropping; (b) the corresponding 3D medical image; (c) watermarking detector

**Table 9.** The NC under cropping

| Cropping ratio | 2% | 4% | 6% | 8% | 10% | 12% | 14% |
|---|---|---|---|---|---|---|---|
| NC(cropping from Z) | 0.91 | 0.91 | 0.84 | 0.84 | 0.77 | 0.77 | 0.71 |
| NC(cropping from Y) | 0.95 | 0.90 | 0.82 | 0.79 | 0.71 | 0.68 | 0.63 |
| NC(cropping from X) | 0.86 | 0.72 | 0.66 | 0.64 | 0.61 | 0.55 | 0.52 |

**(5) Distortion attacks**

Fig. 11(a) and Fig. 11(b) show the slice and the corresponding 3D medical image under distortion attacks with the factor of 13, respectively. The PSNR and NC are 9.83dB and 0.60, respectively. Fig. 11(c) shows that the watermarking can be detected. Table 10 contains the values of PSNR and NC when the image has been distorted. The results show that the scheme is robust against distortion.

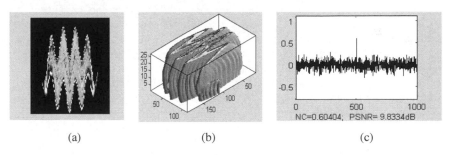

(a)    (b)    (c)

**Fig. 11.** Distortion attacks (factor is 13): (a) a slice under distortion attacks; (b) the corresponding 3D medical image; (c) watermarking detector

**Table 10.** The PSNR and NC under distortion attacks

| Distortion factor | 5 | 7 | 9 | 11 | 13 | 15 | 17 | 20 | 22 | 24 | 26 |
|---|---|---|---|---|---|---|---|---|---|---|---|
| PSNR(dB) | 10.16 | 9.88 | 9.58 | 9.43 | 9.83 | 9.7 | 9.8 | 9.68 | 9.77 | 9.68 | 9.68 |
| NC | 0.42 | 0.40 | 0.52 | 0.44 | 0.60 | 0.55 | 0.56 | 0.58 | 0.58 | 0.66 | 0.63 |

## 5 Conclusion

A novel embedding and extracting algorithm is presented in this paper. The algorithm is based on 3D-DCT. It combines feature vector, Hash function, the third party authentication. The watermarking can be extracted without the original medical volume data. Experimental results show that the algorithm is robust to geometric attacks including rotation, scaling and translation and cropping. Moreover, the content of medical volume data remains unchanged with our proposed algorithm which is one kind of the zero-watermarking technology.

**Acknowledgements.** This work is partly supported by Hainan University Graduate Education Reform Project (yjg0117), and by Natural Science Foundation of Hainan Province (60894), and by Education Department of Hainan Province project (Hjkj2009-03), and by Communication and Information System, Hainan University -- Institute of Acoustics, Chinese Academy of Sciences for Joint Training of Special Support.

# References

1. Coatrieux, G., Lecornu, L.: A Review of Image Watermarking Applications in Healthcare. In: Proc. 28th Annual International Conference of the IEEE: Engineering in Medicine and Biology Society, EMBS 2006, pp. 4691–4694 (2006)
2. Woo, C.-S., Du, J., Pham, B.: Multiple Watermark Method for Privacy Control and Tamper Detection in Medical Images. In: Proc. APRS Workshop on Digital Image Computing Pattern Recognition and Imaging for Medical Applications, pp. 43–48 (2005)
3. Navas, K.A., Sasikumar, M.: Survey of Medical Image Watermarking Algorithms. In: 4th International Conference: Sciences of Electronic, Technologies of Information and Telecommunications, TUNISIA, March 25-29 (2007)
4. Coatrieux, G., Maître, H., Sankur, B., Rolland, Y., Collorec, R.: Relevance of watermarking in medical Imaging. In: Proc. IEEE Int.Conf. ITAB, USA, pp. 250–255 (2000)
5. Rajendra Acharya, U., Niranjan, U.C., Iyengar, S.S., Kannathal, N., Min, L.C.: Simultaneous storage of patient information with medical images in the frequency domain. Computer Methods and Programs in Biomedicine 76, 13–19 (2004)
6. Coatrieux, G., Sankur, B., Maître, H.: Strict Integrity Control of Biomedical Images. In: Proc. Electronic Imaging, Security and Watermarking of Multimedia Contents, SPIE, USA, pp. 229–240 (2001)
7. Wakatani, A.: Digital watermarking for ROI medical images by using compressed signature image. In: Proc. 35th Hawaii International Conference on System Sciences, pp. 2043–2048 (2002)
8. Macq, B., Dewey, F.: Trusted Headers for Medical Images. In: DFG VIII-DII Watermarking Workshop, Erlangen, Germany (1999)
9. Zhou, X.Q., Huang, H.K., Lou, S.L.: Authenticity and integrity of digital mammography images. IEEE Trans. on Medical Imaging 20(8), 784–791 (2001)
10. Cox, I.J., Miller, M.L.: The first 50 years of electronic watermarking. Journal of Applied Signal Processing (2), 126–132 (2002)
11. Wu, Y.H., Guan, X., Kankanhalli, M.S., Huang, Z.Y.: Robust Invisible Watermarking of Volume Data Using 3D DCT[A]. In: Proceedings of Computer Graphics International, vol. 3(6), pp. 359–362. IEEE Computer Society Press, Hong Kong (2002)
12. Liu, W., Zhao, C.: Digital watermarking for volume data based on 3D-DWT and 3D-DCT. In: Proceedings of Int. Conf. Interaction Sciences, pp. 352–357 (2009)
13. Rao, K., Yip, R.: Discrete cosine transform: algorithms, advantages, applications. Academic Press Inc., London (1990)
14. Jeng-Shyang, P., Hsiang-cheh, H., Feng, W.: A VQ-based multi-watermarking algorithm. In: Proceedings of IEEE TENCON, pp. 117–120 (2002)
15. Solachidis, V., Pitas, I.: Circularly symmetric watermark embedding in 2-D DFT domain. IEEE Tranactions on image processing 10(11), 1741–1753 (2001)

# Detection and Analysis of Power System Harmonics Based on FPGA*

Xi Chen and Yonghui Zhang

College of Information Science & Technology, Hainan University,
570228, Haikou, China
fxcxcx@126.com,
zhyhemail@163.com

**Abstract.** With the development of technology, the power quality detect devices become more and more powerful and the measure accuracy increase quickly. This paper analyses frequency and harmonics signal of power system based on the theory of all-phase FFT spectrum by FPGA which has powerful processing function. All-phase time-shifting phase difference correcting spectrum algorithms is used to correct the measurements of power parameters quickly. The paper analyze the real-time data of power harmonics and frequency with high accuracy, the precision of frequency is $10^{-10}$ which can detect harmonic component under 20 degree correctly.

**Keywords:** All-phase FFT, Harmonic Analysis, FPGA.

## 1 Introduction

Power system harmonic and power system frequency are the important power quality parameters in China's power systems. The power frequency is 50Hz which regulated by GB/T15945-1995 "power quality-power system frequency deviation allowable". Power frequency allowing deviation value is 0.2Hz. When the capacity is lesser, deviation value can be extend to 0.5Hz. The waveform distortion and noise interference can reduce the precision of frequency measurement, especially the noise interference is the main reason.

The harmonics in power system produce additional spectrum leakage. Harmonic can cause power line aging, it even can cause a fire on power line. The harmonics produce mechanical vibration on electrical motor and cause physical damage to power electronic devices. When transfer signals in power system the background signal contains a large number of harmonic components. It caused the transmission difficult and the information lost in some seriously situation.

Power voltage and frequency is not stability due to the random power load. For the voltage and frequency instability, a mount of electrical energy lost during the

---

* Supported by Program of International S&T Cooperation[GJXM20100002], Hainan Province Natural Science Fund[808132], Scientific Research in Higher Education Department of Hainan Province [Hjkj2011-08] and 211 Project of Hainan University.

P. Sénac, M. Ott, and A. Seneviratne (Eds.): ICWCA 2011, LNICST 72, pp. 445–454, 2012.

transmission process. According to science statistics, power supply coefficient is just 70% or 80% in some place which shows the serious phenomena.

The theory of all-phase spectrum with good suppression of spectral leakage has high accuracy estimation by consider the input signal divided by all circumstances. In case of no disturbance, all-phase FFT analysis spectral can retain phase information. Due to the frequency and amplitude is liner to phase correction, this character provides a guarantee for frequency and amplitude accuracy measure. In this paper, time shifting and phase difference correction method is used to measure the harmonic and frequency precisely [2].

## 2  Basic Principle of All-Phase Spectrum

The China power supply is three-phase AC which frequency is 50Hz. The actual current has higher harmonics component except fundamental 50Hz. The third harmonic is larger compare with other harmonic component and it is the most harmful harmonic. Harmonic detection is the basic of harmonic management, the harmonic accuracy measure is prior to the harmonic management.

All-phase spectrum analysis need preprocess the sequence data which contain sample point $x_0$ and the length is N, then take the window comprehensive treatment and traditional FFT spectrum analysis. It improved the performance of spectral analysis by weight average offsetting the spectrum leakage[3] [4].

All-phase digital signal data pre-processing can be described as: Suppose a discrete signal's data length is (2N-1), divide this data into the length of N, then get the N data segment. Alignment each piece of data circular by centre point N which function as triangular window. Then overlap and normalize the corresponding phase and obtain a sample of data which length is N. Thus, all-phase method take account of all the possible chance of center sample data. The method can cut off to reduce the error caused by signal truncation [5].

All-phase FFT double window spectrum has better capability of data processing compared to non-window or single- window, it has less leakage and increases the measurement precision.

Frequency spectrum resolution precision and amplitude estimation precision is contradictory, window function can improve the amplitude spectrum estimation errors but it reduce the frequency spectrum resolution. In order to design a window function both has small amplitude estimation error and does not reduce the frequency resolution, we adopted double window function approach in practical applications.

The process as:

A. Sample signal of single-frequency and get the sequence:

$$X_{0=}[X(N), X(N+1),..., X(2N-1)]^T$$

$$X_{1=}[X(N-1), X(N),..., X(2N-2)]^T \qquad (1)$$

$$\vdots$$

$$X_{N-1=}[X(1), X(2),..., X(N)]^T$$

B. Move the sample point first, shift each vector circular. We get the other N data which is N-Dimensional

$$X'_0 = [X(N), X(N+1),\ldots, X(2N-1)]^T$$

$$X'_1 = [X(N), X(N+1),\ldots, X(N-1)]^T \qquad (2)$$

$$\vdots$$

$$X'_{N-1} = [X(N)\ X(1),\ldots, X(N-1)]^T$$

C. The All-Phase data vector can get by added sample points then average the Sum

$$X_{ap} = [NX(N),(N-1)X(N+1),\cdots, X(2N-1)+(N-1)X(N-1)/N]^T \cdot \qquad (3)$$

## 3 Use Time Shifting and Phase Retardation Correction Method Based on All-Phase FFT

Sample two signals with same length consecutively and get the sequence. The sampling data should be preprocessed before FFT spectrum analyze. Then use the difference between the phase Sine signal and its delay signal to correct the spectral.

$$X_1(t)=A\cos(2ft+\theta) \qquad (4)$$

$$X_2(t)=A\cos(2f\ (t-t_0)\ +\theta)$$

A is signal amplitude, f is frequency, $\theta$ is the original phase.

Sample the signal with $f_s$, do Fourier transform and get a sequenced spectrum $X_{ap}(k)$

$$X_{1ap}\ (k)= C_1(\omega_0,k)\cos(\theta+2\pi k_0\ *n/N)+ \qquad (5)$$

$$jC_2(\omega_0,k)\sin(\theta+2\pi k_0\ *n/N)$$

$$X_{2ap}\ (k)= C_1(\omega_0,k)\cos(\theta+2\pi k_0\ *(n-n_0)/N)+$$

$$jC_2(\omega_0,k)\sin(\theta+2\pi k_0\ *(n-n_0)/N)$$

use $\varphi_1$ describe the phase of $X_1\ (k)$

$$\varphi_1 = \theta+2k_0\ *n/N \qquad (6)$$

use $\varphi_2$ describe the phase of $X_2(k)$

$$\varphi_{2=}\theta+2k_0*(n-n_0)/N$$

$$\Delta\varphi=\varphi_1-\varphi_{2=}2\pi k_0*n_0/N \tag{7}$$

the corresponding frequency correction value is :

$$k_{0=}\Delta\varphi*N/(2\pi*n_0) \tag{8}$$

Amplitude spectrum of all-phase FFT is the square of amplitude spectrum of traditional FFT.

## 4  Hardware Design

### 4.1  Acquisition Hardware Description

According to the character of the power system and consideration the real time detection, choose Cyclone II 2C35F672C8FPGA as the central processor. It is support a broad range of external memory interfaces, such as SDR SDRAM, DDR SDRAM, DDR2 SDRAM. The chips has 33,216 LES. The eight-channel 12 bits ADC MAX1308 is used to acquire high accurate power sampling signal. Eight channel's fast conversion time is 1.98 μs.The results can be transformed by RS232 and displayed in PC. Initial angle of current signal usually fluctuated, so the paper choose voltage signal as detect data can get a high-precision[5]. The paper design power parameter detection equipment to analysis harmonic wave and frequent by using FPGA and ADC1308 , meet the needs of power system measurement and have the practical value. This instrument measurement precision of frequency is $10^{-10}$, can analyze harmonic component under 20 degree correctly [6] [7].

### 4.2  The Structure of the Hardware System

This paper adopt FPGA as the main processing chip, it has the character of the programmable components and prospect in digital signal process [8]. For the algorithm design, adopt the superiority of all phase FFT algorithm compare to some other power harmonic detection algorithm, it has high precision [9].

The paper present the whole system framework and how to complete each module. High power voltage signal has been changed into -5 ~ +5V low voltage signal through the conditioning circuit. The signals is sampled by AD and translated into FPGA which has great digital processing capability. For the current signal has some interference the system choose voltage signal as sampling data, processed in all phase pretreatment module, floating point FFT processing modules and so on, we get higher harmonic amplitude, RMS voltage and other power quality parameters, the results can be stored in the data storage module or translated to PC through communication module, it also can be stored in LABVIEW waveform for real-time display, the detector will generate an alarm signal to inform people when the data exceed the national standard.

The harmonic analysis system based on FPGA can be divided into data disposal module, data acquisition module, signal analysis module, communication module, and the PC display module.

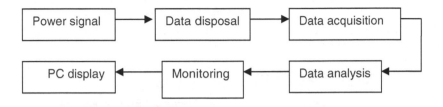

**Fig. 1.** The system structure diagram

The data disposal, data acquisition, pc display are the periphery design of the system. The data analysis and communications monitoring which process internal in FPGA are the core part of the system.

### 4.3  Key Module

#### 4.3.1  FIFO Module

FIFO (First In First Out) is a kind of advanced data buffer, FIFO is used as the data transfer between the different clock speed interface or different data width interface, it also used as data buffer between data acquisition module and data processing module. FIFO can establish a connection between data processing module and the corresponding circuit. In this system it not only can change 50Hz low-speed sampling data into a continuous N point high-speed data, also can used as buffer between two processing module. The data buffer transport a group of data into to data processing modules, transfer the result to next processing module after be completely calculated.

**Fig. 2.** FIFO QUARTUS simulation

### 4.3.2  FFT Module

Fixed-point FFT has a simple structure, but the effective signal could be submerged because of the noise disturb. Sometimes the data could be cut off for this reason. The floating-point FFT has high accuracy, the floating-point structure which each number is represented by single index and digit,  but it consumed supreme resources and its speed is low. This paper adopt the floating-point mode to insure the harmonic detection accuracy, QUARTUS FFT is using flow pattern, ALTERA ATLANTIC interface use I/O agreement, eight road 256 point of FFT operations can be completed within 1 ms by multilayer parallel pipelines technique. The simulation as follows, the Sink Master as input interface, Source Master as output interface.

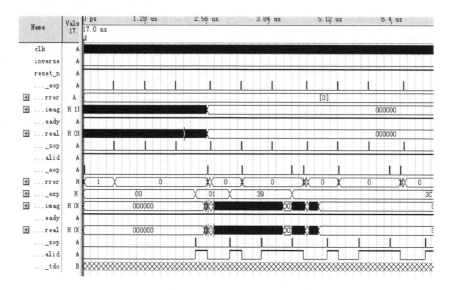

**Fig. 3.** FFT QUARTUS simulation

### 4.3.3  RMS Algorithm Module

Voltage RMS is one of the important power parameters, voltage deviation is a symbol of the power supply system operation whether normal or not. RMS algorithm adopts a discrete algorithm processing module, the formula as follows:

$$Urms = \sqrt{\frac{1}{N}\sum_{i=1}^{N} u^2(n)} \tag{9}$$

N - sampling points of measured signal in a cycle;
U (n) - the instantaneous voltage of sample point;
Urms - the RMS voltage of measured signals

The algorithm is intuitive comparatively. It is compare of multiplier module, accumulator module. The module above adopt 32-bit floating-point mode so the data precision is high. The shortcoming is it take too memory. The algorithm can share the same ALM module which generated by QUARTUS with the FFT algorithm processing module to save some resources and time, [10] [11].

## 5  Measuring the Frequency

The power frequency is measured by the acquisition sample data, the real power frequency is fluctuated all the time. The waveform distortion components in transient periodic process and the noise interference are the reason of low measure precision. In this paper, initial angle disturbance of voltage signal affect measure frequency precision. The frequency is fluctuated at different time in same places. The result shows the maximum deviation is in safe standard.

The maximal deviation is:
 (50. 36785322-50) = 0. 36785322<0.5
The minimum deviation is:
 (50.03545321-50)= 0.03545321<0.5

## 6  Detection of Higher Harmonics

The extensive use of rectifier device which is non-sinusoidal in China's power system can cause a large number of harmonic mixed in AC current. Harmonic will generate additional damage to load, result in power loss and line aging. Power Harmonic detect arithmetic can monitor and record the real-time parameters. The perfect harmonic power detect arithmetic can do real-time monitoring and analyzing .The accurate detection of harmonic is premise to maintain the power normal operation. The design of detect arithmetic has practical meaning and potential development.

The power signal is complicated. It is combine the fundamental signal of 50Hz and other higher frequency harmonic components. The harmonic cause the power factor is low. For the harmonic disturb, the quality of power supply is in low efficiency. The harmonic cause power lost in distribution system and high failure rate of equipment. Analysis the real voltage data to represent the power signal as follows. The wave is showed in MATLAB in figure 4.Despite the complicate harmonic, the waveform is not a smooth sine curve. Because of the noise disturb, UA,UB,UC are not display as the same waveform[12].

Analysis higher harmonic by classical way has spectrum leakage. The strength signal's frequency next line will override the weak signal's frequency main line. FFT can't detect the low frequency signal. So the suppression of spectral leakage trait in all-phase FFT spectrum can be used in detecting the higher harmonics in power system[13] [14].

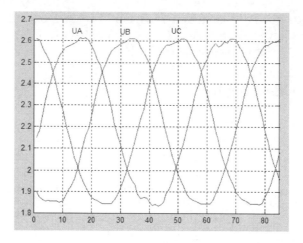

**Fig. 4.** Real three-phase voltage signal in power system

In this harmonic analysis of all-phase FFT can detect the 20th harmonic. We can see the contentment of 50Hz is high and the contentment of odd harmonics is large than the even harmonics. In some research , the universal simulation experiment consider the harmonic amplitude is decreased by harmonic random increased, but by this actual acquisition date, 9th harmonics amplitudes is slightly larger than the 7th harmonics amplitudes.Harmonic's amplitude are not always decreased by harmonic degree increased[15].

All-phase FFT improves the accuracy of higher harmonic analysis. After the treatment of all-phase FFT, the leakage of spectrum is reduced. Figure 5 is harmonics power amplitude spectrum based on all phase FFT. Figure 6 is partial enlargement of Figure 5. It is shows the higher harmonic component clearly. Pay attention to the point A, the same point in both figure 5 and figure 6. Figure 7 is the bar charts of content of harmonics in power system. The result is complied with national standards GB/T15945-1993 quality of electric energy supply [16] [17].

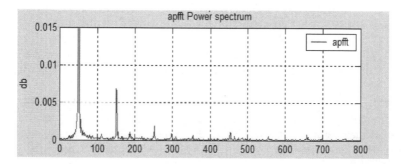

**Fig. 5.** Higher harmonics power amplitude spectrum based on All-phase FFT

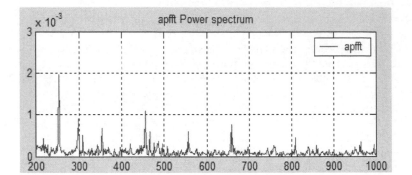

**Fig. 6.** Partial enlargement of Figure5

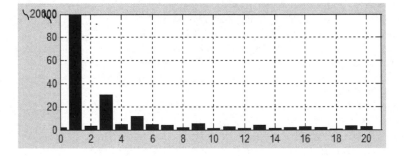

**Fig. 7.** The bar charts of amplitude content of harmonics based on All-phase FFT

## 7 Conclusion

Take the all-phase FFT algorithm to process the real power signal by FPGA, the power frequency and the higher harmonic could be measured accurately. All-phase FFT has the phase correction linear characters which increases the accuracy of the frequency and harmonics detection. The character of all-phase FFT restrain spectrum leakage can be used to detect the weak higher harmonic component in this equipment. Precise harmonic detection is the base of the normal operation of power system, the high accuracy of harmonic detection can monitor and analyze the real-time power signal in the electricity system[18].

Because of the large amounts of harmonics presence in power system, three-phase power frequency waveform is not the smooth sine curve. We measured the RMS voltage power is 386.425V, less than five percent of the require standard. It is visible the dominant part of spectrum is 50Hz frequency, the higher amplitude content is descend in turn, odd harmonic content is larger than the even harmonic content. Due to the all phase reprocess detection methods, spectrum analysis showed the harmonic precision is as high as 20 degree.

# References

1. Andraka., R.J., Phelps, R.M.: An FPGA Based Processor Yields A Real Time High Fidelity Radar Environment Simulator. In: Military and Aerospace Applications of Programmable Devices and Technologies Conference, Andraka Consulting Group, USA, pp. 19–23 (1999)
2. Wei, y.: Correction and application of All Phase discrete spectrum. Master thesis in Tianjin University (May 2007)
3. Deng, Z., Liu, Y.: The frequency estimation of sine wave based on all-phase Spectrum analysis. Data acquisition and processing (7), 449–450 (2008)
4. Xu, j.: Harmonic frequency estimation based on FFT method and MUSIC method. Protection and Control of Power system 1(3), 37–40 (2009)
5. Wang, z., Huang, x.d.: Digital signal spectral analysis of all-phases and filtering technique. Peking Electronic Industry (2009) (in press)
6. Hidalgo, R.M.: A simple adjustable window algorithm to improve FFT measurements. IEEE Transactions on Instrumentation and Measurument 51, 31–36 (2002)
7. Pang, H., Li, D.x., Zu, Y.: An improved algorithm for harmonic analysis of power system using FFT technique. Proceedings of the CSEE 23(6), 50–54 (2003)
8. Zhang, F., Geng, Z., Ge, Y.F.: FFT algorithm with high accuracy for harmonic analysis in power system[J]. Proceedings of the CSEE 19(3), 63–66 (1999)
9. Ferrero: High accuracy Fourier analysis based on synchronous sampling techniques. IEEE Trans. on IM 41(6), 780–785 (1992)
10. Chai, X., Wen, X., Guan, G.: An algorithm with high accuracy for analysis of power system harmonics. Proceedings of the CSEE 23(9), 67–70 (2003)
11. Wang, X., He, Y.: A new neural network based power system harmonics analysis algorithm with high accuracy. Power System Technology 29(3), 72–75 (2005)
12. Dixon, G., Moran, L.: Control System for Three-Phase Active Power Filter Which Simultaneously Compensates Power Factor. IEEE Trans. on Industrial Electronics 42(6), 636–641 (1995)
13. Mack Grady, S.: Understanding power system harmonics. IEEE Transactions on Power Engineering Review 21(11), 8–11 (2001)
14. Grady, S.: Characterization of distribution power quality events with Fourier and wavelet transforms. IEEE Transaction on Power Delivery 1(15), 247–254 (2000)
15. Zhang, S., Yu, D.: Design and implementation of a parallel real-time FFT processor. In: 7th International Conference on Solid-State and Integrated Circuits Technology, vol. 3(10), pp. 1665–1668 (2004)
16. Densem, T.J., Bodger, P.S., Arrillaga, J.: Three Phase Transmission System Modeling for Harmonic Penetration Studies. IEEE Trans. 103(2), 310–317 (1984)
17. Xu, W., Dommel, M.: A Synchronous Machine Model for Three-Phase Harmonic Analysis and EMTP Initialization. IEEE Trans. 6(4), 1530–1538 (1991)
18. Talacek, J., Watson, R.: Marginal Pricing of Harmonic Injections. IEEE Trans. 17(20), 50–56 (2002)

# Author Index